SOVIETICA

MONOGRAPHS

OF THE INSTITUTE OF EAST-EUROPEAN STUDIES

UNIVERSITY OF FRIBOURG / SWITZERLAND

Edited by

J. M. BOCHEŃSKI

PHILOSOPHY AND IDEOLOGY

Z. A. JORDAN

PHILOSOPHY AND IDEOLOGY

THE DEVELOPMENT OF PHILOSOPHY AND MARXISM-LENINISM

IN POLAND SINCE THE SECOND WORLD WAR

D. REIDEL PUBLISHING COMPANY / DORDRECHT-HOLLAND

Yet, I think, my good sir, that it would be better for me to have a musical instrument or a chorus which I was directing in discord and out of tune, better that the mass of mankind should disagree with me and contradict me than that I, a single individual, should be out of harmony with myself and contradict myself.

PLATO, *Gorgias* 482 bc

TO MY TEACHERS AND FRIENDS IN POLAND

WITH RESPECT AND AFFECTION

FROM THE EDITOR

The present volume of the 'Sovietica' series is part of the results of an extensive research program, undertaken by the Institute of East-European Studies of the University of Fribourg (Switzerland) with the help of the Rockefeller Foundation. I would like to express here my thanks.

J. M. BOCHEŃSKI

CONTENTS

PREFACE

The purpose of this study is to describe the development of philosophy in Poland since the end of the Second World War and the development of Marxist-Leninist philosophy which, owing to international political events, has assumed an important role in the intellectual life of contemporary Poland. This task could not have been accomplished without relating post-war developments to those of the interwar period. Consequently, the period studied covers the years 1918–1958.

Yet another extension was necessary. Marxism-Leninism regards sociology as a part of philosophy. Moreover, Marxism-Leninism often resorts to sociology to support or justify some of its philosophical views. Finally, its criticism of 'bourgeois philosophy' is often concerned with social philosophy and sociological theories which supposedly are implicit or explicit in 'bourgeois philosophy'. For this reason it was desirable to consider in this study some theoretical and methodological problems of the social sciences. They are taken into account when they illuminate philosophical controversies or the evolution of Marxist-Leninist philosophy.

Marxism-Leninism is not only a new line of development but also a new point of departure in Polish philosophy. It provides a striking contrast with the established philosophical tradition which originated roughly at the time when G. E. Moore and Bertrand Russell initiated the analytical trend in English philosophy. The contrast can be epitomised by the contradistinction of philosophy and ideology, chosen as the title of this study.

To make this point clear, it was necessary to inquire more closely into some of the philosophical theories of Marxism-Leninism. In view of the fact that the more specifically philosophical parts of Marxism-Leninism are little known, this detailed inquiry might hold some intrinsic interest. It considerably enlarged the scope and length of this study, but also revealed some new facts which shed light on the changes wrought in Marxism-Leninism under the impact of its encounter with academic philosophy.

Considering the ideological nature of Marxism-Leninism, its rise in Poland was bound to lead to sharp clashes of philosophical attitudes and opinions. Owing to political circumstances, these clashes turned into an internecine war, which Marxism-Leninism declared upon the existing philosophical tradition, its methods and techniques, its general programme and particular views. The war was not waged solely by intellectual means and did not respect the procedures necessary in the search for truth. Yet the outcome of this conflict was not the destruction of philosophy by ideology. On the contrary, it was ideology which slowly changed its initial position, reducing its claims, revising its points of view, modernising its outlook, and discovering the value of objectivity, logical consistency and free inquiry.

This dénouement might have been of more general significance were it not for certain restrictive circumstances peculiar to Poland which are to be found in the vigour of the native philosophical tradition. It is no exaggeration to say that the outcome might have been different, if Polish philosophy had not been steeled for generations against any form of irrationalism by a systematic cultivation of logical and other scientific procedures and if it could not draw upon these resources to maintain its steadfastness of purpose and its power of attraction.

Although the Polish case may not admit of any easy generalisation, it seems to prompt some general reflections on the importance of philosophical thinking, its relevance to man's life, and its social function. The controversies and arguments to be recounted and analysed in the following pages transcend a purely theoretical approach to problems of philosophy. If Polish philosophers had failed to bring to bear the whole force of their knowledge upon the problems at issue or to take the utmost advantage of the persuasive power of logical procedures, if they had yielded to the extra-logical pressure or ceased to oppose confused thinking and fallacious reasoning, something more than an abstract argument would have been lost. Conversely, the sustained and successful effort to maintain a certain kind of philosophical inquiry or a certain way of exercising intelligence had repercussions outside the restricted field of philosophy. It undermined and helped to dispel irrational beliefs in the wider area of social life. Although philosophical controversies in Poland were in some respects a contest of specialised skills and knowledge, they were not exclusively such, for they carried risks and implications from which a debate pursued in academic seclusion is usually free. For this reason the developments in Poland seem to have a universal significance.

It is sometimes said that the philosophy of to-day, having become specialised and technically refined, has lost relevance to that with which the common man is concerned. The development of events in Poland does not confirm this opinion. The prevailing philosophical tradition was professional as well as being technically advanced. Its vision, which, to quote Friedrich Waismann, inspires any philosophy worth the name, was derived from science and logic. Yet it has shown itself to have implications for the perplexities and conflicts of the times. The vision not only secured the survival of philosophical thinking, but also helped the general public by providing it with standards of rationality and objectivity as well as by inspiring confidence in the fruitfulness of critical discussion as a means of liberating the mind from errors and prejudices. The philosopher's consistency, persistence and reasonableness were clearly relevant to ordinary opinions and left their imprint on the course of social and political events.

PART ONE

PHILOSOPHY BETWEEN THE TWO WARS

INTRODUCTION

The last sixty years have perhaps constituted the most remarkable period in the history of philosophy in Poland. Never before were so many talents and abilities attracted to philosophy to make valuable contributions in its development. Poland, after the First World War, having hardly regained its own statehood and organised its institutions of teaching and research, became one of the internationally important centres of philosophical studies. Polish logicians and philosophers promoted new trends and opened fresh fields of research. The fame of the Warsaw School was widely known to some because of its mathematicians and to others because of its logicians and philosophers.

When the Second World War broke out some thought that this was the end of a bright but short interlude. Among them was E.T. Bell, the distinguished historian of mathematics. Recalling Alfred North Whitehead's tribute of 1934 to H. M. Sheffer and 'the great school of Polish mathematicians', concluding with the statement: 'there is continuity in the progress of ordered knowledge', Bell wrote: 'Five years less one month later, 'the great school of Polish mathematicians' was being bombed from the air in the progress of ordered ignorance, that is, in the general progress of European civilisation. What had taken twenty years to gather was dispersed and in part obliterated in about twenty days. 'The great school of Polish mathematicians' followed the Vienna Circle into death or exile'[1].

Bell's prophecy turned out to be only partly true and Whitehead's faith in the continuity of the progress of ordered knowledge has been vindicated. Shortly after the end of hostilities of the Second World War the survivors resumed the interrupted development. The losses in human lives and research facilities, suffered by want on destruction and systematic extermination, were grievous but not fatal. First to recover were mathematics and mathematical logic; the first post-war volume of *Fundamenta Mathematicae* appeared in 1945 and the regular publication of this periodical was recommenced in 1947. About the same time mathematical logic resumed its place in the world of learning. At the International Congress of Philosophy in Amsterdam (1948) Polish philosophers did not appear in person, but their contributions were numerous and of the same quality as previously. By the side of the older generation of philosophers there appeared the younger one, which made a promising start and justified trust in the future. Important works, some of them of outstanding value, were published. There was no reason to feel apprehensive that the present would not equal and even improve upon the past.

Just then, however, the course of development was again interrupted by political interference, suppression of free thought and speech, and the imposition of an oracular philosophy, enforced by decrees and administrative measures. The protracted struggle for the rights of reason, intellectual integrity, respect for facts, even the validity of logical thinking, began in earnest. A great amount of mental energy and spiritual resources was spent in the defence of the elementary and well-established truths. The struggle was desperate, philosophical thinking appeared to be doomed. Its outcome in 1956, sudden and decisive, again proved all the apprehensions to be exaggerated. The submerged determination to search for truth and abide by its verdict has re-asserted itself with a renewed strength.

If one looks back at the Polish philosophical scene in the years since 1945, one thing stands out in clear relief. The modern philosophical tradition, which commenced in Poland at the beginning of this century and gathered strength during the following decades, has survived all the disasters and upheavals and contributed to shape the methods and ways of philosophical thinking in the post-war period. It has continued unobtrusively even at times when a different tradition seemed to have won the day and proclaimed its decisive victory over the past and its discovery of the ultimate truth.

This power of survival is probably due to many factors, of which one, however, is of direct interest to the purpose of this study. It should be looked for in the persistence and vigour of the modern Polish philosophical tradition which gave to its followers in the post-war era the strength of deep-rooted beliefs not easily misled or affected by pressure and other more extreme measures. This tradition must be traced back to its source, for it has provided the background of post-war developments and has constituted their formative force and influence.

CHAPTER 1

THE LWÓW SCHOOL

The beginning of modern philosophy in Poland can be given a precise date. It was in 1895 that Kazimierz Twardowski (1866–1938) was appointed to the chair of philosophy at Lwów University and became the founder of modern Polish philosophy [2].

Twardowski belonged to the so-called Austrian school whose head was Franz Brentano. The large circle of Brentanists included psychologists and philosophers of a world-wide reputation: Alexius Meinong, Alois Höfler, Oskar Kraus, Christian Ehrenfels, Carl Stumpf. Twardowski's contributions to the teaching of the school considered to be the most important are contained in his book *Zur Lehre vom Inhalt und Gegenstand der Vorstellungen. Eine psychologische Untersuchung,* published in 1894. They provided a link in the development of thought which, on the one side, led from Brentano's descriptive psychology to Meinong's ontology *(Gegenstandstheorie),* and to Husserl's phenomenology, on the other. Husserl recognised the importance of Twardowski's contribution and, after the publication of *Logische Untersuchungen,* Twardowski's reputation was established in Austrian and German philosophy [3].

When Twardowski arrived in Lwów, he came to a philosophical wilderness. There was much interest in philosophy, but it was taught and pursued in the traditional, somewhat amateurish manner. Twardowski clearly faced the choice of either continuing his own work and returning to Vienna as soon as possible, or staying in Lwów, giving up his own studies, and devoting his life to teaching. He decided upon the latter course. This decision must have been a momentous one for him. It constituted the decisive turning point in the history of philosophy in Poland.

Twardowski's teaching was based on Brentano's philosophy and on its further development, to which other Brentanists and himself contributed. In a certain sense Brentano was a supporter of psychologism; he saw in psychology the basic science of all science. Psychology, as he conceived it, was an empirical discipline, although its empiricism was not of the kind familiar to natural scientists. It did not make any use of experiments and very little of observation; it did not try to reduce psychological phenomena to physiological processes, as was done by G. T. Fechner and W. M. Wundt. Moreover, Brentano agreed with Comte that psychological phenomena cannot be really observed by introspection. Instead, we can directly apprehend them and, by a careful and minute description of what there is before our mind, acquire the knowledge of the phenomena involved. Brentano's psychology is a descriptive science, based on direct apprehension of its subject matter and thus superior, in his opinion, to natural science, which is barred from direct access to what it investigates. In this sense, psychology provides fundamental knowledge for all science. Brentano returned to the thesis of the French rationalist thinkers of the seventeenth century that we know the mind better than we shall ever know matter.

Brentano's descriptive psychology provides a basis for a general method of philosophical investigations. When we perceive a tree outside the window, we cannot be aware of its being there without being aware at the same time of the act of seeing it. This distinction between an act and its object, which although distinct are never given separately and might thus be confused, is fundamental for Brentano's philosophy. Only the act of a representation – and by this term Brentano refers to anything that is apprehended by or is before the mind – constitutes a psychological phenomenon. The object of an act is often a physical thing and cannot be, therefore, a constituent of a mental phenomenon.

Besides the act and object, there is still a third element, which must be distinguished in every mental phenomenon – the content of the act. Brentano did not keep the object and the content of the act clearly apart and the sharp distinction between them is Twardowski's important contribution. The content of the act is the latter's 'quality', by virtue of which the act is directed towards its object and not to something else, as well as that by which it presents the object to the mind in one manner rather than another. To this distinction between content and object Twardowski added two further theses. First, that to every representation there corresponds an object and, second, that there is a necessary relation between a representation and its object. The latter thesis, which for Twardowski was a psychological statement, might have ultimately paved the way for Husserl's transcendental idealism.

Brentano's conception of mental phenomena contained the nucleus of ideas that led far beyond his initial point of departure. They could lead in the direction which Husserl took, or to conceptual analysis and formal logic, to logical analysis of language, to syntax and semantics. The choice of roads depended on what was given paramount attention: the descriptive psychology which dealt with the mental act and its content, or the objects apprehended in the act of representation. This duality in Brentano's initial position became more pronounced owing to Twardowski's distinction. Twardowski took the second course and made extensive excursions, beyond the bounds of descriptive psychology, into the field of logic and the theory of knowledge.

In Poland Brentano's philosophy was thus given a distinctly realistic orientation. While his descriptive psychology provided the means for specifically psychological investigations, carried on by Twardowski himself and by a large number of his pupils, it also constituted a starting point for a wide range of epistemological and ontological research, which undermined and finally destroyed the last vestiges of psychologism, in the above-defined sense, common to Brentano and Twardowski.

Only the acts are immanent to and constituents of the consciousness; the objects, given by means of representations, are outside the consciousness and transcendent to it. The analysis of psychological phenomena, carried by means of descriptive psychology, revealed a whole realm of objects independent from the experiencing subject – of things, meanings, concepts, logical laws, which are

6

neither immanent to the mind nor mere generalisations of the mind's activity. To describe these objects, to differentiate between them, to reveal their structure and relations, became the proper task of philosophy. They are found by the mind, and psychology only helps to establish their reality empirically. Twardowski's writings abound in suggestive psychological descriptions and thorough philosophical analysis, in clarifications and definitions of the philosophical conceptual framework used in the discussion of the questions of psychology, logic and the theory of knowledge (the different kinds of representations, concepts, judgements, sentences, propositions, and the notion of truth). This move forward, away from psychologism, is unmistakable and pronounced in the whole activity of Twardowski. He laid the foundations for the logical conception of science and for epistemology in the etymological sense of this term. Twardowski called his method by a name now very familiar – the analytical method [4].

In his lectures, Twardowski dealt approvingly with the reform of formal logic, initiated at that time, paid much attention to logic and encouraged his pupils to do so. But in an article widely read in Poland at that time, he pronounced himself against the 'symbolomania' in which one of his pupils (Jan Łukasiewicz – unnamed in the article) indulged, so Twardowski thought, too much. Łukasiewicz not only agreed with his teacher that logic had been led astray by psychologism, but was also convinced that it was exact logical analysis that should replace psychological examinations of the origin of concepts as the method of philosophical investigations. Twardowski rejected this suggestion. Logic is not a self-sufficient, autonomous discipline. It is, rather, an instrument to be carefully used for the solution of definite problems. Its concepts cannot be assumed; they must be critically examined and applied in accordance with the results of philosophical analysis. This was the attitude which Husserl took with respect to modern formal logic and to logical investigations on the foundations of mathematics, and which was represented by Roman Ingarden in Poland in the 'thirties. Twardowski's views also influenced Stanisław Leśniewski, who had begun his studies under Hans Cornelius in Germany, but completed them in Lwów. It perhaps explains Leśniewski's initial distrust of formalism which he later abandoned when he found a way of his own to combine Twardowski's standpoint with formal techniques.

However much Twardowski might have been opposed to the traditional philosophy in Poland and abroad – its lack of a method, its terminological confusions and conceptual ambiguities, its failure to find 'empirical' foundations – he was no admirer of scientism. He believed that philosophy could work out a method of its own, appropriate to its subject matter and fully satisfying the requirements of scientific procedure. Philosophy was to him an autonomous science and not a discipline to be made scientific by parcelling out its various problems to particular sciences. He was only a severe critic of the traditional philosophy, and not its liquidator. He was ready to undertake work of reform, and he practised it throughout his life. But his programme was limited and did not include the drastic measures which his former pupils were later to advocate.

The direction in which Twardowski led his followers in Poland required them to undertake painstaking analysis of specific problems which were rich in conceptual and terminological distinctions, and directed rather to the clarification than to the solution of the problems involved. Philosophy, as he conceived and taught it, was unlike its popular conception, impressed upon the popular mind by Poland's romantic poets and messianic philosophers, who more or less identified it with flights of imagination and poetical inspiration. Philosophy became a pedestrian affair, an elaborate and highly specialised technique of thinking, which, being closer than ever before to the hard ground of everyday experience and common sense, could not be followed, as was the case in the past, by educated but philosophically untrained amateurs. A sharp line of division emerged between the old and poetic and the new and scientific philosophy, the division line being concerned rather with the standards of performance than the subject-matter of what was considered to be a philosopher's proper study. Twardowski's school, wrote Tadeusz Czeżowski, was a hard one. It made great demands on the beginner and at first offered little reward [5].

What is known under the name of the Lwów school had thus little in common with a philosophical school of thought; it was a school of philosophical method and thinking. Its members were not linked with each other and with their teacher by a common body of philosophical assumptions and beliefs; they differed widely in this respect. The unity was forged by the common formal standards of clear thinking, precision of conceptual analysis, and by the terminological distinctions and mode of expression.

Twardowski did not proclaim these standards, but practised them himself in his lectures and seminars which covered a great variety of subjects – psychology, logic, history of philosophy, ethics – and thus showed that the method advocated by him admitted of universal application. He sharply differentiated between what can be accepted as a body of philosophical knowledge – the various problems, their different solutions, the arguments for and against them, the basic philosophical trends and schools of thought – and the *Weltanschauung,* the world outlook, which goes beyond what can be known and which accepts certain tentative solutions as final on the basis of global value judgements. He did not reject them altogether, recognising their practical utility, at the same time denying them scientific value. Twardowski's vast knowledge of classical philosophical literature made him abhor all onesidedness born of ignorance or contempt for the achievements of the past and excessive claims of being in possession of the whole truth [6].

The secret of Twardowski's influence and achievement as a teacher lay not only in the power of his mind, his vast and varied knowledge, his didactic talents and efficiency, but also in the Socratic quality of his personality, to which all his pupils testify unanimously. There was an atmosphere of uncompromising integrity about him. His demands for precision and exactitude in philosophical thinking which he practised himself and inculcated in others, sprang from his deep sense of intellectual honesty, and were a reflection of his unremittent concern and respect for truth. To choose a philosopher's life was to him to follow an exacting calling which demanded an effort both of mind and will.

Twardowski·taught as much by example as by his lectures and seminars. He left an inheritance which is not measurable in purely intellectual values, an invisible power which once created pervades the minds of those who have been affected by it and who in turn pass it on multiplied to the others.

Finally, Twardowski was the organiser of philosophical activities in Poland. He devised and tried out the university curriculum and didactic methods of teaching philosophy, which, with minor changes, have been followed ever since. He organised the first psychological laboratory in Poland (1901) and set up in Lwów the first Philosophical Society (1904). He actively supported the decision to start the first Polish philosophical periodical, *Przegląd Filozoficzny* founded by Władysław We ryho in Warsaw in 1898, and he founded in 1911 and edited until his death *Ruch Filozoficzny,* a bibliographical philosophical publication unique of its kind at that time, which kept Polish philosophers informed about philosophical developments at home and abroad. He initiated the translation into Polish of classical philosophical literature and encouraged others to follow his example.

When Twardowski died in 1938, his life work as founder of the school, as teacher and organiser of philosophical activities, had already brought ample results. The philosophical scene in Poland was completely transformed and philosophy flourished. Philosophy became an academic, scientific discipline, taught by his former pupils, at all the Polish universities. The philosophical activities were well organised. There were national philosophical congresses every few years, (the first was held in 1923), philosophical societies meeting regularly in every university centre, and four philosophical periodicals of a high standard were published. There was above all a thriving school of philosophical thinking, vigorous and confident, with an established reputation for its various achievements. The memory of Twardowski was a living force and the record of his achievements an inspiration for further sustained work by all. It was widely felt that Twardowski found the best way to combine abstract pursuit and search for truth with service to the community, or, to use the fashionable expression of the post-war period, he found how science can best serve life.

Twardowski had numerous pupils and followers displaying a wide range of abilities and interests. Between the oldest and youngest among them there was an age difference of more than a generation. Jan Łukasiewicz (1878–1956) and Władysław Witwicki (1878–1948) were Twardowski's oldest pupils. The first excelled in abstract reasoning, the second, a leading Polish psychologist and Plato's masterful translator, displayed a great power of observation and was unsurpassed in subtle and detailed descriptions of psychic phenomena, especially of emotions. The fact that these two men, so different in what they strived for and achieved, came from the same school is telling evidence of Twardowski's breadth of mind and tolerance.

To the same generation as Łukasiewicz and Witwicki belong Kazimierz Ajdukiewicz (born 1890), Stefan Baley (1885–1952), Stefan Błachowski (born 1889), Władysław Borowski (1879–1938), Tadeusz Czeżowski (born 1889), Daniela Gromska, Salomon Igel (1889–1942), Stanisław Kaczorowski (born 1889), Tadeusz Kotarbiński (born 1886), Mieczysław Kreutz (born 1892), Stanisław

9

Leśniewski (1886–1939), Kazimierz Sośnicki (born 1883) and Zygmunt Zawirski (1882–1948). But besides these thinkers, who later became prominent in psychology, formal logic and philosophy, there were also others who were either Twardowski's pupils or came under his influence, though their main interest lay outside philosophy. Among them were Ryszard Gansiniec (1888–1958), a classical scholar, Julian Kleiner (1886–1957), a historian of literature, Zygmunt Łempicki (1886–1943), a German philologist and historian of culture of many accomplishments, Ostap Ortwin (1873–1942), a literary critic, Władysław Szumowski (1875–1954), the holder of the first chair of history and philosophy of medicine at the University of Cracow [7], Bogdan Nawroczyński (born 1882), a professor of pedagogy, and Mieczysław Treter (1883–1944), an art historian and theorist.

The second generation of Twardowski's pupils included Walter Auerbach, Eugenia Blaustein (1905–1944), Leopold Blaustein (1905–1944), Izydora Dąmbska, Maria Kokoszyńska, Seweryna Łuszczewska-Romahnowa, Henryk Mehlberg, Zygmunt Schmierer, Helena Słoniewska, Tadeusz Witwicki. They took their degrees after the First World War, were taught by Twardowski and Ajdukiewicz, and, with some exceptions, belong to a different philosophical formation known as the Warsaw school.

Until recently Twardowski's school was referred to, at least in Poland, as the Lwów-Warsaw school. This was an apt description in view of the continuity in the philosophical development and of the persistence of certain characteristic traits in the philosophical method that have been apparent from the time Twardowski came to Lwów up to the present day. This continuity, which both its supporters and opponents rightly and strongly emphasise [8], is best testified to by the fact that all or practically all the leaders of the new philosophical orientation that emerged in Poland after the First World War were at some time or other Twardowski's pupils and followers. The Lwów-Warsaw school was also a convenient name, because it helped to differentiate the philosophical school from the Warsaw school of mathematicians, led by Zygmunt Janiszewski (1888–1920), Wacław Sierpiński (born 1882), Kazimierz Kuratowski (born 1896) and Stefan Mazurkiewicz (1888–1945), which shortly after the First World War acquired a world-wide reputation, as well as from the Warsaw school of logic, whose undisputed leaders were Leśniewski, Łukasiewicz and Alfred Tarski. Both the mathematical and the logical school were often called, particularly abroad, 'the Warsaw school' without any further qualification.

There is no doubt, however, that Twardowski's conception of philosophy, which he imparted to his pupils and which they at first espoused, differed in many and important respects from that which they evolved in their maturity. The differences are real, deep, and sometimes fundamental, and the passage of time put into relief what in the past was only vaguely seen and understood. Kotarbiński, one of the protagonists in the development of ideas originated by Twardowski, rightly emphasised that it is more correct to speak of the Lwów (Twardowski's) and the Warsaw school than to class them together [9].

To put it concisely, the Lwów school can be described as a period of psychologism and the Warsaw school as that of 'logicism'. By psychologism in this context should not be understood the well known historical trend which tried to reduce philosophy to psychology, the laws of logic or sociology to psychological laws, and historical and cultural events to the state of consciousness of the contemplating mind. As it was indicated above, psychologism stands here for the opinion that whatever is studied by any science must be first given in the representation (in Brentano's sense) and the examination of what is given is the task of psychology.

The pupils who remained most faithful to their teacher and who could still be described as members of Twardowski's school when the Warsaw school came into being, were those whose interests were psychological. Some of them, like Błachowski and Baley, became experimental psychologists; they extended the scope, but adhered to Twardowski's teaching in letter and spirit [10]. Others, and these included perhaps the most original psychologists among Twardowski's followers, contributed to the expansion of descriptive psychology and to the improvement of the methodology of psychology in general. To this group belonged Władysław Witwicki, Igel, Kreutz, and, among the younger, Auerbach and Blaustein, whose life of great promise and high achievements was cut short at an early age in a concentration camp.

Those of Twardowski's pupils who were interested in philosophy followed a path of their own rather than deviating from the road paved by him. Their method was continuation of, but it also differed from, Twardowski's approach both in manner and content. Philosophy in Poland took its now familiar modern form only in the Warsaw school.

If attention is concentrated on the differences, the contrast between the Lwów and Warsaw schools is considerable. They can be differentiated in a fourfold way. The Lwów school represented the pre-logistic stage of development; it showed little, if any, interest in the logical examination of the foundations, structure and methods of the empirical and deductive sciences, (psychology being perhaps the only exception to this rule); it did not attempt to solve any major philosophical problem being content with the preparatory work, with forging a conceptual apparatus and a philosophical vocabulary; and it recognised the existence of a philosophical method irreducible to those of the deductive and empirical sciences.

In contrast to it, the Warsaw school devoted most of its energy to modern formal logic and its applications; showed a lively and unflagging interest in methodology and theory of the deductive and empirical sciences; took up in a modern form some traditional major philosophical questions, in particular in ontology and the theory of knowledge, and tried to solve them with the aid of methods derived from formal logic and the philosophy of language (logical syntax and semantics); and, finally, it denied the existence of an autonomous philosophical method, coming very close to scientism.

Scientism is not used here as term of opprobrium to denote a misguided, if not a straightforwardly naive effort, to imitate in philosophy the language and methods of science. It refers to the philosophical trend, which proclaimed that most, if not all, philosophical problems have a sound core and misleading adjuncts. Furthermore, it believed that if the latter are discarded and the former are either reformulated and re-examined by means of logical methods or handed over to an appropriate science, the philosophical perplexities could be resolved once and for all. Philosophy has no other methods of inquiry but those which are either empirical or deductive (in the technical sense of these terms). Problems which cannot be either clearly stated or investigated by the methods of science lie outside the scope of scientific philosophy. Scientism of the Warsaw school was a methodological and philosophically neutral doctrine. It relied on the methods of science, since only these methods provide warranted knowledge.

Nothing better exemplifies the differences between the Lwów and the Warsaw school than the contrast between the writings of Leśniewski and Łukasiewicz published at the time when they were still Twardowski's followers and those which made them famous at a later period. In the years 1911–1914 Leśniewski contributed four articles to *Przegląd Filozoficzny*, all of them dealing with logical problems. They were examined informally with thoroughness and minuteness, which still deserve high admiration. One of them dealt with Russell's antinomy and solved it by means of what later became known as Leśniewski's theory of semantical categories (theory of types). What is striking in these articles from the present point of view, however, is the absence of symbolism and formal techniques. They were not used at all by a thinker who even among the logicians acquired the reputation of pushing formalism to its extreme and who almost ceased to use ordinary speech when he expounded his logical constructions. These articles were later repudiated by Leśniewski who expressed his regret that such immature contributions, unequal to the problems involved, should ever have been published [11].

Łukasiewicz's development was not less striking. He was appointed lecturer in philosophy at Lwów University in 1906 and moved to Warsaw in 1915, where he taught logic until the outbreak of the Second World War. Practically all his important work was done in Warsaw [12].

Łukasiewicz's first papers, published in *Przegląd Filozoficzny* (1903, 1907), dealt with the problems of induction and with the notion of cause. Notes and reviews, which he wrote at that time, show the interest with which he followed the criticism of psychologism in logic launched by Husserl, Meinong and Höfler. His first major publication was *On the Principle of Contradiction in Aristotle*, followed three years later by *Die logischen Grundlagen der Wahrscheinlichkeitsrechnung*. This period might be considered closed with two essays – *On Science* and *The Concept of Magnitude* [13].

Philosophically his most important contributions of that period were probably *On the Principle of Contradiction in Aristotle* and *On Science*. The latter was twice reprinted twenty years later and its description and classification of different kinds of reasoning were until recently universally accepted in Poland [14]. The former is a historical and systematic study of the principle of non-contradiction in Aristotle, still of a considerable value for a historian of logic, in which with an exemplary clarity the distinction between the ontological, logical and psychological principles of non-contradiction was made and their respective validity discussed. This distinction has also turned out to be of permanent value and has provided the basis from which every discussion – and they became frequent in recent years in Poland – on the status of the principle of non-contradiction used to start. The ontological and the logical principles of non-contradiction are equivalent, but neither of them is equivalent to the psychological principle. The latter states that two beliefs expressed in contradictory sentences cannot exist in one mind. It is clear that this statement is an empirical probability law and not a principle at all.

Łukasiewicz rejected the claim that the principle of non-contradiction in its ontological or logical formulation is a 'first principle' or, as it was put at that time, a 'fundamental law of thought'. It is a logical theorem, whose validity may be doubted. It must be proved, therefore, but such a proof cannot be found either in Aristotle or anywhere else. If the principle of non-contradiction is neither a 'first principle' nor a proved theorem, we must recognise that we accept it for its important extra-logical reasons, of practical and moral nature, namely as a means to guard us against falsehood and lies [15]. Apart from other reasons, striking at that time, but no longer valid today, by which he supported his opinions, Łukasiewicz used Couturat's algebra of logic to show that the principle of non-contradiction is a theorem and not an axiom, a theorem provable in this system. It should be added that Łukasiewicz never again returned to the view on the principle of non-contradiction expounded in his first major work. He recognised that the metalogical principle of non-contradiction must be assumed as an absolute principle, if logic and science in general is to make sense [16].

The study On the Principle of Contradiction in Aristotle is memorable for another reason. It made a reference to the Aristotelian doctrine on contingent propositions, which were to play a considerable role in the discovery of many-valued logics, mentioned the possibility of constructing a non-Aristotelian logic, and shortly discussed the relation between time and the validity of the principle of non-contradiction with respect to the world of experience. The idea of a non-Aristotelian logic took firmer roots in Die logischen Grundlagen der Wahrscheinlichkeitsrechnung, where he came to the conclusion that the principle of bivalence is not absolute. There are sentences which are neither true nor false and to reject them on the ground of Aristotle's principle of bivalence is to transform that principle into a prejudice [17].

All these contributions contained many original ideas, they excelled in clarity of thought, in precision and simplicity of language. They made Łukasiewicz a rising philosophical star in Poland, but not an explorer of new lands. Philosophically he moved well within the area familiar to Twardowski's school and he did not deny its assumptions. Before he became completely absorbed in formal logic, he considered that effective philosophical methods for solving philosophical problems could be found. He changed his opinion only with his first logical discoveries, which convinced him of the inventive and explanatory power of formal logic. His demand for the reconstruction of philosophy by means of formal logic probably began emerging in his mind at the same time as the idea of many-valued logics was born, to solve, as he then thought, some of the philosophical problems which haunted him [18] and to prompt further discoveries in formal logic. This opened a new period in the development of philosophy in Poland.

The differences between the Lwów and the Warsaw school grew up slowly and almost imperceptibly, to become accentuated only in the late 'twenties. By 1930 Leśniewski's system of the foundations of logic and mathematics, which was to avoid the shortcomings of *Principia Mathematica*, was emerging from the privacy of lectures, seminars, and personal contacts into print [19]. Łukasiewicz's investigations on the propositional calculus, Aristotle's syllogistic, many-valued logics, and history of logic, were summarised in a number of articles and reports [20]. Two important text-books of formal logic were published, which, as it were, codified various discoveries made in Poland and abroad, incorporated them into the body of common philosophical knowledge, and set a pattern for teaching of and research in logic [21]. Tarski, who since 1923 made a number of important contributions, clearly joined his teachers as the third leader of the logical school and became responsible for initiating systematic studies in meta-logic and semantics [22]. Kotarbiński's *Elements of the Theory of Knowledge, Formal Logic and Methodology of Science* was just published and showed how the general assumptions of the school were applied in practice and what they could achieve [23]. The leading logicians, Leśniewski, Łukasiewicz, and Tarski, and the most prominent philosophers, Kotarbiński and Ajdukiewicz, were by that time surrounded by a large number of young assistants and followers who had already made their mark in logic or philosophy. The school also had adherents outside Warsaw, in Lwów, Poznań, and Wilno, Kraków jealously guarding its independence both in logic and philosophy, and exercised a considerable influence on the minds of the younger generation studying at the universities or starting their own research. The Warsaw school was clearly the dominant force in academic philosophy and a powerful stimulus in the intellectual life of the country.

The Warsaw school had its logical and its philosophical wing without losing its unity. The unity was the manifestation of a personal union of logic and philosophy, represented by Leśniewski and Łukasiewicz, reinforced by the mutual influence which the pure logicians and the philosophers were exercising on each other. In this respect Tarski, who is a logician and mathematician, represented a new departure which, in the course of time, was to assert itself increasingly in the development of the school. While the older generation of logicians represented the alliance of philosophy and formal logic, the younger generation of logicians combined logic and mathematics, drew away from philosophy and were becoming more and more absorbed in and by the mathematical school. This trend has become very pronounced after the Second World War. Although its origin could be traced already in the 'thirties, it did not affect the unity of the Warsaw school at that time.

CHAPTER 2

THE WARSAW SCHOOL

The first distinguishing characteristic of the Warsaw School to appear, was the spectacular rise to prominence of formal and mathematical logic. This was due to Leśniewski and Łukasiewicz who jointly share the honour of being the founders of the Warsaw school. Its achievements have by now become widely known, even outside the narrow circle of professional logicians. Some of their works have been translated or rewritten in one of the world-languages, others have been competently summarised and reviewed, particularly in the columns of *Journal of Symbolic Logic*. The most important results have been incorporated, after the Second World War, in all contemporary textbooks of logic. There is no need, therefore, to give here another survey of its achievements. For the purpose of this study it is enough to indicate the most outstanding of them and to emphasise those of their features which were philosophically important and became a point at issue in the post-war period.

THE LOGICIANS

From this viewpoint Leśniewski's system still holds its high rank of importance and philosophical significance [24]. In the inter-war period he was a power second to none and he influenced deeply both the logicians, including Łukasiewicz, and the philosophers, among the latter Kotarbiński, who ever since has emphatically recognised his indebtedness to Leśniewski [25]. Tarski, through whom, one may almost say, Leśniewski became known internationally, has also repeatedly testified to Leśniewski's inspiration in his own research [26]. Kotarbiński's and Tarski's tribute could be extended to others. In fact, hardly anyone who spent his formative or mature years at that time in Warsaw escaped being influenced, in some way or other, by this extraordinary mind, extreme in whatever views he held, and whose combined power of criticism and of invention caused both admiration and fear.

Leśniewski's position was based rather on personal contacts than on what he published. For he published little during his Warsaw period and what he did was written in a highly condensed manner; some parts of it could be followed only by those fully acquainted with Leśniewski's ideas and methods. He was a perfectionist for whom nothing, either in his own or other people's work, was good enough. Leśniewski died prematurely and during the war his manuscripts were destroyed. The efforts to reconstruct Leśniewski's system are being made both in Poland and abroad [27].

Leśniewski seemed to have influenced the philosophy of the Warsaw school by some of his philosophical views and by his practice. His practice was an almost ruthless, radical formalism, to which he adhered not for its own sake, but as an

15

instrument of conveying meanings and intuitions otherwise doomed, as he felt, to ambiguities and distortions. Formalism was to him the only effective method of making unequivocal philosophical statements and of consistent reasoning, free from the pitfalls of contradictions. He was thus one of the decisive influences in accepting the view, hotly contested by traditionalistic philosophers, that there is in formalism a creative power that liberates the mind from many evils which beset philosophy in the past.

Leśniewski was able to arouse and to establish respect for formalism by his unusual technical inventiveness and by his deep philosophical insight which he tried to express in a formalised language. During his philosophical apprenticeship in Twardowski's school he was converted to the absolute conception of truth, and became a staunch opponent of any kind of relativism which, following Twardowski, he thought to be prompted by confusion of thought or terminological ambiguities. Formal theories which he constructed were to provide an exact and adequate description of the structure of the world. This prompted the utmost care which he took in every aspect of the construction – semantical categories, axioms, formation and transformation rules, definitions – and the attention which he paid to the deduction of theorems or to the perfecting of matters of detail. Mere formalism of the Hilbertian type or Russell's logicism were of no interest to him. They could be and were interpreted as a play with meaningless symbols or a game of chess [28]. A formalised deductive theory consisted for him of clearly meaningful, intuitively valid propositions. The most important of them were those involving the word 'is' (ontology) and 'part of' (mereology), or involving the concept of class in its distributive and collective sense. Leśniewski's ontology and mereology are deductive theories of objects and relations that hold among them, and correspond in their content to the traditional ontology. They are not metaphysical theories in the sense that they do not make any assumptions about the nature of those objects. For what we know, they might be or might not be material. The axiom of ontology remains true irrespective of whether names of concrete entities, universal or empty names are substituted for its variables (on this account ontology is a more general theory than Aristotle's syllogistic). But the meaning which the axiom ascribes to the term 'is' ('ε') in its main sense makes the propositional function '$x \varepsilon y$' a true expression provided that 'x' does not admit empty or universal names as its value, or, affirmatively expressed, provided that only names of individual objects can be substituted for 'x'. Similarly in mereology the name of a part of an object clearly cannot be objectless. Consequently, ontology and mereology are particularly suited for what is known as nominalism or rather the programme of a nominalistic reconstruction of logic and science. Leśniewski is a precursor, perhaps still unsurpassed, of what later was undertaken by Chwistek, Goodman and Quine.

Leśniewski's examinations of antinomies were of high philosophical importance and exercised a powerful influence in the development of philosophy in Poland. Little of them has been left in writing and they constituted part of the 'oral tradition' of the Warsaw school, based on Leśniewski's lectures and on personal

16

contacts [29]. They inspired the distinction between an object-language and metalanguage, a theory and metatheory, and prompted the emergence of philosophical and theoretical semantics.

In the examinations of antinomies, Leśniewski's starting point was the recognition of the basic difference between an antinomy and an ordinary contradiction. The latter results from an error, from the failure to formulate fully and precisely all our premises and directives of transformation; it can be, therefore, removed by purely technical means. This cannot be done with the former. Leśniewski criticised the way in which antinomies were eliminated in *Principia Mathematica*, because the theory of types was a kind of a police-theory or of prophylactic, as Tarski put it, to guard the deductive sciences against the known and other possible antinomies. It cured the symptoms without touching the cause of the disease.

An antinomy differs from a contradiction in that the former does not result from an error or imprecision, but follows in a valid manner from the premises and rules of inference, which we believe to be true. The elimination of antinomies, of any possible antinomy, requires, therefore, a re-examination of these premises and rules of inference. Leśniewski's system of logic and foundations of mathematics was such a re-examination (It has been shown convincingly that the logical antinomies cannot be reproduced in Leśniewski's ontology) [30]. It included the theory of semantical categories which, technically speaking, corresponds to the role played by Russell's theory of types, but otherwise differs from it. The theory of semantical categories was not added to the system of logic, but the system itself grew out of the theory and owes to it many of its peculiar characteristics. Moreover, the theory of semantical categories is not concerned with logical objects such as individuals, classes, relations; it classifies and orders logical constituents of language, hence its name and immediate philosophical relevance. In concrete applications the signs and expressions belonging to different semantical categories are made apparent by being enclosed in different kinds of brackets, the use of which is as much restricted and fixed as that of other expressions. In Leśniewski's words, the theory of semantical categories did not replace the hierarchy established by the simplified theory of types, which for him lacked intuitive justification, but 'intuitively undermined' such assumptions and consequence relations that together lead to contradictions. As Leśniewski said, he would feel bound to accept the theory of semantical categories, if he wished to speak sense, were there no antinomies whatsoever in the world [31].

After his Lwów period Leśniewski hardly ever said anything on philosophical subjects. Unlike Leśniewski, Łukasiewicz spoke often on these matters. Compared with Leśniewski, Łukasiewicz enjoyed the reputation of being a logician with pronounced philosophical interest. This opinion cannot be accepted without qualification.

Łukasiewicz admired formalistic methods irrespective of what philosophical purpose and intentions they served. Formal logic was not to him a method or an instrument, but an autonomous discipline, to be studied for its own sake. The importance of this discipline was increased in his eyes by the fact that it carried philosophical implications and provided useful techniques for mathematics. But if that were not the case, formal logic would still possess an intrinsic value. Łukasiewicz was critical of Hilbert's formalism, because it deprived formal logic of its independent status, subordinated it to mathematics and transformed it into some kind of mechanical device for getting results [32].

This criticism was prompted by the consideration that formal logic has achieved a degree of precision which mathematics cannot emulate and that by making of formal logic a maid-servant of mathematics the standards of precision achieved by formal logic are being debased. In fact, however, Łukasiewicz shared Hilbert's approach to formalistic methods; he valued them because they did get results. He was fascinated by what can be done with symbols once the appropriate techniques are worked out and he did not spurn any of them, as Leśniewski did, since they were considered in some sense or other philosophically unsound. Łukasiewicz rejected the assumption of the Lwów school which required that basic logical concepts should be philosophically examined before they are accepted and made use of. In a discussion with Adam Żółtowski, representing the traditional trend in philosophy, he said plainly that this was an unfounded presumption of philosophy.

This attitude was probably responsible for the influence Łukasiewicz exercised on the mathematicians in Poland; he provided them with methods that they found useful in their own work. While Leśniewski, who became a mathematician and devoted his life to the task of securing a safe and consistent foundation for mathematics was more or less ignored by the mathematicians, Łukasiewicz, in spite of not being a mathematician *sensu stricto,* did play a considerable role in the development of mathematical thought in Poland. He was particularly influential with the Warsaw mathematical school grouped round the editors of *Fundamenta Mathematicae* [33].

Within classical logic Łukasiewicz's work was concentrated on the propositional calculus and the theory of *A-I-E-O* relations (Aristotle's syllogistic), of which he was recognised an undisputed master and to which he gave their modern form, unsurpassed in simplicity, clarity and formal precision. The publication of *Elements of Mathematical Logic* established his authority in very wide circles in Poland and the appearance of *Untersuchungen über den Aussagenkalkül,* written together with Tarski, marked the beginning of his international reputation. But the full recognition abroad came later, not until the years following the end of the Second World War, when the Republic of Eire generously offered him hospitality in Dublin. His creative power remained almost unaffected by the progress of age and he died like Euler, working and making plans for future work [34].

Łukasiewicz became acquainted with the modern propositional calculus probably through Frege and there is no doubt whatsoever that Frege influenced him deeply, both by his logical and philosophical ideas. Under Frege's influence he became a Platonist in logic, the position which he rejected as 'mythology' in his later years, and to which he again returned later still [35]. He also thought

Frege's calculus to be superior to that of Russell-Whitehead and perfected it considerably, in particular by reducing the number of axioms from six to three (compared with four axioms of *Principia Mathematica* after one had been found deducible from the others by Bernays and Łukasiewicz working independently of each other). He devised a symbolism of his own, based upon a suggestion of Chwistek, the now widely known CN calculus, making it possible to dispense with dots and brackets, and, consequently, constituting an essential step forward in the strict formalisation of logic. He constructed other propositional calculi and their subsequent investigation greatly contributed to the understanding of the structure of formal theories. Łukasiewicz's interest in the propositional calculus was based on the belief that the calculus of propositions is the fundamental logical discipline and the 'deepest foundation' of all deductive sciences. The whole structure of logic rests on it and mathematics rests on logic. If there are different logics of propositions, irreducible to each other – and many-valued logics have established this fact – there must be different calculi of predicates, and, consequently, different theories of sets and different arithmetics [36].

Apart from the axiomatic method, he worked out with Tarski's assistance the matrix method as a general method of constructing formal calculi, investigated the consistency, independence, and completeness of logistic systems, and devised new methods of providing proofs to this effect. He initiated a vast body of investigations on the extended and restricted propositional calculi, as well as on calculi with single axioms (based on Sheffer's stroke, equivalence or implication as primitive terms), and himself achieved important results in this field. While some of his discoveries should be credited to Łukasiewicz himself, others could have been made only because he worked with a team of logicians of great brilliance. One of them was Tarski. Others were Stanisław Jaśkowski (born 1906), Adolf Lindenbaum (1909–1941), Andrzej Mostowski (born 1913), Mojżesz Presburger, Jerzy Słupecki (born 1904), Bolesław Sobociński (born 1906), Mordchaj Wajsberg, all of whom left their mark and contributed to the achievements of the logical school as a whole. The team work was an essential and characteristic feature of the school and one of the secrets of its success. The collaboration was so close and intimate that it is often hard, if not impossible, to say, who should be credited with what. The team spirit without depreciating individual merits, those of Łukasiewicz and Tarski in particular, is a tribute to the disinterestedness and purposiveness of all [37].

The rich crop of particular and general results not only enriched our knowledge of formal structures but also constituted a prerequisite of the emergence of metalogic. This term occurs already in *On the Principle of Contradiction in Aristotle* (1910). Łukasiewicz used it to refer to investigations on the relations between logical principles which may lead, as he suggested, to various logical systems, including non-Aristotelian ones, in a similar fashion as the investigations on the parallel axiom had led to the construction of non-Euclidean geometries [38].

The choice of the term 'metalogic' might have been also prompted by the distinction between 'mathematics' and 'metamathematics' made a few years earlier in Germany to differentiate between two parts of Hilbert's programme. Hilbert tried to show: firstly, that the whole of mathematics can be presented as a system of formulae derived from axioms according to some fixed rules; secondly, that this system is consistent. 'Metamathematics' was the name given to the investigations and arguments which were expected to secure the proof of consistency. As Hilbert conceived it, metamathematics was to make use – apart from other restrictions – only of the very simplest logical operations. Metalogic was conceived differently. Some of its seminal ideas can be traced to Leśniewski's lectures at the University of Warsaw from the early 'twenties onwards and to the stimulus which he provided in scientific discussions. Metalogic grew out of the critical examination of the principles and methods used in the construction of deductive systems, which also included investigations on the consistency of these systems as one of its important tasks. In view of the generality of these examinations they were known at first by the name of 'methodology of deductive sciences'. In the course of time this conception turned out to be too narrow. On the one hand, there arose the need to differentiate between the language of the systems considered and the language in which the methodological investigations were carried out (the language and meta-language); on the other, various special concepts, created for the purpose of investigating the construction and structure of deductive formalised systems, called for critical examination and systematisation (the theory and the meta-theory). In the late 'twenties these facts were widely recognised. The appearance of Łukasiewicz's *Elements of Mathematical Logic* made them more pronounced and the publication of Łukasiewicz's and Tarski's *Untersuchungen über den Aussagenkalkül* showed the metalogic in the process of its creation by the sheer weight and number of results and efforts at their systematisation.

The decisive step was taken by Tarski, who, from the evaluation of methods applied in the construction of deductive theories, passed to investigating these theories as wholes and to the elaboration of concepts necessary for this task. In his papers Tarski avoided the expression 'metalogic' and used instead that of 'metatheory' or 'metamathematics'. This was prompted by his conviction that every deductive theory, and consequently also every logical system, is a mathematical discipline. 'Metamathematics' was, therefore, a more general term than 'metalogic'. As to its meaning, 'metamathematics' in Tarski's sense differed considerably from that in Hilbert's [39].

Łukasiewicz's second major contribution to logic was his research into its history and the encouragement which he gave to others to follow suit. Łukasiewicz's interest in the history of logic dated from the time when he was still a follower of the Lwów school. His acquaintance with modern formal logic constituted, however, a decisive turning point; only then did he realise that the existing works on the history of logic had no scientific value [40]. His most important contributions concern the logic of the Stoics, which he rescued from contemptuous oblivion restoring it to its true greatness, and Aristotle's syllogistic, which he liberated from its distorting accretions accumulated through centuries, and presented in its original formal and modern formalised form. The interest in Aristotle's logic, which had occupied his mind since the early 'twenties, was brought to its fruition in the first edition of *Aristotle's Syllogistic*. He died before the second edition, supplemented by an exposition of Aristotle's modal logic, appeared in print. His life-long concern with Aristotle's logic was closely bound with many of his own discoveries and testified to the fact that historical research is fruitful in more than one respect.

Łukasiewicz found followers and collaborators in Poland, among whom Jan Salamucha (1903–1944) and J. M. Bocheński (born 1902) were the most distinguished. The first examined the concept of deduction in Aristotle and Thomas Aquinas, St. Thomas' proof *ex motu* for the existence of God, Ockham's propositional calculus, and the problems of antinomies in medieval logic [41]. Before the war the second published several contributions on ancient and medieval logic, to become in the post-war period an internationally recognised authority on the subject [42]. Other contributions which were prompted or influenced by Łukasiewicz's historical research, came from Zbigniew Jordan, Maria Kokoszyńska, and Konstanty Michalski [43].

Łukasiewicz conceived the idea that means should be provided to equip an able young man, willing to undertake the task, with the necessary knowledge in classical philology, history and formal logic in order that he might devote his entire life to the rewriting of the history of logic. This idea was not and could not be implemented; the task clearly overreaches at present the strength of body and mind of any single man [44]. But however unfeasible Łukasiewicz's idea was, his insistence and efforts have achieved wonders. Since he spoke for the first time on the logic of the Stoics in 1923, a steady output of studies began to follow, first a trickle in Poland and Germany, later, in particular after the Second World War, a gathering stream all over the world. Many contributors recognised their indebtedness to Łukasiewicz and hardly anyone can ignore what he had to say on the subject [45]. In Poland after the Second World War the interest in the history of logic revived, but little work, based on the study of original sources, has been done so far.

Łukasiewicz's greatest achievement, as is now widely recognised, is the discovery of many-valued logics. The fact that they do arouse considerable controversies – concisely and suggestively summarised in the Introduction to J. B. Rosser's and A. R. Turquette's *Many-Valued Logics* – perhaps only enhances the audacity not so much of the idea itself, entertained before Łukasiewicz, but of working it out and of establishing many-valued logics as consistent formal structures [46]. The main facts concerning the logical discovery are easy to ascertain. The L_3 was established by Łukasiewicz by the matrix method in 1920 [47], that is, before E. L. Post's celebrated paper was published. The L_n followed in 1922, according to Łukasiewicz's own statement, but was not published until 1929, that is after Post's generalisation [48]. The mutual independence of Post and Łukasiewicz is evident from their respective publications, from the differences in the approach, formal in the case of Post, philosophical in that of Łukasiewicz, as well as in their respective treatment of the designated truth-values. In its abstract form the L_n

system was presented in Łukasiewicz's and Tarski's *Untersuchungen über den Aussagenkalkül,* its philosophical origin and implications were examined in Łukasiewicz's *Philosophische Bemerkungen zu mehrwertigen Systemen des Aussagenkalküls.* A primitive base of L_3 was established by Wajsberg in 1929 and the axioms of a full L_3 were given by Słupecki in 1936 [49]. Finally, in the 'fifties Łukasiewicz examined L_4 more closely by the matrix method in *Aristotle's Syllogistic* and *A System of Modal Logic* [50].

The idea prompting Łukasiewicz to construct L_3 originated from his studies of Aristotle's logic and his interest in providing a consistent basis for the thesis of indeterminism. The latter interest is apparent from first to last in his attempts to formulate a theory of contingency which would allow the acceptance of the existence of true contingent propositions [51]. Probably already in 1910, when he wrote *On the Principle of Contradiction in Aristotle*, he came to the conclusion that the thesis of indeterminism and the principle of bivalence, or rather that of the excluded middle, as he then saw it, were incompatible. He stated this view in an address delivered at Warsaw University in 1918 and again in a much fuller form in 1922; the former was recently reprinted, the latter was never published and perished during the Warsaw rising [52]. Besides his indeterministic convictions, at the source of the discovery of L_3 was Łukasiewicz's concern with modal logic. He was prompted by the intuition, which has turned out to be right, that a system of modal logic cannot be accommodated within L_2.

Łukasiewicz's conviction concerning the incompatibility of indeterminism and of the principle of bivalence was strengthened by one of Kotarbiński's studies, first published in 1913. In fact Kotarbiński went further than that and came very close to the idea of a three-valued logic. If a man is free, Kotarbiński argued, *i.e.* is able to make choices and bring about what without his action would not materialise, there must be things in the Universe which may or may not happen, an 'ambivalent possibility', as he described it. A statement about an ambivalent possibility cannot, therefore, be either true or false; it constitutes a 'third kind of propositions', different from those which are true or false. Kotarbiński rejected expressly the principle of bivalence, that a 'given proposition is either true or false', which 'unlawfully passes off for the principle of the excluded middle'. The latter is valid only in so far as it states that contradictory statements cannot be false together, from which it does not follow, however, that one of them must be true. Kotarbiński argued in a Brouwerian manner that if a proposition is proved not to be false, this does not entail that it is true. He concluded: 'Every proposition is either true or false or neither true nor false and *quartum non datur'* [53]. He was not certain, however, whether this assumption does not lead to contradictions and whether the *quartum non datur* principle is not absurd [54]. Kotarbiński's essay was known to Łukasiewicz and according to his own confession strongly influenced his thoughts on the subject [55]. The seeds of L_3 were sown in the Lwów school and more than one mind participated in their cultivation.

As is well known, these seeds go back to Aristotle. Łukasiewicz's discovery carries, above all, the Aristotelian imprint and was prompted by his studies of Aristotle's logic guided by his knowledge of formal modern logic. Aristotle accepted the view that particular statements referring to some future events, *e.g.* the statement 'there will be a sea-battle to-morrow', when pronounced to-day can be neither true nor false. Łukasiewicz drew the conclusion therefrom that they must have a third value different from truth and falsehood. Let us assume, in accordance with Aristotle's suggestion, that: it is contingent that *p* (symbolically : *Tp*) if and only if it is possible that *p* and it is possible that not *p*. In Łukasiewicz's notation this definition can be written as the equivalence (*Q*):

$$Q\,T p\,K\,M p\,M\,N p.$$

Now, if a statement is either true or false, there is no true value of *p* for which *Tp* is true. The right-hand side of the equivalence is a conjunction which for both truth-values of *p* must become falsehood. A consistent theory of contingency requires that the principle of bivalence of our intuitive and classic logic is replaced by a more general principle. There is nothing to prevent us from doing it in view of the fact that the statement: 'for every *p*, *p* is either true or false', is not a theorem but a principle of logic and can be replaced by a different principle, provided that certain conditions are satisfied. On this basis Łukasiewicz proceeded to the construction of L_3, an interpretation of which was to be modal logic, the third value standing for possibility. This attempt failed and Łukasiewicz was the first to see and to recognise it. L_3 can be constructed and proved to be a consistent and complete formal system, but modal logic is not its interpretation. If we consider the theorems of L_3 as those of modal logic, some theorems of L_3 turn out to be inconsistent with the accepted meaning of modal functors, some others could not be interpreted in terms of modal logic. In particular, the theory of contingency cannot be accommodated within a three-valued modal system. If *Tp* is equivalent to *KMpMNp* and *KMpMNp* is true for some values of *p*, say α, then we can assert both *Mα* and *MNα*. However, from these assertions and a theorem due to Leśniewski follows that we have then to assert *Mp*, or, in other words, to admit that all problematic propositions are true. This destroys what Łukasiewicz called basic modal logic, a set of assumptions which must be included in any system of modal logic, if it is to make sense. The rejection of the expression *Mp*, which has to be asserted in a three-valued modal logic is a constituent of the basic modal logic [56].

Twenty years after this failure Łukasiewicz returned to his original idea and by defining certain four-valued matrices he succeeded in constructing a four-valued system of modal logic that renders faithfully, in his opinion, our intuitions associated with modal functors and includes a consistent theory of contingent propositions [57]. The theory of contingency is very ingenious but requires purely symbolical treatment. It assumes the distinction of two kinds of possibility and contingency, for which an appropriate terminology does not exist in ordinary speech (they can perhaps be described and expressed as different degrees of assertibility, associated with respective problematic and contingent statements). By means of a four-valued modal system and two kinds of possibility and contingency the existence of true contingent propositions in Aristotle's sense:

$$Q\,T\,p\,K\,M\,p\,M\,N\,p,$$

can be asserted, with the functor 'M' denoting different possibilities.

There were some other attempts, all made outside Poland – in France, the United States, and the USSR – to find an interpretation or to make use of the L_n in the calculus of probability, quantum mechanics, set theory, and the theory of electronic circuits. Neither was fully successful and neither contributed substantially to the development of the branch of science which was to benefit from it [58]. Thus, at present, the interpretation of L_4 in terms of modal logic is the only example of L_n being something else but a purely formal structure. Moreover, this instance is not yet safely established. Hence some logicians look askance at the many-valued logics, as Leśniewski did. Leśniewski considered as useless such consistent deductive theories as enable us to prove an ever increasing number of theorems which are irrelevant in view of their being unrelated to reality. But the history of science provides numerous examples of abstract theories which had been developed long before any use was found for them. Moreover, there can be little doubt that Łukasiewicz's performance of a 'bold experiment' has fundamentally changed our conception of logic and provided a new insight into the nature of formal structures, including those based on the intuitive bivalent logic.

Łukasiewicz became a logician through search in philosophy for exactitude and precision in speech and thought. In the propositional calculus, greatly improved by his own achievements, he found the unsurpassed model of perfection which every science should strive for and try to emulate. Mathematics was no exception to this rule. As he saw it, modern formal logic was no branch of mathematics, but an autonomous science which set up a new ideal of scientific precision even for mathematicians. Compared with this function any other service that formal logic may render to mathematics, for instance by helping to solve otherwise very important questions of the consistency and completeness of mathematics (written 1929), has a secondary value. By raising still higher the standards of scientific procedure, formal logic makes every branch of knowledge exert itself to raise its own standards and to approximate the ideal model of formal logic. This was in Łukasiewicz's opinion the highest contribution of formal logic to science and philosophy [59].

To train one's mind in the methods of formal logic, wrote Łukasiewicz, is to allow scales to fall from one's eyes. 'One notices distinctions where there is none to the others and one sees nonsense where others look for deep mysteries'. Then comes the realisation that one has not learnt to think logically, precisely, consistently, thoroughly, neither in philosophy nor in science, neither in public nor in personal life [60]. Certain conclusions follow inevitably. Much that has been done in the past in philosophy has no scientific value and to continue in the old habits of thought is simply a waste of time and mental energy.

This evaluation of formal logic made Łukasiewicz despair of philosophy. In an address delivered at the Second Polish Congress of Philosophy (Warsaw, 1927) Łukasiewicz gave the advice to the audience that they should forget the past and start everything again from scratch. If all human disciplines were ordered according to the scientific precision of their methods, philosophy would have to be placed at the bottom. Philosophical systems of the past might have some aesthetic and moral value, they might occasionally have made a true and intuitively justifiable observation, but scientific value they have none. The philosophers' failure to make of philosophy a science results from their neglect of logic. They do not adhere to and do not follow the logical procedure or they base their views on wrong theories of logic. Philosophy has thus fallen into the abyss of vain speculations from which only formal logic, and the axiomatic method in particular, can rescue it.

Not all philosophical problems could be examined in the suggested manner, but not all philosophical problems have a definite sense. Those which are concerned with the essences of the world, with the mythological entities like Plato's ideas or Kant's *Dinge an sich,* cannot be formulated in a comprehensible, clear, and unambiguous manner. Questions concerning the structure of the world – time, space, causality, determinism, indeterminism, teleology – are a different matter; to these questions the axiomatic method can be applied. While the axiomatic method provides an instrument by means of which scientific philosophical theories can be constructed, experience and natural sciences would be used to verify them and to revise continually the basic concepts and assumptions of these theories. The latter would pave the way for a philosophical synthesis, a truly scientific and formally sound view of the world, to guide us in our efforts to improve ourselves and the world we live in [61].

This makes it clear that Łukasiewicz's conception of philosophy substantially differed from that advocated by the Vienna Circle. Łukasiewicz spoke approvingly of Moritz Schlick's and his followers' efforts to revise philosophical method by making use of formal logic, but he emphatically rejected Carnap's reduction of philosophy to logic of science. He was inclined to agree with Carnap that metaphysical propositions are meaningless, if they claim to convey knowledge about something which is over and beyond all experience (the essence of things, or things in themselves). But this is the Kantian understanding of metaphysics; there remain factual problems concerning the structure of the world which are metaphysical, whether they are so termed or not. The latter are not syntactical questions, as Carnap suggested. It is hard to see at all, how by investigating the structure of language, its formation and transformation rules, the problems as to whether the world is or is not finite in space can be solved. The same applies to the question of causality, determinism, and many others. These are questions of fact and their solution is not a matter of language. One can again agree with Carnap that there is a formal mode of speech correlated to a material mode and that some errors might be avoided by translating sentences expressed in the material mode into those clearly syntactical. But to say that by such a translation we get rid of the misleading impression, inherent in the material mode of speech, that a 'material' sentence refers to some extra-linguistic reality where no reference of this kind is in fact involved, is a dogmatic, unjustifiable statement. The sentence: 'the evening star and the morning star are identical' is correlated with: "the words 'evening star' and 'morning star' are synonymous"; their meaning, however, is quite different. The former refers to the extra-linguistic, the latter to the linguistic reality. The matter of fact involved in the former was resolved after long years of observations and could not have been decided upon by an examination concerned with the usage or by the reflections upon the meaning of the words referred to in the latter.

Finally, Carnap's view that logical and mathematical sentences are tautologies which do not say anything about the world cannot be accepted either. There are various systems of geometry and logic but one and only one of them does apply to the outside world, irrespective of the fact whether we are at present able to state which of them does. When a formal *a priori* structure is applied to reality it must be treated as any other hypothesis, *i.e.* to be verified by experience. When this is achieved, a geometrical or logical system does convey some knowledge about the outside world. Carnap's logic of science and the *Wiener Kreis* doctrine in general, Łukasiewicz stated, were risky philosophical speculations which would soon become obsolete [62].

The critical attitude to the logical positivism of the Vienna Circle was presumably reinforced by Łukasiewicz's return to Platonism in logic. Łukasiewicz discovered that formal logic displays certain paradoxical features. On the one hand, formal logic is neutral; it does not commit anyone to any particular view in ontology or in the theory of knowledge, and it can be combined with empiricism or rationalism, with realism or idealism. On the other hand, a formal logician accepts, in practice, the nominalist viewpoint. The expressions and sentences with which he deals, are considered to be names of man-made inscriptions. This should commit him to finitism; only a finite number of inscriptions can be given at any time. Finitism makes, however, the validity of logic dependent on certain empirical facts, which is unacceptable, and is actually incompatible with the logician's practice. There is no longest logical thesis, as there is no largest natural number. Moreover, it can be easily shown that in the two-valued propositional calculus the class of all theorems is infinite in Dedekind's sense. The nominalistic outward appearances of formal logic mask metaphysical problems concealed in the foundations of logic [63]. How should they be solved?

The answer belongs to philosophy and not to logic. Łukasiewicz never said that it is either too complex or impossible to give a theory which would do without postulated abstract entities, but he was inclined to accept their existence on the ground of what is implied by logical constructions and by the insight they provide. We believe that there are shortest possible axioms of various calculi which are to be found. In general, the logician only discovers formal structures. They appear to his mind 'as if they were a concrete and palpable object, made of the strongest material, a hundred times stronger than concrete and steel'. Nothing can be changed, created, arbitrarily decided by the logician, who by his efforts gains the knowledge of 'permanent and lasting truths'. Personally Łukasiewicz believed that they were the thoughts of God [64].

Łukasiewicz was a man of few philosophical ideas and those which he held in one period of his life seem to have differed sharply from those expounded by him in another. The one exception was his unshakeable conviction in the truth of the thesis of indeterminism. In other respects he oscillated between the extremes. Philosophically Łukasiewicz was influential in considerably strengthening certain tendencies. He has done much to inspire the respect for the use of formal logic in philosophical investigations, implying some restrictions on the range of problems discussed and a sharp distinction between what can be scientifically examined and what does not lend itself to such treatment. He also strengthened the methodological orientation of Polish philosophy and its absorption in the problems of science. He was a moderate supporter of scientism; he believed and inspired trust in the methods and achievements of science, both in their theoretical and practical aspects. In general, he seems to have been a power in so far as some intellectual trends were concerned and to have exercised little influence in matters concerning the philosophical programme and methodological procedures. What he wished philosophers to accomplish was not feasible. He underrated the difficulties of reducing philosophical problems to the form which would provide a possibility of their solution by a purely deductive method, and also those connected with the verification of axiomatised philosophical systems. Practically nobody tried to put these ideas into effect. What was widely accepted was Łukasiewicz's criticism of the state of philosophy, his diagnosis of its causes and his belief that much could be improved by sharpening the philosopher's tools with the assistance of formal logic.

Tarski (born 1902) from the beginning enjoyed the advantages and disadvantages of his intellectual background. Unlike his teachers he was by training a mathematician and logician, and only afterwards a philosopher [65]. In his philosophical views he was influenced by Kotarbiński, to whom the collection of his pre-war papers, translated into English, is dedicated. But what he took from philosophy he repaid with interest.

Already his first contribution [66], in which he showed that, granted the use of functions with propositional variables and of the universal quantifier, all the propositional functors can be defined in terms of the equivalence (Leśniewski adopted Tarski's discovery in his protothetic), secured him recognition and his reputation has been rising ever since. While for Leśniewski logic and metalogic constituted an organic whole, and Łukasiewicz associated them closely together, Tarski early realised that their respective domains differ not only by the degree of abstraction but also by methods appropriate to each of them. The rise in volume and importance of metalogical research, as well as construction of the conceptual framework and methodological tools in metalogic, are bound indissolubly in Poland with Tarski's name.

The shift of interest towards metalogic, which took place everywhere after the publication of Gödel's celebrated paper, in Poland only enhanced the tendency previously initiated by Tarski. Tarski moved through the unexploited land of metalogic, improved whatever he touched, framed new notions, discovered new methods and ideas, gathered a rich harvest of 'incidental' results from the application of his analysis to a variety of subjects belonging to logic, mathematics and applied mathematics. In the late 'twenties he was the first, or one of the first, to introduce an informal axiomatic method to metalogical investigations. Those on the concept of truth in formalised languages, first published in 1933 but dating back to 1931, are based on an axiomatised metatheory. The power of the new methods was made apparent and the importance of a general metatheory of deductive systems enhanced when Tarski showed that some mathematical problems might be solved by metamathematical methods and that the examination of classes of deductive systems (calculus of systems) opens new vistas to the knowledge of formal structures [67].

Metalogic passed through several stages of development. At first, it was not clearly differentiated from logic itself and under the name of methodology of deductive systems was mainly concerned with the investigations of the consistency, completeness and independence of axioms. When it emerged from this stage to the status of an autonomous discipline, it was conceived as the study of the formal aspects of formalised deductive systems (formalised theories). After the publication of Carnap's *Logische Syntax der Sprache* (1934), these investigations used to be called 'logical syntax'.

Outside Poland, in particular in the Vienna Circle, metalogic and any metatheoretical examination were identified with logical syntax. This carried certain important philosophical implications. They were connected with the construction of various artificial formalised languages by means of which philosophical problems were to be examined and elucidated. The construction of artificial formalised languages was based on the assumption, prompted by the identification of metalogic with logical syntax, that its object-language (in this case – the ordinary speech) can be specified by its formal characteristics. In other words, it disregarded the fact that the expressions of everyday language and scientific discourse have a meaning, denote something or refer to some state of affairs, and that they are true or false. Artificial formalised languages which eliminated these semantical notions were consequently bound to be fragmentary and to constitute an inadequate medium for the examination of philosophical problems. As this was not at first realised by the inventors of artificial languages, certain serious philosophical errors became inevitable.

Tarski's important contribution to philosophy in Poland, and later also to philosophy in general, was his early recognition of the fact that logical syntax (he then called it 'morphology of language') constitutes only a part, though an important one, of metatheoretical investigations. The decisive step was taken in 1931 when he supplemented the concept of syntax by that of semantics. While logical syntax investigates formal characteristics of formalised theories, the subject matter of semantics is the relation between the expressions of language and the objects which they denote or to which they refer, that is, between language and extra-linguistic reality. In Tarski's words, the 'semantical concepts (*i.e.* of theoretical semantics) serve to set up the correlation between the names of expressions and the expressions themselves.' [68] The idea of semantics is general; it applies equally to the ordinary speech and to formalised theories. Theoretical semantics (semantics of the formalised theories) was in fact established after the need of semantical concepts was revealed by the examination of ordinary speech.

The term 'semantics' was taken in Poland from grammar or rather from that part of it which is called descriptive or historical semantics and which deals with the questions how it came about that words mean something and designate something, how their meanings change in the course of time and how they can be divided into classes according to what they mean or designate [69]. The term was adopted from grammar, but its use was prompted by extra-linguistic considerations. These emerged from the examination of antinomies, particularly those of the liar, the Grelling and Nelson antinomy of heterological terms and Richard's antinomy of definability, all of them resulting from the usage of 'self-referring' terms. They drew attention to the logical analysis of language and to what Kotarbiński called 'semantical relations'. Already in the late 'twenties a rudimentary logical theory of language (philosophical semantics) was worked out; it included the examination of the concept of meaning, designation, name, expression, definition and semantical categories as its main elements [70]. These studies were greatly influenced by Husserl, and, above all, by Leśniewski's penetrating criticism and original ideas. In particular Leśniewski devoted to the examination of antinomies much of his inventive energy and Tarski took advantage of Leśniewski's views on this matter [71]. Once again antinomies turned out to be a blessing in disguise. While antinomies of classes, and, above all, Russell's antinomy, inspired efforts to construct a consistent formalised system of logic and mathematics, the antinomy of the liar was the starting point for the rise of philosophical and theoretical semantics.

The important conclusion which emerged from the examination of semantical antinomies stated that a semantically closed language and one within which the laws of logic hold, must be inconsistent and provide a breeding ground for antinomies. It should be understood that a semantically closed language is any natural or artificial language which does not differentiate between expressions about which we speak from those in which we speak, *e.g.* between object- and meta-language. In a semantically closed language the object- and meta-language coincide; the former thus contains its own semantics.

Semantics is a relative concept. While we can speak of semantical concepts in general – such as meaning, denotation, reference, definition, truth – semantics is always related to a particular language and each language has its own semantics, not to be confused, under the penalty of inconsistencies or errors, either with the language itself or with its structure (syntax), the form, arrangement and composition of the expressions of this language.

Once this is recognised, semantical antinomies can be, in principle, eliminated and semantics of any particular language constructed in a logically unobjectionable manner. There is, however, an important difference in this respect between natural and artificial languages. The logically unobjectionable and materially adequate use of semantical concepts depends on the structure and the vocabulary of the object language. We can construct the semantics of a language by exact methods if and only if this language is exactly specified, and, as a matter of fact, only formalised languages are exactly specifiable [72]. Strictly speaking only languages of logical systems are at present formalised. But these languages have been successfully applied to mathematics, theoretical physics, and also to some branches of biology. Outside this field, and this includes, of course, everyday language which provides means of scientific and philosophical discourse, the use of semantical concepts can have only an approximate character. Both the vocabulary and the structure of everyday language are not formally specifiable and depend on extra-linguistic factors. Apart from the structure, it has, as it were, 'depth'. On this account Tarski doubted at first (1933) whether a consistent and fruitful use of semantical concepts, in particular that of a true sentence, can be made in everyday language [73].

This feeling was not shared by philosophers. Neither a scientist nor a scholar nor a philosopher can do without semantical concepts. They would have to keep silent if they were to dispense with terms such as 'meaning', 'denotation', 'definition', 'true' and 'false statement'. The realisation that they might get involved in contradictions did not prevent them from using these terms. To be provided with a general theory of semantical concepts, their exact definitions and general characteristics, gave the scientist and philosopher a firmer hold of these concepts in the examination of their own problems. Theoretical semantics was, therefore, accepted as a discipline of considerable philosophical significance. In particular, as has already been mentioned, theoretical semantics spared philosophy in Poland committing some errors to which other philosophers of language fell victim. The question of the correct usage of language was never dissociated from its semantical aspects and absorbed by the syntax of language [74].

The philosophical significance of theoretical semantics was the more obvious owing to the fact that Tarski's demonstration of the uses of semantics was made in connection with his efforts to provide a satisfactory definition of truth. His semantic conception of truth is universally known and widely accepted; only some of its salient features will, therefore, be considered.

As his starting point Tarski accepted the classical conception of truth, also known under the name of the correspondence theory of truth, which was in agreement with the tradition of the Warsaw school. The Warsaw school, however, went further and accepted what used to be called the 'absolute conception of truth' [75]. By this qualifying term several things were meant. The expression 'every true proposition is absolutely true' meant the same as 'no proposition is relatively true'. Since the relativistic conception of truth implies that in the sentence ' 'p' is true', the term 'true' is not a full predicate, the absolute conception of truth can also be described as the view which holds the contrary opinion, namely that in the expression ' 'p' is true' the term 'true' is a full predicate. Finally, the absolute conception of truth claims that a proposition is true if and only if it states what is the fact (and not what somebody says or thinks to be the fact). The explication of this last meaning inherent in the absolute conception of truth might involve its supporters in considerable difficulties, and this is the point where Leśniewski's stimulating and original ideas on the matter and Tarski's partial definition of truth – the (T) schema – prove their usefulness. Tarski's partial definition of truth states in a clearer and unambiguous manner what the supporters of the classical conception of truth (in its Aristotelian version) in general, and those of the absolute conception in particular, had in mind [76].

In the summary of main results obtained in his celebrated essay *The Concept of Truth in Formalized Languages,* Tarski expressed the view that the only way of overcoming confusions and contradictions resulting from the application of semantical concepts to everyday language is to reform this language. He wanted this reform to be done in a manner which would finally make the language of everyday life closely resemble formalised languages. In a later essay he approached this subject from a slightly different angle. Perhaps, he said, nonformalised languages with an exactly specified structure could be constructed to replace everyday language in scientific discourse or at least in a comprehensive branch of empirical science [77].

Tarski's suggestion was not followed in Poland, where analytical trends prevailed over the tendency to construct formal artificial languages. The philosophers did not share Tarski's gloomy evaluation of the position prevailing in colloquial speech. In their opinion the worst confusions and the more obvious antinomies can be avoided by fully accepting and carefully adhering to Tarski's distinctions between the object- and meta-language, as well as by applying self-imposed restrictions in the use of semantical concepts. Subsequently, partial reform and not a total reconstruction was undertaken. With the differentiation of various levels of discourse and the distinction of the syntactical structure and semantical aspect of the ordinary speech, philosophical problems appeared in a new light and had to be re-examined. The impact of theoretical semantics on philosophy was lasting but of necessity limited in scope. To use Tarski's own words, theoretical semantics could be applied 'only with certain approximation'. The situation with which philosophy was confronted after the publication of *The Concept of Truth in Formalized Languages* did not differ essentially 'from that which arises when we apply laws of logic to arguments in everyday life' [78].

Leon Chwistek (1884–1944) was the most colourful and the least influential logician of the period between the two wars. His unconventional, if not eccentric, personality set him apart and made him tread a path of his own. His intellectual background differed from and his interests seemed to be only marginally connected with what was being done in the Warsaw school.

Chwistek spent most of his life in Cracow which, with Warsaw and Lwów linked by the ties of a common school of philosophical thinking, was the third centre of logical research. While in Warsaw logic, being an autonomous discipline, kept close to philosophy and philosophy to logic, this was not the case in Cracow. The philosophers there adhered to more traditional ways and only mathematicians showed interest in modern formal logic. Among the latter the most distinguished was Stanisław Zaremba (1863–1942), one of Chwistek's teachers [79]. The greatest credit for spreading knowledge of modern logic in Cracow was due to Jan Śleszyński (1854–1931), also a mathematician and Chwistek's teacher, whose lectures on logic published in book form by S. K. Zaremba, the son of the eminent mathematician, were widely read in Poland even when it was supplanted by better and more comprehensive textbooks. Being the concern of mathematicians, logic became a branch or an instrument of mathematics. The conviction that formal logic provides no useful knowledge but only a method was one of the ideas firmly established in Chwistek's mind.

Chwistek's personality is very apparent in everything he wrote. Although he was likeable and entertaining in personal relations, as a writer he excelled in a style that was both malicious and combative. He uttered forceful and not always just opinions of other people and their views. His knowledge was wide but often superficial. He did not take enough care to present the views which he wished to criticise in a scrupulously objective manner. He used the names of trends with which he disagreed, *e.g.* that of Cantorism, not as descriptive but as qualifying, invective-like terms. There are pages upon pages in his books and articles in which he came close to journalism, which are *geistreich* but rambling. Chwistek indulged sometimes in modes of expression and habits of thought that the Warsaw school set out to eradicate from academic philosophy.

It would be wrong, however, to draw the conclusion that Chwistek exercised only harmful influences. His merits were as numerous as his demerits; those who saw clearly the latter did not disregard the former [80]. The ultimate reason why he did not play a role commensurate with his achievements in Polish philosophy was the fact that he attached greater significance to certain philosophical problems than did the Warsaw school and other Polish philosophers under the influence of this school.

Chwistek was probably the only philosopher in Poland who not only watched and followed the dispute concerning the foundations of mathematics between intuitionism, formalism, and logicism, but also took a serious interest and part in it. When a young man he attended a lecture given by Henri Poincaré in Göttingen after which he remained under the spell of 'constructivist' ideas [81]. This was the starting point of a long and sustained effort recorded in a number of contributions, the final result of which is the system presented in English in *The Limits of Science*.

Chwistek was the first Polish logician to gain recognition abroad by his criticism of *Principia Mathematica*, in particular of its theory of types and its extra-logical axioms (those of infinity and reducibility). In this connection he worked out the theory of constructive types, based on the reduction of the notion of class to that of propositional function (Chwistek was the first to see that this can be done), and the simplified theory of types. The latter was very important as a working semi-intuitive tool, particularly in relation to the theory of sets. To-day they belong to the history of logic, the second having been incorporated into the body of common knowledge. From the point of view reached by Chwistek some years later, the simplified theory of types has outlived its usefulness. The principle involved was to be included in a more comprehensive theory which replaced the hierarchy of types within a language by a hierarchy of languages [82].

As Chwistek saw it, the problem of establishing consistent foundations for mathematics required the reconciliation of several not easily reconcilable principles. First, the principle of nominalism: to recognise the existence of only such objects as are given in immediate experience and with respect to which no serious question or doubt can be raised. These are clearly some objects of the physical world. The implementation of the principle of nominalism is a prerequisite for showing that in the impressive structure of mathematics no more complicated and less obvious operations are ultimately involved than those of laying brick on brick. Second, the principle of constructivism or *la règle de Poincaré*: never to consider any objects or a class of them which are not capable of construction. It is true that a great majority of mathematicians has become reconciled to un-constructive objects and that the assumption of the existence of such objects does not need to lead to contradiction (*e.g.* Russell's universal class of real numbers), but the presence of these metaphysical, idealistic suppositions is a fundamental flaw in the whole structure [83]. Third, the principle of formalism: without formalisation there is no construction of deductive theories by exact methods. The only alternative to formalisation is the use of everyday language with its confusions and pitfalls. Everyday language can never be made accurate and Poincaré was wrong and Hilbert was right when he wished to transform the entire content of mathematics into symbolic formulas derived from axioms in a mechanical manner. Fourth, the principle of 'completeness': every part of classical mathematics, irrespective of the way in which it has been acquired, should be included in the system. Such a hypothesis as Cantor's actually infinite has its source in fantasy. It should be shown that what is really of value in it can be absorbed in a system based on the above enumerated principles.

This was the plan on whose implementation Chwistek was engaged since 1928 and in this undertaking he was assisted by three collaborators, Jerzy Herzberg, Władysław Hetper, and Stanisław Skarżeński, none of whom survived the war. The first step was the creation of what Chwistek called 'elementary semantics', which, besides its name, has nothing in common with semantics in Tarski's sense. Chwistek claimed that in Hilbert's metamathematics there is contained an intuitive semantics, *i.e.* the rules for the construction of the simplest possible expressions from given elements (letters or signs). This intuitive semantics is formalised and expanded into a system of syntax in terms of which the propositional calculus and the theory of classes are constructed. On this basis the axiomatisation of classical mathematics which assumes no non-constructive objects is finally undertaken. If successful, and this matter must be left to the mathematician to judge, it would provide a proof of the consistency of mathematics. In this, more than in anything else, lies the importance of Chwistek's system. The opinion has been expressed that Chwistek's work represents the most important attempt ever made to establish such a proof [84].

The question might be asked why Chwistek undertook this enormous task and what philosophical significance he attached to it. He himself answered this question at length. The proof of consistency would put it beyond any possible doubt that a rationalistic view of the world can prevail against confused metaphysics and stem the rising wave of anti-rationalism. He traced the origins of modern anti-rationalism down to Hegel and among its representatives counted Nietzsche, Bergson, Husserl, the pragmatists, and many eminent scientists –

33

such as Weyl and Eddington – who became affected by the intellectual atmosphere which he considered hostile to rational thought. A rational view of the world is based on simple and clear truths derived from experience and exact reasoning, and ultimately on what Chwistek called 'sound reason', not to be confused with common sense. While common sense accepts what seems 'obvious and inevitable in a given society', sound reason prompts both criticism and constructive thought. Hume, Comte, Marx, and Mach were its great exponents. Chwistek's work, as he conceived it, was to turn the scale against anti-rationalism and restore sound reason to its place in human affairs. From this viewpoint he considered everything else done in philosophy in Poland as unimportant and ultimately irrelevant. This verdict was neither just not right. In many respects he was closer to the Warsaw school than he cared to recognise.

This review of the work accomplished by the four leading Polish logicians in the period between the two wars cannot close without a short mention of the mathematicians. The period under discussion witnessed a considerable expansion of mathematics in Poland, particularly in the domain of the theory of sets and topology [85]. The theory of sets is perhaps the most 'philosophical' branch of mathematics. The concept of class and its obscurities fall within the region where the logician, the philosopher and the mathematician meet to clarify their ideas, to revise the premises, and to make more precise the modes of reasoning they use in common. The concept of class is not the only one of this kind; the theory of relations or the notion of probability provide other examples. The wide application of statistical methods in more or less exact sciences drew attention to the mathematical theories of probability, which, with the use of statistics, come into play sooner or later.

Among the pure mathematicians, who either directly contributed to logic or whose works were widely read by students of philosophy, the names of Sierpiński, Kuratowski, Mazurkiewicz, Wilkosz (1891–1941) and Mostowski should be mentioned. As the first three were the leaders of the Warsaw mathematical school there is little wonder that the philosophers, the logicians, and the mathematicians were often lumped together into a single group to be known in the world outside as the Polish or the Warsaw school. Although confusing, this single name has the merit of throwing into relief the close and fruitful collaboration that existed at that time between the three sciences and in various ways contributed to the development of each of them.

THE PHILOSOPHERS

From the moment he began teaching philosophy at Warsaw University in 1918 Tadeusz Kotarbiński has been the most influential philosopher in Poland. Kotarbiński's intellectual leadership has been enhanced by the moral authority which he commands and which is not limited to the academic circles.

Kotarbiński's starting point was 'philosophical minimalism': the relinquishing of the consideration of great philosophical issues in order that basic philosophical concepts might be clarified and defined and scientific habits of mind firmly established. Philosophy has no methods other than those used in the deductive and empirical sciences. In a certain sense, there are even no philosophical problems. What is called 'philosophy' is a composite whole consisting of disparate, unrelated parts: psychology, logic, the theory of knowledge, methodology, ethics, aesthetics, metaphysics, philosophy of history and of Nature, sociology. It is better to give up the term 'philosophy' altogether. Specialisation is a prerequisite of making philosophy a scientific discipline [86]. The subject which Kotarbiński has chosen for himself and in which he excels is logic, the theory of knowledge and methodology. 'Logic' in this context means 'modern formal logic', which Kotarbiński accepted as a model of precision and applied in his inquiry in the elucidation of concepts and problems selected as his particular concern.

However, Kotarbiński soon left the narrow limits which he set for himself and others. In a number of essays published between 1920 and 1935 and in *Elements of the Theory of Knowledge, Formal Logic and Methodology of Science* [87] – perhaps the most widely read and the most important philosophical book of the period between the two wars – he examined various problems of the philosophy of language, logic, methodology, physics, psychology, and the humanities from the viewpoint called by him 'reism' and later 'concretism'. In its inception reism was a semantical doctrine intended to help in the elimination of pseudo-problems and in the formulation of the real ones in a clear, precise and materially valid manner. In the course of time the volume of research on various special problems, undertaken by means of semantical analysis, made of Kotarbiński a system builder. The main characteristics of his system are nominalism and materialism. While nominalism is an essential part of reism conceived as a semantical doctrine, materialism is not. As Kotarbiński himself later discovered, there were reists before him. One of them was Leibniz and another was Brentano; the latter was a dualist and the former a spiritualist [88]. Those in Poland who supported reism were not always materialists, just as all materialists were not reists.

The shortest and most precise way of describing semantical reism is to say that it provides a philosophical interpretation of the only axiom of Leśniewski's ontology [89]. This axiom states the necessary and sufficient conditions for the function '$x \, \varepsilon \, y$', in which 'ε' stands for 'is' in its main existential meaning, to be true. These conditions may be interpreted to mean that a singular proposition is true only if its subject is a genuine non-empty name. But the question, which names are genuine and non-empty and which are not is an extra-logical question, and reism is a semantical answer to it.

The thesis of semantical reism states that only names of concrete objects, either corporeal or sentient, are genuine names. All the others are apparent or quasi names. For instance the name of a relation is an apparent, objectless name, and it cannot function as subject in a sentence implying the consequence that a certain object is a relation. If the sentence: 'the relation of being a spouse is symmetrical' (R) is considered to be a substitution of the function '$x \, \varepsilon \, y$', in which the functor 'ε' carries its main meaning, the sentence (R) is false. We often use, however, the sentence (R) as some kind of shorthand expression, which stated fully would say: 'for all A and B: if A is a spouse of B, then B is a spouse of A'. This sentence contains no apparent names and is a meaningful and true statement. As it stands, a shorthand expression is neither true nor false. Its truth or falsehood can be ascertained only upon its being translated into a sentence which contains only genuine, non-empty names or variables admitting these and only these names as their value.

What has been explained on the example of the category of relations applies equally to other categories. 'Properties', 'events', 'facts', 'meanings', 'propositions', 'classes', are apparent, objectless names and sentences which imply the existence of properties, events, facts, meanings, propositions, and classes are meaningful but false, unless they are considered to be shorthand expressions. Shorthand expressions must be translated and reduced to their 'normal form' before they can be stated to be true or false. A reistic analysis of language consists in the examination of expressions which seemingly have a correct syntactical structure, but literally understood are misleading and false; in finding their semantically correct translation, which will enable us to see what problem they involve, what solution there might be, and whether they are true or false. In this manner also pseudo-problems can be eliminated and new problems revealed.

A reistic analysis of language was demonstrated in *Elements of the Theory of Knowledge, Formal Logic and Methodology of Science* on a variety of problems, including those concerning the concepts of time, space, mind, matter, as well as the concepts encountered in the humanistic studies and historical sciences. Its publication aroused many controversies and it was from that moment that reism acquired the character of a full-fledged philosophical doctrine.

The semantical doctrine of reism is a method by which all ostensible references to abstract entities can be shown either to be meaningless or reducible to expressions which imply or assume the existence only of concrete objects. This is the nominalistic programme in its modern form, initiated in the Anglo-Saxon world by Quine in 1940. Nominalism as an assumption of the philosophy of science is the view that the only values for variables admissible in the language of science are to be concrete objects or individuals, that is, entities of the lowest type in the sense of the simplified theory of types, which, of course, does not exclude using general terms in this language. Semantical reism does not say anything about these concrete objects. To say what these objects are, we have to leave the ground of semantics and go into that of ontology [90].

The ontological doctrine of reism is also called 'somatism'. The main thesis of somatism states: 'every object is a thing'. 'Thing' is a defined term and means 'a physical or sentient body' (in the non-exclusive meaning of 'or'). 'Physical' can be further analysed. 'Physical' in Kotarbiński's sense means the same as 'temporal, spatial, and resistent'. The term can be thus applied both to solids in the meaning of common sense physics, to an aggregate of such solids, to particular parts of solid bodies, and to something that is not solid in the popular sense, for instance, to an electro-magnetic field. 'Sentient' is not further analysed. 'A sentient body' designates animals, men, and also what is referred to by the term 'soul' or 'mind'. The thesis of somatism entails the thesis of pansomatism: 'every soul is a body'. Pansomatism does not prejudge whether the soul is identical with the whole organism or with one of its parts. It only holds firmly to the statement that if something is a soul, this something is a body or part of it. On the strength of pansomatism we can say there are only bodies in the Universe.

Somatism (ontological reism) has been described as materialism without matter; to formulate its assumptions it does not use the concept of matter at all. This was probably prompted by the consideration that the term 'matter' cannot be assumed as a primitive term, that it would have to be explained and defined. But this would require analysing the concept of matter and this concept belongs to physics and not to philosophy. It was not possible to take it over from physics, because the physical concept of matter was made vague by modern discoveries; it was not clear either how the physical concept of matter could be applied to sentient bodies.

These considerations also explain other peculiar features of somatism which is a materialistic doctrine in a certain sense of this term, and not in another. Somatism is clearly a monistic materialism; it implies that the statement: 'no soul is a body', is false. It is not a materialistic doctrine, if materialism is understood to mean: 'psychical phenomena are physical phenomena' or 'mind is merely the highest product of matter'. In its literal meaning the former statement is false – no object is a phenomenon whether psychical or physical – and in another, to be explicated from this abbreviated statement-like expression, it is again a scientific and not a philosophical question. The latter statement does not necessarily follow from the thesis of somatism. Other possibilities are left open and a supporter of somatism will wait for the verdict of science on this matter.

The same applies to the mechanistic or dialectic hypotheses, with either of which materialism is usually closely associated. A supporter of ontological reism is committed to neither of these hypotheses. The first of them would imply that man is a machine, and experience does not show man to be a machine; the second is a reaction to naive myths about the creation of the world and to Hegel's idealistic historiosophy, of which it did not manage entirely to free itself[91]. In the theory of knowledge reism leads to the view called 'radical realism', which is very similar to that of sensational realism. Sentences with the names of sense-data or elements (in Mach's sense) as subjects are either false or nonsensical. Such sentences are false, because no object is a sense-datum, an element or a complex of elements. A radical realist considers critical realism, phenomenalism or naive realism as a learned speculation which does not stand the test of semantical analysis. He is inclined to recognise that things he perceives may be rough or soft, sweet or bitter, white or black, in the same way as they are spatial and temporal. He is, therefore, close to the commonsense view that ascribes the primary and secondary qualities to the physical objects. What he affirms about the objects directly observed, is not necessarily truly affirmed.

37

There is a difficulty here – that of criteria which allow to distinguish a true empirical statement from a false one – but this difficulty is common to all possible theories [92].

Radical realism presupposes the reistic interpretation of psychological statements. To put it in the briefest form possible, the latter claims that all psychological statements are reducible to the schema: 'A experiences this: P', where 'A' is a name variable and 'P' is a variable admitting as substitutes any expression that refers to bodies of the outside world, including the body designated by A. Every psychological statement is based on extraspection, and never on introspection. What we call 'introspection' is in fact and on closer examination, a perception, an experience stimulated either by external or internal senses. The latter is the case when 'P' stands for an enunciation referring to the body of A [93].

Applied to various kinds of psychological statements, in particular to those in which what A experiences refers to other people's experiences (other minds), the reistic interpretation of psychological statements meets serious difficulties. These are linguistic and extra-linguistic, resulting either from the complexities involved in the translation of psychological statements into the reistic language or from the peculiarities of what for the sake of brevity is referred to as psychological phenomena. The former difficulties become also very apparent when reism is applied to praxeology, the theory of effective action, to which Kotarbiński has devoted much time and attention [94].

Kotarbiński has also a pronounced interest in ethics. One of his first publications was a critical study on utilitarianism in John Stuart Mill's and Spencer's ethics. Later other philosophical questions somehow outweighed this interest and only after the Second World War he returned to it to defend the individualistic conception of morals without religion and sanctions. Although he was influential also in this respect, he did not evolve any theory of morals and was content with the elucidation of concepts and with the disentangling of moral issues involved in social problems. He surveyed them with the zest of a social reformer, supported by the impartiality and serene detachment of a philosopher free from irrelevant prejudices, anxious to understand human nature, and deeply concerned with the dignity of man. He has lived in accordance with his views and convictions, showing forebearance to others and making high claims on himself. This has made him not only a mind respected for its achievements, but also a man loved by everyone who came in contact with him.

Ajdukiewicz has kept closer to the minimalistic programme in philosophy than Kotarbiński. His main object of interest has been logic and methodology to which later the theory of knowledge has been added. It is very difficult to summarise his writings and still more difficult to say in general terms what his views are. He is at his best as the painstaking analyst of a specific issue, which he takes great trouble to formulate and which is followed by a closely reasoned argument intended to elucidate the issue involved and to clarify the terms in its formulation. Being a philosophers' philosopher, he is a model of clarity and precision as a teacher. He is the author of many textbooks which are among the best written in Poland. He put into these textbooks much that he had learnt from others as well as what he had found himself without claiming the credit for what was new in them [95].

His main contributions to the development of philosophy in Poland in the period between the two wars can perhaps be summed up as follows. He was a trenchant critic of the nominalistic programme, which gained him the reputation, not entirely unjustifiable, of being a Platonist. He formulated the view known as 'radical conventionalism'. Having become converted to realism in the theory of knowledge – at the time of writing his essays on radical conventionalism he was, as he himself stated later, at the cross-roads of epistemological idealism and realism – he applied semantical concepts in the examination of the idealist argument, which contributed to the elucidation of the idealist paradox and initiated new methods in the examination of the problems of the theory of knowledge in general [96].

Radical conventionalism was the most widely known and the most spectacular of Ajdukiewicz's contributions. Poincaré contended that some empirical problems are insoluble unless some principles, which experience can neither prove nor disprove and which are neither true nor false, are accepted. Ajdukiewicz went a step further. According to him, all propositions accepted by us and constituting our 'view of the world' are not unequivocally determined by the data of experience, but also depend on the choice of language and its universe of meanings *(Begriffsapparatur)*, in terms of which our 'view of the world' is formulated. This happens in a language, which is closed and connected. In such a language, to put it briefly but imprecisely, everything can be said in an unequivocal manner and everything said is somehow determined by any other valid statement of this language [97].

A closed and connected language is clearly modelled on an ideal language of the formalist philosophers, like Carnap. It is not, however, an artificial language, since its structure cannot be specified solely in terms of its syntax. The empirical rules of meaning introduce sentences whose assertibility depends on extra-linguistic reality. Such a language is an essentially open language and it is hard to imagine how it could ever be connected. Ajdukiewicz soon realised that his closed and connected language was not a discovery but an invention; no natural or artificial language, as rich as his, could ever fulfil the requirements imposed upon it. He gave it up and overboard with it went the thesis of radical conventionalism. Without at least two untranslatable closed and connected languages, the thesis of radical conventionalism becomes groundless [98].

Although the idea of a closed and connected language turned out to be a fiction, it was an important contribution to the development of philosophy in Poland. At the source of Ajdukiewicz's examination stand some of Tarski's results, in particular those concerning the difficulties of providing an adequate and formally correct definition of a true statement in ordinary language. Consequently, Ajdukiewicz did not use the concept of truth and introduced only a rule of meaning which governs the use of the term 'true'. This rule does not belong either to logical syntax or to logical semantics, but to what later Ch. W. Morris called 'logical pragmatics'. This rule lays down that if a sentence *p* of the language L is an assertable sentence with respect to the rules of meaning of the language L, the user of the language L will accept also the statement: ' 'p' is true'. Although the concept of truth in the sense of logical pragmatics was not meant to replace the semantical concept of truth (in this sense radical conventionalism does not entail the relativism of truth), the limited usefulness of the former puts into relief the importance of the latter. The definition of the concept of truth in terms of logical pragmatics reinforced the realisation that the use of the predicate 'true' is not determined solely by the rules of meaning of the language in which it is applied. More generally, philosophical questions are partly of a linguistic and partly of an extra-linguistic nature. For Ajdukiewicz himself this was the starting point for the examination of the idealist position in the theory of knowledge, in which a true proposition is defined as a proposition determined by the rules of meaning. Ajdukiewicz's first contribution can be, therefore, described as the strengthening of the realistic and anti-linguistic trend, if by the latter is understood the reaction against the reduction of philosophical problems to purely linguistic questions. This can be seen, for instance, in Kokoszyńska's paper *Syntax, Semantik und Wissenschaftslogik,* in which she criticised Carnap's views on language and his reduction of philosophy to logic of science. Her criticism was based on Tarski's contributions to the philosophy of language and on the consequences to be drawn from Ajdukiewicz's investigations, which put into relief the importance of semantical and pragmatical rules for a unique characterisation of a language.

Ajdukiewicz also contributed to the realisation that the meaning of an expression is relative to the language in which it occurs not only in the obvious and trivial manner, but also in the sense that the meanings of expressions of a language constitute a structure determined by interrelated rules of meaning. Ajdukiewicz attaches great importance to his differentiation of these rules (axiomatic, deductive, empirical), but this seems to be less important than the above mentioned more general fact [99]. His insistence that language has a structure and that this structure is not exclusively formal or syntactical (for people speaking a language with the same syntax but different meaning rules would not understand each other) turned out to be fruitful. It contained the ideas from which logical pragmatics and the conception of semiotic as an instrument of philosophical inquiry were evolved.

Like other conventionalists before him, Poincaré in particular, Ajdukiewicz was impressed by two strangely contrasting facts: the 'porosity' and inadequacy of everyday language and the effective use to which language can be put by a logician or a scientist. This suggested that the search for the necessary conditions of mutual understanding – of which scientific language provides a striking example – and the elucidation of the problem of meaning in general cannot be successful unless language is considered as a structure and its structural features, formal and informal, are investigated. The view that language has a structure of its own again emphasised the importance of the linguistic aspect of philosophical problems and provided this belief, novel at that time, with a rational explanation.

Finally, very much worth emphasising is Ajdukiewicz's effort to provide a definition of meaning which does not use the concept of designation or reference. There were three reasons which prompted Ajdukiewicz to undertake this course. One has been already mentioned – the danger of antinomies resulting from using semantical concepts in semantically closed languages. The second was the observation that all terms and expressions of a language have a meaning, but not all of them designate something, and that two expressions with different meanings, *e.g.* 'the highest peak in Europe' and 'the highest peak in Switzerland', might denote the same object. The third was the controversy with Kotarbiński about universals and Ajdukiewicz's critical evaluation of the reistic assumption, held in common with logical atomism, that the concept of meaning is closely bound with that of designation. Furthermore, Ajdukiewicz rejected the view, held by logical positivists, that the vocabulary and logical syntax are sufficient to characterise a language and provide a basis for definition of meaning associated with the expressions of this language. He discovered the missing factor in the conditions under which an expression has a definite meaning, the correlation between the conditions and expressions being made explicit in empirical meaning-giving rules, the way the expressions are used and asserted, which is the basic concept of logical pragmatics. We shall return to Ajdukiewicz's theory of meaning in Part III.

Zawirski was a philosopher of great versatility. He moved with ease over the fields of logic, mathematics, physics, philosophy and combined historical with systematic interests. He has done much to keep philosophers in Poland familiar with the latest developments in mathematical logic, mathematics and physics and its philosophical implications. There was a streak of the metaphysician in him in the sense that he was attracted by wide conceptions and generalisations, for which no adequate empirical support could be given, but which fill in the gaps in our knowledge of the world and make it intelligible. He seemed to have been worried by what useful purpose philosophy might serve if it does not provide us with a *Weltanschauung*. On the other hand he was fully aware of what happens when speculations are given free rein. His apprenticeship in the Lwów school and his training in science had the upper hand, but he sympathised with the tendency to extend the scope of philosophical thought instead of restricting it to the minimalistic programme.

When the sharp distinction between a metaphysical assertion and a scientific statement, made by the Vienna Circle, broke down, Zawirski felt that perhaps metaphysics could be revived as a hypothetical-deductive discipline, to which the axiomatic method should be applied. This metaphysics presupposed as much knowledge of mathematics and natural science as he himself possessed. The man who tries his hand at metaphysics should be able to examine the relation between the calculus of probability and many-valued logics; to say in what way intuitionistic mathematics differs from classical mathematics; and to analyse the dispute of determinism and indeterminism in atomic physics.

These subjects were mentioned on purpose, because these and similar questions were discussed by Zawirski in his publications. He was, above all, a philosopher of science and he exemplified the interest in the theory and methodology of science, which was one of the characteristic features of the Warsaw school. Outside Poland he will perhaps be remembered as a historian of scientific concepts. His book in French on the evolution of the notion of time was his greatest work and probably his most valuable contribution to science [100].

In the period between the two wars Czeżowski incarnated all the characteristics of the Warsaw school. He avoided problems which could not be precisely formulated or examined by exact methods. His papers were mostly concerned with specific problems of traditional formal logic. Although he was free from any taint of psychologism, he retained a lasting interest in some psychological questions. He showed an increasing appreciation for the historical and evolutionary approach to philosophical concepts and to scientific methods.

This has become very marked since the war; his historical interests have considerably widened to include the history of logic. The war has affected him also in other respects. While he pays as much attention as ever to the strict rigours of the philosophical craftsmanship and practises them, as in the past, in short papers dealing with specific questions of inductive logic, probability reasoning, theory of science and its relation to philosophy, he no longer excludes problems in which the same standards of precision cannot be achieved.

Adam Wiegner (born 1889) had no connections with the Lwów school. His first contribution dealt with Leonard Nelson's important and little known examination of the problems of knowledge [101]. Wiegner's main interests were, however, logic and methodological problems of psychology. He published an important little book concerned with an analytical definition of psychological phenomena in which he examined a number of fundamental psychological concepts, such as those of introspection, of psycho-physiological isomorphism, and of behaviour. He continued this line of investigations with a paper on the philosophical significance of the Gestalt psychology [102]. He has published little but as a teacher he exercised a beneficial influence.

The role and importance of the Warsaw school cannot be judged alone by the achievements of its most prominent representatives. Also outside the school there were thinkers whose contribution to the development of philosophy in and outside Poland was considerable. The importance of the Warsaw school should be measured by its contribution to the intellectual life of the country and by the influence it exercised on the development of philosophy. In this respect it had no rivals. Practically everybody came under its spell and influence. The conception of philosophy, of its subject-matter, task, and method, the standards of philosophical thinking established by the leading exponents of the Warsaw school have been universally accepted. Although the school existed without interruption for less than twenty years, there emerged a living tradition, oral and written, which has turned out to be an intellectual force, with a considerable power of resistance and of attraction, that survived the test of historical catastrophes and upheavals.

Kotarbiński's philosophical views were firm and settled but as a teacher he has emulated Twardowski in liberalism and tolerance. Among his pupils were logicians – Alfred Tarski, Bolesław Sobociński, and Henryk Hiż; psychologists

– Walter Auerbach, Irena Filozofówna, Edward Geblewicz and Estera Markin; philosophers of law – Rafał Wundheiler; historians of modern thought – Mieczysław Milbrandt (1915–1944), Antoni Pański and Jakub Rajgrodzki; physicists – Aleksander Wundheiler; those who were to make their names in the philosophy and history of art – Mieczysław Wallis, sociology – Aleksander Hertz and Stanisław Ossowski, and the science of morals – Maria Ossowska. There was a group of influential methodologists – Janina Hosiasson-Lindenbaum (1899–1942), Janina Kotarbińska and Edward Poznański. All of them in the particular field of his or her interest tried to practise and to improve the methods learnt in the period of their apprenticeship in the Warsaw school. There was finally J. F. Drewnowski (born 1901), who became one of the moving spirits behind the initiative of transplanting modern formal logic to Thomism [103].

Ajdukiewicz's pupils excelled in the methodology and the theory of science. They included Izydora Dąmbska, Maria Kokoszyńska, Seweryna Łuszczewska-Romahnowa, Henryk Mehlberg and Zygmunt Schmierer. From Wilno came Jan Rutski who under Czeżowski's guidance made his way from law to philosophy [104].

Some of these names do not now need any introduction even outside Poland. Hosiasson-Lindenbaum's contributions on induction and probability, Kokoszyńska's on the concept of truth, Mehlberg's on the epistemological problems of physics are known to those interested in these particular subjects. Of the achievements of some of the others, especially of Ossowski and Ossowska, we shall speak again in discussing the course of events in the post-war period.

For a description of the Warsaw school in a general manner only methodological terms are appropriate. From whatever viewpoint it is considered, one cannot find a body of beliefs, substantial enough and held in common, that would justify calling it a school of thought in the traditional meaning of this term. Semantical reism is closely associated with the nominalistic programme, with realism in the theory of knowledge, and materialism in ontology. But reism was not the creed of the school, it was supported by some of its members and criticised by others. Those who adopted semantical reism did not always combine it with materialistic views or feel committed to the nominalistic programme. While the view that philosophical problems are partly a question of language was widely held, nobody ever went to the length of supporting the opinions of the Vienna Circle. Indeed the main thesis of the *Wiener Kreis* that all meaningful philosophical problems belong to logical syntax, was criticised sympathetically but firmly on semantical and other grounds, and this criticism proved to be justified [105]. It was agreed in Poland that in philosophy there may occur what Carnap called pseudo-object questions, which because of their formulation seem to refer to extra-linguistic reality while in fact they refer to the object-language and should be considered as logical or syntactical problems. But the view that all questions of philosophy can be shown to be syntactical was firmly rejected. Problems of ethics, and, in general, those concerned with values and norms, were never altogether banished as unscientific. The boundary lines which divided scientific from unscientific questions in philosophy were much more determined by the manner of the procedure than by the substance of the problems involved. There was, therefore, no finality about these boundary lines. It was felt that this was a reasonable attitude and one in keeping with the requirements of scientific progress. There is a body of beliefs held in common at every stage of scientific development which are surrounded by some kind of no man's land where what is true for one person is not necessarily true for another. The former makes for the consolidation of the knowledge already acquired, the latter for its further expansion. This applies even more to philosophy. All qualified persons assent to a true scientific statement and only some qualified persons assent to what is held to be a true philosophical statement. The distinction is only too familiar from the history of philosophy.

The views that were held in common were of a very general nature and they thus determined only an attitude to philosophical problems, a method of their solution, and a technique of which this method took advantage. The attitude was anti-irrationalistic, the method scientific (in a sense to be defined), and the technique logistic.

The anti-irrationalistic attitude was prompted by a staunch realism, belief in the absolute conception of truth, concern with and respect for facts, particularly those established by science, demand for clarity and precision of expression. Its negative aspect was a sound and firmly established distrust towards abstract speculations of an illusive simplicity and deceptive clarity and the rejection of any knowledge acquired by other means than those of experience or exact reasoning.

The method was scientific in view of the fact that in the evaluation of philosophical analysis it applied the same criteria of validity as those used in the deductive and empirical sciences. If other sources of knowledge, often claimed by philosophers (intuition or any other kind of direct insight into the essence of things), are discounted, only provable *(sensu stricto)* propositions and those testable by experience constitute valid knowledge. In principle, the methods of philosophy are those of science. This qualification is necessary in view of the fact that the relation between philosophy and language is closer than between science and language. Since philosophical problems are partly linguistic, this requires not only a greater clarity and precision of expression than is often the case in science, but also calls for an advanced technique in dealing with these partly linguistic and partly factual problems.

The new technique was provided by modern formal logic. Modern formal logic constitutes an unsurpassed model of exact reasoning and an instrument of disentangling involved, complicated and otherwise uncontrollable arguments. It is also the foundation on which new techniques can be worked out. This has been proved over and over again in the distinction between different levels at which our language can operate, and, consequently, between concepts and theorems of different levels; in the examination of language in terms of its syntax, semantics, and logical pragmatics; in the creation of a science of language. Philosophical technique must, therefore, either look to formal logic for guidance, or apply it in practice or study its procedure to improve and evolve better analytical means. Philosophical method cannot be scientific without being logistic.

The methodological unity of the Warsaw school was the result of a long development, to which the logicians, the mathematicians and the philosophers contributed. It took advantage of errors and achievements at home and abroad; it could not have become what it was in a vacuum, without keeping in close touch with what was happening in the world outside. The influence of the great thinkers of the past, of Leibniz, Hume, Mill and Bolzano, of those closer in time or contemporary – Frege, Schröder, Brentano, Poincaré, Duhem, Husserl, Hilbert, Einstein, Russell, Whitehead, Bridgman, Weyl, Neurath, Carnap, Popper, and many others, was considerable. The purpose of this survey is not, however, to trace these influences, but to describe the final outcome of outside impact and local genius.

CHAPTER 3

OTHER SCHOOLS AND OTHER PHILOSOPHERS

After Warsaw and Lwów, Cracow was the next most important centre of philosophical studies in Poland in the period between the two wars. Like logic, philosophy developed there under influences which differentiated Cracow philosophers from those of the Warsaw school.

When Twardowski was beginning to teach in Lwów, the University of Cracow was dominated by historians of philosophy, Father Stefan Pawlicki (1839–1917) and Maurycy Straszewski (1848–1921), and was under the pronounced influence of Christian philosophy, represented at that time by Father Marian Morawski (1845–1901). Later both these trends remained strong and were felt. In particular, the University of Cracow continued to be the best school for historians of philosophy.

A new development was started by Władysław Heinrich (1869–1957), who since 1905 for more than half a century held a dominant position in Cracow University. Heinrich studied under Avenarius and his main interest was psychology [106]. As a teacher of philosophy and its historian he gave to philosophy a distinctly scientific orientation. This trend was also represented by Tadeusz Garbowski (1869–1940), a zoologist by education and vocation, who was appointed to the second chair of philosophy in Cracow.

The rise of interest in the philosophy of science was also due to other factors. For a long period the chair of physics at Cracow University was held by distinguished scientists of international renown. Zygmunt Wróblewski (1847–1888), who together with Karol Olszewski (1846–1915) first liquefied oxygen, was succeeded by August Witkowski (1854–1913) and the latter by Marian Smoluchowski (1872–1917). Smoluchowski had pronounced philosophical interests and his contributions to statistical physics led him to the examination of the concept of probability, chance, natural law, determinism, in short, of philosophical problems of physics, for which he won international reputation [107]. Philosophical interests were shared by Władysław Natanson (1864–1937), another distinguished physicist, who combined knowledge of physics, history and philosophy with a considerable literary talent.

In the period between the two wars physicists outside Cracow made important contributions to the philosophy of science. The most eminent among them was the Warsaw theoretical physicist Czesław Białobrzeski (1878–1953), who exercised a considerable influence before and after the Second World War, Leopold Infeld (born 1898) and Szczepan Szczeniowski (born 1898), both theoretical physicists. Borderline questions between science and philosophy were approached from the viewpoint of biology by Ludwik Hirszfeld (1884–1954), and of medicine by Władysław Szumowski, Ludwik Fleck (born 1896) and Tadeusz Bilikiewicz (born 1901).

The leading Cracow representatives of the philosophy of science were Joachim Metallmann (1889–1942), Bolesław Gawecki (born 1889), Zygmunt Mysła-kowski (born 1890), and among the younger Zygmunt Spira; Aleksander Birkenmajer (born 1890), a historian of science and philosophy, should also be mentioned in this group. Metallmann was its outstanding figure. He combined philosophical education with knowledge of physics, chemistry, and biology. He differed from the methodologists of science of the Warsaw school by his method, modelled on the traditional manner of philosophical analysis, familiar from the writings of A.N. Whitehead or Emile Meyerson, whom Metallmann highly appreciated. Towards the end of his life he drew nearer to the Warsaw school and tried to acquire a command of the methods provided by modern formal logic.

Metallmann's most important contribution was his book on determinism in natural sciences, in which he carefully distinguished three types of natural laws (causal, statistical, and morphological), mutually irreducible to each other, and concerned with basically different phenomena (events, classes of events or characteristics, co-existence of different characteristics). Consequently, he differentiated three meanings the term 'determinism' may have in science, the terminological distinctions being based on different kinds of regularities in Nature.

Two other schools of thought had very numerous adherents in Poland in the period between the two wars, Catholic philosophy and traditionalistic philoso-phy, the two often coalescing by a personal union. The first included August-inianism and Thomism. It was taught at the university Theological Faculties, in the Roman-Catholic seminaries, and in the Catholic University of Lublin founded in 1918. Although it has produced some outstanding scholars, it seemed to exercise little influence on academic philosophy. It was widely felt that a philosopher follows every argument wherever it may lead and a Catholic philosopher, by his own admission, is not always willing or able to comply with this basic requirement [108].

There were, however, some Catholic philosophers whose specialised knowledge secured for them a high rank and a recognised position in the world of learning. Among them were Konstanty Michalski, the eminent mediaevalist, Jan Sala-mucha and J. M. Bocheński, logicians and historians of logic, Paweł Siwek, an authority on Spinoza, Józef Pastuszka, a historian of philosophy, J. F. Drew-nowski, a logician and methodologist, Stefan Świeżawski, a historian of metaphysics. In the 'thirties a group of Thomists, led by J. M. Bocheński, J. F. Drewnowski and Jan Salamucha, set up the so-called Cracow Circle, which advocated the adoption of modern formal logic and its application to Thomistic philosophy as well as to theology [109].

The Cracow Circle was strong because of its thinkers but weak in numbers; the opponents of modern formal logic and of new philosophical trends, originating from formal logic, were clearly in a great majority among the Catholic philoso-phers. Their recognised representatives: Father Jacek Woroniecki (1879–1949), Piotr Chojnacki (born 1897), Bishop Kazimierz Kowalski (born 1896), Jozef

Pastuszka (born 1897) and Bishop Jan Stepa (1892–1959), were supporters of traditionalistic philosophy. The same can be said of the leading lay Catholic thinkers: Witold Rubczyński (1864–1938), a metaphysician and moral philosopher, Bugumił Jasinowski (born 1883), a historian of philosophy, Bohdan Rutkiewicz (1887–1933), a philosopher of science, Stefan Harassek (1890–1952) and Wiktor Wąsik (born 1883), historians of philosophy in Poland.

The differences of opinion between the Cracow Circle and the traditionalists were ostensibly concerned with the question whether or not scholastic logic was still unsurpassed by anything that modern thought may offer, but in fact the issue lay deeper. The traditionalists could not deny that logic had made some progress since Thomas Aquinas, and their hostility to modern innovations was prompted by suspicions and misgivings about what purpose this progress served.

These suspicions towards the uses of modern logic were clearly expressed at a conference held in Cracow in 1935, at which the modernisers were represented by Bocheński, Drewnowski, and Salamucha, supported by Łukasiewicz, and the traditionalist trend by Chojnacki and Pastuszka. The main argument of the latter was that the formalism of modern logic was not philosophically neutral, but entailed a certain intellectual attitude, with which nominalism, positivism, conventionalism, physicalism, pragmatism, and relativism were closely associated. The modernisers, whose standpoint was ably and forcefully presented, did not succeed in dispelling these misgivings and making their views prevail. They did, however, manage to launch publicly their ideas and start a new development, which has ever since had some supporters in Poland and begun to spread abroad. A few years ago a warm tribute was paid by Michalski to the members of the Cracow Circle for their contribution to the modernisation of the whole field of medieval studies [110].

It should be remembered that at the time of the Cracow conference there were only three chairs of Catholic philosophy in the entire world from which modern logic was taught – at the *Angelicum* in Rome, at the *Institut Supérieur de Philosophie* at Louvain, and at the Theological Faculty of Cracow University. The first of them was held by Bocheński, the second by Robert Feys, and the third by Salamucha. Since then the number of Thomist scholars active in the field of modern logic and history of logic has considerably increased. In their name Philotheus Boehner recognised the pioneer work accomplished by the Cracow Circle [111].

The term 'traditionalistic philosophy' did not designate any organised group, like the Thomists and Catholic philosophers in general. It was a descriptive colloquialism used and applied to all those who for various reasons were opposed to the use in philosophy of the methods of science, in particular those based on modern formal logic. What was implicitly or explicitly common to the traditionalistic philosophers was their belief that each discipline, including philosophy, has its own method and standards of precision, which cannot be replaced by those taken over from some other discipline without exposing itself to some fatal effects. In the case of philosophy the application of the methods of science results either in an arbitrary elimination or in a serious misinterpretation of some essential philosophical problems. Second, and this opinion was not held by all traditionalistic philosophers, philosophy cannot do without vague, inadequately defined and highly abstract concepts, or dispense with the modes of reasoning that escape formal control. 'Elastic notions' are sometimes methodologically valuable, a metaphor or analogy is often more enlightening than a strict formal proof. What the adherents of scientific philosophy considered as a fatal weakness inherent in the traditional way of philosophical thinking, the adversaries of the scientific methods felt to be its essential feature, its strength and virtue.

The supporters of the second thesis formed the militant wing of traditionalistic philosophy and were inspired by the Hegelian tradition or the tradition of the so-called national philosophy. The militant wing constituted a minority of traditionalistic philosophers. It included first of all those inclined to treat the Warsaw school and similar movements abroad as a transient fashion, upon which the old tendencies would reassert themselves and the examination of the neglected and essentially philosophical problems would be resumed. Many of the adherents of traditionalistic philosophy belonged to the oldest generation at that time active in Poland and were reputed for their thorough knowledge of some particular period or trend in the history of philosophy. In this respect each of them contributed to and has a place in the history of philosophy in Poland. The best known were Benedykt Bornstein (1880-1948), Henryk Elzenberg (born 1887), Wincenty Lutosławski (1863-1954) [112], Piotr Massonius (1863-1945), Michał Sobeski (1877-1939), Mścisław Wartenberg (1868-1938), Adam Żółtowski (1881-1958).

There was no clear-cut line of division between the scientifically- and traditionally-minded thinkers, since between the two extremes there were other groups and individuals in some respects closer to the former and in other respects to the latter (e.g. Helena Kończewska (1887-1959) and Jan Leszczyński). But the division was real and important. The younger people who studied in the interwar period, were trained in the shadow of this division and had to make their choice between the two main trends – the modern and the traditionalistic. With very few exceptions, their choice was in favour of the former.

Husserl's phenomenology has exercised a powerful influence in Poland. This concerns, however, almost exclusively, the first phase of Husserl's philosophy of essence, expounded in *Logische Untersuchungen*. Husserl's devastating criticism of psychologism in logic, his analysis of meaning and his phenomenologically-descriptive method of what is 'given' were incorporated into the common body of philosophical knowledge, accepted and used in philosophical investigations. Husserl's criticism of nominalism and empiricism found fewer supporters, and his phenomenological method by means of which he strived to establish a final basis for all science and philosophy had only one. He was Roman Ingarden (born 1893), one of Husserl's most prominent followers and one of the most original minds in Poland in the first half of this century. Ingarden was and has remained a phenomenologist, but he did not follow Husserl into transcendental idealism. He came early to the parting of the ways with Husserl and devoted his energies to ontological studies through which he made his way back to realism in the theory of knowledge [113]. The old issue: idealism *versus* realism, is the subject of what seems to be his life work and of which the two first volumes appeared in 1947–1948 [114]. What he did before the last war, now appears to him as a preparatory study, the nature of which he did not fully realise at that time and which had to precede coming to grips with the main issue.

In the period between the two wars Ingarden's activities followed two main lines. He evolved a theory of literary works and he extended it later to other kinds of art works (music, painting, architecture, film) in a number of books and essays [115]. They were not concerned with aesthetic values or aesthetic experience, although they might or did lead to them; they were, as Ingarden put it, 'aesthetically neutral'. What Ingarden was interested in was the formal structure of a work of art, its mode of existence and in what its mode of existence differs from that of concrete real objects. Ingarden established a whole realm of such non-autonomous intentional objects (in Husserl's sense) whose specific formal structure and existence were contrasted with the objects of the external world and indirectly revealed and elucidated the ontological status of the latter. In another series of studies Ingarden examined the autonomous concrete real objects, the objects of the outside world, and subjected their formal structure and mode of existence to a searching phenomenological analysis [116].

Ingarden combined these ontological studies with criticism of what he called the 'logistic reconstruction of philosophy', as practised in the Warsaw school and the Vienna Circle. His share in the critical examination of Kotarbiński's reism, in particular of Kotarbiński's reistic interpretation of psychological statements, has already been mentioned. He turned later to the logical positivism of the Vienna Circle [117]. Ingarden's criticism was not limited to the pointing out of inconsistencies or unresolved problems, which he extricated from their concealment behind the imposing structure of the doctrine; he saw in them the result of an exaggerated reliance on formalistic methods, cut off from the intuitive sources of philosophical knowledge, without which the most perfect formal instrument must ultimately reveal its insufficiency. As Ingarden saw it, the scientific current in philosophy, initiated by the Vienna Circle, often dodged great theoretical issues instead of facing them.

Ingarden was the first or one of the first who noticed that the verification theory of meaning supported by the Vienna Circle was untenable. He pointed out that on principles accepted by the Vienna Circle metalogical assertions, that is, the whole logic of science, were meaningless as much as any other meaningless statement rejected by logical positivists on account of its being unverifiable. Moreover, verifiability and unverifiability were no criteria of meaning. If a statement is said to be unverifiable, we must first somehow apprehend its meaning to reach the conclusion that it is not verifiable. More generally, to carry out any logical analysis we have to be in possession of some knowledge distinct from the knowledge about the physical world and irreducible to what can be learnt by the methods of the empirical sciences. This is the reason why metalogical statements are unverifiable, and, therefore, meaningless in Carnap's sense. The procedure of verification cannot be described in physicalist terms, the meaning, an immanent attribute of a statement, is not something physical and thus must be independent of the method of its verification. The logical reconstruction of philosophy, undertaken by the Vienna Circle, led to the liquidation of philosophy, resulting from the acceptance of some unproven dogmas, as a matter of fact, of a metaphysical nature. What logical positivism set out to eliminate from philosophy, it cannot achieve without destroying itself in the course of this elimination and without invalidating any kind of philosophy, including the logic of science.

S. I. Witkiewicz (1885–1939), a philosopher by vocation and not by education, was not attached to any particular school, either in Poland or abroad. Apart from Chwistek, he was the most colourful personality on the Polish philosophical scene. A painter, playwright, literary and artistic critic, writer, explorer of various *paradis artificiels,* he turned finally to philosophy which for a few years before his death – he perished by his own hand at the beginning of the war – became his chief preoccupation. Compared with philosophy, art, literature, morals, seemed to be immaterial and somehow futile in their failure to face the ultimate issues of human existence [118].

To say the least, Witkiewicz is not easy to read and understand, his 'theoretical structures display errors of spelling' to use Kotarbiński's dictum. He was ignored by many and admired by a few, but the latter belonged to the most prominent Polish thinkers. He was not content with a plural reality which according to Chwistek obtrudes itself upon us [119], and tried to get at what is behind it, the reality more real than any of its manifestations. Thus he was led to an ontology growing up and groping into a metaphysical system whose originality and depth aroused admiration of those who in principle were hostile to metaphysical speculations.

Witkiewicz called it 'biologic materialism', and others 'materialistic monadology'. He thought that only something extended in time and space could exist, but this something is not purely material in the ordinary sense from which life and consciousness emerge by an interplay of mechanical changes. Witkiewicz's materialism was anti-mechanistic and anti-dialectical. Everything in the world that exists autonomously is either an individual alive or an agglomeration of such individuals. Sentient bodies are clearly the former, the so-called inanimate objects cannot but be the latter (otherwise biological materialism would have become primitive animism); they are inanimate but comprise sentient individuals. These somewhat startling opinions were reached by accepting the common sense view as the starting point, by comparing various theories intended to make intelligible this view, by eliminating from these theories what seemed to be extravagant, by inferences from the most general premises which led to the 'inescapable' conclusions in the sense that upon their rejection we would have been faced by something incomprehensible. It is in these various procedures, arbitrary as they may be, from which materialistic monadology emerges as the only solution left, that Witkiewicz showed the power and penetration of his mind. He acted as a stimulus by the manner he carried on his mental struggles – the laying bare of the logical consequences of what he believed to be the case – and not by the results which he obtained. The latter fall to the ground as soon as anyone dissents from the premisses to which Witkiewicz assented.

It is perhaps not surprising that philosophy of life had no supporters among academic philosophers. Its Polish representatives were scholars who being eminent in some other disciplines contributed to philosophy on the sidelines. Life-philosophers incarnated more than anybody else the anti-rationalistic tendencies in modern culture, denounced by Chwistek in his *Limits of Science*. They wished to return to some more fundamental life experiences and to explore knowledge revealed in them, which they set against the soul-destroying analytical spirit of philosophy and barren scientific rationalism.

Life-philosophers in Poland were under the preponderant influence of German life-philosophy – of Dilthey, Spranger, Heidegger – to a lesser extent of Bergson and later for a short period of French existentialist thinkers. The most original among them was Zygmunt Łempicki, who being a historian of German literature included in his studies also borderline problems between literature and philosophy and often crossed the line into the field of philosophy of culture. Other exponents of life-philosophy were J. M. Rozwadowski (1867–1935), professor of linguistics, Bogdan Suchodolski (born 1903), an educationist, and also Stefan Kołaczkowski (1887–1940), a historian of literature. Suchodolski abandoned philosophy of life and by way of existentialism has finally become a Marxist-Leninist.

Methodologically, life-philosophers and the adherents of traditionalistic philosophy on the one hand, the Warsaw school on the other, stood poles apart. Philosophy of life and existentialism include strong irrationalistic ingredients and renounce scientific method in the above defined sense. Łempicki, Rozwadowski, Suchodolski left hardly any mark on academic philosophy in Poland. Their influence was much greater among the literary and artistic circles.

In the academic world sociology was the successful rival to philosophy of life conceived as a philosophy of culture. In the person of Florian Znaniecki, a life philosopher in his youth and an empirical sociologist in his mature age, the two trends merged and produced a theory of culture closer to experience and facts of social life. Znaniecki was a determined 'dualist' and proclaimed the existence of a sharp contrast between the natural sciences on the one hand, the humanities, the social or cultural sciences on the other. He was criticised from both sides, by life-philosophers in the name of the humanities and by the Warsaw school on behalf of the natural sciences.

While life-philosophers emphasised the differences of the subject-matter and methods which in their opinion separated the natural and the cultural sciences, an opposite tendency appeared in one of the disciplines that uncontestably should be counted as part and parcel of the cultural sciences. In the philosophy of law a trend against the splitting up of various branches of study and for their gradual fusion became clearly perceptible.

Philosophy of law is not a well defined subject. It is used here in the sense introduced by Leon Petrażycki, who differentiated between jurisprudence, the so-called dogmatic jurisprudence in particular, and the theory or philosophy of law. The first deals with the logical interdependence of legal norms, the second examines their origin and foundations in the facts of social life. This is a rough distinction which will later become a little more precise. It is clear that the theory or philosophy of law, as defined by Petrażycki, is closely associated with social psychology and sociology.

Leon Petrażycki (1867–1931) was the dominant figure in the philosophy of law in the inter-war period. He spent most of his life in Russia, where he taught at the Kiev and Petersbourg universities; N. S. Timasheff calls him justly a Russo-Polish scholar. He returned to Warsaw after the restoration of Polish independence in 1918 and until his death he held a chair at the university there. He wrote in German and Russian; his main works were only later translated into Polish. In Russia he created an entire school, from which came P.A. Sorokin, Max Laserson, G. D. Gurvitch, N. S. Timasheff. In Poland he had not only a large number of followers among legal thinkers, among whom the most prominent was Jerzy Lande (1886–1954), but also influenced the methodologists of the Warsaw school, above all Kotarbiński, by his ideas and theories in the field of social and political sciences [120].

For Petrażycki law was not solely or even mainly a body of precepts, supported by the social controls which a politically organised society applies for the enforcement of these precepts. This is an important but a secondary and, as it were, negative aspect of law. Its primary function is to determine people's behaviour by implanting in them certain permanent dispositions. This can be achieved because there exist what Petrażycki called 'legal experiences' or 'legal phenomena'. They differ from other experiences, in particular those of moral nature, by their imperative-attributive character. In the case of a legal experience what I feel to be my obligation I also experience as somebody's right. Legal norms should not be looked for in the outside world or in the realm of abstract entities; their peculiar content manifests itself in human experience. Only a part of legal experiences become 'objectivised' to make up a body of law in the practical sense, a system of prescriptions recognised as being obligatory and considered justiciable. The latter can be examined by means of logical analysis, the former require the methods of psychology, social psychology and sociology, which must also be applied to the examination of causal relations between legal and other social phenomena. Petrażycki and his followers initiated the investigations and studied the relations between law on the one hand, morality, political and economic organisation on the other. They threw new light on the social function of law and its role in the evolution of human societies.

Unlike morality, law creates in man not only the concept of obligation with respect to others but also that of other people's obligations to himself. By providing him with a sense of his rights, law makes of man a citizen. Since law might supplant old dispositions, change motives of behaviour and implant new ones, jurisprudence is an important instrument of social evolution. If it is rightly used, it brings about self-adjustment of individuals within the society and thus paves the way for progress which can be evaluated by the decrease of the use of force and violence [121].

Czesław Znamierowski (born 1888) was concerned, above all, with the logical analysis of legal concepts. His interests are wide and include philosophy, sociology, political science and law. He is a great admirer of British empirical philosophers; he translated into Polish Hobbes, Hume, Bertrand Russell, G. E. Moore. His interest in law seems to be basically of a moral nature, and he has lately become a moral philosopher.

In the inter-war period he was more attracted by logical problems of law, to which he applied the methods of modern formal logic. He was at that time the only legal thinker who had acquired a thorough knowledge of modern formal logic and tried to do in law what the Warsaw school was doing in philosophy. At first distrusted, he has eventually won the day. 'Logic for lawyers', and this means modern formal logic, has been flourishing in Poland in recent years. Many share credit for it, but its originator was Znamierowski.

Using logical means Znamierowski declared war on conceptual confusions, terminological ambiguities and abstract entities, with which the traditional jurisprudence has been burdened. Unlike Petrażycki, who in a positivistic fashion recommended going back to psychological and social facts, Znamierowski saw the remedy in the reconstruction of the legal language, in unequivocal definitions, and in the application of the deductive method, which would replace the man-made tangle of hopelessly intricate and involved problems by a simple theoretical construction.

With some exceptions, the Warsaw school was interested in analytical and systematic philosophy, and not in its history. The capital of historical studies was Cracow University. Cracow was also the seat of the Polish Academy of Science and Learning, which encouraged such studies and set up a commission for research on the history of philosophy in Poland. Most of the historians of philosophy either received their education in Cracow or were in some way or other connected with Cracow University. Its leadership was recognised by Władysław Tatarkiewicz (born 1886), the most eminent historian of that period, who himself held the chair at Warsaw University.

Tatarkiewicz, who is also a moral philosopher, a historian of art and aesthetics [122], gave the first Polish universal history of philosophy from Thales to the outbreak of the Second World War, of which the two volumes appeared in 1931 and the third, comprising philosophy in the twentieth century, in 1950 [123]. It is an impressive achievement, clear in construction, rich in information, concise in style, elegant and vivid in the presentation of problems and personalities. It conveys admirably the movement of philosophical thought, its conquest of partial truths which are criticised, rejected and taken up again in reconstructed and expanded form.

Heinrich wrote an outline of the history of philosophy, which covers antiquity and the Middle Ages [124]. It is more modest in scope than Tatarkiewicz's three-volume work and scholarly austere. It is a history written by a philosopher who, relying exclusively on his own research, reflects on the history of his subject in order to clarify his own views.

The historian who won an international reputation for his studies on the philosophy of the fourteenth century was the learned mediaevalist Konstanty Michalski (1879–1947). He was the teacher of many historians, among whom were the already mentioned Salamucha, the historian of logic; Świeżawski, the historian of metaphysics; and Marian Heitzman. The latter together with Bogdan Kieszkowski made philosophy of the Renaissance their special subject of historical studies [125].

The most versatile and original historian of Greek philosophy was Adam Krokiewicz (born 1890). He translated the writings of Lucretius, Sextus Empiricus and Plotinus, wrote on the doctrine of the Stoics, Sceptics and of Epicurus, to whom he devoted a large monographic volume.

Besides Krokiewicz many classical scholars gained high reputations for their studies on ancient philosophy. Tadeusz Zieliński (1859–1944) is best known abroad for his book on Cicero, *Cicero im Wandel der Jahrhunderte,* first published in Leipzig in 1897 and since then reprinted several times; but in Poland he is remembered above all for his series of books on Greek and Roman religion, and for another series on the literary and political history of ancient Greece and Rome. Tadeusz Sinko (born 1877), the highest Polish authority on classical scholarship in the period between the two wars, is the author of a monumental history of Greek literature (published 1931–1948), which no student of ancient philosophy can ignore. Jan Sajdak (born 1882), translator of Minucius Felix and Tertullian, edited a collection of Polish translations of Patristic literature (24 volumes in the period 1924–1947) and was an authority on Gregory of Nazianze [126]. Jerzy Siwecki, a classical scholar and historian of ancient philosophy, who won distinction at an early age, was killed in action in 1939.

Hindu philosophy had in Stanisław Schayer (1899–1942) an internationally known scholar. Schayer and Adam Kunst published important studies on Indian logic. They were both students of Łukasiewicz [127].

Among the historians of the modern era Ludwik Chmaj (1888–1959), Narcyz Łubnicki (born 1904), and Adam Żółtowski distinguished themselves by the scope of their knowledge and the penetrating insight of their contributions. The first was an authority on Cartesianism and the Reformation in Poland, the second – on positivism and dialectical materialism, the third – on German idealism and the so-called national philosophy. Żółtowski, together with Wartenberg and Łubnicki, was the most prominent representative of the historians of philosophical thought for whom the historical and systematic interest in a given system – that of Hegel, Kant, and positivism respectively – coalesced and provided an opportunity for expounding their own views.

A considerable number of the historians of modern philosophy trained in the inter-war period perished during the war. Those whose premature death is particularly mourned include Bolesław Miciński (1911–1943), Mieczysław Milbrandt, killed in action, Antoni Pański and Jakub Rajgrodzki, murdered in the Wilno prison and the Warsaw ghetto [128].

CHAPTER 4

MARXIAN TRADITION

By 'Marxian tradition' is meant 'Marxian view of history' or 'Marxian philosophy of history'. This Marxian tradition should be differentiated from the philosophical doctrine of dialectical materialism, as well as from Marxism-Leninism. The distinction will become clearer in the course of tracing the origin and development of Marxian tradition in Poland.

Marxian tradition in Poland dates from the last two decades of the nineteenth century. At that time a group of young and able men, which included Stanisław Krusiński (1857–1886), Bronisław Białobłocki (1861–1888), Ludwik Krzywicki (1859–1941), Kazimierz Kelles-Krauz (1872–1905), Leon Winiarski and for a short period Edward Abramowski (1868–1918), became acquainted with the works of Marx and popularised his economic, sociological and historical views in Poland. The most important among them was Krzywicki. Unlike some of the others who died young and, except for Abramowski, were rather sociological and literary journalists, Krzywicki lived long, turned away from journalism in his youth and became a social anthropologist, educationist and organiser of social research in Poland. He was very active in the inter-war period and exercised a considerable influence both through his personal qualities and his achievements. At an early age Krzywicki took part in the activities of the first Socialist organisations that were formed in Poland. Later in his life he withdrew from public political activities, but his sympathies clearly remained with the Socialist movement.

Krzywicki was one of the team who translated the first volume of *Capital* into Polish and was the editor of the whole work. The translation was published in Leipzig in 1884 by private contributions under Krzywicki's personal supervision [129]. One year later Engels' *The Origin of the Family, Private Property and the State* appeared in Paris in Krzywicki's translation. About this time most of the important works of Marx and Engels were translated into Polish [130]. Lewis H. Morgan's *Ancient Society* was also translated (Warsaw 1887). Krzywicki again participated and provided the book with a comprehensive explanatory appendix.

Krzywicki's first publications were journalistic in character; they explained in a popular form the main economic, social, and historical ideas of historical materialism. He used them to criticise other social and economic views, based on Comte's positivism and Spencerian evolutionism, which at that time were widely accepted among the Polish educated classes. Krzywicki was a materialist, but he never indicated that historical materialism required a metaphysical foundation. So far as he was concerned, and this equally applies to his contemporaries who supported the Marxian view of history, historical materialism was a self-sufficient hypothesis [131]. In this Krzywicki was in agreement with

Marx for whom the materialistic dialectic was a conceptual framework for the examination of the historical and social reality. The external world – Nature – entered the sphere of Marx's reflection only as a part of social reality, in its relation to man, and not in itself, as it is investigated in the natural sciences.

In his exposition and popularisation of historical materialism Krzywicki showed great independence of mind. He always held firmly to the view that historical materialism is a method of investigating and of explaining the course of social and historical events, it is a means of research in various social sciences, and not one by which man can or should interfere in the historical process. This might be called the scientific version of historical materialism which is characterised by the predominance of its cognitive content over its voluntaristic aspect; historical materialism is conceived by it rather as a key to knowledge than as a key to action. The cognitive content of historical materialism has been incorporated into the scientific tradition, and has become a permanent, almost truistic, part of the methodology of the historical and social sciences. Krzywicki has the credit of having understood it at the time when the issues involved were much more confused than they are at present. He has thus decisively influenced the way in which the Marxian theories were accepted in Poland. The opinion later defended by Plekhanov against Lenin, that the 'value of the materialist conception of history is primarily methodological' [132], was established in Poland at the time when the views of Marx first became known there.

Krzywicki influenced the formation of the Marxian tradition in yet another manner. To use a term only later introduced, he never conceived of historical materialism as a doctrine of economic materialism. Historical materialism involved, in Krzywicki's opinion, mutual interaction between the economic base and the superstructure. He was expounding this view before Engels wrote his famous letters to Konrad Schmidt, Joseph Block, Franz Mehring, and Heinz Starkenburg (1890–1894) and before Plekhanov formulated his theories on this matter in *The Development of the Monist View of History* (1895) [133].

According to Krzywicki, historical materialism explains the origin and the appearance of social and political ideas in a society at a given stage of its development and does not deny that once formulated these ideas exercise a powerful influence upon the productive forces and relations of production which brought them into being. Being functionally a secondary and dependent phenomenon, the ideas may become later a factor of primary importance. Without them there would be no social development. They only make possible the purposeful activity of great masses of people and talented individuals. Since the ideas can enter into various combinations in the human mind they are thus also conditioned by the mind. The power of the mind is, however, limited in so far as only such ideas assert themselves which somehow correspond to the material conditions. The latter limit the range of socially effective ideas, make the selection between what is utopian and non-utopian, between what can and what cannot modify the social and economic base.

Not only the ideas which are reflections of and prompted by the forces latent in a society can exercise an influence on the economic base, but also those 'wandering in time and space'. Krzywicki accepted the fact of the diffusion of ideas, of their passing from one society to another or from one historical epoch to another. He also recognised the existence of a 'historical substratum' in each society, by which he understood the habits, manners, beliefs, sentiments, political and legal institutions, moral and philosophical ideas, accumulated from the past and constituting a modifying medium of social evolution. Thus, there is no general pattern of change, which can be applied to every society. Since the conditions of change vary from one society to another, social evolution takes different forms and proceeds in various ways.

While Krzywicki remained throughout an evolutionist, he somehow modified the classical evolutionary doctrine and came close, in particular in his later works, to the functional approach which his compatriot Bronisław Malinowski helped to formulate [134]. Guided by the idea that there is no single pattern of social evolution, Krzywicki reached the conclusion that historical materialism has no universal application. It is, for instance, an unsuitable means of research for the investigations of primitive communities. His social anthropological studies, to which he devoted much of his energies in later life, show no trace of the Marxian view of history. They are based on a vast accumulation of facts, examined meticuously for any empirical generalisation which they might yield [135].

In 1938 a collective volume devoted to Krzywicki's life and work was published in Warsaw (he was to celebrate his eightieth birthday the following year), which included the essay *Ludwik Krzywicki as Theorist of Historical Materialism* by Oskar Lange, a prominent Marxian scholar. Among Krzywicki's contributions to the Marxian tradition Lange singled out the restrictions implicitly imposed by Krzywicki on historical materialism which limited its application to mass social phenomena. The materialist-historical method cannot be applied to such disciplines as the history of art, of literature and philosophy, unless the artistic, literary and philosophical ideas are of social nature, *i.e.* express certain aspirations of a mass movement and are closely bound up with the social structure of the society in which this movement takes place. In particular, historical materialism cannot be applied to individual works of art and thought. Lange concluded that clear realisation of its limits, indicated by Krzywicki, would have protected historical materialism from some futile and abortive applications which did not increase its scientific reputation [136].

Marxian tradition in Poland, as shaped by Krzywicki, included three characteristic features. It emphasised the cognitive content of historical materialism, it combined the materialistic conception of history with a multifactorial analysis of social change and with an empirical approach to socio-cultural processes. It did not operate with humanity at large and was not committed to the belief in the existence of what P. A. Sorokin called 'unilinear perpetual trends' in the development of mankind. Since the factual evidence contradicted the assumption that such trends are operative, Krzywicki concentrated on the repeatable features of socio-cultural change (or systems of such features) and in this respect was in advance of most sociologists of his time [137].

In the inter-war period the Marxian tradition was sharply differentiated from

Marxism-Leninism. The latter was not considered to be a philosophical school or a philosophical system, but a 'view of the world and a code of life precept of militant Communism' [138]. Marxism-Leninism did not arouse any considerable interest but it was not ignored either; information concerning the development of Soviet philosophy and historical sciences were appearing in scientific periodicals [139]. On the other hand there was no doubt that the Marxian tradition constituted a part of the scientific body of knowledge; its assumptions and particular views were examined in the same manner as those of other philosophical systems. To use Professor Butterfield's words, one did not need to be a Marxist to recognise important services rendered by Marx and Engels to the study of historical process [140].

Apart from the writings of Marx and Engels published for clearly political purposes, either in Poland or in the Soviet Union, there appeared a new translation of *Ludwig Feuerbach* and of *Socialism: Utopian and Scientific*. The first volume of *Capital* was again translated, a selection of Marx's correspondence with Kugelmann was published in Polish for the first time [141]. There is little trace, however, of any serious interest in Marx and Engels; the intellectual stir, produced in 1880–1900, was an event which never recurred in Poland.

Krzywicki, universally recognised as the leading authority on historical materialism, became the head of the Institute of Social Economy, set up in 1920. He was engrossed in his social-anthropological studies and in organising social research especially on the working and living conditions of the working classes [142]. His collaborators, Stanisław Rychliński (1903–1945) in particular, followed in his footsteps. There were really only two men, Oskar Lange (born 1904), an economist, and Stefan Czarnowski (1879–1937), a sociologist and historian of culture, who represented the Marxian tradition and tried to develop and to apply in their work the assumptions of historical materialism.

Czarnowski, former lecturer at the *École Pratique des Hautes Études* in Paris, was trained in Durkheim's school and he remained a Durkheimist throughout his life. He was in many ways a remarkable man, little known in Poland outside a narrow circle of sociologists and even not by all of them. Only after his death some of his works, originally published in various periodicals and thus lost, were republished in book form in 1939 [143]. His collected works did not appear until 1956; they are an aid to a full appreciation of Czarnowski's learned and original mind [144]. His international reputation was based on his sociological studies on religion published in French [145].

Czarnowski's interests were wide and varied. They included sociology of religion, sociology of literature, sociology and history of culture, problems of sociological methods. His historical knowledge was comprehensive, detailed and accurate, particularly authoritative in matters concerning the ancient Greeks, Celts and Gauls. In his studies he followed the method of the Durkheim school which, however, satisfied him less and less and he came increasingly under the influence of historical materialism. His recent biographer suggested that towards the end of his life he came both politically and intellectually very close to Marxism-Leninism without having been able to reject entirely his former scientific beliefs and pass the threshold of Marxism-Leninism [146]. Whatever Czarnowski became politically, he was neither a Marxist-Leninist nor close to Marxism-Leninism in his scientific work. In what he wrote, Czarnowski combined Durkheim methods with those of the classical Marxian tradition and revealed historical materialism at its best. All the main features of the Marxian view of history, as interpreted by Krzywicki, are found again, improved and enriched, in Czarnowski's works.

Czarnowski's sociology of culture, in which the influence of historical material-ism is most pronounced, is based on the assumption that social phenomena are both material and socio-psychical. Whenever we are inclined to see in them purely psychical forms and contents, we find, upon closer examination, that they are insolubly bound up together with material facts. Also conversely, there are no material facts *sensu stricto* in social life, matter is 'socialised', transformed by and associated with respective collective representations. A 'spiritual' or a 'material' culture is an abstraction to which nothing in social life corresponds. At the origin of culture stands the division of labour; it diversifies and perfects productive processes. The development of culture is based on the work of the great masses of people. It is a necessary condition of any spiritual achievement and in our own times creates a new, proletarian culture. Mass social phenomena and class conflicts – not great individuals – are the driving force of history and of cultural evolution.

All these statements are familiar and Czarnowski's claim to originality is not based on the fact of having made them. It results from the manner in which this dry skeleton of the half-Marxian, half-Durkheimian constructions is covered with the living flesh of social, political, and cultural facts, with human ideas, feelings and strivings. The dry skeleton is not there from the very beginning but it appears at the end to support the whole construction emerging from an abun-dance of particular facts: from the etymology of the names 'Paris', 'Reimes' or 'Bourges', the descriptions of Berber villages and their architecture, the discovery of old Spanish and Marseilles coins in Soissons, the inferences prompt-ed by the tools of the ancient Gauls, and a mass of other equally well as-certainable evidence. What the factual evidence suggests is explained by a general statement, which, however, is not claimed to be universally valid, but only with respect to a particular period or to a particular major event in the history of ancient Greece, the Roman Gallia, and medieval France. Within the materialis-tic conception of history Czarnowski practised the functional and multi-factorial sociological analysis, which differentiated seemingly similar events (*e.g.* the diffusion of tools, the cultural survivals), showed the variety of their component factors, their role and determination in a wide but concrete context of mutually interdependent social facts. The ultimate determination of cultural phenomena by social and economic conditions of life was thus firmly set in this context, to work its way, as it were, from within and to be extricated from it only by abstraction.

Neither Krzywicki, nor Czarnowski examined the connections between the Marxian view of history and Marxian philosophy more closely. Even the term 'dialectical materialism' does not occur in their writings. In the philosophical circles there prevailed the opinion that Marx did not leave any specifically philosophical doctrine. He was known as one of the members of the Hegelian Left, concerned with matters that belonged to the history of social and economic thought, to the methodology of the historical and social sciences, that is to say, with subjects that only marginally touched upon the questions in the centre of a philosopher's interests. Engels was considered to be clearly a progeny of Hegelian philosophy and thus discounted as a serious thinker. He aroused only a historical interest and instructively exemplified the strange fortunes of a speculative philosophical system, like that of Hegel, gradually transformed by its supporters into the exact opposite of what it had been at its inception. It appears, there was only one man who thought highly of Engels' dialectical materialism and considered it as a philosophically significant and acceptable doctrine.

Stefan Rudniański (1887–1941) was with Edward Frauenglas (1905–1939) the most prominent Polish historian of philosophical thought in the eighteenth century. While Frauenglas was a pure historian, Rudniański's interest was guided by his philosophical preferences. He became an authority on French materialism because he was a materialist himself and wished to serve the cause of its popularisation. He had some original ideas about the sources of French materialism and expounded the view that a continuous line of development can be traced from Descartes' *Discours de la méthode* and *Des Passions de l'âme*, through Spinoza and metaphysical materialism, to Feuerbach and the dialectical materialism of Marx and Engels. In 1910 he published a little book which in a popular form presented the metaphysical and epistemological aspects of dialectical materialism. This book was republished only in 1958 and in the meantime forgotten. He wrote a report on philosophy in the Soviet Union and examined the relation between the theory and practice in dialectical materialism. Rudniański was a member of the Communist Party of Poland [147].

The view was expressed that Chwistek was the only Polish philosopher who before the war declared himself for dialectical materialism and Marxism-Leninism [148]. This view, allegedly based on *The Limits of Science,* is contradicted by what Chwistek actually said.

Two things about Chwistek stand out clearly. First, he was a materialist. Second, his admiration for Marx was not matched by his knowledge of the works of Marx and Engels. What Chwistek did know about Marx and Marxian materialism was second-hand and came from the writings of Plekhanov, Deborin, Bukharin, and Lenin [149]. Chwistek admired Marx because his philosophical and sociological doctrine was entirely based, as Chwistek claimed, upon what he called the principles of sound reason. Marx's method did not differ essentially from the constructive methods of the exact sciences and his sociological thinking rested on one of those truths which are not subject to change, namely that the road of progress is marked by blood, violence and revolutions.

This does not mean, however, that Chwistek espoused the Marxist-Leninist version of dialectical materialism. One of the reasons to support this opinion is the fact – slight as it might appear to some people – that in 1935 he described

Bukharin as one of the foremost contemporary Marxists. His unorthodoxy is further testified by the esteem, as high as that he bestowed upon Marx, in which he held Hume, Comte, and Mach. On the other hand, Hegel was considered by Chwistek to be the man responsible for contemporary anti-rationalism. From Hegel comes the plainly absurd idea that motion can be understood only in terms of moving thought, which vitiates dialectical materialism and makes its supporters cite 'in one breath . . . . improbable Hegelian nonsense and important scientific theories'. The dialectical method is responsible for entirely unnecessary confusion of thought. Marx's thesis of universal mutability or that of the dependence of intellectual life upon physiological processes is sound. The thesis that a special method is necessary to understand the changes and dependence in question is wrong. To suppose that the adherents of the dialectical method do mean what they say would imply that they cannot be taken in earnest.

Chwistek accepted dialectical materialism without the dialectical method and without any other metaphysical ingredients, *i.e.* materialism based upon experience and exact reasoning. He called it 'dialectical' because it emphasises change and mutability, one of the truths of sound reason that was lost and is made prominent by Marx. What Chwistek said of Marx is true enough and close to what Marx seemed to have wished to impress upon philosophical thinking of his times. Chwistek is not alone in evaluating the contribution of Marx to philosophy in that manner. This does not, however, make Chwistek a supporter but a critic of the Marxist-Leninist dialectical materialism.

CHAPTER 5

SOCIOLOGY AND SOCIAL PHILOSOPHY

Krzywicki was the Nestor of Polish sociology, but its founder as an academic discipline and its undisputed chief exponent was Florian Znaniecki (1882–1958). Znaniecki's school as much dominated the sociological thinking in Poland in the inter-war period as the Warsaw School did in philosophy. Before Znaniecki began to teach, some studies in social philosophy and much sociological journalism were published in Poland but sociology as such did not really exist[150]. Znaniecki provided a definition of the subject matter of sociology, gave it its method and research techniques, organised its teaching, set up the Polish Sociological Institute (1927) and the first Polish sociological periodical *Przegląd Socjologiczny* (1930). The inter-war period witnessed a lightning growth of the interest in sociology, a considerable expansion of sociological studies and research activities (in particular in the ecology of towns, in rural sociology, in social stratification and mobility), an increasing output of sociological publications, a steady rise in the status of sociology as an academic discipline. Before the war Poland enjoyed the reputation of being one of the most highly organised and productive centres of sociology in Europe [151].

The various achievements of Polish sociology in the inter-war period have been described in Polish as well as in English [152]. What is intended here, is to explain the epistemological and methodological assumptions of Znaniecki's sociology in view of the role which they have played in post-war developments.

Znaniecki came to sociology from philosophy where his main interest was philosophy of value, the relations between action and knowledge, the individual and the community, personality and culture. What he published (1910–1912) was at once recognised in Poland to be of considerable importance for the study of society [153]. He went to the U.S.A. and he was exposed there to a quite different influence of considering the same problems from the empirical instead of the philosophical viewpoint. This influence was in some respects decisive. 'If William I. Thomas had not asked me to collaborate with him on the *Polish Peasant*', wrote Znaniecki in his last work, 'I would probably have remained all my life a philosopher, and never have turned to sociology as an inductive science'[154]. The above-mentioned celebrated work – *The Polish Peasant in Europe and America,* came out in 1918–1920 and was described by H. E. Barnes and H. Becker as a major event in the history of American sociology. It was based on what now is called 'personal documents' – verbatim statements, life histories and letters of the peasants, which were published together with their analysis and interpretation.

Znaniecki was led by his philosophical studies to the conviction that sociology is not a natural science, a part of biology or psychology, but a humanistic discipline, one of what he called the 'cultural sciences'. Cultural reality exists objectively, as much as the natural does, from which it differs by the fact that its elements have been produced and are maintained in existence by conscious human agents. His studies in the U.S.A. inspired him with the belief that this humanistic discipline might be made empirical. These two convictions, as Znaniecki himself indicated, constitute the main pillars of his sociology whose first outline was expounded in Polish in *The Introduction to Sociology*, summarised in English in *The Object-Matter of Sociology* and re-stated in *The Method of Sociology*.

In the past century two philosophies concerning the relation between the individual and society were struggling with each other – social realism and social nominalism (atomism). The first of these assumed the existence of society, or of any part of it, as an objective reality, irreducible to a collection of individuals. Sometimes it also assumed that the individual has no existence apart from his social existence or that of society. Social nominalism or atomism asserted that only the individual exits as an empirical entity, and society is a construction and a shorthand expression to designate various combinations of interacting individuals. Sometimes it also claimed that the individual is only a biological entity and suggested that any sociological statement (*i.e.* a statement that refers to interacting individuals) is reducible to a physiological one, in the same manner as the latter is in principle reducible to a statement of chemical and physical relations. Durkheim showed, and Znaniecki follows him in this respect, that these two philosophies are not necessarily mutually exclusive. The claim that social phenomena have an objective reality and are irreducible to those in which only separate individuals are involved does not imply that society as a whole is objectively real. On the other hand, the assertion that social phenomena are ultimately founded in interacting individuals and can only be studied in that manner does not commit us to the claim that the facts of interaction are not objective; they are independent in some sense from the plurality of interacting individuals. 'Objectively real' means in this context 'to appear within a frame of relationships'. In this sense both a falling snowflake and David Copperfield are objectively real; intersubjectively valid statements can be made both of the falling snowflake and of David Copperfield [155].

Objectively real social entities differ, however, from those a physicist or a biologist has to deal with. A social investigator is not concerned with the individuals and their groups as biological or physical entities, or as a collection of such entities, to be studied like natural objects – forests, an animal organism or an animal herd. A social individual is a person, and a 'person' means a 'social image of an individual as directly experienced by other individuals and reflectively by himself'. He cannot be conceived without considering the expectations of other individuals concerning his actions and without his own expectations with respect to the actions of others. A person conforms to patterns, exercises certain varying functions, assumes a status, considers other individuals as persons and is considered by them as a person. An individual socially performs a number of different roles – the term, introduced by G. H. Mead, is new but the idea is old – and is a different person each time, every role being defined in a structurally closed social system, which is functionally or causally connected with other systems. A social investigator must apply what Znaniecki termed 'the humanistic coefficient' and others called simply 'the social factor'; he does not approach the social individual and social groups as 'directly given' objects of his experience, but in the same fashion as he considers languages, religions, works of art, philosophic and scientific theories, as things that have meanings and values, different meanings and values in different circumstances. In other words, a social investigator must consider social individuals and their groups as related to somebody else's experience and discover by controlled observation and other empirical means 'how they appear and what they mean' in the experience and thought of experiencing persons within the frame of definite social relationships (social systems) [156].

In this manner there disappears the essential unrelatedness of the individual and the community which no naturalistic social theory can ever bridge and which the orthodox social realism and social atomism either ignored or decreed out of existence. The person and the group constitute two aspects of what Znaniecki called a 'social system'. The subject-matter of sociology as one of the cultural sciences is social systems in which persons and groups are involved, their recurrent characteristics, their relations and changes, their structural and other laws. Four social systems, functionally related to each other, were singled out by Znaniecki – social actions, social relations, social roles, and social groups; they constitute the four main domains of sociological studies. Being a general theory of what is sometimes called 'human relations', sometimes 'social relations' and more recently 'social actions', sociology assumes the same basic role among cultural sciences as is performed by physics for natural sciences. Cultural order in general has been defined by Znaniecki as an order of relationships among all kinds of human actions in a similar manner as natural order is the totality of relationships among all kinds of natural objects [157].

The method of investigating social systems is to be empirical and inductive. Since, however, social systems are never directly given, but are constituted in the social consciousness of the individuals participating in those systems, and the content of social consciousness cannot be either observed or experimented with, the method of personal documents has acquired a particular importance. Statistical methods had for Znaniecki only a subsidiary usefulness. Controlled observation, diaries, autobiographies, and later also questionnaire responses provided him with his basic research material. In its analysis, interpretative technique was preferable to the quantitative. Znaniecki applied in it a conceptual framework which was rich and varied, though somewhat vague, more intuitive than analytic [158].

Znaniecki expounded the assumptions of his sociology and applied them to particular sociological problems in a number of books, about a half of which were published in English and the other half in Polish. Perhaps the most important are those in which he expanded his theory of cultural sciences – *Social Actions* and *Cultural Sciences*; applied it to the sociology of education, in what was the first attempt (1928–1930) at a complete sociological theory of education, published in a two-volume work in Polish *Sociology of Education*; and used it to enlarge the scope of social inquiry by initiating the sociology of science in two remarkable studies *The Men of the Present and the Civilisation of the Future* (in Polish) and *The Social Role of the Man of Knowledge*. They are all works concerned with the problems of sociological theory; they provide a theoretical framework rather than an empirical inquiry on investigated problems.

Znaniecki's sociology had a liberating effect in Poland. It enforced a final and general retreat from the extensive speculative systems of the last century, which being an all-inclusive repository of knowledge taken over from various social sciences, were to transcend and illuminate all of them. This task was to be achieved by providing a truly universal synthesis of social and historical knowledge and by laying bare the deep underlying causes of anything that happens in history and society. Znaniecki's sociology was a decisive influence in Poland in rejecting this conception of sociology which generated systems perhaps suggestive in their message but of little cognitive value.

Owing to Znaniecki there began the period of monographic studies on specific issues, in particular in the field of rural and urban sociology, sociology of occupational groups, and of education. Various research institutes (Sociological Institute, Institute of Social Economy, Institute of Rural Sociology, Institute of Social Relations, Institute of Rural Culture) vied with each other in assembling and publishing collections of autobiographies and other personal documents, which brought up striking factual revelations about the industrial workers, the unemployed, the emigrants, and the peasants. The task of making sociology an empirical science was undertaken on a broad front. Abstract and inconclusive disputes ceased, and specific issues concerning facts and empirical generalisations were discussed. The personal documents method was further elaborated by Józef Chałasiński (born 1904). He was Znaniecki's most prominent pupil and author of many studies, above all of a notable work in rural sociology *The Young Generation of Peasants* [159]. The method raised many methodological problems and enhanced the importance of the conceptual framework in determining factfinding techniques as well as of analytical procedures in the examination of the results of inquiry.

Two questions were thus brought to the surface – the problem of the validity of the explanations concerning the facts revealed by personal documents and that of the research worker's personal or social equation. It was methodologically naive to assume that the consistency of the findings with the data guaranteed by itself the validity of the former. Findings could have been enlightening, significant and plausible, but the question of their validity required more refined techniques of research and analysis than was at first realised. The questions involved in the choice of a particular conceptual framework by a social research worker were even more complicated; they raised serious and difficult problems which partly passed unnoticed [160]. The important fact was, however, that the personal documents method, despite its shortcomings so obvious today, was not entirely unsuccessful; that it did provide some knowledge and insight, based on experience, into particular classes of social phenomena; and that considerable progress and expansion of sociological knowledge in general could not be denied. From this viewpoint it was probably immaterial that some empirical acquaintance with and understanding of social phenomena was achieved by unrigorous methods. At that time they were the best available.

Znaniecki's sociology reveals a striking paradox which seems to pervade the whole of contemporary sociology. In principle, it is based on the realist conception of social reality; without reifying it, it claims its objectivity, its independence from individual human agents, and its irreducibility to a collection of individuals. On the other hand, the personal documents method is based on the modified nominalist conception of society. This conception is modified because it assumes not only the plurality, but also the interaction of the human individuals. In present-day sociology this paradox has been enhanced by the appearance of statistical and sociometrical methods which are practically useless unless they are supplemented by the method of case study. This paradox makes it clear that the ontological status of social phenomena, as defined by Znaniecki, conceals unresolved problems and fails to give a satisfactory answer to the question, what are the social phenomena which a sociologist refers to and a social research worker claims to investigate.

This paradox is far from being solved and it offers a challenge to the theoretical and empirical sociologist. While it might prompt the claim that methods based on the nominalist conception should be abandoned, it is clear that to follow this claim is not possible at the present moment. The 'nominalist' methods are the only available techniques of empirical investigations and they have proved their usefulness, despite being unrigorous, in providing us with much reliable knowledge about social groups and types of social behaviour. On the other hand, the rejection of the realistic conception of social reality would probably imply the acceptance of a naturalistic philosophy of society, with little gain and guidance for research, which the hypothesis of the humanistic coefficient (the social factor) did provide. This hypothesis with its programme of investigating the manifestations of the social factor turned out to be heuristically fruitful.

NOTES TO PART I

1. Bell (1), 572.
2. There is no full biography of Twardowski, but his former pupils wrote much about him. See Ajdukiewicz (18) and (37); Czeżowski (3), Czeżowski (22), 9–16, Czeżowski (23); Kotarbiński (15), T. 2, 891–899, 926–927, Kotarbiński (28); Słoniewska (1) and (2).
3. Twardowski's role in the development of Austrian and German philosophy is examined in Ingarden (10).
4. In this respect Twardowski's two studies: *Wyobrażenia i pojęcia* (Representations and Concepts) and *O czynnościach i wytworach* (On Acts and Their Products), published in 1898 and 1911 respectively, were of considerable importance in the development of Polish philosophy. Twardowski came very close to the view established in modern times by Frege, Peano, and Russell that the logic of propositions is logically prior to the logic of classes. See Czeżowski (23), 7–8; Ajdukiewicz (37), 32.
5. Czeżowski (3), 16.
6. Czeżowski (22), 10–11; Czeżowski (3), 14–15; Słoniewska (1), 58–63.
7. The Chair of the History and Philosophy of Medicine, founded at Cracow University in 1920, was the first of this kind not only in Poland but also in Europe (Szumowski (2), 1115). Similar chairs were set up at the University of Warsaw, Poznań, Wilno and Lwów. In 1924 a periodical *Archiwum historii i filozofii medycyny* devoted to the history and philosophy of medicine was started, eighteen volumes of which appeared up to 1947.
8. Łukasiewicz (9), 607; Czeżowski (22), 9–16; Schaff (15), 37.
9. Kotarbiński (15), T. 1, 733–749; T. 2, 203–206.
10. See Baley (1), Słoniewska (2).
11. Leśniewski (3), 182–183.
12. The most complete bibliography of Łukasiewicz's writings is Gromska-Mostowski (1) or Bibliografia (1).
13. Łukasiewicz (1), (2), (3), (12). For a summary of the content of these and Łukasiewicz's other contributions published at that time see Borkowski-Słupecki (2), 7–21.
14. An outline of the classification in question is to be found in Łukasiewicz (1), 169–170. Łukasiewicz divided all reasoning into two types: deductive and reductive, according to whether the antecedent is known and the consequent is sought, or, conversely, the consequent is known and the antecedent is sought. Each of the two types is further subdivided, the deductive reasoning into inference and demonstration, the reductive reasoning into verification and explanation. Let (q?) and (p?) stand for a sentence that is put as a question. Then the subdivision can be schematically described in the following manner:
Inference: (q?) (p and if p then q).
Demonstration: (q?) (q and if p then q).
Explanation: (p?) (p and if p then q).
Verification: (p?) (q and if p then q).

Łukasiewicz's classification was revised and improved in Ajdukiewicz (28).
15. Łukasiewicz (1), 142–154. This view was recalled by Schaff forty years later in support of the Marxist-Leninist 'logic of contradiction'. According to Schaff, Łukasiewicz doubted the validity of the ontological, logical and psychological principle of non-contradiction and saw in ethics its only justification (Schaff (7), 261). This claim has no foundation in Łukasiewicz (1) and was quickly corrected by Ossowski (8), 30.
16. Łukasiewicz (10), 67–68; Łukasiewicz (18), 15. See Sobociński (7), 11.
17. Łukasiewicz (1), 6, 136; Łukasiewicz (2), 56–57.
18. They were the problems of determinism and of the freedom of will. See Łukasiewicz (4).
19. Leśniewski (3), (4), (5).
20. Łukasiewicz (9), (10), (11), (13); Łukasiewicz-Tarski (1).
21. Ajdukiewicz (2), Łukasiewicz (10).
22. Tarski (5).
23. Kotarbiński (3).
24. A different opinion was suggested by Grzegorczyk who claimed that Leśniewski somehow missed the opportunity, first, by delaying the publication of his system at the time when it would have had a chance of influencing further development; second, by continuing his efforts on the formalisation of the whole of logic and mathematics when under the impact of Gödel's results the interest shifted towards metalogical research (Grzegorczyk (7)). Grzegorczyk's assessment is not endorsed by other mathematical logicians. See Fraenkel–Bar-Hillel (1), 185–188. The assessment of Leśniewski's system that follows stresses its philosophical importance which is not affected by what has happened in the research on the foundations of mathematics.
25. Łukasiewicz (10), 9. Kotarbiński paid a warm tribute to Leśniewski's inspiration in the introduction to Kotarbiński (3) and later often recognised his philosophical debt to him. See Kotarbiński (15), T. 2, 738, 834; Kotarbiński (24), 4–5.
26. Tarski (5), 24, 54, 155, 215, 333, 402.
27. Leśniewski' system consists of three parts: the prototthetic, ontology and mereology, whose elements are respectively expounded in Leśniewski (4), Leśniewski (5) and (3), chapter 11, Leśniewski (3). So far as ontology is concerned, Kotarbiński (3) and Sobociński (1) are important sources. A concise description of Leśniewski's system is to be found in Sobociński (2), 11–13. The work of reconstruction of Leśniewski's system was undertaken by Słupecki (Słupecki (11) and (13)) and abroad by Sobociński and Lejewski. See Sobociński (4) and (5), Lejewski (2), (3), (4). Sobociński's and Lejewski's contributions both elucidate Leśniewski's system by solving a variety of its problems and reconstruct its particular parts.
28. Compare Łukasiewicz's opinion in Łukasiewicz (18), 6, which sounds very much like that of Leśniewski. Leśniewski's evaluation of earlier systems intended to establish a safe foundation for mathematics is to be found in Leśniewski (3), chapter 1–3.
29. Leśniewski (2) and Leśniewski (3), chapter 2–3. It was mentioned before that Leśniewski had repudiated his paper of 1914, but it was studied and extensively used by others. See, *e.g.*, Kotarbiński (3), T. 1, 175–177. Practically all the expositions of Leśniewski's views on antinomies and the manner in which they should be resolved refer to the 'oral tradition'. See Kotarbiński (15), T. 2, 834; Kotarbiński (16), 191; Tarski (5), 155, footnote 1; Sobociński (3), 95, footnote 2.
30. Sobociński (3).

31. As we know from Leśniewski himself, the theory of semantical categories was established in 1921, but the foundations for it were laid much earlier, namely in his presymbolic Lwów period. Leśniewski's theory of semantical categories is explained in Słupecki (11), 45–47, Słupecki (13), 9–11.
32. Łukasiewicz (9), 607.
33. See Mostowski (10), 1–2. A similar evaluation of Leśniewski and Łukasiewicz, as well as of the role they played in philosophy, logic and mathematics in Poland, was given by Sobociński. See Sobociński (7), 42–43.
34. Łukasiewicz's contributions to logic made in the post-war period are briefly described in Prior (2).
35. Łukasiewicz (6), Łukasiewicz (9), 607, Łukasiewicz (18), 4–7, 15. When he could still have been described as a member of the Lwów school, Łukasiewicz considered logical and mathematical structures as a 'free creation of the mind'. See Łukasiewicz (12), 30–31.
36. Łukasiewicz (19), 99–100. Chwistek made *en passant* a remark in one of his lectures that it did not matter whether the functor is written between or in front of its arguments. This idea was seized upon by Łukasiewicz and worked out into a new system of symbolic notation. See Sobociński (7), 16–17. Chwistek himself did not claim the authorship of the new symbolism and gave credit for it to Łukasiewicz (Chwistek (3), 110). The formal advantages of the CN calculus were at once appreciated in Poland, also outside the circle of logicians. See the review of Łukasiewicz (10) in Kotarbiński (15), T. 2, 810–813.
37. The collective character and team work of the Warsaw school is very apparent in Łukasiewicz-Tarski (1) or Sobociński (1). Some references to it can be also found in Leśniewski (3). For the survey of Łukasiewicz's and of the Warsaw school achievements in the field of the propositional calculus in their relations to the progress made elsewhere see Church (1), 155–166; Borkowski-Słupecki (2), 21–29. – Lindenbaum perished at the hands of the Germans, Presburger and Wajsberg are missing, presumably murdered by the Germans.
38. Łukasiewicz (1), 6.
39. See Tarski (4), 138–140, and Tarski (5), chapter 8, in particular § 2, also chapters 3 and 5. For reasons given, Tarski's description of the origins of metalogic is closer to the facts than the short and sometimes misleading 'Terminological Remarks' in Carnap (1), 9.
40. Łukasiewicz's criticism aimed in particular at K. Prantl, *Geschichte der Logik im Abendlande,* 4 Bde, Leipzig, 1855–70, and, so far as Aristotle was concerned, H. Maier, *Die Syllogistik des Aristoteles,* 3 Bde Tübingen, 1896–1900. But in the case of Aristotle Łukasiewicz showed that gross errors were committed by practically all historians and logicians, including the most eminent ones.
41. Salamucha (1), (2), (5), (6), and Sobociński (8). Salamucha was shot by the Germans together with the wounded whom he refused to leave alone in a Warsaw hospital during the rising of 1944.
42. Bocheński (5), (7), (9), (12). Bocheński's pre-war contributions are listed in Bocheński (5).
43. Jordan (2), Kokoszyńska (1A), Michalski (1).
44. Łukasiewicz (9), 616; Bocheński (6), 1063.
45. See, *e.g.,* the bibliography of works concerned with ancient formal logic in Bocheński (7), 112–116, to which Boehner (1) should be added. Heinrich Scholz, the author of *Geschichte der Logik,* was with Łukasiewicz the second protagonist of the revival of the history of logic in our times. Scholz kept in close touch with

the Warsaw school, in particular with Łukasiewicz.

46. They will be denoted by the symbol 'L$_n$', where n is a natural number or n is aleph zero.

47. Łukasiewicz (5) and (6). In Łukasiewicz (4) the discovery of L$_3$ is stated to have been made in the summer of 1917.

48. Łukasiewicz (11), 72; Łukasiewicz (10), 67–70.

49. Wajsberg (1), Słupecki (1). See also Słupecki (2), (3), (5).

50. Łukasiewicz (21). No reference is made to non-Polish contributions because they lie outside the scope of this study. With the exception of Post and the intuitionist school, whose purpose and manner somehow differed from that pursued in Warsaw, the investigations on L$_n$ were carried out before the war exclusively in Poland.

51. Łukasiewicz (20), 207–208.

52. Łukasiewicz (4). Łukasiewicz felt that the second of these addresses was important enough to reconstruct it and he did it in 1946. A copy of the manuscript is in possession of the writer.

53. Kotarbiński (15), T. 1, 150–159, 122–140.

54. Kotarbiński (15), T. 1, 168. In a note attached to the 1957 edition of his essay published in 1913 Kotarbiński said that he did give up 'logical indeterminism' one year after the initial publication of his essay, largely under Leśniewski's influence. See Kotarbiński (15), T. 1, 13, footnote 1.

55. Ajdukiewicz (8), 158–159; Greniewski (8), 94.

56. Łukasiewicz (11), 59; Łukasiewicz (20), 156.

57. Łukasiewicz (21), Łukasiewicz (20), 158–180. The qualification of Łukasiewicz's success is prompted by his own observation to the effect that some consequences of his four-valued modal system look paradoxical. In this connection Łukasiewicz remarked that when the propositional calculus had first become known some of its theorems, still referred to as the 'paradoxes of implications', also aroused fierce opposition. By now they are universally accepted.

58. Mostowski (10), 3.

59. Łukasiewicz (9), 609–612. When Łukasiewicz was asked to address the Congress of Philosophy in Prague (1934) on the significance of logical analysis for knowledge, he simply surveyed the most important logical discoveries and emphasised the precision achieved by logic. See Łukasiewicz (14).

60. Łukasiewicz (9), 614; Łukasiewicz (17), 124.

61. Łukasiewicz (8), Łukasiewicz (9), 612–614; Łukasiewicz (17), 125–126.

62. Łukasiewicz (17), 126–129.

63. Łukasiewicz (17), 119–121; Łukasiewicz (18), 4–7.

64. Łukasiewicz (17), 121; Łukasiewicz (18), 15.

65. 'Perhaps a philosopher of a sort', as he described himself (Tarski (3), 41).

66. Tarski (5), chapter 1.

67. Tarski (5), chapter 7 and 12.

68. Tarski (5), 252. A short summary of Tarski's celebrated essay was first published in Polish in 1931 and in German in 1932. The full text in Polish appeared in print in 1933 (Tarski (1)), and in German in 1935 (Tarski (2)). Outside Poland it was almost ignored at that time.

69. Kotarbiński (3), T. 1, 22, 85–86; Doroszewski (1).

70. Elements of semantics were included in Ajdukiewicz (2) and Kotarbiński (3). Some semantical concepts were discussed in Ajdukiewicz's, Kreczmar's, Ossowska's and Ossowski's papers published in the early 'thirties. Kotarbiński (15), T. 2,

221–224 provides some information concerning the history of semantics in Poland.

71. Tarski (5), 155, footnote 1, 402.
72. For a very clear definition of the conditions under which a language can be exactly specified see Tarski (3), 18.
73. Tarski (5), 165.
74. Apart from philosophers of the traditional school of thinking, including Marxist-Leninists in the post-war period, who considered the philosophical application of semantics as trivial, I do not know of anyone in Poland subscribing to Bergmann's view, published in 1950, that 'formal semantics is philosophically not important' (Bergmann (1), 29).
75. See Kotarbiński (3), T. 1, 167–173; Kokoszyńska (4) and (7).
76. At the time of writing his essay on the concept of truth Tarski agreed in principle with what he called Leśniewski's intuitionistic formalism, which, as says a note to the English translation of his pre-war papers, 'does not adequately reflect his present attitude' (Tarski (5), 62). If I understood him correctly (Tarski (3), 27–28), Tarski no longer considers himself an adherent of the absolute conception of truth. His (T) schema states what is the meaning of the classical conception of truth and does not raise the claim of being the only acceptable definition of a true statement.
77. Tarski (5), 267; Tarski (3), 19.
78. Tarski (5), 37.
79. Chwistek (3), 70–73 refers to Zaremba and summarises some of his ideas.
80. See, e.g., Ajdukiewicz (8), 160–161.
81. The lecture and the impression it made on Chwistek is described in Chwistek (3), 78–79.
82. Chwistek (3), 154.
83. 'I must confess', Chwistek wrote, 'that systems of symbolic logic, worked out with extreme accuracy but based upon idealistic presuppositions, are much less clear to me than are trivial descriptions in which everyday language is employed' (Chwistek (3), 273).
84. Chwistek (3), chapter 7; Myhill (1), 119.
85. See Marczewski (1), where a short survey of the development of mathematics in Poland in the years 1918-1939 is to be found.
86. Fragmenty Filozoficzne (1), Przedmowa; Kotarbiński (15), T. 1, 435–445; Kotarbiński (3), T. 2, 281–283.
87. Kotarbiński (3). The essays mentioned were reprinted in Kotarbiński (15), T. 2, 7–136.
88. Kotarbiński (15), T. 2, 110–113, 154–155.
89. I do not refer to the shortest axiom of ontology but to its original formulation which can be found in Kotarbiński (3), T. 1, 295. See also Lejewski (4). Kotarbiński said recently that the origins of reism were of intuitive nature and that reism was an answer to the difficulties he experienced in understanding what was meant by the object-property inherence relation. Only later he found in Leśniewski's ontology a powerful logical instrument which gave him a chance to expound and express precisely the main reistic assumptions (Kotarbiński (24), 3–5). What is said in the text above should not be understood as a denial of Kotarbiński's autobiographical information.
90. Quine (1), 119–123. Within the Warsaw school Ajdukiewicz was the most incisive critic of reism.
91. Kotarbiński (15), T. 2, 76–89; Kotarbiński (3), T. 2, 244–246; Kotarbiński (9),

495–496; Kotarbiński (17), 18–20.

92. Kotarbiński (15), T. 2, 97–103; Kotarbiński (3), T. 1, 122–133; Kotarbiński (9), 493–495.

93. The reistic interpretation of psychological statements, the most controversial part of reism in Poland, is briefly explained in Kotarbiński (9), 496–500. Kotarbiński expounded his views on this matter in a paper published in 1922 and reprinted in Kotarbiński (15), T. 2, 40–59. In the discussion that followed Ingarden and Helena Lelesz were Kotarbiński's main opponents. The discussion is summarised in Jordan (1).

94. Kotarbiński dealt with problems of praxeology in numerous articles. See Kotarbiński (15), T. 1, 331–386, 395–397, 422–449; Kotarbiński (1), (2), (5), (8), (13). The difficulties encountered in praxeology formulated in the reistic language are indicated in Dąmbska (11), 147.

95. Ajdukiewicz (3), (19), (21), (27).

96. The examination of the idealist argument by means of semantical concepts belongs mainly to the post-war period but it originated with a paper published in 1937. See Ajdukiewicz (10).

97. The concept of a closed and connected language is defined in Ajdukiewicz (5), 120–129.

98. Ajdukiewicz (6), 278–282. Ajdukiewicz abandoned the conception of radical conventionalism in 1936. See Ajdukiewicz (26), 316–317.

99. Ajdukiewicz (5), 113–118; Ajdukiewicz (26), 295.

100. Zawirski (2). For details see Gawecki (6).

101. Wiegner (1).

102. Wiegner (2), (3).

103. Many of them are no longer alive. Markin, Auerbach, Pański, Rajgrodzki, Hosiasson-Lindenbaum perished at the hands of the Germans, Milbrandt was killed in the Warsaw rising, and A. Wundheiler died in the U.S.A. Tarski, Sobociński, and Hiż are teaching in American universities, and Poznański at the Hebrew University in Jerusalem. For a fuller list of Kotarbiński's pupils see Fragmenty Filozoficzne (1), 5.

104. Rutski was killed in action in 1939 and Schmierer perished in a concentration camp. Mehlberg is in the U.S.A.

105. In the 'thirties much has been written about the Vienna Circle. See Kotarbińska (3) and the literature quoted there.

106. See Gawecki (7). Heinrich was the teacher of many psychologists now active in Poland, among whom are Stefan Szuman, a scholar of high and varied accomplishments, and Włodzimierz Szewczuk, author of a valuable book on Gestalt psychology.

107. See in particular Smoluchowski (1), T. 3, 87–110 and Mises (1), sixth lecture.

108. A short characterisation of Catholic philosophers can be found in Bocheński (3), 247–248. See also Woroniecki (1), 50–55.

109. See Bocheński (3), 245.

110. Michalski (2).

111. Boehner (1), XIII.

112. Lutosławski is the author of *The Origin and Growth of Plato's Logic with an Account of Plato's Style and of the Chronology of His Writings* (London, 1897), which greatly contributed to the final establishment of the chronology of Plato's dialogues.

113. Ingarden (12), T. 1, 1.

114. Ingarden (12).
115. Ingarden (6), Ingarden (22), T. 1, 3–226.
116. Ingarden (1), (2), (5).
117. Ingarden (3), (4).
118. The publication of a volume of essays and recollections commemorating Witkiewicz and his various achievements (Kotarbiński-Płomieński (1)) was delayed for several years because of the prohibition of the Communist authorities.
119. This particular Chwistek's theory is outlined in the last chapter of Chwistek (3).
120. See Opałek-Wolter (1), 11–13; Kotarbiński (3), T. 2, 261–264; Kotarbiński (15), T. 2, 326–327.
121. A concise summary of Petrażycki's various theories is to be found in Lande (2), 843–908.
122. The history of art and aesthetics were highly developed disciplines in the period between the two wars. For selective bibliography, see Wallis (3).
123. Tatarkiewicz (5).
124. Heinrich (1).
125. Heitzman teaches now in the U.S.A. and Kieszkowski disappeared without trace.
126. For details see Hammer (1), 35–58.
127. Bocheński (12), 485.
128. It is not possible to mention all who contributed to the history of ancient, medieval and modern philosophy. A fuller survey can be found in Bocheński (3), 225–256.
129. See Krzywicki (5), T. 1, 287–288, T. 2, 231–235. The Polish translation was preceded by that in Russian and French (1872). The first English edition of *Capital* appeared in London in 1887.
130. They included *Socialism: Utopian and Scientific* (Geneva 1882), *The Manifesto of the Communist Party* (Geneva 1883), *The Civil War in France* (Geneva 1884), *Wage, Labour and Capital* (Paris 1886), *The Poverty of Philosophy* (Paris 1886), *The Eighteenth Brummaire of Louis Bonaparte* (Paris 1889), *A Contribution to the Critique of Political Economy* (Paris 1889), *Ludwig Feuerbach* (Riga 1890), *The Peasant War in Germany* (London 1902), *The Class Struggles in France, 1848 to 1850* (Warsaw 1906).
131. Compare Hertz (1), 74–76.
132. Plekhanov (1), 24.
133. Krzywicki met some Russian emigrants in Paris in 1885 from whom he heard of Plekhanov's *Our Differences* (Krzywicki (5), T. 1, 301–308). So far as I am aware, Krzywicki's interpretation of historical materialism was worked out before 1890.
134. See Znaniecki (7), 222–223; Lutyński (2), 792–800.
135. Krzywicki (1) and (4), T. 1. See also Krzywicki (2), 217.
136. Lange (1), 109. Lange's essay was reprinted in 1947.
137. Znaniecki (5), 248. Krzywicki's hostility to speculations and all-embracing sociological theories constructed without sufficient factual evidence was widely considered as his greatest contribution to the development of sociology in Poland. See Bystroń (1), 235.
138. Kotarbiński (15), T. 2, 748.
139. Rudniański (3), 199–231; Bachulski (1) and the literature quoted there; Reutt (1).
140. Historical materialism is examined in Kotarbiński (3), T. 2, 244–246; Kotarbiński (15), T. 2, 88; Engels' opinions on chance – in Kotarbińska (1); social determination of knowledge in Ossowska-Ossowski (1), Ossowski (1), 7–10. Lande's essay on the sociology of knowledge *(O tak zwanej socjologii wiedzy. Czasopismo*

Prawnicze i Ekonomiczne 30, 1936, 470–523) was not available to me. This essay was not reprinted in Lande (2).

141. *Marks i Engels w Polsce* (1), 27–39. Full original editions of the works of Marx, Engels, and Lenin, as well as Soviet scientific publications and periodicals not easily obtainable from the Soviet Union, were available to university undergraduates and other persons. See Assorodobraj (2), 119–120.

142. Chałasiński (13), 26–27.

143. Czarnowski (2).

144. Czarnowski (3).

145. The most important of them was Czarnowski (1).

146. Assorodobraj (2), 117–124, 151–156. It is clear from what good and reliable judges of men say about Czarnowski (see Ossowski (2), Kotarbiński (15), T. 2, 905–910) that he was a man of tender heart, sensitive to injustice, intolerant only of violence and oppression, which aroused in him a strong urge to action. His political and social views were radical and kept on becoming more and more so. When he died he was mourned not only by his intellectual friends, but also by Warsaw workers, among whom he was active as a devoted educationist, and who came out in great numbers to pay him the last tribute.

147. Rudniański (2), Rudniański (3); Szaniawski, I. (1), 267.

148. Zawirski (6), 333, Zawirski (7), 31.

149. Chwistek discusses Marx's doctrine and dialectical materialism in Chwistek (3), 45–52.

150. Ludwik Gumplowicz (1838–1909), who can be described as the first Polish sociologist in the modern sense of this term, left Poland for Austria to teach at the University of Graz. He exercised hardly any influence on the development of sociology in Poland and has been even better known abroad than in his native country. Krzywicki never taught sociology and his scientific work was concerned mainly with social anthropology. Czarnowski was trained in Paris in the Durkheim school and began to make his mark in Polish scientific life from 1926. J. Bystroń, who held the chair of cultural anthropology at the University of Poznań and Cracow, combined anthropology with sociology only later when he came to Warsaw.

151. Abel (1), 104.

152. Chałasiński (5) and (13), Znaniecka (1), Barnes-Becker (1), Vol. 2, 1069–1078.

153. Bystroń (1), 257.

154. Znaniecki (10), VIII. Znaniecki paid a high tribute to W.I. Thomas' contribution to sociology in Znaniecki (5), 237–238.

155. See Znaniecki (10), 148–151.

156. Znaniecki (9), 205–206.

157. Znaniecki (10), 387–400.

158. This did not contribute to the establishment of good relations between the Warsaw school on the one hand, Znaniecki and his followers on the other. See, *e.g.*, Kotarbiński (15), T. 2, 743, 905–906.

159. Chałasiński (1).

160. The personal documents method was critically examined after the war in Szczepański (4). In his reassessment, Szczepański made use mainly of the results of the discussions on this method obtained by American sociologists, but he also referred to criticism and suggested improvements that were put forward in Poland by Stanisław Grabski.

PART TWO

THE PERIOD OF RECONSTRUCTION AND
THE RISE OF MARXISM-LENINISM

INTRODUCTION

The development of philosophy in Poland after the Second World War can be divided into three distinct periods. The first was the period of reconstruction which ended some time in 1949. It was marked by the rise of Marxism-Leninism as one philosophical trend among others which existed at that time in academic philosophy. Marxism-Leninism as a philosophical doctrine had a handful of supporters mostly outside the universities. They were regarded as philosophical and sociological journalists rather than as professional philosophers. In their activities they tried to dispel what they called the 'misinterpretations of Marxism-Leninism' and the widespread intellectual distrust of this doctrine, which was regarded as obsolete and wildly speculative, suspected of serving purely political aims under the guise of ostensible theoretical interests, and repudiated by many on moral grounds [1]. For their part, Marxist-Leninists showed moderation in their publications concerning more specifically philosophical problems, kept on the defensive and adopted a conciliatory attitude towards other schools of thought with the exception of Christian philosophy.

While emphasising their distinctive characteristics, Marxist-Leninists also professed themselves to be the inheritors and supporters of the rationalistic and scientific tradition in philosophy. They spoke highly of the Warsaw school and logical positivism, and indicated, at least verbally, their willingness to apply modern logical, semantical and syntactical methods to Marxist-Leninist theories. Philosophical discussions were outspoken and free. In the conditions of freedom of thought and expression the Marxist-Leninist claim of having a philosophy superior to any other and of being in possession of the whole truth could have neither been made nor substantiated. The contrast between what Marxist-Leninist and non-Marxist philosophy had to offer was striking to the informed and uninformed reader alike, and the contrast was not in favour of Marxist-Leninists.

Towards the end of 1947 the scientists and scholars on the one hand and the Marxist-Leninist circles on the other lived in a watertight isolation. The former, Ossowski explained, considered Marxism-Leninism as 'journalism which did not deserve serious consideration', the latter ignored scientific progress accomplished since Engels' death and showed no interest in 'bourgeois science', except for the sake of polemics. What deserved a thorough inquiry, Ossowski commented, was the astonishing ossification of the philosophical and sociological Marxist-Leninist doctrine, which contrasted strangely with its political and social outlook. Marxism-Leninism was an embodiment of the 'unity of the opposites'. It had a revolutionary programme of action, proclaimed respect for science and creative thought, declared war on superstitions and prejudices, but its theory was speculative and antiquated, still lingered in nineteenth century problems and atmosphere, and turned its back on science and empirical evidence. The puzzling combination of the Marxist-Leninist revolutionary social practice with an obsolete doctrine constituted a problem to be explained sociologically. Ossowski set out to accomplish this task in two impressive essays [2].

Ossowski's critical examination of Marxism-Leninism was one of the many attempts undertaken by non-Marxist scholars to discuss the foundations of the Marxist-Leninist doctrines [3]. Although only some received an answer, the efforts of others were not wasted. In particular, Ajdukiewicz's skilful performance played a considerable part in modifying Marxist-Leninist orthodoxy at a later date. The most comprehensive examination of Marxist-Leninist philosophy as a whole were two essays produced by Łubnicki. His criticism can ultimately be reduced to laying bare the incompatibility of Marxian positivism and naturalism with what it retained from Hegel's philosophy.

It was generally pointed out that these Hegelian survivals have been taken over and put into relief by Marxism-Leninism, which revives metaphysical disputes of the last century and presents their solutions, now only of historical value, as a final and scientifically valid theory of the Universe, society, history, and man's place in Nature. Marxism-Leninism abounds in vague and equivocal concepts, ambiguous and untestable assumptions, fallacious arguments, incompatible ideas derived from antiquated science, logic, and methodology. If the meaning of Engels' various statements were examined, their implications analysed and concepts made unequivocal, many misconceptions would have disappeared. Since this has not been done, the valuable trends in the Marxian tradition – its rejection, in principle, of speculative philosophy, its insistence that only experience and reason provide valid knowledge, and that philosophy can contribute to an effective action, transforming social and historical reality – are submerged by naive and uncritical conceptions, accepted on the strength of practical considerations rather than of logical arguments.

The second period is known under the name of the 'times of the cult of personality' or the 'Stalinist period'. Its commencement was not initiated by any new development in the realm of thought. It was closely bound up, to use Schaff's words, with the 'progress of the class struggle and of the socialist construction in our country'. The event that ushered in the new era in philosophy was the setting up of the Polish Workers' United Party at the end of 1948 [4]. Following it Marxism-Leninism was announced to be the Party's and the State's official doctrine, enforced by all the administrative means at the disposal of the authorities. Marxism-Leninism could no longer be freely discussed and criticised in public, the validity of its foundations and the main body of its doctrine were placed beyond suspicion and possible human doubt, unless the revision or re-adjustment was made by the highest Marxist-Leninist authority in or outside the country. The Stalinist period in philosophy and science commenced in 1949 and was officially inaugurated at the First Congress of Polish Science, held in Warsaw early in 1951.

The Stalinist period was not, as might be thought, a period of complete stagnation. Much was happening beneath the surface which in the course of time has shaken the very foundations of Marxism-Leninism in Poland. The Stalinist period was unfruitful in the sense that it did not produce anything philosophically significant and impeded any development of philosophical inquiry. It ended as it commenced, namely by political events of a revolutionary character. These events took place, however, after Marxism-Leninism had already been changed out of recognition from within, and abandoned by its most promising exponents who have returned to the Marxian tradition. Marxism-Leninism disintegrated in Poland and left very few holding on to the flotsam and jetsam of the intellectual shipwreck. The first signs of what was forthcoming appeared in 1954 and the following year the disintegration was practically complete. The whole structure was so badly damaged by the moving ground of critical thought beneath it that it could not stand the slightest strain and collapsed at the first stress. It was the beginning of the third period, now in progress, which in some respects is reminiscent of the first. It cannot be described in general terms since it has not yet acquired any characteristic features.

Social and political strains and stresses, to which philosophy in Poland was exposed, were present from the first moment of peace, but only later began to weigh heavily upon and to restrict philosophical inquiry. The first three or four years witnessed a considerable degree of freedom and during this time there was a remarkable display of energy to make good the ravages of war in every sphere of national life.

It would be wrong to assume that the work of reconstruction was guided exclusively by the purpose to recreate and preserve the past. The institutions of teaching and research were provisionally reconstructed on the model of the inter-war period because they had passed the test of experience and proved their worth. The spirit that was to animate them was, however, greatly changed. The experiences of war and occupation deeply affected all and induced a considerable majority of scholars and scientists to adopt a new attitude toward their work, toward their social function and obligations. This basic change in the social attitude of the man of science constituted an important factor in post-war developments. To describe the impact of war on the world of science and learning in Poland it is not necessary to go into all the social changes which the last war brought in its wake everywhere, and which in Poland were considerably intensified by the migration of population, vast war destruction and post-war misery, international and social upheavals. What is of interest in this context can be confined to the effects of war on the mind of the man of science and to the conclusions he drew from them in the redefinition of his social function.

The experiences of war and occupation have shaken the conviction that Western Civilisation is a secure and solid rock providing in itself a bulwark against a return to the savagery of the past. Civilisation has turned out to be a thin and precarious crust. Its achievements do not provide safety at a time of crisis, but make a determined barbarian, lurking behind the mask of modern civilisation, thorough and efficient to a degree unimaginable in the more primitive ages. Moral ideals, standards of personal and public behaviour are incapable of restraining the outrages of men and whole nations dominated by the lust for power. They can be rejected or denied, they may give way under stress and reveal unsuspected, latent possibilities of human nature. Civilisation cannot be left to care for itself. It is a feeble growth which must be kept alive by the constant active co-operation of all.

The outbreak of barbarity occurred within Western Civilisation that has claimed its moral superiority over those preceding and co-existing with it. The events have proved this claim unjustifiable. Moreover, they have proved that this civilisation is affected by some deep-rooted ills, some social and spiritual sickness. The source of the disease must be traced and diagnosed to prevent its recurrent outbreak. For some more fortunate nations this may be a problem of conscience and a means of regaining spiritual comfort; for others it is a matter of sheer biological survival.

The first conclusion to be drawn from what the experiences of war and occupation implied was that the man of science could not and should not keep aloof from political, social, and, in general, the practical problems of his time. The memory that in the inter-war period Polish scientists and scholars had often remained in their ivory tower of pure science resulted in a sense of guilt. They felt that they were thus co-responsible, if only by default, for the catastrophe that befell their country; they failed to realise what was in store for them and others and to act accordingly. This must not happen again. It is a moral obligation and a social responsibility of scholars and scientists to take an active interest in the whole scale of human values and to contribute as much as they can to the elimination of evils, conflicts and maladjustments of our civilisation, which afflict their own community and that of mankind at large.

To be realistic this conclusion had to be more closely defined in the two spheres to which it was to be applied. The responsibility towards humanity at large could be fulfilled only by international scientific co-operation. This idea had in the Polish world of science and learning numerous and eager supporters. The scientist, wrote Chałasiński, has acquired a position of influence never enjoyed by him before. The fate of the world was once in the hands of high priests and military leaders, it passed later on to those of statesmen and politicians, industrialists and financiers; at present, scientists, scholars, intellectuals have also gained the invisible power of exercising influence on the course of events. They should consolidate and strengthen it by fact-finding research, providing information and helping to create a world-wide public opinion [5].

Considerable hopes were aroused in connection with national and international scientific and cultural bodies, above all with UNESCO. UNESCO was considered to be a palpable sign that science has become actually universal and international. Motions and appeals for organising international co-operation of scientists on various projects were submitted to UNESCO [6].

The sociologists were in particular anxious that the chance of studying the effects of large-scale experiments carried out by Nazi Germany on the living body of society in the occupied countries and Germany itself, and of mass post-war migrations, should not be lost. A detailed programme of such social research on an international scale was prepared by Ossowski, who also urged that the regime of national-socialism should be investigated both for theoretical and practical reasons. If an epidemic, argued Chałasinski, had killed as many people as the Nazi had all over Europe, would not all the laboratories in the world be busy trying to discover its germ and cure? [7]

In all these suggestions the international character of the planned research was emphasised. The illusion that there exists only one way of looking at and thinking of social problems can be effectively destroyed by international co-operation of sociologists on definite common problems facing the world at large. There are questions, like that of the proper use of scientific knowledge, which are truly universal and require studies on the level of human civilisation, common effort and understanding. A new revolutionary era of the atomic age has begun. All previous revolutions have taken the communities involved unawares and un-prepared to deal with what lay in store for them. The present one does not need to be a blind force, the adjustment might be made by rational foresight and purposeful self-adaptation in the light of what has become known about social attitudes on the one hand, technological and economic change on the other [8].

Scholars and scientists have above all a social responsibility to their own com-munity. Knowledge means deeper insight into the phenomena of nature and society. It also means the power of betterment, the taking advantage of change, which is not always beneficial, for the benefit of society. The power of better-ment results from the common effort of the scientists to achieve what could not be attained without science. This is the essential social responsibility of the man of science and to this subject was devoted a widely noted editorial article in the first issue of the new monthly *Życie Nauki* [9].

Życie Nauki was the organ of a group of scientists and scholars, active in Cracow from 1945, interested in what they called 'the science of science'. Many distinguished scientists suggested in the past that a separate discipline to deal with various problems of science in its theoretical and practical aspect should be created. In pre-war Poland this idea was supported by a number of eminent scientists who set up a debating group in Warsaw (*Koło Naukoznawcze*), meeting regularly from 1928. The Cracow circle continued this tradition. 'The science of science' was to combine investigations on science from methodologi-cal and historical viewpoints, to consider its organisational, technological and socio-technological aspects, as well as the role science plays or may be made to play in the life of man. The theoretical interest was reinforced by the pronounced desire, born out of the experience of hunger, poverty, cruelty, and degradation suffered during the war and occupation, of improving the material and spiritual well-being of the people. To this objective politicians, social reformers, and scientists could and should contribute their respective share.

The editorial in *Życie Nauki* was not a pronouncement against pure science, but against pure science for its own sake, conceived as a means of satisfying individual intellectual curiosity. It stressed its independence from and its op-position to dialectical materialism on the one hand, and the Catholic world view on the other, on account of their speculative foundations. The attitude of scien-tific humanism was advocated by *Życie Nauki* on the ground that science is of social origin, has ever remained a social phenomenon and is essentially a social activity. Science often owes its development to social needs and should recognise their claim upon itself. It depends on social conditions and social support; the scientist's impartiality and objectivity is a product of the social character of science which is also apparent in the increasing role played by teamwork and planning in scientific activities. Once this is recognised, the cult of pure science as a private concern, with a purpose in itself, determined merely by love of knowledge, is no longer acceptable. 'Science for science's sake' must be replaced by 'science for the sake of society'[10].

Scientific humanism advocated the adoption of the scientific attitude, as contrasted with the traditional, irrational, or non-scientific outlook, the willing acceptance of the services which science can render to social betterment and progress, and an active participation in the whole range of social and cultural activities that benefit the community. It recognised the supreme importance of the social and political sciences, whose development should secure for them the same place with respect to social and public life as physics and chemistry have assumed with respect to technical problems. Scientific humanism was a programme of integrating the scholars and scientists into the life of the community, of considering its needs in their research, and of imbuing the whole social life with the spirit and values of science. Science searches for an optimal solution of a given problem from which all would benefit, since all have the same needs. Political solutions consist in asserting the interests of one group against those of another. Scientific humanism did not urge the scientist to become a politician, but to replace, whenever possible, the political ways of solving social problems by those based on scientific method[11].

The programme of scientific humanism was criticised by different people on various grounds: philosophical, metaphysical, religious, political; Marxist-Leninist and Catholic writers repudiated it, each for reasons of their own[12]. There were scientists and scholars who, fearing the interference and control of political authorities over science and scientific institutions, preferred the ideal of pure knowledge with no utilitarian obligations. They argued that recognition of those obligations was the thin end of the wedge which may ultimately destroy the autonomy of science. But the number of supporters of scientific humanism was considerable and included many names which carried weight and authority in the country.

There arose, however, the question of what could actually be done apart from the propagation of scientific humanism, popularisation of knowledge, and the organisation of professional associations. From this practical point of view two matters assumed great importance: first, the reorganisation of the educational system; second, the problems of the planning of science and of giving social guidance to its progress. These two problems received in the course of time a practical solution, although in a manner that was neither anticipated nor desired by those who raised them.

While the former of these problems will be touched upon briefly later, the latter deserves consideration now, because it throws some light upon the new social attitude of the scientists. The idea that science should be planned was almost universally accepted and the only difference of opinion seems to have been that some accepted it with eagerness and others as a matter of necessity. The reasons for the acceptance of a planned science were not of ideological but of a practical nature. Two of them were perhaps most important. In war-devastated Poland the whole system of teaching and research institutions had to be rebuilt and re-organised. Moreover, science was expected to provide assistance in the general reconstruction of the country. Both these tasks had to be accomplished with very limited and inadequate human resources. Thus planning of scientific activities seemed to have been an obvious answer to the problems involved. Second, the planning of science seemed to be required in view of the increasing role of team work in scientific research. Team work is involved in the common research of many individuals, and in the co-operation of various groups investigating the same subject in its different aspects. Both forms require planning in some way or other. Jan Rutkowski (1886–1949), a distinguished economic historian, who already before the war had been deeply concerned with the questions of the organisation of science, of university teaching and lecturing, and of training young scientists, and Jan Drewnowski, an economist, were the most prominent exponents of this point of view [13].

It was fully realised by those who advocated the planning of science that it involved a point of principle of paramount importance, that of freedom of science and of scientific research. What freedom of science means and what are its prerequisites was discussed by Ajdukiewicz with his usual precision and incisiveness [14]. Ajdukiewicz examined the concept of the freedom of science in general terms and did not consider whether or not the planning of science has any bearing on the freedom of thought. The latter problem was taken up by Rutkowski.

Rutkowski assumed, which later turned out to be an error of judgement, that nobody wanted to use planning as a means of imposing unscientific dogmas and of prescribing methods of research. The planning of science which does not strive to achieve such aims might also come into conflict with scientific freedoms and Rutkowski recognised this clearly. An inappropriate use of planning might be as disastrous, in Rutkowski's opinion, as the failure to apply it where it is advantageous. Planning should be used in establishing the priorities of research, in organising team work in both its forms, in the organisation of research institutions and their territorial distribution. It would be an error to plan everything and to try to embrace in the plan every scientific worker and every scientific activity. The planning should be applied in accordance with the requirements of the problems involved, and not as a matter of principle; it should take into account the differences in mental dispositions of research workers who can not always adjust themselves to team work, although as individuals they can achieve valuable results; and it should, therefore, include the proviso that planning means leaving possibilities of research outside the planned area. Being a supporter of the planning of science Rutkowski recognised that there was a clear case for individualism in the cultivation of science, for allowing the scientist and scholar to follow his particular line of research. It is clear that no discovery or original work, extending the existing knowledge, can be foreseen and planned. We can make plans how a particular problem should be tackled and possibly solved, but we cannot plan scientific progress [15].

Rutkowski also recognised that the problem of who is to be the planner is of crucial importance. There were various schools of thought on this matter. It was clear, however, that the planning of science required the setting up of a supreme scientific body responsible for the development of science as a whole. The conference summoned by the Academy of Science and Learning, held in Cracow early in 1946, which accepted the principle of planning, recommended that this supreme scientific body should be elected by scientific associations.

The problems of the organisation and planning of science held the uppermost place in the preoccupations of the Cracow circle, because the group assembled round *Życie Nauki* was scientifically-minded. 'Science' meant for it 'empirical science'. It found congenial trends and ideas, above all, in the Anglo-Saxon world. *Życie Nauki* showed little interest in the humanities and in the problems of humanistic values. This was the ground chosen by *Myśl Współczesna*, founded and published in Łódź. It was the most influential periodical in the years 1946–48 and its contributors included the most distinguished men of learning. It was to be the organ of progressive intellectuals, irrespective of their political views, who repudiating any doctrine wished to induce by a free discussion and encounters of different minds the revival of creative thought in Poland. Progressiveness was not to mean a total rejection of the past but an active support for the social reforms and changes in the social structure. Among the questions with which *Myśl Współczesna* wished to deal, those concerning the relations between science and social life and the development of international intellectual co-operation were given pride of place.

In contradistinction to *Życie Nauki*, for *Myśl Współczesna* 'science' meant, above all, 'the humanities'. *Myśl Współczesna* was much closer than *Życie Nauki* to the whole range of the intellectual life of the country and often moved close to the ground where politics, philosophy, ethics, and social sciences meet. Kotarbiński's admirable essay on practical realism provides an instance in point [16].

Problems of personal and social values were directly and indirectly the main concern of *Myśl Współczesna*. This was the period in Polish internal life characterised by an intense search for new intellectual orientations. The search was inspired by a sturdy sense of realism and by the awareness of the limitations imposed on the country by the realities of history and political power. Within the thus confined area the place for reason, the value of the human person, social progress and justice, finally, for the hope and the expansion of every kind of intellectual energy was to be found.

During the first three years of its existence *Myśl Współczesna* remained faithful to its declared editorial policy, later denounced as 'eclectic' by Marxist-Leninists. The views of logical positivism, reism, and Marxism-Leninism were presented and analysed, problems of sociology and ethics were discussed from various viewpoints. Polemical exchanges of opinion on the relation between logic and dialectics, sociology and philosophy, Marxian and non-Marxian sociology took place there. While the weakness of the Marxist-Leninist philosophical assumptions were laid bare and the inadequacy of various Marxist-Leninist theories was openly discussed, a revision of the presuppositions accepted in the humanities before the war, particularly those in historiography, was undertaken. Translations of articles by Soviet philosophers and scientists were published along with reviews of important books which appeared in the Western world. Whatever other shortcomings Marxist-Leninists might have displayed, their contributions to the debate on the indicated issues were not yet reduced to monotonous repetitions of a few clichés.

Chałasiński's numerous essays published in *Myśl Współczesna* deserve special attention, because they expressed very clearly the new intellectual attitude which tried to assert itself at that time. As a sociologist Chałasiński was well qualified to express what was in the mind of scholars and scientists striving to define their social obligations and to secure for themselves a position in society that would permit them to discharge their responsibilities with respect to science and to the community. As a sociologist he had no difficulty in recognising the fact that science does not develop in a social vacuum, that it is dependent in various ways on the social structure, more generally, on the social environment, and that institutional changes in the latter may have advantageous or disadvantageous consequences for scientific activities.

The widely felt urge and demand for the 'engagement' of the intellectuals in the social and political issues of the time found in Chałasiński one of its most influential protagonists. He came out very early in the day as a sharp critic of the intellectuals' detachment, of their isolation from the life of the community, which, in his opinion, had been a characteristic feature of the Polish intelligentsia in the pre-war period. To this subject he devoted a brilliant, hard hitting essay, partly historical, partly sociological, bitter in tone, sometimes extreme and not quite just in its indicting observations, but on the whole driving home salutary truths and revelations about the way of life and hierarchy of values of the pre-war Polish intelligentsia [17]. But with a highly critical attitude to the past and with the acceptance of the social responsibility of the intellectual he combined the claim to freedom from any political and social dogma; he wished to be committed by his own free choice and in a manner compatible with his scientific standards. The 'social engagement' of the intellectual was not to be an uncritical adherence to a doctrine, which in the case of Marxism-Leninism, as he repeatedly stated, was obsolete, out of touch with the social and cultural trends and the aspirations of the mass of the people [18].

Chałasiński's objective was to work out an ideological frame of reference and a hierarchy of humanistic values which would throw light on what should be done in terms of practical life and simultaneously provide guidance in social and historical research. It was clear to him as much as to a Marxist-Leninist that what a sociologist or a historian says in abstract terms does not remain an abstract idea, but is also a factor that shapes social or historical consciousness and thus changes in some way or other cultural reality. In the social sciences there exists a close interaction between the observer and the observed; what the observer says might precipitate or prevent something from happening or affect it in various ways [19]. A social scientist must become aware of those contingencies. One way of gaining control over what he does is to clearly determine his 'social equation', his ideological frame of reference which governs his practical preferences and guides in the choice of his theories. The second way of exercising control is to submit one's theories to empirical tests, to be prepared to reject them once the proof is given of their inadequacy. The fact that a social scientist holds certain political or social views is unobjectionable and unavoidable. What is objectionable might be the way of holding them, the way being either doctrinaire or empiricist.

Chałasiński's ideological framework was based on two concepts, those of class and nation. The concept of nation is, according to him, a moral idea. 'Moral' is not used here in its ordinary meaning. Znaniecki called a group 'a moral union' when it becomes conscious of itself, tries to control its own evolution and sets for itself a collective task [20]. Chałasiński used the term 'moral' in the same sense. The idea of the nation is based on the recognition that Nature made all members of the community equal in some respects and that all have the same claim to participation in the national cultural inheritance. This moral idea has been and still continues to be a driving force in history; it is independent of the material conditions of life and unaccountable in terms of economics or those of class and class relations. In general, it is not possible to explain social change and historical process without resorting to moral ideas; the strong urge to establish a moral justification for human action, including economic activities, is written plain and large on the pages of human history. Max Weber's discovery of the connection between the rise of capitalism and protestant ethics has revealed only a particular case of a general regularity.

It is futile to search for the origin of the anti-capitalistic tendencies prevailing in modern society in the development of the proletarian consciousness. These tendencies are, in a certain sense, older than the capitalistic system, are a manifestation of the people's protest against injustice and spring from the moral conscience inherited from ancient times, which strives for the establishment of social life on the basis of mutual assistance, of equal rights and duties and, generally, of the primacy of moral and social values over the economic ones [21].

The division of the community into social and economic classes as well as the class struggle are social facts. A community, however, in which only various forms of class consciousness were operative, could never become a nation; the class struggle, in the course of which one class asserts its domination over other classes, comes into conflict with the idea of the nation.

Socialism is a revolutionary ideal born out of the conflict and clash of the economic principles, epitomised in the concept of class, and the moral principles expressed in the idea of the nation. It is a revolutionary ideal since it indicates the road of transcending the contradictions and resolving the tension between what the social life actually is and what it should be in accordance with man's sense of right and wrong. Its overwhelming power over the mind of men does not depend on any predetermined pattern which allegedly holds sway over historical events. 'To be ashamed of misery and injustice, one must have the sense of human dignity', and this sense is born and constantly invigorated by one's identification with the people at large and the recognition of the common moral bond uniting individuals into a community [22].

Chałasiński's social philosophy was formulated in opposition to the Marxist-Leninist ideological interpretation of social development. What Marxist-Leninists say about the determination of moral concepts by the material conditions of life is an unverifiable metaphysical speculation. Owing to Krzywicki, the Marxian tradition in Poland has been freed from the 'dogmatic system of historiosophical metaphysics' and reduced to the status of methodological rules, useful and fruitful in historical sciences. Metaphysical dogmas of Marxism-Leninism are unacceptable to a modern social scientist of an empirical orientation. A theory of cultural processes, based on the concept of class and class struggle, is unworkable; various essential social relations would then have to be disregarded or misconstructed. History is irreducible to economic history. For what we call economic phenomena are a part of a more comprehensive whole which is unaccountable in economic terms and can be comprehended only by means of specifically historical categories.

The Marxian conception of man rightly emphasises that there is no man in general, no universal and unchanging human nature, but overlooks that the 'concrete man', a man of a definite class and society, is also the inheritor of a definite tradition which as much as the other factors determines his being. *Homo historicus* of Marxism-Leninism is a metaphysical abstraction comparable with that of *homo aeternus* in Christian philosophy. It is the source of the erroneous assumption that man and society can be changed at will to comply with any predetermined pattern. It results in the conception of social technology which imposes social reforms by administrative measures, irrespective of what the state of society is and of what is objectively feasible. Faith in the administrative omnipotence of the State is not enough to carry out social reforms. Sociologically this faith is unjustifiable [23].

Chałasiński's sociological-journalistic activities were a declaration of faith of a progressive liberal intellectual with his adherence to reason and experience, freedom and social justice. His views were shared by many of his fellow-scholars. The general principles underlying the liberal attitude were just then being restated in a more detached manner by some leading philosophers and some moral and social scientists [24]. There was not only a philosophical but also an ideological abyss that divided the small body of Marxist-Leninists from the academic community.

But seen against the background of the prevailing social and political conditions in the country the ideology of progressive democratic liberalism led some observers to infer unexpected consequences. Again, Chałasiński's journalistic activities provide the best help in tracing the course of intellectual evolution. Liberalism had no social support in Poland; there was no class, as in France or

England, to transform an 'abstract philosophical conception' into a social and political force. With his truly remarkable insight into the historical situation Chałasiński came to the conclusion that liberalism was doomed to defeat. Individualism, to which liberalism was pledged, had a better chance of survival in the Catholic Church; the Church with its religious and moral authority and its institutional organisation throughout the country was an effective social force, actually capable of defending the dignity of the human person. The liberals were committed to social justice and social progress, but it was wishful thinking to suppose that these could be promoted and implemented by a mere pressure of ideas and personal convictions. Marxist-Leninists controlled all the levers of power in the State and were thus in a position not only to preach but also to put into effect what they considered to be social justice and social progress. Faith in reason alone is not enough, the idea of a good society which disregards what is historically possible and feasible leads only to futile protests and helpless declarations of praiseworthy intentions. It was no wonder, therefore, Chałasiński concluded, that the intellectuals were deserting the liberal, anti-metaphysical and ahistoric creed, to join one or the other of the philosophies firmly grounded in the community and thus commanding real power, that is to say, either the Catholic or the Marxist-Leninist philosophy of life. Their struggle would dominate the social and political scene in Poland and determine the historical and social evolution [25].

In the course of time this assessment led Chałasiński to the total repudiation of the liberal outlook, no longer relevant, as he felt, to the human problems of modern societies. An intellectual, thrown upon his own resources, is helpless in the modern world. He should adjust his beliefs and attitudes to the nature of the struggle by which the world is faced and which is dominated by the conflict between two conceptions of the nation, the socialist and the bourgeois ideals. The latter, inspired by the pursuit of profit, corrupts science, and, by making of war an instrument of internal and external policy, leads to gigantic slaughters and mechanised horrors of the capitalist civilization. The former wisely controls and organises the efforts of men, directs them to constructive ends, abolishes the danger of war, and restores to scientific knowledge its deep human meaning and social function.

The man of science has to make a choice and act accordingly. He does not need a reflective and critical philosophy, but one interpreting the experiences of man who creates the history of his nation. This philosophy is to be found in Marxism-Leninism and Chałasiński became one of its most distinguished converts. The Marxist-Leninist theory of the revolutionary transformation of society is 'scientifically irrefutable'. It provides a social and ideological framework to which science and teaching have to adjust themselves [26].

Chałasiński was not alone in drawing these conclusions. Some of the scholars and many literary intellectuals followed his lead.

CHAPTER 6

THE PHILOSOPHICAL REVIVAL

Poland suffered grave losses of human life during the German occupation and these included more than two thousand scientists, scholars, artists, men of letters, and members of the professional classes, who were either shot by the firing squads of the German army or perished in concentration camps [27]. Philosophers constituted a large group of those who were deliberately exterminated. The generation which grew up in the inter-war period might be described with some reason as a missing generation [28]. In the Warsaw rising (1944) many graduates and young research workers, some of them of great promise, were killed in the fighting against the Germans or fell victim to atrocities inflicted upon the population of the devastated but unconquered city. Many libraries were destroyed or removed to Germany. Individuals suffered similar losses to their private book collections and to manuscripts of works prepared for publication.

The war left Poland not only in ruins, but also with changed frontiers. There were six universities in Poland before the outbreak of the war, of which four have remained within her post-war boundaries – the universities in Warsaw, Cracow, Poznań, and the Catholic University in Lublin, colloquially called 'KUL'. Of these, the University of Warsaw ceased to exist physically, and only one, Cracow University, was untouched by the devastation of war. To these, four others were added immediately after the war to make, at present, eight in all. New universities were set up in Łódź, Toruń, Wrocław, and in Lublin, where a State university exists side by side with KUL.

The situation after the Second World War was not unlike that after the First. At that time Twardowski's pupils scattered throughout Poland and were appointed to the chairs of philosophy at practically all the universities. The same happened after the Second World War. Leśniewski's, Łukasiewicz's, Kotarbiński's and Ajdukiewicz's disciples moved to the old and new universities to teach there in the manner they had been taught themselves in Warsaw and Lwów.

For the first two post-war years Łódź was the intellectual capital of Poland. Many leading members of the Warsaw school taught logic, methodology, ethics, sociology and aesthetics at Łódź University before most of them moved back to Warsaw. The Warsaw school was strongly represented at the new universities in Wrocław and Toruń. The chairs of logic and philosophy at Cracow and Poznań University were also held by members of this school. Generally speaking, the Warsaw school regained its academic ascendancy and no other trend could effectively challenge it. Its past achievements were admired, its intellectual standards were accepted, its philosophical methods were applied in university teaching and adopted by the younger generation of philosophy students irrespective of what particular philosophical views they had adhered to or were to adhere to in the future.

The end of hostilities of the Second World War was followed by an upsurge of energy. Teaching was resumed at once, contacts with international philosophical bodies were re-established. The philosophical associations were revived at the old and founded at the new universities. Some old textbooks were republished, often in mimeographed form, and new works soon started appearing.

There were five philosophical periodicals in Poland before the war: *Przegląd Filozoficzny* (Warsaw) and *Kwartalnik Filozoficzny* (Cracow), which published contributions on any philosophical subject; *Ruch Filozoficzny* (Lwów) which provided abstracts and bibliography of philosophical publications, both Polish and foreign; *Studia Philosophica* (Lwów) for the publication of articles in one of the 'world languages'; and *Collectanea Logica* a periodical devoted entirely to logic and its history, founded in 1938, of which the first issue was ready on the outbreak of the war and was destroyed during the siege of Warsaw in 1939 [29]. Of these five periodicals the first four were revived in the period 1946–1948.

Sociology had a more difficult start. Of all the research institutes existing before the war only the Sociological Institute was revived in Łódź in 1945. Under its auspices the publication of *Przegląd Socjologiczny* was resumed in 1946. The Institute of Social Economy, the Institute of Rural Economy and the Institute of Social Affairs lost their leading members, who either died or perished and there were no successors to take their places. Of the older generation of sociologists Czarnowski died before the war, Krzywicki during the war, and Znaniecki was away in the U.S.A. from whence he never returned. Thus, the responsibility for the fortunes of sociology has fallen squarely on to the shoulders of the younger generation brought up during the inter-war period. The ranks of sociologists shrank considerably owing to the heavy and tragic losses [30].

The revival of sociology was, however, remarkable, nourished by a widespread interest in the theoretical and practical aspects of sociology [31]. Some of the ablest undergraduates were attracted by it and the departments of sociology, whose number increased from three before 1939 to five after the war, were busy with hundreds of students. The programme of teaching was closely integrated with social research and some large-scale projects were launched.

Łódź became the most important sociological centre of teaching and research after the war. This was due to Chałasiński and Szczepański (born 1913) who have both been teaching there. Round them a large group of young research workers has grown up, some of whom soon began to make a name for themselves in Polish sociology.

Warsaw was the second sociological centre. The head of the sociology department has been Ossowski, the outstanding authority in Poland on the theory and methodology of the social sciences. In response to public needs he organised a research organisation at Warsaw University. It was Ossowski who with some of his students and assistants undertook field work in the Western territories.

The sociological and philosophical revival was a reassertion of trends existing before the war and the first works published continued the developments interrupted by the invasion of the country in 1939. Among the first post-war publications were new textbooks in formal logic which continued to be considered the best introduction to philosophical thinking and an indispensable instrument in every field of knowledge. The rising temperature of philosophical discussions, increasingly distorted by political considerations, gave to the diffusion of logical knowledge a special importance. Articles on logic, its function and purposes, published at that time, had a ring of Socrates' teaching. They emphasised that there is no knowledge without making our speech and thoughts precise and no chance of avoiding errors without the ability to differentiate a valid from an invalid reasoning; that confused thinking is misleading in a variety of ways and that logic sharpens our criticism and points out right courses of action. The confusion created among the uninformed by the claim of Marxist-Leninist philosophy that besides formal logic there existed dialectical logic, the former being the particular case of the latter, produced the demand for the popularisation of logic. This was not forgotten, but teaching of logic was considered a more important task than its popularisation. The latter was expanded and developed only in the 'fifties, when some excellent books of this kind were published, in particular, Grzegorczyk's *Popular Logic* and *Decision Problems*. A popular book on logical errors commonly made in everyday life and scientific practice, on the lines of L. S. Stebbing's *Thinking to Some Purpose*, appeared in 1957. Lively written and abundantly illustrated by examples from topical discussions, it was a great success and had soon to be reprinted [32].

Four logical textbooks of different levels and for different purposes appeared in quick succession. Kotarbiński's *Course of Logic* [33], clear, precise and easy to follow, is an elementary introduction to formal and inductive logic, and to general methodology. Originally written for law students, though it is useful for any beginner, it became the pattern for many similar textbooks published in the following years [34]. Wiegner's *Elements of Formal Logic* [35] is narrower in scope, but within these limits it is more advanced. It is strictly confined to formal logic for the use of students at the Faculty of Arts and for students of philosophy in particular. The most comprehensive are Mostowski's *Mathematical Logic* and Czeżowski's *Logic* [36]. In the early 'fifties Ajdukiewicz and Greniewski produced their own courses of logic of which the first has won a high and deserved reputation for its lucidity, originality and outstanding didactic qualities [37].

As yet Mostowski's *Mathematical Logic* and Czeżowski's *Logic* are the most important book-form logical publications in the post-war period. As its title indicates, *Mathematical Logal* presents logic as a means of investigation on mathematical theories in general and on the foundations of mathematics in particular. It is rich in content, highly readable, and inspires a feeling of awe and admiration for the tidy ways of logicians' procedures. It includes an introduction to the theory of models, gives much space to metalogic, reviews some recent Gödel's, Tarski's and Mostowski's — metalogical results, and ends with Gödel's celebrated theorem of incompleteness and its philosophical implications concerning the concept of truth in mathematics. Czeżowski's book is wider in scope; in it philosophical interest predominates over the consideration of the usefulness of logic for mathematical research. Besides the exposition of the classical part of formal logic, it includes the elements of general syntax and semantics, of many-valued logics and probability calculus. A concise and highly instructive survey of the history of logic puts its modern expansion in proper perspective and also shakes up the impression of finality and completeness which modern formal logic might misleadingly convey. Mostowski's and Czeżowski's textbooks supplemented each other and together supplied the knowledge necessary for an informed discussion of questions concerning the philosophy of logic.

Ajdukiewicz published an introduction to the theory of knowledge and metaphysics, in which he analysed and elucidated various concepts of these two disciplines and gave a lucid survey of epistemological and metaphysical theories [38]. His own attitude to some of these questions was more closely defined in a number of articles on the relation of logic to experience and on the language of epistemological idealism [39].

Ajdukiewicz conceived an ingenious idea of applying some results obtained in the philosophy of language to the theory of knowledge. The advantage to be gained from this application is derived from the fact that it is possible to infer from statements formulated in terms of semantical or pragmatical metalanguage statements about things and occurrences referred to in some expressions of the former. Thus, for instance, given the premiss: 'The statement 'the flame of sodium is yellow' is true', we can infer: 'The flame of sodium is yellow'. In a similar fashion we can use statements about epistemological sentences, or shorter, epistemological meta-statements, as premises for the conclusions about things and facts referred to by the sentences which occur in the epistemological meta-statements. These inferences are valid provided that the metalanguage comprises besides the names of sentences and expressions also these sentences and expressions themselves. In other words, the necessary condition of valid inference is that we use the metalanguage of semantics and not that of syntax, hence also the name 'semantical epistemology'.

To see the advantages to be gained from the application of semantical-like methods to the theory of knowledge, and, in particular, to the dispute between epistemological idealism and realism, another preparatory step must be made. The epistemological reflection may be expressed in terms of two basically different languages. We can use a vocabulary which includes only names of representations and no names of objects represented by these 'thoughts'. This is a syntactical-like metalanguage. We cannot formulate in this syntactical-like metalanguage any problem of the object language, that is to say, to assert anything about the objects designated by the expressions of the object language. On the other hand, we can also express the epistemological reflections in a semantical-like metalanguage, *i.e.*, use a metalanguage that contains the object language. In this case we are able, in principle, to resolve any problem concerning the objects referred to by the expressions of the object language in the same manner as is done by the scientists or any man that speaks the object language. In a semantical-like epistemological metalanguage we have no difficulty in passing from statements about linguistic expressions to those about things described by these linguistic expressions.

Ajdukiewicz suggested and tried to show that the idealist philosophers employ a syntactical-like language and are, therefore, forever barred from being able to assert anything about the things and occurrences designated by the object language. If they do make such assertions, *e.g.*, *esse* is *percipi*, their assertions cannot be valid, though *''esse' is 'percipi' '* is a valid sentence of their language. For to assert that *esse* is *percipi* they would have to make use of the expressions of the object language, which their metalanguage does not contain and in which the assertion is evidently false. The two sentences: *''esse' is 'percipi' '* and *'esse* is *percipi'* are not equiform and they conform to different sets of rules of meaning. In the object language things are said to exist whether they are or are not perceived or thought of, their being does not depend on their being known. What an epistemological idealist says, purports to refer to the designata of the object language, but it does not, since in his syntactical-like metalanguage there is no valid manner of passing from syntactical statements to the object statements about spatio-temporal extra-linguistic entities.

It also follows that an epistemological idealist cannot use the expression 'true sentence' in the sense determined by the correspondence theory of truth. The assertions: 'The sun is shining' is true and ''the sun is shining' is true', have different meanings. For the latter implies that the sun is shining (what an epistemological idealist cannot state), and the former only indicates that the sentence 'the sun is shining' complies with the meaning rules of the language (which for an epistemological realist is a necessary but not sufficient condition of its being true). In the sense which an epistemological idealist àttaches to this term a sentence is true or false if its acceptance or rejection is respectively required by the rules of the language. Conformity with these criteria of truth is usually described as the coherence conception of truth.

Czeżowski provided another textbook-type survey of metaphysics, of its historical origin, its concepts and problems [40]. Czeżowski makes two points. First, that metaphysics is a historically relative concept; what belonged to metaphysics at some time, becomes later a scientific problem as was the case, *e.g.*, with the concepts of time, space, matter, or continuum. Second, that it is not easy to formulate a generally valid criterion by which we can recognise a statement being metaphysical. Consequently, Czeżowski is less concerned with the disqualification of metaphysical statements than with the explanation of the difference between knowledge and mere supposition, between science on the one hand, metaphysics, religious faith or *Weltanschauung* on the other, as well as of their various respective functions in man's life. It is not an unpardonable error to make a metaphysical statement. It is a much more serious philosophical offence not to recognise it for what it is.

The question whether there is a criterion or a set of criteria by which the metaphysical character of a given statement can be tested, was taken up by Mehlberg in a number of studies [41]. Generally speaking, both science and metaphysics include unverifiable statements, from which, however, the conclusion should not be drawn that there is no fundamental difference between science and metaphysics. The axioms of geometry, considered as physical hypotheses, are unverifiable; but a physicist does not hold them to be true in the manner which is peculiar to a metaphysician when he utters with conviction the statement: 'only matter exists'. It is not advisable to restrict excessively the meaning of the expression 'a testable statement', because this tendency leads to the condemnation as metaphysical of large parts of science whose further developments have shown them to contain valuable knowledge. A statement might be testable in various ways and Mehlberg tried to distinguish various types of testable statements in the light of Carnap's, Popper's, Kokoszyńska's, Kotarbińska's, and his own investigations (directly and indirectly, positively and negatively, finistically and inductively, probabilistically and axiomatically testable statements). The concept of confirmability is rich and varied in possibilities and it might be made precise without inflicting an injury on the development of science or implying certain views about the external world unacceptable to common sense [42]. The latter point was exemplified in Mehlberg's essay on the idealist interpretation of atomic physics. Mehlberg attempted in it to show that idealist conclusions frequently drawn from the quantum physics by physicists and philosophers of science are closely related to the concept of verifiability or testability and that this concept is of crucial importance in the epistemological disputes between epistemological idealism and realism in the interpretation of microphysics [43].

Mehlberg differentiated various epistemological viewpoints in empirical science by means of the methodological concept of testability. Kokoszyńska tried to define these viewpoints on the ground of Ajdukiewicz's theory of language. The language is determined by its rules of formation and rules of acceptance, including empirical rules of acceptance in the case of an empirical language. The former provide the basis for the definition of a sentence, the latter for that of an accepted sentence or a theorem of the considered language. It can be shown that the positivism or physicalism of the Vienna Circle, Kotarbiński's realism, Hume's idealism and J. S. Mill's empiricism differ by their conception of a theorem of the language, or, otherwise expressed, that the differences among them can be determined in terms of logical pragmatics. A similar conclusion seemed to have been reached by Grzegorczyk in a more general way when he tried to show how the semantics of a language depends on its pragmatics [44].

The semiotic concept of a theorem of a language and that of a statement true in this language are not co-extensive. Kokoszyńska adheres to the so-called classical or Aristotelian conception of truth. She has done much to disentangle different ideas inherent in the relativistic theories of truth and to refute them one by one [45]. This allowed her to make more precise the so-called absolute conception of truth, widely accepted in the Warsaw school, and to distinguish its legitimate and unwarranted use. The absolute conception of truth does not imply the view that there are empirical statements which in no circumstances, e.g., given our own or other people's future experiences, could be rejected, corrected, or changed. The absolute conception of truth is perfectly compatible with the relativity of knowledge, which, speaking freely, makes manifest only the fact that our empirical knowledge grows and improves and that no limit to this growth and improvement can be set. Consequently, a statement p true with respect to empirical data at the time t_1, may not be true with respect to empirical data at the time t_2. A statement p is true with respect to the language L in which it is formulated. An empirical language L changes and becomes richer together with the extension and improvement of experience data. The fact that a statement p is true at the time t_1 and is no longer true, or no longer true without some qualification, at the time t_2, does not involve any contradiction or relativisation of the concept of truth, since the language L, in terms of which the statement p is formulated, is in fact in each case a different language.

Five large volumes which appeared in the early post-war period constitute a category apart by the scope of their respective subjects and the excellence of their achievements. All of them are works of a long fruition which dates from pre-war times, they were written during and completed after the war. Some of the manuscripts had a miraculous escape from the destruction of war, others were saved at the risk of their authors' lives.

The first to be considered is Tatarkiewicz's *Philosophy of the Nineteenth Century and Contemporary Philosophy,* which constitutes the third volume of his *History of Philosophy* [46]. It was withdrawn from circulation by order of the Communist authorities almost as soon as it was published in 1950. However, it reached a vast number of readers by devious ways and when the ban was lifted in 1956 practically the whole first impression was found to have been 'sold out'. The severe criticism to which it was subject was due to the fact that Tatarkiewicz did not comply with the requirements established by A. A. Zhdanov in his speech delivered at the conference convened to review G. F. Alexandrov's *History of Western European Philosophy.*

Tatarkiewicz's work deals with modern and contemporary philosophy from 1830 to 1939 (it includes a summary of the philosophical views of Marx and Engels as well as those of Lenin and Stalin, which is one of the best Polish presentations of Marxian and Marxist-Leninist philosophy) and tries to describe more closely the main lines of its development. Tatarkiewicz carried out this task with thoroughness and erudition which still make his work unique in world literature. It is more comprehensive and provides more information than Bocheński's *Contemporary European Philosophy,* the only other publication of this kind [47]. The development of philosophy in the traditional sense is supplemented by four additional chapters devoted to philosophical problems of formal logic and mathematics, physics, psychology and sociology as they emerged from the investigations of the specialists in these sciences. No interpretation and evaluation of the established facts is offered, this being thought to be impossible to achieve at a stroke. Since, however, to be described, facts have to be ordered, grouped together and related to other facts of the past and the present, certain general features of the development emerge and enable us to find bearings in the enormous philosophical production of the last few decades.

The most important of them is the firmly established fact that the beginning of this century constitutes a dividing line between modern and contemporary philosophy. The latter is characterised by a 'real flood' of works opening new fields of research, unusual penetration and high technical standards. Contemporary philosophy has been 'professionalised' and acquired an international character. There is a mutual interdependence of philosophies evolved in different countries and an increasing effort at co-operation. Contemporary philosophy displays also some mutually exclusive features. On the one hand it is analytic to a degree unknown in the past, on the other it indulges in vertiginous constructions of a Husserl or a Whitehead. It is professional and incomprehensible to the layman, and yet sometimes ready to offer its offices to mass political or social movements. It parcels up philosophical investigations into small and specialised fields of research and thus liquidates philosophy in the traditional sense, and at the same time philosophical problems of great generality and metaphysical nature crop up in the empirical and deductive sciences which used to pride themselves on their freedom from philosophical speculations. A new era has begun, but what this era is and where it leads to is still far from being clear.

By a strange coincidence, it was the manuscript of the treatise *On Happiness* for which Tatarkiewicz risked a shot in the back to save it from the gutter where it was thrown during a personal search in 1944 [48]. This book is not an essay in practical wisdom in the manner of Russell's *The Conquest of Happiness*. Tatarkiewicz was interested in theoretical questions, he wanted to ascertain what meaning the term 'happiness' had to different people at different times, on what psychological phenomena the sense of happiness depends, and what are its external and internal necessary conditions. His investigations are concluded by an examination of the ethics of happiness. The procedure adopted by Tatarkiewicz is analytic, descriptive, critical, and not didactic, instructive, and therapeutic. It is an important contribution to moral philosophy notable for its analytic acumen, historical knowledge and breadth of view.

Two more important works on moral philosophy were published in the first post-war years – Ossowska's *Foundations of the Science of Morals* and *Human Motivation* [49]. Ossowska is a moral scientist trained in the Warsaw school. The term 'moral scientist' is no slip of the pen. She wished to initiate a science of morals, free from value judgements, purely descriptive and analytic. Ossowska was not the first to conceive this idea and she recognised her debt to such scholars as Max Weber, Durkheim, Lévy-Bruhl, Hobhouse, Westermarck, Schlick and many others. But she brought to this task a considerable logical and methodological skill, combined with a sturdy common sense and a rare ability of understanding other people's minds. She claimed, not without reason, that scholars who had preceded her, had not been quite clear about what the science of morals is and what they had wished to achieve. Its task is not to reduce ethics to psychology, social psychology or sociology; it is not to provide an empirical substitute for normative ethics; nor to provide a history of moral ideas and moral precepts. As Ossowska saw it, a science of morals is a complex of disciplines, in which at least three constitutive parts should be distinguished: the foundations of the science of morals which deals with the analysis of moral concepts, above all those of moral evaluation and moral norm; the psychology of morals in which besides such problems as psychological origins of morals, types of moral behaviour and its pathology, questions concerning the psychological basis of moral evaluation and the motives of morally qualified behaviour assume the chief place; and the sociology of morals, whose main task is to investigate the social differentiation of morals, its relations to other aspects of social life, its evolution and so-called progress. The unity of the science of morals is provided only by its subject matter. The method applied in each of its main fields of research must be different. It is the method of philosophical analysis, supported by logic and semantics in the first; of psychology, including experimental psychology, in the second; and the sociological and historical methods in the third [50].

Ossowska's works deal with problems which belong to the first and second part of the science of morals, with the question of an adequate analytical definition of moral evaluation, with the concept of motive and with various theories of psychological motivation, with the concept of human nature, psychological and 'factual' hedonism, egoism and altruism, sympathy, moral sense, conscience, and remorse. They sometimes fail to achieve what they set out to do. For instance, the attempt to define the concept of moral evaluation is not successful, but the reasons of the failure are enlightening and instructive. They always provide a great wealth of careful terminological and conceptual distinctions, help to clearly formulate the investigated problems, reveal new ones, and open new approaches of inquiry.

Tatarkiewicz's and Ossowska's contributions to moral philosophy were the most prominent among many others. In contradistinction to the inter-war period, the interest in the questions of morals became very pronounced after 1945. Znamierowski's major work, in which he expounded his psychological theory of moral evaluations and norms, was ready for publication in 1946. Its printing was delayed and subsequently prohibited by the Communist authorities [51]. With the exception of Marxist-Leninists, philosophers of various schools of thought contributed to philosophical and other periodicals numerous articles dealing with the problems of axiology, ethics, and science of morals [52].

The work which overshadows all those previously mentioned is Ingarden's *Controversy over the Existence of the World*[53]. It would be premature to assess it at the present moment; no more than a part of the undertaking which Ingarden set himself has been so far completed. For the time being, therefore, its importance must be evaluated on a provisional basis; only the setting of the problem can be considered, the suggested manner of its solution, and the general significance of its initial results. From these points of view Ingarden's work on the controversy over the existence of the external world is impressive and prompted the comment that we have in it one of the most significant publications of the present time [54]. It is deplorable that it has been published only in Polish.

The controversy over the existence of the external world is the ancient problem of idealism *versus* realism. Since Descartes, it has been widely assumed that the controversy is an epistemological problem. In Ingarden's opinion this is a wrong assumption; the question whether the external world is independent from the pure consciousness or rather created by it, is a metaphysical one. The doubt

99

about the independent existence of the external world might arise on the ground of epistemological reflexions. It may be, moreover, prompted by ontological considerations; it is inevitable that we have to start from the *cogitationes* of the philosophising subject and what we call real objects are transcendent to the consciousness. Whatever the origin of this doubt, the questions it puts are essentially existential and neither epistemology nor ontology can provide the ultimate reason for what must necessarily exist.

To give an idea about the way which Ingarden has chosen to solve the dispute between idealism and realism – as a matter of fact, 'idealism' and 'realism' should be in the plural in this context, because a whole host of various idealisms and realisms is involved in the dispute – two points must be briefly discussed. The controversy is a fundamental one in philosophy; practically nothing philosophically significant can be done unless the controversy is resolved, one way or another. On the other hand, no solution is in sight and the further we go the more intractable the issue becomes, owing to the absence of a systematically and analytically established conceptual framework. It also grows more complicated by the accretions and confusions brought to it by thinkers who before such a frame of reference is ready at hand tried to solve it, as it were, hastily and prematurely. Finally, the lack of a firm solution of the fundamental philosophical question suggests that sometime and somewhere a serious error must have been made. There is little hope of ever discovering it or of making any progress towards the solution unless an attempt is made to see the essential points involved in the dispute between idealism and realism. For this purpose a preparatory work must be undertaken on a broad front. It includes the questions of ontology, metaphysics and epistemology. Only upon the completion of these inquiries can the dispute be clearly formulated and the way of resolving it marked out. The published part of Ingarden's work did not reach the end of the ontological investigations.

The method applied is 'transcendental'. Its starting and only point of support is what is given to pure consciousness and what is apprehended in it by immanent perception. Also pure consciousness alone can reveal the cognitive reasons for the acceptance of any non-immanent object in its actuality. The choice of the 'transcendental' method was dictated not only by Ingarden's deference to Husserl – whose philosophy is, in Ingarden's opinion, one of the most important attempts ever made to solve the issue of realism *versus* idealism [55] – but also by the consideration that it is the only method available in and appropriate to this kind of investigation.

The methods of science provide no assistance. A physicist may consider the question whether matter, in some way given in sense experience, is in fact some kind of substance, whether it is composed of atoms, electrons, protons, and neutrons, which have the kind of reality that belongs to objects of experience and are the 'carriers' of physical processes, or whether there is no material substratum of these processes, nothing that changes and what it changes from and to, only complexes of events. An ontologist is interested in problems of quite a different nature. He will ask, for instance, the question whether a process with no material substratum is possible at all and whether there is not a necessary relation between the 'form' of the process and the 'form' of the thing involved in it. The physicist deals with facts, the ontologist with 'pure possibilities and necessities'[56]. Again, a physiologist is interested in finding out what process in the nervous system is causally or otherwise related to a definite psychological phenomenon. Once this is established, he is satisfied with the mere fact that it is so. A metaphysician wants to know how these facts are essentially and necessarily related to each other. A mere fact is not enough to him; he wishes to investigate whether there is any existential, necessary structure and relation by which the facts are bound up together and constitute an intelligible whole. To adopt the method of science in ontology and metaphysics, or to make statements about the non-immanent objects without testing them by the 'transcendental' method, would lead nowhere or result in dogmatism of traditional metaphysics. The 'transcendental' method is as much justified and appropriate to its realm of problems as observation and experiment are in natural science.

Here the point is reached where doubt about Ingarden's method raises its head. He makes the claim that by means of it he is able to ascertain what is beyond and over experience and what by its very nature is not accessible to scientific knowledge. Some will doubt whether the controversy over the existence of the external world can ever be solved in that manner. The doubt persists in spite of the way in which Ingarden proceeds with his task, elucidating what he finds, making numerous subtle and enlightening distinctions, pressing hard and effectively upon the sources of information to which he restricted himself. A rich and comprehensive general theory of objects emerges from these investigations, to limit what might exist by ascertaining what is possible and to circumscribe it by revealing what is necessary. Whatever misgivings one may have, no final verdict is, however, possible until the whole undertaking is completed. There is no use pretending that the existence of the external world holds no mystery whatsoever, and, if there is any, that it can be easily explained away as apparent problems created exclusively by the imperfections of speech.

The Catholic University in Lublin – the only Catholic university between Fribourg and Seoul – was the first university in Poland to resume its activities after the end of hostilities. In 1946 a separate Faculty of Christian Philosophy was established at the University. Following the example of Louvain and the French Catholic universities, Christian philosophy has not been confined there to Thomism; all trends in contemporary Catholic philosophy can be taught. Christian philosophy was also one of the subjects at the Theological Faculties of the Warsaw and Cracow universities, which were later closed down to be replaced by a Theological Academy. The Catholic University in Lublin with its Faculty of Christian Philosophy, where both lay and clerical students could study, has become, however, the main centre of Christian philosophy in Poland, competing with Warsaw University as to the number of philosophy students [57].

The University of Lublin has its own philosophical association and its own publications, including a series of philosophical works. In 1948 there began to appear *Roczniki Filozoficzne,* a periodical organ of Christian philosophers,

101

which has continued to be published, though intermittently, even when the Communist authorities closed down non-Catholic philosophical periodical publications. In 1958 a quarterly *Zeszyty Naukowe* KUL started appearing. The latter is not exclusively a philosophical publication, but it gives much space to philosophical subjects. Also the Catholic weekly *Tygodnik Powszechny* and the monthly *Znak,* both appearing in Cracow, have made their columns available to popular philosophical articles. This was a sign of the times. One of the by-products of the Marxist-Leninist political ascendancy was an increasing popular interest in and demand for philosophical journalism, which has been flourishing in the weekly press representing various world-outlooks. In the Catholic press philosophical journalism has assumed perhaps an even more prominent place than in the others, such as *Kuźnica* and *Odrodzenie* or later *Nowa Kultura* and *Przegląd Kulturalny.* Distinguished Catholic writers and prominent scholars contributed to this activity in Catholic publications.

Like the others, Christian philosophers were above all anxious to provide new textbooks and introductions to Christian and Thomistic philosophy, to its metaphysics and ontology [58]. Pastuszka, who belongs to the Augustinian school of contemporary Catholic philosophy, continued his comparative studies on modern philosophical trends and published a large work on general psychology based on the principles of Christian philosophy [59]. Świeżawski, a prominent lay Catholic thinker, carried on his studies in history of metaphysics [60]. Adam Krzyżanowski published a treatise on Christian ethics [61]. Philosophy of law and formal logic had in Jerzy Kalinowski and Józef Iwanicki able representatives [62]. History of logic, philosophy of science and of Nature attracted much interest (Stanisław Kamiński, Antoni Korcik, Kazimierz Kłósak, Stanisław Mazierski). In the early 'fifties the tradition of the Cracow Circle (a group of prominent Thomist logicians known under this name) was resumed at Lublin University. Under Kalinowski's leadership discussions and studies were undertaken on whether, and in what way, Thomist metaphysics could benefit by the application of modern methodology, logic and semiotic [63].

Catholic philosophers were the first to provide an informative and critical survey of Marxism-Leninism, of its philosophical, moral, sociological views, of its theories of State and society. This was done in a popular form and for polemical purposes, but in a fair and objective manner, with a good knowledge of the Marxist-Leninist doctrine, as was recognised by its chief representative [64]. The naturalistic conception of man and society, Marxian ethics and historiosophy were, obviously enough, the main points of controversy and polemics. Later dialectical materialism became the subject of vigorous, pertinent and sometimes incisive criticism, in which Kłósak excelled [65].

Existentialism had only a peripheral hold on Polish post-war philosophy and professional philosophers dismissed it as a pretentious and strange combination of an intellectual and literary fashion, moral protest and social reaction against 'impersonal' philosophies, which disregard what might be most important to an individual, the dread and anxiety of human existence [66]. Existentialism never acquired respectability in academic philosophy and had in Bogdan Suchodolski its only supporter, who soon abandoned it in favour of Marxism-Leninism [67]. Catholic thinkers and literary circles showed a greater interest in and appreciation of existentialism. The writers' interest was soon damped in the course of a mounting ideological pressure denouncing the corrupt bourgeois art in general, existentialism in particular [68], but Catholic thinkers were more persistent.

The latter differentiated between various kinds of existentialism. They criticised Sartre for his 'philosophy of nihilism' as firmly as the Marxist-Leninists did, recognised in Heidegger a deep and powerful mind, who, particularly in his later works, showed the way to the recognition of transcendental being, and gave to Marcel, a continuator of Saint Augustine and Pascal, a high rank. As in some other countries, for instance in England, France and Germany, Christian philosophy in Poland was more deeply affected by existentialism than was academic philosophy. The tendency to evolve a Christian existentialism, which refers directly to Thomas Aquinas and has only loose connections with its modern version, is represented by Albert Krąpiec and supported by Świeżawski [69].

One more work must be briefly mentioned. Kreutz, a psychologist from Twardowski's school, wrote a critical assessment of modern psychology, in particular of various psychological methods, in an effort to remedy its methodological shortcomings [70]. A considerable part of it, in which the testing techniques are analysed, is now obsolete, but its searchingly critical scientific spirit is worth noting. It was the last psychological book published in Poland for many years. Soon after its publication psychology was 'ideologically and methodologically reconstructed' to perish in the process [71]. A dialectically materialistic psychology, based on Pavlov's theories, which was to replace the 'idealist psychology', failed to materialise leaving the ideological planners with a gaping void on their hands.

It is perhaps not unjustifiable to say that the philosophical development in the first three or four post-war years was hopeful and showed signs of vigour. Philosophy was not confined by any dogma, the inquiry could follow the line of its choosing and came up with what results were obtained. There were ugly war scars, but no incurable wounds. There was a determination to make good the losses of war and time, and considerable progress in this direction was made. The old schools revived, but a critical spirit in assessing the past could be felt. What remained unchanged was the continuance of the scientific trend with its skilful philosophical techniques, reinforced by realistic, rationalistic, and a common sense attitude. The past achievements, recognised at home and abroad, provided the foundations on which future developments could be safely built. The postwar revival of philosophy was the resumption of a tradition. The coming years were to prove its strength and power over the minds of its followers and of all, including its adversaries, who have come in contact with it.

FORMAL AND MATHEMATICAL LOGIC

One of the most important and spectacular features of post-war development was the swift recovery of logic. Polish logicians have again been in the vanguard

103

of logical research and as a team are second only to the American school of logic [72]. Closely associated with the recovery was the division of modern logic into two branches, formal (or philosophical) and mathematical logic ('Philosophical logic' is a term of pre-war origin and now not in use). The division was formally recognised in the early 'fifties [73], but it became apparent much earlier. It came to light in the approach, selection of subjects and emphasis given to various logical theories in textbooks, including their titles, published by Mostowski and Czeżowski. One of its manifestations was the incorporation of mathematical logic, in the sense defined below, into the Polish Mathematical Institute set up towards the end of 1948. The Institute has the departments of theoretical and of applied mathematics, and mathematical logic constitutes a section of the former.

The division into formal and mathematical logic was brought about by the specialisation and division of labour. Some of the logicians with mathematical training have acquired highly specialised formal techniques which they apply in the solution of mathematical problems, in the investigations of new fields of mathematical research and in the inquiry on the foundations of mathematics. Gödel's discovery that no formalised system, which is of interest to the mathematician, can be complete, radically changed the direction of the research on the foundations of mathematics and transformed it into a complex of clearly mathematical problems to be solved by methods technically different from those generally applied in formal logic, such as decision procedures, the theory of recursive functions, or algebraic methods. The foundation problems of mathematics have become still more specialised by their being diversified and considered separately for particular branches of mathematics (*e.g.* the arithmetic of natural numbers, the theory of sets or that of real numbers). The sequel of Gödel's discovery was that logic applied to the study of the foundations of mathematics ceased to be a purely logical discipline and has grown into a branch of 'applied mathematics'. This is the development against which Łukasiewicz once warned the logicians and which has been brought about by their discoveries. These discoveries turned out to be the rock on which the hopes of solving the problem of truth in the deductive sciences, once and for all, by means of constructing formalised logical and mathematical theories were wrecked. The concluding sentence of Mostowski's *Mathematical Logic* emphasises this dramatic development and lets it be understood that the curtain has fallen on a whole era in the history of the foundation problem [74].

Thus, the division of logic into formal and mathematical became inevitable. The methods used in the study of the foundations of mathematics cannot be understood unless the logician turns into a mathematician. These methods are not, as a rule, applicable to the problems in which a formal logician is interested. On the other hand what a philosophically-minded formal logician is concerned with, namely a general study of formal structures and the application of formal logic to natural languages, no longer attracts much attention on the part of a mathematical logician. The latter lost interest in them once he realised that the understanding of the notion of truth in mathematics cannot be reached by the construction of formal systems embracing the whole of intuitive mathematics. Formal logic ceased to be the common ground on which a philosopher and mathematician used to meet to investigate deductive sciences and to search for the solution of the foundation problem of mathematics. The division of formal and mathematical logic is not absolute, but the difference in methods and interests is apparent. Modal logic, logic of imperatives, contrary-to-fact conditionals are examples of questions which hardly any mathematical logician would care to take up.

Mathematical logic has in Andrzej Mostowski an undisputed leader. With him works a group of logicians, some of whom, like Henryk Greniewski, Stanisław Jaśkowski and Jerzy Słupecki had already made a name for themselves before the war, while others – Andrzej Grzegorczyk, Jerzy Łoś, Helena Rasiowa, Juliusz Reichbach, Czesław Ryll-Nardzewski, Roman Sikorski, Roman Suszko, Wanda Szmielew – belong to the younger generation. Some of them are clearly mathematical logicians, others work both in the field of mathematical and formal logic.

Słupecki discovered the functionally-complete axiomatic system of the three-valued propositional calculus, solved the decision problem of the Aristotelian syllogistic, and gave an exposition of Leśniewski's protothetic and ontology [75]. Jaśkowski formulated a system of the so-called logic of discussion and investigated the theory of modal and causal functions [76]. Łoś started as a formal logician. He investigated various axiomatic presentations of Aristotle's syllogistic (those of Łukasiewicz, Śleszyński, and Słupecki), subjected the validity of Mill's method of agreement and method of difference to scrutiny on the ground of an axiomatised partial language of physics, and dealt with the formalisation of intentional functions [77]. Suszko did research on the possibility of extending the idea of natural deduction to rich formalised languages, tried to apply some of his results obtained in mathematical logic (in which he follows the semantical line) to the theory of knowledge, and is interested in some purely philosophical problems of the foundations of mathematics [78]. Grzegorczyk, who has done some outstanding work in mathematical logic, came to it from philosophy and has retained a pronounced interest in the latter [79]. Ludwik Borkowski, Jerzy Kalinowski and Tadeusz Kubiński can be described as pure formal logicians. Their investigations are concerned with matters of direct philosophical significance, those of definitions, propositional calculus, modal logic and logic of imperatives [80]. But there seems to be a strong trend among the logicians towards mathematical logic in the above indicated sense. It attracts the ablest minds and clearly predominates over formal logic. This position provides a striking contrast to that before the war.

Unlike formal logic, mathematical logic suffered hardly any ideological and political interference even at the worst times of the Stalinist period in Poland. The main lines of its development can, therefore, be briefly described without reference to the evolution of the Marxist-Leninist doctrine. It is true that the results obtained in mathematical logic were sometimes presented as a confirmation of the materialistic views on mathematics, namely, that the latter is a natural science [81], but this pronouncement was an appendage to and not a guiding principle of research, which was free from any preconceived assumptions. What Mostowski and the others probably had in mind was the rejection of the neo-positivist doctrine which sharply separated the empirical and formal sciences. Carnap's neat classification of truths into analytic and synthetic, the former being tautological and conventional in the sense that they are obtained by arbitrarily agreed upon transformation rules, was challenged by Łukasiewicz in 1936. It had been challenged for the same reason for which Mostowski and some other logicians rejected it, namely on the ground that logic and mathematics do say something about reality. Without any further additions there is nothing peculiarly materialistic about this perfectly sound, though somewhat constringent view.

The starting point of the mathematical investigations concerning the foundations of mathematics was the realisation that Gödel proved the futility of the great undertaking to make intuitive mathematics coincide with a formalised system of mathematics. If that had succeeded, the nature of mathematical concepts and the notion of mathematical proof would be definitely clarified. On the other hand, if the class of true mathematical theorems and that of provable ones within a formalised system have been shown never to be co-extensive, a new way of solving the basic foundation problems of mathematics must be found. This explains why Gödel's discoveries occupy the central place in mathematical logic [82]. In the light of the incompleteness theorem the formalised logical and mathematical systems are only of a subsidiary and historical value.

One of the points in Hilbert's programme was the contention that the scope and content of mathematical entities are defined in a unique fashion by the set of axioms established in the branch of mathematics in which these entities occur. The incompleteness of any sufficiently rich system of axioms makes it clear that this view is unacceptable any longer. Each such system has numerous mutually non-isomorphic models. Consequently, an axiomatic system does not define a single notion, but a whole class of them, let us say, not one but a whole class of notions of natural numbers. This consequence involves no contradiction; it is, however, hardly acceptable.

There arose the need, therefore, to ascertain the limits of the applicability of the axiomatic method as a means by which the nature of mathematical notions can be investigated. In this respect the concept of model has proved very fruitful and a general theory of models or structures determined by sets of axioms has been developed. In these investigations general algebraic notions are applied, and thus what is called the algebraisation of logic has been initiated. Finally, models themselves were conceived as some kind of algebraic entities and incorporated into modern abstract algebra to be investigated by methods appropriate to this branch of mathematics. The research on models led to unexpected results and established for the second time a close connection between logic and algebra. It applies both ways. On the one hand problems concerning formal structures (deductive theories) can be formulated as algebraical problems to be dealt with by algebraic methods (algebraic logic); on the other, some general algebraic results can be obtained from studies in the theory of models (logical algebra). This idea was compared with Descartes' discovery of analytical geometry. In algebraic logic and logical algebra the correspondence between certain entities of abstract algebra and classes of all models of a certain kind takes the place of the relation between points and numbers in analytical geometry.

Algebraisation of logic is not by any means a trend restricted to Poland, although its inspiration was native [83]. Its origin goes back to Tarski's calculus of systems and has been closely connected with the investigations on Gödel's completeness theorem, which has become the subject of numerous studies (Łoś, Rasiowa, Sikorski, Reichbach).

Within the theory of axiomatic systems the investigations on many-valued logics have undergone a radical change. The discovery of many-valued logics was made on the ground of philosophical considerations and they also guided Łukasiewicz's later research in this field. It was done by the matrix method, by which the number of truth-values and the manner for establishing values of compound sentences were fixed. On this basis the deduction of logical theorems was undertaken. It was discovered, however, that matrices constitute a special case of models, determined by a peculiar type of axioms, which might be repre- sented in the form of algebraic systems. Thus the so-called non-classical calculi have been absorbed by algebra to be studied by algebraic methods (Mostowski, Rasiowa and Sikorski).

The second main line along which the problems of clarifying the nature of mathematical notions is approached is the constructivist trend. It is free from the philosophical assumptions of Brouwer's intuitionism, and it is not associated with the revision of logic by bestowing a different meaning on the logical con- stants from that usually accepted. The constructivist trend is bound up with the problem of decision, *i.e.* with the method of effectively deciding whether a given sentence is a theorem or not, and with the efforts to distinguish constructive and non-constructive mathematical entities. The relevance of this distinction to the foundation problem of mathematics is obvious. On the other hand, the question how far the constructivist programme can be carried out and whether the classical results can be obtained in constructive mathematics, has an inherent interest. The theory of recursive functions constitutes the main development line of constructive mathematics. A particular field of application of this theory is the so-called computable analysis, studied by Grzegorczyk, Mazur and Mostowski.

So far as the clarification of the notion of mathematical proof is concerned, the investigations are more or less concentrated on decision problems and decision methods in various branches of mathematics (Grzegorczyk, Janiczak [84], Jaśkowski, Mostowski, Szmielew). They strengthen the constructivist trend in view of the fact that in proofs of undecidability for a class of problems the use of recursive functions is essential. On the other hand the importance attached to decision problems is not unrelated to the recognition of the failure to establish the foundations of mathematics by means of formalised mathematical systems.

The investigations on the foundations of mathematics are not concerned any longer with one problem and do not constitute a single undertaking. There are instead foundation problems approached from different directions and attacked by different, though inter-related, methods. The problems themselves have no direct philosophical relevance. They are essentially mathematical problems. The question, therefore, arises whether any philosophical question of the foundation of mathematics has actually remained, or, otherwise expressed, whether the mathematical investigations on the foundation problems have no philosophical assumptions to be further elucidated and critically assessed.

Mostowski has clearly recognised that it is not possible to re-establish the foundations of arithmetic and to explain the nature of mathematics in general by the exclusive means of mathematical methods [85]. Ultimately the problems involved have a philosophical character. Mostowski has also felt that what he calls the 'materialistic philosophy of mathematics' is, in principle, the right solution. This materialistic philosophy is, however, either purely negative or extremely vague. It says what mathematics is not. It is not a set of tautologies in the formalistic or neo-positivistic sense; it is not a mere game, consisting of manipulations with symbols, formation and transformation rules. On the positive side it says that mathematics either corresponds in some way to reality or is an ontological theory whose development is closely connected with the natural sciences and with what Marxist-Leninists prefer to call 'the history of the relation between man and Nature'. These assumptions are clearly inadequate. They are not strengthened by an attempted revival of John Stuart Mill's view, according to which mathematical concepts are empirical generalisations based on experiments and the accumulated experience of many generations [86]. This view is trivial, if it means that experience has played an important role in the development of mathematics, and it does not seem to provide much enlightenment when it is intended to state something more than that.

To close this short survey a few words should be added on the history of logic. The interest in this subject aroused by Łukasiewicz's and his pupils' investigations in the inter-war period has remained alive after the war. Both Czeżowski's *Logic* and Greniewski's *Elements of Formal Logic* include chapters on history of logic from the modern viewpoint, of which the first in particular is worth noting [87]. More specialised inquiry includes the general history of logic and the history of logic in Poland. In the 'fifties a considerable number of studies dealing with various detailed problems of ancient logic and logic in modern times were published, but no more ambitious work, comparable with Łukasiewicz's *Aristotle's Syllogistic* or Bocheński's *Ancient Formal Logic* and *Formale Logik*, appeared [88]. The history of logic in Poland is a new undertaking, started after the war. It has some achievements, though of limited interest, to its credit [89].

By far the highest rank should be accorded to Kotarbiński's *Lectures on the History of Logic* [90]. It is not a continuous and exhaustive survey of the whole subject for which the preparatory work has yet not been accomplished. It is, however, a remarkable achievement, one of the most comprehensive accounts of the history of logic from the modern viewpoint in existence so far.

CHAPTER 7

THE BEGINNING OF MARXIST-LENINIST PHILOSOPHY

When the war ended and various philosophical trends which had existed in Poland before 1939 were resuming their interrupted development, Marxist-Leninist philosophy was non-existent. Marxism-Leninism has always taken pride in the fact that it was not an academic philosophy and that it has combined theory with practice, philosophy with ideology, political doctrine with political action. If we take Marxist-Leninist philosophy in this larger sense into considera-tion, we still cannot find a single Marxist-Leninist of intellectual distinction who had something significant to say, either among the living or the dead. The Polish Communist Party had political leaders but no philosophers or ideolo-gists. Julian Marchlewski (1866–1925), who came closest to this category, left one contribution of some value, which dealt with the reception of physiocratic ideas in Poland in the eighteenth century.

After the death of Czarnowski and Krzywicki, Oskar Lange was the only eminent representative of the Marxian tradition; he accepted Marxism-Leninism politi-cally, but theoretically he was no Marxist-Leninist [91]. Moreover, the Polish Marxian tradition, originated by Krzywicki, was suspect to the Marxist-Leninists from the very beginning, and was soon repudiated altogether for the sake of the purity of the Marxist-Leninist doctrine. There was nothing in the past to sustain the efforts of those who were anxious that Marxism-Leninism should strike roots in Polish intellectual life.

When in 1949 Schaff read a paper on the development of Marxian philosophy in Poland at a meeting of the Polish Academy of Science and Learning in Cracow, he had to present his subject as the history of the 'ideological struggle within the workers' movement', that is, as a chapter of political history. 'Marxism', he explained, for various reasons had not produced any prominent philosophers. Schaff found serious faults with Rosa Luxemburg and Marchlewski, who, in the public mind, were held to be the leading Polish representatives of the Marxist-Leninist theory, for having misunderstood the Marxist-Leninist dialectics. Krzywicki was not a consistent Marxian thinker and he committed fundamental theoretical errors. Abramowski, whose writings exercised at that time wide influence, Kelles-Krauz and Brzozowski, were deserters of 'revolutionary Marxism'. Only the victory of the People's Democracy after the war, Schaff concluded, had opened a new era in the development of Marxian philosophy in Poland [92].

However, this new era was hardly noticeable. In the first post-war years there was only a handful of Marxist-Leninists in Poland acquainted with the theoreti-cal aspects of the doctrine, and there was still a considerable doubt as to what they should be considered, for they lived in the half-world of politics and of philosophical and literary journalism. There was no chair of Marxist-Leninist philosophy at any university for the lack of a suitable candidate; the first one in Warsaw was set up only in 1948. The four leading Marxist-Leninists at that time were Julian Hochfeld, Władysław Krajewski, Adam Schaff and Stefan Żółkiewski, of whom only the third had philosophical training, received in the Soviet Union. Hochfeld had been a politician and journalist who after the war turned to sociology to become a Marxist-Leninist authority in this subject. Krajewski can perhaps be best described as a populariser of dialectical materialism. Żółkiewski, a historian of literature by education, is, above all, a politician and a prolific journalist on cultural problems in their political aspect. Questions of political strategy and tactics in the cultural field are included in what the Marxist-Leninists call 'Marxist-Leninist methodology' and in this sense Żółkiewski is a Marxist-Leninist methodologist.

Around 1950 this little group was reinforced by the accession to Marxism-Leninism of Józef Chałasiński, the sociologist, Tadeusz Kroński (1907-1958), a historian of philosophy, Czesław Nowiński, a law scholar, Bogdan Suchodolski, a versatile writer whose special subject is philosophy of education and history of culture, and Tadeusz Tomaszewski, a psychologist. About the same time there appeared a numerous group of young people, supporters of Marxism-Leninism, who received their philosophical education in post-war Poland. Among them Bronisław Baczko, Helena Eilstein and Leszek Kołakowski soon distinguished themselves. Only the latter supplied Marxist-Leninist philosophy with some intellectual force, with specialised philosophical knowledge, and originality of thought. After a few years, however, their road and that of the orthodox Marxist-Leninist philosophy have parted; they became 'revisionists' in the Marxist-Leninist parlance. Marxist-Leninist philosophy has again been reduced in influence and numbers to little more than what it had been at its starting point.

Adam Schaff (born 1913) has been from the beginning and still remains the leading and perhaps the only Marxist-Leninist philosopher in Poland [93]. He studied economics and political science in Lwów and Paris, and philosophy at the Philosophical Institute of the Soviet Academy of Science, where he received his Ph. D. in 1944. After the war he was lecturer at the Communist Party Political School in Łódź and became associate professor of contemporary economic doctrines at Łódź University in 1947. One year later he was appointed by the Minister of Education to the first chair of Marxist-Leninist philosophy at Warsaw University. When the Polish Academy of Science was set up, Schaff became head of the Philosophical Committee, and later of the Institute of Philosophy and Sociology. Schaff has always combined theoretical or ideological with political activities – he joined the Communist Party of Poland in 1931 – and is a full member of the Communist Party (PZPR) Central Committee. Since 1948 he has been closely associated with practically everything that happened to philosophy in Poland. In fact, for a few years he wielded some kind of dictatorial power on what used to be called 'the philosophical front'. The expression is apt and fittingly describes what was happening in the world of science and learning at that time.

Schaff holds a central position in the evolution of the Polish version of Marxism-

Leninism because of his versatility and the leadership he has been giving to the small body of Marxist-Leninists. In contradistinction to the others who have been concerned with some selected subjects – history of philosophy and social thought, ethics, philosophy of science, sociology, political science – Schaff has displayed a wide range of interests and with the exception of aesthetics he has devoted his attention practically to all traditional philosophical subjects. He has an easy pen and has written a stupendous number of articles, pamphlets, and books. He has also been the man who at the recurrent internal crises of the Communist Party laid down the line to be followed in philosophy and the humanities in general. He has so far weathered all the storms without losing his exposed position for a single moment.

In the first post-war years Marxism-Leninism was not only weak in numbers. Also the knowledge of the doctrine, displayed by its followers and protagonists, was poor, fragmentary and superficial. Poets, writers and literary critics, like Jerzy Andrzejewski, Jan Kott and Adam Ważyk, who found in Marxism-Leninism a revolutionary intellectual force, identified it with the European tradition of rationalism from Descartes to Carnap. To be a Marxist-Leninist meant to discover and to extricate the rational kernel of what was progressive in the bourgeois culture. Marxism-Leninism was supposed to continue the positivistic tradition of thought, or still further back, that of d'Alembert, Voltaire, Diderot and the whole French Enlightenment. To choose Marxism-Leninism was to proclaim confidence in science and social reforms, to be sceptical and critical with respect to opinions unconfirmed by experience [94].

The early converts to Marxism-Leninism – some poets and writers, journalists and publicists, literary critics and artists – were entirely ignorant of the content of the Marxist-Leninist philosophy. They became converted to it as a faith that promised to change the surface of the Earth and the nature of man, to establish peace in the world and social justice in society, by the alliance of political power and reason. No genuine philosophical question was involved in the conversion. The only part of the Marxist-Leninist doctrine of which they seemed to have had some vague knowledge, was historical materialism. Historical materialism made it certain that the march of progress would continue and that the inexorable laws of history would assert themselves in the revolutionary struggle that was engulfing the whole surface of the Earth. Historical materialism encouraged the identification of what was inevitable with what should be preferred and endowed the intellectuals with a sense of mission. The Kingdom of Reason was just round the corner and they, the inheritors of the French Enlightenment, which was resuming in their persons its predetermined course, were the vanguard of Reason.

Such a reputation was securing to Marxism-Leninism some obvious advantages in the short run, and some serious disadvantages in the long run. It helped to gain a political foothold among a section of the intellectuals but handicapped the chance of retaining their allegiance in the more distant future. It was also harmful to Marxist-Leninist philosophy, since it encouraged and spread misconceptions about its fundamental tenets.

The confusion was not confined to literary and artistically-minded intellectuals who were in fact responding to what the best qualified exponents of Marxist-Leninist philosophy were saying. Żółkiewski was an admirer of the Warsaw school and the Vienna Circle, of Carnap, Reichenbach, Neurath, Popper, Hempel, Woodger. It is difficult to find, he wrote, a greater precision, simplicity, and courage of thought than in these writers. The leaders of the Warsaw school – Leśniewski, Tarski, Kotarbiński – 'taught how to think'. They were the great force that in the past prevented the young generation from yielding to the allurements of the idealist constructions in the humanities, imbued the minds of the young with respect for empiricism, and were an embodiment of the superiority of the scientific habits of thought over the intuitionistic conceptions of culture inspired by Dilthey, Spranger and Znaniecki. Similarly, Schaff recognised the skill and importance of Kotarbiński's, Łukasiewicz's and Ajdukiewicz's contributions to philosophy. Polish Marxist-Leninists openly deplored the poor knowledge of formal logic in the Soviet Union and advocated the co-operation of Polish logicians with Soviet dialecticians, from which both sides would benefit and astonish the world by their common achievements. In the pronouncements of its chief representatives Marxism-Leninism was declaring itself for the continuation of the Polish philosophical tradition, its intellectual kinship with this tradition, and its willingness to adopt the techniques of modern logic and methodology [95].

There were also some followers of the Marxian school of thought who denied that there was any specifically Marxist-Leninist philosophy at all. They took seriously Marx's opinion that 'when reality is depicted, philosophy as an independent branch of activity loses its medium of existence'. Modern materialism no longer needs any philosophy; it is identical with positive science, philosophy as knowledge of the 'great totality of things' is superfluous. Engels, they argued, would have been surprised, if he saw that his own materialism was still expounded in spite of the great scientific discoveries made in the twentieth century or that anybody appealed to his authority in the discussions on the structure of matter. What Marx and Engels said about matter and the world was relative to the knowledge of their times; permanent only was their attitude to reality, the attitude of a man of science, who rejects all *a priori* conceptions, and is guided by facts alone. The laws of dialectics provide no knowledge about the motion of matter; they should be conceived as some very general methodological rules, which in fact have been accepted in scientific procedure. A scientist who adheres to this procedure fulfils all the requirements of dialectical materialism. To look for a class-determined division in physics, biology, and mathematics was an infantile disorder of Marxism-Leninism. There is only one science, validated by the same rules of procedure and the same concept of truth. The formulations of modern materialism must be tested by logical and semantical methods, devised by neo-positivist philosophy. If these formulations turn out to be inadequate and unacceptable by the standards of logic of science, they should be revised and accordingly adjusted. To evade this test and not to abide by its verdict, would show that materialism is no longer science, but a declaration of faith [96].

These opinions came from a supporter of the original Marxian doctrine. He did not intend to expound orthodox Marxism-Leninism, but to put forward an argument for its revision. But faithful adherents of Marxism-Leninism could not have assumed that Marxist-Leninist metaphysics may be reconciled with Carnap's logic of science unless they entertained some misconceptions about Marxism-Leninism or logic of science or both. Similarly, the view, expounded at that time, that historical materialism is the most fundamental Marxist-Leninist assumption and dialectic materialism is its generalisation [97], could only result from an inadequate knowledge of Marxism-Leninism.

Philosophical confusions and doctrinal errors were not infrequent in Marxist-Leninist writings published in the post-war years. Thus, one writer took the tertium of Łukasiewicz's three-valued logic for a conjunction of contradictory statements, hailed Marx and Engels as forerunners of many-valued logics and demanded that dialectics, the 'logic of contradiction', should at last be expressed in terms of many-valued calculi [98].

At that time Marxism-Leninism could have been learnt from three sources. First came the translations of the works of Marx, Engels, Lenin, Plekhanov, and Stalin. They were followed by surveys and critical evaluations made by non-Marxist philosophers. Finally, came books on Marxism-Leninism prepared by its Polish supporters.

As early as 1945 the Communist Party set up the publishing house *Książka* (later *Książka i Wiedza*) which was entrusted with the task of making available translations of the so-called classics of Marxism-Leninism. Among the first to appear were some works of Stalin, *Problems of Leninism* and *Dialectical and Historical Materialism*. His collected works in thirteen volumes, published in the years 1949–1951, also preceded the appearance of the collected works of Lenin (1950–1957). On the other hand, *A Contribution to the Critique of Political Economy* of Marx appeared for the first time after the war in 1953 and the three volumes of *Capital* in the years 1950–1957. The mass production of the so-called classics of Marxism-Leninism did not start until 1948. In the years 1945–1950 over eleven million copies of various works of Marx, Engels and Lenin were made available, of which 10.8 million appeared in the three years 1948–1950 [99].

The second and probably more important source of information was surveys and critical evaluations of Marxist-Leninist philosophy prepared by non-Marxist philosophers and philosophical journalists. The first of such surveys in a popular form was provided by the Catholic writers in 1945. Soon after a comprehensive critical essay for philosophers was published by Łubnicki, a historian of positivism and a positivist philosopher himself. Łubnicki also gave a review of post-war developments in Soviet philosophy [100].

Łubnicki's essay is a competent presentation of dialectical materialism and of the Marxist-Leninist theory of knowledge. It concentrates on basic assumptions, shows the way in which they were obtained, and illustrates their applications. He also critically examines these assumptions, reveals their ambiguities, and points out what, in his opinion, is philosophically significant and valuable in them. Łubnicki ignores almost entirely the ideological and political aspect of Marxist-Leninist philosophy. He emphasises the importance in Marxist-Leninist thinking of the assumption concerning the social and class determination of philosophy, but he does not accept the implications of this premiss in the critical evaluation of Marxist-Leninist philosophy. He examines the latter in the light of facts and logic, and disregards its political and ideological justification. A major error of Łubnicki's essay is his approval of the restrictions imposed by Marxism-Leninism on the validity of the principle of non-contradiction, which he holds to be in agreement with the assumptions of the many-valued and intuitionistic logics [101].

The third source from which Marxist-Leninist philosophy could have been learnt, and the last to come, were monographic studies prepared by Polish Marxist-Leninists. In the course of time quite a number of them were published, but they were mostly popular pamphlets and booklets, intended to reach the widest possible circle of readers and to serve propaganda purposes [102]. Philosophically significant were Schaff's *Introduction to the Marxist Theory* and *The Origin and Development of Marxist Philosophy* [103]. They still constitute the best and most comprehensive exposition of Marxist-Leninist philosophy written by a Polish Marxist-Leninist for the use of philosophers.

Introduction to the Marxist Theory was first published in 1947 and quickly sold out; it had four more editions in the next few years. It had a mixed reception, more favourable among non-Marxist than Marxist-Leninist readers [104]. The former were pleasantly surprised by the absence of some most objectionable Marxist-Leninist views, the not entirely unsuccessful effort to write in a clear language, and the moderate tone, favourably contrasting with the apodictic and vituperative pronouncements of Zhdanov's speech on philosophy, which had just reached Poland. The latter were clearly disappointed by the speculative and antiquated character of the doctrine presented in Schaff's book and by those of its features that appealed to non-Marxist readers. This book, wrote a Marxist-Leninist reviewer, could have been written many years ago and anywhere in the world [105].

Schaff's *Introduction to the Marxist Theory* is not an original work. With one or two exceptions to be later considered, it is a free paraphrase of the classical Marxian and Marxist-Leninist literature, copiously interspersed with long quotations from the same sources. This is one of the main causes of its philosophical weakness. Schaff adopts various concepts of Marx, Engels, Lenin and Stalin in their original form, without elucidating and defining their ambiguous meaning or examining their compatibility. Consequently, each phrase is in a certain sense clear, but their sequence is not, and his arguments either fail to carry conviction or on closer examination turn out to be no arguments at all. Often they are like the Cheshire cat's smile – a grin without a cat.

Schaff's book introduces a new conception of philosophy, which combines elements previously sharply differentiated in Poland. Marxist-Leninist philosophy, Schaff declares, is an ideology, a world outlook, and an ordered set of scientific statements. What is a world outlook, he does not say precisely, but that it is something more than an ordered set of scientific statements is beyond doubt. A world outlook is supposed to be a coherent and all-inclusive system of knowledge about the world, society, and man, which helps its believer to find his bearings in life, guides his action and somehow determines his value judgements. It comprises, therefore, both some scientific knowledge and an ideology. The term 'ideology' in this context has not its technical, Marxist-Leninist meaning. 'Ideology' means 'social and personal ideals' or 'ideals that inspire, prompt and govern human behaviour'[106].

The component of scientific knowledge within a world outlook functions in a different manner than it does taken separately as an ordered set of scientific statements, describing a segment of reality. In the former, the component of scientific knowledge is closely associated with emotional experiences, it purports to support some and exclude other value judgements, it is imbued with a personal belief and conviction. In the latter, knowledge is intersubjective, free from value ingredients, ordered and supported solely by logical relations and empirical evidence.

The difference between an ordered set of scientific statements and a world outlook is considerable and unbridgeable. The discovery of a logical error in the structure or of a factual one in the results of experiments and observations, which falsify a hypothesis or a generalisation, upsets a scientific system. It necessitates adjustments and replacements of the falsified hypothesis by another one which stands up better to the test of experience. This is not the case with a world outlook, for which the test of falsification by experience or of logical incompatibility and contradiction is not necessarily decisive. It is claimed or assumed by implication that it is not any particular part but the totality of the world outlook that is confirmed by experience. 'Experience' and 'confirmation' do not carry in this context the same meaning as they have with reference to scientific knowledge. In the case of two mutually exclusive scientific systems we can, as a rule, indicate facts which could really resolve the difference of opinion. There are no such facts that would resolve the difference of opinion between two conflicting world outlooks. We believe in the latter in a manner different from that we believe in the former. The logic of a scientific system and that of a world outlook are incomparable. The first is recognised by those who can think and are properly qualified; the second invariably only by those sharing the same kind of life experience. Their respective concepts of truth are also widely different. For science, truth is the warranted assertibility. True in the sense accepted in the world outlook is what partakes in the all-pervasive internal coherence apprehended in a total life experience.

One of the characteristic features of scientific philosophy is a self-imposed restriction to consider only such opinions as can be examined by the methods of the deductive and empirical sciences. It differentiates, therefore, sharply between a world outlook and scientific philosophical problems. It holds that thus philosophy gains a firmer ground for its investigations, from which advantages can be drawn for the examination of various conflicting world outlooks.

Schaff's definition of Marxist-Leninist philosophy has abandoned the above distinction and thus created a permanent conflict between Marxism-Leninism and the overwhelming majority of Polish philosophers. Besides the rejection of the principle of non-contradiction, the Marxist-Leninist conception of philosophy was the second major obstacle which prevented their recognition of Marxism-Leninism as a philosophically significant system. Marxist-Leninists have substantiated this opinion by being utterly insensitive to the objections of terminological ambiguities, logical inconsistencies and incongruities, empirical unverifiability of their particular statements or theories. Such objections were often qualified by them as evasions of the real issue, conscious or unconscious designs to conceal the position taken in the dispute, verbal smoke-screens and ideological masks of socially and politically reactionary ideals placed under the protection of logic. What was important for them, was where a given statement leads to, what are its implications and what final conclusions in terms of their world outlook can or could possibly be drawn from it. If they directly or indirectly denied or questioned whatever Marxist-Leninists believed to be true, the statement was declared as false and harmful.

To Polish philosophers this procedure lacked the true philosophic spirit. What they felt to be so unphilosophical in Marxist-Leninists was their stubborn refusal to examine their assumptions, to search themselves for objections to their views, to consider in earnest any objection actually raised, and to follow the argument wherever it might lead. Instead, they were turning a blind eye to anything that might reveal their theories to be wrong or inadequate, every criticism was brushed aside on the pretext that it misrepresented the Marxist-Leninist views and did not apply. This habit of thought was not only regrettable in the opinion of Polish philosophers, but also strongly suggested that a Marxist-Leninist was hardly ever engaged in an inquiry. Before he started reasoning, he already knew the conclusion. If the truth is known in advance, a philosophical examination is reduced to a search for arguments. This was not philosphy, as it was conceived in Poland, but the propagation of a faith.

In *Introduction to the Marxist Theory* Schaff shows how the Marxist-Leninist conception of philosophy operates in practice. In Schaff's opinion the justification of dialectical materialism, of its theory of knowledge and metaphysical suppositions, can only be established by a critical assessment of idealism, and this he proceeded to do [107]. But if he meant what he said, he could not achieve his aim in that manner. A most devastating criticism of a rival theory is not sufficient to establish the justice of the views denied by this theory. It might lead to the rejection of some opinions or to the laying bare of the dubious character of what the adversary asserts; the validity of a different theory is not, however, thus established. In particular, any theory of knowledge stands or falls by its success or lack of success in answering the questions that constitute its object of examination, that is to say, by its success or lack of success in explaining how we know what we admittedly do know. In other words, a theory of knowledge is satisfactory if it successfully accounts for the knowledge given before it sets out to explain the manner in which it has been acquired. The proof, however unobjectionable, that somebody else failed to achieve this purpose, is not enough. It does not make one's own theory true or probable and it does not transform a mere announcement of a belief into a valid theory of knowledge.

Schaff's method of exposition is throughout dogmatic and deductive. The first principles – the laws of dialectics – are introduced in the manner familiar from Engels' *Anti-Dühring* and Stalin's *Dialectical and Historical Materialism*. Since the 'dialectics of the brain is only the reflection of the forms of motion of the real world, both of nature and history', Schaff considers dialectics interpreted as methodological rules and dialectics conceived as laws of nature as two equivalent or indistinguishable conceptions. This in itself justifies the claim that dialectics is an absolutely necessary assumption for the natural sciences, for physics and biology in particular, and that it is the only scientific manner of inquiring into the phenomena of Nature and society [108].

Dialectics purports to be the science of the most general laws of motion and development of Nature, and Schaff subscribes to this dogma. Non-Marxist philosophers seized upon this formulation in the Stalinist period, since it tended to neutralise dialectics by placing it in the realm of abstractions too elevated to exercise any harmful influence on their actual work [109]. Following the example of Engels and Stalin, Schaff establishes his claim by way of providing some illustrations taken from everyday life or based on sham scientific interpretations that drew protests from his own supporters [110]. On this basis he proceeded to the examination of various theories and statements and what turned out to be compatible with the laws of dialectics he recognised as valid and true, otherwise as invalid and false. Thus the biological theory of evolution is found to be in fact an anti-evolutionary and anti-dialectical distortion of our views about life and its development, which a truly scientific research has refuted over and over again. In a similar manner formal logic is reduced to the status of a dead branch of knowledge, to be tolerated on account of its limited uses but in every respect inferior to the more universal and inventive dialectical logic. Finally, to give the last example, Hume's account of causation is quickly disposed of as self-contradictory and altogether unacceptable in view of the fact that if it were valid the world would have to be conceived either as a chaotic welter of events or as something kept in order by God's constant intervention [111].

The latter point has an inherent interest. Bertrand Russell and Richard Mises argued that the concept of cause and the so-called law of causality are a relic of a bygone age. The expressions 'the same event' or 'equal circumstances' do not admit of a precise definition. In scientific practice there are, strictly speaking, no repeatable events, since no single event or occurrence can be completely isolated. Causal expressions are the surviving residue of a pre-scientific and naive world picture in which there exist events whose occurrence is dependent on some other well-defined events. As soon, however, as the scientist describes the antecedent sufficiently fully to calculate the consequent with some exactitude, the antecedent turns out to be so involved with other events that its recurrence is highly unlikely. There is nothing to be properly called 'cause' and 'effect' in a system that is not isolated, and whether a system is or is not isolated we cannot know in advance [112].

The assumption that there are, strictly speaking, no isolated systems and that we are not entitled to say in advance whether a system is or is not isolated, might be described as a modern and scientific version of the first law of dialectics. It entails the opinion that the concept of cause and causal relation is otiose. Marxist-Leninists drew, however, from their principle just the opposite conclusion.

If Hume's account of causation is accepted, it is clear that all inferences concerning the future are invalid and the belief that causal laws describe universal uniformities is unjustifiable. We have no reason to suppose that the sun will rise tomorrow or for that matter that the so-called socialistic formation must succeed the so-called capitalist system. The expectation of the experienced uniformities to continue in the future is one of the inferences drawn from the premiss about the existence of universal necessary uniformities; the rejection of the latter deprives the former of their justification.

Repeated attempts have been made to show that Hume was wrong and that causal laws state something more than the uniformities of coexistence or succession, that is to say, that they state the necessary uniformities. A theory of causation that constantly bears in mind its practical application to social and political events is in particular anxious to prove Hume to have been wrong. This probably explains why Marxism-Leninism treats Hume's account of causation as a hostile statement, specifically directed against itself. The argument of the alleged self-contradiction in Hume's examination of causation or of its making science impossible, though untenable on purely theoretical grounds, is supported by the ideological consideration. The rejection of universal necessary uniformities, entailed by Hume's views, would namely invalidate the Marxist-Leninist version of scientific socialism.

Schaff's manner in which he disposes of some theories in order to replace them by others better suited to his world outlook, closely resembles what for brevity sake might be called 'Lenin's deductive method'. It seems to be little more than an extension of Lenin's standard procedure to philosophical questions.

It was justly pointed out that Lenin was no philosopher and no social scientist. His mind was never engaged with realities unless he dealt with politics. Outside politics 'he was not trying to find solutions to difficult problems, he was not making hypotheses and weighing the evidence for and against them; he was merely defending his heritage of ideas, polishing his intellectual armour and sharpening his weapons for the war of words'[113]. For this purpose his 'deductive method', of which *The State and the Revolution* is the best instance, was well suited. In *The State and the Revolution* Lenin did not try to analyse facts that would throw light on the nature of society, on the function of the State and on the purpose of the government. He assumed that what Marx and Engels said on the subject was all one needs to know, provided that their views are given their 'original' and 'authentic' meaning. With a collection of extracts from Marx and Engels ready at hand, Lenin annihilated all his opponents, one after another, merely by showing that what they were asserting was incompatible with Marx's and Engels' original views. This was, in his opinion, a crushing retort to his adversaries. Lenin thought and acted like the man to whom Engels referred in his polemics against Dühring. When a man feels to be in possession of the ultimate truth and of the only scientific procedure, 'it is only natural that he should have a certain contempt for the rest of erring and unscientific humanity' [114].

Whatever virtues Lenin's method might have in the political struggle, it is out of place in philosophy. To start from an arbitrary principle and to assert that what disagrees with its implications is false, only leads to a clash of conflicting opinions. It provides no means of resolving the differences and of examining the validity of various views. What one side considers to be self-evident or proven, is far from being either self-evident or proven in the opinion of the other, to which it may appear as a dogmatic pronouncement or a groundless prejudice.

The picture of Marxist-Leninist philosophy that emerged from the first contacts with its literary production was that of a philosophical system with no cognitive value, making use of the terminology peculiar to the idealist philosophy of the nineteenth century and of a scholastic method in the examination of philosophical problems [115]. This evaluation did not tell, however, the whole truth about Marxist-Leninist philosophy, in which, according to some opinions, puzzling paradoxical features and incongruent components co-existed side by side.

On the one hand, it was clearly a philosophy traditionalistic in its method, untouched by logical and other modern developments, ignorant of and unable to deal with the new problems considered in Polish philosophy. They could not be even formulated in terms of Marxist-Leninist philosophy without its conceptual framework being modernised and considerably enriched. It was an uncritical philosophy, unwilling to subject its assumptions to a searching scrutiny and to revise them in the light of new scientific facts and theories. In this sense it was dogmatic, speculative and obsolete. Its views on mathematics referred to mathematics at its pre-Cauchy stage, on philosophy – to the system of Parmenides and his unknown modern supporters, on logic – to the state at the time of Kant, on social anthropology and sociology – to the development reached by Marx and Lewis Morgan. In physics, biology and psychology Marxism-Leninism was more concerned to show that whatever valuable new knowledge has been acquired it can be deduced from Engels' dialectical doctrine than to investigate what are its philosophical implications and significance. Marxist-Leninist views on formal logic, and on the principle of non-contradiction in particular, invalidated the distinction between truth and falsehood and logically justified the claim that any statement whatsoever is as much acceptable as any Marxist-Leninist theorem. A philosophical system with such nonsensical implications could be of no interest. The political origin and justification of some Marxist-Leninist theoretical theses about the structure of the world was clearly recognisable. Its denial of the possibility to reach objectively valid knowledge, especially in the domain of the social sciences, was traced to the same source [116].

Marxist-Leninist philosophy cut a poor figure and was widely considered as not much more than a philosophically embellished dilettantism for the use of a fighting political organisation, aware of the importance of a political philosophy and a world outlook in the struggle for power. Seen against the background of Polish modern philosophy, Marxism-Leninism did not appear as one among the other philosophical trends, to be treated with them on an equal footing. Schaff complained of the 'wide-spread prejudices against dialectics', of the 'suspicions' that it violates common sense, and of academic philosophy keeping its distance from Marxism-Leninism. To a philosopher, wrote Hochfeld, Marxist-Leninist literature is only a 'propaganda leaflet' [117]. Philosophy held a key position in the ideological reconstruction of science in Poland, and the majority of Polish philosophers showed a strong resistance to consider Marxist-Leninist philosophy in earnest. Kotarbiński explained the reasons for this resistance plainly and bluntly. Marxism-Leninism is a world outlook for mass consumption, some times simplified by philosophical amateurs and reduced to the level of mere propaganda by their political zeal. For philosophers, who observe more fastidious standards and more vigorous procedures, this is not enough. A doctrine, that recognises the existence of objective contradictions *sensu stricto* leads to absurdities. It neither can nor should be accepted [118].

On the other hand, Marxism-Leninism had certain traits that commended it to many Polish philosophers. These traits came from the original Marxian doctrine; integrated into Marxism-Leninism, they provided a striking contrast with other parts of its philosophical content. Marx was a pronounced realist in the theory of knowledge, an empiricist in science, an anti-irrationalist firmly opposed to speculative philosophy, which claims to be in possession of important knowledge acquired by other means than observation, experiment and reason. He was a positivist who wished philosophy to investigate the nature and development of scientific thinking and of the naturalistic view of the world.

The Marxian positivistic component in Marxism-Leninism was emphasised by Kotarbiński, Łubnicki, and Ossowski in their respective criticism of the whole Marxist-Leninist doctrine. Besides positivism this Marxian component also included the fertile and important method of historical materialism. The critics of Marxism-Leninism had no doubt that historical materialism has transformed modern historiography and social science, and constituted a common property of civilised mankind. Finally, there was the influence of Marx's doctrine on world history. Marx might have been wrong in his prophecies of what was bound to happen, but these prophecies were and continued to be one of the important causes of what did or would happen. The Marxian inheritance commanded the respect of the philosopher, historian, social scientist, and it must be considered in the evaluation of Marxism-Leninism claiming to be its heir. The Marxian component somehow moderated the evaluation of Marxism-Leninism and kept the hope alive that the scientific core of Marxian tradition may prevail in Marxism-Leninism over the ossification and accretions of a different provenance [119].

This turned out to be an error of judgement so far as the immediate future was concerned. One of its causes was the mistake, made by practically all the critics of Marxism-Leninism, in Poland and elsewhere, of considering the Marxian tradition and Marxism-Leninism as a coherent whole, a single and continuous trend, based on the assumptions formulated by Marx and Engels. There is no doubt that Marxism-Leninism is based on the teaching of Marx and Engels and that it is its continuation in a certain sense. But this continuation has brought about some novel features which necessitate the distinction between Marx and Engels on the one hand, Lenin and Stalin on the other.

Marx wanted to know the world in order to change it. His successors assumed that the world had been made known by Marx and what remained to be done was to complete the second part of Marx's programme. For Marx, truth was to be discovered by scientific means; for his successors truth was to be made by successful action, by forcing the world to conform to a preconceived truth. Instead of the theory being a guide to action, action became a guide to the theory. The doctrine has been put to new uses, although its content has been left unchanged [120].

The cognitive content of Marxian teaching was reduced to the premiss of a voluntaristic programme of how to remake social and historical existence. For a voluntarist the truth and adequacy of thought to reality are proved by the process of changing the latter and by mastery over it. Science and philosophy have no autonomous function; they are a subsidiary means of transforming man and society. Lenin did not regard philosophy as theoretical knowledge, governed by its own standards of procedure and criteria of truth, but as one of the social forces, determined by the economic evolution of society, which in turn shapes or can be used to shape social-political development. He combined with this conception of philosophy the belief that the world is knowable and that truth can be discovered in certain definite social and political conditions, which he strived to bring about by his activities. With Stalin the second component of Lenin's views receded into the background and the first assumed the predominant role. From the Marxian thesis that our conception of the world is a product of social activity, Lenin and Stalin drew the conclusion that by adapting the conception of the world to the requirements of action the desired kind of social activity might be induced to serve the purpose imposed upon society. While Lenin restored the 'revolutionary content of Marxism', Stalin identified 'revolutionary Marxism' with the 'theory and tactics of the dictatorship of the proletariat'.

Marxism-Leninism has become a doctrine which cannot be described any longer by its content, and still less by the kind of philosophy it favours, of arguments it uses, of views it holds as true. It is a programme of action, a collection of ever adjustable rules on how to change society and to control social processes by the use of power. These rules also include those which determine the content of the doctrine in the manner conducive to the achievement of some practical aims set by the policy makers. The term 'voluntarism' applies to this attitude, since the will takes the place of reason as the primary, all-determining factor.

Neither the transformation of the Marxian tradition in the hands of Lenin and Stalin, nor its implications with respect to science and philosophy, were at that time understood in Poland. The proclamation of Marxism-Leninism as the supreme and unchallengeable truth and its enforcement by administrative measures came, therefore, as a shock [121].

121

SOME PECULIAR CHARACTERISTICS OF THE POLISH VERSION OF MARXIST-LENINIST PHILOSOPHY

At first, the Polish version of the Marxist-Leninist philosophy did not differ substantially from its Soviet model. There were, however, certain minor deviations and shifts of emphasis which instead of disappearing persisted and tended to increase the original distance from the orthodoxy. In the course of time they have produced a markedly different Marxist-Leninist philosophy from that which exists in the Soviet Union.

The first and one of the most important was the problem of the relation of dialectics to formal logic. In view of the strength and high reputation which formal logic has enjoyed in Poland, Polish Marxist-Leninists could never think of entirely dismissing it as the so-called metaphysical mode of thought. The tendency in this direction, latent in Soviet philosophy, was put down to a poor knowledge of formal logic in the Soviet Union. After some hesitations as to what attitude he should take in this matter, Schaff pronounced himself, in his *Introduction to the Marxist Theory*, in favour of Plekhanov's 'logical dualism', the coexistence of formal and dialectical logic one alongside the other. Although he qualified the stand taken by the stipulation that it was provisional and for the purpose of discussion, he also added that there was no question of depriving dialectics of such powerful technical tools as formal and mathematical logic. What remained undecided was the division line between the subject-matter of dialectics and formal logic or between the fields of their respective validity. The solution of this question, Schaff explained, rather in reference to the Soviet Union than to Poland, would have a salutary effect on the progress of logic and the advancement of science [122].

This tentative solution was later re-inforced by philosophical developments in the Soviet Union. On the other hand, Schaff was exposed to a heavy pressure of arguments of all kinds, put forward by Polish logicians and philosophers, to abandon the untenable view of 'logical dualism' and to recognise that dialectics has nothing to lose and everything to gain by the acceptance of the principle of non-contradiction. This protracted tug-of-war will be examined in one of the succeeding chapters, but its outcome can now be stated. Schaff became finally persuaded (1955) that Marxist-Leninist philosophy was misled by Hegel and mistook contraries for contradictories. A dialectical contradiction is not a logical contradiction, and, consequently, formal logic must be recognised as the only universally valid logic [123].

The second slight difference between the Soviet and Polish versions of Marxist-Leninist philosophy concerned the principle of *partijnost'*. This principle assumes the social determination of knowledge and its varying validity which depends on the social location of particular social classes. In the course of social and historical development different classes occupy a social location that is situationally adequate for the knowledge to be valid or as valid as is possible under the existing circumstances. It is claimed that at present only the proletariat provides a social location that favours progress of undistorted and genuine knowledge. This knowledge has been attained by the proletarian party, that is, by the Communist Party, which is by definition the most conscious and advanced part of the proletariat. *Partijnost'* is usually defined as 'to be in agreement with the objective truth', provided it is understood that 'objective truth' is what is declared by the Party leadership to be true in each particular case. A non-Party scholar and scientist may also rise to the 'objective truth', when he is in accord with the Party, accepts its authority to determine what is and what is not knowledge and to settle scientific questions recognised by the Party to be its concern.

In *Introduction to the Marxist Theory* Schaff passed over the principle of *partijnost'* in silence. He mentioned only briefly the doctrine of the class determination of science and explained its meaning in terms of the Marxian theory. Marx confined the class determination of knowledge to philosophy, the social and historical sciences, and Schaff followed in his footsteps. He accepted the Marxian view that what matters in philosophy, political economy, sociology, history, jurisprudence, political science, is a general conceptual framework, which lends to isolated facts, opinions and partial theories their meaning and significance. These general conceptual frameworks are a social product and reflect the forms of social consciousness and class interests of social groups in which they originate.

Since there are two main classes in a modern society, the bourgeoisie and the proletariat, there is, therefore, a bourgeois and a proletarian science, the latter being more progressive and objective than the former. The working class has nothing to lose and everything to gain from the advance of knowledge, which is not the case as far as the bourgeoisie is concerned. The implications of scientific progress may threaten or endanger the position of the ruling class. The class interests of the bourgeoisie then act as an obstacle to the progress of knowledge and prevent those who wittingly or unwittingly are exposed to their influence from seeing objectively the forces and laws shaping the historical, political and social existence.

Dialectical materialism provides an example in point. The laws of dialectics are rejected on the pretext of their being deduced from Hegel's mystic schemes. In fact they are rejected for their social implications. The 'law of the transformation of quantity into quality' implies that changes occur both by evolution and by revolution and this conclusion is unacceptable to a man of science associated by many links with the ruling class and its interests. The same applies to the opposition which the dialectical 'logic of contradictions' has encountered. The recognition of the fact that objective contradictions are inherent in the phenomena of nature justifies a revolutionary practice. The defence of the principle of non-contradiction aims at depriving the supporters of this practice of what theoretically justifies their course of action [124].

It is not possible to say what were the reasons which persuaded Schaff to leave out the principle of *partijnost'* in his first presentation of Marxist-Leninist philosophy. Whatever these reasons were, Schaff soon abandoned the position adopted in *Introduction to the Marxist Theory*. He extended indiscriminately the class determination of knowledge to all science, to history, political economy, sociology, philosophy on the one side, mathematics, physics, and biology on the other, and supplemented it by the principle of *partijnost'*. The latter was, in his opinion, only a logical conclusion of the former. There is no 'pure science'; every science is necessarily class-bound and class-determined. If it is class-determined, its partisan character follows therefrom as a consequence [125].

The extension of the class determination to all science was accomplished by a simple syllogism: if all science is ideology, and all ideology is class conditioned in its content, then all science is class conditioned in its content. The first premiss is not invalidated by the fact that there are sciences ideologically neutral, since this neutrality is not absolute but relative with respect to place and time. Physics and biology were once neutral; they are not so any longer. So far as physics is concerned, this can be seen by placing Einstein's theory of relativity, Heisenberg's indeterminacy principle or the theory of quanta in the full context of modern life in which they function as weapons in furious ideological disputes. It becomes then clear that certain solutions of the problems of physics serve the cause of progress, and others that of reaction. The struggle for the recognition of Michurin's biology is clearly of the same nature. Moreover, Russell the mathematician and Russell the philosopher or Einstein the physicist and Einstein the philosopher are one and the same person. Their authority in mathematics and physics lends weight to their philosophical views, and the latter have rendered great services to the bourgeoisie in its struggle against Marxism-Leninism. The most abstract investigations are connected, in one way or another, directly or indirectly, with the continuing class struggle [126].

The alleged distorting influence of ideology on science was made somehow clearer by Eilstein. She started with distinguishing the social and epistemological roots of idealism (in the Marxist-Leninist sense) in a manner closely modelled on Lenin's 'sociology of science'. Fideism is a component part of the bourgeois superstructure, since it provides the exploiters with an effective means of exercising control over the masses. Fideism, or more specifically theism, is a belief intrinsically connected with idealism *sensu largo*, with the opinion that there are real entities which are not material in the world. Thus idealism *sensu largo* is strengthened by any epistemological view which either implies or does not explicitly exclude the idealist conceptions. Idealism in physics, which scientists like Bohr, Born, Einstein, Heisenberg, Jordan, Pauli, Schrödinger support, is one of them. The idealist views of these scientists are not totally groundless, they have some foundations in the facts established by atomic physics. But these facts admit both a materialist and an idealist interpretation. If the latter is accepted, this should not be explained by an impartial weighing up of evidence and arguments, but by the scientist's ideological dependence on the bourgeois superstructure. In assessing the validity of philosophical theories in physics the key is provided by the analysis of ideology, to the influence of which their protagonists are subject in one way or other [127].

It is perhaps not difficult to understand why in Schaff's opinion the partisan character of science and philosophy is entailed by their being class-determined.

His claim is comprehensible once it is accepted that according to the Marxist-Leninist doctrine the Party is the most conscious part of the working class, incarnates its class consciousness and translates its content into deeds and ideas. What is more difficult to comprehend is the extraordinary claim that by being consciously class-determined and partisan in character Marxist-Leninist philosophy provides the only truly objective and undistorted reflection of reality [128].

It does not seem possible to account for this irrational conception of objectivity in other terms than those of psychology. The principle of *partijnost'* not only transfers the authority to settle scientific questions to the hands of those holding power and opens the door to establishing truth by political decision, but also makes of philosophy a means of discrediting the adversary, of demolishing the basis of his 'social and intellectual existence'. The sense of power, which this technique may provide, is taken to be the result of having risen to a higher level of knowledge and prompts the claim of objectivity, obtained by the adherence to and the consistent use of the principle of *partijnost'*.

When a Marxist-Leninist discovers a class bias, class prejudice or interest behind every view with which he disagrees, he enters a state of mind in which he believes he is in possession of knowledge superior to any other. His knowledge is not 'the phantom formed in the human brain', mere 'ideological reflexes and echoes of the life process', which Marx set out to exorcise. Compared with those who blindly follow their prejudices and are obliged to say what they say without being able to understand the reasons that make them do it, Marxist-Leninists have reached a higher degree of comprehension. Since everybody is in a varying degree deceived without knowing it and only Marxist-Leninists are aware of this fact, as well as of the cause of everybody's deception, Marxist-Leninists constitute a body of the elect whose vision of truth is neither veiled nor obscured by pretentious and futile aspirations to achieve the impossible, the impartiality and objectivity of pure science. They are the only ones who can look the truth in the face, they are the first to see the human world not in the distorting mirror of an ideology but as it actually is. In the kingdom of Hegelian freedom the claim that only a consistently partisan attitude secures a genuinely objective knowledge seems to lose the ring of a deadly contradiction [129].

The psychological description of the mental processes by which a Marxist-Leninist arrives at the statement, that his knowledge is the only objective one in virtue of being partisan, does not yet establish the truth of what he says. The gnawing doubt that what he holds is absurd does not cease to persist. Some young Marxist-Leninists complained that it was an unenviable task to face the undergraduates with the statement that Marxist-Leninist philosophy is objectively true and partisan together. Schaff himself did not manage to silence entirely this doubt and while adhering to the principle of *partijnost'* he seemed to have felt its irrationality and ideological character in the pejorative sense of this term [130].

The contention that all knowledge is class-bound and class-determined in its content can be regarded either as a statement that itself is class-bound and class-determined in its content, and thus an expression of the class-interest of a particular group, a 'mere ideology' in Marx's sense, or as a piece of genuine and objective knowledge. In the former case, the contention cannot claim objectivity, in the latter it reduces to absurdity the statement that all knowledge is class-bound and class-determined. For if the contention is objectively true, it follows that there is some knowledge which does not reflect the class interests of a particular group, is not class-bound and class-determined in its content.

Marxist-Leninists never removed this contradiction from their system, nor even faced it squarely. It was a source of intellectual uneasiness within their own ranks, and one of the most disreputable characteristics of Marxist-Leninist philosophy to others. To the latter it meant that Marxist-Leninists were saying a final farewell to reason and taking flight from science based on the inter-subjective, public, and social rules of procedure to the realm of the irrational and the arbitrary, subject to no control but the unpredictable intuitions of the initiated. It was pointed out that the opponents and not the supporters of the principle of *partijnost'* could claim the authority of Marx in their favour [131].

This principle is not only logically but also epistemologically unsound. The principle of *partijnost'* seems to imply that there is a body of absolute knowledge which only a Marxist-Leninist can discover or comprehend. In his *Introduction to the Marxist Theory* Schaff made a distinction between the unchanging core of the Marxist-Leninist system and its parts which are subject to modification and adjustable to the requirements of the social and political development. He did not specify this unchanging core of absolute knowledge, contained in Marxist-Leninist philosophy, except by saying that it is expressed in certain assumptions of the view of the world, presumably those of dialectical materialism, and in some methodological rules [132]. Thus, however, some new difficulties have been made apparent.

Dialectical materialism purports to be an empirical generalisation of the historical development of science and of what particular sciences learn about the order and laws of Nature. As an empirical generalisation dialectical materialism cannot be an immutable principle. On the other hand, if it is a metaphysical principle, the question arises how to justify the claim that it holds good for natural phenomena and settles problems of science. The identification of the principle of *partijnost'* with any other Marxist-Leninist theorem must fail for the same reason. There is no such theorem that would satisfy the requirements of being an empirical generalisation and a statement immune from correction. The requirements are clearly incompatible. An unchanging principle must be a metaphysical one, but then the claim of its empirical origin and empirical relevance must be given up. If it is empirical, it cannot be immutable and the claim that it must be adhered to unconditionally and unreservedly has to be abandoned.

The principle of *partijnost'* cannot consist in fixed principles unless they are factually vacant. Such principles purport to cover all the facts and by covering all the facts they lose the logical connection that exists between a genuine statement of law and statements of fact referring to particular cases of law. The

126

absence of this connection marks an all-embracing statement not only as a false hypothesis – a false hypothesis is a meaningful and genuine statement of law, falsified by particular statements of facts – but a sham law statement. The claim to the validity of the latter cannot be maintained unless it is ambiguous enough to be verified by any evidence and data of experience. It thus loses the character of a genuine theory and acquires that of a pseudo-theory. The usefulness of a sham law statement is not theoretical; it is useful in the practical sense, or, more precisely, in the sphere of political life. It allows us to make changes and to contend that no change has been made.

The principle of *partijnost'* is not what it is presented to be – an epistemological principle that assures that the world is viewed from the 'right' social perspective. It is a moral and political principle. It is political since it reserves to a politically selected group the right to decide ultimately what is true and what is false. It is a moral principle, since its adherents must believe something to be true and something else to be false on account of its having been declared to be true or false by the authority. It is inspired by the 'instrumentalist' conception of philosophy. Philosophy is reduced to the function of a means which helps to shape man and society. Thus, the principle of *partijnost'* provides the essence of what was called above the 'voluntaristic interpretation of the Marxian doctrine' [133].

The mistaken view that the disclosure of the social origin of an opinion may amount to a proof of its falsehood, prompted a debunking technique which in Poland, as much as elsewhere, became very common in Marxist-Leninist writings and was transformed into a general method of resolving philosophical and other differences of opinion. The conviction that by unveiling the secret or hidden motives of human behaviour, sentiments and thoughts, the latter can be shown to be meaningless, 'unreal', and, as it were, laughed out of court, is not peculiar to Marxist-Leninists alone [134]. Nobody, however, but Marxist-Leninists reduced the philosophical argument to a debunking technique. If it could be shown by a more or less arbitrary interpretation that a philosophical view 'implies' or 'is implied', 'supports' or 'is supported' by the 'idealist outlook', this view was thus 'proved' to be socially conditioned by the class interests of the bourgeoisie and thereby dismissed as an ideological distortion. The same procedure was applied to provide 'proofs' of the truth of some other opinions. If they supported or followed from the 'materialistic outlook', they served the interests of the proletariat and were true. The debunking technique of Marxist-Leninists undermines and finally destroys objective criteria of validity and thus reinforces the tendency towards dogmatism, irrationalism and oracular philosophy [135].

The contention that the truth and validity of a view or a theory depends on its social origin was strongly challenged by logical and historical arguments. There is a wide measure of agreement that class-determined presuppositions, conscious and subconscious, play a part in the social and natural sciences by influencing or conditioning individual scientific workers. The inference that there is no scientific objectivity is, however, unwarranted. Chałasiński referred to the history of science and civilisation to provide some supporting evidence for this opinion. There is continuity in scientific advance, although different social classes contribute to it, either in turn or simultaneously. It is impossible to maintain that only the bourgeoisie has created the social and philosophical thought of the nineteenth century; it is certain that the bourgeoisie benefited from the achievements of Greek antiquity and the Renaissance. Scientific procedure has at different times and in different political systems served the interests of different social classes, not all of them, it must be conceded, in the same measure. But what has been conquered by science and technique, whether it is the art of writing and reading, of printing or logical thinking, is at the disposal of all. Science has been in the past a powerful factor in levelling down class differences. The twentieth century tendency to subordinate science to military requirements and political interests or to a social class to secure its hegemony over the others is a retrogressive development [136].

This argument is not by itself decisive; a Marxist-Leninist may accept it without changing his original conviction. Much stronger is the logical argument, commonly called the 'genetic fallacy' argument, put forward by Czeżowski, Lange and Ossowski. According to this argument, Marxism-Leninism confuses the social and psychological origin of a belief with its logical validity [137].

A universal and personal standard of truth is not based, as Marxist-Leninists seem to believe, on the scientist's protestations of impartiality and objectivity, and it is not made illusory by the discovery that social, moral, political and even some scientific opinions are determined by class interest, or, more generally, by historical and social circumstances. The validity of scientific statements depends on the adherence to scientific procedure, to appeal to facts, verification of predictions, and the test of consistency with other already confirmed statements. This procedure is unaffected by personal or class motivation, conscious or subconscious, by what psychology or sociology may reveal about the origin of any particular statement. Any statement stands or falls according to the rules of scientific method, which is intersubjective, public, and social; it rules out of court arbitrary ideas and thoughts inspired by some hidden motives and establishes what is confirmable or verifiable by the co-operation of many minds. If the scientific method fails, as it sometimes does fail in morals and sociology, the only conclusion to be drawn is that these disciplines do not consist of scientifically valid statements. The fact that a statement originates in the class consciousness of one class rather than another has no logical significance and does not provide a criterion by which scientific statements can be distinguished from non-scientific ones.

The rules of testing and verifying the validity of scientific statements, irrespective of whether they are inspired by partial or impartial motives and ideas, provide the best possible guarantee against class prejudices and other irrelevant presuppositions. Whatever successfully passes the public and social test of validity, can claim scientific value, though necessarily a relative one, liable to revision in the light of further progress of scientific knowledge. The hypothetical character of scientifically valid statements is not to be confused with the absence of objectivity. The former results from the inconclusiveness of evidence at every stage of scientific development, the latter is based on observing the established procedure with respect to the evidence available at the time.

These arguments were not accepted by Marxist-Leninists and in 1949 the distinction between a bourgeois and a proletarian science was proclaimed a dogma, which could not be publicly challenged. They were not made in vain, however, they helped to keep critical thought alive, and slowly undermined the dogma. When more favourable circumstances prevailed in 1956, they were re-stated and substantiated with an invigorating freshness by Eilstein and Kołakowski, former supporters of the Marxist-Leninist dogma, and placed within a more general social framework by Ossowski [138].

The third peculiarity of the Polish version of Marxist-Leninist philosophy concerns dialectical materialism. In Schaff's account of its historical origin there is apparent a pronounced tendency to minimise or to eliminate, whenever possible, Hegel's share in it. This is worth emphasising for two reasons. Polish Marxist-Leninists later became divided on the issue of Hegel's philosophy and something like a Hegelian and an anti-Hegelian wing made its appearance. The Hegelian wing included, primarily, those interested in the history of philosophical and social thought (Baczko, Kołakowski, Kroński). The Hegelian wing was not only motivated by respect for Hegel's historical dialectics but also by the desire to find an escape from the intellectual straight-jacket imposed on the Marxist-Leninist historians by Zhdanov's pronouncement. On the other hand, those interested rather in the theoretical aspect of Marxism-Leninism, though by no means all of them (e.g., Krajewski, Ładosz, and, above all, Nowiński are Hegelians in the above indicated sense), were inclined to deplore the Hegelian influence on the Marxist-Leninist thought and were anxious to erase any trace left by it. Schaff belonged to the anti-Hegelian wing. His anti-Hegelian attitude played a certain role in his final rejection of the view that there exist 'objective contradictions' and that consequently the validity of the principle of non-contradiction must be restricted.

It is true that under Stalin the anti-Hegelian trend in Soviet Marxism was conspicuous and its reflection in the Polish version of Marxism-Leninism was to be expected [139]. But there is little doubt that this influence was at least strongly reinforced by native considerations. What Chwistek said of Hegel in *The Limits of Science* represented truly the widely held opinion on Hegel's philosophy among Polish thinkers. The intellectual climate of Polish philosophy was decidedly hostile to speculations of Hegelian metaphysics, Hegel's doctrine was thought to be pernicious, his method fantastic and capable of producing any farrago of nonsense. Moreover, Hegel's view on the State and the State's supremacy over the individual was totally rejected, the terms 'Hegelian' and 'totalitarian' being used almost synonymously. For practical and theoretical reasons the connections between Hegel and Marxism-Leninism were disadvantageous [140]. Schaff was exposed to these influences and his attitude exemplifies the effect of the pressure exercised by non-Marxist thought on Marxism-Leninism in Poland.

The most objectionable principle of Hegelian dialectics was the 'triad', the negation of the negation which, having been stripped by Marx of the 'veil of mystery in which it was wrapped by the old idealist philosophy', was proclaimed by Engels to be an 'extremely general, and for this reason extremely comprehensive and important, law of development of Nature, history and thought'. This law, to quote more of what Engels said, 'holds good in the animal and plant kingdoms, in geology, in mathematics, in history and in philosophy' and concerns a 'very simple process which is taking place everywhere and every day, which any child can understand' [141]. While Hegel applied the triad to abstract entities, Marx, and following him Engels, saw through the 'mystification which dialectics suffers in Hegel's hand' and declared it to be the law that governs the phenomena of Nature. Marx expressly recognised, however, that Hegel was the first to 'present its (dialectics') general form of working in a comprehensive and conscious manner'. Those who said that Marxian speculations about dialectical development are derived from Hegel and his triad were certainly right [142].

Schaff simply denied this to be the case and based this denial ultimately on the fact that Hegel's dialectics is speculative and irrational, that of Marxism-Leninism rational and empirical. Hegel's laws of dialectics are 'different' from those laid down in Marxism-Leninism, because instead of to ideas they apply to the material world, to self-developing matter instead of self-developing thought [143]. This difference has been denied by nobody but neither does it imply, as Engels carefully and strongly emphasised, that thus Hegel was simply put aside. What is common to the Hegelian and Marxist-Leninist dialectics is the substitution of bogus laws of Nature, whose mode of operation is identical irrespective of the realm of being to which they apply, for genuine laws of Nature. Thus, they are not only a nuisance, but also a menace. While the laws of dialectics purport to be a contribution to physical, biological, psychological, sociological and logical theories, they are actually factually vacant phrases and only pretend to be generalisations of scientific observations. The emptiness of the claim to empirical relevance can best be seen from the fact that these alleged generalisations of observations are quite useless in the description of natural phenomena. They neither make more comprehensible nor predictable anything that actually happens in the world of experience. If they have any meaning, the scientist has no use for it [144].

Schaff returned to the subject of the relationship between the Hegelian and Marxist-Leninist dialectics after Stalin's death. Stalin's greatest contribution to the Marxist-Leninist theory, Schaff wrote, was his expurgation of dialectics from the last remnants of Hegelianism. Stalin's teaching on dialectical materialism in *Dialectical and Historical Materialism* is an improvement upon Engels' formulation of the laws of dialectics. Stalin stopped 'coquetting Hegel', did not mention the negation of the negation, and finally ousted it from among the principles of Marxist-Leninist dialectics. The time has clearly come to cut Marxist-Leninist philosophy free from even a semblance of any connection with Hegel's philosophy. What Lenin had begun in *What the 'Friends of the People' Are* was thus completed by Stalin in *Dialectical and Historical Materialism* [145].

Hegel's ancestry is visible not only in the negation of the negation, but also in other laws of dialectics. In Schaff's opinion, Stalin's *Marxism and Problems of Linguistics* and *Economic Problems of Socialism in the USSR* contain further repudiations of the Hegelian inheritance. The law of transition from an old quality to a new by means of an explosion, wrote Stalin in *Marxism and Problems of Linguistics*, 'is not always applicable to . . . . . social phenomena of a basis or superstructural character'. Schaff also felt that in *Economic Problems of Socialism in the USSR* Stalin no longer insisted, as he did before, on the development being a 'disclosure of the contradictions' which reveal a struggle of opposite tendencies operating on the basis of these contradictions. The emphasis in Stalin's last work, Schaff argued, is on the development by way of gradual changes, on the adaptation of the old to the new, without the destruction of the former by the latter [146].

Schaff claimed that this reformulation of dialectical principles removes the inconsistency between the law of the unity and struggle of the opposites on the one hand, the principle of non-contradiction on the other, or between dialectics and formal logic. If change is the 'adaptation of the old to the new', change does not imply contradictions, in the strict sense of this term, being inherent in social and natural phenomena. Dialectics would not require imposing restrictions on the validity of the principle of non-contradiction; formal logic and dialectics could be reconciled [147]. Thus, the expurgation of Marxism-Leninism from the most objectionable Hegelian influences did mark a certain progress of Marxism-Leninism back towards reason and common sense.

HISTORICAL MATERIALISM

The survey of historical materialism is the best part of Schaff's *Introduction to the Marxist Theory*. He was praised by Ossowski for having tried to remove, to a certain extent, the ambiguities and to explicate the meaning of the basic concepts, and by others for having renounced economic determinism [148]. The final result is not, however, satisfactory. This is due partly to the difficulties of the subject, and partly to the acceptance of incompatible premises.

Schaff takes as his starting point Stalin's highly controversial pronouncement that historical materialism is an extension of the principles of dialectical materialism to the study of social life. Historically it is not true. Engels noted in the preface to *Anti-Dühring* that only after the dialectical laws had been discovered to operate in history, he undertook the task of convincing himself that they also govern the 'apparent fortuitousness of (natural) events' [149]. The formulation of historical materialism preceded that of dialectical materialism.

Moreover, it is more than doubtful whether Marx was ever anything more than a historical and philosophical materialist. In a striking passage in *Capital*, to which very early attention was drawn in Poland [150], Marx emphasised the enormous distance dividing man from the animal kingdom. What is 'exclusively human' in man was to Marx not easily reducible to matter; he was a conscientious scholar, reluctant to content himself with some 'indications' of a general nature to consider his point satisfactorily proven. Marx accepted the assumption of

131

philosophical materialism. It is impossible to separate thought from matter, man's consciousness from his body. Marx further assumed that matter was primary and thought secondary and this he found confirmed by the course of history. 'Consciousness', Marx wrote in *The German Ideology*, 'can never be anything else than conscious existence, and the existence of men is their actual life process'. The latter is the man's struggle to secure his subsistence. Men must be in a position to live in order to be able to 'make history'. The production of the means to sustain life is, therefore, man's first historical act. Marx did not think that any further assumptions were necessary to support historical materialism. If there were, they should be looked for in the science of Nature [151].

In a sense Żółkiewski was right when he wrote that dialectical materialism is a generalisation of the Marxian theory of history and culture. It does bear the marks of minds disdainful of abstract subtleties. It takes a bold, breath-taking leap of thought to contend that if the material world is primary and mind secondary it follows that the material life of society is also primary and its spiritual life secondary [152]. The term 'material' has in the antecedent and the consequent a different meaning, and even if it had the same there still remains a considerable gap between the material and social reality large enough to make us stop and reflect over what is involved.

Philipp Frank wrote recently that close ties have always and everywhere existed between man's picture of the physical Universe and his picture of an ideal human society. Political and religious trends, particularly in our own century, have favoured such interpretations of the results of science that would or could support their ideologies. This is a sociological fact which once revealed can be investigated and helps to relieve the picture of the Universe from its ideological preconceptions [153].

There is a great deal of these preconceptions in Stalin's account of dialectical materialism. Dialectical materialism in Stalin's exposition is a transparent introjection of the class struggle, of the order of succession of social-economic formations, of the inevitable revolutions, even of Party strategy and tactics, into the structure of the Universe, from which they are derived as laws of Nature [154]. Stalin's Universe and its laws are a 'socio-cosmic' conception and it is little wonder that he was able to deduce from it any sociological, political or historiosophical thesis he desired. In this manner historical materialism is no longer a mode of critical thought and a conceptual framework for the analysis of social and historical reality, as was the case in *Capital* or *The Eighteenth Brumaire*. It emerges from Stalin's hands as a component part of the scientific view of the world, founded on the science of Nature and validated by experience. At least this is the outcome if circular thinking is cheerfully ignored.

The deduction of historical materialism from the universal laws of the external world has, however, serious disadvantages. In dialectical materialism a historical and transitory state of society is hypostatised into a metaphysical state of affairs. Although this metaphysical state of affairs is supposed to be dynamic, involves both evolutionary and revolutionary changes, its laws of development themselves cannot change; they must remain immutable and apply to every state of society. To assume that the laws themselves are changeable would allow laws to be dispensed with altogether. If the change of laws is admitted as a scientifically valid explanation, everything is explained in advance, no theory or hypothesis is any longer needed. An assumption that purports to explain everything provides no explanation of anything.

On the ground of an empirical sociology one can argue that the laws of social, economic, and historical development differ or operate in a different manner according to the social and other conditions prevailing in a given society. This explanation fails, if it is assumed that these laws are inherent in the structure of the Universe. For instance, why should the passing of slow quantitative changes into abrupt qualitative changes, which makes social revolution an inevitable phenomenon, apply to the capitalist and not apply to the socialist society? In this respect Marxian historical materialism as a purely sociological and historical hypothesis with its distinction of the 'pre-historical' and 'historical' phase in the development of mankind, is superior to Stalin's 'socio-cosmic' approach. It is of the very essence of the Marxian historical dialectics that the passage from the present class-divided to the future classless society results in a complete change of the laws of historical development. Marx could make this claim, since his dialectical principle is not a general principle, applicable to any imaginable realm of being, but specifically related to human society. He did not extend it beyond human society and its history, or, more precisely, beyond the capitalist society. Stalin's metaphysics makes of the change of social laws a phenomenon to be explained and difficult to account for.

The unitary pattern within which historical materialism has been placed offers another major difficulty. According to Marx, the stage of history is set in the 'kingdom of necessity'. This is no figure of speech. In *Capital* Marx tried to show how capitalistic production 'begets, with the inexorability of a law of Nature, its own negation'. This inexorability is established by several stages, of which the first is concerned with the relations between the individual on the one hand, and class and society on the other.

For Marx the 'real individual' cannot be conceived outside class. His nature coincides with what he produces and with how he produces and this means that he cannot be conceived outside society, and in society outside the classes which came into existence in the wake of the division of labour. The class asserts 'an independent existence over and against the individuals, so that the latter find their conditions of existence predestined, and hence have their position in life and their personal development assigned to them by their class, become subsumed under it'[155]. In a class-divided society the individual is strictly determined in what he is and in what he does by his class role. In contradistinction to the Hegelians and also to Feuerbach, Marx found the 'essence' of the individual in the '*ensemble* of the social relations' which bind him up with other individuals within his class and with those outside it, in the latter case by the mediation of inter-class relations [156]. The individual is like a knot in a net, a point of the intersection of the chords, without an independent existence outside the net, moving always with it and never on his own. This opinion will be referred to by the name of the 'thesis of sociological determinism'.

The thesis of sociological determinism is one of the basic assumptions in *Capital* and Marx warned his readers about it at the very outset. Particular persons should not be blamed for their actions depicted in the pages of *Capital*. They are only 'personifications of economic categories, embodiments of particular class-relations and class-interests', creatures of social relations, for which they are not responsible. Marx makes use of this assumption repeatedly in the following pages to describe the actions of the capitalist as determined by 'external coercive laws', over which to lament is of no avail. Individuals act under compulsion, they function as the 'wheels' of the social mechanism. As Popper justly said, Marx looked upon human actors on the stage of history 'as mere puppets, irresistibly determined by economic ties'[157].

It is important to extricate the assumption of sociological determinism from its application in the Marxian analyses of social and historical processes, because otherwise the abstract concepts of instruments of production, productive forces, relations of production, mode of production, acquire the character of disembodied forces that compel events to happen and the historical process to move in its predestined direction. Marx wished them to be always related to concrete groups and classes of individuals, as their *modus operandi*. The question then arises, however, in what way the relations between abstract concepts, in terms of which social and historical processes are described and explained, compel the individuals to act in the manner in which they are supposed to act. The thesis of sociological determinism provides the answer. The individual as such, that is to say, outside his class, can be disregarded; the state of society and its development is exclusively determined by its class structure and class struggle. The social and historical laws govern the 'movements' of the social classes as majestically and imperturbably as Newton's laws do those of the heavenly bodies.

The thesis of sociological determinism also makes clear why so many people feel that the Marxian sociological and historiosophical doctrine deprives the individual of freedom, and with freedom, of genuine responsibility (although in a classless society the man regains, or rather conquers freedom by having liberated himself from class determination, and thus confirms Marx's prediction that the social animal in man can develop into an individual only in society).

It is clear that a man cannot be morally responsible unless he is capable of acting freely. On the other hand, if man's actions were entirely unpredictable, like a throw of a dice, to hold a man responsible for them would be neither reasonable nor justified [158]. Responsibility presupposes some kind of determinism and a place for freedom must be found within it. The concepts of an individual's freedom and of determinism cannot be considered as mutually exclusive.

Marx's thesis of sociological determinism assumes more than some kind of determination of the individual's actions. The individual is strictly determined in his action by class and inter-class relations. What Marx's capitalist does, 'does not depend on the good or ill will of the individual capitalist', his actions are a mere function of capital, of the external coercive laws, 'endowed in his person with consciousness and a will'. His private conscience is of no avail, since he cannot help playing the role assigned to him by the existing state of social conditions. He could not act otherwise than as he does, whether he is aware of it or not.

Freedom is incompatible with this strict determinism, with having to act under internal or external compulsion, which makes it impossible to will and to act in this rather than in another way. The freedom which the critics of the Marxian doctrine have in mind consists in the freedom of choice. The latter and determinism do not exclude each other, but strict determinism does exclude freedom of choice. In a strictly determined world the man has no real alternative, he is neither free nor morally responsible for his deeds. Even when he fully understands the forces which make him do what he does, this knowledge does not somehow liberate him from being under compulsion. A man who falls down from a mountain peak is not made free in his fall by the knowledge that what happens to him is in agreement with the law of gravity. It is doubtful whether this knowledge is of any comfort to him, although it seems to be to some people, should what they say be accepted at its face value.

In Stalin's 'socio-cosmic' conception of dialectical materialism the thesis of sociological determinism is strengthened and made immune to any criticism limited to social and historical facts. It cannot be argued any longer that the thesis of sociological determinism is a sociological hypothesis to be tested or a historical interpretation, a selective point of view, justifiable by what it can reveal and achieve, but as arbitrary as any other historical interpretation. It becomes a piece of the unique cosmic pattern, an instance of how the cosmic forces operate in and through men and society, and bring about the succession of certain states of affairs. Marx's words that it is of no avail to lament over historical necessity acquire a new dimension. Dialectics of Nature and dialectics of society and history confirm each other, because all dialectical laws themselves are subject to the first law of dialectics. They constitute an 'integral whole', depend on and are determined by each other [159].

Stalin's 'socio-cosmic' conception of dialectical and historical materialism comes into conflict, however, with the views established on the ground of practical and political premisses, deduced from the 'revolutionary content of Marxism', rediscovered by Lenin and developed into the voluntaristic outlook of Marxism-Leninism. Marx recognised the existence of a revolutionary force in society, identified by him with the industrial proletariat, ultimately brought into being by the dialectical relation between Nature and man. It is a natural force in so far as men are creatures of Nature, but no cosmic force, which it becomes, if Stalin's view is accepted.

Since Lenin wrote *What is to be Done* not even the industrial proletariat as a whole, but only its most conscious and advanced part, the Party, has become the carrier of the revolution. Later the Soviet State and, with the Soviet State, the Soviet Army were assigned the role of the demiurge of history, which is responsible for the revolution spreading over the surface of the Earth [160]. Thus, however, the carrier of the revolution can hardly be conceived as a natural force in the Marxian sense, and still less as a cosmic factor. The revolution becomes a human goal and purpose imposed on social reality by free human agents, who act in accordance with their knowledge and ideals, instead of being mere 'wheels of social mechanism', working, as Marx suggested, 'with iron necessity towards inevitable results'. Marxist-Leninists actually regard this view as morally cynical and factually erroneous [161].

This implies, however, that whatever limiting conditions of intelligent actions there might be in any definite historical and social situation, the latter does not determine one single path of development, but leaves open at least more than one major alternative of action. The contingent and the unforeseen enters thereby on the social and historical scene. Furthermore, since knowledge, skill, intelligence, and other unforeseeable human factors assume an important role in the development of events, economic determinism is reduced to the status of being one among the many determinants of social and historical events. The role of the individual in history, which is justly denied on the assumption of economic determinism, must again be admitted. With the acceptance of the voluntaristic principle, for which social and historical reality is as much a creation of a purposeful activity as of circumstances independent of human will, leadership becomes indispensable.

Thus Marxism-Leninism includes incongruous and incompatible principles, which cannot be simultaneously held, unless it is only a sum total of plausible beliefs, claiming no scientific validity. If that were the case, the incompatibility of various Marxist-Leninist tenets would be no unusual occurrence. Probably all of us, at some time or other, adhere to beliefs which either are contradictory or lead to a contradiction. Contradiction and incompatibility condemn to absurdity, however, a body of beliefs which claims universal validity and purports to be a scientific system of 'objectively true' statements. This claim is made with respect to Marxism-Leninism, and in particular with respect to its sociological and historical content. It is, as Schaff claims, 'an exceptionally consistent and complete theory'. The question, therefore, arises how to deal with the contradictions and the problems resulting from the acceptance in the system of theses derived from the principle of strict determinism and the voluntaristic principle. The first excludes the existence of free human agents, the second assumes that at least some of them may successfully strive for what they feel to be best in a world of the contingent and unforeseen.

In Schaff's exposition the incongruity and incompatibility of various parts of historical materialism in its Marxist-Leninist version do not disappear but grow more pronounced. The social phenomena, Schaff states repeatedly, are subject to natural necessity, take place independently of the will of man. The social processes proceed with an elemental and inexorable power of the phenomena of Nature; this applies equally to the change of one economic-social formation into another and the general order of their succession. In particular, socialism is an objective social necessity which inevitably results from the capitalist formation [162].

On the other hand Schaff declares economic materialism to be a distortion of Marxism-Leninism, foreign not only to Lenin, Plekhanov, and Stalin, but also to Marx and Engels. He extols the 'creative power of human thought', which changes gradually and indirectly the economic basis, and ultimately the whole social reality. He recognises the importance of ideas which have a considerable effect on the economic structure, and in general of the 'spiritual factor' in the social development. In Schaff's opinion Marxism-Leninism is not guilty of the one factor fallacy. The social development is not reducible to the operation of economic forces, which are essentially forces of Nature and which man is powerless to influence [163].

How can these two collections of assertions be held together? Schaff does not try to answer this question in earnest and is satisfied when he is able to ascertain that they were actually held by one or other of the so-called classics, and to support his contention by a pertinent quotation from the writings of Marx, Engels, Lenin, Plekhanov, or Stalin. He does not analyse these quotations to discover their meaning and to test their mutual consistency. He refuses to discuss the substance of any objections or to consider the phenomena themselves. The authority of the so-called classics of Marxism-Leninism justifies the truth of the statements and constitutes a sufficient reason for the rejection of any objection that questions the justice of the claims made by his authorities.

Schaff's method is exegetic. What agrees with a body of assertions assumed to be true, is true, and what disagrees with it, is false. Schaff faithfully follows Lenin's 'deductive method'. It assures him easy victories over opponents, but the results are unsatisfactory unless the conclusions are believed in advance or accepted on other grounds. The procedure is that of a political controversialist, the subjects discussed are philosophical and methodological. The exegetic method has later become very common and widely used by Polish Marxist-Leninists. Schaff, however, set the pattern and was the first in Poland to offer it as a method of what was to replace a genuine philosophical argument.

Schaff compared Lenin's 'deductive method' to the procedure applied in mathematics and logic. A mathematician rejects a theorem if it is incompatible with already proved theorems and which added to the system makes it contradictory. He also accepts p as true if $\sim p$ is not a theorem of the system. This defence of Lenin's 'deductive method' clearly ignores the difference between a mathematical or logical theorem on the one hand, an empirical and philosophical statement on the other. Neither in the empirical sciences nor in philosophy can the truth of p be inferred from the falsehood of $\sim p$. So far as empirical science is concerned, this manner of reasoning was ultimately rejected some three centuries ago after Galileo had subjected Aristotle's physics to his memorable criticism. No man of science and hardly any philosopher would today consider in earnest Engels' advice, endorsed also by Lenin, to the effect that science can benefit from going back to Hegel's school, whose great contributions to the natural sciences Engels put higher than those of Newton and Laplace [164]. Philosophers of an empirical and scientific turn of mind stopped supporting their arguments by Schaff's procedure at least since Locke, for Lenin's 'deductive method' has invariably led to dogmatism in two meanings of this term: to the acceptance as certain of assertions that are doubtful, and to the acceptance as true of assertions which should be rejected in view of their having been shown inadequate or invalid.

The salient feature of Schaff's presentation of historical materialism is his insistence on the 'creative power of human thought', on man's capability of remaking social reality and of subjugating natural and economic forces by means of his knowledge of the respective laws. A few years later, after the publication of Stalin's *Economic Problems of Socialism in the USSR*, Schaff self-critically observed that his former view on the matter smacked of the error of subjectivism[165].

According to Schaff, Marx and Engels neither denied nor underestimated the reciprocal interactions between the economic basis and the ideological superstructure; they recognised the importance of social consciousness and, in general, of a considerable number of intermediate factors operative between the basis and the superstructure; they accepted the reciprocal actions and reactions exercised and suffered by the economic basis, ideology, and the intermediate factors, which result in an intricate, if not intractable, web of mutual interdependence. As a matter of fact, Schaff's interpretation is only a paraphrase of Plekhanov's views to be found in *The Development of the Monist View of History* and *Fundamental Problems of Marxism*.

The prominence given to Plekhanov's opinion was not prompted, however, by theoretical considerations, by the opinion that pure economic materialism is an inadequate method of research and explanation. The role of consciousness in social development was put into relief only by Lenin and Stalin; it reflected their political experiences and the requirements arising from the prevailing social conditions [166]. Plekhanov's interpretation of historical materialism in which the economy of society and its psychology were conceived as 'two sides of one and the same phenomenon, that is to say, of the struggle for existence'[167], best fitted the requirements of the political situation. The latter called for a theory which would justify both the Marxian thesis: 'the social existence of men determines their consciousness', and the new one emerging in the Marxist-Leninist practice: 'the social consciousness of men determines their existence'. The shift of emphasis and the changes from Marxian determinism to Marxist-Leninist voluntarism were dictated by the demands which practice imposed upon theory. Under the pressure of political demands alterations and adjustments were made in the 'scientific outlook', which, although changed out of recognition, still remained the ostensible guide to action. Such 'theories', conforming solely or mainly to the transitory political requirements, were called 'mythologies' a few years later. 'In this capacity', wrote Kołakowski, 'the theory instead of fulfilling its practical function owing to its cognitive value loses its cognitive function in favour of its practical role, ceases to be a justification and becomes a sanction for practice, stops being a theory and turns into a mythology'[168]. Schaff's presentation of historical materialism has really nothing to do with the development of its cognitive content but only, or at least mainly, with the development of the Party line on historical materialism as the basis of the Party's strategy and tactics.

Schaff's *Introduction to the Marxist Theory* was something more than a systematic survey of the Marxist-Leninist doctrine written by an ardent believer and a faithful Party member. It exemplifies an attitude to philosophy and thinking in general, for which thinking is never an autonomous cognitive activity and a pursuit of knowledge for its own sake, but is always closely integrated with and subordinated to the struggle for survival and to some basic preoccupations of man's life, above all, to the conquest of power and its consolidation. In Marxism-Leninism philosophy has become a means to this end. Political power secures the control over man's overt action, ideological power – over man's mind and conscience. In the Marxist-Leninist language the expressions 'philosophical or ideological struggle' carry the meaning which the term 'struggle' commonly conveys. Marxist-Leninists treat philosophy seriously because they think that it allows them to extend and fortify the system of social and political power. In the long run, it is one of the main devices by means of which power may be effectively held.

Schaff's book was actually an introduction to philosophical struggles in the indicated sense and in this respect it had a twofold significance. It introduced to Poland Lenin's exegetic method and it announced the appearance of a new type of philosopher. This new type can generally be termed 'political scholar', since it was not confined to philosophy. It does not merely indicate the fact that scientific criteria of eligibility for scientific research were not always decisive for academic appointments. The more important characteristic of a political scholar was his belief that his particular discipline is not autotelic, but only a means to some higher ends, served by the Party, to which he either belonged or which he supported. Consequently, he believed that thought, of which the Party does not approve, must be wrong, and that it was his duty to subordinate his views to the Party, that is, to its ideological considerations and political ends. This made of him a suitable person for being entrusted with the responsibility for the establishment of officially approved theories, methods, and ideological interpretations in various branches of science and in the humanities. In the Stalinist period practically each of them had an ideological leader, with vast administrative powers, who, as the expression current at that time put it, commanded on this particular front.

This development had very little in common with Marx. Marx differentiated between what he said as 'a Party' and 'a scientific man'. Only Lenin ridiculed and rejected 'non-partisanship in philosophy' and in his inimitable manner supplied it with Marx's authority [169]. The appearance of political scholars is closely bound up with the principle of *partijnost'*. A political scholar accepts ultimately as true what the Party leadership decides to be true and rejects as false what the Party leadership decides to be false, and this is the essence of *partijnost'*. In non-Marxist language we can say of him that he considers himself above all a member of the movement, in his hierarchy of values the good of the Party comes before that of science.

The political scholar is a relatively new but not an entirely unknown phenomenon. Znaniecki differentiated various types of scholars and scientists and investigated their respective social roles. One of them was the religious scholars and the sacred school, the social form of their organisation [170]. The characteristics of the religious scholar and his role performed within the sacred school bear a close resemblance to the political scholar and to the ideological school respectively. These similarities were put into relief by the introduction of the concept of institutional Marxism-Leninism, derived from Durkheim's views on the social origin and function of religion [171].

The distinctive characteristic of religion in Durkheim's sense is that in religion thought and action are inseparably joined together. The religious phenomena in Durkheim's sense are those which consist in obligatory beliefs connected with some practices relative to objects (sacred things) given in these beliefs [172]. The obligatory character of beliefs held in common and of collective practices associated with them differentiates religious phenomena from the legal or moral, which lack either the former or the latter kind of obligatoriness. In this conception of religion the content of the beliefs has a secondary importance; they fulfil their function if they are considered to be sacred, *i.e.* beyond doubt, are held in common, and command an unconditional subordination on the part of all group members. By compelling conformity they endow the group with cohesion, which no other means would secure. This is the social purpose which the obligatory beliefs and practices serve. Unlike other collective representations, the compulsion of religious beliefs is experienced as a force which resides both outside the individual group members and within them. They act, therefore, as an effective restraint against non-conformity and every kind of social behaviour that injures the group cohesion.

Durkheim's concept of religion also applies to beliefs and practices that are not religious in the common meaning of the term. From the sociological point of view, every combination of beliefs and practices can fulfil the religious function provided that they concern some important aspects of man's life experience. Marxist-Leninist ideology satisfies this requirement which has enabled it to be transformed into a body of beliefs endowed with the compulsory power of a religious creed (in Durkheim's sense). The institutionalisation of the Marxist-Leninist ideology secures considerable social advantages for it enables it to compel conformity. But as a result its cognitive content must suffer accordingly. To fulfil its social function the doctrine must be immunised from change and adjustments, and by being exempt from criticism and rational examination the doctrine is bound to lose touch with the realities of present-day science and to become more and more dogmatic as well as ossified.

The religious function of a doctrine (in the above defined sense) is incompatible with its cognitive role, no single doctrine can act in both capacities without either its scientific or religious function grievously degenerating in the process. The scientist's maxim: *de omnibus dubitandum,* is a useless and harmful precept for a prophet, the obedience expected from a believer conflicts with the basic obligation of a scientific worker, who owns obedience to no authority, neither to Caesar nor to God. The technique effective in political strife is out of place in science. The untouchable authority of a political leader is of decisive importance

140

in achieving political success and constitutes a fatal impediment to the advance of knowledge. Moreover, a political discussion differs from a scientific one. The aim of the former is not only to establish that one is right, but also to 'destroy' the opponent by exposing the social and existential foundations of his thinking, and thus discrediting his general outlook and theories. The weaker the opponent the better for ourselves. In a scientific discussion the stronger our opponent the better the truth. The adversary in a scientific discussion is first and foremost our ally in the common pursuit of discovering what is actually the case.

A doctrine which merges religious and scientific functions is a retrogressive social phenomenon. The separation of these two functions has been attained after a long historical struggle, fraught with tragic events, and completed in the social sciences only recently. A scientific doctrine may be made to serve a religious end, but this does not promote either science or social well-being and progress. Science has other uses which may effectively help in the solution of practical problems without jeopardising or impeding scientific advance. The operation of religious beliefs (in Durkheim's sense) in the realm of scientific knowledge is not only responsible for the anachronistic and mythical content of Marxism-Leninism, but also for inducing peculiar psychological attitudes, modes of behaviour and standards of moral judgement on the part of the believer and those toeing the line. Their most far-reaching effect is the undermining and final destruction of the urge to search for truth [173].

Marxist-Leninists did not challenge the basic facts of this analysis, that is, they agreed that their doctrine fulfils a religious (in Durkheim's sense) and a cognitive function [174]. What they refused to accept was the incompatibility of these two functions. They not only contended that the religious and cognitive functions of Marxism-Leninism are compatible, but also that their combination is beneficial both to scientific and to social progress. The two functions 'are organically bound together', they constitute a 'dialectical unity' and they cannot, therefore, hamper each other. Once the proletariat has acquired political supremacy, the proletarian ideology is forever emancipated from being conceived in what Engels called 'false consciousness'.

If every science is partisan, and this a political scholar sometimes believes with a fervour immune from any doubt, his partisanship accomplishes openly and consciously what others hypocritically conceal or do unwittingly. Moreover, he thus best serves science. A scientific worker is invariably socially conditioned and politically inspired in some way or other. Only those who let themselves be led by the Party of the proletariat have an uninhibited interest in the advance of science. The ideology of a progressive class always promotes and encourages the development of knowledge in every possible manner. There might exist certain psychological factors which can sometimes induce an undue caution in the revision of theoretical assumptions in view of the fact that for Marxism-Leninism there is no pure theory, every abstract thesis affects practice. Since, however, the theory is determined by the material conditions of existence and must ultimately correspond to what these conditions dictate, the theory is bound to be changed, every incongruity be sooner or later eliminated and replaced by what more faithfully corresponds to the changing social and economic basis, whatever psychological factors might come into play. There may be temporary deviations and errors in the theoretical formulation of ideology, but these are transient and all discrepancies are inevitably and finally removed by the pressure of freely and benevolently developing social relations of production. The theory itself guarantees the readjustment of the doctrine and the re-establishment of the correspondence between its cognitive content on the one hand, and the material conditions of existence on the other [175].

It will be noted that with these assumptions the theory becomes irrefutable. Since its being undogmatic is one of its premises, it is unassailable and impregnable as much from within as from without. Everything confirms it, and nothing can falsify it. It provides an explanation for itself, for anything that might happen, for any objection raised against it. It accounts for regularities and chance events, for what is predetermined and what is a man-made deviation or an error of judgement. It can never be wrong.

In 1949 this confession of faith became a dogma, guarded by another dogma, namely that it is a scientifically established fact. It was impossible to dispute and critically examine it outside the philosopher's study [176].

NOTES TO PART II

1. Some moral and social doctrines of Marxism-Leninism were considered as objectionable and destructive by writers and philosophers who differed widely and fundamentally in practically every other respect, for instance, by the Rev. Piwowarczyk and Krzyżanowski on the one hand, Chałasiński and Kotarbiński on the other.
2. Ossowski (5) and (7).
3. Schaff (21), 5. Compare Dembowski (5), Żółkiewski (11).
4. Ajdukiewicz (15), Chałasiński (9) and (16), Kłósak (5), (8), (9), (10), Kotarbiński (15), T. 1, 676–679, T. 2, 501–516, Łubnicki (1), (2), (7).
5. Chałasiński (14), 362.
6. Białobrzeski (3); *Wniosek Polskiego Instytutu Socjologicznego do* UNESCO (1).
7. Chałasiński (14), 359.
8. Ossowski (4), 2.
9. Choynowski (1).
10. Choynowski (1), 9–14. It is clear that Choynowski was strongly influenced by the British scientific humanists of the 'thirties, but the attitude which he expressed was widespread in the country at the time.
11. Choynowski (1), 14–16; Choynowski (2), 333. It is no wonder that Marxism-Leninism was strongly opposed to scientific humanism.
12. Choynowski (2), 322–325.
13. Rutkowski (1), (2), (3), (4); Drewnowski, J. (1), (2).
14. Ajdukiewicz (12).
15. Rutkowski (2), 366–368, 371–374. Most of the demands for restricting the planning of science, advocated by Rutkowski, were later rejected by the Communist authorities. The errors committed were belatedly recognised by a considerable number of Communists. See, *e.g.*, Schaff (28), 17–21, 29–32. 85–87.
16. Kotarbiński (15), T. 1, 680–698.
17. Chałasiński (2).
18. Chałasiński (2), 11–14; Chałasiński (9).
19. This point was forcefully stated by Ossowski before the war. See Ossowski (1), 7–8.
20. Znaniecki (2), 570.
21. Chałasiński (12), 194–198; Chałasiński (8), 418. The same conclusion, based on an accumulation of a vast historical evidence and an impressive comparative analysis of class structures at various times and in various societies, was reached in Ossowski (15), 157.
22. Chałasiński (12), 198–199, 201–208; Chałasiński (17), 21–22.
23. Chałasiński (3), 14–16; Chałasiński (7), 142–143; Chałasiński (12), 194–195.
24. Kotarbiński (15), T. 1, 676-679, 680–698; Łubnicki (4) and (5); Ossowska (3); Ossowski (6); Suchodolski (2) and (3); Znamierowski (2).
25. Chałasiński (7), 152–174.
26. Chałasiński (21), Chałasiński (19), 30–47.
27. For a comprehensive but not exhaustive list of those who died or were killed in the period September, 1939–March, 1946, see Olszewicz (1).

28. See Gromska (1).
29. What remained was burnt down during the Warsaw rising of 1944. The story of *Collectanea Logica* is told in Sobociński (2), 7–10.
30. See Bartoszewski (1); Chałasiński (13), 52.
31. See Abel (1).
32. Słupecki (6), Sośnicki (1), Kaczorowski (1) and (2), Grzegorczyk (8) and (10), Malewski (3).
33. Kotarbiński (6), published in mimeographed form in 1947. A mimeographed reprint of Kotarbiński (3) appeared at the same time.
34. See Kalinowski (3).
35. Wiegner (4).
36. Mostowski (2), Czeżowski (11).
37. Ajdukiewicz (27), Greniewski (5).
38. Ajdukiewicz (21). Ajdukiewicz (19) is a reprint of the book published before the war.
39. Ajdukiewicz (13), (24), (16), (17), (23).
40. Czeżowski (9). Czeżowski (1) is a post-war edition of the book published before the war.
41. Mehlberg (1), (3), (4). See also Kotarbińska (3) and Ajdukiewicz (11).
42. Compare Popper (5), 36. The consequences of conceiving the concept of verifiability in a too narrow manner persuaded the younger Marxist-Leninists in Poland that logical positivism of the Vienna Circle was a false and harmful doctrine. It leads to subjective idealism in the theory of knowledge, to conventionalism and agnosticism in the theory of science (Kołakowski (2), 305). This verdict, based on Cornforth's criticism of logical positivism, pronounced at the end of 1951, referred to the developments of the 'thirties and ignored entirely later publications of logical empiricists. Gierowski drew attention to this shortcoming of Cornforth's criticism, but his comment was ignored. See Gierowski (1), 21.
43. Mehlberg (2) and (5).
44. Kokoszyńska (3); Grzegorczyk (1), (2), (3).
45. Kokoszyńska (4) and (7).
46. Tatarkiewicz (5), T. 3.
47. The German version of Bocheński (4) appeared in 1947 and precedes Tatarkiewicz (5), T. 3.
48. Tatarkiewicz (4), 8. *Es gibt keine polnische Kultur mehr,* was the comment of a German officer who carried out the search. Two chapters of Tatarkiewicz (4) were translated into English (Tatarkiewicz (3)).
49. Ossowska (5) and (9).
50. Ossowska (5), 1–11. The idea of a science of morals was almost simultaneously criticised from the Catholic and Marxist-Leninist point of view. See Keller (1), Keller (2), T. 1, 16–26; Fritzhand (3).
51. See Znamierowski (10), 15.
52. Czeżowski (12); Indan (1); Ingarden (15); Kotarbiński (15), T. 1, 699–707; Krzyżanowski (1); Lande (1); Ossowska (1), (6), (7), (8), (10); Pieter (1); Szaniawski, K. (1); Znamierowski (1), (4), (6), (7), (8).
53. Ingarden (12).
54. Bocheński (11), 130.
55. This evaluation does not imply the acceptance of Husserl's transcendental idealism, which Ingarden specifically rejects.
56. An ontological inquiry in Ingarden's sense is an *a priori* inquiry into the content

of ideas. See Ingarden (1), 162.
57. Pastuszka (5), 275.
58. Chojnacki (1), Świeżawski (4).
59. Pastuszka (1), (2), (3), (4).
60. Świeżawski (1), (2), (5).
61. Krzyżanowski (1).
62. Kalinowski (1) and (2); Iwanicki (2).
63. A.B.S. (1), 132.
64. Piwowarczyk (1); Schaff (1).
65. Kłósak (1), (3), (5), (8), (9), (10), (11).
66. Kotarbiński (15), T. 2, 512–514.
67. Suchodolski (1), (4). Other minor contributions are Milbrandt (1), Kroński (9), 347–370.
68. Ważyk (1), 106–110. Ważyk's article was the first and the only major attack on existentialism, and on Sartre in particular, which was made in Poland; it appeared to be due to Zhdanov's speech in June, 1947. Later existentialism was often referred to in derogatory terms in Marxist-Leninist contributions, but only concurrently with other symptoms of the decaying Western culture, since existentialism had no prominent adherents in Poland.
69. Pastuszka (2), 29-37; Sawicki (1); Krąpiec (1); Świeżawski (6), 494–495.
70. Kreutz (2).
71. For details see Choynowski (4) and (5), Hornowski (2).
72. Beth (1), 29.
73. Ajdukiewicz (29), 270-272; Ajdukiewicz (25), 55–58. See also Stonert (1), 252–253.
74. Mostowski (2), 373.
75. Słupecki (5), (4), (7), (8), (11), (12).
76. Jaśkowski (7), (8), (9).
77. Łoś (1), (2), (3).
78. Suszko (1), (2), (7).
79. Grzegorczyk (6), (9), (11).
80. Borkowski (1) – (6); Kalinowski (2), (5).
81. Mostowski (9), 16, 42.
82. Mostowski (1), 231–232; Mostowski (6), 1–4; Mostowski (9), 30–31.
83. Łoś (8), 152–156.
84. Janiczak, a young man of outstanding ability, committed suicide in the early days of the Stalinist period in Poland (June, 1951). The number of suicides was apparently high at that time. Janiczak was not the only man of talent and promise who perished in this manner.
85. Mostowski (9), 18, 42.
86. Such an attempt in a popular form and for didactic purposes is made in Wilkosz (1). See also Suszko (5), 153–154.
87. Czeżowski (11), 205–235; Greniewski (5), 344–460.
88. Korcik (1) – (6); Kamiński (1) – (6); Leśniak (1); Greniewski-Wojtasiewicz (1).
89. Ziemski (1); Ziemski-Spirało (1); Średzińska (1); Narbutt (1).
90. Kotarbiński (16).
91. This can be clearly seen from Lange (2).
92. Schaff (11), 597–598.
93. His short biography is to be found in Żółkiewski (6A).
94. Kott (1), T. 2, 70, 77, 338–339.
95. Żółkiewski (1), (3), (5); Schaff (3), 335, 347; Wudel (1), 344; Suszko (3), 391.

96. Marx-Engels (1), 15; Engels (1), 31; Konrad (1), 10. Compare Hochfeld (1), 78–81, 87, whose language and sequence of thought are, however, very hard to follow and understand. Konrad perished in a Party purge, or, to use Kołakowski's words, 'has been withdrawn from historical circulation, murdered by the missionaries of great historical justice' (Kołakowski (16), cz. 1, 11).
97. Żółkiewski (2).
98. Wudel (1), 343, 350, 361, 367.
99. Bromberg (1), 83.
100. Łubnicki (1), (2), (7), (8). See also Iwanicki (1).
101. Łubnicki (1), 148.
102. Krajewski (7), Krajewski-Temkin-Hekker (1), Lider (1), Litwin (3), Schaff-Brum (1), Wagner (1).
103. Schaff (6) and (12).
104. Compare W. Sobociński (1), Piwowarczyk (2) and Ossowski (7), 5 on the one hand with J. Górski (1) or Hochfeld (1), 77 on the other.
105. J. Górski (1), 292.
106. See Schaff (6), 7, 17; Schaff (12), 40, 44.
107. Schaff (6), 31. Elsewhere, and in order to refute a view with which he disagreed, Schaff recognised that such a procedure cannot help to prove anything. See Schaff (14), 199.
108. Schaff (6), 78.
109. See, *e.g.*, Kotarbiński (6), 121.
110. Schaff (6), 117 and Eilstein (2), 199; Sejneński (1), 32–33. Konrad (1), 10 spoke of the transformation of dialectics into 'mysterious rites'. See Ossowski (7), 4–5, whose criticism was favourably commented upon by Krajewski (3), 49.
111. Schaff (6), 97, 102, 108, 129, 140, 146–147. Kłósak has convincingly shown that Schaff had extremely inaccurate, fragmentary and antiquated ideas about modern theories of evolution. See Kłósak (5), 80–86.
112. Russell (4), 180–199; Mises (2), 151–154.
113. Plamenatz (1), 250, 248. See also Wolfe (1), chapter 29.
114. Engels (1), 36.
115. Choynowski (1), 17; Choynowski (2), 330–331; Ossowski (5), 503–504.
116. The objections summarised above were actually made in the critical assessment of Marxism-Leninism, published in the years 1946-1948.
117. Schaff (6), 73; Schaff (7), 263; Hochfeld (2), 605.
118. Kotarbiński (15), T. 2, 509, 515–516.
119. Kotarbiński (15), T. 2, 502, 514; Łubnicki (1), 156, 179; Łubnicki (2), 86; Ossowski (5), 504–505, 512.
120. This was realised by Bukharin. See Bukharin (2), 12–19.
121. Kotarbiński (21), 34.
122. Schaff (6), 142–143.
123. Schaff (23).
124. Schaff (6), 71–72, 107–108, 135.
125. Schaff (5), 4; Schaff (12), 71.
126. Schaff (12), 46, 53–63. These were grave words in Poland at that time. They stated as plainly as possible, without using actual threats, that the neutrality of non-Marxist scholars was no longer sufficient and that it could not be tolerated, since no genuine neutrality was possible. – It should be emphasised that no Polish physicist ever attacked Einstein, either his physical or philosophical theories. What is more, ideological distortions and factual errors in the Soviet criticism of

Einstein were gently but firmly pointed out by Infeld at the time when a more reasonable attitude to Einstein's views did not yet prevail in the Soviet Union. See Infeld (4). The position in biology was different, for some leading Polish biologists were for 'Soviet creative Darwinism' and against 'formal genetics of Mendelism-Morganism'. In their opinion, criticism of Lysenko exemplified the class struggle in science and the ideologically-conditioned blindness of the bourgeois science. See Dembowski (1) and (2), T. Marchlewski (1), Skowron (1), Skowron-Wróblewski (1), Petrusewicz (1) and (2).

127. Lenin (3), 336–337 and Eilstein (2), 195–198. Four years later Miss Eilstein came to the conclusion that Marxist-Leninist philosophers themselves had been under the pressure of 'ideology' (the inverted commas are hers) in the pejorative meaning of this term, 'that is to say, under the pressure of prejudices and taboos of an extra-scientific origin' (Eilstein (9), 168). The source of numerous errors committed by contemporary Marxism-Leninism, she wrote elsewhere, was the intrusion of social and political considerations into what can be resolved only by scientific procedure (Eilstein (8), 80).

128. Schaff (12), 67; Schaff (22), 29.

129. See Lenin (3), 553.

130. Eilstein-Kochański (1), 151; Schaff (22), 12–13, 28–29; Konrad (1), 10.

131. Ossowski (14), 71–74. Ossowski's essay was at that time suppressed by the censorship.

132. Schaff (6), 20. Schaff's insistence on the unchanging core of Marxism-Leninism was described as dogmatism not only by its opponents but also by its active supporters. See W. Sobociński (1), 430; J. Górski (1), 297–300.

133. This was later recognised by Schaff who, however, did not conclude therefrom that the principle of *partijnost'* must be rejected. This principle was only distorted by Stalin and means should be found to prevent the recurrence of a similar development. See Schaff (29) and (30). On the other hand, former supporters of Marxism- Leninism, such as Kołakowski, reached the conclusion that the only effective means was a return to the respect for and practice of scientific procedure. See Kołakowski (11).

134. See Popper (1), Vol. 2, 203.

135. This method applied to the problems of ethics, physics and sociology, can be seen at work in Fritzhand (3), Eilstein (2) and Wiatr (1) respectively.

136. Chałasiński (11), 6; Chałasiński (18), 12.

137. Czeżowski (22), 305–309; Lange (2), 750–751; Ossowski (7), 8; Ossowski (14), 71–74.

138. Kołakowski (11); Kołakowski (13); Kołakowski (14), 69–83; Eilstein (8), 79–80, 94–98, 103–107; Ossowski (14), 78–99. See also Malewski (1).

139. For details see Baczko (9); Wetter (1), 134–135, 155–156, 182.

140. J. Górski (1), 293–295. Górski wrote in the theoretical organ of the Communist Party and his views reflected the concern felt in Communist political circles. Górski criticised Schaff for doing too little to expurgate Marxism-Leninism of its Hegelian ingredients.

141. Engels (1), 151–152, 157; Engels (2), 26.

142. Łubnicki (1), 131; Zawirski (7), 13; Ajdukiewicz (21), 143-144.

143. Schaff (6), 77, 112. Schaff followed Plekhanov who tried to exonerate even Hegel from the objection that Hegel used the triad as a method of proof. See Plekhanov (2), 100.

144. Kłósak (5), 86–88; Kłósak (10); Ajdukiewicz (15), 48. Compare Acton, H. B.

(1), 89–90.

145. Schaff (19), 68. Schaff probably referred to Lenin (1), Vol. 1, 101–110. After Stalin's death some Soviet philosophers re-opened the discussion in order to reinstate the negation of the negation among the laws of dialectics. See Wetter (1), 355–365. Some passages in Lenin's writings were found to support the view that Lenin, after all, did accept the negation of the negation as a 'development, so to speak, in spirals' (Lenin (3), 25). This interpretation found some enthusiastic support in Poland. See Krajewski (9).

146. Stalin (2), 38; Stalin (3), 59; Stalin (1), 573. Schaff ignored the fact that in the quoted passages Stalin's pronouncements apply solely to social phenomena in so-called socialist conditions. – Lysenko's assumption was that every change results from a leap. First public criticism of Lysenko's theory in Poland took the line that this assumption was not always valid. See Petrusewicz (2), 85–90.

147. Schaff (19), 68–69, 99.

148. Ossowski (7), 5; Sobociński, W. (1), 433.

149. Stalin (1), 569; Schaff (6), 165; Engels (1), 15–16. Stalin's view can be found in Lenin (1), Vol. 1, 60, but Lenin was more cautious and spoke of philosophical materialism and its extension to the knowledge of human society.

150. Marx (4), Vol. 1, 177–178; Piwowarczyk (1).

151. Marx (2), 92; Marx-Engels (1), 14, 16.

152. Stalin (1), 578. See Acton, H. B. (1), 141–144.

153. Frank (4), 12–16.

154. Stalin (1), 573–575. This aspect of dialectical materialism could hardly have been publicly mentioned, but became one of the reasons for the poor opinion in which it was held. See Eilstein-Kochański (1), 149.

155. Marx-Engels (1), 49.

156. This is the sixth thesis on Feuerbach, Marx-Engels (3), Vol. 2, 366. Each individual, wrote Bukharin, is basically 'filled with the influences of his environment, as the skin of a sausage is filled with sausage meat . . . . . a collection of concentrated social influences, united in a small unit' (Bukharin (1), 98).

157. Marx (4), Vol. 1, 10, 270, 364, 592; Popper (1), Vol. 2, 94.

158. Ossowska (5), 200-202; Ayer (2), 274–284. This view was vigorously stated by Moritz Schlick in *Fragen der Ethik*.

159. Krajewski (3), 65.

160. Schaff (6), 272, 274.

161. See, *e.g.*, Lukacs (1), 586–587.

162. Schaff (6), 199, 208, 222, 235, 240.

163. Schaff (6), 154–155, 179–180, 184–188.

164. Engels (2), 154–155; Lenin (3), 560.

165. Schaff (18), 9.

166. Schaff (12), 245–249; Schaff (19), 53. It should be noted that the concept of social consciousness or of the consciousness of the masses is not an empirical concept in Marxism-Leninism. It is a normative category, a postulated state of affairs, not to be confused with what could be found by empirical research.

167. Plekhanov (2), 206–207.

168. Kołakowski (12), 137.

169. Marx-Engels (4), 322; Lenin (2), 346, 349–50, 361–362, 365. During the Stalinist period the principle of *partijnost'* was found in *Capital* and Marx was presented as its supporter. See Brus (1), 46.

170. Znaniecki (8), 98–111.

148

171. Ossowski (5), 505–506.
172. Durkheim (1), 47.
173. Ossowski (5), 509–511; Ossowski (7), 17–18. Compare Ossowski (14), 78–99; Ossowski (12), 22–23.
174. Hochfeld (1), 92–93; Schaff (7), 248.
175. Schaff (7), 250–253.
176. Ossowski's essay published in Ossowski (14), 69–77, is an instance in point. It was refused publication at the time it was written (1950).

PART THREE

THE YEARS OF MILITANCY

INTRODUCTION

The years 1948–1954 witnessed a radical change of the philosophical scene in Poland. This change became very pronounced towards the end of 1951 and the developments of the ensuing three years gave the impression that the change was permanent. At that time it was not difficult to believe that the philosophical tradition which had originated with Twardowski and had been developed by the Warsaw school had come to an end to be superseded by an entirely new orientation and way of thinking.

The most spectacular characteristic of this period was the dominant position which Marxist-Leninist philosophy seemed to have assumed in intellectual life in general, and in science and philosophy in particular. To describe this position as dominant is an understatement. To judge by outward appearances, nothing else existed and Marxism-Leninism accomplished a complete intellectual conquest. This characteristic was combined with another. Since at that time, as its followers themselves later recognised, Marxist-Leninist philosophy degenerated into a collection of textbook maxims, in the period under discussion philosophical production was reduced to an abstruse logomachy. The battle of quotations and the repetition of threadbare clichés supplanted logical analysis and rational argument. These were the years of solemn boredom, and also the years of establishing philosophical truths by oracular pronouncements and Government decrees. A codified doctrinaire rationalism gave no scope to intellectual curiosity, knowledge and inventive skill.

Marxist-Leninist philosophy of the first post-war years was in some respect superior to its later developments. It then had an open-mindedness and a readiness to see philosophical problems, to argue and to understand a different viewpoint to an extent which later it failed to display. The border-line dividing philosophy and ideology, however precarious, was recognised, and some arguments to support Marxist-Leninist philosophy were produced. Invectives and invective-like vocabulary, open partisanship and partisan militancy, were almost entirely absent. Marxist-Leninist philosophy during the period of dominance, of the 'monopoly of a single school', as it was commonly called, lost these characteristics and took pride in this distinction extolled as an indication that it had achieved a higher stage of development.

The dominant position which Marxist-Leninist philosophy secured for a few years was not won by the sheer numerical preponderance of its adherents. It is true that in the period under discussion Marxist-Leninists were no longer a handful of politicians, journalists, and ideologists, active outside the universities and the world of learning. Many of them were appointed to university chairs. Their ranks increased by the adherence of some non-Marxist scholars and scientists, and, above all, by a large and growing number of younger people, some of them of outstanding ability. Finally, the following of Marxism-Leninism was strengthened by the reassertion of the regularity that seems to govern the relations between beliefs and action, to which L. J. Russell has drawn attention [1]. The rejection of one system of ideas and the acceptance of some other is not always due to a rational recognition of the latter being superior to or sounder than the former. Sometimes the particular kind of social life and activities in which people participate determine their intellectual choice and preference. They are inclined to endorse beliefs and ideas that justify and provide a theoretical support for the life they live and for the functions they perform. The intrinsic power of beliefs which rationalise behaviour, eliminate conflicts, and restore coherence between intellectual outlook and activity, cannot be overestimated.

There were also other factors that tended to create a misleading impression about the strength and the preponderance of the Marxist-Leninist school of thought. Practically everybody who spoke up in public had to argue in terms of the Marxist-Leninist conceptual framework, irrespective of whether he did or did not accept it. This too created the semblance of a nearly universal acceptance of Marxist-Leninist philosophy, in some form or other, from which the conclusion might have been drawn that except for those keeping silent everybody else was either an adherent of Marxism-Leninism or about to become one. Such suggestions were actually voiced and opinions were expressed that a decisive shift of influence in favour of Marxist-Leninist philosophy took place [2].

This turned out to be an optical illusion. Whatever numerical gains, real or apparent, Marxist-Leninist philosophy could have claimed at the time, they were short-lived and did not compensate for the loss of prestige. This prestige was never high and it dropped dangerously low during the Stalinist period. The loss in reputation, Schaff explained some years later, did not result from any hostility towards Marxism-Leninism, but from serious errors of its supporters. He exemplified these errors by what he described as various dogmatic absurdities, of which Marxist-Leninists were guilty and which they tried to impose on linguistics, biology, chemistry, and physiology, by their evaluation of the theory of relativity or of Hegel's philosophy, and by some interpretations of historical materialism. In each case, Schaff pointed out, a sharp and sudden change of view, first in one direction and then in the opposite, was accompanied by loud protestations that only the most recently announced opinion was in agreement with the Marxist-Leninist doctrine. This practice, he concluded, confused the followers and estranged others from Marxism-Leninism [3]. This assessment draws attention to some important reasons though it does not mention all of them.

The ascendancy of Marxism-Leninism was in fact an apparent one, secured, above all, by administrative means, and it vanished as soon as the latter were abolished or restricted in 1956. The ascendancy of Marxism-Leninism was based on the repressive powers at the disposal of the State [4]. Deprived of this support the ascendancy turned out to be a hollow claim.

It was not without reason that the setting up of the Polish United Workers' Party at the end of 1948 was described as a turning point in the development of

Marxist-Leninist philosophy in Poland. It was from that moment that the State began in an increasing measure to fulfil the function of the dictatorship of the proletariat as it was understood at that time, that is to say, to use force and suppression in the Socialist construction [5]. This construction included an 'ideological offensive' which was carried along two lines. The opponents had to be rendered harmless and institutional changes introduced to secure to Marxist-Leninist doctrines the commanding position in the whole field of the scientific, artistic, and cultural life of the country. This took place from 1948 onwards. From that moment methodological and ideological upheavals were announced by decrees, scientific theories were made and unmade at political meetings, political leaders were promoted to the status of leading scholars and philosophers, opponents were considered to be non-existent since they were prevented from voicing their opinions in public or removed from their university chairs. By 1949, having been made one of the instruments by which society was to be transformed, philosophy became engulfed by this avalanche of changes. It came under Party supervision and received from the Party the directives concerning its *ordre de bataille*. Those who assumed the command on the 'philosophical front' could subsequently rely on the full assistance of State administration in carrying out any measure thought to be necessary. These extraordinary powers were used effectively but with moderation, at least as far as the philosophers and the sociologists were concerned [6].

CHAPTER 8

THE ROAD TO ASCENDANCY

To make the further course of events comprehensible, the main institutional reforms and changes in the informal organisation of scientific life must be briefly described. Among the former the reform of the higher education system and the setting up of the Polish Academy of Science were the most important.

The reform of higher education was a problem which attracted much attention even during the German occupation and it was taken up as soon as the war was over [7]. While the most urgent task of the universities was to resume teaching at the earliest moment in order that a start on filling up the gap caused by the war and the war losses could be made, this was clearly recognised as a provisional arrangement pending a thorough overhaul of the whole system. The demand that the doors of the universities should be thrown wide open as a matter of right to all who deserved it because of their abilities, was widely accepted. Moreover, the work of reconstruction and future expansion required that provisions should be made for training an ever increasing number of young men and women both for the professions and for scientific research. The pre-war set-up of the universities was considered to be unequal to these tasks.

It was realised that a university being a social institution has to express the characteristics of the social order in which it exists. Whatever social order was to prevail in Poland, it was certain that it would not be liberal capitalist democracy. It was, therefore, also certain that the type of liberal university, on which the establishments of higher education in pre-war Poland had been largely modelled, was bound to disappear. There were powerful academic groups which opposed this idea for fear that this would facilitate the replacement of scientific standards in teaching and research by political and ideological ones and the imposition of restrictions on the autonomy of universities by State administration, which was increasingly becoming an administration of a Communist State. However valid these fears might have been, they failed to appreciate the temper of the times. In Poland, perhaps more than anywhere else, a liberal university would have been an anachronism [8]. It was unimaginable that after the cruel experiences of war the universities wished to or keep aloof from social needs, social struggles and tensions, unsullied by contact with the realities of life, when the dangers and precariousness of this course had just been so clearly demonstrated by the fate of science in Nazi Germany and occupied Europe.

A new conception of a university, which would reflect social needs, and, on its part, help to spread the moral, social and intellectual values created by disinterested pursuit of knowledge, could not have been formulated in any other manner than by experience, the method of trial and error, the competitive co-operation of the universities as they strove to perform their re-defined function. The general direction in which the universities should evolve could be fixed in advance, but the means had to be left undetermined until the best and most effective ones were found in practice. It was certain, however, that the universities would at once have to take into account the new responsibilities arising from the widening of the basis of recruitment for higher studies. It would not be enough to train the undergraduates for the professions and scientific careers. They would have to be helped in realising how best to play their part as citizens outside the universities [9].

Excluding a small but vocal minority, the prevailing and strongly held view was that the autonomy of the establishments of higher education should remain untouched in the educational reform [10]. The developments in Nazi Germany provided new confirmation of the traditional belief that unless the right of scientific communities to follow their own judgment in the discharge of their duties is safeguarded, science suffers grievous harm. Moreover, the trend towards centralisation, in particular in the economic sphere, was visible all over the world and in Poland it was, for various reasons, a necessity that was widely accepted. This trend was in itself a powerful argument against delegating university self-rule to a higher authority. The dangers of centralisation must be counteracted by the strengthening of the role and weight of public opinion, and universities are important centres where public opinion is formed. They could not perform their new social function unless they were autonomous in their formal and informal organisation. Freedom from restrictive external controls, whether they were imposed by the State or a political Party, was essential for the effective functioning both of the State and of the universities. Subjected to political exigencies, science and teaching would degenerate and fail to play their social and cultural role [11].

These views voiced in public discussions and at various meetings were endorsed at the conference convened by Cracow University and the Academy of Science and Learning at the beginning of 1946 [12]. The conference, and later the Academy, failed, however, to take practical steps and produce anything more tangible than an expression of opinions. Soon the initiative slipped out of the hands of the learned societies and university bodies [13]. A few months after the Cracow conference the Council of Higher Education Establishments was called into being by a Government decree and its members were appointed by the Prime Minister. The Council, under the chairmanship of W. Sokorski, Secretary of the Central Commission of Trade Unions, also a Government appointment, was entrusted with the preparation of the reform bill for Government approval. The work of the Council was carried out behind closed doors, and its provisions were not officially known until the bill was published as a decree in October, 1947.

Although the decree left many matters of detail untouched, it was of fundamental importance. It gave to the Minister of Education, and, through him, to the Communist Party, unlimited powers to do practically anything he liked. He could change the organisation of universities, determine the content of teaching, introduce new subjects, transfer the professors and the teaching staff from one university to another, and appoint new lecturers and professors. Nominally he was advised in what he did by the Central Council for the Affairs of Science and Higher Education, but in fact the Central Council had no effective power. It was conceived in such a manner that it could act in support, but it was unable to set its own views against those of the Minister. There was nothing that could stop the Minister from establishing his dictatorial rule over the universities [14].

This was what actually happened and in the following years the formal and informal organisation of the universities was gradually changed; by the end of 1951 it was altered out of recognition. Apart from considerable and beneficial increased opportunities for university studies, which, in this respect, put Poland among the leading countries of Europe, all the other proposals concerning the educational reform mentioned in the preceding public discussion were either ignored or given aninterpretation far from the intentions of those who put them forward.

A university was no longer a self-governing scientific community. It was controlled by a Rector who himself was appointed by the Minister and could be dismissed by him at any time. The heads of the departments were elected by their colleagues, but they too had to be approved by the Minister. The composition of the Senate and of the faculty councils was greatly extended, which meant, in practice, the neutralisation of the influence that a member of the Senate or a faculty council could exert by his own authority and exposed the traditional university organisation to an outside pressure.

Dialectical and historical materialism became a compulsory subject for all undergraduates and it was not possible to take a degree without having passed an examination in this subject. The curricula were fixed by the Minister and a strict control over their application was enforced. The changed curricula ensured that the teaching of all subjects conformed to the official doctrine of dialectical materialism and included specific fallacious theories which enjoyed the support of the Communist Party.

The Minister took advantage of his powers over the teaching staff to remove some professors and to appoint others, to abolish old chairs and to set up new ones. The selection of appropriate candidates for chairs and lectureships, combined with the setting up of new chairs, can, in all circumstances, stimulate a new school of thought or a new branch of science. The wide powers, which the Polish • Minister of Education possessed, not only provided the opportunity of achieving this purpose, but also made it possible to establish a virtual monopoly of the Marxist-Leninist way of thinking in the whole field of science and scholarship. He neither needed to wait for the chairs to fall vacant, nor was he uncertain which particular school of thought offered best prospects of scientific progress. The process of changing the 'worldview profile' of the universities was accomplished swiftly. It did not take long before Marxism-Leninism was established as the dominant university *Weltanschauung,* pervading practically every branch of knowledge [15]. The teaching of the Marxist-Leninist doctrines and the inculcation of the Marxist-Leninist outlook in the minds of the younger generation became as important a function of the university as the training for professions.

Finally, the institution of joint chairs was introduced. A jointc hair comprised one or more subjects of instruction and its personnel consisted of several professors, lecturers, and auxiliary scientific workers. Each such chair had its director, appointed by the Minister. He was responsible for the work of the joint chair as a team, and supervised the didactic activities and scientific research of its members. The institution of joint chairs was to strengthen what was described as 'planned activity' in university teaching and to enhance the 'ideological influence' of the so-called progressive professors over the others [16].

Viewed against this background, it is perhaps easier to understand how it was possible that the teaching of non-Marxist philosophy and sociology could be suddenly discontinued. Some philosophers and sociologists, among them Ingarden, Ossowski, Ossowska, and Tatarkiewicz, were given leave of absence and the right to teach was withdrawn from them. Other philosophy and sociology chairs were transformed into chairs of logic and of the history of social thought respectively.

This did not mean that formal logic was recognised unreservedly nor that it was considered to be entirely immune from any ideological entanglements. The dividing line between the materialist and the idealist philosophy also passed through logic, though it was concerned only with the theory of logic and its philosophical applications. Marxist-Leninists laid down two demands on formal logic: that it does not exceed the narrowly drawn bounds of its subject-matter and that its foundations are revised in accordance with the requirements of dialectical materialism [17]. The first of these demands was strictly enforced. Excursions into the field of philosophy, the theory of knowledge or methodology were considered as an infringement upon the rights of dialectics. Logic was 'put in quarantine' and restricted to the teaching of formal calculi [18].

Philosophical subjects, other than formal and mathematical logic, could be taught only by Marxist-Leninists. Since they were few some new appointments were made. Moreover, the study of philosophy was concentrated at Warsaw University. Outside Warsaw there were exclusively 'service chairs' of logic and no philosophy courses were given apart from those in dialectical and historical materialism, the compulsory subject of instruction for all undergraduates.

Within the above described bounds the development of formal logic was little hampered or interfered with. There was at least one chair of logic at every university and logic was a compulsory subject in almost all curricula of undergraduate studies. Logic benefited from the patronage of the State though perhaps on a less munificent scale than other sciences, and was assured of State support in the future in order that it might carry on its tradition of the past [19]. The Philosophical Committee of the Polish Academy of Science, set up in 1951, included a section of logic, over which Ajdukiewicz presided. The resolution, passed at the First Congress of Polish Science, that a periodical devoted entirely to logic should be started, was implemented, though with some delay and on a modest scale [20]. Meetings of logicians could be organised, at which plans for future activities were worked out, purely logical papers were read and discussed. The first meeting of this kind was held in Warsaw at the end of 1952, *i.e.* at the time when the prospects for philosophy looked grim [21].

159

The fate of sociology was worse. Non-Marxist philosophers could take refuge in giving lectures on formal logic. There was no corresponding refuge in sociology. Even the most trusted among the sociologists were not trusted enough to be able to lecture on their own subject. Since there was not a single trained Marxist-Leninist sociologist the teaching of sociology ceased entirely until 1956 [22]. The sociologists could do two things. They could either critically examine the so-called bourgeois sociology – provided that the verdict was a foregone conclusion – or study the history of social thought. In the latter case they enjoyed a somewhat greater degree of freedom in their studies and hence the history of social thought became their favourite subject. This was the course taken by the leading sociologists and their numerous pupils. In this manner they succeeded in holding, as it were, the second line of defence and in saving something from destruction.

In the autumn of 1950 the Institute for the Training of Scientific Cadres, attached to the Central Committee of the Polish United Workers' Party, closely modelled on the Soviet Institute of Red Professors, was organised in Warsaw. It evolved from a Party school, set up in 1948, at which distinguished Party members used to teach. In 1950 the school assumed the name of the Institute for the Training of Scientific Cadres, later changed to that of the Institute of Social Sciences, and the first full three year course of study was inaugurated.

The Institute had three departments, each of them with several chairs of philosophy, political economy, and history. The philosophical department had three joint chairs: of dialectical and historical materialism (subdivided into three sections – historical materialism, philosophy of science, and aesthetics), of the history of philosophy, and of the theory of the State and law. The number of 'aspirants' in philosophy who studied at the Institute amounted to some eighty persons by 1954.

Students of the Institute must have been graduates of an establishment of higher education (this condition was not always essential) and have had at least four years of work in the Party behind them. They were supposed to be taught and to teach themselves in order to gain experience, to write a thesis which would complete their graduation and secure them the title of a candidate of science [23], and throughout their studies combine intellectual work with work for the Party. The objective of the Institute was to train teachers of philosophy and the social sciences for the universities and other higher schools, to prepare for research work, and to supply this new type of scholars who, without being themselves physicists, chemists, biologists, physiologists, historians, sociologists, were to direct the development of these sciences in the light of dialectical materialism. Since the students of the Institute were to devote themselves, above all, to the elaboration of ideological matters, their task was to develop what was called the progressive tradition of Polish science and to become the intellectual elite and leaders of the country [24].

Admission to the Institute for the Training of Scientific Cadres became the main channel of obtaining a teaching appointment in philosophy and the social sciences at the universities and of securing the opportunity for research in these fields. Later similar opportunities were created in the philosophical department of Warsaw University and at the Polish Academy of Science, but in these cases too the degree of candidate of science, which opened the road to a teaching or research appointment, had to be taken in Marxist-Leninist philosophy, for no other philosophy was officially in existence. Under these circumstances it was almost a miracle that a new generation with a thorough knowledge of subjects other than Marxist-Leninist philosophy – general methodology, methodology of the social and historical sciences, philosophy of science – grew up at all [25].

The second major institutional change that was to assure to Marxism-Leninism a dominant position was the setting up of the Polish Academy of Science. The Academy came into being chiefly for political and ideological considerations. But from 1956 it had shaken off much of its initial inspiration, had settled down to more normal forms of existence and activities, which are associated with the institutions of this kind, and its important role in the advancement of science and scholarship in Poland is beyond doubt.

The setting up of the Polish Academy of Science was formally based on the resolution passed by the so-called Congress of Polish Science, held at Warsaw, in July, 1951. The Congress, carefully prepared for almost two years, was conceived as a major ideological campaign. Hundreds of minor and major conferences were held in preparation for the Congress. Eminent representatives of Soviet science participated in these conferences, read papers, took part in the discussions, and conveyed to their Polish colleagues their own experiences in transforming science according to Marxist-Leninist principles [26]. The purpose of these elaborate preliminaries was to make every scientist and scholar familiar with what was called 'progressive methodology', that is, with the application of dialectical materialism and its various theories to particular natural and social sciences. The Congress was to endorse and publicly proclaim the achievement of this objective and to become the beginning of a new development in the history of science in Poland, then firmly based on ideological and methodological principles of Marxism-Leninism.

The Congress was a huge gathering of scholars and scientists, divided into eleven sections and some sixty sub-sections. At the committee meetings reports and evaluations of the position existing in particular branches of science and learning were to be read, discussed and accepted. This did not always go according to plan, since the opposition was still considerable. With very few exceptions the reports were never published. The joint report on philosophy and sociology is known only from a summary and the names of its authors have remained, officially, anonymous.

It is not possible to assess the real results of the preparatory work for the Congress. According to the official account, the discussions at the meetings preceding the Congress invariably showed that the principles of dialectical and historical materialism were victorious in every branch of science and learning. The superiority of the dialectical method was recognised, the duty of everybody to acquire thorough knowledge of it was emphasised, and the opportunity of benefiting from the achievements of Soviet science was eagerly seized upon [27].

There is little doubt that some successes were scored. The most spectacular among them were some self-confessions of past errors, combined with the adherence to the orthodoxy of Marxism-Leninism [28]. These successes were offset by equally resounding failures. Thus the linguists refused to acknowledge any value for their research either in the Marxist-Leninist doctrines or in Stalin's pronouncements on linguistics [29]. Jerzy Konorski, one of the most distinguished Polish physiologists and an internationally known authority on the theories of Pavlov, under whom Konorski studied before the Second World War, could not be persuaded to accept these theories as a dogma from which the solution of every possible physiological, psychological, medical, and philosophical problem could be deduced [30]. The philosophers of the Warsaw school refused *in corpore* to accede to the Marxist-Leninist evaluation of philosophy in Poland in the inter-war period and to follow the dialectical method in their research and teaching [31]. The general trend of developments in the following years strongly suggests that the ideological and methodological turning point, officially announced as an important achievement of the Congress, was an illusory or at least a grossly exaggerated event.

The setting up of the Polish Academy of Science was a permanent achievement of the Congress. This should not be understood to mean that, had the Congress not taken place, the Academy would not have been set up. The Academy came into being by the decision of the Central Committee of the Communist Party [32], and what the politicians decided the scientists and scholars for their own reasons, only partly concurrent with the aims of the Party, formally resolved at the Congress.

The political purpose in setting up the Academy was threefold. The Party wished the scientists to co-operate within an organisation that was to be clearly committed to the Marxist-Leninist conception of science, that is to say, to a conception recognising the priority of political considerations in scientific research. The Academy was to provide the organisational framework for the planning of science which would take into account not only problems arising from scientific development but also fully meet the present and future needs of the State and of the national economy. It was assumed that this task could not be achieved unless there existed a supreme body that co-ordinated, organised, planned and controlled research work on a national scale. Last but not least, the Academy was necessary for ideological and educational reasons. Polish scientists and scholars, said Jan Dembowski, President of the Academy, were trained on Western models and they failed to appreciate the progressive methodology of Marxism-Leninism. The Academy, as he put it, was to play a very real part in introducing the scientists and scholars to this new and superior approach to science [33].

On their part, the scientists and scholars did not disapprove of all of these aims. On the one hand, they recognised the need for a supreme scientific body in the country that would be responsible for organising and planning research, for safeguarding scientific standards and for the advancement of knowledge. They also saw in the Academy an opportunity of participating in the reconstruction

162

and development of their country and of contributing to scientific progress. On the other hand, they were afraid of the harmful effects that a one-sided emphasis on the practical applications of science could have on scientific advance. They had misgivings about the planning of science that, by being conceived too rigidly, might stultify inventive and creative minds. They were convinced that no useful purpose could be served by concealing facts and silencing critical opinions. They were acutely aware of the fact that dogmatism is the greatest obstacle in the path of scientific advance [34].

Thus, the scientists approved of some of the objectives pursued by the Party and disapproved of others, though their joining of the Academy purported to commit them indiscriminately to the politicians' acceptable and unacceptable aims. The incompatible purposes which the Academy was to serve in the expectation of the politicians and the scientists somewhat explain its chequered fortunes in the first years of its existence.

The Academy came into existence in April, 1952, when the President of the Republic appointed its first Praesidium and also the first members. The statutory rules laid down that no change in the Praesidium could be made and no new officers elected without the approval of the highest authority in the State. This practice continued for a few years. But in June, 1956, the General Assembly of the Academy met and held a memorable debate. The Praesidium resigned and in January, 1957, the first genuine elections of the Praesidium took place. Kotarbiński was elected its Chairman and important changes in the activities of the Academy were made.

Among the first members of the Academy, appointed by the State authorities, there were some striking omissions, by no means accidental, and some purely political personalities with no academic qualifications or scientific achievements. It was to be a general principle that a member of the Academy should be a scholar or scientist of distinction in a particular field of knowledge. A Party scholar was exempted, if necessary, from this requirement. But the membership of all the four sections of the Academy included many leading scientists and scholars in every domain of learning. The latter constituted an overwhelming majority and could, in principle, have a decisive voice in the Academy. Yet in the first few years of its existence this was not the case.

The Academy became the chief promoter, endowed with considerable powers of enforcement, of the 'progressive methodology' in every branch of knowledge. It supported and disseminated fallacious theories, such as Lysenko's and Lepeshinskaya's, and held them up as the highest scientific achievements. It enforced further centralisation of science in order to tighten political and ideological control over scientific activities. It lent its authority to the distinction between 'bourgeois' and 'progressive Soviet science' and encouraged giving precedence to ideological considerations over respect for facts and the requirements of logic. In general, the Academy started as a force for increased centralisation and ideological regimentation, for a stricter political control and orthodox submission of science and learning to the doctrine of Marxism-Leninism. During the initial period of its existence the Academy often made pronouncements unworthy of the supreme scientific body in the country. It submitted declarations of homage to those who were destroying science, cultivated the cult of the 'most outstanding man alive', took political decisions concerning the truth of scientific theories. It did not do anything to protect scholars who were removed from their university chairs and did not speak up for those subsequently arrested and held in prison for many months without any reason whatsoever [35].

The explanation of this state of affairs should be sought in the contrast between the Academy's fictitious façade and the reality concealed behind the trappings[36]. To an outside observer the Academy was a self-governing scientific community composed, in its majority, of the leading scientists and scholars in the country. In reality the Academy was controlled from the outside, from the offices of the Communist Party. The decisions taken there were passed on to the body of men in the Academy who enjoyed the full confidence of the Party to carry them into effect. They formed the Scientific Secretariat of the Praesidium, and, through the Praesidium, which 'rubber stamped' (this is Professor Infeld's expression) what the Scientific Secretariat prepared for its formal approval, controlled the Academy. Besides the Scientific Secretariat of the Praesidium each section of the Academy had its own Scientific Secretariat, composed in the same manner, which in its respective field exercised a closer supervision over the implementation of the principles accepted at the higher level. The members of the Scientific Secretariats were almost exclusively members of the Party, who often owed their scientific position to Party membership. While nominally the Praesidium and the General Assembly were the highest authority in the Academy, the 'commanding heights' were held by the network of the Scientific Secretariats. The latter were representatives of the supreme power in the State and against this power no majority vote of the Academy members could prevail. Behind the formal, statutory structure of the Academy, there was hidden an informal and more important one, with a delegated, but real and effective power of decision. It was not subject to control by the members, and, though it ruled the Academy, could not be held responsible or be called to account for its action [37].

The outcome of the discrepancy between the façade and the reality was that the decisive voice on particular scientific matters within the Academy belonged to persons with little if any competence and knowledge of the branch of science which was subject to their control. The bodies that effectively ruled in the Academy were composed of men who were described as 'laymen', 'learned politicians', or 'scholars by Party appointment'[38]. Political scholars, who made their appearance in 1948, managed by means of the Academy to establish themselves in a commanding position over the whole field of science and scholarship. This was in keeping with the tenets of the Marxist-Leninist doctrine. According to this doctrine the leadership of the Party is the highest authority even on scientific matters. A political scholar does not recognise the demand for the freedom of science if this means freedom from Party control [39].

The informal organisation of the Academy accounted for much of its unusual activities, but did not explain everything. Science can be described as a system of research techniques and logical procedures for acquiring knowledge. But science is also a socially organised activity. In this capacity science is exposed to the impact of other social processes, has definite connections with other social factors, such as system of power and awards, class structure, cultural values, and generally depends in various ways upon the society of which it forms a constituent part. Consequently, science can be affected not only directly, but also indirectly, that is, by the processes taking place in its social environment.

In an article which caused a considerable stir at the time Chałasiński pointed out that the ideological superstructure in Poland in the Stalinist period exercised a disintegrating influence upon the ethos of science as a social activity. It replaced the distinction between professional competence and incompetence by that between conformity and non-conformity to the truth imposed by a non-scientific authority. The priority of politics, the subordination of any consideration to political exigencies and expediency, made nonsense of the rationality of science. Its universalism was invalidated by the stipulation that the ability to discover truth is dependent on holding the correct kind of political beliefs and upon rank in Party hierarchy. Freedom of thought and speech, freedom to publish and publicly defend one's views were restricted and with it the scientist's main means of exercising influence, the power of persuasion and reasonableness, was taken away from him. The defence of freedom and autonomy of science was equated with the 'nostalgic voice from the previous century'[40]. A public disagreement with opinions on scientific matters, imposed by political authorities, was treated as a politically hostile statement [41]. A whole social mechanism of chain reactions was put in motion which tended to discourage the scientist, either individually or collectively, to actively oppose the misuse of science for political purposes. Finally, resignation from the Academy meant giving up the opportunity of exercising any moderating influence whatever with no apparent gain of any kind. In such a dilemma no conclusive argument could be produced for this course.

On its foundation the Polish Academy of Science absorbed the two greatest and most influential scientific societies in the country – the Academy of Science and Learning in Cracow and the Warsaw Scientific Society. This was followed by a sustained effort to absorb or to oust, in some way or other, all the remaining scientific societies. The regional scientific centres were gradually compelled to restrict their activities, and found themselves under severe pressure to surrender their academic status and to transform themselves into bodies for the popularisation of science [42]. Also plans of reorganising the specialised societies were envisaged. This was partly the question of integrating their activities into those of the Academy and partly that of neutralising the authority of professional competence which they represented in public opinion. Specialised scientific societies, stated Jan Dembowski, President of the Academy, erred by their exclusiveness, resulting from the demand of academic qualifications from their members, and no longer corresponded with the needs of the country. They should throw their membership wide open not only to the young, but also to 'working people, rationalisers and shock workers'. Their perspicacity and good judgment, unburdened by the routine of academic thinking, would discover the weak points which escape the mind of a scientist [43].

These ideas were enforced mainly in professional technical associations, but some scientific and scholarly societies also suffered from them, and, in some cases, had to discontinue their activities altogether. Among the latter was the Sociological Institute in Łódź, after the war the main sociological association in the country. It was revived in 1956 and about the same time the sociologists formed a section within the Philosophical Society, later transformed into the re-established Polish Sociological Association [44]. The Philosophical Society was little affected. While during the Stalinist period the Society as a whole could not initiate any activities on a national scale, the regional organisations met regularly and were probably the only platforms for genuine philosophical discussions, held in closed circles, in which various schools of thought could be heard and argue with each other. They managed somehow to survive the period of repressions and to carry on their normal existence. The Society has greatly increased its activities since 1956 [45].

The Polish Academy of Science enforced a strict censorship of all scientific publications. This was facilitated by the centralisation of the nationalised publishing industry. Since 1950 a central commission, later known under the name of the Central Office of Publications, was supervising all publishing activities and controlled them more and more rigorously. The Central Office of Publications was the only supplier of print and the only distributor of books. Thus it became impossible to publish anything without official approval [46]. Within the framework of this organisation the Academy proceeded to establish its own detailed system of censorship over the content of scientific publications.

The printing of scientific publications was entrusted to a handful of publishing houses, of which the most important was 'Polish Scientific Publishers' *(Państwowe Wydawnictwo Naukowe)*, set up in 1951, and responsible for the production of nearly three quarters of all scientific books and periodicals. The responsibility for the form and content of any publication passed from the hands of the author or the sponsoring society into those of the publishing houses and the supervisors appointed by the Academy. This system of control had nothing to do with the accepted practice of editors and publishers, who have their advisers or independent referees passing scientific books and papers for publication. The control of the Academy also invariably applied to manuscripts qualified for publication by appropriate committees appointed by scientific bodies.

The censorship of the Academy was mainly political and ideological. For these reasons some manuscripts were refused publication and others were held up for years waiting for a decision which was not forthcoming [47]. The censorship was anonymous and there was no appeal against its verdict. The author was advised by the publishing house that he should leave out some passages, change the wording of others, or supplement his manuscripts in some definite manner. He had either to accept the advice or give up the publication [48]. The censorship, sponsored by the Academy, not only suppressed freedom of thought, but also humiliated the author and abased the value of the written word [49].

The censorship was not restricted to new works and current periodicals. The re-edition of books written a long time ago was also censored and the text altered or tampered with. The most notorious instances were the fate of Józef Nusbaum-Hilarowicz's *Idea of Evolution in Biology* and J. H. Pestalozzi's *Wie Gertrude ihre Kinder Lehrt,* both published under the auspices of the Academy [50].

It was an established rule that each book had its officially appointed scientific editor, who together with the censors was held responsible for the content of the publication. Since the work done on the manuscript by the censors and the editor often changed the text out of recognition, the authors lost interest in giving to their manuscripts the final and finished form before sending them to the publisher. The mechanism created for the exercise of ideological control over scientific publications produced a peculiar situation. The author supplied a substitute of a book, and the work itself was emerging at the writing desk of the ideological supervisors, helped by the editors employed by the publishing house [51].

The publishing activities of the Polish Academy of Science have also considerable and notable achievements to their credit. With the large financial means at its disposal the Academy launched a comprehensive publishing plan. It included the publication in Polish translations of a great number of famous works from English, French, German, and Russian literature. Students of law, economists, educationists, philosophers each had their separate 'Libraries of World's Classics'. The largest of them, 'The Library of Philosophy Classics', now numbers over fifty works. The responsibility for the choice of works to be translated and for the translation has been in the hands of a committee composed of the most competent persons to be found in the country. Philosophers and sociologists who at that time were forbidden to teach have been among its members [52]. The circulation of philosophy classics reached very large figures. For instance, eight thousand copies of the translation of Kant's *Kritik der reinen Vernunft* were published, of which three quarters was sold almost immediately [53].

The last aspect of the Academy's activities to be briefly considered is the creation of a wide network of scientific research institutes, covering many fields of knowledge. More than eighty bodies ranging from fully-fledged and well organised institutes, staffed with numerous research workers, to commissions meeting occasionally for some definite purpose, have been established. Practically every scholar and scientist has been connected in some way or other with a working body and participates in the research organised by the Academy [54].

Such a huge and complicated organisation has its merits and demerits, and it can serve various purposes. It might be used as a means of control that has nothing to do with the aims and interests of science; there is little doubt that initially the effort to concentrate all research work in the institutes and other bodies of the Academy was undertaken to achieve this end among others. It might also provide an organisational framework for the most effective use of human and material resources for the benefit of science. In some branches of

167

science, in which team work, expensive equipment, a considerable outlay of money play an increasing role, such a centralisation of research is necessary and in fact practised all over the world. There is evidence that the network of the Academy institutes has actually stimulated research by providing vast opportunities either for individual or collective efforts.

Since 1956 one of the institutes of the Academy has been the Institute of Philosophy and Sociology. At the time when the Academy was set up, all the energies of the Marxist-Leninist philosophers were concentrated on the reorganisation of philosophy as an undergraduate study. Since an institute has a statutory obligation to carry on research, philosophical research had to conform to Marxist-Leninist principles, and no Marxist-Leninist could be spared for this purpose, the intention of organising the Philosophical Institute was at first abandoned [55]. Some of its functions were provisionally taken up by the Philosophical Committee, set up in May, 1952.

The Philosophical Committee was a supervisory body and had three sections: dialectical and historical materialism, history of philosophical and social thought, and formal logic. With the exception of Ajdukiewicz and Kotarbiński, other non-Marxist philosophers did not sit on the Committee. Schaff, the leading Marxist-Leninist philosopher, was appointed its chairman. The primary function of the Philosophical Committee was to provide an ideological authority and leadership in transforming the teaching of philosophy and philosophical research to the established Marxist-Leninist pattern. The Committee assumed supervision over the Editorial Board of the 'Library of Philosophy Classics' (without interfering with its work). It published *Myśl Filozoficzna,* a periodical devoted exclusively to Marxist-Leninist philosophy. It also watched *Studia Logica,* the supervision being rather nominal than real; no Marxist-Leninist ever contributed a single article to this periodical.

In 1953 it was decided to set up the Seminar of Philosophical Sciences comprising two sections, namely of logic and of history of philosophical and social thought. With the organisation of the historical section in the Philosophical Seminar two serial publications were started *(Archiwum Filozofii i Myśli Społecznej, Studia Mediewistyczne),* of which the first number appeared in 1957 and 1958 respectively. Finally, in 1954, the Philosophical Committee was considerably enlarged by the co-option of representatives of the provincial universities. Kotarbiński and Ajdukiewicz were members from the beginning and now they were joined by Czeżowski and Kokoszyńska. Other prominent non-Marxist philosophers still remained outside it and the Philosophical Committee continued to be dominated by Marxist-Leninists [56].

In 1956 the Institute of Philosophy and Sociology was formed and a number of changes for the better took place. Schaff was appointed director of the Institute, and Ajdukiewicz became his deputy. Kotarbiński assumed the chairmanship of the Scientific Council. The Philosophical Committee fell into abeyance. The Institute of Philosophy and Sociology has seven seminars or departments concerned with the history of modern philosophy and social thought, the history of ancient and medieval philosophy, logic, dialectical materialism with a section for the philosophy of natural sciences, the theory of culture and social change, social research, the theory and history of moral philosophy, and philosophical bibliography and documentation.

To complete the description of conditions in the universities, scientific institutions, and philosophical publications, under which Marxist-Leninist philosophy could make the claim of having obtained the dominant position in the intellectual life of the country, a few further details must be added. They concern the philosophical periodicals and scientific contacts with the outside world.

In 1949 there appeared the last philosophical books of the non-Marxist writers and no others could be published until 1955 [57]. This did not apply to the textbooks of formal logic, the translations of the classical philosophical works, a few translations of the contemporary Catholic thinkers, which the publishing house *Pax,* owned by the so-called progressive Catholics, managed to bring out. The prohibition was also extended to non-Marxist philosophical periodicals (except the Catholic *Roczniki Filozoficzne),* which were declared to be objectively a weapon in the struggle against Marxist-Leninist philosophy [58].

In 1949 the last volume, the forty fifth in succession, of the main Polish philosophical periodical *Przegląd Filozoficzny* was published. *Kwartalnik Filozoficzny,* another periodical established after the First World War, managed to bring out one number, devoted to Descartes, in 1950, but then the order to discontinue publication was enforced. *Ruch Filozoficzny,* a bibliographical philosophical periodical, stopped appearing in the middle of 1950, and *Studia Philosophica,* published in French and English, appeared for the last time in 1951. *Nauka Polska,* a yearly publication devoted to the development and organisation of science, could produce only one volume in 1947. Sociological and psychological periodicals *(Przegląd Socjologiczny, Kwartalnik Psychologiczny,* and *Psychologia Wychowawcza)* shared the fate of the philosophical ones. They too stopped appearing in 1949.

About the same time the content of various periodicals, which were not to be banned for the time being, changed abruptly and radically. This was particularly noticeable in those with a liberal editorial policy, of which *Myśl Współczesna* and *Życie Nauki,* both of interest to philosophers, provided examples. They became, to all practical purposes, exclusively Marxist-Leninist periodicals.

It was also at that time that the peculiar Marxist-Leninist style in philosophy, militant and offensive, confusing argument with invectives, with invective-like qualifying terms and sweeping condemnations, made its first appearance in Poland. It firmly established itself when *Myśl Filozoficzna,* the Marxist-Leninist philosophical periodical, was started at the end of 1951. The intrusion of political considerations into philosophical argument was clearly discernible towards the end of 1948, and it increased gradually in volume and insistence. It too reached its culmination in *Myśl Filozoficzna,* which announced in its first number that it would not be inspired by academic objectivism and philosophical detachment [59].

Finally, about the same time, Polish scientists and scholars were made aware of the importance to be attached to the struggle between proletarian international-

169

ism and imperialist cosmopolitism, the latter being a peculiar and most rabid form of bourgeois nationalism [60]. Cosmopolitism was the ideology of capitalism in the era of imperialism, which under the guise of universal values tried to impose upon the world an ideology hostile to proletarian patriotism and to protect the capitalist domination. Contemporary cosmopolitism was a conscious and elaborate expression of the reactionary aspirations of international imperialism, above all, of American imperialism. On the other hand, internationalism was another name for the peaceful co-operation of nations which without losing their national identity were striving towards the common good of making socialism a reality. Internationalism was perfectly compatible with patriotism. It accepted the principle that every nation, whether large or small, could contribute to the cause of progress, that is to say, of progress towards socialism, provided that it took the right road leading to this goal. The right road was marked out by the scientifically established laws of historical development. The support of socialism implies the support of proletarian internationalism, and the rejection of capitalism implies the rejection of imperialist cosmopolitism [61].

It is not true, therefore, that there is only one science, neither socialistic nor capitalistic. First, there is no impartial science and to expect science in a society based on class struggle to be impartial is, as Lenin put it, 'silly and naive'. Second, there is a progressive science inspired by internationalism and working for the benefit of man, and a reactionary science, cultivated in the capitalist countries and preparing the destruction of mankind. There is no third course, for neutrality is in such circumstances either hypocritical or mendacious [62].

Cosmopolitism might take two different forms. It might consist in playing the part of admirers and disciples of capitalistic science or in ignoring or underestimating one's own national contribution to the progress of civilisation. Accordingly, there are two ways of combatting cosmopolitism. The first is to discover in the history of one's nation the progressive revolutionary tradition, the groping progress towards Marxism-Leninism and the proletarian ideology. The second is to reject the grovelling attitude towards West-European capitalistic science and culture, to recognise that 'to-day Moscow is the capital of political and scientific progress', and that Soviet science provides an inspiring model of progressive science to all nations. The first Soviet model which the scientists were urged to accept, to bear witness to the victory of proletarian internationalism over cosmopolism in Poland, was the new biology of Michurin and Lysenko [63].

It is unnecessary to dwell on these views for they are familiar from elsewhere. What is of interest is the use made of them in the framing of the policies for the development of science and in philosophical discussions. For the suppression of some philosophical schools of thought was sometimes justified as a measure intended to protect the national culture against the evils of cosmopolitism [64].

Those who were responsible for the formulation and implementation of the policies of the Academy assumed the distinction between cosmopolitan and international science as the basic principle in all their decisions. This not only

170

resulted in declarations of admiration for the progressive Soviet science, in advocating and in establishing close cultural and scientific relations with the Soviet Union, but also in maintaining these relations to the exclusion of contacts with the world outside the Soviet sphere. Very soon after the Academy was set up, the recommendation to sever all contacts with science that was not international was formulated and implemented [65].

In philosophical discussions the distinction between cosmopolitism and internationalism rendered immediate and valuable service in establishing Marxist-Leninist philosophy in its dominant position. It was impossible to deny that the philosophical schools of thought other than Marxism-Leninism developed in close connection with Western European philosophy, had their origin in and drew their stimulus from its developments. It followed from the doctrine of cosmopolitism that non-Marxist philosophy reflected a hostile ideology and that to continue its cultivation was a political act directed against national interests. To criticise the logic of such a verdict was to stand condemned by one's own words.

The doctrine of cosmopolitism helped to increase the political pressure upon the philosophers and to induce one more inhibition to the freedom of expression. It also opened the flood-gate through which a mounting stream of translations from the Russian and of Russian publications began to pour into Poland. Biology and economics were probably the first to experience a pronounced effort to impose upon them the ideological theories accepted in Soviet biology and economics. This was accompanied by a vast and indiscriminate supply of translated articles, pamphlets and books on these subjects published in the Soviet Union. Anything whatsoever that happened to come into the hands of the publishers was published in translation [66].

The position in philosophy was at first different. Soviet philosophical articles and essays, translated and published in Polish periodicals, were initially few in number and carefully selected. Whatever opinion could have been formed about them, they did not offend intellectual standards accepted in Poland, prior to the establishment of the Marxist-Leninist dominance strictly adhered to by everyone. When a deviation from this rule occurred in 1947, it was unfavourably commented upon by Marxist and non-Marxist alike [67]. This wise discrimination was abandoned with the proclamation of the dogma of two sciences, the cosmopolitan and the international. The eagerness with which anything Russian was seized upon to be extolled and admired rendered poor service to the reputation of Soviet philosophy.

For a few years contacts outside the Soviet part of the world were restricted to the point of complete severance. Some philosophers who sent their contributions to the international congress of philosophy, held in Brussels in 1953, were publicly censured [68]. Opportunities of obtaining books and periodicals published in the non-Soviet world were largely limited to those who were to use them for the purpose of ideological polemics. Philosophical developments outside the Soviet world were generally known only by hearsay or as reflected in the distorting mirror of Marxist-Leninist criticism, from which, to recall

171

Schaff's observation, academic objectivitism and philosophical detachment disappeared. Isolated from the exchange of ideas, non-Marxist philosophy was expected to offer less resistance or to become submerged by the expanding Marxist-Leninist philosophy.

CHAPTER 9

THE INSTRUMENTALIST CONCEPTION OF PHILOSOPHY

Towards the end of 1951, at the time when most of the institutional changes just described had already been accomplished, there appeared the first number of *Myśl Filozoficzna*, introduced in its editorial as a 'clearly Marxist' publication. This description turned out to be perfectly true. *Myśl Filozoficzna* never published articles which either questioned the established Marxist-Leninist assumptions, or made a critical evaluation of them from without, or put forward opinions incompatible with the tenets of Marxism-Leninism. Practically the only deviation from this rule was some infrequent contributions on neutral subjects, and some authorised or unauthorised revisions in the interpretation of the Marxist-Leninist principles, whose validity remained unquestioned. The latter started appearing towards the end of 1955 and were the first symptoms of the forthcoming basic change, *i.e.*, of the abolition of the 'monopoly of a single school'. There would have been nothing unusual in the fact of *Myśl Filozoficzna* being a purely Marxist-Leninist publication, if for six years it were not the only Polish philosophical periodical.

Initially, *Myśl Filozoficzna* appeared four times a year, but from 1955 it became a bi-monthly. Altogether twenty nine issues were published, each of them containing three hundred or more pages. About the middle of 1957 the publication of *Myśl Filozoficzna* was discontinued and replaced by *Studia Filozoficzne*. The change of title was an outward sign of the clear breach with the editorial policy of *Myśl Filozoficzna*. While the appearance of the latter periodical might be taken as the commencement of the period characterised by the monopoly of Marxist-Leninist philosophy, the disappearance of *Myśl Filozoficzna* marked its end. This should be understood as a convenient rough approximation.

Myśl Filozoficzna was edited by Schaff in consultation with an editorial board, on which, for a short time, both Marxist-Leninist and non-Marxist philosophers were sitting. There were at first some stormy meetings of the board, at which its non-Marxist members frankly expressed their opinions on the editorial policy of the periodical and the content and style of its contributions. They insisted that the articles published in *Myśl Filozoficzna* failed to achieve scientific standards; that they criticised in an unfair and offensive fashion philosophers and philosophical trends which were scientifically far superior to anything *Myśl Filozoficzna* was able to produce; that its one-sidedness and exclusion of any other standpoint but Marxism-Leninism could not be reconciled with its claim to being a scientific publication; and that in view of its content, dominated by social and political problems, it was not a philosophical periodical at all. The Marxist-Leninist members of the editorial board rejected this criticism as a defense of bourgeois pseudo-objectivism and of its reactionary ideological function. The two sides spoke different languages and any understanding between them was out of the question at that time [69].

The description of *Myśl Filozoficzna* as a 'clearly Marxist' philosophical periodical meant several different things. Above all, it indicated that *Myśl Filozoficzna* set out to be an organ of 'consistent' and 'militant materialism'. In pursuing this aim, *Myśl Filozoficzna* was anxious at its inception to apply Lenin's advice, given to the editors of the magazine *Pod Znamenem Marxisma*. His advice was that in the circumstances under which *Pod Znamenem Marxisma* started appearing, the joint work of Communist and non-Communist was necessary in combatting 'philosophical reaction' and the 'philosophical prejudices' prevailing in the Soviet society at that time. *Myśl Filozoficzna* was confronted by circumstances not dissimilar from those experienced by the editors of *Pod Znamenem Marxisma*, but the philosophical prejudices, referred to by Lenin, which they were to combat were of a very different nature. The failure of *Myśl Filozoficzna* in its endeavour to secure the support of non-Communists for the establishment of materialism as the dominant popular philosophy was largely due to its conception of philosophy and of the purpose philosophy was intended to serve. This conception was at variance with what philosophy was understood to be among professional philosophers, including the materialistically-minded members of the Warsaw school.

The differences between the Marxist-Leninist and the modern conception of philosophy, represented by the Warsaw school in Poland, have been already touched upon. Marxism-Leninism refuses to recognise any line of division between the world outlook and philosophy *sensu stricto*. For the Warsaw school this line of division was of primary importance.

Philosophy, as understood in the Warsaw school, is an attempt, free from ulterior motives, at exact knowledge obtained by rigorous investigations (as contrasted with speculations) of particular problems arising from the efforts to understand the structure, procedure, and validity of the positive sciences. These investigations require a specialised technique and a mastery of auxiliary disciplines, among which formal logic is most important. They also lead to the discovery of new fields of research, such as the philosophy of language, whose bearing upon philosophical problems and their solutions cannot be overestimated.

Philosophy which abandons speculation, follows scientific procedure, and is governed by the cognitive purpose, presupposes a definite state of mind, known since Descartes as methodological scepticism. While offering a solution, the philosopher is aware of its tentative and provisional character, his mind is open to new evidence, receptive to objections and anxious to search for them himself. A rational philosophical inquiry involves a constant revision of the foundations of knowledge and results in hypothetical statements and probabilities, though rigorously stated.

Philosophical views clearly differ from beliefs which constitute a *Weltanschauung*. They differ as to their respective subject-matter and the reasons for which they are held. A world outlook is concerned with the Universe as a whole, its structure, its ultimate ground and cause. Such beliefs are assumed to be true, but their validation is not determined solely or even mainly by the theoretical criteria of truth and falsehood. In a world outlook the Universe is considered in its relation to man, under the aspect of its bearing on human behaviour, and his place in the natural order. We accept one rather than another synoptic picture of the world because of the presence within it of specific values, incorporated, as it were, in the structure of the world as described in the preferred world picture.

This also applies to the theories of high generality, in principle concerned with the observable facts, but undecidable at a given stage of knowledge. The question whether living matter has developed from inorganic matter is answered 'yes' or 'no' and qualified as probable or improbable in accordance with the conviction this answer seems to imply with respect to human behaviour, individual and collective. Although some theoretical considerations are involved in what is held to be probable or improbable, the respective views on the origin of life are accepted or rejected in accordance with whether they are felt to uphold or degrade the dignity of man, affect his place in Nature in one way or another, and lead to different appreciations of the worth of ends to be attained. Similar considerations influence our opinions in the dispute on determinism and indeterminism in physics, as the recent discussions between physicists and non-physicists alike amply testify. Under the influence of such considerations a hypothetical statement, assumed tentatively or heuristically, is converted into a subjective certainty to lend its authority to a belief concerning the role man should play in the world and to a way of life considered to be desirable [70].

In this sense it might be said that world outlooks are concerned with the ultimate questions of human life. A world outlook supports beliefs conducive to specific actions; beliefs conducive to specific actions prompt the acceptance of a world outlook. A *Weltanschauung*, wrote R.B. Perry, evokes a 'characteristic practical response and inspires a characteristic faith'[71]. A world outlook is ultimately based on considerations of a practical, moral, social, and political nature. It is the work of an intelligence that serves the purpose of life, its brevity, urgency, and the practical necessity of reaching conclusions on evidence that is theoretically unsatisfactory, incomplete, and inconclusive.

It is clear, therefore, that a *Weltanschauung* may conform to scientific knowledge to a varying degree, but there is no scientific world outlook. Science and world outlook are prompted by different motives, serve different purposes, and are assessed by different criteria of validity. The sense of certainty associated with beliefs is rooted in man's whole life experience which helps to bridge the gap between what is assumed in a belief and the paucity of its supporting evidence. Beliefs capable of inspiring sustained action may sometimes produce thereby their own evidence which nourishes further exertions. This explains the power of resistance, which a world outlook displays to unfavourable theoretical evidence. While the latter concerns a particular aspect of a *Weltanschauung*, a self-fulfilling belief adds strength to the whole of it and invigorates steadiness of purpose. There is a sharp contrast between the certainty of beliefs and the rational assent given by a mind disciplined to see coolly and steadily what may be held to be valid or true on the ground of logic and experience.

Marxism-Leninism is clearly a *Weltanschauung*. It starts with the belief that the world is wholly material and that various realms of being are different forms of matter in motion governed by the laws of dialectics. On this ultimate metaphysical datum, in which the mind may rest for ever, a unified world picture is built, various philosophical views and scientific theories are assessed, accepted or rejected according to their compatibility or incompatibility with the basic assumption. Thus, for instance, not only objective idealism, monistic or dualistic spiritualism are brushed aside for obvious reasons, but also phenomenalism turns out to be a totally false doctrine. For if the world and its laws were not fully knowable, if our knowledge of these laws were not 'authentic knowledge' having the validity of 'objective truth', the basic assumption of the Marxist-Leninist outlook could not be an 'objective truth'.

Once this assumption is accepted, the materialist conception of history becomes obviously true, which is not correct but immaterial in this context. If living matter sprang from inorganic and mind emerged from living matter, then the material life of society is primary and its spiritual life is derivative and secondary, dependent, in the mode of its existence, on the former. But the material life of society is its mode of production, which, therefore, determines the political and social institutions, various social theories and ideas, in fact man's whole manner of thought. To change the latter it is necessary and sufficient to change the former and the effectiveness of this practical rule is safeguarded by the structure and laws of the Universe. The belief in the unity of Nature as a whole supports the belief that definite economic and social policies, intended to bring about a desired state of society, can be determined with 'scientific accuracy' leaving no room for doubt or uncertainty.

Action needs confidence and trust, which cannot be secured by the weighing up of evidence in a detached manner, by considering various possible standpoints and hypothetical alternatives. This trust and confidence is drawn from practical beliefs, though in Marxism-Leninism, as much, for that matter, as in any other *Weltanschauung*, they are projected on to the outside world, from which they are derived as the 'objective truth' concerning the nature, structure and laws of the Universe.

The identification of the *Weltanschauung* and philosophy *sensu stricto* was apparent in Schaff's *Introduction to the Marxist Theory*. At that time, however, this was a characteristic feature of one philosophical school of thought, competing with others for recognition and support. The position changed when Marxism-Leninism achieved supremacy and exclusiveness, for that meant the suppression of philosophical inquiry in the proper sense of this term.

The Marxist-Leninist conception of philosophy was widely felt to be a step backwards to a stage of development that in Poland had been overcome half a century earlier. The chances of its acceptance were not improved by the manner of its imposition and by the particular form which it assumed at that time. For in the period of the 'monopoly of a single school' the Marxist-Leninist conception of philosophy was simplified still more. This simplification resulted from the emphasis laid upon the social function and the instrumentalist character of philosophy.

According to Marxism-Leninism the highly specialised character of present-day philosophy is a symptom of its degeneration. It is a barren scholasticism, which bears no relation to the real world, to problems of real life, to knowledge as a guide to action and to the improvement of life conditions by the means available to control Nature. It is a philosophy divorced from the masses of the people, unintelligible to the layman, the domain of esoteric disputes among the elect. They rack their minds to complicate the simplest issue and obscure the most obvious truth. They juggle with a multitude of new terms and invent new techniques which lead nowhere and discover nothing. The make-believe of scientific procedure is a sophisticated mask to disguise the support that the modern bourgeois philosophy gives to Bishop Berkeley's subjective idealism and religion. This is an escape from reality and its problems. It faithfully reflects the disintegrating processes which take place in bourgeois society in the epoch of imperialism [72].

The remoteness of bourgeois philosophy from life, its abstract and specialised character, are contrasted with Marxism-Leninism which knows no breach between academic philosophy and the needs and beliefs of mankind. Marxist-Leninist philosophy belongs to the masses of the people, provides a rallying point for their aspirations, shapes their attitudes, determines their ideals and guides them in their struggle for social betterment. The propagation of this philosophy and its way of thinking is a truly philosophical undertaking. Philosophy fulfils its social function and its proper task if it provides a system of beliefs which promote collective endeavours and concerted actions in the struggle for human emancipation and control over the blind forces of Nature [73].

The emphasis on the social function of philosophy makes of it an instrument that serves some definite purpose. Instrumentalism is a conception of science according to which a scientific theory is not valued for its cognitive content and its ability to free the mind from errors and prejudices, but as an effective instrument for calculation and prediction [74]. Similarly, the Marxist-Leninist conception of philosophy can be described as instrumentalist. Stalin contributed greatly to its establishment. 'The specific features of the basis', wrote Stalin, 'consist in that it serves society economically. The specific features of the superstructure consist in serving society by means of political, legal, aesthetic and other ideas and provide society with corresponding political, legal and other institutions'. Philosophy belongs to the superstructure and constitutes the ideologically most sensitive scientific discipline. As a component part of the superstructure philosophy is an 'active force'. It assists its basis in consolidating itself and helps to eliminate the old basis and the old classes by destroying their world outlook and ideologies [75].

The instrumentalist conception of philosophy has its origin in the voluntaristic interpretation of the Marxian doctrine, which Lenin originated and which Stalin imposed in his version of Marxism-Leninism. In accordance with what

177

has been said in the preceding pages, voluntarism should be understood to be the setting up in an arbitrary fashion of a normative scheme to which social reality is made to conform. The instrumentalist conception of philosophy fits in and is an appropriate means for carrying such a scheme into effect. A world outlook is a system of views which supports beliefs conducive to action of a definite kind. The instrumentalist principle reduces the world outlook to beliefs considered to be useful for the realisation of a predetermined scheme. An act of will defines the content of the world outlook, the direction and manner of action in the course of which 'thought' is compared with the 'real processes in the world outside' and the discrepancy between them adjusted by subsequent actions. Finally, to use Marx's expression, to the 'thought' striving for realisation there corresponds 'reality' striving towards 'thought'.

The Marxist-Leninist instrumentalist conception of philosophy assigns to the latter two fundamental tasks. It is to serve the socialist construction in the country and the cause of socialism in the world [76]. In this manner philosophy as conceived by Marxism-Leninism becomes a means of inducing appropriate attitudes in the ruled and of exercising control over them by the rulers. The proper name for such activities is propaganda, and Marxism-Leninism was thus described in Poland as long and as soon as a spade could be called a spade [77].

The term 'propaganda', applied to the Marxist-Leninist doctrine, was, naturally enough, strongly resented by its supporters, although it was refuted by a stroke of the pen and explained away as a symptom of class hostility and intellectual *hybris*, which was outraged by a philosophy that meets the needs of the people and helps them to liberate themselves from oppression and superstition [78]. 'Propaganda' was a term applied specifically by Marxist-Leninists to some trends of bourgeois philosophy, for instance to empirio-criticism and conventionalism. Duhem, Dingler, Le Roy, Poincaré consider as absurd the existence of the outside world, independent of the human mind. However, they do not in earnest deny the existence of an objective reality, they do not actually believe what they say and write. Their strange views are restricted to their studies outside of which they behave as any other human being and refute their idealist speculations at every step. This inconsistency can only be accounted for sociologically. Its function is to throw the door open to every kind of irrationalism and religious obscurantism, which in turn serve and protect social reaction. When scientific laws are reduced to the status of convenient conventions, religious dogmas become immune from rational criticism. To depreciate the value of science is to make it helpless against superstition, to provide means for the defence of religion and to put science on an equal footing with theology. This was the reason that Lenin called the conventionalists 'scientific salesmen of the theologians'. For they help to confuse truth and falsehood and to mystify fantastic beliefs by presenting them as justified by positive science. Confusion and mystification are the essence of propaganda and modern bourgeois philosophy confuses and mystifies [79].

For Marxist-Leninists propaganda did not consist in a peculiar technique of making people accept some beliefs, but in the content of these beliefs. If they were 'reactionary', they were propaganda, irrespective of whether they were honestly held and presented for free acceptance or rejection. 'Progressive' views, whatever their content and way of propagating them, are never propaganda. To speak of the propaganda of truth is self-contradictory. In this conclusion there was more naive self-righteousness than avowed cynicism, which makes it almost impervious to argument and persuasion.

The instrumentalist conception of philosophy is well suited to the role which Marxism-Leninism was anxious to play in creating and consolidating 'socialist consciousness' or in forming a 'socialist nation'. It also fitted in well with the function assigned to philosophy in the struggle for power in the world.

Having conceived philosophy as a political instrument, Marxist-Leninists ascribed to their own conception a universal character. Philosophical instrumentalism may not be the doctrine to which all philosophers subscribe, but it is the manner in which philosophy is actually, consciously or unconsciously, practised by them. This, Marxist-Leninists contended, can be clearly seen from the history of philosophical thought and from the contemporary events on the world scene. The world divided itself into two camps, the socialist camp and the imperialist camp. The front on which the struggle between them was fought included ideologies in general and philosophy in particular. In the field of philosophy the ideological struggle was most intense and assumed the form of the conflict between dialectical materialism and idealism. This dispute had been carried on throughout history, but in contemporary philosophy the polarisation was complete and the differentiation took its extreme form. On the one hand, materialism found in dialectical materialism its absolutely consistent and final formulation, on the other idealism, concealed under the guise of logical empiricism and misleading by the misuse of symbolism and elaborate pseudo-scientific logical and linguistic techniques, reached the very heights of subtlety, formal precision and perfection[80]. The hard and fast division of the two main philosophical trends was a product and a reflection of the progressive political division of the world without which it cannot be understood.

The philosophical division provided the basis for the evaluation of various philosophical schools and thinkers. When in any doctrine an idealist content was discovered, this doctrine stood at once condemned as reactionary, and therefore false, by what it said. There was no need to refute it any longer. None of its arguments had to be assessed on its own merit and none of its solutions to be examined for the purpose of discovering or indicating how a better one could be found. The valuation of a thinker or a school followed a strict procedure as easy to handle as the method of solving an elementary equation.

The Marxist-Leninist division of philosophical schools into materialist and idealist does not provide an unequivocal and exhaustive principle of classification that would give us a clear bearing in the great variety of views to be found in contemporary philosophy. As is well known, Marxism-Leninism accepts, in principle, Engels' definitions of 'materialism' and 'idealism'. According to these definitions, those who assert the primacy of spirit to Nature comprise the camp of idealism, and those who regard Nature as primary belong to the school of materialism. Lenin thought that to use the terms 'idealism' and 'materialism' in any other way could only give rise to confusions and he strongly discouraged any deviation from the proposed definitions. Polish Marxist-Leninists adhered to his advice, though occasionally not without some embarrassment. They agreed that considered from the viewpoint of the 'philosophical struggle' it was best to respect the 'root distinction', established by Engels and Lenin, and to recognise that the epistemological differences within the idealist camp, in Engels' sense, were of secondary importance [81].

'Nature' in the above context probably means the 'material world' or 'matter' in the common sense meaning of this term. Matter has filled the Universe from eternity and will fill it for eternity, it is neither created nor destructible. To be a materialist is to assert that the Universe has not been created and this is equivalent to saying that God does not exist. On the other hand, an idealist assumes world creation in some form or other, and, in the last instance, the existence of God.

If we apply Engels' criteria of division to such systems as the neutral monism of Bertrand Russell, known from the *Analysis of Matter*, or to Kotarbiński's pansomatism, it is clear at once that they are not idealists. Neither of them assumes the existence of God, though they would deny that God's existence has been or could be disproved, if it means something more than the incompatibility of God's existence with what we know about the world. Neither of them is a creationist, unless the 'creation' of the Universe is a scientific term of modern cosmology. Finally, neither of them assumes that the spirit is primary and in the case of Russell this is made explicitly clear by his criticism of Hegel's and Bradley's doctrines.

On the other hand, neither Russell nor Kotarbiński are materialists in Engels' sense. Russell denies that the traditional separation between mind and matter is metaphysically defensible. Both mind and matter are logical structures composed of hypothetical 'neutral stuff', in which they are 'brought together' without being subordinated one to the other. Russell recommends the acceptance of the 'neutral stuff' on the grounds of economy and comprehensiveness of theoretical exposition and refrains from the contention that the 'neutral stuff' can be demonstratively established [82].

Kotarbiński is not a materialist in Engels' sense either, nor, for that matter, in Russell's, whose views are incompatible with the thesis of ontological reism. He would agree with the opinion that the question of mind-matter relation is a crucial one for materialism and would add that with the present state of knowledge there are several solutions of this problem, all equally entitled to be called materialist. He once referred explicitly to Engels' criterium – the primacy of matter over mind – which he calls 'genetic materialism' and from which he dissociated himself. Why should mind, he asked, in some initial form of development not be as eternal as matter itself? Materialist philosophers are inclined to single out one of the many alternatives, for reasons which are not always relevant to the problem in hand – in Engels' case natural theology was the target – but the answer should be left to science to find [83].

There are other systems which cannot be accommodated within Engels' classification, reflecting some salient features of the nineteenth century philosophical discussions now of exclusively historical interest. Attention was drawn to this fact in Poland and was supported by numerous examples [84]. At that time they made no impression on Marxist-Leninists and only recently the justice of the criticism was recognised in varying degrees by the present and former adherents of Marxism-Leninism [85]. The matter in question is in itself of minor importance if it were not an illuminating example of the Marxist-Leninist approach to philosophical problems.

Engels' criteria helped Marxist-Leninists to sharpen to the utmost the differentiation of philosophy into its polar materialist and idealist extremes. The complete polarisation secured for dialectical materialism its unique position, delimited it from any other trend, whether monistic or pluralistic, materialist or idealist, and inspired it with militancy and a sense of mission. In the case of dialectical materialism Hegel's precept that 'Negation is just as much Affirmation as Negation' was vindicated. By refuting one philosophical school after another and finding them all more or less failing in truly materialistic principles, by discovering that even thinkers commonly considered to be materialists had more in common with Bishop Berkeley than with dialectical materialism, Marxist-Leninists actually accomplished the polarisation of philosophy of which they spoke. They made reality conform to what they decreed it to be and thus convinced themselves of the fact that the class character of dialectical materialism was the only reason why other philosophers did not adopt its standpoint. A Marxist-Leninist found his assumption of the class character of philosophy and of its division, according to the class interests involved, confirmed and verified in whatever direction he looked. Thus, it was an 'objective truth' that philosophy is nothing but a weapon in the struggle between capitalism and socialism, and any criticism of dialectical materialism is nothing but a hostile, class determined political act. The defence of capitalism might not be explicit. Capitalism can also be defended by the support of views which achieve this purpose by implication, and this includes direct or indirect criticism of dialectical materialism. 'He who in the present period fights against dialectical materialism in any way, that is to say, against the philosophy which is the foundation of the proletarian ideology', Schaff wrote, 'defends by the same token the capitalist superstructure, and, consequently, capitalism as a whole' [86]. *Myśl Filozoficzna* was able not only to proclaim this doctrine, but also to effectively impose it.

Explained in terms of its own theory, the rise of Marxism-Leninism in Poland should be conceived as the process of a new superstructure coming into being, conditioned by and corresponding to the socialist basis. This new superstructure, a Marxist-Leninist would say, is not 'passive, neutral, indifferent to the fate of its basis', but having come into being grows into an active force and increasingly plays an important role in consolidating the economic structure of society. The superstructure may assist the consolidation of the basis in a twofold way. Firstly, by formulating and propagating the ideas that reflect the basis.

Secondly, by overcoming the surviving remainder of the old superstructure. The power of the superstructure is creative and destructive, the full use of this power necessitates taking advantage of both its capacities.

These assumptions help us to understand the plan of action drawn up and published in the first issue of *Myśl Filozoficzna*. The plan set five tasks whose order and content were as follows. First, the propagation of Marxist-Leninist philosophy among the masses of the people. Second, the discovery of the regularities which govern progress towards socialism and the establishment of the ideological and methodological foundations that would promote the development of particular sciences. Third, studies on the progressive tradition in the history of social and philosophical thought in Poland which would reveal how the past has prepared the ground for the victory of Marxism-Leninism. Fourth, the training of cadres which would create a new philosophy and science. Fifth, the overcoming of the influence and the survivals of bourgeois philosophy in Poland [87].

It should be remembered that in its early stage of development Marxism-Leninism did not claim exclusive rights to truth, it saw advantages in the plurality of philosophical trends, and thought highly of the contribution to the development of philosophy made by some of them. It recognised the value of critical discussion as an indispensable condition of the search for truth and of the effort to understand the world in which we live.

At the stage now under discussion Marxism-Leninism emphatically repudiated its former position. A new basis has won victory over the old, a new superstructure has come into being, and the new superstructure cannot 'take over' philosophical trends corresponding to the old basis in order to incorporate them into its own body of ideas. The old, *i.e.*, the bourgeois philosophy must be 'overcome' and 'smashed', since it reflects the interests of a hostile class, misrepresents and mystifies the 'objective truth'. A new superstructure, whose function is to protect and consolidate the socialist basis, cannot assimilate ideas incompatible with this function [88].

This argument goes beyond the thesis of historical materialism which does not imply that the different superstructures are mutually exclusive in every respect. The unique character of the superstructure, called into being by the socialist basis, is justified by a different and *ad hoc* principle.

The *ad hoc* principle in question was formulated by Zhdanov. It states that with Marx and Engels there begins a completely new period in philosophy. For Marx and Engels created a 'new philosophy, differing qualitatively from all previous philosophical systems'. It may be developed and enriched, as it has been in Marxism-Leninism, but its foundations, based on 'objective truth', are incorrigible. The discovery of Marx and Engels was the end of the search for principles by means of which a universal explanation of the world could be given. The relation of Marxist-Leninist philosophy to any previous or contemporary system is like that of modern chemistry and astronomy to alchemy and astrology. Philosophical views and ideas which ignore or oppose Marxism-Leninism are of no value whatsoever. They should be looked upon as nothing but freshened up idealist merchandise, produced by the 'philosophical lackeys of imperialism' for the comfort and support of their 'frightened masters'[89].

Myśl Filozoficzna fully accepted Zhdanov's principle and proclaimed that in our epoch Marxist-Leninist philosophy is 'the highest expression of scientific objectivity'. Two consequences should be drawn from this statement. First, that the tenets of Marxism-Leninism provide the absolute criteria by means of which the truth and falsehood of any particular view should be established. This conclusion especially applied to science and provided the basis for the acceptance of some and the rejection of other theories in physics, chemistry, biology, physiology, psychology. Second, all non-Marxist schools of thought in philosophy were declared to be a variety of idealism [90]. Since they all ignored the assumptions of Marxism-Leninism, their mutual resemblance was more important than their respective differences. The only recognised differences between them were either of a historical character or were concerned with their respective range of influence.

It is an established principle of the Marxist-Leninist historiography that the same system of beliefs can be reactionary or progressive under different concrete historical conditions. This principle is applied in particular to pre-Marxian times, but it is also extended to cover the post-Marxian period, preceding the establishment of Marxism-Leninism as a part of the socialist superstructure. For instance, Marxist-Leninist critics of Kotarbiński's views recognised that these had once been progressive, while either Thomism or phenomenology have always been reactionary. In the post-war period, however, Kotarbiński's views impeded the progress of philosophy, and, objectively, were playing a reactionary role [91].

A more important difference, which Marxism-Leninism recognised, was the strength of particular schools of bourgeois philosophy. A battle order for the 'ideological struggle', announced by *Myśl Filozoficzna*, required a careful assessment of the adversary's resources and power of resistance. The existence of four main opponents was recognised – Thomist, or more generally, Christian philosophy, phenomenology, the Warsaw school, and Znaniecki's school in sociology [92].

While surveying the social and intellectual scene in post-war Poland, Chałasiński and Kotarbiński came to the conclusion that two and only two world outlooks were firmly rooted in Polish social reality, combining a universal and comprehensive system of beliefs with mass social support. They were the Christian and the Marxist-Leninist world outlooks. However different their respective principles were, they had a common pragmatic approach to life and its problems; they wished to change and improve the world. This urge can be transformed into a steady, confident, and consecutive endeavour, if people believe more than they know or if they assume to be known what in the theoretical sense is uncertain. In Poland academic philosophy has been governed by theoretical interest, and did not produce, therefore, a world outlook, at least not a universal one, which might appeal to a great number of people. On the other hand, the Christian and Marxist-Leninist world outlooks were ready to take what William James called a 'living, forced and momentous option'. Where theoretical considerations enjoin to suspend judgment, they were ready to take risk, to act and to create the actuality of what they postulate in their respective beliefs. The Christian and the Marxist-Leninist world outlooks make an appeal to a deeply-rooted need in the average man, to which large numbers respond, so securing them mass social support [93].

Marxist-Leninists contrasted their own 'scientific philosophy' with the Christian 'obscurantist' world outlook. The suggestion that there exists wide-ranging correspondence between certain fundamental categories of thought in Soviet philosophy on the one hand, and those of Thomism on the other, was received by them as an outright insult to be answered by an outpouring of vituperation and abuse [94]. But Marxist-Leninists looked at Christian philosophy in a manner not dissimilar from that of Kotarbiński. They saw the strength of the latter in its appeal to the masses, little interested in the more philosophical content of the Christian world outlook. Only a handful of Catholic intellectuals was concerned with philosophical questions. In academic philosophy the Christian school had no influence and was tolerated rather than accepted. Philosophically, it was not, therefore, a serious opponent to Marxism-Leninism. No proof was necessary to show that it was the most extreme version of 'objective idealism'. It did not hide its opposition to dialectical materialism, its fideism, hostility to science, and its socially reactionary character. Marxist-Leninists came to the conclusion that they would demean themselves by dealing with Christian philosophy in a serious manner.

Christian philosophy was recognised, however, as a social and ideological threat to Marxism-Leninism. The source of this threat should be sought in its hold and influence upon the masses of the people exercised through the Catholic Church. Thomism was the philosophy of the Church and its strength was a function of the power of the Church in the country. When the masses of the people adopt the scientific outlook and abandon religion – and according to the Marxist-Leninist assumptions this was bound to happen in a socialist society that was just round the corner – Christian philosophy would lose its foothold and vanish from the intellectual scene without any efforts on the part of Marxist-Leninists [95].

Phenomenology was classed with Christian philosophy and described as a variety of objective idealism or as a notoriously idealist and reactionary doctrine. Marxist-Leninists ignored the fact that in the hands of Ingarden phenomenology has become a method of philosophical inquiry combined with a clearly realistic standpoint in the theory of knowledge. From their viewpoint this was immaterial and the fame of Husserl's transcendental idealism justified equalling any phenomenology with objective idealism of the most objectionable kind. Ingarden was denounced as unfit to teach philosophy in the People's Poland [96].

Because of the small number of phenomenologists in Poland, phenomenology could have been philosophically ignored, if Ingarden had not exercised a considerable influence on the theory of art, and, in particular, of literature. Although Żółkiewski, the Marxist-Leninist authority on this subject, summarily dismissed Ingarden's contributions as contaminated by their Husserlian origin and reflecting the prescientific stage of the 'science of literature', others did not share his opinion and Ingarden's philosophical views were critically examined from the Marxist-Leninist standpoint [97].

The two most serious and influential opponents of Marxism-Leninism in the field of academic philosophy, whom Marxism-Leninism singled out as its main target, were the Warsaw school and Znaniecki's sociology. Marxist-Leninists had to recognise that the differences of opinion and approach between themselves and the philosophers of the Warsaw school were considerable and that the latter were in no mood to throw up the sponge. They also recognised that the Warsaw school enjoyed supremacy in academic philosophy and a wide reputation for its achievements. The view was widespread that, if any school of thought in philosophy deserved the qualification 'scientific', this was the Warsaw school. Marxist-Leninists questioned and rejected this claim – there was no scientific philosophy outside dialectic materialism – but could not deny that the 'appearances' justified it and that it was supported by a wide circle of people, in and outside the universities, including some Marxist-Leninists.

The Warsaw school constituted an opponent that was not easy to deal with. Marxist-Leninist philosophy was one of those traditionalistic trends which the Warsaw school, from its inception, tried to eradicate from academic philosophy and to replace by scientific methods and specialised philosophical thinking. The discussions of 1946–1948 clearly showed that the application of these methods to Marxist-Leninist philosophy threatened it with destruction. To hem in and to isolate the Warsaw school, to prevent it from exercising an influence that was considered to be fatal to dialectics, to its position and prospects, became the chief objective of the announced plan of suppressive action [98].

In the same manner as the 'overcoming of bourgeois philosophy' meant its forceful elimination, similarly the 'overcoming of bourgeois sociology' was an euphemism for the suppression of sociology to the benefit of historical materialism, which was to enjoy the privilege of monopoly. Marxism-Leninism did not recognise the existence of sociology as a separate discipline, but considered it in the nineteenth century fashion as a branch of philosophy, and in its own system identified or subordinated it to historical materialism. According to Marxism-Leninism, a sociologist is always committed to a definite philosophy, whether he is or is not aware of it, and he cannot make a single step without resorting to some philosophical principles [99].

The term 'sociology', as used by Marxist-Leninists, did not refer to the present-day empirical sociological inquiry, but to the speculative grand scale systems of the past, like those of Comte, Spencer, or Marx. The subject-matter of sociology in the Marxist-Leninist sense of this term is society as a whole. Its task is to discover the laws of functioning, growth and decay of society, of the succession of various historical formations. Sociology in its nineteenth century garment was described by Znaniecki as a 'vain dream of ambitious philosophers' [100]. We give it to-day the name of 'philosophy of history' rather than that of 'sociology'.

In these circumstances Znaniecki's school became inevitably an incontrovertible opponent of Marxism-Leninism. Znaniecki was the founder of modern empirical sociology in Poland, which dominated sociological thinking in the inter-war period and continued to do so after the war. When Marxist-Leninists described Znaniecki's school as 'openly idealist' they had in mind its modern conception of social research, its highly critical attitude to the speculations of the past, which included Marx's social philosophy and philosophy of history, as well as some of its peculiar characteristics differentiating it from other trends in modern sociology. The question whether these peculiar characteristics of Znaniecki's sociology justify the qualification 'idealist' must be, for the moment, left undecided. It should be emphasised, however, that at the time when this objection was raised it was to some extent irrelevant. Neither Znaniecki's nor any other school of modern sociology, whatever principles it was based on, could be reconciled with historical materialism or Marxist-Leninist sociology as it was conceived in the Stalinist period.

It seems to be advisable to precede a more detailed survey of the Marxist-Leninist criticism directed against particular schools of thought with some general remarks on its form and technique, which differed considerably from those universally accepted in philosophical discussions. These remarks may appear severe but their severity falls short of what at a later stage Marxist-Leninists themselves said about their methods of criticism. They did not hesitate to expose their shortcomings in a manner that reflects credit on them [101].

The technique of criticism was exegetic. As already mentioned, it invariably consisted in showing by some means or other that the writer's views were incompatible with the tenets of Marxism-Leninism and consequently false. The problems raised and their solutions were not examined for themselves, for it was assumed either that there was in them no question worth investigating or that they had been already solved in Marxism-Leninism. When the incompatibility of the criticised view with Marxism-Leninism was established, what remained was to find for it an appropriate condemnatory term – of subjective idealism, conventionalism, agnosticism, or a combination of them all. To complete the refutation some ready made social and political implications of these false and harmful trends were recalled. In that manner the adversary was regarded as annihilated, for his errors and his ideological offences, for which he was objectively responsible, were thus clearly revealed. 'Criticism of other doctrines' commented Kołakowski, once a Marxist-Leninist himself, 'was not meant to persuade anyone, effectively and rationally, but became a part of a ceremonial ritual and could successfully combine ignorance of the subject with contempt for those whom the criticism concerned' [102].

It was often easy to show that a particular view was not acceptable from the Marxist-Leninist standpoint, but this was not always the case. To achieve this purpose Marxist-Leninists sometimes misconstrued fundamental theses of the position criticised and presented them in such a manner that the accounts were little short of caricature [103]. To a considerable extent it could not have been otherwise once the exegetic method was accepted. Many problems which Marxist-Leninists had to consider were never examined in the Marxist-Leninist school. They were only vaguely known to its supporters whose main interests were problems of the world outlook and not those of philosophy in the stricter sense. They could not be formulated in terms of the Marxist-Leninist doctrine, since it lacked an appropriate conceptual framework and terminology. This concerned, above all, problems of logic, logical syntax, semantics, the theory of knowledge, but also of general methodology, philosophy of science and modern sociology. Marxist-Leninists confidently assumed and stubbornly adhered to the view that the conceptual framework established by the founders of the doctrine in the last century was sufficient for the formulation and solution of any problem whatsoever, and that nothing was worth considering if it could not be formulated in terms of this framework. Thus Marxism-Leninism had its own range of philosophical *Scheinprobleme*. However, the division line between real and pseudo-problems was not determined by some methodological principle, but by a historical accident – the time of origin of the Marxian doctrine [104].

In these circumstances criticism using the exegetic method, having constantly to translate problems from a richer conceptual framework into a poorer one, was somehow forced into simplifications, mistranslations, and misconceptions about what the criticised views actually stated. A loose, uncommon or, arbitrary use of technical terms, such as 'idealism', 'conventionalism', 'agnosticism', added to the confusion. The formulation of the criteria of validity in terms of the alleged political and social significance encouraged breakneck deductions and conferred upon the whole procedure an air of irrelevance. If consistent thinking has no inherent value, but needs justification by some ulterior motive, arguing becomes futile and consistency is oddly out of place.

The presuppositions implicitly accepted in a rational discussion require that the problem to be considered should be seen in its whole setting, its difficulty appreciated, its questions analysed and clearly formulated, before the argument and the solution are examined and evaluated. This means that not only the views criticised but also those of the critic must be subject to a searching analysis. The idea that the opponent in the discussion is also a participant in a common endeavour militated, however, against the Marxist-Leninist conception of the partisan character of philosophy. This conception determined the form of the 'ideological struggle', a term that was substituted for that of 'discussion' and 'argument'.

According to Zhdanov, the principle of *partijnost'* imposes the duty to subject the opponents of Marxism-Leninism to 'ruthless criticism', to emulate Lenin's *Materialism and Empirio-Criticism*, in which Lenin saw through the manoeuvres of reactionary professorial philosophy and used against it a language as sharp as a 'piercing sword'[105]. Most Marxist-Leninists in Poland followed Lenin's and Zhdanov's example. The technique of criticism described above was enriched by an expressive use of language giving free vent to scorn and derision, disdain and contempt, felt by the Marxist-Leninist critic towards the criticised author. The terms 'idealism', 'fideism' and many other lost their descriptive and classificatory function. They became, as Kotarbiński put it, 'dynamic name callings' and warnings to the offender to mend his ways [106]. The critic did not conceal

187

his intention of hurting, giving offence and 'annihilating' his opponent by disparagement and denigration.

The technique and the form of Marxist-Leninist criticism gave it a unique and unmistakable imprint. Its objections were difficult to formulate in an unequivocal language, its arguments hard to follow or incomprehensible, but its conclusions left no doubt that the opponent asserted a farrago of self-evident and undiluted nonsense. Moreover, he was either a wicked man or a fool, a submissive tool in the hands of some cunning masters who served some sinister purpose.

Eristically, the instrumentalist conception of philosophy and the exegetic method were highly effective. They put every opponent at a disadvantage and on the defensive from the start. He stood, as it were, in the dock and had to prove his innocence, if he could. This was, in fact, impossible to achieve. The powers of the best trained and disciplined mind are unequal to the task of dealing with the 'objective significance' or 'political and social implications' which are arbitrarily established and ascribed to a particular view in the theory of knowledge, ontology, or philosophy of science. They are like the many heads of the mythological hydra. Disposed of in one instance, they can be conjured up in some other.

The results of these methods fell far from what Marxist-Leninists expected from them. They made the 'ideological struggle' ineffective and harmed the critics more than their victims. While the exegetic method could successfully silence the opponents of Marxism-Leninism, it left them masters of their own minds. It inflicted a more grievous harm upon the Marxist-Leninists themselves. The rigid and schematic patterns of thought, the rejection of anything that did not fit in with them, the disparagement of what could not be accommodated within the Marxist-Leninist conceptual framework as scholastic conundrums, barred the way of invention and stifled creative intelligence [107]. The examination of philosophical problems of any kind almost entirely vanished from the pages of *Myśl Filozoficzna,* and, in general, from the Marxist-Leninist philosophical production. Marxist-Leninists did not venture to think for themselves. For if they deviated from the line of orthodoxy they too would have to face the question of the 'objective significance' of what they said. They more or less identified themselves with the official line and followed it wherever it led, without any apparent qualms or doubts. In a discussion of the non-Marxist views they adhered to a set pattern, which, as a rule, did not involve any genuine philosophical thinking, for it was a foregone conclusion that a non-Marxist thinker could not be right. The self-imposed restrictive rules on independent thinking made the Marxist-Leninist doctrine more and more antiquated, and estranged the most enterprising minds among its supporters. Instead of increasing, the attractive force of Marxism-Leninism was waning.

The world of Marxist-Leninists, which they claimed was one of common sense and science, was a strange one to a philosopher of a materialist, empiricist and nominalist turn of mind. It teemed with hypostatisations, substantialised or reified concepts. Matter, dialectical laws, objective reality and other abstract entities seemed to have been directly accessible to them and known by acquaintance as are chairs, tables or trees to other men. Socialism and capitalism, progress and reaction, were like Homer's gods, fighting each other, struggling for the salvation of man's soul, inciting and helping men to accomplish good or evil deeds. In our scientific age these gods of the Homeric epics were also penetrating into the most hidden crannies of the human brain to dictate what the brain produced, to mislead the thinker, and to use him as a means of mystifying others. These disembodied forces, haunting the world of men, were either of a benevolent or a malevolent disposition. Dialectical materialism was like the magician's occult knowledge that was giving the power over the disembodied forces to exorcise the malevolent spirits and to invoke the benevolent ones. When these strange times were over even the staunchest supporters of orthodoxy felt relieved and could not look back without shocked astonishment.

CHAPTER 10

CRITICISM OF THE WARSAW SCHOOL

As the Warsaw school was recognised by Marxist-Leninists as their most formidable academic opponent, the best Marxist-Leninists writers participated in the concerted action directed against the school [108]. It started in 1951 and continued for about three years before it was abandoned.

Marxist-Leninist criticism was carried out in a series of studies dealing separately with the views of Twardowski, Kotarbiński and Ajdukiewicz. The plan to extend this series to cover the works of Leśniewski, Łukasiewicz and Tarski never materialised. The latter were charged specifically with the responsibility for imposing upon formal logic some erroneous philosophical ideas which, in the opinion of Marxist-Leninists, exercised an unfavourable influence upon the development of logic [109].

Marxist-Leninists did not think much of Leśniewski and Łukasiewicz. The latter in particular was held in low esteem because of his religious convictions. Tarski was treated more kindly, though he was blamed for having reconciled himself 'easily and lightly' with the 'impossibility of differentiating truth and falsehood in colloquial language', or for expounding a theory which made the concept of truth in everyday language meaningless [110]. The view imputed to Tarski cannot be found in his celebrated essay. Tarski is believed to have shown that the possibility of a consistent use of the expression 'true sentence' in everyday language seems to be questionable and that the possibility of constructing a correct definition of this expression is, therefore, also doubtful [111]. Only if we assume that without a correct definition of 'true sentence' we cannot tell truth from falsehood, would the view ascribed to Tarski have followed from what he actually stated. But Tarski never made this assumption which is clearly a falsehood.

The gravamen attached to the Warsaw school as a whole can be reduced to three objections. The Warsaw school cultivated idealist semantics and made of language, abstracted from its insoluble connections with thought, with its social function as a means of intercourse between people, and, consequently, with the social history of man, the sole object of philosophical inquiry. Having made of language a source or the source of knowledge (Marxist-Leninists vacillated between these two versions without being aware that they were different), the Warsaw school believed that philosophical problems, and, in particular, the issue of idealism *versus* materialism, were questions of language that could be resolved by a linguistic analysis. Consequently, the Warsaw school was inclined to make the truth and falsehood of philosophical and scientific statements dependent on the rules of language, laid down arbitrarily, that is, by conventions. Finally, and this is in fact a conclusion implied by the two preceding objections, the Warsaw school was a congeries of foreign influences. The doctrine of the school was intimately bound up with English logical empiricism (Bertrand Russell), Austro-German neo-positivism (Schlick, Carnap, Neurath, Reichenbach, Frank and others), and the American cross-breed of pragmatism and neo-positivism (Ch. W. Morris). Since the idealist semantics and the semantical philosophy were the most perfidious, subtle and refined variety of the idealist reaction to dialectical materialism, the Polish progeny of these various trends could not be something different. The reputation enjoyed by the Warsaw school of having made an original contribution to philosophy was without foundation. This reputation was a myth to conceal, under an elaborate disguise, a cosmopolitan subjective idealism of foreign origin [112].

The characteristics common to the Warsaw school as a whole did not prevent its particular representatives from holding opinions which differed considerably from each other. Marxist-Leninists recognised this fact but they claimed that these differences only made more pronounced what was revealed by the general circumstances. The leading members of the Warsaw school were idealists both on account of having supported the common doctrine of the school and in their own right.

The Marxist-Leninist analysis of Twardowski's views revealed two levels in them, described as those of a concealed and an overt professorial obscurantism, an idealist and positivistic theory of knowledge and a neo-scholastic metaphysics. They were blended together to form an eclectic jumble that was one more attempt to reconcile positivism and religion, science and theology [113].

To follow the Marxist-Leninist criticism, Twardowski's basic standpoint must be recalled. It can best be described as psychologism, *i.e.,* the conviction that psychology is the fundamental philosophical discipline. The emphasis placed upon the epistemological priority of the cognitive consciousness provided a basis for philosophical investigations. This empirical basis was contrasted with that of traditional metaphysics which used to lay down some abstract principles and to deduce from them what and how it is experienced.

The assertion of the priority of the cognitive consciousness established descriptive psychology as an autonomous discipline, irreducible to physiology, and the analysis of mental acts, which revealed their intentional character, led to the world of objects and made these objects the proper subject matter of philosophical inquiry. This initial standpoint could and did pave the way, in the course of time, for epistemological idealism, but Twardowski did not follow this line of development. Although he contributed by his investigations to the transformation of descriptive-psychological methods into Husserl's transcendental analysis of pure consciousness, Twardowski himself inclined towards epistemological realism and was increasingly opposed to the emerging transcendental phenomenological method. Everything that is known must first be represented by mental acts, but the existence of objects, given in representations, is not dependent on these acts, on the cognising subject or pure consciousness. On the other hand, descriptive psychology refuted the view that conceived the content of mental acts as a 'psychological reflection' of their object. This was one of the important reasons why there was the need for philosophical investigations, which, making use of psychological descriptions, went beyond them and required specialised reflective techniques for the examination of the world of objects.

In the opinion of Marxist-Leninists this particular variety of psychologism was a continuation of subjective idealism from 'Berkeley and Hume to Avenarius and Twardowski'. To accept the epistemological priority of the cognitive consciousness, which Lenin and his followers failed to differentiate from the ontological priority, was to adopt an idealist principle. Twardowski abstracted thinking from matter, denied that matter is primary and mind secondary and that consciousness is a reflection of the external world. Under the disguise of empiricism and by means of a method that was to eliminate metaphysical speculations, Twardowski dismissed fundamental philosophical problems and materialism. Marxist-Leninists were not quite certain, whether Twardowski's ideas should be classified as a dualistic conception of the mind-body relation or a positivist 'senseless jumble of materialism and idealism' on the lines of Avenarius' empirio-criticism. They were sure, however, that Twardowski, prompted by the 'hatred of materialism', tried to destroy it by a declaration of war on metaphysics. In this respect he did not differ from Mach and Avenarius. His teaching was not, therefore, a 'reaction against idealist metaphysics', which, on the contrary, it either directly or indirectly supported, but a 'reaction against materialism'[114].

A common theme of the Marxist-Leninist criticism directed against particular thinkers of the Warsaw school was that upon the rejection of the naive, common sense view of the external world, including the copy theory of knowledge, everybody is entitled to create for himself another realm of being, from which God, disembodied spirits, immortal souls, and ideal entities cannot be dislodged. The criticism of Twardowski made much use of this assumption and found its justice confirmed by Twardowski's general theory of objects, and, in particular, of intentional objects.

Twardowski's theory of objects is an ontological – what Meinong called *eine daseinsfreie Wissenschaft* – and not a metaphysical doctrine. He took a neutral attitude to problems of metaphysics and he claimed validity for his theory of objects irrespective of whether we adopt an idealist or realist standpoint in the theory of knowledge. Twardowski did not inquire into the nature of the external causes of our experiences, sensations, representations, and judgments, and was convinced that such an inquiry would not modify his psychological and ontological investigations [115].

Twardowski's theory of objects has serious difficulties and might lead to contradictions, which prompted its sharp revision by logical and philosophical means undertaken by Leśniewski and Kotarbiński. In the development of the Warsaw school Twardowski's theory of objects was the starting point of further investigations and prepared the way for much that came later, often in opposition to the initial ideas of the founder of the school. Historically, Twardowski's theory of objects, Leśniewski's ontology and Kotarbiński's reism constitute a consecutive development of the same philosophic problem. This immanent development of thought passed unnoticed by Marxist-Leninist critics. They examined Twardowski's views outside their historical settings and looked at them rather as a theory to be refuted than as a formulation of a problem to be solved. The objections which they raised against his theory of objects were not concerned with its shortcomings, but concentrated on some of its other aspects, offering an opening to criticism better suited to the purpose of the exegetic method.

Twardowski's concept of object is of great generality. Things of the external world given in experience, intentional objects, which in some cases seem to coincide with things without being identical with them, abstract entities, anything at all that can be represented, are objects in Twardowski's sense. If we say that things exist and that mental or ideal objects are not things, the latter cannot exist unless they are contradictory objects [116]. Mental or ideal objects are not, however, pure figments of imagination, they are objective and real in some sense of these terms. If they do not exist, they subsist, and their subsistence is revealed by the descriptive analysis of mental acts. According to Marxist-Leninist criticism, Twardowski's intentional objects and his theory of objects in general provide the link between his idealist and positivistic theory of knowledge and 'fideistic metaphysics'. It is 'fideistic metaphysics' since it merges with theology and paves the way for the belief in God and the immortality of the soul [117].

This claim was substantiated by reference to a popular article, written by Twardowski in Vienna at an early stage of his career. He argued in it that our internal experience makes the belief about the thinking mind being a spiritual entity more probable than Büchner's and Haeckel's opinion which identifies the thinking subject with the brain. If we accept the former belief, we are faced with the question of how the soul came into being and the only satisfactory answer is that God created it. In this article Twardowski referred to psychology and internal experience; he did not make any use of his theory of objects. The latter was established by means of investigations to be accepted or rejected irrespective of whether we do or do not believe in God.

This was not how the Marxist-Leninists looked at the matter. They assume that every item of being is essentially determined by universal interrelationship. The same applies to what men believe, think and do. Moreover, by the same principle of universal interrelationship, thoughts and actions must be related to determinate social conditions and also be examined from the viewpoint of their social consequences. Various views, held by a thinker, are intrinsically related and support each other. If his views are erroneous, it is possible to trace them down to a common source and to identify one single fundamental error that pervades all his assumptions and conclusions, the propounded issues and their proposed solutions. The opinion according to which the sources of possible error are not manifold and do not vary from one problem to another, but, on the contrary, may and should be reduced to a unique source, will be called the 'monistic fallacy'.

An instance of the monistic fallacy is the Marxist-Leninist view on the far-reaching and all-pervading consequences of the belief in God. It is not possible

193

to accept the evidence of science and to believe in God. The only scientific belief about God is that he does not exist. A scientific mind is an irreconcilably atheistic mind. 'The neutrality of a philosopher in this question', wrote Lenin, aiming his criticism at Mach and Avenarius, 'is in itself servility to fideism'[118].

The views of a man who believes in God's existence cannot be valid, true and scientific, however rigorously they are formulated and established. They cannot be taken at their face value and their examination cannot be restricted to what they explicitly state in any particular case. They must be evaluated with respect to the thinker's world outlook and their true meaning be revealed by laying bare the purpose which they serve within this outlook. When this is accomplished, it becomes evident that whatever he says, be it an examination of the conditions conducive to visual illusions, or an analysis of the term 'percept' or the adherence to genetic empirism or the formulation of a general theory of objects, is affected by or distorted for the sake of his belief in God. His views need not be considered on their own merits, since they are only an instrument that serves the purpose of justifying this belief. The evidence for such a contention is often left to the reader's intuitive insight and unsupported by demonstrative grounds in its favour. This was actually the course adopted by the Marxist-Leninist critics with respect to Twardowski's theory of objects [119].

Twardowski's theory of objects was simply dismissed as a barren scholastic exercise and a worthless professorial artifice, unrelated to any genuine philosophical problem, whose sole purpose was to establish the realm of *entia rationis,* the supremacy of spirit, and, finally, the whole of theology. The elaborate construction, set up on empirical psychological foundations, had one supreme objective, namely, to provide the proofs of the immortality of the soul and of the creation of the world by God (Twardowski never spoke of such proofs and never indicated that they could be provided), to secure *treuga Dei* between science and religion, philosophy and the Church [120].

Thus, the legend about Twardowski was exploded and his life work shown in its true light. The man who was presented and honoured as the founder of scientific philosophy in Poland stood revealed as a philosophical 'obscurantist of the extreme kind', who indulged in the prevailing prejudice against materialism and was a supporter of clericalism and the Church [121].

Twardowski's philosophy, argued his Marxist-Leninist critic, was firmly rooted in the tradition of medieval theological discussions, from which it borrowed its technique of careful conceptual distinctions and precise terminological definitions, its analytical and constructive skill. These, in principle praiseworthy, habits of thought were used to produce a learned philosophical gibberish, with no sense of relevance for genuine philosophical issues, and to oppose the growing influence of dialectical materialism. In the Warsaw school this medieval theological tradition was merged with modern positivistic and logistic trends. The facility with which it was achieved provides an illuminating testimony to the bourgeois partisan character of the whole Warsaw school. In the face of a common class enemy, dialectical materialism, the irreconcilable tendencies joined hands and supported each other [122].

Kotarbiński is a materialist. Nothing is a soul or a mind, every soul is a body. His materialism, or somatism, as he prefers to call it, is not in principle committed to the mechanistic hypothesis, of which Kotarbiński personally is not in favour. Mechanistic theories are not universally adequate, if by mechanistic theories are understood explanations formulated in terms of the spatial and temporal distribution of gravitating bodies, of the direction and velocity of their motions. Kotarbiński is not only an empiricist, suspicious of abstract entities – properties, relations, propositions, classes, numbers – but also a consistent nominalist, who spares no pains to restrict himself to a nominalistic language. A consistent materialistic outlook, as he understands it, should be formulated in terms of a nominalistic language under the penalty of transgressing its own principles. Tirelessly Kotarbiński exposes various substantialisations of modes of behaviour, hypostatisations of name-like expressions, and reifications of immanent representations or intentional objects. He shows how sentences involving references to a hypostatised or abstract entity can be translated into equivalent sentences containing no such references [123].

Kotarbiński is a radical realist in the theory of knowledge. The qualification 'radical' indicates that he denies the existence of sense data. His radical realism includes the 'principle of tolerance' with respect to the question whether the secondary qualities – to use for brevity's sake the non-reistic language – are subjective modifications of the sentient body or characteristics of external objects. Although nothing is whiteness, sweetness or bitterness, a radical realist may say that a white or sweet or bitter thing exists now, here or there, and generally that things may be coloured, smelling, sounding, tasting, these statements being either true or false. Radical realism is not incompatible, therefore, with what a supporter of the copy theory of perception is inclined to say about the objects of the external world [124].

Kotarbiński is an atheist, and his materialism leaves no loophole for believing in the existence of disembodied spirits and God, the creator of the Universe. He is an empiricist in ethics and in his investigations of moral and social problems follows in Hume's footsteps in trying to base his conclusions on a 'cautious observation of human life' as it appears 'in the common course of the world'. His open-mindedness on the questions of morals is restricted only by few convictions, such as that truth, honesty, justice, kindness, modesty, care of the weak, are intrinsically good for man, and that they should not be treated lightly. His examinations of moral issues are inspired by a sympathetic understanding of human beings and by a keen appreciation of the qualities of the human personality. This may not tally with the popular idea of a materialist philosopher, but is not incompatible with the materialistic conception of man, unless materialism is equated with considering man to be a complicated mechanism or a piece of animated matter.

According to Marxist-Leninists, it would be a serious error to describe Kotarbiński as a consistent materialist. This follows syllogistically from the premisses that only dialectical materialists are consistent materialists and Kotarbiński is not a dialectical materialist. The latter premiss is easy to establish. A dialectical materialist considers matter as primary, mind as secondary. Kotarbiński's pansomatism is not equivalent to that assumption, disregards its importance, does not legislate away the possibility of panpsychism (matter might always have been sentient), and rejects as meaningless the assertion 'every psychical phenomenon is identical with some physical phenomenon'. Moreover, the 'principle of tolerance' in the theory of knowledge militates against the copy theory of perception, for it allows for deviation from it. The principle in question constitutes an agnostic infringement upon the thesis of knowledge being a true reflection of the external world [125].

The materialistic content of Kotarbiński's views, Marxist-Leninists said, is a variety of the metaphysical materialism in Engels' sense, *i.e.*, it is an anti-dialectical materialism. It does not contribute anything to the modern materialistic philosophy and judged by its standards it is an anachronism. Over and above their materialistic content Kotarbiński's views include elements incompatible with materialism, namely, conventionalism, agnosticism, nominalism and an idealist semantics. Engels revealed 'real idealism', concealed under the surface of metaphysical materialism, in Feuerbach's philosophy. Kotarbiński shared Feuerbach's fate at the hands of his Marxist-Leninist critics.

Kotarbiński's 'real idealism' reveals itself in a threefold way: in his semantical reism, which is one of the trends of idealist semantics; in his somatism and pansomatism which are a conventionalist doctrine; and in his nominalism which undermines the scientific world outlook and promotes the interpretation of scientific theories in terms of subjective idealism. It should be remembered that the objection of cultivating an idealist semantics was also raised against the Warsaw school as a whole. The first reason for describing Kotarbiński's views as an eclectic compromise of materialism and idealism will be, therefore, considered at a later stage. Also the objection that nominalism is an anti-materialistic doctrine will be examined together with other Marxist-Leninist views on universals.

The assertion that Kotarbiński is at heart a conventionalist is solely based on his own statement to the effect that somatism and pansomatism are hypotheses which he accepts according to his inclination [126]. It is hard to say what else his assumptions could have been. 'Every soul is a body' and 'every object is a body' are not analytic statements, for their denials are not self-contradictory. On the other hand, they do not refer to a finite class of individuals, that is to individuals to be found in an interval of time and a defined region of space, but to all individuals, irrespective of these restrictions. They are strictly universal statements, as distinguished from those merely numerically universal, in Popper's sense. Being synthetic they cannot be *a priori* valid, they must be tested and be corrigible in the light of fresh evidence. Consequently, they are tentative universal statements or conjectures held on insufficient grounds. In this sense they can rightly be described as hypotheses [127].

A hypothesis in the above sense, argued the Marxist-Leninists, is a much too flimsy foundation for a world outlook. 'To be held on insufficient grounds' means, in their opinion, the same as 'to be held arbitrarily', and to accept something according to one's disposition is to accept it by the *fiat* of one's whim. They clearly hold a belief to be a mere state of mind, a purely psychological fact with no objective significance [128]. The factual and terminological confusions, of which this argument makes use, are apparent.

To believe in *p* is a state of mind, in which we are ready to assert *p*. But seldom, if ever, do we believe something with no reason whatsoever and our disposition to believe *p* varies in degree, according to the nature and extent of evidence for *p*. The evidence might be irrational or rational, and in the latter case it can have a wide range of reliability. A reliable or warranted belief is not arbitrary or dependent on anybody's whim. As long, however, as the evidence is not con- clusive, it remains a belief, accepted according to one's inclination, that is to say, according to one's knowledge of the subject-matter and one's ability to bring the evidence to bear upon a belief. A warranted belief *p* induces the state of mind of believing what *p* states to be the case [129].

The distinction between the belief in the psychological and epistemological sense does not satisfy Marxist-Leninists. For they seem to assume that dialectical materialism in an 'objective truth' which is superior to a warranted belief. More- over, to say that a world picture is based on a warranted belief is to concede that it cannot be absolutely true and a perfectly faithful reflection of reality deter- mined by the nature of the external world. If this viewpoint is accepted, it might appear that Kotarbiński abandons the claim to knowledge of objective reality and resorts to an arbitrary logical construction. This construction combines conventionalism with subjective idealism. For in somatism, based on semantic reism, genuine questions of fact are resolved by linguistic conventions and 'laws of Nature' are replaced by a free creation of the mind [130].

Underlying this criticism is a conception of knowledge which may be called 'epistemological absolutism'. According to this conception only absolutely certain knowledge is genuine knowledge, to be sharply differentiated from true or warranted beliefs, which being corrigible and sometimes false are unreliable knowledge or no knowledge at all in its proper sense. This is not to be under- stood as a linguistic rule. An epistemological absolutist does not wish to say that in the use of the verb 'to know' he follows the rule: what is not true cannot be said to be known. For there can be no doubt that the verb 'to know' is sometimes used in conformity with this rule irrespective of whether the speaker is or is not an epistemological absolutist. What the latter asserts has nothing to do with linguistic rules alone. An epistemological absolutist believes as a matter of fact that that which is known cannot be false and that to deny it is to make a self-contradictory statement. This again should not be understood to mean that whatever is known is an analytical truth. For some epistemological absolutists would not restrict knowledge, as they understand it, to necessary, that is, analytic truths. When they say: 'what is known must be true', they mean: 'what is known is indubitable'. The conclusion to be drawn therefrom is that if what was held to be certainly true proves to be a falsehood, it was not knowledge but a belief mistaken for knowledge, for it is impossible to know what is not the case. Knowledge provides incontrovertible truths, belief is a state of mind, supported

197

merely by the individual's fallible sense of being right. Consequently, though held to be warranted, it may turn out to be false and since no genuine knowledge can ever be false, no belief is genuine knowledge, whatever evidence it may claim. For if one can believe something to be true and admit without contradiction that what is believed may be subject to doubt or false, what is believed cannot be knowledge. It would be self-contradictory to say that what is known may be false.

Epistemological absolutism is an ancient doctrine, at least as old as the philosophy of Parmenides and Plato's *Theaetetus*. From the first moment of its appearance it was faced by numerous serious difficulties which it tried to avoid by restricting the scope of what can be certainly known. Plato, the Stoics, Bertrand Russell, or G. E. Moore, however different were their respective starting points and conclusions, all took this course. In the case of Marxism-Leninism no such restrictive measures seem to have been taken. Absolutely certain knowledge is attainable not only in logic, mathematics, and, generally, in the deductive sciences, but also in natural science and philosophy. This is a position hard to defend and to justify. For there is a strong *prima facie* case for asserting that it is very doubtful whether there are any indubitable empirical statements. If there are any, the question of how to find and distinguish them from those which are mere beliefs, acquires a crucial importance. Generally stated, the basic difficulty, by which epistemological absolutism is confronted, is as follows: what is the procedure for distinguishing certain knowledge from mere belief, by what criterion can the former be differentiated from the latter, and what is the difference between merely believing something to be true which is eventually found to be false and falsely believing to know when one does not know.

We can, of course, accept a linguistic rule for the use of the term 'certainly true', by which it may be predicated of propositions even if there is no effective means of discovering whether they are certainly true. There are such rules probably in all natural languages to serve didactic, moral, and some other purposes, to keep before the mind's eye the intrinsic value of truth in man's search for knowledge. But the meaning of 'true' or 'certainly true' governed by this rule does not refer to a characteristic of particular propositions, but rather to 'absolute truth' of the metaphysician from Plato to Frege. It provides us with the conviction, of which William James wrote, that there is a truth to be discovered by experiment and studies, which inspires us with the determination to strive for it in our thinking lives. It is an idea that regulates behaviour without determining the sought for characteristics of knowledge. For what is claimed as 'knowledge' in any particular case hardly ever comes close to this elevated ideal, and is, as a rule, corrigible, capable of being improved upon, made more reliable. 'Truth and error, like all concepts, which are expressed in polar opposites, have absolute validity only in an extremely limited field', wrote Engels [131]. This is a sound observation and Marxist-Leninists are right in recalling it frequently, although often solely by way of an introduction to the inclusion of their own views in the limited field corresponding to the first of the above mentioned polar opposites.

For the purpose of obtaining reliable knowledge we need some general method for discovering whether a proposition is true. There can be no doubt that we can with some success distinguish what can from what cannot be proved, as well as warranted beliefs from unwarranted ones, and warranted beliefs from each other according to their respective degree of justification, the nature and extent of evidence in their favour. But we do not know how to proceed in order to discover what is certainly true among various competitive views, all of which, outside logic and mathematics, are liable to be false. To say that in the case of knowledge we know that we know, provides no solution, for it either involves a *regressus in infinitum* or renders the answer circular (in the manner similar to the Platonic Socrates' proof to the effect that *Theaetetus'* definition of knowledge being a rationally justified belief was circular). If a false or a corrigible belief is mistakenly held to be certainly true, this error can be ascertained in due course by a *post mortem* examination. But an examination of this sort can only reveal what was not certainly true, without being able to indicate by what it should be replaced and how we should set about it. To equate reliable knowledge with what is certainly true does not seem to secure any advantages over the opinion that we have always to start with beliefs held on inconclusive grounds, which we test, refute, and replace by others in the light of the available evidence. While no advantages are gained in this course, many and considerable disadvantages are incurred.

It has been pointed out that strictly universal synthetic statements, for instance of reism, somatism, and pansomatism, are necessarily conjectures. The same applies to the assumptions of dialectical materialism, which, too, are clearly strictly universal synthetic statements. The claim that they are not conjectures but incontrovertible truths cannot be established otherwise than by an *a priori fiat*. For if they were certainly true, we could not know it. What can be logically inferred from them does not depend on whether they are or are not certainly true. Their explanatory power is not affected in the slightest by the finality attached to them, and, in this respect, nothing would be changed if instead of being proclaimed certainly true they were held to be but warranted beliefs. The advantages to be drawn from the identification of knowledge with infallible knowledge lie outside the sphere where the search for truth is pursued. Only when metaphysical beliefs function, in a disguised form, as moral and political rules, is their epistemological significance affected in accordance as to whether they are considered to be certain knowledge or warranted belief. For in the former case their effective regulative power gains considerably from being endowed with the privilege of infallibility [132].

It has been said that a critical and scientific attitude is not so much opposed to the dogmatic and pre-critical attitude as superimposed upon the latter. For criticism presupposes beliefs accepted on inconclusive evidence, which, to be tested, refuted and improved upon must be initially held, as it were, dogmatically. Moreover, to pursue the efforts of establishing more and more reliable beliefs and conjectures, we must have an understanding of what being certainly true is. The failures of attaining certainty result in the delimitation of the two realms of rationality, of rational certainty restricted to the deductive sciences, and of warranted beliefs never conclusively established and comprising practically all the knowledge outside the deductive sciences [133].

If this view is accepted, epistemological absolutism should be considered a residue of the pre-critical stage in philosophical and methodological thinking. This concerns both its identification of genuine knowledge with certainly true knowledge and its disposition to assert dogmatically what can only be tentatively, though rationally, asserted.

In the opinion of Marxist-Leninists, Ajdukiewicz was the most consistent representative of the Warsaw school. In Kotarbiński's reism and pansomatism the conventionalist and idealist ingredients are concealed and have to be extricated from their intricate and misleading shell, in Ajdukiewicz's radical conventionalism they are striking. Moreover, Ajdukiewicz stood closest to the neo-positivism of the Vienna Circle. He can be credited with the distinction of having produced the crowning achievement in the development of thought which started with Bertrand Russell's logical atomism, and which through the logic of science of the Vienna Circle attained its perfection in Ajdukiewicz's radical conventionalism. Ajdukiewicz's views provide the best opportunity of studying the idealist semantics and the semantical philosophy, for which the Warsaw school gained its reputation [134].

Before the Marxist-Leninist criticism of the idealist semantics is examined two preliminary points must be taken up. They concern the relation of the Warsaw school to the Vienna Circle and the movement of logical empiricism in general, and the meaning attached to the term 'idealist semantics', of which so much use, clearly derogatory in its expressive function, was made by the Marxist-Leninists. At that time, apart from its technical sense, different in the Marxian and non-Marxian tradition, 'idealist' also meant 'being incompatible with Marxism-Leninism and reactionary', or 'unscientific' *tout court*.

The assertion that the Warsaw school was not a native growth but one of foreign inspiration, mainly implanted by the Austro-German neopositivistic revival, disregards the time factor. The Warsaw school never published a programme like *Wissenschaftliche Weltauffassung: Der Wiener Kreis* (1929) that marked the international appearance of the Vienna Circle. Nor was it ever formally organised and active as a collective body as the Vienna Circle was in the 'thirties, publishing a periodical of its own and various series of monographic publications, arranging international meetings and congresses of like-minded thinkers. The Warsaw group was an informal body which in the late 'twenties, roughly at the same time as the Vienna Circle, acquired collectively distinctive characteristics. The endowed it with some cohesion and group identity, apparent to outsiders [135]. Both the Vienna Circle and the Warsaw school existed much earlier than the time of their public appearance would indicate, each of them little aware of the existence of the other and each following its own course of development. Mach, Russell and Wittgenstein are recognised as thinkers whose influence on the Vienna Circle was the most significant. In the case of the Warsaw school the influence of Brentano, Frege and Russell was predominant. The origin and the formative years of the Warsaw school, already reviewed, testify to the fact that the influence of these and many other thinkers, duly recognised by those who benefited from it, did not preclude the school from following its own line of development [136].

The co-operation between the Vienna Circle and some thinkers of the Warsaw school established in the 'thirties had a stimulating effect on both sides and increased the channels of mutual influence. Jørgen Jørgensen, a logical empiricist himself and its historian, emphasised an especially lively and fruitful exchange of thought between Carnap, Gödel and Tarski [137]. Among those who on the Polish side participated in the international meetings (Prague, Paris, Copenhagen) and contributed to *Erkenntnis* were Ajdukiewicz, Chwistek, Hosiasson, Jaśkowski, Kokoszyńska, Łukasiewicz, and Zawirski. These contacts led to the recognition of the kinship between the two schools and also of their mutual differences [138]. At the International Congress of Scientific Philosophy in Paris (1935) and at the Second International Congress for the Unity of Science, held in Copenhagen in 1936, these differences became pronounced [139]. They did not affect the high reputation which the Vienna Circle, and later logical empiricism, continued to enjoy in Poland before and also after the war [140].

Nobody in Poland accepted the conception of philosophy propounded by Carnap in *Logische Syntax der Sprache*. The replacement of the 'inextricable tangle of problems which is known as philosophy' by the logic of science was expressly rejected by Łukasiewicz who analysed and criticised it at length. On the other hand, problems in which, for instance, Kotarbiński was interested were declared by Carnap to be of non-cognitive character. The epistemological controversies concerning the reality of the external world or the disputes about the universals between the nominalists and the realists were rejected by Carnap as battles about pseudo-statements, dealing with pseudo-problems [141]. Ajdukiewicz opposed Carnap's view that a language is unequivocally determined by its vocabulary and syntactical rules. Signs or words and expressions of a language must be used according to definite rules if they are to have meaning, that is, if they are to serve the purpose of communication. He called them meaning rules of the language and the manner in which he conceived them led ultimately to the establishment of pragmatics. His ideas were opposed by the Vienna Circle and objections were raised that Ajdukiewicz was trying to infect a formal study of language with psychologism [142]. Tarski's investigations, initiated in 1929 and inspired by Leśniewski's lectures delivered ten years earlier, revealed that the concept of truth can be defined only in terms of a language essentially richer than that considered by the logical syntax of language, since it must contain both the expressions of the object language and the terms used in the structural description of the language. Only on the basis of this richer metalanguage can various concepts, such as meaning, naming, denotation, connotation, extension, and truth be defined in a materially adequate and formally correct manner. These various concepts are the subject-matter of semantics which was unknown to and for a few years disregarded by the Vienna Circle [143]. All these questions were not minor quarrels dividing thinkers in agreement on all essential principles – like the differences between Schlick, Neurath, Carnap, and Hempel on the subject of the protocol-sentences – but reflected some basic differences.

These differences originated in the philosophical background and resulted from an immanent development of thought, different in Vienna and in Warsaw. A staunch adherence to epistemological realism was an unmistakable trait of the Warsaw school. There was associated with it a conception of truth that conceives it not as the correspondence between a sentence and an experience but as that between a sentence and a fact or occurrence. With the logical theory of correspondence, as distinguished from the epistemological one [144], there was combined the emphasis upon the referential function of language, upon the existence of the extra-linguistic reality, from which language should not be divorced, since it does not constitute an independent realm. Consequently, if everyday language is not sufficiently precise for the purpose of philosophical investigations, its revision cannot be undertaken as if there were no extra-linguistic occurrences to determine the structure of language and as if the latter could be artificially reconstructed on some premises of its own. The same applied to formal logical systems. For the Warsaw school the acceptance of Carnap's 'principle of tolerance' was inconceivable. To paraphrase Carnap's saying [145], there are morals in logic, and there are not only internal but also external problems of existence. The conventionalist interpretation of logical and scientific systems ignores the fact that these systems reveal something about the external world, and, if they do, it is the philosopher's or logician's business to set up prohibitions instead of being satisfied with decisions concerned merely with the efficiency of the instrument used. An abstract linguistic or logical instrument might be in some way effective and yet be useless as a means of establishing a system of clearly true propositions.

The epistemological attitude which characterised the thinking of the Warsaw school exercised a restricting influence upon what was common to the movement *sensu largo,* to which both the Vienna Circle and the Warsaw school belonged. It is widely accepted that this movement should be described rather by a common tendency to make philosophy a scientific discipline and by a common technique of investigation, derived from formal logic and procedures used in science, than by common views and principles. These common methodological conceptions and techniques were bound, however, to produce vastly different results, for the manner of their application was determined in Vienna and Warsaw by different epistemological presuppositions. This was what actually happened. If the methodological aspect and the general purpose are disregarded, the increasing divergence of definite views, held by the Vienna Circle and the Warsaw school, becomes predominant. They were clearly two independent branches within the same movement, each of them with a distinct character and contribution of its own. Their differences did not preclude co-operation which reflected their endeavour to emancipate philosophy from parochialism. To say that the Warsaw school was nothing but a Polish version of the Viennese neo-positivism, eclectically enriched by some English and American ingredients, is not an adequate account of the philosophical development in Austria and Poland in the inter-war period.

Marxist-Leninists propounded the above assertion as self-evident and made practically no attempt to substantiate it by showing the similarity or identity of particular views held by the Vienna Circle and the Warsaw school respectively[146]. The basic differences escaped their notice and when they could not be ignored, as in the case of Ajdukiewicz's criticism of Carnap's syntactical theory of meaning, its nature and import were misunderstood and declared to be minor family differences of opinion, insignificant in comparison with the fundamental affinity of the two schools [147]. This appraisal of the Viennese and Warsaw thinkers was dominated by the evaluation of their views in terms of the alleged social and political significance, which was the same in both cases. Since the Vienna Circle propagated its views with considerable zeal and the impact was felt all over the world, an evaluation in terms of the social and political significance was bound to assign the role of leader to the Vienna Circle and that of the follower to the Warsaw school [148].

The term 'semantics' is used by Marxist-Leninists so broadly that like some other of their technical terms it becomes meaningless. They do not differentiate semantics from logical syntax, or fail to appreciate the difference [149]. Consequently, what they say about semantics may be occasionally true, if 'semantics' means 'logical syntax', but false if 'semantics' has its proper meaning. For the same reason their critical arguments are often irrelevant, and conclusions hardly ever follow from premises. They make confusions worse by using 'semantics' in a non-technical sense of this term, in which any examination of language, including terminological definitions, is called 'semantics'. Finally, they do not discriminate between semantics in Tarski's sense and the 'general semantics' of Alfred Korzybski and Stuart Chase, as if to accept the former logically implied the acceptance of the latter [150]. In Tarski's own words, they confuse a 'sober and modest discipline which has no pretensions of being a universal patent-medicine for all the ills and diseases of mankind' with that claiming to be a 'remedy for decayed teeth or illusions of grandeur or class conflicts'[151]. The fact that Korzybski adopted the term 'semantics' after it had been used by Polish philosophers is not convincing proof that his and Tarski's semantics are the same thing. There is not a word to be found in the Marxist-Leninist writings on the subject which would allow one to say with confidence that they realise the difference between the sober kind of semantics and the adventures in pseudo-science, also practised under the name of 'semantics', and that they are aware of the criticism which the practitioners of the former made of the latter [152].

If the term 'semantics' is used with all these connotations, we never know what we are talking about. There is then no wonder that Ajdukiewicz's contribution to semiotic by supplementing syntax with a rudimentary pragmatics was dismissed as a minor 'semantical' modification; the significance of Tarski's semantics for our systematic knowledge of language was disregarded, and Carnap's views on language in *Introduction to Semantics* and *Meaning and*

Necessity were held to be an immaterial reformulation of those pronounced in
Logische Syntax der Sprache [153].

Marxist-Leninists recognise 'semantics' as a legitimate discipline provided that
it satisfies the conditions specified by Stalin in *Marxism and Problems of
Linguistics* [154]. Semantics is a means of making thought and speech precise. It is
concerned with the 'meaning aspect of linguistic expressions', and as such, it
constitutes a branch of linguistics. A specifically materialistic semantics never
separates language from thought or thought from language (Marr committed
the latter error), nor a study of language from the investigations of the physiological processes of thinking. Thinking always proceeds along two parallel lines,
thinking always being accompanied by its linguistic expressions and a significant
use of language involving thoughts and ideas. The insistence on the 'unity' of
thought and language seems to be prompted by the belief that should there be
thoughts unexpressed or which cannot be expressed in words, it might suggest
that thinking and understanding are an inner mental process which is concealed
underneath its linguistic expressions and goes on behind it, something rather
spiritual than material. The correlated linguistic expressions, which are clearly
something material, do not invalidate this suggestion but blunt its sharp edge.

Moreover, language is an instrument of communication and of understanding.
To separate language from the world of Nature and society, to divorce a study of
language from the social history of man, is to fail to study language in a scientific manner. Language being primarily a social phenomenon embraces all fields
of man's activity and reflects in its vocabulary, in its semantical and pragmatical
rules, the social and historical changes of the society which uses this language.
The manner in which the world is depicted by means of language is, therefore,
dependent on the social determination of language, and to treat language, freed
from this dependence, as an adequate model either of the world or of thought is
to fall into the snares of idealism.

A materialist semantics seems to merge with what Carnap called 'descriptive
pragmatics', the examination of the historical, social and psychological (physiological) determinations of the language within the community in which this
language is used [155]. This comprehensive study of language would require the
co-operation of specialists of numerous disciplines – descriptive semantics and
comparative philology, social history, social psychology and sociology, history
of literature and history of science, methodology and logic. At the present
moment such a scheme is utopian, hardly connected with what is and can be
done in a scientific study of language. At present not much more than an examination of various types of discourse, the clarification of the concepts
required for this examination and the formulation of principles underlying such
studies can be undertaken.

This is ignored, however, by the Marxist-Leninist critics of contemporary
studies of language by logical methods. They look into the distant future and
come to the conclusion that theoretical and general semantics in Tarski's sense
or Carnap's pure semantics are idealist. Tarski, Carnap and their various
followers, including the Warsaw school thinkers, do not consider the 'meaning

aspect' of language in its relation to the psychological (physiological) processes of thinking, they treat language in false abstraction and disregard its function as a social means of communication and expression of thought. These two omissions are characteristic features of every idealist semantics.

The third reason why Tarski's and Carnap's semantics, as well as that of Ajdukiewicz and Kotarbiński, was considered to be idealist, is a little more specific but also more bedevilled by the variety of meanings in which the term 'semantics' is used by Marxist-Leninists. They say that semantics which treats language as an autonomous realm, to be investigated without reference to extra-linguistic reality, is necessarily idealist [156].

The first two objections raise a very dubious point. It is yet to be shown, instead of taking it for granted, that a study of language, if it is to yield valuable results, neither should nor could be separated from the social history of man and from the psychology (physiology) of thinking [157]. Protagoras ignored them entirely when he gave the first classification of the parts of speech and of tenses. Generally, grammar and logical syntax seem to provide the evidence that the separation of language from extra-linguistic considerations can increase our knowledge in a limited field. The grammarian would not have been able to examine the *consecutio temporum,* if at every step he had to consider the dependence of language upon the higher activities of the nervous system and the transformations of society. The changes of the linguistic syntax and vocabulary in their social and historical settings are studied by the philologists and nothing would be gained by duplicating their research. The fact that the communicative function of language is not considered in the logical syntax does not reflect unfavourably upon it. No progress could be made, if everybody dealt with everything. Evidently, it would be a serious error, if it were denied that language is a means of communication, but this no sane person would ever dream of doing. The communicative function of language does require the examination of the relation between thought and language. In so far as this question concerns the philosopher, it is investigated by semantical methods, and, above all, in pragmatics. The term 'pragmatics' was only coined later, but the interest in the problems of pragmatics is older than this term. The questions of pragmatics were discussed by the Warsaw school thinkers in their numerous contributions published in the inter-war period, and especially by Ajdukiewicz [158]. Marxist-Leninists, who subjected Ajdukiewicz's writings to severe criticism, seemed to have been entirely unaware of this fact. Ajdukiewicz concentrated on the problems of the usage of language, its dependence on circumstances and the wider context in which the speaker is placed. In these studies Ajdukiewicz could not and did not separate language from thought. The puzzling question is how his Marxist-Leninist readers could have ignored it.

The assumption that underlies the philosophy of language is the inseparability of thought and language. This does not mean that there are no thoughts which fail to acquire a linguistic expression, that bare thoughts 'free of the linguistic material' do not exist (a point, which Stalin made in his pronouncement on linguistics and which from then on was incorporated into the body of beliefs accepted by all Marxist-Leninists). The essential connection between thought and language, emphasised by the philosophers of language, is a narrower one. They point out that only thoughts which can be expressed in language, and this means 'communicable to others', are philosophically significant. Moreover, if the inseparable connection between thought and language were not assumed, one of the important reasons which has prompted the philosopher to study language would disappear. For the investigations of language began as investigations of thought and thinking, the former being an expression of the latter and better suited for study in view of its public character which thought does not possess.

The sociological principle, which, according to Marxist-Leninists, should never be forgotten in 'semantical inquiry', might be true, but whether it is true or not is hard to decide, since practically no corroborating evidence is ever provided. Neither is it clear why the protest against divorcing language from thought and the firm adherence to the pronouncement: 'There is no language without thought', should immunise us against the virus of idealism. It appears that the Wittgensteinian question as to whether language and thought are or are not distinguishable, as well as whether language is or is not an adequate model of the world, should be discussed on their own ground. The philosophic and sociological problems should be kept separate until more is known about them.

While the first two Marxist-Leninist objections against 'idealist semantics' seem to be off the point, the third is self-contradictory. For it is self-contradictory to assert that 'idealist semantics' treats language as an autonomous realm and investigates it without reference to extra-linguistic reality. If the term 'semantics' carries its technical meaning, semantics is the study of the relations between words and compound expressions on the one hand, and their designata or referents, things, facts, non-verbal occurrences, on the other. Therefore, semantics can never treat language as an autonomous realm, divorce it from extra-linguistic facts and lose track of the outside world. This particular Marxist-Leninist objection against 'idealist semantics' does not make sense, unless it confuses 'semantics' with 'logical syntax' and 'syntactical theory of meaning'. In this case, however, the objection of being idealist does not apply to semantics, but to syntax. To find fault with logical syntax on account of its failure to consider non-verbal occurrences is as unreasonable as to take exception to the theory of numbers for not considering continuous magnitudes [159].

The Marxist-Leninist idea of semantics was not only vague and confused, but also bore a very remote resemblance to what semantics was and how it was practised in the Warsaw school. Consequently, the same discrepancy can be observed when the Marxist-Leninists proceeded to the criticism of the application of semantical methods to philosophical problems, to the criticism of 'semantical philosophy', as they used to call it. Their contention was that 'idealist semantics' having abstracted language from its natural integument made of the 'bare linguistic material' its sole subject-matter of investigation. An erroneous theory of language led to an erroneous philosophy, 'idealist semantics' was transformed into à 'semantical philosophy', infecting the latter with idealism and conventionalism. The chief purpose of 'semantical philosophy' was to show that the dispute between materialism and idealism was a meaningless controversy, and, generally, that fundamental differences dividing various world outlooks could be satisfactorily resolved by linguistic analysis. The Viennese invention of 'semantical philosophy' is a modern incarnation of Mach's teaching. In his own time Mach tried to combat 'natural-scientific materialism' by eliminating metaphysics from natural science. In a similar manner 'semantical philosophy' claims to have transcended the dispute of materialism and idealism and thus made dialectical materialism an obsolete doctrine. The metaphysical agnosticism of Mach, of the Vienna Circle, and of the Warsaw school was not a genuine philosophical attitude. It is a sophistical artifice which provides the basis for formulating a reactionary ideology masquerading as a scientific method [160].

The relation of Marxist-Leninist philosophy to the 'semantical philosophy' of the Warsaw school was presented in terms of polar opposites. While Marxist-Leninists recommended that philosophers should attend to the nature of thought, of knowledge, of the world as a whole, the Warsaw school thinkers investigated the use of language, which, in their opinion, offered panacea for philosophical controversies and disputes between different world outlooks. For instance, Kotarbiński considered that the essential fault of idealism was its wrong semantical conception and that the most effective remedy for it was better semantics, namely, semantical reism. Thus, he suggested that the differences of opinion about matters of fact were only linguistic disputes to be settled by a revision of the rules of language. The latter were conceived as conventions accepted for didactic purposes, and arrived at by arbitrary decisions. The revisions of the rules of language accomplished in semantical reism made it possible to dispose of a great many philosophical questions which proved to be pseudo-problems arising from linguistic confusions. Among questions relegated to oblivion by means of semantical methods were fundamental problems of philosophy, such as the problem of the mind-body relation [161].

Some presuppositions underlying the general Marxist-Leninist appraisal of linguistic philosophy do not differ from those widely accepted in the Warsaw school. They found expression in the critical attitude, assumed by the Warsaw school, to some doctrines of the Vienna Circle and to Carnap's logic of science. While emphasising the fruitfulness of the approach to philosophical problems by way of the study of language, the Warsaw school firmly refused to identify philosophy with the latter. For the truth of a proposition is not determined, either exclusively or even mainly, by linguistic criteria. While we can employ different languages subject to different syntactical and other rules, the choice between them cannot rest on a convention, if the language is to serve adequately the cognitive purpose. It is the subject-matter under investigations which should determine the choice of language. Ultimately knowledge increases and its concepts are clarified under the impact of new experience. It is new experience that prompts revision of some part or of the whole structure of language, and not *vice versa*. The clarification of the formal structure of language may be helpful, but it is not a substitute for the study of the empirical reference of language.

These ideas seemed also to inspire some of the Marxist-Leninist criticism, paradoxically directed against the Warsaw school. Various factors were responsible for this paradox, but probably one of the most important was methodological conservatism. It revealed itself in arbitrary prohibitions concerning the manner of investigating the use of language, in a dogmatic legislation of some principles and procedures, and in the utter inability to understand novel views and to follow their application. The Marxist-Leninist criticism of Kotarbiński's reism, of Ajdukiewicz's semantical epistemology and radical conventionalism will illustrate these points.

It is evidently true to say, as the Marxist-Leninists did, that Kotarbiński's semantical reism is logically prior to somatism. But the formulation of semantical reism was prompted by somatism and was to provide a language adequate to some insight into the nature of reality. The non-verbal facts were Kotarbiński's starting point and determined the semantical revision of language. The procedure, novel at that time, with which semantical reism supplied him, consisted in the use of its rules for the reformulation of some classical philosophical problems in a manner which, whatever other disadvantages it might have had, was clear and precise. Although Kotarbiński was not the first to notice that traditional philosophy was plagued by misunderstandings about language and that correct use of language cannot be taken for granted, he was certainly one of the first who devised a general method of dealing with the linguistic aspect of philosophical problems. While his analytical procedure was applied to thought and knowledge as expressed in language, its justice was ultimately based on ontological assumptions and matters of fact. Kotarbiński never entertained the idea that thought and knowledge are merely the use of language [162]. To affix the derogatory label of idealism and conventionalism to reism is to miss the point and to mistake unctuous sermonising for a competent argument.

The brunt of the Marxist-Leninist criticism concerned with 'semantical philosophy' was borne by Ajdukiewicz. It was Ajdukiewicz who was alleged to have reduced philosophical inquiry to the concern with the use of language, to have identified philosophy with the syntactical analysis of language, and to have made of language 'the only subject-matter of investigation'[163]. As it stands, this assertion is not only incorrect, but also absurd in its implications.

It is true that Carnap once propounded the view that the philosopher should apply himself solely to the logical analysis of language. But Carnap differentiated logical and object questions, the latter being concerned with extra-linguistic objects, their properties and relations, to be studied by empirical methods. Only the former are questions concerned with linguistic expressions, refer to sentences, terms, and theories (which, of course, refer themselves to objects), and have language as its exclusive subject-matter of investigation.

Ajdukiewicz never embraced Carnap's theory. At the time when Carnap's views, expounded in *Logische Syntax der Sprache*, held wide sway in the world, the most significant single contribution of the Warsaw school to philosophy was its staunch defence of the position that the meaning of linguistic expressions is not determined solely by the syntactical rules of language and is not, therefore, ultimately a matter of convention. Consequently, philosophy could not be replaced by the logic of science. This contribution was due to Tarski and Ajdukiewicz; the former supplied the semantical method of investigation and the latter the pragmatical approach to the definition of meaning [164]. Neither semantics nor pragmatics can, or do, abstract language from its reference to non-verbal reality. They both bring out the intimate connection, severed by Carnap, between language and non-linguistic occurrences to be considered in philosophical investigations.

To substantiate the claim that Ajdukiewicz reduced the dispute between the idealist and materialistic world outlooks to a controversy about language to be resolved by purely linguistic methods, Marxist-Leninists referred to his semantical epistemology. Semantical epistemology consists in the application of modes of procedure modelled on semantical methods to epistemological problems, of which Ajdukiewicz took advantage in a series of studies intended to refute transcendental and subjective idealism in the theory of knowledge [165]. Marxist-Leninists argued that semantical epistemology rests on the assumption that every epistemological object sentence can be translated into a 'sentence about sentence', and this implies, that epistemology can be reduced to the logical syntax of language. Consequently, the question whether things exist independently of the experiencing mind or are rather a bundle of qualities whose existence depends on their being known is decided by purely verbal means and on the ground of linguistic considerations [166].

The Marxist-Leninist criticism of semantical epistemology seems to be uninformed and the conclusions reached unjustifiable. The translation of epistemological sentences into 'sentences about sentences', mistakenly identified with syntactical sentences (which are only a subclass of the former), and the alleged reduction of epistemology to the logical syntax of language constituted no part of Ajdukiewicz's objective. Not every metalinguistic sentence is a syntactical statement, and not every epistemological sentence is translatable into the metalanguage. In epistemology there are real object sentences, not merely pseudo-object ones, which do not concern words or sentences but extra-linguistic objects. Semantical epistemology does not undertake, either, the programme of translating sentences of the material mode of speech into sentences of the formal mode (by which, for instance, Carnap tried to show that though the theses of phenomenalism and realism in the theory of knowledge seem to be incompatible as long as they are formulated in the material mode, there is no inconsistency between them any more upon their being translated into the formal mode). Ajdukiewicz did not reject this method of translation altogether since there is little doubt that it is often an effective method of formulating, in a meaningful and clear manner, the essence of a given problem which appears ambiguous and confused as long as it is discussed in the material mode of speech. But he did not consider translatability into the formal mode as the 'touchstone for all philosophical sentences' by means of which they are either shown to be syntactical or are relegated outside the realm of meaningful expressions [167]. Semantical epistemology is a study of the problems of knowledge in their logical and linguistic aspects. It is concerned with sentences and not with judgments or sentence utterances which report directly what is experienced. The examination of epistemological sentences does not abrogate the right of these direct reports to priority in reflecting our experience of the world and does not legislate them away as unreal or non-existent. On this account semantical epistemology cannot resolve any non-linguistic question concerning the 'relation of experience to reality'. It can, however, lay bare the structure and rules of meaning by which the language of different epistemological standpoints is determined and draw conclusions concerning the validity of claims made by the representatives of these standpoints.

The relevance of this new method, in particular of its application to the dispute with epistemological idealism, is apparent. The thesis of epistemological idealism has a paradoxical characteristic; it offends our common sense and is supported by an argument extremely hard to refute. While it is doubtful whether semantical epistemology provides its final refutation, it does account for its puzzling quality and undermines the tenability of the idealistic thesis.

On the other hand, the test of practice, on which Marxist-Leninists rely, is unlikely to make any impression on a staunch idealist. Berkeley did not intend to refute the beliefs of common sense, to persuade ordinary men that they are mistaken when they claim to see a chair and to sit on it or to deride Newton for having discovered the law of gravity. What Berkeley said has no bearing on how the world appears from the common sense viewpoint, does not cause any events different from those expected by Newton to occur, and, generally, is not falsified by whatever facts of experience are established by the common or scientific man. On this account the argument of practice leaves the idealist undisturbed. He must be challenged on his own ground, that is, his intention of describing familiar facts in a simple manner, free from confusion and puzzles, for which he blames the realist philosopher, must be shown to be failing to accomplish this task. This is what semantical epistemology set out to achieve. It points out that the idealist manner of description cannot possibly fit familiar facts for it can never reach them on account of the vocabulary and linguistic rules that determine the language of the idealist [168].

The permanent contribution to the philosophy of science, made by conventionalist philosophy, is its clarification of the relation between theory and observation. According to conventionalist philosophy, no theory is unambiguously determined by experience. Most philosophers would agree with this opinion, although they would differ in what manner the ambiguity is in fact or should be either reduced or removed. Ajdukiewicz's radical conventionalism is an extension of the non-controversial central idea of conventionalist philosophy to every statement. He believes that no part of our knowledge of the world is unambiguously determined by experience alone. This is the less extreme formulation of radical conventionalism, to which Ajdukiewicz continues to adhere upon the rejection of its more extreme version.

To be communicated, the content of experience must acquire verbal articulation, be expressed in some language. This happens, *e.g.*, when somebody looking out of the window and observing a regular fall of white flakes utters the sentence: 'it is snowing'. Such direct reports raise the question, what is the reason for sentence utterances expressing and conveying something of the speaker's experience. For it is clear that the experience itself is much richer than its verbal articulation and that the speaker fails to express and convey it in all its fullness. A direct report is selective in what it refers to and communicates to others. But granted that we should distinguish what is communicable from what C. I. Lewis called the 'adventitious and purely personal' in reported experience, the question remains, how the identifiable content of experience can find its way into the expressions uttered by different speakers and be understood by all. For their situational context is never exactly the same and even that of the same speaker changes with every movement in space and time. Every individual report is, therefore, ambiguous in its referential meaning and varies in this respect from one speaker to another. This was what so much impressed Poincaré, when he emphasised the infinity of facts that a report of experience can suit [169].

Ajdukiewicz took the view that it is not the experience alone that determines the objective, communicable content of expressions, but also some definite meanings, phrase- or sentence-meanings, with which the sentence utterance is endowed. Linguistic expressions are the vehicles, as it were, of the concepts which constitute and determine their meaning. The totality of meanings of a language, which form a complicated pattern of interrelated categories, is called the conceptual apparatus of this language [170]. The central idea of radical conventionalism in its weaker version can now be formulated a little more precisely. Our knowledge of the world is determined by experience and the conceptual apparatus of the language in which experience is directly or indirectly reported and verbally articulated. The choice of conceptual apparatus may be made in one way or another, and in this sense its choice is a matter of convention. The choice of conceptual apparatus determines the kind of questions, which we are able to put to Nature, and thus also the perspective from which Nature and the world in general is viewed [171].

What Ajdukiewicz calls 'meaning' is close to what Frege called *'Gedanke'*, the objective content of thought as distinct from the content of particular acts of thinking and judging, the 'common property of many' which is independent of the individual's privacy of feeling and imagery [172]. The mode of existence of these objective contents, apprehended whenever we understand an expression, is a problem that he did not undertake to resolve in all its complexities. The question he set out to answer was how expressions and sentences have a definite meaning and how the 'community of meanings', their objectivity of some sort, is established within a language. Science and everyday life presuppose that thoughts and knowledge can be communicated. A satisfactory theory of meaning should provide the necessary conditions of mutual understanding and thus explain the fact that the meaning of an expression may be something communicable [173].

From this viewpoint the theories of meaning existing at that time were inadequate; they failed to achieve the indicated objective. If the meaning of a sentence is ultimately reduced to the content of the 'given' in the immediate experience, as Carnap suggested about that time, or to Schlick's *Konstatierungen* or Neurath's protocol-sentences, fixed by convention, its communicability becomes doubtful. On the other hand, the attempts to show that language mirrors, as it were, the logical structure of the world, that expressions have meaning because they denote objects, and that to learn the meaning of an expression is to discover what it denotes, provide at best only a partial solution of the problem. Ajdukiewicz pointed out that the meaning of an expression should be distinguished from its connotation, if it has got one, which is not always the case. A meaningful expression may have no denotatum and two expressions with a different meaning may denote the same object. These things had been known to Frege but at that time they were not common knowledge, as they have become to-day. At the time when Ajdukiewicz tried to formulate a systematic theory of meaning, the view that all significant expressions are of one variety and that they are all cast in one basic mould, to which Professor Ryle gave the name " 'Fido' -Fido principle" [174], was still prevalent.

Ajdukiewicz's belief that it is incorrect to identify the meaning of an expression with its denotatum provided one of the important reasons why he felt that the establishment of semantical relations between linguistic expressions and the extra-linguistic reality is an inadequate basis for a theory of meaning. He concluded that neither a purely syntactical nor a semantical theory of meaning is able to explain the communicative function of language [175].

The objective content, the identifiable common constituent of expressions spoken or written by different persons, is communicable owing to the fact that we follow in the use of expressions certain specifiable meaning-giving rules of language. The examination of the contextual usages of an expression advocated by various analytical thinkers as the best means of establishing its meaning, is done in a haphazard manner and cannot provide a basis for systematic investigations on the structure of language. Its replacement by the study of meaning-giving rules offers a more fruitful approach. If adequately specified, they constitute the necessary conditions for communication and mutual understanding. The evidence for the existence of these rules is provided by the fact that we accept some sentences and reject others, either conditionally or unconditionally, because they do or do not conform to the way they should be formulated. We refer to these rules if we claim that a word has been misused or used in the prescribed sense. Three different kinds of rules are characteristic to every language, axiomatic, deductive, and empirical meaning-giving rules [176].

Each conceptual apparatus is bound up with a definite set of meaning-giving rules, to which the meanings of the expressions of a language conform. The latter make explicit the structural relationship, the interrelatedness of the former. We can expand the conceptual apparatus by adding new rules of meaning and the rules can be enriched by the introduction of a new concept. The rules of meaning of the language *S* together with data of experience determine a set of sentences of this language, which will be called 'theses of the language S'. The theses constitute a component and restrictive part of the knowledge that can be gained by making use of this language. Given certain data of experience there are problems which cannot arise at all unless the change of the conceptual apparatus and of the corresponding rules of meaning is accomplished. These circumstances acquire a special significance in the so-called closed and connected languages. In such a language all the rules of meaning, including the empirical ones, are unequivocally determined, and its conceptual apparatus cannot be enlarged and enriched [177]. The set of theses of a given language, that is to say, the set of sentences of a given language which are determined by its meaning rules and data of experience, is called the 'world picture' or the 'world perspective' of that language [178].

The concept of the world picture leads to three important conclusions. The effort to gain new knowledge does not place the man 'so to speak, in front of a heap of factual material'. His world perspective and conceptual apparatus are restrictive and selective, though not absolutely, since both the rules of meaning and the conceptual apparatus may be altered. Second, we never accept an isolated sentence, but a whole system of them, interrelated by their conceptual apparatus and rules of meaning associated with the latter. Third, no world perspective can be singled out as true and none of its sentences can be accepted as true or rejected as false except by those who make use of this world perspective. For each world perspective has its own rule of meaning that determines the use of the word 'true'; it applies only to sentences of which this world perspective is composed. Nobody can, as it were, step out of his world perspective to predicate truth and falsehood of sentences belonging to another world perspective [179].

The last of these conclusions applies only to world pictures formulated in terms of different closed and connected languages. Open languages, that is, languages which can be enriched and expanded by the addition of new concepts and meaning-giving rules, confront us with a different situation. An open language does not preclude the possibility that on the foundations of the same data of experience there might coexist different but not incompatible world perspectives, whose respective advantages must be evaluated by means of some other criteria than those of agreement with reality only. They are the criteria of consistency, completeness, rationality and empirical testability. The task of an epistemologist is to give his attention to the changes introduced into the conceptual apparatus and the corresponding world picture of science and to investigate the reasons which prompt these changes.

Ajdukiewicz did not provide the definition of the term 'true sentence' which would do justice to the intuitions expressed by the correspondence theory of truth. He did not deny, either explicitly or implicitly, that this definition cannot be given at all, and, in fact, he took care to differentiate between the expressions: 'true sentence in the language S' and 'sentence accepted as true by the speaker of the language S'[180]. The meaning-giving rules are essentially rules of pragmatics, and the definition of a 'true sentence' cannot be given in terms of pragmatics [181]. The question, however, arises whether a radical conventionalist cannot do without the classical concept of truth, which, he might add, is by no means unambiguous and in everyday language fraught with the dangers of antinomies. The answer to the above question seems to be in the affirmative.

The Marxist-Leninist critics were not interested at all in Ajdukiewicz's theory of meaning and concentrated on its epistemological consequences. This was not the best course to take if the philosophical issues involved were to be seriously examined. For Ajdukiewicz formulated the thesis of radical conventionalism, in its stronger and weaker versions, on the basis of his theory of meaning and it is not really possible to dissociate one from the other.

Marxist-Leninists emphasised two points in Ajdukiewicz's theories, one of which led to the conclusion that radical conventionalism was a trivial and the other that it was an absurd doctrine. Both arguments were inspired by some erroneous ideas about Ajdukiewicz's conception of language and about what can or cannot be inferred from it.

They argued that according to radical conventionalism our picture of the world is determined not only by experience, but also by the conceptual apparatus. The choice of the conceptual apparatus is 'utterly arbitrary'. Therefore, ran the conclusion, any picture of the world is also an 'utterly arbitrary creation of the mind'. If a mass of terminological distinctions, elaborate definitions, and logical subtleties is overlooked, there remains a trivial core, undistinguishable from Berkeleyan idealism. No amount of logical finesse can conceal the fact that radical conventionalism is a variety of subjectivism and relativism of an extreme kind [182].

On the other hand, if radical conventionalism is right, the criteria of a meaningful use of expressions of the language S also determine the truth value of the sentences in the language S. A sentence p, formulated in conformity with the rules of meaning valid in the language S, is a true sentence in the language S. Moreover, according to radical conventionalism the conceptual apparatus and the rules of meaning, associated with it, are arbitrary. We can choose them, therefore, in such a manner that in the language S_1 '$\sim p$' is a thesis of the language S_1. The sentence $\sim p$ is, therefore, a true sentence in the language S_1. This is, however, absurd, and, if it were not, a still greater absurdity follows from it. For if 'p' is a true sentence in the language S and '$\sim p$' is a true sentence in the language S_1, and the truth of a sentence consists in its agreement with reality, it would follow that not only the picture of the world but the world itself too is a free creation of the mind, changeable at will according to the language we choose for its description [183].

The doctrine which Ajdukiewicz's critics proved to be trivial, false and utterly absurd, bears no resemblance to radical conventionalism. They made use of some of its concepts in a manner which is precisely excluded by radical conventionalism. The doctrine against which they turned was trivial, false, and absurd, but this doctrine is not that of radical conventionalism, and the easy victory over it was that over a man of straw. Their argument also failed to reveal the reason which prompted them to reject Ajdukiewicz's theories.

The epistemological conclusions of radical conventionalism are clearly incompatible with the Marxist basic conviction that knowledge is an authentic reflection of the outside world, having the validity of 'objective truth'. The concern with truth is one of the central preoccupations in the Marxist-Leninist approach to philosophy. Any view that seems to question in any manner the possibility of discovering 'permanent' or 'objective truth' is rejected forthwith. In particular, truth does not depend in any way on the language in which it is expressed, on its logical structure, on precise definitions and careful considerations of the use of words, since this would make of truth something arbitrary and dependent on human conventions. 'Convention', as Marxist-Leninists understand this term, is synonymous with 'something utterly arbitrary' or 'freely invented'. This is a confusion against which Poincaré warned in his polemical exchanges with Le Roy, who was inclined to consider a convention as a pure creation of the mind, unrestrained in any manner by experience. For Marxist-Leninists it is self-evident that if conventions played any role in the formulation of knowledge, knowledge would lack objective validity and would be a subjective product of our fancies and whims.

Epistemological absolutism, which again appears to inspire Marxist-Leninist criticism, is responsible for treating lightly all the linguistic and logical considerations involved in the search for truth. For truth reveals itself in the faithful correspondence between things and occurrences on the one hand, judgments and sentences on the other, and this relationship is invariant with respect to the signs and symbols in terms of which this correspondence is stated. Truth is something that is already there and is something to be discovered by observing, thinking, and acting, by subjecting the conclusions obtained again and again to the test of observation, thought and action. Seen against this background of the absolutist conviction, radical conventionalism appears as a futile and abortive attempt to apply human inventions and constructions to what cannot be thus discovered. Radical conventionalism may neither deny nor imply the denial of the existence of 'objective truth', but this is a 'useless and empty declaration', since it does not try to indicate how to discover it or even how to differentiate a true proposition from a false one. Conventionalism is a betrayal of science and philosophy. It gives up the attainability of absolute truth and surrenders it to an agnostic scepticism and irrationalism [184].

The reasons why epistemological absolutism is a barren doctrine have already been briefly touched upon and its clash with radical conventionalism provides an opportunity to add one more comment. The common characteristic of the absolutist tendency in philosophy is not only the conviction that a given system has attained the highest knowledge and certainty, corrigible in detail and infallible in its essential features, but also that all other philosophical systems are collections of false beliefs. This conviction may vary, however, in intensity and the supporters of epistemological absolutism may show very different degrees of dogmatism. If in Marxism-Leninism this conviction is revealed with excessive self-confidence, this seems to be partly due to some of its methodological peculiarities. For the pursuit of those aspects of the 'objective truth' which have not yet been discovered is so severely restricted by various prohibitions, imposed either uncritically or in ignorance of the actual procedures practised in logic, methodology, and natural science, that ultimately nothing new can be discovered and a few ossified and useless dogmas remain in the field. This is bound to happen when all the approaches leading to the re-examination of the sources of knowledge and of the accepted criteria of warranted beliefs are closed one by one.

These prohibitions are made impregnable by being presented as means of salvation from doctrines hostile to the search for knowledge, whose unmasking and destruction takes precedence in importance over the efforts of discovering what is the 'objective truth'. The philosophical ogres of idealism, conventionalism, agnosticism, semantical philosophy, operated by some unidentifiable causal agents, referred to by invidious epithets, hamper a genuine understanding of what Marxist-Leninists disagree with and prevent them from seeing what are the issues whose solutions they wish to criticise. The Marxist-Leninist criticism of radical conventionalism, in which one misunderstanding or misconception supports another and helps to produce more and more startling paralogism is an illuminating instance of these habits of thought and of their methodological roots.

Ajdukiewicz's patient and detailed answer to the criticism of his views and Schaff's final retort closed the long drawn out controversy between Marxism-Leninism and the Warsaw school [185]. Its outcome was not encouraging. Not a single member of the Warsaw school was persuaded that the objections against his particular views or against methods common to the school as a whole were either pertinent or justified. The outsiders and also some Marxist-Leninists were unwilling to accept the verdict that thinkers who differed from Marxist-Leninist orthodoxy were thereby shown to be entirely wrong and to have nothing but nonsense to say. For the fact that the criticised views failed to satisfy the Marxist-Leninists was not proof that these views were mistaken. The conviction that a statement is true or false does not logically imply its truth or falsehood. What the Marxist-Leninists kept on repeating, namely, that they themselves were right and their opponents wrong, implied nothing but that this was their view.

Marxist-Leninists recognised their failure more in sadness than in anger. In his final summing up Schaff stated that no useful purpose would have been served by continuing the discussion, since the leading representatives of the school persisted in upholding their respective positions. The most significant advantage gained from the discussion was a greater precision in defining the standpoint of Marxism-Leninism and that of the Warsaw school, which disclosed their irreducible irreconcilability [186]. While all the initial objections against the Warsaw school were upheld, namely its bourgeois liberal mentality, its socially reactionary and philosophically idealist and conventionalist character, a note of moderation was conspicuous in the final summing up.

It is hard to say whether, and, if so, to what extent, the intellectual temper

216

cultivated in the Warsaw school contributed to this outcome. If it can be believed that absence of dogmatism, tolerance, diffidence of final solutions and incontrovertible truths can be conveyed and affect the opposite intellectual attitudes, the role played by the thinkers of the Warsaw school must be considered as one of the decisive educational influences that was increasingly civilising the philosophical and intellectual climate in Poland during the Stalinist period.

CHAPTER 11

PHENOMENOLOGY FROM THE MARXIST-LENINIST

STANDPOINT

When we pass from the Marxist-Leninist criticism of the Warsaw school to that of phenomenology we might expect arguments and evaluations which would command a wide measure of consent outside the Marxist-Leninist school of thought. In Poland Husserl's *Logische Untersuchungen* was a widely studied and influential work. Polish thinkers owed much to Husserl's criticism of psychologism in logic and he inspired their interest and first studies of semantical concepts [187]. This could not be said of Husserl's later philosophical works, commencing with *Ideen zu einer reinen Phänomenologie und phänomenologischen Philosophie,* and of the elaborate speculative system that followed the latter. Husserl's transcendental idealism found no supporters in the small circle of Polish phenomenologists, including Roman Ingarden, Husserl's eminent pupil. Ingarden did not accept the view often expressed by Husserl in his oral pronouncements: *Streichen wir das Bewußtsein, so streichen wir die Welt* [188].

Broadly speaking, and with some qualifications, the phenomenological method was not accepted in Poland as a reliable method for acquiring knowledge. Its application to some fields of experience and for specific purposes caused no apprehension. Leopold Blaustein's use of the phenomenological method as a reflective analysis of various kinds of representations or Ingarden's studies in which he applied this method to the examination of literary and other works of art, were admired for their incisive insight and fruitful probing of particular kinds of experience. But the universality of the phenomenological method was challenged and its assumptions were questioned, since they failed to conform to, if not defied, the accepted criteria of validity. It was emphasised that various claims of the phenomenologists did not stand up under critical examination by scientific procedure. There is, for instance, no eidetic science, independent of all knowledge of fact and based on pure intuition, in which essences are apprehended just as individual objects are in empirical intuition. In particular, Kotarbiński criticised the phenomenological theory of intentional objects, according to which for every O, if somebody thinks of O, there is something that is O. At the time when Marxist-Leninists subjected phenomenology to criticism, Kotarbiński analysed various concepts employed in the humanities, teeming with intentional objects, hypostatised expressions, idealisations, abstract entities and reified constructions. He showed that descriptive phrases used in these disciplines do not imply the existence of appropriate denotata and that under certain conditions they may be significant, although there is no abstract entity that answers to these phrases. Incidentally, these conclusions deeply shocked some of the Marxist-Leninists [189].

The expectation that in view of the speculative character of phenomenology Marxist-Leninist thinkers might justify its rejection in a genuinely philosophical manner was not fulfilled. On the whole, their interest was once more limited to the social and political implications of the phenomenological doctrine. They wished to locate phenomenology on the intellectual map determined by the reference frame of the two pairs of polar opposites, namely, materialism and idealism, Marxist-Leninist and non-Marxist philosophy; as well as to find the co-ordinates which would describe more precisely the position of Ingarden's phenomenology on this map.

If materialism with its conception of reality prior to and independent of the mind is put at one extreme, Husserl's transcendental idealism constitutes the other. For according to Husserl, pure consciousness, and not Nature, as the totality of natural objects, must be reckoned as an absolute. The whole spatio-temporal world, including man, is a 'mere intentional Being . . . . which has the merely secondary, relative sense of a being for consciousness'. To make the latter absolute, is simply nonsense. 'An absolute reality is just as valid as a round square'. The world of natural objects is 'posited' by consciousness in its experiences, but 'over and beyond this, it is just nothing at all'[190].

It is right to call this view, as Marxist-Leninists do, an extreme idealism, only the qualification 'subjective', which they add and which is accepted in order to avoid further confusion, is misapplied. For Husserl emphatically warned against misconstruing pure absolute consciousness as an individual, psychologically conceived agent. Marxist-Leninists ignored this warning. Their differentiations of subjective and objective idealism run along various lines of divisions, but they are never similar to those traditionally accepted. Subjective and objective idealism in the traditional sense are in their terminology subjective idealism [191].

The 'phenomenological secession' resulting from Husserl's failure to persuade his followers about the truth of transcendental idealism marked the emergence of objective idealism within the phenomenological school [192]. Objective idealism, as Marxist-Leninists understand it, does not exclude epistemological realism. Not every realist is a materialist, and a 'non-materialist' realist is an 'idealist realist', in short, an objective idealist [193]. Objective idealism as a metaphysical doctrine comprises both spiritualistic monism and any metaphysical dualism. It is also sometimes equated with the belief that the world is created by God – on this account Twardowski was classified as an objective idealist – or with what Marvin Farber calls the 'party of religion in philosophy'[194]. The latter comprises thinkers whose philosophy directly serves the purpose of demonstrating God's existence, and also philosophers of various tendencies, who, either consciously or not, support this purpose by undermining the authority of science.

There is, indeed, much circumstantial evidence that idealism, either directly or by implication, provides philosophical justification for religious belief. This is very apparent in the views of many idealist thinkers. In Berkeley's philosophy the 'reduction' of Nature to spirit leads to Theism and without the appeal to God's will and perception Berkeley's theory of knowledge would not be tenable. R. P. Perry clearly recognised that idealism is a form of spiritualism and that this is its message to modern times. But he also emphasised that 'while the burden of idealism is a religious interpretation of Nature, its cardinal principle is a theory of knowledge'[195]. This cardinal principle reflects the preoccupation of philosophy from the time of Descartes in establishing a foundation for our knowledge of the world that is impregnable to doubt. It is not irrevocably committed to or overshadowed by the endeavour to substantiate the claims of faith. To see the connections between idealism and Theism is one thing, to identify them quite another. The latter presupposes the conviction that there is a philosophical procedure by means of which God's existence may be proved or disproved (Marxist-Leninists assert that they can disprove the existence of God). But the validity of such procedure is at least a moot point, contested by those who consider both Theism and anti-Theism to be theological doctrines, outside the reach of philosophy.

Objective idealism, as Marxist-Leninists understand this term, is a bundle of miscellaneous and heterogeneous opinions. It has no classificatory function and it does not circumscribe adequately any single historical trend of philosophical thought.

Objective idealism, Marxist-Leninists asserted, was represented in Poland by Neo-Thomism and Ingarden's phenomenology [196]. It is true that Ingarden refused to adopt Husserl's view that the world is created by the constitutive activity of pure consciousness. He also opposed the neo-positivistic standpoint, and professed realism in the theory of knowledge. He sharply differentiated between an autonomous and a non-autonomous (intentional) individual object: while the latter does not, the former does transcend 'its givenness' or our knowledge of it. Thus, however, the Husserlian world of natural realities is no longer reducible to mere intentionality [197]. This did not exonerate Ingarden from being an objective idealist. For Ingarden recognised that there are real entities, other than things, in the world, which, therefore, clearly is not exclusively material. There are various levels of existence. Besides bodies there are ideas or essences, intentional objects, and values, all of them real, though each of them in a different sense. With Ingarden's 'phenomenological realism' we are *en plein idéalisme,* without a mask or mystification [198].

The thinking of Polish Marxist-Leninists on the phenomenological method has been under considerable influence of Georg Lukács' views and Lukács' criticism of the phenomenological method follows a peculiar course of its own. In agreement with thinkers of very different orientations, such as Farber and Bocheński [199], he considers the phenomenological method as a distinct sort of reflective analysis and a legitimate one within certain definite limits. Its proper field of investigations are intentional acts and intentional objects, and in this capacity it has proved its usefulness in Husserl's examination of questions of 'pure logic'. Outside this field, however, transformed into a universal method and a universal philosophy, phenomenology reveals its inadequacy to 'objective reality'. This became increasingly clear when Max Scheler made use of it in his studies concerned with ethical and sociological problems, and Heidegger and Sartre applied it to the 'ultimate questions of philosophy'. Lukács examined in a detailed and incisive fashion existentialist philosophy and interpreted it as a product of an illegitimate extension of the phenomenological method. The existentialist thinkers have put the phenomenological method to uses for which it is not designed, and consequently distorted the issues involved. Lukács does not criticise the phenomenological method on its own original ground, but, as it were, carried out its *reductio ad absurdum*. If it is conceded that existentialism results from the application of the phenomenological method outside its proper field and that existentialism is an absurd and false doctrine, the validity of Lukács' thesis should be recognised [200].

Polish Marxist-Leninists could not follow in Lukács' footsteps, however much they were impressed by his *reductio ad absurdum* and his impressive analysis of existentialism. They accepted his thesis that phenomenology was a powerful influence reinforcing the irrationalistic trends in philosophy, either indirectly, by inspiring such movements as existentialism, or directly, by its basic assumptions concerning the limited validity of science [201]. But existentialism as a philosophical or quasi-philosophical doctrine did not exist in Poland and Ingarden's phenomenology, concerned mainly with 'pure acts and objects of thought', with questions of ontology, theories of value and of art, would have been impervious to this kind of refutation. Ingarden made it clear also that his concept of existence had besides an ontological and metaphysical meaning, closely related to that accepted in the philosophical tradition, also an empirical sense, clearly distinct from the existentialist uses of the term 'existence', familiar from Heidegger's writings [202].

This raised difficulties in finding an effective way of criticising Ingarden's phenomenology. Phenomenology, as much as idealism, is immune from the pressure of arguments brought to bear upon it by accepting the standpoint of science and experience. From the phenomenologist's point of view such arguments raise assumptive questions; they take for granted what phenomenology puts in doubt, they identify science in general with science of experience, sensory seeing with seeing described by Husserl 'as primordial dator consciousness of any kind whatsoever'. The intuition of the phenomenologists cannot be dislodged from its stronghold of being the ultimate source of justification for all rational statements, including those of science, by an argument based on an explicit or implicit denial of this intuition. Moreover, the phenomenologists insist that the method of science is also dependent upon deeply concealed and uncritically accepted 'subjective ground'. This was made clear by Husserl in the opening chapters of *Ideen zu einer reinen Phänomenologie und phänomenologischen Philosophie* and his followers have considered this view of Husserl as irrefutable. The position taken by a phenomenologist is similar to that of an empiricist who would reject as fanciful speculation any argument against his standpoint based on the assumption that questions concerning the mind or matter may be decided otherwise than on the basis of empirical evidence alone. The impregnability of the phenomenological method to criticism from without has been further strengthened by Ingarden's clear recognition, stated more clearly than it had been done by Husserl, that science on the one hand, ontology and metaphysics on the other, have distinct tasks and that their respective methods are equally legitimate, provided that each of them is restricted to its own field.

221

More controversial and more easily refutable was Ingarden's claim that, in principle, metaphysics may obtain absolute knowledge, while science can never reach beyond what is uncertain and contingent [203].

Thus, the phenomenological method can be effectively challenged only on its own ground and Marvin Farber has shown that this can be done successfully without destroying its specific and necessarily limited merits. The first step is to firmly establish the fact that whatever else any reflective procedure – like the phenomenological method – may be, it is not outside the natural order. Consequently, its temporal quality and reference, with everything that this recognition implies, cannot be denied. In this manner, what C. I. Lewis called the 'thin experience' of intuition is enclosed by the 'thick experience' of everyday life [204]. The phenomenological subjectivistic procedure is thereby assigned the role of a methodological expedient. It becomes one particular type of reflective analysis among others, to be assessed by the results obtained, instead of being a self-contained study of the whole of reality, providing absolute knowledge, subject to no control, unique in its method, *toto coelo* different from other kinds of reflections. The drawing of distinctions between phenomenology conceived as a method and as a universal philosophy does not abolish the value of any contribution that the phenomenological method may make towards the philosophical understanding of the mind's activities and removes the discrediting claim that thereby a final and complete explanation of man and his knowledge of the world is given [205].

The criticism of phenomenology from within requires one concession. The critic must accept the desirability of the Cartesian method of universal doubt, as the means of freeing the mind from unwarranted beliefs and dogmatic assumptions, or of its phenomenological version that enjoins us to suspend beliefs and to bracket judgments as the first step towards the discovery of a new range of problems. If this concession is not made, the usefulness of reflective analysis and its function within a larger context of human existence cannot be either understood or appreciated. This is, however, a concession which the Marxist-Leninists seem to be unwilling to make. They would be ready to say that Descartes had every reason to search for the Archimedean point to support philosophical constructions, but there is no need for it any more, since the Archimedean point has been found. The very idea that one can entertain a philosophical doubt, and, in particular, a doubt about the existence of the world, that it may provide the subject of a philosophical controversy, and that anybody can try to resolve it by the examination of what this controversy is about, was described as an 'utterly ridiculous' undertaking and a parody of philosophical circumspection [206].

If a philosophical doctrine is unassailable from without and for some reason or other the possibility of its criticism from within is disregarded, its content must be ignored and the doctrine may be examined only in terms of the beliefs and aspirations which it is supposed to express, and from the viewpoint of its social significance. This was the course taken by the Marxist-Leninists with respect to Ingarden's phenomenology.

In his critical studies on modern philosophical trends Georg Lukács argued that subjective and objective idealism (in the Marxist-Leninist sense) are not different in their social significance and this opinion was accepted by the Marxist-Leninists in Poland [207]. An undisguised and thorough-going idealism can thrive only in times free from tensions and open conflicts. Lukács recalled Goethe's comment on the incident during which students had broken windows in Fichte's home. 'This is a very disagreeable way', Goethe was reported to have said, 'to take cognisance of the reality of the external world'. In modern times such window-breaking takes place on a world-wide scale. Since Nietzsche, bourgeois philosophy has been made aware that man has got a body, not only a soul; his body having been rediscovered he experiences all the joys and dangers of his bodily existence. The realities of the time have invalidated the assumptions of idealism of the extreme sort and to save its conclusions a third way, distinct from materialism on the one hand, and from subjective idealism on the other, became indispensable. It recognises the reality of the body and of the external world without making concessions to materialism and without losing any essential ingredient of the idealist moral and social outlook. This is the key to the understanding of such figures of modern thought as Nietzsche, Mach, Avenarius, Dilthey, Bergson, and Scheler. At its face value the third way is not idealism; it asserts that there is no consciousness without being. But it also asserts that there is no being without consciousness and by making being dependent on consciousness it is not materialism but objective idealism.

Phenomenology exemplifies the manner in which idealism can emerge from epistemological non-materialist realism. The intuition of essence starts from what is given in inner experience and does not inquire into its social and historical preconditions. Thus, the mind ossifies into a formal agent, emancipated from causal dependence on the extra intellectual circumstances of existence. Finally, it proceeds to conjure up a false and irrelevant ideal of the mind, alien to the world of contingent empirical facts, which is irreducible to the categories of essence and logically necessary structures. For to demand certainty from empirical statements is to deprive them of factual content. The vision of the world and human existence, inspired by the phenomenological procedure, is divorced from reality. The phenomenologists embrace the Kantian conception according to which the content of an object of thought is the same as that of an actual object. They lack, therefore, the capacity, as it was put, 'to grasp concrete being'[208]. The conception of the mind as an autonomous agent, unconditioned by and abstracted from all social actuality, operating with the appearance of logic and rigour, opens the door to irresponsible intuitive claims, which are supposedly based on the insight into essences, but which fly in the face of factual evidence. Thus, there arises the 'logical myth' of a world independent of consciousness in spite of the fact that its structure and characteristics are recognised as being 'determined by the individual consciousness'. The phenomenologists under the guise of formalistic formulations only seem to go beyond the epistemology of subjective idealism and its ontology. These appearances, however, make objective idealism less objectionable and more congruent with the temper of the times.

In one of his impressionistic essays, written shortly before the war and published in 1947, Ingarden said things which fit into Lukács' explanatory framework. In his essay Ingarden argued that man is raised above the animal level by the magical potency of intentional experience (in the phenomenological sense of the term 'intentional'), which discovers essences, ideal structures, and values, permeates the world with significance, bestows meaning on natural objects and makes the world as a whole what it appears to be in man's life. It is intentional experience that somehow creates the world satisfying the needs of the human spirit, gives man an ideal commanding his devotion and provides a purpose worth striving for [209].

It should be noticed that the pure consciousness of Ingarden's essay, whose creative power is extolled, somehow hovers in the air, unaffected by any apparent connection with the physical and biological reality, or with its claims upon men. In principle, the author recognises that pure consciousness is no disembodied spirit and that man has got a body subject to natural laws, but the latter is left in the background and plays no effective role [210]. It is hard not to be sensitive to the appeal of Ingarden's vision, which combines a certain grandeur of thought with a sense of tragic heroism inherent in an intensely human experience of life. On second thought, however, the conclusion may be reached that Ingarden fails to answer some searching questions that occur to sober minds who are anxious to secure evidence instead of being subject to the pressure of noble sentiments and who wish to be governed by facts rather than by inspiring thoughts and intuitive insights. What Ingarden presented as knowledge based on intuition of essence lacks positive evidence, and it is in the nature of the case that it can never produce it. This essay provided the testimony which revealed, in the opinion of Marxist-Leninists, the real purpose of Ingarden's major work *Controversy over the Existence of the World* published after the war [211].

They argued that the Cartesian method of universal questioning, by means of which Ingarden establishes the preliminaries for the formulation of his problem, is nothing but a transparent subterfuge. It led Husserl first to a neutral position with respect to the issue of idealism *versus* realism, and later paved the way for his transcendental idealism. In Ingarden's case the Cartesian doubt helps to discover the alleged Archimedean point of his procedure, namely, pure consciousness, whose existence cannot be put in question, and its *cogitationes*, which provide necessary knowledge. On this foundation Ingarden constructs his ontology, and, with its assistance, eliminates not only subjective idealism but also materialism. The refutation of materialism is in fact the supreme task of Ingarden's work. True to Husserl's transcendental objectivism, Ingarden rejects monistic materialism as an epistemologically naive and dogmatic assertion, which accepts the existence of the world in its alleged unquestionable obviousness. The certainty which apparently can be obtained in the examination of pure thoughts and pure acts is a baseless claim and a trap for some ulterior metaphysical purpose. In this manner any opinion adopted beforehand might be presented as absolutely founded in pure consciousness. There is hardly anything that Ingarden cannot prove as a 'pure possibility' by his *a priori* analysis of the content of ideas, whether it be God or the devil. This exemplifies the arbitrariness of his procedure and the scholastic conceptual muddle in which his mind is bogged. Ingarden's ontology with its emphasis on the absolute reliability of the intuition of essence gives support to religious faith, which also appeals to the certainty of inner life. In his own work there are indications that the controversy over the existence of the world would be resolved by the acceptance of its reality as God's creation. For according to Ingarden God is also the ultimate ground of all values, effected by man's intentional acts in the created world [212].

It should be remembered that the critical comments on Ingarden's phenomenology are rationalisations superimposed on evaluation concerned with the social significance of objective idealism and of phenomenology as a particular instance of it. In the last resort, it is evaluation in terms of social significance, and not rationalisation, that claims to establish a valid case against phenomenology in general and Ingarden's phenomenology in particular. The objections raised against the latter are worth, however, a moment's attention, for they throw some light on the philosophical assumptions of Marxism-Leninism itself.

Although some of the Marxist-Leninist arguments against the phenomenological method are not new, they seem to be both relevant and right. Marxist-Leninists are not alone in their doubt as to why the analysis of essences should be immune from error while such reputed sources of knowledge as perception or memory are not. The questions whether the intuition of essence actually performs what it claims to achieve and whether it is a procedure that provides reliable knowledge were asked insistently and persuasively before. The suspicion that knowledge derived from intuition and pure consciousness might provide intellectual support for false doctrines goes back to John Stuart Mill. In Poland as much as anywhere else there were numerous thinkers who pointed out the dangers resulting from the elevation of intuition, whether Bergsonian or Husserlian, to the position of a source of indubitable knowledge that secures an unassailable foundation for philosophy, morals, politics, and religion. There was a large measure of agreement that it might be an excellent instrument for consecrating all deep-seated prejudices.

What is valid in the Marxist-Leninist criticism of the phenomenological method is, however, subsidiary to the main objection concerning the Cartesian method of doubt. It is this method that Ingarden tries to elaborate and apply to the controversy over the existence of the world. It is also the method that is generally approved and in some way or other cultivated by the whole of modern philosophy. For the position of a modern philosopher does not differ radically from that of Descartes when he set out in search of the philosopher's stone. Uncritical assumptions and dogmas dressed up as certain knowledge, whether they appear as beliefs of philosophers, presuppositions of science, or habits of thought, continue to be one of the main obstacles to the search for truth. For that reason the Cartesian device of methodological scepticism has become a standard constituent of a philosopher's intellectual equipment and an accredited route to knowledge.

Marxist-Leninists seem to take a different view and to reject the Cartesian principle. At best, it was a device for establishing the rights of reason against the encroachments of religion and theology, for the secularisation of the criteria of truth and for the emancipation of knowledge from authority. But in the theory of knowledge Descartes initiated a development in the wrong direction and was responsible for settting up almost unconquerable obstacles to knowledge about the world as a whole and about man as its integral part. To follow Descartes' lead in epistemology is to fall into the trap of idealism [213]. There is no room for the Cartesian principle in the controversy over the existence of the world, because there is no such controversy among sane men, undeluded by idealist inventions, who have never thought that the world could not be real.

Marxist-Leninists start, therefore, with the assumptions that the outside world is independent of the mind and that the mind is able to acquire an objective knowledge about the world by somehow comparing thought with the real processes in the external world. These assumptions might be, of course, true but they must be shown to be true, and this purpose cannot be achieved unless they are doubted and questioned. In other words, to be shown to be true they must be conclusions emerging from prior critical and reflective examination instead of being assumptions from which other conclusions can be safely drawn. The latter approach to the controversy over the existence of the world is dogmatic, as contrasted with the sceptical, the critical and the transcendental in Descartes', Kant's, and Ingarden's sense respectively [214].

The dogmatic approach was in the case of Marx and Engels an understandable development. It was a reaction to the wild speculations of post-Kantian idealism and, in particular, of Hegelian idealism. On reading Engels' *Feuerbach and the End of Classical German Philosophy* one still experiences the feeling of elation and the liberating effect of the discovery that after all 'Nature exists independently of all philosophy'. Some believe that the attitudes of mind, which are symbolised by the names of Parmenides and Hegel, are deeply ingrained in human nature and that there is always a Father Parmenides to every generation of philosophers. He calls forth in others the dogmatic and uncritical assertion denying any contribution of the mind to the determination of what is given, real, or valid in experience [215]. To discover the source from which this sort of dogmatism springs and from which it draws its renewed strength, does not amount to the justification of the dogmatic claims. Common sense metaphysics breaks down sooner or later, when tested by the criteria of consistency, agreement with reality, and requirements of intelligent action. It cannot survive these tests unless it denies the possibility of some questions which can be asked, declares others to be illegitimate and eliminates the difficulties by an increasing number of prohibitions concerning the object and manner of philosophical inquiry. These prohibitions make of common sense metaphysics an impregnable stronghold but also one that is a prison to its defenders. The fetters of common sense may be as oppressive as those of idealism.

The objection that Ingarden's phenomenology is a cunning device, similar to that of Berkeley, for refuting materialism and justifying God's existence, is based on a misconception about what Ingarden's ontology is and what it can achieve. Again it should be remembered that Ingarden differentiates ontology, a study of pure possibilities, from metaphysics, which deals with existential questions. At the level of ontological reflective analysis, concerned with the controversy over the existence of the world, there is no room for existential statements and since materialism is an existential metaphysical hypothesis, this hypothesis can neither be argued for nor against, neither proved nor disproved on the basis of ontological conceptual investigations and revisions alone.

Ingarden's transcendental method is in fact incompatible with 'absolute materialism', for it takes as its Archimedean point pure consciousness, to be apprehended in 'immanent perception' and whose mode of existence, though left undetermined, excludes its being something clearly physical. This pure consciousness is essentially man's consciousness, and not that of God. The idea of God being the ultimate ground of the reality of the world as a whole is mentioned marginally, but not explored as a distinct approach to the problem, discussed exclusively on a human level [216]. It is true that moderate materialism (this is Ingarden's terminology) excludes some possible existential relations between consciousness and matter, namely, those which would deny either the priority of matter or the dependence of consciousness on the latter. These again are existential metaphysical questions which cannot be resolved on the ground of ontology. Moreover, Ingarden's ontological examinations concerned with the mode of existence of pure consciousness, i.e., with what the idea of its existence considered as a pure possibility implies, lead to the conclusion that there might be some necessary relations between pure consciousness and the mind [217]. If that were actually the case, the essential connection of the mind and body within the real world, over which the controversy takes place, could jeopardise the whole transcendental method of procedure and its Archimedean point of departure. For the existential relations that would bind pure consciousness with the mind, and through the mind with the body constituting a part of the world, would deprive the being of pure consciousness of its primary and independent character. Ingarden's work ends on this note, and he did not indicate what the solution of this question might turn out to be [218].

The opinion that Ingarden's phenomenology is an introduction to theistic metaphysics cannot find any support in what he said in his published work so far. More controversial is his attitude to materialism. His transcendental method is incompatible with 'absolute materialism'. But Marxist-Leninists reject it too, under the name of 'vulgar materialism'. So far as consciousness is concerned, 'absolute' or 'vulgar materialism' is epitomised in the famous dictum that the brain secretes thought in the same way as the liver secretes bile (the emphasis being put on 'the same way'). 'Absolute materialism' includes, however, 'absolute realism', that is, speaking freely, the thesis that the knowledge of the world is not in any way relative to and dependent upon consciousness. 'Absolute realism' is not necessarily implied by materialism, but for

Marxist-Leninists it is the opinion of 'any healthy person', which they regard as the foundation of their theory of knowledge. Since 'absolute realism' is one of the pure possibilities which are excluded by Ingarden, his ontology does refute materialism, but materialism of a particular sort [219].

On the other hand, Ingarden did not consider materialism as a metaphysical doctrine that is concerned with the nature of the world and with the determination of the materialist criteria by which 'real' or 'existent' can be truly and correctly predicated, since these matters go beyond the limits of ontological investigations. Although it seems to be clear that he is not a materialist, it is at least premature and possibly wrong to say that he refuted materialism in the metaphysical sense of this term. The question whether the world is entirely material or entirely spiritual or both material and spiritual is undecided, and, apart from occasional references to various possibilities, not even touched upon.

The central motive of all modern philosophy is to view the world 'under the form of knowledge'. This observation was made in connection with the rise of idealism from Berkeley onwards, but it equally applies to other philosophical trends [220]. The concern with epistemological problems, of which the idealist tradition is only one branch, dominates modern philosophy. If it ventures beyond the theory of knowledge into the domain of metaphysics, it remains primarily an epistemology and becomes a metaphysics by implication.

The Marxist-Leninist criticism of Ingarden's phenomenology indicates that Marxist-Leninist materialism is the exact opposite of the initial standpoint, method and strategy applied by modern philosophy. For its cardinal principle is not a theory of knowledge but a metaphysics. It is metaphysics first and foremost, and a theory of knowledge only by implication. This offers some advantages in the criticism of other trends of thought. What the latter present as their views on the nature and structure of the world is tentative, hypothetical and inferred knowledge which Marxist-Leninists confront with assertions claiming some kind of direct acquaintance and absolute validity. The position is reversed when the controversies move from the field of metaphysics to that of epistemology. For Marxist-Leninists encounter serious difficulties in giving an account of how they arrive at the knowledge which they claim to possess and in justifying what they assert. These difficulties considerably increase with the conjoining of materialistic metaphysics and 'absolute realism'. For by denying that knowledge is relative to the mind, Marxist-Leninist thinkers put reality beyond the reach of the mind. The denial of the fact that knowledge is relative to the mind is forced upon Marxist-Leninists by their implicit endorsement of the idealist argument. The epistemological idealists argue that if knowledge of the external world is relative to the mind, the external world is completely dependent upon the mind. As Marxist-Leninists reject the conclusion, they feel obliged to reject the premiss. There is, however, no dilemma here, for if the realist is right the conclusion does not follow from the premiss, and one can accept the latter without being committed to the former.

Having recognised the justice of the idealist argument, Marxist-Leninists are compelled to consider any concession to the view that recognises the relativity of knowledge to the mind as a repudiation of materialism. A Marxist-Leninist materialist has to reject any limitations on the likeness or similarity or coincidence of knowledge and reality [221]. This gives him a unique position in two different meanings of this term. He is looked upon by others as a naive epistemologist, holding a view clearly untenable and, upon closer examination, absurd. On the other hand, and from his own vantage point, everybody but himself is an idealist. All thinkers but the Marxist-Leninists are tarred with the same idealist brush, they all, whether be it Berkeley or Russell, Kant or Hegel, Comte or Carnap, 'create' or 'construct' reality [222]. Idealism is the common denominator of all philosophical standpoints and tendencies, however different they might be in other respects, for they are related by their fundamental epistemological assumption. This assumption makes Husserl and Ingarden, logical positivists and the Warsaw school thinkers members of one single philosophical family, all stricken by the same fatal disease.

CHAPTER 12

CRITICISM OF ZNANIECKI'S SOCIOLOGY AND THE
DECLINE OF SOCIAL INQUIRY

If Alexander the Great really cut the Gordian knot, observed Felix Kaufmann, this might have been the cause of the relations between Aristotle and his former pupil becoming strained in later years. For there is nothing less congenial to the scientific way of thought than to dispose of a theoretical difficulty by an arbitrary action instead of undertaking its solution by the accepted rules of procedure.

Historical materialism in the Marxist-Leninist interpretation, which is also called 'Marxist-Leninist sociology', is one such attempt at cutting through the Gordian knot peculiar to sociology. The Marxist-Leninist doctrine claims the discovery of conclusively verified knowledge which forms the final basis of the social sciences in general and of sociology in particular. To raise an unconditional claim to truth for knowledge of matters of fact is to ignore elementary rules of scientific procedure. No empirical science is able to establish incontrovertible and self-evident truths, with which anybody who is not bemused by irrelevancies must concur.

There is a tendency among sociologists, stated Julian Hochfeld, to look at the Marxian doctrine as one of numerous sociological theories and to consider it on an equal footing with the others. It is maintained that one can justly speak of the Marxian and non-Marxian approach to sociological problems in the same manner as in other cases a procedure could be described as Durkheimian or non-Durkheimian. It is believed that the division of sociological theories into Marxist-Leninist and non-Marxist is not legitimate, since some non-Marxist theories are closer to the Marxian standpoint than to any non-Marxist doctrine. Hochfeld assured his readers that nothing could be further from the truth than these views. They ignored the fact that the difference between the Marxist-Leninist and the 'bourgeois sociology' was the same as that between truth and falsehood, between a truly scientific sociology and one given to arbitrary constructions whose purpose was to falsify social reality in the interest of the bourgeoisie [223].

There were several reasons why the attacks on non-Marxist sociology showed a degree of virulent belligerency which some other disciplines, for instance psychology or the philosophy of education, were spared. Deep and wide social changes of the sort that had taken place in Poland tend to stimulate the interest in social inquiry outside the narrow circle of professional social scientists and thus heighten the social significance of sociology. Social problems which emerge in the wake of extensive reforms give rise to opposing views and parties advocating different methods of solution. Even when these parties cannot expect to resolve their differences by rational arguments, such arguments are extensively used for they fortify convictions and convert them into a real social force [224]. An inquiry concerned with problems of human conduct, either individual or collective, has some direct relevance to practical problems. It might harm the interests and offend the convictions as well as the prejudices of those in power, affect the attitudes of the people at large and thus infringe upon what the politicians claim as their exclusive preserve. The latter are not, as a rule, inclined to accept the existence of an alternative to their own views with an equal or better claim to rational justification. The subordination of matters concerned with sociological problems to political considerations is made easier by the fact that both the theoretical assumptions and the findings of social research exhibit a high degree of indeterminacy which becomes manifest when they are to serve as the basis for 'predictions' or projected action. A sociologist encounters considerable difficulty in establishing his scientific position in society and in the world of learning, and in being recognised as a person with an authority of his own, based on an expert knowledge, superior to that which may be acquired by men of action with wide experience of human affairs. His authority can and has been challenged over and over again by politicians, journalists, writers and fellow scholars, who all claim to possess the requisite sociological knowledge to be competent and reliable arbiters on matters of social import.

This also accounts for the fact that sociologists in Poland have exhibited perhaps a weaker power of resistance to outside pressure upon their discipline than scholars in some other subjects. Unlike a mathematician or a philosopher, a sociologist can hardly live in the seclusion of his study. His work is closely bound up with the life of the community to which he belongs and from which he cannot isolate himself without some of his essential functions being affected by this withdrawal. Thus, as Chałasiński put it, he may feel that to surrender to conformism is a high, but not an excessive price to be paid for 'getting out of the social void'[225]. This attitude applied to a considerable group of Polish sociologists. They found themselves in between the convinced Marxist-Leninists and those, who, like Ossowski, rejected any compromise with truth on moral and social grounds.

The attitude of the 'middle group' exercised some influence on the development of events, which was partly favourable and partly unfavourable to the Marxist-Leninist plan of action. The immediate effects were of the former sort. For in order to play an effective role in social development and to bring their knowledge to bear upon its course, the sociologists of the 'middle group' had to become a part of the power structure in society, which in Poland meant a more or less close accommodation to or identification with the Communist Party as the constituted power [226]. The self-adjustment required not only some kind of ideological allegiance but also the acceptance of some definite views on sociology, its subject-matter, purpose and methodology, implied by the Marxist-Leninist social theories. These theories did not favour, however, the development of sociology and subsequently turned out to be a revolt against reason and science. This was not an entirely unexpected outcome, but one that could not have been foreseen either. Thus it happened with the co-operation of some sociologists, sociology, unlike philosophy, ceased to exist for a few years.

What Marxist-Leninists call 'bourgeois sociology' should be identified in Poland with Znaniecki's sociology, for his school had dominated the sociological scene in Poland before and after the war. Outside it there was no trend of importance that was in a position to offer an alternative conception of social inquiry.

The Marxist-Leninist opposition to Znaniecki's sociology sprang from two main, closely related considerations. The first was prompted by the sharp distinction between the modern, empirical conception of sociology and that underlying the socio-philosophical and historiosophical systems of the past. Znaniecki was a champion of the former and a determined opponent of the latter. The second reason for the Marxist-Leninist hostility was some characteristic features of Znaniecki's views.

There is not the slightest doubt that Znaniecki did reject the 'old synthetic conception of sociology', as he referred to it. The only future for sociology was in becoming an empirical and inductive science, which limits its units of study and tries to answer specific questions of fact. He was not alone in pursuing this aim, but he made it familiar and universally accepted in Poland. Znaniecki did not question the legitimacy of the powerful intellectual and moral interest in obtaining a view on a grand scale that would comprise and provide some understanding of all the civilisations, interpret their development, and discover some possible direction of the whole historical evolution of mankind. He compared this justifiable interest with that in metaphysical systems which aim at interpreting the natural world as an intelligible whole. But metaphysics neither can nor does replace physics. In the same manner the philosophy of history and socio-philosophical systems do not make history and sociology otiose. Znaniecki advocated the establishment of a sociology which does not misjudge its possibilities and instead of entertaining grandiose ambitions pursues limited objectives, restricts its inquiries to units of study capable of being empirically investigated, and to specific social structures, amenable to rational analysis. As he conceived it, sociology should be concerned with four major subjects, constituting a coherent whole, which he described as the theory of social actions, of social relations, of social roles, and of social groups. Znaniecki emphasised that this conception of sociology as an independent discipline with a distinct field of data of its own and distinct research techniques has been approached from different points of view by numerous sociological writers, Ch. H. Cooley, Georg Simmel, Alfred Vierkandt, Leopold von Wiese, Max Weber, R. M. MacIver, R. E. Park, E. W. Burgess, and many others. It needed only systematisation and consolidation [227].

This conception of sociology was called 'little sociology' in the Stalinist period. The tag had clearly a malicious meaning and was a term of dismissive abuse. It was said that its social and class purpose was to keep problems of social progress out of sight or within the limits that would be harmless to the capitalist system, and thus, in the 'objective sense', to protect the latter. Viewed from a different standpoint, 'little sociology' favoured an extreme and sterile form of empiricism or pseudo-empiricism, which has been the characteristic, above all, of many

American social research studies [228]. The objection that 'little sociology', with the assistance of elaborate research techniques, was producing a chaotic jumble of unrelated facts, an accumulation of discrete small-scale discoveries without rhyme or reason, of banal findings and trivial conclusions, lacking any global significance and theoretical orientation, alternated with another, to be later considered, namely, that far from being empirical and hostile to speculations it was actually itself a product of idealist speculations. The pseudo-empiricism peculiar to 'little sociology' was contrasted with the sociology of Marxism-Leninism with its balanced combination of theory and facts, theoretical studies and empirical research.

The objection of narrow empiricism was aimed at 'bourgeois sociology' in general and was meant to exemplify the alleged disintegration of science in decrepit capitalist society rather than to discredit Znaniecki and his school. For Znaniecki's thinking was dominated by the conception that combines a searching interest in empirical data with the ideal of a rational science. Znaniecki deplored the 'absorption in concrete data as such, apart from their significance for scientific generalisation', which he viewed as perhaps the greatest check on the progress of sociology. He dissociated himself from the tendency of making enormous surveys, of an indiscriminate use of questionnaires, of an appalling waste of resources and energy spent on collecting various materials and on interviewing thousands of people, without being guided by a clearly conceived theoretical purpose and a verifiable hypothesis. He refused to dignify this procedure by ascribing it to scientific circumspection [229]. Without delving any deeper, for instance, to examine from this viewpoint Znaniecki's opinions on the role of statistical methods in sociology or his ideas about 'analytical induction', Marxist-Leninists could have extracted from his writings a comprehensive compendium of observations on the harm inflicted upon sociology by the presumption that nothing but facts matter. Moreover, no wide reading in recent American sociological literature was necessary to ascertain that the neglect of theory has been more and more realised in the United States since the late 'thirties and that the radical empiricist camp in sociology has not been alone in the field there any longer. So far as the situation in American sociology is concerned, Marxist-Leninists and their supporters seem to have been behind the times [230].

The platitude that sociology needs both empirical research and theoretical studies does not settle the dispute between the Marxist-Leninist and the 'bourgeois sociology'. For when they speak of the desirability of theory, they use the same term in a different meaning. As Marxist-Leninists understand it, a sociological theory is an all-embracing philosophical system that would apply and account for vast ranges of social behaviour and include universal laws of social change in all its multifarious aspects. A theory of this type is not what a modern sociologist understands by it.

A modern, scientifically minded sociologist is aware of the fact that the search for such a theory is an unrealisable goal at the present state of knowledge and that it would have to run far ahead of the means available for its construction.

233

It would have to move by bold leaps and to start from scanty evidence to arrive by short-cuts to vast generalisations which turn out to be beliefs held before the investigations commenced. Being of a high degree of abstraction, with few if any partial hypotheses and special theories to relate the facts encountered in empirical research with the general theory, all-embracing systems would provide no guide in research and in the solution of general problems. This means that they would have no heuristic and cognitive value, if thereby is understood empirical verifiability, the consolidation of knowledge already acquired and the guidance in the acquisition of new knowledge. This point was strongly emphasised by Znaniecki and, later, by R. K. Merton and Talcott Parsons.

Theories the need of which is recognised by modern sociology, are what Merton calls 'theories of the middle range'. They are intended to be 'logically interconnected conceptions which are limited and modest in scope, rather than all-embracing and grandiose'. Their name is to indicate that they are intermediate to working hypotheses of routine research and general theories from which a great number of empirically confirmed uniformities of social behaviour could be deduced. Theories of the middle range would provide the basis for making sociological research in any particular field cumulative, help to remedy the present dispersion of effort and to remove the confusion resulting from the steadily growing mass of empirical generalisations which nobody notices and considers in his own research in a similar or closely related domain of social inquiry [231].

Without going beyond the methodological level, there is a sense in which Znaniecki's sociology may be declared to be incompatible with Marxist-Leninist sociology. The central point of disagreement is the difference of opinion concerning the empirical content of a sociological theory. Znaniecki refused to accept mere 'juggling with concepts' as a theoretical construction with a valid claim to empirical relevance, because it can refer to some empirical data, some favourable instances, supposedly providing its verification. 'Outside of the lunatic asylum', he wrote, 'there are no theories unsupported by facts'. An appeal to facts to illustrate the meaning of some abstract assertions does not transform their status of pseudo-empirical theories into genuinely empirical ones.

Long before Popper discovered and made precise the logical ground on which a scientific and a non-scientific theory, that appeals to observation and experience, can be clearly differentiated, non-scientific and pseudo-empirical theories were considered with an instinctive distrust by working scientists. Znaniecki rightly observed that the latter do not differ from the former by a complete absence of confirmation or verification. It is the nature of this confirmation or verification. that matters and helps to solve what Popper called the 'problem of demarcation' [232].

Znaniecki also came very close to Popper's solution of the demarcation problem for he insisted that a method that avoids 'conclusions which might be challenged and thus lead to the formulation of new problems' is unproductive. A sociologist strives for universal uniformities, but he is not afraid of counter-instances. The latter raise new problems, invalidate former generalisations and stimulate the search for a more efficient theory. 'The exception is thus an essential instrument of scientific progress', which should not be accepted meekly, as a necessary limitation resulting from the discrepancy between the world of facts and rational theories, but as the very source of creative science that constantly 'supplements or supplants the theory that has met with the exception by a new theory . . . and thus turns defeat into victory, strengthening and widening the sway of reason'. Znaniecki referred to physics, chemistry, and biology, as the sciences which invariably accept counter-instances. He wished sociology to emulate this particular method of natural science, called by him 'analytical induction' or 'logic of scientific research' and sharply differentiated from 'enumerative induction' which he thought to be unproductive or even obstructive to the 'dynamic ideal of knowledge'[233].

Znaniecki's methodological approach clearly implied that Marxist-Leninist sociology was not a sociological theory in the proper sense of this term, but a speculation, marked by the disparity between rare and meagre data on the one hand, and the extent of the conclusions on the other. The conclusions greatly overstep their supporting evidence and the data are barely sufficient to illustrate the argument. Znaniecki's point of view also implied that Marxist-Leninist sociology was deprived of empirical and cognitive significance, though this did not mean that it lacked any significance whatsoever or that it should not be studied as a social fact of the highest importance. This was the attitude taken by Durkheim to socialism. Durkheim refused to examine socialism as a theory of social facts but instead considered it as a social fact and object of sociological inquiry. In his numerous writings published in the immediate post-war years, Chałasiński, Znaniecki's most prominent pupil, adopted the same attitude with respect to Marxism-Leninism.

It should be clear that Znaniecki's views could not be tolerated by Marxist-Leninists as soon as they elevated their own theories to the position of an incontrovertible truth. Znaniecki's name alone personified for some time every possible error of 'bourgeois sociology' and epitomised the essence of opinions to be found in the works of its most prominent representatives [234].

This brings us to the second main reason for which Marxist-Leninists repudiated Znaniecki's sociology altogether, namely, to its philosophical presuppositions, general orientation and theoretical content. To discover in what respect the Marxist-Leninist doctrine is incompatible with Znaniecki's sociology it is best to begin with the Marxist-Leninist criticism of the latter.

The Marxist-Leninist refutation of Znaniecki's sociology was accomplished in a simple manner. It was argued that the humanistic coefficient is identical with the Berkeleyan principle 'esse is percipi'. Znaniecki denied the objective existence of any object, either in Nature or in social reality, and he reduced it to the content of individual consciousness. Znaniecki dematerialised mountains and rivers, society and its classes, made the world of dreams and imagination indistinguishable from the world of stubborn facts and hard realities. Whatever stability is revealed in the fluid world, created by the consciousness, it owes it to the objective and immaterial values which, in Znaniecki's opinion, determine the attitudes of men, make man a definite human person, bind human persons into social groups and ultimately account for the whole of social and cultural reality, conceived as a web of interacting persons, groups and their mutual relationships. Values function in Znaniecki's system in the same capacity as God does in Berkeley's Universe. They represent the element of objective idealism, interwoven into the fabric of subjective idealism, which provides the guiding principle of Znaniecki's conceptions and the foundation for the whole theoretical structure. The social significance of the latter is clear once their philosophical principles are laid bare. It hardly needs repeating that Znaniecki's sociology, being an elaborate idealist construction, is a bourgeois reaction to dialectical materialism and the proletarian movement. Znaniecki formed an alliance with all the forces whose chief purpose in life was to stem and counteract the expansion of the revolution by spreading confusion in the minds and blurring the differences dividing materialism and idealism in the social sciences [235].

In the inter-war period Znaniecki's sociology was criticised, by Kotarbiński in particular, for its ontological and methodological dualism, namely, for its distinction between natural and cultural reality, methods of natural and cultural sciences, which were considered by Znaniecki as irreducible to each other [236]. After the war Szczepański, Znaniecki's pupil, tried to revise the theoretical assumptions on which Znaniecki's ontological and methodological dualism is based in order to reduce, if not eliminate altogether, the irreducible cleavage of natural and cultural reality [237]. The method of personal documents was subject to severe criticism, both in Poland and in America, and the criticism was recognised as pertinent and irrefutable. Consequently, other more critical and reliable techniques were devised which reduced Znaniecki's favourite method to a subsidiary or auxiliary status [238]. Znaniecki's sociological system includes restrictive provisions which, if accepted, would relegate some important sociological issues, such as the problems of class structure, outside the realm of sociology. They also formally forbid the use of any data which are not social in Znaniecki's sense, that is, are not determined by the humanistic coefficient [239]. These limitations prompted by circumspection or by the requirement of theoretical coherence, could be justly criticised from the Marxian or any other viewpoint. But it cannot be said that Znaniecki incarnated Berkeleyan idealism in sociology or that the humanistic coefficient is equivalent to the idealist principle 'esse is percipi' without grossly misconstruing what he put down in writing in an unequivocal manner.

While introducing the humanistic coefficient, Znaniecki explicitly stated that he was not interested in the dispute between idealism and realism in the theory of knowledge. 'The attitude of the positive scientist, the specialist in any field', he wrote, 'is uniformly realistic', and he emphatically and repeatedly identified himself with this attitude. The world studied by the natural sciences is a 'world of things connected into systems by natural forces' and independent of man. On

236

this point there is not the slightest ambiguity either in Znaniecki's mind or in his writings [240].

The humanistic coefficient is a means of differentiating two main types of order or reality discovered in human experience: the natural and the cultural. The objects of the latter – a poem, a ceremony, a factory, a painting – cannot be studied in the same manner as a stone or a tree or any object supposed to exist independently of any human being. For if anybody tried to do so, he would fail entirely to understand the cultural objects and the role they play within their respective systems. They would disappear, as it were, and the investigator would be confronted by a disjointed heap of natural things, entirely dissimilar from the reality which he tried to comprehend. The nature and role of cultural objects are 'determined not merely by the characters these elements possess as natural things but also (and chiefly) by characters which they have acquired in the experience of people during their existence as cultural objects'. These acquired characteristics constitute their meaning. To differentiate natural objects from cultural objects Znaniecki called the former 'things' and the latter 'values'. Things neither are nor become values by themselves, independently of any conscious human agent. To be or to become values, objects must belong to somebody's active experience. This active experience gives them a meaning and makes them what they are, always relative to a conscious agent. This principle of relativity of cultural objects was called 'humanistic coefficient' by Znaniecki [241].

The humanistic coefficient does not imply that cultural objects are entirely dependent on the conscious agent, for they have an objective order of their own and are constituents of an independent reality. The distinction between things and values has nothing to do with differentiating between what is objective and what is subjective in human experience. It should be remembered that Znaniecki uses the term 'value' in an unusual manner to denote certain categories of objects such as social individuals, their collectivities or social groups, and institutions, as well as what common speech calls 'valuable'. Anything that is the object of certain activities, is referred to as desirable or undesirable, useful or harmful, in general, that has an axiological significance or a meaning pointing to its structural dependence in the system of which it forms a component part, is a value in Znaniecki's sense. A sacred vessel has a meaning within a cultural system, in this case, in a particular religion, since it is linked with certain words, representations and behaviour of the worshippers. Similarly, the buildings and machines of a factory have a meaning apprehended by those who man them and by anyone prepared to understand their use. The inner order of a cultural system raises it above the arbitrariness of individual experiences and endows it with an objective validity recognised and complied with by all who participate in it. There is, therefore, nothing subjective about values, they are intersubjectively established, experienced by any number of people, whose experiences can be tested. Furthermore, values take genetic precedence over things; we learn first about values in life, and only later, if ever, we take cognisance of things [242].

The question arises whether Znaniecki's sociology, having been cleared of the objection of subjective idealism, is not found guilty on the second count, that of

237

objective idealism. It appears that provided a suitable meaning is given to the term 'objective idealism' the Marxist-Leninist objection should be recognised as valid.

Although cultural reality seems at first to be superimposed on that of natural objects, the order of priority should be in fact reversed. This was done by Znaniecki in his last work *Cultural Sciences* in which he argued that cultural reality should be considered as primary and natural reality as secondary, abstracted from the former in the course of the development of natural sciences. While cultural reality is primary, its knowledge expressed in terms of a comprehensive theory has evolved, for various reasons, only after that of natural reality (the natural sciences) has reached an advanced stage of maturity. On this account natural reality has overshadowed and assumed priority over that of cultural objects. This leaves the existence of the natural sciences and of the activities of the scientists unaccounted for. For science itself is not a part of the natural order, investigated by the scientist, and requires, therefore, the cultural sciences, and, in particular, sociology conceived as a general theory of human actions as its foundation. Scientists who specialise in investigating natural phenomena and develop theories that have no direct reference to men take themselves for granted as conscious active thinkers, and thus fail to notice that their own activity presupposes the existence of cultural reality and of its specific order, which is unaccountable in terms of the natural sciences [243].

If this viewpoint is accepted, it becomes clear that whatever ontological status is assigned to values by reflective analysis of social behaviour, much of cultural reality is non-material. Even material cultural objects, let us say, a mine or an architectural monument, have meaning and are values, which are not material and which make them what they are. It was evident to Znaniecki that the objective form of an activity – what has later been called 'pattern' – oriented to non-material aspects of culture cannot be described in terms of actions dealing with material objects alone, and thus he saw no chance of reducing sociology to a naturalistic discipline. The proper subject-matter of sociology is non-material objects and their systems which, as Znaniecki emphasised, though non-material are 'as real as material ones, if not more so'. For instance, we cannot seriously deny reality to the Tree of Knowledge of Good and Evil experienced and identified in imagination and thought by innumerable generations in the course of centuries. In the indicated sense the Tree of Knowledge is an empirical datum more real than any of the trees in the Amazon basin or in the Siberian Taiga, which never was or will be observed by any human individual [244].

Znaniecki thought that the peculiar nature of cultural objects becomes incomprehensible if the validity of causation with respect to the actions of human agents, considered as elements of cultural reality, is not restricted and replaced by the principle of spontaneity. For granted the primacy of cultural reality, the problem whether a certain activity is free or determined is insoluble. Any naturalistic explanation of why the human agents act as they do is barred by the very assumption of cultural reality being primary. An action is entirely defined by the system of values within which it occurs and which it constructs or maintains in being. This does not mean that any stimuli provided by non-cultural objects can simply be ignored or denied; they are, however, relative to pre-existing spontaneous tendencies [245].

It is clear, therefore, that the world as unreflectively experienced and reflectively known consists of material and non-material entities. There are objects which being real are neither sensuous nor material, and whose structural organisation is not causally determined (nor, for that matter, logically or teleologically). The order intrinsic to cultural systems is irreducible to the natural one and lies outside the range of natural phenomena. Acquaintance with the latter presupposes the familiarity with the cultural order, and, on the theoretical level, the knowledge of natural reality cannot do without categories of the cultural sciences. For knowledge of the world of Nature is itself a social and cultural activity, comprehensible and to be accounted for in terms of the social and cultural sciences.

Although Znaniecki's theories do not appeal either to spirit or to ideal essences as the ultimate constituents of the world, they can be called 'idealist'. This qualification would differentiate them from those to be described as materialistic and naturalistic [246]. Thinkers who try to avoid metaphysics, stated Znaniecki, cannot accept the 'existence of a spiritual world outside and above the material one'. Znaniecki would refuse to define the 'true essence' of cultural objects as no concern of his and as essentially an extra-scientific question. Cultural reality was for him an empirical datum in a world by no means timeless and spaceless. He wished its investigations to be restricted to the study of factual relationships among cultural objects and to the discovery of the order in these relationships, without asking questions which a student of culture could not and should not answer [247].

It is not quite clear whether Marxist-Leninists had exactly this in mind when they described Znaniecki's theories as objective idealism. For in their own social theories they make use of concepts referring to entities hard to accommodate within a system of purely material objects and whose reduction to purely material constituents is by no means certain. Still, from the viewpoint of a naturalistically oriented sociology, Znaniecki's theories can be rightly described as idealist in the sense indicated above, to be ranged against the Marxist-Leninist standpoint.

Whatever else might be said about Marxist-Leninist theories on man, Nature, and culture, their ultimate purpose is clear and unequivocal and based on convictions diametrically opposed to those of Znaniecki. For Marxist-Leninists man is a natural being, like all other animal species, who exerts himself to make his life secure. He is also a social being who only by collective actions can make his life enduring. By self-adjustment, inventions and discoveries he can assert himself against Nature and gain an increasing control over his environment. Culture is nothing but a collective name for the instruments and means discovered by man to transform the natural environment and bend it to his needs. These exertions bring in their wake knowledge of Nature, the natural sciences, the social sciences, and philosophy, whose content and functions are determined by technical means primarily invented for the practical purpose of life. In the natural and social sciences there is laid up the sum total of knowledge about the world which is ultimately the knowledge about man himself, about his origin and progressive development to the stage reached at the present time. Philosophy is the final synthesis by means of which man traces back his natural history in relation to the world, recognised as the independent factor that determines his being but that is also transformed by man's action in his struggle for existence. Philosophy helps to discover the principles by means of which man's behaviour may be controlled and his efforts rationally directed in the further struggle for the improvement of his conditions.

From this standpoint Znaniecki's belief about the primacy and priority of cultural reality over natural reality is fundamentally wrong and turns upside down the actual recorded natural history of man. Its non-naturalistic conception of man is bound to assign an undue importance and effectiveness to man's will, wishes, and aspirations, as if man's past and future depended solely on himself. Such a suggestion amounts to substituting an arbitrary principle for a patent fact that man is a natural being, Nature is prior to man, and the laws of Nature are indifferent to man's hopes and strivings. These critical observations were not used against Znaniecki, though they could have been applied, since they are all contained in the Marxian tradition.

Simultaneously with the condemnatory verdict on Znaniecki and his school, the Marxian tradition of social thought in Poland was re-evaluated from the Marxist-Leninist viewpoint. Separate studies on its representatives, Krusiński, Kelles-Krauz, Abramowski, Brzozowski, and Krzywicki, revealed that there was little in their life work from which Marxism-Leninism could learn and benefit. Their main common errors were the identification of the Marxian thought with sociology and economics, its separation from dialectical materialism and a patent 'anti-revolutionary' attitude of mind. Only Krusiński, least known of them all, passed muster and was accepted without undue reservations and also without enthusiasm, since he was not an important writer. Krzywicki's merits as a populariser of Marxian thought were not ignored, but he was declared to be a confirmed revisionist in his interpretation of historical materialism, thus unacceptable as a forerunner of Marxism-Leninism. There was not a single good point in the remaining representatives of the Marxian tradition. They were responsible for the delay and obstructions to the development of revolutionary, *i.e.* Marxist-Leninist thought in Poland. They were individualists, anarchists, and disguised enemies of the proletariat, who only by mistake could have been ranked among the precursors of the Marxist-Leninist tradition [248].

Finally, Czarnowski was found only partially acceptable. He owed the rescue of his name and writings to the political activities in which he participated towards the end of his life. His sociological contributions did not satisfy the Marxist-Leninist requirements for they are Durkheimian in spirit and method. Durkheim was supposedly committed to an ahistorical standpoint, ignored the class structure and class conflicts, preached social solidarity, and represented objective idealism in sociology and social philosophy. Czarnowski's contributions to the history of culture and of social thought were considered to be a remarkable achievement but they too displayed serious theoretical errors. They failed to comply with the standpoint of Marxist-Leninist historiography, of which more will be said later [249]. Czarnowski was, however, exceptionally treated; the first and complete edition of his works, a valuable and, on the whole, scholarly publication, was published even before greater tolerance and respect for thought had again prevailed.

Thus a clean sweep was made of everything past and present and Marxist-Leninists were left alone in the field to begin again from scratch. The work of destruction confronted them with formidable problems of organising research and teaching on entirely new lines. It can be said at once that they failed in both these spheres of activity.

The dispute between Marxism-Leninism and sociology was essentially a clash between the nineteenth century's and the modern conception of the social sciences. There was little doubt that there was no Marxist-Leninist sociology in the sense of the latter and no doubt whatever that Polish sociology represented the empirical and modern trend in the social sciences. Three out of the four leading Polish sociologists in the post-war period, Chałasiński, Szczepański and Szczurkiewicz, were not only Znc .iecki's pupils, but also shared his views on sociology, and applied his conceptual framework, his theories and methods in their own work. After the war Chałasiński and Szczepański re-established Znaniecki's school of thought and made it dominant in the universities. The fourth leading sociologist, Stanisław Ossowski, followed a path of his own, but he also cultivated 'little sociology'. At the time when freedom of discussion still prevailed, he gained prominence for his learned and effective defence of modern sociology against Marxist-Leninist criticism.

Ossowski was a particularly formidable opponent. He combined wide and thorough sociological knowledge with a mind trained in the Warsaw school [250]. His attachment to reason, to the requirements of logic and to the respect for facts is unyielding and uncompromising. These qualities have assured him considerable intellectual stature, made him an influential teacher and an authority in his subject, widely recognised in intellectual circles. It was Ossowski who from the defence of 'little sociology' passed on to the criticism of Marxism-Leninism and made numerous suggestions as to how its various parts should be revised to be adjusted to the state of contemporary knowledge and to satisfy the accepted standards of validity. While Chałasiński's initial critical attitude to Marxism-Leninism concerned mainly its socio-philosophical content and its social message, Ossowski was interested in the Marxian social theories, in their incorporation and application, in a revised form, to sociological inquiry.

Stanisław Ossowski and Maria Ossowska have associated themselves with this development of modern sociological thought which instead of ignoring the existence of Marx has been deeply concerned with the issues raised by him. Émile Durkheim and Max Weber were the most prominent figures of this trend in the past and Ossowski and Ossowska have continued it in Poland. They are not Marxian, if by this qualification is to be understood the acceptance of the whole body of the Marxian doctrine in its original form. They believe, however, that Marxian ideas hold an important place in modern sociology and provide a fruitful point of departure for the formulation and investigation of many sociological problems. In particular, this concerns the Marxian theory of economic and social classes and of class conflicts. Interest in Marxian thought inspired Ossowski's inquiry into the concepts of class and social structure, resulting in 1957 in a remarkable book *Class Structure in Social Consciousness*, and in Ossowska's investigations on the plurality of morals, which coexist in the same community and are found to be related to its class stratification [251].

The importance attached to the teaching of Marx leads to the conclusion that a further development and application of Marxian ideas require their reformulation in terms of the conceptual framework of modern sociology. Ossowski and Ossowska did draw this conclusion and by doing it they greatly jeopardised their position. To transgress the line dividing the sacred and the profane is dangerous in any society, but in some more than in others. Revisionism, of which Ossowski was accused, was presented not only as a sacrilegious deed, but also as a political crime [252].

At the time when Marxist-Leninists decided to establish the supremacy of their doctrines in sociology to the exclusion of any other, academic sociology – as represented by Chałasiński, Ossowski, and Szczepański – was entangled from their viewpoint in the 'old theoretical and methodological errors', retained the conceptual framework of the past, and was engaged in criticising and revising the foundations of Marxism-Leninism. Each of the non-Marxist sociologists was subjected to severe public censure, Chałasiński and Szczepański for being continuators of Znaniecki's theories, Ossowski for the incompatibility of his views with Marxism-Leninism [253].

The hardest blows fell on Ossowski in view of his stubborn adherence to his scientific standpoint which he refused to abandon either in speech and writing or in his teaching activities. His articles were banned from publication and he was removed from his university chair by being sent on enforced leave of absence. Ossowska shared the same fate.

The fortunes of Chałasiński and Szczepański were different. They were not removed from their university chairs, but instead of teaching sociology, which ceased to exist as an undergraduate study – it was replaced by historical materialism and the teaching of this subject was reserved, naturally enough, for Marxist-Leninists alone – they taught the history of social thought. This proscriptive measure was not relaxed even for Chałasiński, who was accorded an official bill of intellectual health. For about the same time Chałasiński made a public, oral and written, self-criticism of his former views, supported the Marxist-Leninist criticism of Znaniecki's sociology, and professed himself basically in agreement with the assumptions of Marxist-Leninist sociological theories. He justified his conversion to Marxism-Leninism by a comparison of the conscience of the intellectual, which is divorced from the course of history, to the magnetic needle of a compass that is out of order. The course of history showed that there is no middle road between socialist revolution and crimes of capitalism. An intellectual cannot avoid making a choice between them in the great social and political conflict that divides the world in the era marked by the struggle between imperialism and socialism. Chałasiński's self-criticism, held up as example to others, helped Marxist-Leninists in proclaiming that the victory over 'bourgeois sociology' was achieved in open discussion [254].

On the other hand, Chałasiński's conversion, nullified a few years later, provided a protective screen for the teaching centres in Warsaw and Łódź, where under the guise of studying the history of social thought students were learning sociology and followed its development in the outside world. When sociology was rehabilitated in 1956, it emerged from its hiding places with a large group of trained young sociologists prepared to undertake teaching and research. They have at present made of sociology one of the most thriving academic disciplines in Poland. Chałasiński was also one of the leading spirits during what, in the period 1954–1956, was called the 'thaw'. From the position of authority, which his conversion enabled him to retain, he launched a very effective campaign against the distortions of the intellectual life and the decline of science under the system of the 'monopoly of a single school'. His rediscovery of some simple but long forgotten truths pushed the Marxist-Leninist doctrine on its downwards course and to its final destruction, as a dogma, in the fire of the ensuing free discussion.

The decision to reject altogether every sociological achievement accomplished by 'bourgeois science', was announced towards the end of 1951. There was nothing in existing sociology, either in Poland or abroad, of which Marxist-Leninists wished to take advantage, whether in the field of theory and methodology or research findings and techniques. The whole conceptual framework was to be reformulated, theories recast, new methods and techniques devised. This was to be accomplished by taking dialectical and historical materialism as the only guiding principles. Social research was to be remodelled on the pattern of Engels' *The Condition of the Working Class in England* and Lenin's *The Development of Capitalism in Russia*, since these two works showed that the adequacy and validity of a method was determined by the fact whether it yielded significant contributions to our knowledge of the 'objective social development'[255].

Marxist-Leninists seem to think that the nature of social facts determines in a unique fashion the conceptual scheme to be adopted in their investigations. Furthermore, since concepts necessarily correspond to the things they designate, there exists an objective adequacy between the conceptual framework in terms of which social facts are described and these facts themselves. Therefore, it is the social theory that determines which method is right and appropriate, and what kind of results it should yield. This view on the relation between theory and method puts the cart before the horse.

For there is no *a priori* reason to suppose that there is one and only one method which is appropriate to a given subject matter, and the history of science seems to suggest that, on the whole, methodological pluralism is preferable to methodological monism. No theory can, in principle, exclude a particular method. Methods are rules of procedure, adopted either by a conventional decision or on the ground of observations of what scientists do to arrive at warranted conclusions. A method is the product of a resolution stipulating which is the best way of dealing with a particular class of scientific statements. Finally, to say that a theory determines its own method is to run a considerable risk. For if a method is recognised as adequate, if it yields results in agreement with what the theory lays down, the question arises what useful purpose a method, adequate in this sense, would serve apart from illustrating the justice of the preconceived ideas.

There seems to be concealed in Marxist-Leninist thinking a misconception not only of what is a method, but also of what is a theory, and what is their relation. A theory is not for them an instrument of thought, one of the means of discovering truth, but something that, in the sense of the Aristotelian realism, necessarily corresponds to and reproduces, as it were, the realm of reality described by this theory. The thesis of methodological monism, the view that there is a unique method, appropriate and absolutely valid, in each field of inquiry, follows from the Aristotelian realistic presuppositions. But to consider the relation between the subject matter, theory, and method in any empirical discipline in that manner (described on the preceding pages as 'methodological essentialism'), is to turn back the clock many centuries. In particular, the relation between theory and method in an empirical discipline is exactly the opposite of what Marxist-Leninists conceive it to be. Whatever general considerations we have in mind in advance, which may suggest a certain procedure and technique, an empirical theory is defined in terms of a method, that is, in terms of rules of procedure to which the scientist is pledged and which state the conditions for the acceptance and rejection of propositions.

Marxist-Leninists are confronted by a considerable, if not insoluble, difficulty when it comes to the question what method is appropriate to the subject matter of a materialistically conceived sociology. While rejecting the personal documents, public opinion and attitude research, the method of representative sampling as applied so far in Poland and elsewhere, Marxist-Leninists emphatically stated that it was not their intention to abolish social research altogether. They only wished to dissociate themselves, in the manner indicated by Lenin in his polemics against Russian 'empirio-monists', from such methods which abandon 'objective facts' and 'objective situations', independent of the social consciousness of men, and investigate 'facts constituted in the subjective consciousness' or 'subjective views of individuals'[256]. They did not explain what were the 'objective facts' which they had in mind and which they contrasted with the 'subjective' ones, or in what way they wished to establish them. A clue to their ideas was provided when a research project was in preparation and its technique was discussed. The rules of procedure were devised in such a manner that the conclusions to be reached were known beforehand and could not fail to confirm the investigator's presuppositions. The distinction between the 'objective' and 'subjective', 'true' and 'false' social facts was determined on the grounds of Marxist-Leninist theory and empirical research was not intended to test and to modify, possibly to falsify and eliminate, any of its assumptions. If empirical research could not do any of these things, it could only show that the theory agreed with appropriately selected or interpreted evidence. The fallacy inherent in this procedure escaped the notice of the Marxist-Leninist social scientists [257].

Their understanding of objectivity seems to suggest that an 'objective' social fact is a 'true' one in some metaphysical sense of this term. What Max Weber said on this matter may help to elucidate this point. Sociology was for Weber a science which aims at the interpretative understanding of social actions, *i.e.*, of 'all human behaviour when and in so far as the acting individual attaches a subjective meaning to it'. Action is social if the acting individual takes account of the behaviour of others. The 'meaning' of which this definition makes use, either denotes what in the given case a particular agent or a plurality of agents take it to be or a pure type of meaning attributed to a hypothetical agent or agents in some kind of action. Over and above it, there is no other 'objective' or 'correct' meaning which can be empirically ascertained and it is this which distinguishes an empirical sociology from dogmatic disciplines. The latter seek to establish the 'true' and 'valid' meaning which is independent of any agent and associated with the object itself [258].

A social inquiry based on the assumption that there is an 'objective meaning' attributable to social actions, distinguishable from the 'subjective' one, irrespective of whether it is ascertainable in the consciousness of any single individual, has to assume the existence of the former axiomatically and to become a deductive theory [259]. Moreover, since 'objective meanings' are determined, according to Marxist-Leninists, by economic factors, which are the decisive constituents of social reality, the latter should be regarded as independent variables in social inquiry. A materialist social theory consists of statements that are either somehow inferred from the economic ones or provide a sociological interpretation of economic statements. This is a Marxian idea, for in Marx's investigations economics and sociology are complementary, they dovetail and present the same argument on two different planes [260].

The Marxian idea gave to Marxist-Leninist sociology its sense of direction and the guiding principles of its procedure. The fundamental principle of the materialist deductive sociology was Marx's famous assertion that it is the social existence of men that determines their consciousness. It was an absolute principle, neither in need of elucidation and verification, nor amenable to correction or to justification on further grounds. It provided the basis for the general rule that what is found in the social consciousness of men should always be related to the conditions of material life, by which should be understood the productive forces and the relations of production.

Marxist-Leninists supplemented this fundamental principle by a number of rules to be followed in any social inquiry. Three of these rules deserve attention, for they had disastrous effects on the further fortunes of sociology.

The first rule stated that the sociologist should take economic conditions as his point of departure and consider them in their dynamic aspect, that is, to examine the class conflict arising from the prevailing class structure. For social facts unrelated to their economic causes are left precariously in the air and inspire false and reactionary sociological conceptions.

The second rule concerned the determination of the social context, defined in terms of its mode of production, with respect to the scale of social progress. This means that the type of socio-economic formation, to which the given context belongs, should be established and thus the dynamic possibilities of social change be included in the description and interpretation of the investigated phenomena.

The third rule supplemented the second by the demand that the investigations of social facts in their dynamic aspect should lead to the discovery of new regularities – material, socio-psychological, and ideological – maturing in the womb of the community in which the investigated phenomena take place. The importance of the third rule was enhanced by the demand that sociology should play an active role in the construction of socialism and accelerate its advent.

It was the second and the third rule which made havoc of social inquiry and put an end to sociological thinking for a few years. For the requirements of relating social data and conclusions drawn therefrom to a unilinear scale of social progress reduced sociology to little more than a thinly disguised propaganda activity. The role which sociology was assigned to play in adjusting the social conditions to the stage of development prescribed by the universal laws of history, endowed sociology with a direct political significance and made of it one of the chief instruments for moulding minds [261]. Marxist-Leninist sociology was expected to substantiate the claim that what ought to happen was actually taking place.

It should be borne in mind that the assumed unilinear scale of social progress provided a very poor standard of measurement. Only a few points were marked on it and in such a manner that it was never clear how they applied in any definite set of circumstances. Each of the Marxian stages of the universal evolution covered many centuries of history which have remained unexplored and unmarked on the scale. The considerable difficulties in the evaluation of past events in terms of social progress, by which a historian of social, economic or philosophic thought was confronted, were nothing compared with those encountered by the sociologist concerned not with the past but with contemporary events. His task was not to use the universal laws of progress as guiding principles in ordering and interpreting past events, but to show how they worked here and now in the process of transforming the capitalist economic basis into the socialist mode of production and thereby changed entirely the whole social consciousness of men.

In the case of the sociologist the paradoxical features of the situation were pronounced and inescapable. On the one hand, there were the postulated historical laws, which made progress inevitable. On the other, the same laws allowed considerable latitude to men in deciding in each particular case what path and form progress should take. Thus, while the sociologist was obliged by his methodological rule to trace the path of social progress in the course of its realisation, the path described by him was in fact determined by the decision of the policy makers. These decisions had to be taken, however, not for what they were, that is, for the resolutions made according to a plan and directed towards the goal which the policy makers assigned to themselves. They were presented as the work of the ineluctable laws of history and progress, of which the policy makers were the chosen instrument. The sociologist did not describe, therefore, how things were actually happening, but how they should have occurred, if countless external forces did not incessantly interfere with the will of the policy makers who were the sole determinant of social processes, acting with a perfect knowledge of all the effects, intended and unintended, of their decisions. Moreover, the sociologist was expected to help in the creation of facts, and this function he could perform only 'dialectically'. This meant that instead of finding out what were the facts, he tried to conjure them up, to induce certain social attitudes and patterns of behaviour, which in due course would bring about their own verification. He acted on the assumption of William James, that some facts cannot come to pass at all unless they are preceded by the desire for their existence. To encourage faith in a fact was to help to create this fact, for anticipation and forecast precede observation. Thus, however, the actual social conditions and their image were increasingly diverging and social knowledge was more and more replaced by figments of imagination and social myths [262].

The sociologist could not discharge his function of providing confirmation that the policy makers were successful in administering the universal laws of progress unless he accepted the policy makers' criteria of significance and valuation and subordinated his work to political control and expediency. He did not concentrate on what the facts were, what the problems arising from them were, and what the correct solution of the latter were, but on what it was appropriate to say. This meant that he remained a social scientist only by name and instead of his proper social role he performed that of a propagandist. A number of sociologists did assume this role, this having been concealed from their sight by their ideological identification with the constituted power, but only sometimes and to certain extent. This was not always the case. Some sociological political scholars of the extreme sort enunciated the subordination of sociology to politics as a binding and methodologically fruitful principle of their discipline. Social inquiry would be doomed to failure if it did not take the achievements of the revolutionary practice, the policy and directions of the Communist Party as its point of departure, its guiding principle of research and criterion of validity of its conclusions. The leaders of the Party are by the same token the leading theorists of social life; they enrich sociological theory by new ideas and generalisations. The resolutions and directives of the Communist Party provide the framework for social research, which can thus achieve results theoretically important and significant from the viewpoint of practice [263].

This was not a self-fulfilling prophecy but a 'tombstone on the grave of sociology'[264]. The five years that followed the adverse verdict on modern 'bourgeois sociology' were barren and nothing was done to substantiate the claim that there was an alternative to it, based on the Marxist-Leninist principles of dialectical and historical materialism. Marxist-Leninists did not develop a single branch of

social research, whether it be the sociology of primary groups, of social stratification or of criminal behaviour, urban or rural sociology, industrial sociology,
sociology of education or that of knowledge and science. Theoretical sociology
has fared no better. The Marxian theory has been reduced by Marxist-
Leninists to aphorism, versicles, and mottos. Lack of terminological precision
and of well-defined concepts, abuse of reified expressions and metaphors were
conducive to slovenly misuse of reasoning. Marxist-Leninists evolved a peculiar
style of their own which placed the reader in a strange position. He read
phrase upon phrase which did not appear to have any definite meaning and he
was at a loss to follow the writer's sequence of thought. He was baffled by a
host of terms with a scientific sound but used with an offensive intention.
Notwithstanding these peculiarities, Marxist-Leninists adopted a contemptuous
attitude to any genuine scholarship and knowledge, if it denied, disagreed or
did not confirm their assumptions. Finally, they professed their adherence to
empiricism in theory, but in practice repudiated it and showed an unconcealed
hostility to empirical methods [265].

This was widely and full-heartedly recognised about the middle of 1956, and
the consensus of opinion included Marxist-Leninists. What began as the criticism of Znaniecki's sociology, stated one of the numerous critics of the Stalinist
period, ended in the complete destruction of empirical sociology, in a legacy of
ignorance in practically every branch of social inquiry, and in an intellectual
standstill, unrelieved by a single original work. The cause of these developments
was diagnosed and reduced to the absorption of science by ideology, to the
production of reified historical forces superior to human volition, of myths and
evaluations based on extra-scientific considerations and serving a political
purpose. In the absence of freedom of thought and speech, all these distorting
influences could not have been rationally and effectively challenged. The
'monopoly of a single school' established and enforced by various administrative
measures, destroyed creative thought and, like Cronus, in fear of being
dethroned, devoured its children as soon as they were born [266].

The final upshot of the five years during which Marxist-Leninist sociology
dominated the Polish scene was not only the collapse of its monopoly but an
almost general denial that a distinctly Marxist-Leninist sociology existed at all[267].
Marxist-Leninist sociology was established by a 'notorious and egregious
breach of the elementary rules of methodological rationalism', committed by
men who were 'surely not Marxists'[268]. A sociological statement is either valid
or invalid, true or false, and this is established by methodological rules and
procedures of universal application. From the methodological viewpoint there
are no distinguishing characteristics in Marxist-Leninist sociology. On the other
hand, since Marx published his discoveries sociology has made considerable
progress and accumulated a mass of findings, hypotheses, and theories, which to
qualify as Marxian or non-Marxian does not make sense. Specifically Marxian
ideas have been either incorporated into the body of accepted knowledge, or
restricted and more precisely formulated, or, finally, discarded by the advance of
science. When the ideas of a scholar become a constituent part of accepted

knowledge, he achieves his greatest possible triumph. The disappearance of a separate Marxian school should not be regarded therefore as a signal defeat but as a signal victory.

There remain two orientations in sociology, struggling with each other, the idealist and the materialist, but this difference of opinion concerns the philosophical foundations of sociology and does not affect the practice of working social scientists. They may differ in their interpretations, or, more generally, in their intellectual attitudes, but their methods, techniques, data, and results of empirical research are essentially the same. Marxism-Leninism as a distinct, compact and all-inclusive school of thought, whether in economics, sociology or philosophy, is an untenable conception. Its existence can be asserted if it refers to a political and religious phenomenon (in Durkheim's sense), but in the realm of science, though not yet defunct, it is doomed to extinction [269].

Since the revolution against reason and science broke down, symbolically speaking, in October 1956, Polish sociologists have been busy making up for lost time and their return to the scientific ways of thinking is amply apparent in numerous publications. This does not mean that all, or even an appreciable proportion of them, have abandoned a materialistic outlook on history, society, and man. They have remained committed, as a rule, to the Marxian philosophical ideas in a loose sense of this expression, to the stimulus imparted and to the perspectives opened by Marx's genius, who, in Kołakowski's words, is 'a vibrant philosophical inspiration affecting our whole way of looking at the world' [270].

1. Russell, L. J. (1), 405.
2. See, *e.g.*, Schaff (21), 4–5.
3. Schaff (28), 92–93.
4. At the beginning, Party members on the university teaching staff were themselves diffident as to whether they could be a match for their non-Marxist colleagues. They had to be encouraged by the assurance of Party support through the State administration. See Rybicki (1), 43, 48.
5. Schaff (21), 10; Hochfeld (3), 110–115; Żółkiewski (11), 44.
6. *Sesja* (2), 154; Ossowski (16), 220.
7. Antoniewicz (1).
8. Szczepański (8).
9. Chałasiński (11), 4.
10. M. Jaroszyński, professor of administrative law at Warsaw University, was the spokesman of this minority. See, *e.g.*, Jaroszyński (1).
11. Chałasiński (11), 3, 5.
12. *Tezy dyskusyjne* (1), 99–102. For a fuller summary of the agreed views about what the prospective reform of higher education should achieve see Leśnodorski (1), 242–248.
13. This development of events is described in Wojciechowska (1), 519–521.
14. This was described as an achievement of the first order since it enabled the 'seizure of control over the process of change towards socialism' (Jaroszyński (2), 48, 58).
15. The fact that the imposition of Marxist-Leninist doctrines and of political scholars on the universities was one of the important purposes of the educational reform was clearly stated by the Minister of Education. See J. K. (1), 342; Krassowska (2), 1; Żółkiewski (11), 54. Although Marxist-Leninist scholars themselves recognised their inadequate academic qualifications, their appointment to university chairs was urged on account of their political beliefs which in spite of their academic deficiencies would make them a driving force of progress. See Piotrowski (1), 496.
16. Dembowski (3), 27.
17. Schaff (15), 40-41; Schaff (12), 28–29.
18. Kotarbiński (10), 228.
19. Stonert (1), 253.
20. *Obrady* (1), 367. The first volume of *Studia Logica,* dated 1953, appeared at the beginning of 1954 as a yearly publication. Although articles on logic continued to be published in *Fundamenta Mathematicae,* and occasionally also in other mathematical periodicals, *Studia Logica* could not cope with manuscripts waiting for print (Kotarbiński (10), 227). There was no volume of *Studia Logica* for 1954 but two volumes appeared in 1955, one in 1956, two in 1957, and two in 1958.
21. Grzegorczyk (5), 347. At the first meeting the discussion was concerned with the problems of definition and the classification of reasonings (Ajdukiewicz (28), Kotarbińska (5)). The logicians never ceased to demand that the restrictions imposed upon them should be removed. See, *e.g.*, Ajdukiewicz (25), 58–67; Ajdukie-

wicz (29), 269–272; Grzegorczyk (5), 340–343. At the conferences of logicians held in following years logic was expanding and crossed the boundary line which was to separate it from the realm assigned to dialectics. See *Konferencja* (1), 43; Suszko (6), 232; Kokoszyńska (9); Łuszczewska-Romahnowa (4); Czerwiński (4); Greniewski (7). The delimitation of the subject-matter between logic and dialectics and the subordination of the former to the latter was finally abolished in 1956.

22. At the time when the teaching of sociology was discontinued some two hundred undergraduates were reading sociology as their main subject of study (Chałasiński (15), 589).

23. Three volumes of such theses were published in the years 1955–1956, and one of them was an opening volume in the philosophical series.

24. Bierut (1), 505; Schaff (15), 47.

25. This group includes Czerwiński, Giedymin, Lazari-Pawłowska, Malewski, Pawłowski, Pelc, Przełęcki, Szaniawski.

26. Dembowski (3), 29; Dembowski (5), 11.

27. See, *e.g.*, Dembowski (3), 29–31; Żółkiewski (11), 61.

28. Orthwein (1), 98–99; *Obrady* (1), 361–364; Chałasiński (20); Baley (2) and (4); Suchodolski (5) and (6); Tomaszewski (1) and (2).

29. Lewicka-Strelcyn (1), 305; Klemensiewicz (1), 187.

30. Konorski paid the penalty for having refused to join the cult of Pavlov by not being appointed a member of the Academy. See Chałasiński (32), 28. Physiologists in other People's Democracies were warned before their visits to Poland to shun him. See *Biologia i polityka* (1), 90. Konorski was elected a member of the Academy in 1956. The announcement of his election mentioned Konorski (1) as his important contribution to science, that is, the work that previously found no favour with Marxist-Leninists.

31. Schaff (15), 32, 40; *Obrady* (1), 354–355; *Życie Nauki* (1), 531.

32. Jabłoński (2), 5.

33. Dembowski (3), 34–35; Żółkiewski (8), 30–31; *Sesja* (1), 78–84; Jabłoński (1), 14, 22.

34. *Sesja* (2), 53, 79–81; Chałasiński (32), 16; Ajdukiewicz (12) and (32).

35. Chałasiński (32), 10; *Sesja* (2), 67–68, 79; Jabłoński (2), 14–15.

36. What follows is based on the disclosures made at the meeting of the General Assembly, held in June, 1956. See *Sesja* (2); Jarnuszkiewicz (1); Chałasiński (32).

37. This informal organisation of the Academy can be discerned in the plans made in Żółkiewski (8), 34–38. The way in which the informal organisation operated has been described by Infeld and Chałasiński. See *Sesja* (2), 43, 88–89; Chałasiński (32), 8–18, 25–32.

38. Jabłoński (2), 16, 19; Chałasiński (32), 16, 25–32.

39. Hochfeld (3), 112–115; Schaff (21), 10, 13, 17; Werfel (1), 43.

40. This was Professor Dembowski's expression (Dembowski (3), 23) which in the conditions prevailing at that time was hard to answer and damning for those to whom it referred. Similar accusations against those defending the autonomy and freedom of science were raised in Żółkiewski (11), 51.

41. Particular examples of this technique are described in *Sesja* (2), 67, 80.

42. A detailed description of the tug-of-war between one of the regional societies and the Academy was published in 1957 (Wojciechowska 1). This particular effort at further centralisation was ultimately unsuccessful owing to the changes in the Academy accomplished in 1956.

43. Dembowski (3), 39–40.
44. Chałasiński (31), Nowakowski (1). In 1957 the Sociological Society numbered seventy four members and in 1959 this figure rose to one hundred and fifty.
45. At the beginning of 1957 the Philosophical Society numbered nearly three hundred and fifty members.
46. Bromberg (1), 33–38.
47. Among the books whose publication was held up for years – as is stated in their respective prefaces – were Znamierowski (9) and (10), Krokiewicz (7).
48. Particular cases of this kind, based on personal experience, are described in Chałasiński (30), 5; *Biologia i polityka* (1), 66.
49. See Wojciechowska (1), 536, where the bitterness and resentment at the censorship and its methods are described.
50. Nusbaum's work first appeared in 1910. When it was republished in 1952 the editors were not satisfied with adding a new chapter, which would bring the history of evolutionism in biology up to date, but corrected the text throughout in such a manner that nobody knew what was the original text and what was re-written. The work, with Nusbaum's name as its author, was lengthened by about one-third, brought into line with the so-called new biology of Lysenko and Le-peshinskaya and expurgated of what was described as 'errors and wrong views'. Only one young philosopher raised a protest against the manner in which Nusbaum's book was republished. See Kochański (1). – The translation of Pestalozzi's work that reappeared in 1955 simply left out two chapters for they lacked, according to the explanation of the editors, pedagogical interest or had a fideistic content. By then circumstances were greatly changed and the indignation was publicly and strongly voiced. See Csorba (1).
51. Dembowski (3), 42; Budzyk (3), 124–126; Bromberg (1), 25.
52. 'The Library of Philosophy Classics' includes the works of Plato, Aristotle, Lucretius, Marcus Aurelius, Plotinus, Francis Bacon, Berkeley, Locke, Hume, Hobbes, Herschel, Bentham, Descartes, Spinoza, Leibniz, Kant, Fichte, Hegel, Feuerbach, Mandeville, Condillac, Holbach, Mably, Morelly, Rousseau, Voltaire, Condorcet, De la Mettrie, Meslier, d'Alembert, J. S. Mill. Works of some Polish and Russian philosophers of the past also appeared in this series (Staszyc, Śniadecki, Lomonosov, Belinsky, Chernyshevsky, Dobroljubov, Dembowski, Kamieński, and many others).
53. After the end of hostilities the Academy of Science and Learning in Cracow started the publication of a series of philosophical works in Polish translation which included the first Polish translation of Hume's *A Treatise of Human Nature*. Outside the 'Library of Philosophy Classics' there appeared in the 'fifties the translation of the works of Thomas More, Campanella, Galileo, Pascal, Rousseau, Voltaire, Diderot, St. Augustine, Thomas Aquinas, Russell, Dewey, James, Bergson, Gilson, and many others.
54. Dembowski (5), 12. By the end of 1955 nearly 2,600 research workers were permanently employed by the various institutes. This figure did not include the personnel of the Institute of Nuclear Research.
55. Fritzhand (5), 332.
56. *Komitet* (1), 388.
57. Kotarbiński (8), published that yea⁻, made the first breach, through which later an increasing stream of non-Marxist publications began to flow.
58. Schaff (21), 8.
59. Schaff (15), 26.

60. Schaff (10), 139.
61. Schaff (10), 137–149; Schaff (12), 107–116.
62. Hoffman (2), 56.
63. Schaff (10), 149–151; Michajłow (1); Dembowski (1), 361. This happened at the beginning of 1949. The cult of Lysenko, the 'greatest biologist since Darwin', came two years later.
64. Schaff (15), 38–39.
65. *Sprawozdanie* (1), 8–9.
66. Bromberg (1), 85, 87.
67. Bychowski (1), whose more objectionable passages were deleted in the translation. For the critical comments see *Kronika* (1), 462–463.
68. Czeżowski (19), Elzenberg (3), Tatarkiewicz (11). See E.S., B. K. (1), 237.
69. *Posiedzenie* (1); *Posiedzenie* (2); A. Z. (1). The members of the editorial committee, which replaced the editorial board, were as follows: Schaff, Chałasiński, Hochfeld, Baczko, Kołakowski, Sosnowski, Suchodolski. The first six issues of *Myśl Filozoficzna* were favourably reviewed in *Voprosy Filosofii* which in particular stressed that Polish Marxist-Leninists were perfectly capable of coping with the Warsaw school and of 'routing' the 'idealists' (*Voprosy Filosofii* (1)).
70. See Frank (3), 354–360.
71. Perry (1), 246.
72. Schaff (14), 213–218. The source of these views, common to Marxist-Leninists everywhere, was Zhdanov (1), 83–84.
73. *Myśl Filozoficzna* (1), 11; Schaff (15), 21.
74. Popper (2), 360–365.
75. Stalin (2), 47, 9; Schaff (15), 22–23.
76. *Myśl Filozoficzna* (1), 7–8, 10; Schaff (15), 19, 23–26; Baczko (2), 247–248.
77. Chałasiński (9), 8; Kotarbiński (15), T. 1, 678-679; Ossowski (14), 84–85.
78. Baczko (2), 287–288.
70. Schaff (20), 207; Kołakowski (4), 336-337, 351–355. The fact that conventionalism might be a dangerous instrument in the hands of those anxious to uphold the existing order of society was emphasised by Chwistek, who, however, did not ascribe this intention either to Poincaré or to other conventionalist philosophers (Chwistek (3), 234).
80. Schaff (12), 28–38; Schaff (14), 214, 333, 375; Schaff (16), 213, 254–255. In their views on logical empiricism Polish Marxist-Leninists were strongly influenced by Maurice Cornforth's *Science versus Idealism* and *In Defence of Philosophy* which were translated into Polish. Their knowledge of logical empiricism was based more on Cornforth's books than on a study of the original works of logical empiricists.
81. See, *e.g.*, Kołakowski (6), 75–76.
82. Russell (5), 10.
83. Kotarbiński (15), T. 2, 69–96, 87–88.
84. Kłósak (11).
85. Kołakowski (17), 619–620; Kroński (9), 244–245.
86. Schaff (15), 24.
87. Schaff (15), 32–33.
88. Schaff (15), 30–31.
89. Zhdanov (1), 79–83, 91, 96–97.
90. *Obrady* (1), 353, 367.
91. *Obrady* (1), 352; Baczko (2), 289; Baczko (3), 132–133; *Myśl Fizoficzna* (2).

92. Schaff (15), 35, 44; Schaff (14), 375–376; *Myśl Filozoficzna* (1).
93. Chałasiński (7), 152–155; Kotarbiński (15), T. 2, 501–516.
94. See Kołakowski (6), 67–74, 214–240. The statement about the similarities between Marxism-Leninism and Christian philosophy comes from Wetter (1), 556.
95. Schaff (15), 35–36; Schaff (14), 377–381.
96. *Obrady* (1), 352; Rybicki (1), 45.
97. Żółkiewski (7), 61–62. Żółkiewski does not subscribe to this evaluation any longer. See Żółkiewski (13). The interest in Ingarden as an art theorist has considerably increased in Poland in recent years. See Morawski (1), Pelc (2), Gierulanka-Połtawski (1), Kmita (1).
98. *Obrady* (1), 354–356; Schaff (15), 36–38.
99. Schaff (15), 43; Schaff (7), 255-258.
100. Znaniecki (2), 551.
101. See, *e.g.*, Kołakowski (12), 53–68; Schaff (36), 31, 34.
102. Kołakowski (12), 68.
103. *Obrady* (1), 355; Kotarbiński (15), T. 2, 183, 192–193; Ajdukiewicz (26), 312–313, 327–328.
104. Compare Kołakowski (12), 61–67.
105. Zhdanov (1), 87–88.
106. Kotarbiński (15), T. 2, 192, 199; Kotarbiński (7).
107. Schaff (36), 34.
108. Schaff (16) and (20), Baczko (2) and (3), Kołakowski (4), Chałasiński (22), Holland (1).
109. Schaff (15), 37, 40; Suszko (6), 233.
110. Schaff (14), 87, 95; Schaff (20), 222; Holland (1), 308–310.
111. Tarski (5), 165.
112. *Obrady* (1), 352–353; Schaff (16), 209–212, 254–255.
113. Holland (1), 310. This diagnosis follows closely Lenin's evaluation of positivism and empirio-criticism as represented by Mach, Avenarius, Petzold and their adherents.
114. Holland (1), 269–271, 310–312. Readers familiar with Lenin's *Materialism and Empirio-Criticism* will easily recognise that Holland again closely followed Lenin's criticism of Avenarius' views on the mind-body relation (Lenin (2), 76–84).
115. Ingarden suggested that the method of investigation used by Twardowski was essentially that of phenomenology. His neutral attitude to metaphysical problems corresponded to what later became known as 'phenomenological reduction' (Ingarden (10), 23).
116. Kotarbiński (15), T. 2, 7.
117. Holland (1), 278–289.
118. Lenin (2), 351.
119. The monistic fallacy, conceived as a methodological rule in historical inquiry, is most clearly formulated in Kołakowski (6), 72, 117–118, 144–145.
120. Holland (1), 271, 281–283, 294, 300.
121. Holland (1), 288, 295, 311.
122. Holland (1), 300–301.
123. Kotarbiński (9), 495–496; Kotarbiński (15), T. 2, 184–188, 194–195.
124. Kotarbiński (3), T. 1, 128–133; Kotarbiński (9), 493–494.
125. Baczko (2), 267. Baczko considered the rejection of the sentence in inverted commas as an implied or disguised support for psychophysical parallelism which of course it is not.

126. Kotarbiński (3), T. 1, 123–124.
127. The question whether these hypotheses are metaphysical beliefs in Popper's sense lies outside the scope of this study.
128. Baczko (2), 262.
129. Compare Kotarbiński (15), T. 2, 193–194, 201–202.
130. Baczko (2), 255, 257, 262, 278–279.
131. Engels (1), 177–178.
132. Polanyi (1), 7–11.
133. Popper (4), 177–178.
134. Schaff (14), 271–273; Schaff (16), 209–210, 216, 243, 253.
135. See, *e.g.,* Nagel (2), 241–246.
136. Compare Ajdukiewicz (8), 161; Kotarbiński (15), T. 2, 747–748.
137. Jørgensen (1), 54.
138. Carnap (1), XIII–XVI, 280–281; Łukasiewicz (17), 126–130; Ajdukiewicz (8), 151; Zawirski (7), 6–7.
139. See Jaśkowski (2), 278–279; Zawirski (3), 283–284 and also: Kokoszyńska (1) and (2A).
140. See Ajdukiewicz (11), Kotarbińska (3) and (4).
141. Carnap (1), 301, 310–311.
142. Based on Ajdukiewicz's information given orally to the author.
143. See, *e.g.,* Carnap (5), IX–XII, 29.
144. The distinction is Russell's. See Russell (6), 289–290.
145. Carnap (1), 51–52; Carnap (7), 206–208, 220–221.
146. The only exception was Ajdukiewicz's radical conventionalism, which in Schaff's opinion was an extension of Carnap's 'principle of tolerance' to the whole field of knowledge. See Schaff (14), 332, 357.
147. Schaff (14), 272; Schaff (16), 251.
148. Schaff (16), 209, 212; Schaff (20), 209; Baczko (2), 251; Holland (1), 298–301.
149. Ajdukiewicz emphasised this point in his polemical exchanges with Schaff but his efforts were of no avail. See Ajdukiewicz (26), 306.
150. See, *e.g.,* Baczko (2), 252–253; Baczko (3), 24–25.
151. Tarski (3), 17.
152. Nagel (2), 327–330, 347–348; Gardner (1), 281–288; Black (1), 223–246. The first public recognition that 'general semantics' and the philosophical and logical semantics differ in some important respects is to be found in Buczyńska (1).
153. Schaff (16), 255; Schaff (14), 358–359, 366–367.
154. Stalin (2), 15, 29–30, 49–51; Schaff (16), 214–215, 223; Schaff (14), 10–11. See also Schaff (2), 13–15; Schaff (32), 24–35.
155. Carnap (2), 6; Carnap (6), 78–80.
156. Schaff (16), 216, 224–225; Baczko (3), 18–21; Holland (1), 307–308.
157. This was pointed out in Kotarbiński (15), T. 2, 189; Ajdukiewicz (26), 296–297.
158. They are reviewed in Kotarbińska (6).
159. Semantics might be 'idealist' in another sense. Semantics may be conceived as a general discipline, which applies to a comprehensive class of freely invented languages, not necessarily of the lowest type. In general or pure semantics, abstract entities are admitted as designata which seems to commit it to Platonic realism or idealism in the Marxist-Leninist sense. But the usefulness of semantical methods making use of abstract linguistic forms is doubtful when they are applied to languages of communication or languages of science. Moreover, this objection could not be raised against the Warsaw school semantics which was invariably concerned

with a single historical or ethnical language, and, in the case of Kotarbiński, was clearly and consistently nominalist in character.

160. Lenin (2), 353; Schaff (16), 215–216, 254–256.
161. Baczko (2), 254–255; Baczko (3), 56.
162. Kotarbiński (15), T. 2, 189–190, 201–202.
163. Schaff (16), 217.
164. This was already recognised in the 'thirties. See Carnap (2), 8; Nagel (2), 246.
165. Ajdukiewicz (10), (16), (17), (23).
166. Schaff (16), 226–228, 247.
167. Ajdukiewicz (23), 10; Carnap (1), 301, 313–315.
168. Ajdukiewicz (26), 308–310; Ingarden (12), T. 1, 23, 148–149.
169. Poincaré (1), 117.
170. Ajdukiewicz (5), 129.
171. This weaker version of radical conventionalism, as applied to physical theories, was discussed in popular form in Ajdukiewicz (14).
172. Frege (1), 62.
173. There is some apparent similarity between the starting position of Ajdukiewicz and that of C. I. Lewis in *Mind and the World Order*, but their respective methods of solving the problem of communicability are essentially different.
174. Ryle (2), 256.
175. Ajdukiewicz (5), 105.
176. Ajdukiewicz (5), 113–116; Ajdukiewicz (22), 182.
177. The concept of a closed and connected language is defined in Ajdukiewicz (5), 120–123. This definition is not reproduced here since Ajdukiewicz has recognised that it is of no use in the examination of any existing language (Ajdukiewicz (26), 317).
178. For the concept of world picture see Ajdukiewicz (6), 278; Ajdukiewicz (22), 316–317.
179. Ajdukiewicz (6), 278–285. It must be recalled that a thesis of one closed and connected language cannot be translated into a thesis of another and *vice versa*.
180. Ajdukiewicz (6), 278–279; Ajdukiewicz (22), 324–325.
181. The differentiation between the semantical and the pragmatical approach to the problem of meaning is clearly, though marginally, made in Ajdukiewicz (5), 105.
182. Schaff (16), 231–233.
183. Schaff (16), 234–235, 237–240; Kołakowski (4), 358–359. Ajdukiewicz forestalled these objections and showed why they do not apply but they remained unnoticed by his critics. See Ajdukiewicz (6), 270–271, 278–279.
184. Kołakowski (4), 336–337, 358–360; Baczko (2), 263–264. Conventionalism is for Marxist-Leninists exactly the opposite to what it is to some other philosophers who see in it the quest for certainty in knowledge and an indication of progress in the logical foundations of any science. See, *e.g.,* Quine (4), 250.
185. Ajdukiewicz (22), Schaff (20).
186. *Myśl Filozoficzna* (2), 337; Schaff (20), 201, 211–212; Schaff (21), 14.
187. See, *e.g.,* Kotarbiński (3), T. 1, 85–87; Kotarbiński (16), 206–207; Ajdukiewicz (2), 9; Czeżowski (11), 226.
188. Quoted in Ingarden (12), T. 1, 173.
189. Kotarbiński (15), T. 2, 25–36, 161–182. The reaction of Marxist-Leninists can best be seen from Baczko (3), 45–66 and also from Chałasiński (22).
190. Husserl (1), 153, 168.
191. Kroński (1), 47; Kroński (2), 330.

192. According to Kroński (2), 321, the 'phenomenological secession' rejected what Husserl called *Epoche* and by this step abandoned Husserl's subjective idealism. This is not correct.
193. Kroński (1), 34, 54–55; Kroński (2), 329.
194. Kroński (1), 54; Schaff (14), 161; Farber (1), 619.
195. Perry (1), 113, 119.
196. See Schaff (15), 35–36; Schaff (14), 377–378. Kroński was somewhat uneasy about putting Neo-Thomism and phenomenology into the same class and conceded that perhaps neither of them can be called 'objective idealism'.
197. It appears most improbable, Ingarden writes, that the solution of the controversy between realism and idealism suggested by Husserl is correct (Ingarden (12), T. 1, 13). The justification of this assertion is scattered throughout his work. Ingarden's critical attitude to positivism and neo-positivism is very apparent in his various parenthetical remarks and comes out most clearly in his examination of the 'class conception of the individual object', which conceives it as a 'bundle of compresent qualities' (Ingarden (12), T. 2, 193–205). So far as intentional objects are concerned see Ingarden (12), T. 2, 263.
198. Kroński (1), 49, 53–54; Kroński (2), 318–319, 321, 330.
199. Farber (1), 609–614; Bocheński (8), 22–35.
200. Lukács (1), 573–577.
201. Lukács' influence is particularly apparent in Kroński's writings. Husserl's views on science, its lack of 'scientific grounding' and its supposed dogmatic standpoint are fully endorsed in Ingarden (12), T. 1, 27–39.
202. Ingarden (12), T. 1, 67.
203. Ingarden (12), T. 1, 58–59.
204. Lewis (1), 30.
205. Farber (1), 591–600, 609–616.
206. Kroński (2), 318.
207. Lukács (1), 572–574; Kroński (2), 330–331.
208. See Bocheński (11), 153; Farber (1), 611–612; Lukács (1), 589–590. It may be incidentally observed that this objection does not fully apply to Ingarden's phenomenology. Ingarden was aware of the fact that 'objective reality', as conceived in the phenomenological school, was reduced to the status of a twin brother of the 'bracketed reality'. This was one of the reasons why he differentiated ontology and metaphysics, a distinction which Husserl, strictly speaking, was unable to make, and supplemented the former by the latter. See Ingarden (12), T. 1, 53, 57, 67–71, 175.
209. Ingarden (11), 5–14.
210. The recognition of physical reality, its irreducibility to intentional existence, which is emphatically stated in the essay in question, is again strongly underlined in Ingarden (12), T. 2, 260–268.
211. Kroński (2), 319. The other source of arguments to support the Marxist-Leninist evaluative interpretation of Ingarden's phenomenology was his numerous works on the theory of art in which he advocated 'formalism'. This term was to indicate that Ingarden recommended that the ontological structure of a work of art should be carried out in abstraction from any social significance it might possibly have. Since the insistence on this significance was a fundamental principle of the Marxist-Leninist theory of art, 'formalism' was decreed to be a hostile view and Ingarden one of the main opponents of Marxism-Leninism in this particular field of research.
212. Kroński (1), 45–46, 52–53; Kroński (2), 320, 324, 327–329.

213. Kołakowski (6), 106–107; Baczko-Kołakowski (1), 91. This view on the Cartesian method of universal doubt is shared by those who take Marx's second thesis on Feuerbach as their point of departure in the theory of knowledge. See Kołakowski (18), 12.

214. Ingarden (12), T. 1, 158–159. This is the main passage in Ingarden's work which in the opinion of his critics shows that the refutation of materialism is the main purpose of his work.

215. Lewis (1), 9.

216. Ingarden (12), T. 2, 822, 825. This is emphasised throughout the work. See in particular T. 1, 155–156.

217. Ingarden (12), T. 2, 725–825.

218. Ingarden (12), T. 2, 844–846.

219. Ingarden (12), T. 1, 157–160, 286–296, T. 2, 837.

220. Perry (1), 118–119, 126–129.

221. This is no longer accepted by the younger Marxist-Leninists.

222. Schaff (14), 296–297; Baczko (11), 10.

223. Hochfeld (3), 131.

224. Znaniecki made some incisive observations on these matters a few years before they acquired a topical interest in Poland. See Znaniecki (8), 69–78.

225. Chałasiński (34), 142–143.

226. Many of Znaniecki's and Merton's comments on the predicament of specialists in the field of social, economic, and political knowledge, in their relations with the Government and its agencies, apply to Polish sociologists and account for what happened, both when they originally tried to adjust themselves to the prevailing circumstances and when later they led the revolt against the conformity. See Znaniecki (10), 412–419; Merton (1), 207–224.

227. Znaniecki (5). 90–100, 130–139.

228. Chałasiński (20), 76, 78. Hochfeld made similar charges and expressed them in such abusive language that he deprived them of all plausibility. See Hochfeld (3), 113. The best balanced evaluation of American sociology is to be found in Szczepański (7).

229. Znaniecki (5), 26–28.

230. Merton (1), 85-86 and the literature quoted there, Parsons (2), chapter 11 and 17. Chałasiński who was widely read in American sociological literature emphasised its false theoretical assumptions rather than their total absence. See Chałasiński (20), 80.

231. Merton (1), 5–6, 85–101.

232. Popper (4), 155–163.

233. Znaniecki (5), 229–234.

234. Hochfeld (3), 147; Chałasiński (20), 84–85; Schaff (17), 234.

235. Schaff (17), 223–227, 231–248, 253–254; Kowalski (1), 15–20, 26–27.

236. The distinction between the natural and cultural sciences in Znaniecki's sense is not identical or even related, as Schaff suggested, to that of the idiographic and the nomothetic sciences of Windelband and Rickert (Schaff (22), 160-161). Znaniecki expressly rejected the view that there are sciences, including history, which would not combine the generalising and individualising way of thinking. See Znaniecki (5), 23–26, 259.

237. Szczepański (1) and (2).

238. Znaniecki himself accepted the verdict that the method of personal documents was 'methodically defective'. See Znaniecki (10), 238. The criticism made in Poland and

the United States was summarised in Szczepański (4). Szczepański has also done a great deal to transplant in Poland new sociological methods and research techniques worked out abroad. See Szczepański (5). The Marxist-Leninist criticism of the personal documents method, to be found in Schaff (17), is behind the times and falls short of that accomplished by 'bourgeois sociology'.

239. Znaniecki (5), 217–218.
240. Znaniecki (5), 34–36, 155, 172–173.
241. Znaniecki (10), 132–136; Znaniecki (5), 36–43; Znaniecki (9), 205–207.
242. Znaniecki (5), 267–268; Znaniecki (8), 192–194.
243. Znaniecki (10), 7, 115.
244. Znaniecki (5), 55, 207; Znaniecki (10), 140.
245. Znaniecki (5), 295–296; Znaniecki (10), 198–204.
246. This is the meaning of 'idealism' in which this term is used in White (1), 357–372.
247. Znaniecki (10), 132, 138, 151.
248. Schaff (12), 285–397; Schaff (8) and (9); Antoszczuk (1); Baczko (1); Hoffman (1); Kuziński (1); Osiadacz (1). On the other hand, Białobłocki, a contemporary of Krusiński and Krzywicki, was elevated to the rank of the first revolutionary Marxist literary critic in Poland. See Sandler (1) and the ensuing discussion in Osiadacz (2), Sandler (2).
249. *Obrady* (1), 358–359, 364–365; Assorodobraj (2), 126–139.
250. Precision of speech and thought was not one of Znaniecki's strong points and this caused considerable frictions between Znaniecki and the Warsaw school. Without naming any of the Warsaw school thinkers, Znaniecki often retaliated. See, *e.g.*, Znaniecki (5), 238–245; Znaniecki (8), 147–148. Ossowski, Szczepański and Znamierowski represented the tendency of emulating in sociology the example of the Warsaw school. Chałasiński has remained close to Znaniecki in this respect.
251. Ossowski (15), Ossowska (12).
252. Ossowski was accused of being a supporter of Gomułka's ideology just at the time when the latter was arrested and waiting for trial. See Hochfeld (3), 127. This accusation exposed Ossowski to great personal danger and he was lucky not to have suffered more than he did.
253. *Obrady* (1), 357–358; Hochfeld (3), 119–129; Schaff (17), 227–231, 241–248.
254. *Obrady* (1), 360–364; Chałasiński (20) and (22), 314; Schaff (17), 228, 248–249; Schaff (28), 48.
255. *Obrady* (1), 364–365; Hochfeld (3), 129, 153; Schaff (17), 232, 257. See also Szczepański (6), 261–265. Szczepański's determination to exercise a moderating influence was skilfully performed but not particularly successful.
256. Lenin (2), 331–332; Schaff (17), 227–231.
257. Hochfeld-Nowakowski (1). This article reads as if it were a malicious satire on the Marxist-Leninist research techniques, written by a determined opponent of Marxism-Leninism, but this effect was, of course, not intended.
258. Weber (2), 80–81.
259. See, *e.g.*, Bauman-Wiatr (1), 70–71; Hochfeld-Nowakowski (1), 248–249.
260. Schumpeter (1), 18–19, 45.
261. See Chałasiński (34), 146.
262. This term was introduced by Kott (Kott (1), T. 2, 350–351) and widely used since 1956.
263. Hochfeld (3), 106–109, 112–115.
264. Nowakowski (1), 326.
265. Some representative examples of quasi-sociological contributions published at

that time are provided by Chałasiński (23) and (24); Hochfeld (4), (5) and (6); Wiatr (1); Bauman-Wiatr (1); Litwin (2) and (4). The question often asked by Marxist-Leninists why practice did not prevent their theories and actions from wandering astray, was answered in Malewski (1), which is a notable contribution to the methodology of the social sciences.

266. Szacki (2), 38; Bauman-Wiatr (2), 8, 15–17; Schaff (26); Chałasiński (27) and (28).
267. Those who did not endorse this view have resigned themselves to the use of the expression 'historical materialism' and 'Marxist-Leninist sociology' as the name of a particular school of thought within sociology whose existence they no longer deny. See Schaff (28), 41–43; Wiatr (2), 209–213; Wiatr (3), 192–194; Hochfeld (8), 121.
268. Kołakowski (14), 174.
269. Bauman-Wiatr (2), 10–18; Kołakowski (14), 170–173.
270. Kołakowski (14), 174.

PART FOUR

FORMAL LOGIC AND DIALECTICS

INTRODUCTION

One of the fundamental and perhaps one of the most important principles of Marxist-Leninist philosophy is the assumption that internal contradictions are inherent in all things and in all phenomena of Nature. 'In its proper meaning', wrote Lenin, 'dialectics is the study of the contradictions within the very essence of things'[1]. The formulation and the context make it clear beyond any possible doubt that for Lenin there was nothing phenomenal (in the Kantian sense) about the contradictions; they are inherent in the *Ding an sich.*

From the historical viewpoint it would be untrue to say that any science, including mathematics and formal logic, is invariably free from contradiction. Consistency is not an inalienable privilege providentially granted to science; paradoxes, antinomies, and contradictions do appear in the advancement of knowledge. The history of the infinitesimal calculus, the theory of sets and of classes, or the development of semantical concepts testify to the fact that contradictions did occur in the past and continue to appear in the present. It is accepted, however, that the appearance of contradictions is a symptom of the imperfection of our knowledge and that they must be resolved if the distinction between truth and falsehood is to retain its meaning. It is also a matter of historical record that the resolution of contradictions results from or is followed by the expansion of scientific knowledge. For both these reasons, consistency is one of the supreme goals pursued by every science.

If we are to believe Lenin, this goal can never be achieved, nor is it worth striving for. Knowledge and contradiction are not mutually exclusive, but mutually inclusive. This truth is revealed by dialectics which 'is the theory of how opposites can be and commonly are identical, how they become and under what conditions they remain identical, when transforming from one to the other'[2].

A dialectical contradiction is defined either in terms of the so-called unity and struggle of the opposites or in terms of logic. We are told that as long as we consider things as static and lifeless, we do not run up against any contradictions in them. The 'position is quite different as soon as we consider things in their motion, their change, their life, their reciprocal influence on one another. Then we immediately become involved in contradiction'[3]. A body in motion does and does not occupy a given position, a changing object is and is not such and such at the same time. Change and motion are a contradiction, the principle

$$(x, \varphi) \sim (\varphi x . \sim \varphi x)$$

does not apply to them. Consequently, it is not true to say that contradictory statements are never true together. If X is the class of changing or moving bodies, then

$$(x, \varphi)(\exists \psi): \varphi x . \supset . \psi x . \sim \psi x.$$

263

Since it is 'possible to assert and deny the same', we obtain the dialectical metalogical principle of contradiction

$$T`\varphi x` . T`\sim \varphi x`\ [4].$$

For the same reason

$$(x, \varphi)(\exists\psi): \varphi x . \supset . \sim (\psi x \vee \sim \psi x),$$

from which follows the dialectical metalogical principle of the non-excluded middle

$$\sim (T`\varphi x` \vee T`\sim \varphi x`).$$

Finally, the principle of identity is no longer valid. With respect to moving and changing bodies 'abstract identity is totally inadequate' and must be replaced by the dialectical 'inclusion of difference within identity', the 'inseparability of identity and difference', the unity or identity of the opposites [5].

Thus, Marxist-Leninist philosophy appears to deny or to restrict the validity of formal logic, or at least the validity of some of its laws, as well as of their corresponding semantical formulations. It accepts Hegel's doctrine who rose above 'a fundamental prejudice of hitherto existing logic' and recognised in contradiction the truly essential and profound determination of being.

In this manner Marxist-Leninist philosophy has exposed itself to an easy criticism and to the objection of absurdity. A logically trained philosopher has no use for a system that denies the principle of non-contradiction. Let us assume that two sentences like 'p' and '$\sim p$' are true together. Then by means of a well known formula of propositional calculus

$$p . \supset . \sim p \supset q$$

we can by applying the detachment rule twice derive from these contradictory premisses an arbitrary sentence 'q', i.e. any sentence whatsoever. The rejection of the principle of non-contradiction results in complete arbitrariness of thought – true and false statements turn out to be equally valid. Moreover, if contradictory statements were true together, and a statement is true if it corresponds to what it asserts and false otherwise, no statement would be true or false and the difference between truth and falsehood would disappear. This, however, would be the end of philosophy, of science, of any rational thinking.

The disclosure that Marxism-Leninism has a logic of its own, in which the principle of non-contradiction is no longer valid, raises the question whether the admissibility of contradictions does not destroy the rational basis of any discussion. With the rejection of the principle of non-contradiction and of the excluded middle no reasoning, no argument, no confrontation of views is in fact possible. We can neither establish our own point, nor disprove that of our opponent, because in this procedure we have to make use of the rejected principles by pointing out the contradictions within the stated opinions or with the accepted premisses or with statements of fact. *Contra principia negantem,* the schoolmen of the Middle Ages used to say *non est disputandum.* Notwithstanding their declarations, Engels and Lenin also provided testimony in their writings that they were unable to dispense with the laws of logic.

With the rejection of the principle of non-contradiction Marxist-Leninist philosophy itself would face destruction. A Marxist-Leninist may reject the thesis that consciousness determines being, but he is logically bound to accept it, and for that matter any other statement with which he disagrees or which he specifically denies. He can escape this conclusion only by rejecting logic altogether. If he succeeds in actually achieving it, that is, if he actually disregards every rule of logic in his thinking and not merely says that he does, a Marxist-Leninist would reach mentally the point of no return. Not a philosopher but only a psychiatrist could be of help to him then.

The contention that Marxism-Leninism has a logic of its own, different from that commonly used, cannot be accepted in earnest. A Marxist-Leninist is not indifferent to the contradictions in his own system. He does not consider a contradiction as a valuable addition to his doctrine, but, on the contrary, declares it superior to any other by virtue of its being free from contradictions. The principle of non-contradiction must, after all, possess some merits [6].

Marxism-Leninism claims that it is a theory as well as a guide to action. In considering Marxist-Leninist solutions of abstract problems the question of what they imply in practice cannot, therefore, be overlooked. Change and motion, Marxism-Leninism contends, involve contradictions. A horse-race, a flood, a war, are certainly instances of change and motion. When a Marxist-Leninist goes to a horse-race does he bet on a horse because he assumes that it will both win and lose the race? Does not a Marxist-Leninist engineer act on the assumption that the flood might carry the bridge away or does he rather believe that the flood will and will not destroy it at the same time? Would not a Marxist-Leninist general be shot if in war he failed to apply the law of non-contradiction to his enemy's anticipated movements? Can a single example of sound reasoning that rejects this principle be given at all? [7].

To accept contradictions as a significant and permissible means of describing facts is to frustrate one of the main purposes of speech, expressing thoughts and conveying knowledge. A man who contradicts himself or utters contradictory statements may make audible sounds, but from the point of view of communicating facts it is as if he never opened his mouth. 'He utters words but does not say anything'[8]. If, as Marxist-Leninists contend, there is any 'profundity' in a conjunction of contradictory statements, in saying something and unsaying it, in combining expressions which cancel each other, this 'profundity' must remain forever inexpressible. If it is inexpressible, we can call it 'profundity' or by any other term. Without being aware of it, a Marxist-Leninist seems to inhabit a world more strange, more personal and more barred from communication with any other human being than Wittgenstein's world of the *Tractatus Logico-Philosophicus*. The approach to Wittgenstein's world leads through questions that can be put and answers that can be given. A Marxist-Leninist offers no Wittgensteinean ladder, the inexpressible faces us from the start. In spite of this fact a Marxist-Leninist follows just the opposite course to what No. 7 of the *Tractatus* enjoins us to.

It is the law of Duns Scotus which is responsible for making a system of statements, that includes a pair like 'p' and '$\sim p$', 'over-complete', *i.e.*, co-extensive with the set of all meaningful sentences of this system. There arises, therefore, the question whether a propositional calculus could be constructed which is rich enough to make reasoning possible and which does not permit the inference of an arbitrary statement from two contradictory premisses. This question has been successfully solved by Jaśkowski [9].

Jaśkowski's D_2 system, the so-called 'logic of discussion', contains many theorems of ordinary logic, is not consistent in the ordinary sense, that is to say, accepts statements of the 'p' and '$\sim p$' form, and is not 'absolutely inconsistent', *i.e.*, cannot be shown to be equivalent to the set of all the meaningful statements. Since the law of Duns Scotus is not a valid theorem of the 'logic of discussion', the inference of an arbitrary statement from two contradictory premisses is unjustifiable.

The usefulness of the 'logic of discussion' for Marxist-Leninist philosophy is, however, doubtful. An assertion of the 'logic of discussion' is a statement which contains terms with an ambiguous meaning and which can thus be asserted in a different sense by various participants in the discussion. Strictly speaking, 'p' and '$\sim p$' are not contradictory statements. They do not assert and deny the same or in the same respect. The law of non-contradiction is a theorem of the 'logic of discussion'. Also the formula

$$p . \sim p \supset q$$

holds in it [10].

It follows, therefore, that if one of the disputants asserts two statements, contradictory in the ordinary sense, to be true together, he is bound to accept any other arbitrary statement and his system becomes again 'over-complete'. The 'logic of discussion' does not allow any disputant to contradict himself, and thus it cannot grant what the dialectical law of contradiction seems to demand [11]. A Marxist-Leninist would not gain anything from the acceptance of the 'logic of discussion', unless he changed the meaning of what he calls 'contradiction'.

The philosophical purpose behind the 'logic of discussion' differs from that by which Marxism-Leninism is inspired. The recent developments in logic, such as Gödel's incompleteness theorem, the discovery of antinomial risks inherent in any semantically closed language, various antinomies and elaborate techniques intended to deal with them, impose considerable restrictions on the language and theoretical constructions. These restrictions are associated with formally complicated procedures and the abandonment of more ambitious schemes. They result in a more careful treatment of concepts, a more precise use of language, the ruling out of some word combinations from the domain of meaningful sentences. The advantages gained by these developments are as conspicuous as their disadvantages. Among the latter one of the most far-reaching is the tendency, as Professor Ryle put it, to become 'excessively microscopic', to 'stick too closely to the grindstone and go too little out into the wood' [12]. The possibility of formulating a comprehensive view of the world, construction of which requires a rich language and a high degree of freedom in using different logical procedures, moves further and further away. Jaśkowski wished to remedy this position and his 'weaker' logical system goes a little way in this direction. While contradictions *sensu stricto* are as much inadmissible in Jaśkowski's 'weaker' logic as in any other logical system, it does not exclude every kind of 'contradictory statements' and provides a guarantee against inferences that would involve us in asserting falsehood [13].

Unlike the 'logic of discussion' which was meant to be a particular subsidiary instrument of dealing with paradoxes and antinomies, Marxism-Leninism does not shun them. It accepts them as its starting point and considers them as an important part of knowledge of the external world to be incorporated in a comprehensive view of the world. If contradictions are inherent in the essence of things and phenomena of Nature, the inconsistencies in our knowledge need not necessarily be regarded as a falsehood.

The burden of this truth-destroying view, stubbornly defended for a few years, turned out to be too heavy for Marxist-Leninists in Poland. Faced by logicians and philosophers for whom no inconsistent theory could be significant, valid and true, Marxist-Leninists were at once driven to the defensive. They could spread and popularise their views among the philosophically uneducated and naive, but those with scientific training could not be really persuaded to accept Marxist-Leninist philosophy as a sound and justifiable system of beliefs. A Marxist-Leninist was tainted with absurdity through the mere enunciation of his fundamental principles [14].

Consequently, the relation of dialectics to formal logic became the main question at issue between Marxist-Leninist and non-Marxist philosophy. Very early in the day it was recognised by both sides that a satisfactory solution of this problem was a prerequisite of finding a common language in all other matters. Its orthodox solution, the rejection of the principles of non-contradiction and the condemnation of the whole of logic to oblivion, would create an abyss which nothing could bridge [15].

In this respect Polish Marxist-Leninists remained entirely isolated, unaided by anybody outside their own small circle of believers. Also those logicians who were not unsympathetic to some Marxist-Leninist opinions concerning the theory of logic, were clearly not on the side of Marxism-Leninism in so far as its views on the principle of non-contradiction and, in general, its attitude to formal logic were concerned. All 'over-complete' systems, wrote Greniewski, in agreement with every self-respecting logician, are equally useless and valueless [16].

267

CHAPTER 13

THE SUPERIORITY OF DIALECTICS

Prior to a closer examination of the arguments in support of the Marxist-Leninist views on formal logic and the principle of non-contradiction certain terminological distinctions must be made.

We often use the term 'logic' as an abbreviated form of the expression 'formal logic', but this is not by any means always the case. 'Logic' is sometimes used as the collective name denoting a historically developed subject of teaching consisting of a great variety of topics such as elements of formal logic, the theory of knowledge, methodology, psychology, sometimes metaphysics and recently also syntax and semantics. The only principle unifying all these various topics is the fact that they are taught by philosophers who hold the chair of logic at universities. 'Logic' probably has this broad meaning in all languages, and it is certainly used in this sense in Poland [17].

While this usage of the term 'logic' could be justified by some precedents, its widespread adoption at the present time reflects the high repute that logic now enjoys, even among thinkers who are not actually interested in formal logic. The usage is, however, misleading and inappropriate. It is misleading because it makes logic and philosophy indistinguishable. It is inappropriate because it tends to blur the important difference between the formal approach, peculiar to logic, and the non-formal analytic procedures applied in philosophy. It is simply untrue to say that a philosopher and a logician do or try to do the same thing. Deductive reasoning plays a considerable role in philosophical investigations. These investigations pursue, however, an objective entirely foreign to a logician. To make use of the rules of valid inference and to study them for their own sake are two basically different activities.

To define 'traditional logic' is perhaps more difficult than to say what is the object of logic in the broad sense of this term. A modern logician often applies the term 'traditional logic' to all systems of the past that were not conceived and presented on the pattern set by *Principia Mathematica*. This might be sufficient for practical purposes, but strictly speaking it is incorrect or at least misleading, for we would have to consider some parts of ancient logic to be a part of modern logic.

In the past the view was common that what we now call 'traditional logic' dealt with the forms of thought. Since Descartes already knew that our thoughts have no extension, it is clear that what was intended to be a definition was in fact a metaphor, which was not always harmless. It did lead sometimes to the so-called psychologism in logic, and psychologism was a mark of the decay of logic in modern philosophy.

The above definition of traditional logic can be accepted provided that 'forms of thought' are interpreted to mean 'forms of inference'. What seems to be the most general characteristic of logical investigations and what differentiates them from other studies on the 'forms of thought' is exactly the concern of logic with the rules or forms of inference. This concern is an important indication of whether some examinations belong to the field of logic, helps to establish its origin and the various periods of its development. Just for this reason, Bocheński is inclined to speak of Zeno's or Plato's logic, but not of that of the Pythagoreans, and his periodisation of the history of logic is based on the varying techniques of investigating rules of inference applied in different times [17a].

While some logicians prefer to consider modern formal logic as an entirely new discipline, which differs from the Aristotelian class logic as much as 'the railroad from the oxcart', others recognise in traditional logic the direct progenitor of modern formal logic with the same subject-matter, broadly speaking. The latter agree, however, that traditional logic differs from modern logic in three important respects. As a rule, traditional logic was not formal; its subject-matter was only a fragment of that investigated by modern formal logic; and the methods of traditional logic, compared with those applied at present, were at a pre-scientific stage of development. For all these reasons traditional logic could have been of little use, if any at all, either to philosophy or to science, to mathematics in particular. Many great philosophers of the past testified to this fact. On the other hand, the usefulness of modern formal logic is widely recognised by representatives of the empirical and deductive sciences. It provides a method which enables us to obtain knowledge that commands assent of all qualified persons.

Since the discussion of the relation of dialectics to formal logic requires a sharp distinction between the terms 'logic', 'traditional logic' and 'modern formal logic', the meaning of the last of these terms must be at least delimited. For this purpose Alonzo Church's initial definition might provide a starting point. According to Church, formal logic is concerned with the analysis of propositions and of proofs with attention paid to the form and in abstraction from the matter of content [18]. 'Form' in this context means as much as 'structure', and 'structure' can in turn be explained to mean 'arrangement' or 'order' in which things are found or put together. We can now restate Church's definition and say that formal logic is concerned with the relations that are revealed among objects of any kind when only their form is considered. The theory of the *A-E-I-O* relations in the field of universal terms, *i.e.* the logic of Aristotle as rediscovered by Łukasiewicz, Frege's, Russel's and Whitehead's, or Łukasiewicz's propositional calculus provide the simplest examples of what is meant by a system of modern formal logic.

Whenever Engels, Lenin, and Plekhanov discussed logic, the term 'logic' had the above indicated broad meaning, the various ingredients – metaphysics, the theory of knowledge, and methodology in particular – entering into it in different proportions. It is a common theme of *Anti-Dühring, Dialectics of Nature, Philosophical Notebooks,* and *Dialectic and Logic* that – in Marxian or Marxist-Leninist materialism – logic, the theory of knowledge, and dialectics either converge or become identical. There is no need of three words, Lenin wrote, for what is a single discipline. Engels called this single discipline the 'science of thought'. It is 'like every other, a historical science', it assumes different contents at different times. It must be, therefore, distinguished from the 'philistine' conception of logic which tries to establish the 'laws of thought' as 'eternal truth'. Thus, logic in the broad sense, either dialectical or non-dialectical is not a new kind of logic in the strict sense, different from traditional or formal logic, but something not to be compared with the latter [19].

Engels, Lenin, and Plekhanov also used the term 'formal logic', but what they then had in mind had nothing in common with modern formal logic. They spoke of formal logic, but referred in fact to traditional logic. Engels drew his knowledge of 'formal logic' from Hegel's *Wissenschaft der Logik* and *Enzyklopädie der philosophischen Wissenschaften*; Lenin derived it from the same sources, to which some histories of philosophy and some of Aristotle's works should be added. Plekhanov was the most advanced of the three, since apart from Engels' and Lenin's sources he also studied Überweg's *System der Logik* (first published in 1857) and Tredelenburg's *Logische Untersuchungen* (first published in 1870).

The idea of traditional logic which we find in the writings of the founders of Marxism-Leninism was mainly inspired by Hegel and had the imprint of his conception of logic. Hegel's objection to traditional logic was that it was infused with the wrong kind of metaphysics. He set about correcting this error and by his enrichments he accomplished the complete divorce of logic from science. Engels, Lenin, and Plekhanov admired Hegel for this achievement and saw in him a great reformer of logic instead of its grave-digger. They had not the slightest inkling of another reforming trend initiated by George Boole and Augustus De Morgan about the middle of the last century, which was gathering strength at the time when Lenin and Plekhanov were philosophically most active. The direction in which Engels, Lenin, and Plekhanov wished traditional logic to develop was just the opposite of the one it has actually taken to resume its progress and to be transformed into modern formal logic.

The pronouncements of Engels, Lenin, and Plekhanov, which are still quoted with awe and respect to support the present-day views on the relation of dialectics to logic, as a rule confuse different meanings in which the term 'logic' is used. On the one hand, they compare dialectical logic in the broad meaning with non-dialectical logic in the narrower and more technical sense of this term. On the other, 'formal logic', to which their pronouncements refer, means in fact 'traditional logic', to be sharply distinguished from 'modern formal logic'. Consequently, what Engels, Lenin, and Plekhanov said about the relation of dialectical and non-dialectical logic in the past is not only open to objection, but also irrelevant to present-day problems. Whatever the relation of dialectics to formal logic might be, the pronouncements of Engels, Lenin, and Plekhanov provide no help to its elucidation and evaluation.

This remains unnoticed by Marxist-Leninists in general, those in Poland in particular. The same terminological confusions, of which Engels, Lenin, and Plekhanov were guilty, are very àpparent in their own writings whenever they discuss logical matters. 'Formal logic' remains for them an ambiguous term, to denote both traditional and modern formal logic. Their comments on the former interfuse with those on the latter and it is hardly ever possible to decide which of them they have in mind. The considerable advance beyond traditional logic achieved in modern formal logic is largely ignored and little appreciated. While Engels could not know that traditional logic was not formal, because at that time formal logic did not yet exist, and Lenin could have become acquainted with it, had he wished and tried hard, there is no such excuse for a contemporary Marxist-Leninist philosopher.

The task of presenting and defining the Marxist-Leninist views on the 'dogma of traditional logic', the principle of non-contradiction, was undertaken by Schaff [20]. He set about it with an apparent effort to dissociate these views from their Hegelian anti-rationalistic tradition and to accommodate them to what he considered to be the requirements of scientific thinking.

Three different stages might be distinguished in Schaff's argument intended to justify the contention that the ontological principle of non-contradiction is false and that its logical and semantical formulations must be, therefore, rejected. The first tried to establish the epistemological superiority of dialectics over formal logic. The second discussed the foundations of formal logic and placed their dialectical revision within a more general trend of thought, the aim of which is to clarify the foundations of logic. The actual criticism of the ontological principle of non-contradiction followed last. Schaff did not distinguish these three stages and in his argument they were interwoven with each other. It appears, however, that his argument becomes somewhat clearer if the three stages in question are kept separate.

Two main considerations were put forward by Schaff to support the thesis concerning the superiority of dialectics over formal logic. The first of them emphasised that the cognitive value of logical laws is *nil*. Thus, the law of identity, to which he gave the form $A = A$, but which he wants to be read: for all A (A is A), is either false or trivial. It is false if it implies that nothing changes; it is trivial if it means no more than it says. A law that does not add anything to our knowledge is an empty tautology, as was rightly pointed out already by Hegel. Finally, if the law of identity is interpreted to mean that the meaning of any term should be kept invariable throughout the inference in which it is used, the law of identity is reduced to a mere linguistic rule [21].

The conclusion to be drawn from this analysis is familiar and goes back to Engels and Lenin. A theory like dialectics that enables the examination of how concepts and propositions change and are transformed in the actual process of thinking, which reflects the ever changing and moving phenomena and things of Nature, is richer and more significant than that concerned with mere forms of thought or rules of inference. 'Dialectics', wrote Lenin, 'is living many-sided knowledge, with the number of sides eternally increasing, with an infinite number of shadings of every sort of approach and approximation to reality'. On the other hand, 'the old logic' is sterile, deserving only contempt and ridicule [22]. The 'merely formal logic' is content with 'enumerating the forms of motion of thought, *i.e.* the various forms of judgement and conclusion, and placing them side by side without any connection'. Ordinary logic, Engels argued, is common to men and the higher animals, dialectical thought is 'only possible for man, and for him only at a comparatively high stage of development'[23]. It is, therefore, clear that the former should conform to the latter, and not conversely. Dialectics is superior to formal logic, it is the most important mode of thinking for present-day science.

The second argument in favour of dialectics is also based on extra-logical considerations. Briefly, it says that dialectics does and logic does not reflect the regularities in the external world, or, more specifically, that the former lays bare the source of motion in Nature, the source being the struggle of the opposites, without resorting to supernatural factors, which by implication the latter is unable to do. Thus dialectics solves one of the most difficult problems of science and establishes its theoretical superiority over formal logic [24].

Both Schaff's arguments display terminological confusions of the various meanings of the term 'logic'. In the first of them 'dialectics' means the same as 'logic' in the broad meaning of this term and is compared with 'logic' in the sense of traditional logic, the science of the 'forms of thought', the 'childish play of solving jig-saw puzzles', as it was once described by Lenin. The latter is 'static', while dialectics is 'dynamic'. With the tacit assumption that only a 'moving thought' can comprehend and adequately describe change and motion the conclusion is reached that traditional logic and its mode of thought are inapplicable to physical and social reality.

Hegel, Engels, Lenin, and Schaff seem to be essentially in agreement that well defined concepts are an inadequate instrument to describe what continually changes, what 'simultaneously is itself and something else'. From this follows that the 'abstract and refined conceptual framework', worked out by bourgeois philosophy, is merely a subtle ideological weapon that conceals the rejection of the materialist tradition for the sake of idealism. On the other hand, a truly scientific procedure makes use of 'dialectically elastic concepts' and thus obtains a theoretically correct and adequate knowledge. The demand for the abandonment of scientific procedure is made in the name of science. 'Science' stands here for something quite different from what is commonly called by this name and from what it is to a man who studies science in its own right [25].

The objection that the truths of traditional logic are trivial is familiar and to some extent true. Many laws of traditional and formal logic do seem to convey very little knowledge about reality. They are, however, an indispensable condition for speaking with precision about anything at all, including dialectics. The much ridiculed law of identity is an example in point. It is always risky to use a term in two different meanings and it is a serious error to do it in an inference. This danger is by no means always easy to see; Marxist-Leninist writings provide some instances of this. Moreover, the laws of logic which say only little about reality constitute an integral part of an immense, abundant, and diversified system of theorems or rules. There is no reason to underestimate either the intricacies or significance of logical calculi. Even the simplest of them –

the propositional and functional calculus – includes theorems neither self-evident nor trivial. Every mathematical proof may be considered as a substitution of one or more laws of the propositional and functional calculus. The theory of relations has its own intrinsic interest and many applications, neither trite nor uninformative. Aristotle was aware of the existence of relations but he did not realise that their logic cannot be accommodated within the theory of classes. While some laws of logic may give the impression of triviality, formal logic includes many theories of great simplicity combined with a high degree of abstraction, which makes them difficult to discover and easy to comprehend once the discovery has been accomplished. It also includes numerous difficult and complicated theorems, derived from the fundamental ones and providing important knowledge about reality, which to obtain otherwise would be extremely hard, if not impossible.

The second argument in favour of dialectics displays terminological confusions even to a higher degree than the first. In the indicated passages dialectics is called the 'logic of contradiction'. But logic means there not only the theory of knowledge, psychology, or methodology, as was the case in the previous argument, but also metaphysics. In the second argument the term 'logic' is clearly used in its broadest sense, in which practically anything might be called a problem of logic.

Let us assume that dialectics does solve the metaphysical problem of the origin of motion. It does not follow therefrom that the dialectical conception of logic is theoretically superior to traditional or formal logic. The problem of the origin of motion is not a logical one and whatever the flaws of traditional or formal logic might be, the fact that it disregards it is not one of these flaws. The objection is pointless and irrelevant, a classical example of Hegelian logic or metaphysics – from which it was borrowed by Lenin [26] – since for Hegel logic and metaphysics were the same thing.

It is confusing to argue that dialectics is superior to formal logic since it can claim the solution of the problem of the origin of motion, and that it is, therefore, entitled to make and unmake the laws of logic. On this basis one could hold the view that biology is superior to physics, because the former does and the latter does not investigate organic matter. While some reasons can be produced to support the view concerning the superiority of biology over physics, for instance, that biology assumes the laws of physics and supplements them by some others of its own, 'superiority' would then carry a different meaning from that suggested with respect to the relation between dialectics and formal logic. In particular, it would not imply that physics should change and make its laws conform to what the biologist finds to be the 'laws of movement' of organic matter. A logically posterior science cannot dictate what the laws of a logically prior science should be, but has to accept them as they are and, if need be, to try to do its best by them. Schaff's argument about the superiority of dialectics over formal logic seems to suggest that exactly the opposite course is the correct one.

Although the suggestion that formal logic should conform to dialectics, and not the other way round, conflicts with the established scientific procedure, it is in keeping with the fundamental premises of Marxist-Leninist philosophy. The 'dialectics of the brain' is according to Engels only the reflection of the forms of motion in the real world; the basic 'laws of motion' are always the same irrespective of whether they refer to the motion of physical bodies, human society or thought [27]. On this assumption it might not appear bizarre that the laws of logic should be deduced from those of dialectics, which is the 'science of the general laws of motion'.

This particular assumption of Marxist-Leninist philosophy provides an example of the usefulness of the law of identity which the dialectical philosophers have declared to be trivial and dispensable. The term 'motion' has been taken over from physics, where it has a precise and well-defined meaning; it can be applied outside physics, in logic, history, or sociology, only metaphorically. If the dialecticians use the term 'motion' in the sense accepted in physics, they should explain what the expression 'change of place' means with respect to mental or social phenomena. On the other hand, if they prefer to apply the term 'motion' to any kind of change, and not specifically to that of place, they should be aware of the fact that the term in question loses its precise sense, ceases to be a scientific term and acquires the ambiguity peculiar to the words loosely used in colloquial speech [28]. Marxist-Leninists do not adopt either of these courses. 'Motion' does not have for them its clear meaning familiar from physics, and is still considered to possess all the precision of the scientific term a physicist may justly associate with it. This is clearly the error that results from the failure to keep the meaning of the terms used invariable.

The metaphorical usage of the term 'motion' applied equally to the changes of physical bodies, human society, history, or thought, is harmless as long as the metaphor is recognised for what it is. It becomes the source of misunderstandings of the crudest kind, when the metaphor is taken to be literally true. No metaphor can provide the basis for precise investigations. For when we speak of the movement of a physical body we wish to say that its position relative to some frame of reference is changing. Now, no thought or social change has a position whose movement can be observed and described in terms of their spatial-temporal co-ordinates. To be applied to human society or thought in some other than metaphorical sense, the concept of motion would have to be appropriately defined, and we do not find such a definition in the writings of Marxist-Leninists. If we try this course ourselves, we are at once faced by the difficulty that the kind of change we have in mind when it concerns human society or thought is a structural and not a spatial change. What relation there might be between these two kinds of change, it is not easy to see.

The same must be said of the 'laws of motion'. This expression has a well-defined sense in physics, but in logic, psychology or sociology it can be at most a figure of speech. When Marx spoke of the 'natural laws of movement' which a society may discover in its development, he made a similar use of a picture language as when he referred to the 'Furies of private interest'. As the term 'motion' has in logic and sociology a metaphorical meaning, we could only

274

speak of the 'laws of metaphorical motion', but this expression simply does not make sense [29].

The argument that the laws of logic have practically no cognitive value, that they are responsible for the distortions of our view of reality in the manner made familiar by Zeno's paradoxes, or that they are useless in acquiring new knowledge, is to justify the contention that formal logic, being an inferior discipline, should be subordinated to dialectics. Dialectics, forcing its way beyond the narrow horizon and sterile ground of formal logic, provides the reasons for deciding in each case which laws of logic should be accepted and which rejected or restricted in their application. Generally speaking, formal logic applies to things which do not change or are at rest, and loses its relevance whenever change and motion are involved. Since things constantly change or are in motion and remain unchanged or at rest only occasionally, dialectics has an incomparably wider application than formal logic and contains a more comprehensive view of the world. Although they are in a certain sense complementary, they should not be treated on the same footing, dialectics being hierarchically superior to formal logic [30].

The thesis of 'logical dualism' suggests that an Eleatic and a Heraclitean world exist side by side, with formal logic applying to the former and dialectics to the latter. The division results from a misconception of what logic is and what it can do. For obvious reasons formal logic is not responsible for keeping Zeno's 'arrow in flight' poised motionless in the air or for considering 'things as static and lifeless, each one by itself, alongside of and after each other'[31]. To use Zeno's argument as evidence for the distortions which formal logic apparently imposes on change and motion, as Marxist-Leninists do, is to mistake a particular application of the principles of identity, non-contradiction, and the excluded middle, with these principles themselves.

There is nothing in the principle of identity that would limit its application to what does not change or move. In the formula: (A) (A is A), or better: $(p) . p \supset p$, every suitable expression can be substituted for the variable. 'If a body is in motion, then a body is in motion' is as good an example of the identity law as 'a table is a table'. The law of identity neither confirms nor denies change or motion. Logic is not a science about bodies in motion or at rest; it is altogether indifferent to such matters and applies equally to both. An inference is a substitution of a logical formula, formally valid if the formula is valid, but its truth and falsehood, its correspondence with reality, is determined by extra-logical considerations, which do not belong to logic and for which logic cannot be responsible.

The same applies to the principle of non-contradiction and of the excluded middle. The sentence 'A moving body either remains or does not remain in the position x at the time t' is a correct substitution of the law of the excluded middle. Whether it is true or false, is a matter which does not belong to formal logic; it is a question of physics. If by means of logical formulae we come to the conclusion that motion is a series of stationary states, not our logic but our physics should be blamed. Since the question of whether we dismiss motion as

275

an illusion or accept it as real must be decided on extra-logical grounds; since, moreover, formal logic applies both to stationary and moving bodies, both changing and unchanging, there is no reason to accept two logics, a formal and a dialectical logic, based on different principles [32].

If logic is subordinated to dialectics, the accepted order of priority is reversed. For it is assumed, as a rule, that formal logic provides the basis for all science and that it logically precedes any other discipline. This claim is made for several related reasons. Formal logic is the simplest instance of a discipline constructed in accordance with certain intelligible principles stated beforehand and strictly adhered to. These principles are of such generality, clarity and precision that they serve as a universal model of theory construction. Consequently, in any deductive theory logic is presupposed. Logical terms are applied without definition and logical laws made use of in proofs without their validity being examined.

Deductive method and deductive reasoning are not restricted to deductive sciences. Logical argument plays an important and, according to some methodologists, an all-important role also in the empirical science [33]. Only deductive reasoning makes possible the discovery of what a hypothesis implies and a hypothesis cannot be critically examined, to be disconfirmed or confirmed by the failure if its refutation, unless all its implications, including its remote and not easily perceptible consequences, are clearly realised. It is logical reasoning that leads our steps from the level of theory to the level of facts and helps to discover whether the latter confirm the former. Logic is presupposed as much by the deductive as by the empirical sciences.

In general, no argument whether in science or in everyday life can do without logical concepts and every valid inference is made in accordance with some logical laws. The use of logical concepts and laws might not be consciously made, but this does not invalidate their fundamental role. There are probably few men who are aware all the time of all the logical laws they apply in their inferences, but everybody resorts to them from time to time to verify a proof or to discover the source of errors. A Marxist-Leninist is no exception to this rule and the recognition of this fact ultimately led Schaff also to the rejection of his view on the superiority of dialectics over formal logic.

Formal logic can be described as a study of forms on which valid inferences are based. A proof is a sequence of propositions and to ascertain whether the conclusion is arrived at by valid inferences we do not need to and, for certain reasons, should not consider the content of the propositions in question. To study these structures in a precise manner we must investigate various types of propositions and relations among them in abstraction from their content, *i.e.* to restrict ourselves to the investigation of propositional forms.

Marxist-Leninists recognised that formal logic is solely concerned with the 'formal aspect of the processes of thought' and they also somewhat grudgingly conceded that this is a reason for its success. The formalism of formal logic has achieved its highest perfection in mathematical logic, by which they understood, in agreement with the view more and more widely accepted in Poland, various logical methods applied in the investigations of the structure and foundations of mathematics. The achievements of mathematical logic, in Poland and elsewhere, could not have been denied. The fact that mathematical logic has grown out of formal logic was, for instance, for Schaff an important factor in the philosophical evaluation of formal logic itself [34].

The formal character of modern logic sharply differentiates it from dialectical logic, which, unlike the former, considers also content. This, Marxist-Leninists thought, was not necessarily a handicap and did not imply that dialectical logic was a discipline inferior to formal logic. There are logical systems that are formal without being formalised, the abstraction from the content varies and displays a variety of degrees. To paraphrase Plekhanov's dictum, paying to formal logic the homage which is its due leaves a dialectician free to pay homage also to dialectics. Formalism, which is desirable in one branch of knowledge, may be less or not at all desirable in another field. Since 'dialectical logic' means here 'logic in the broad sense', his opinion is basically true.

Although logic to be formal must abstract from content, this does not release it from the obligation of testing the correspondence of its formulae with the observable relations and matters of fact. Formal logic, Schaff argued, would be a futile game and not a serious scientific investigation if it did not pass this test successfully. His moderation in this respect was persuasive in a manner which a more extreme militancy would have failed to obtain [35].

Marxist-Leninists were neither the first nor the only philosophers who demanded some kind of verification of logical insights concealed behind its symbolical garment. Before the war Leśniewski was the logician who was probably most acutely aware of the problems involved and Łukasiewicz never forgot them though he perhaps failed to pay them enough attention [36]. Among philosophers the phenomenologist Ingarden was the most incisive and by far the most competent critic of formal logic and its philosophical claims. He urged incessantly that the relation between reality and logical assumptions should be carefully studied. After the war Ajdukiewicz discussed the problem of the relations between formal logic and experience and indicated various possible approaches [37]. Schaff's demand was, therefore, nothing new, but none of the Marxist-Leninist opinions on formal logic gained a greater number of supporters among logicians and philosophers than the view concerning the necessity and urgency of examining the objective validity of formal logic. It might be said that the support for it was practically unanimous [38].

It is, however, one thing to request the test of formal logic by observable phenomena and quite a different matter to say exactly how it should be done. The verification of formal logic confronts us with problems of considerable difficulty. Schaff's ideas on the subject were simplified in the extreme. What he conceived to be a verification differed essentially from the logician's view on the matter and though they seemed to speak of the same problem they really spoke of two different things [39].

Schaff did not approach the verification problem of logic on its own ground and felt that the issue can be satisfactorily resolved by examining the interpretations of logical formulae in ordinary language. As a matter of fact, he did not see any difficulty at all in answering the question as to whether logic applies to reality. He followed in Lenin's footsteps and in the simplest, most common expressions, like the sentence 'Fido is a dog' or 'John is a man', saw a convincing proof that reality involves contradictions *sensu stricto* and that in general does not adhere to the laws of logic. These sentences apparently reveal that the 'singular is the general', that the opposites are identical, and that everything simultaneously is itself and something else. What is revealed by the analysis in the linguistic expressions, is abundantly confirmed by natural science in the realm of facts. 'Objective nature' also shows us the transformation of the singular into the general, the interfusion and transition of the opposites [40].

The error which these views involve, results from the confusion of logical types and of identity with class membership or class inclusion. 'The singular is general' is a perfectly true sentence if it is understood to mean " 'being singular' is a general characteristic". Otherwise it is a meaningless sentence-like composition of words. No contradiction is involved in the sentence 'John is a man'. John remaining identical with himself may be a member of the class of men, of husbands, soldiers, or whatever it might be, without helping to establish the dialectical law of contradiction. The same thing might be a member of different classes and no contradiction arises therefrom unless the classes are considered to be identical or the inclusion relation is taken to be that of identity, for which, however, there is no warrant.

While a fallacious logical analysis of language is the apparent source of the fanciful conclusions, a more fundamental error is hidden a little deeper. To test formal logic by observable phenomena it is not enough to find an interpretation of the former in ordinary language and to examine how it corresponds to the external world. For various reasons, of which only one will be briefly mentioned, this course encounters insuperable difficulties. Ordinary speech is too vague and imprecise to be reduced to simple elements and to fit unambiguously logical formulae, in order that their correspondence with reality may be directly ascertained. Between the interpretation and the experienced reality there lies always a screen of vague meanings inherent in the expressions of ordinary language and this screen prevents seeing clearly what the language only dimly conveys. This should be borne in mind when at the third stage of his proof Schaff tries to show that in the light of his interpretation the principle of non-contradiction does not apply to things or phenomena of Nature.

Simplified ideas about the manner in which formal logic might be shown to correspond or not to correspond to observable matters of fact are not independent of what Marxist-Leninists believed to be the foundations of formal logic. In their opinion formal logic is always based on the principles of identity, of the excluded middle and of non-contradiction [41]. By testing these principles we can, therefore, test by one stroke the whole of formal logic. Only many-valued logics include certain deviations from this rule. Since, however, they still remain purely abstract constructions they can be left aside for the moment.

By saying that the three above-mentioned principles constitute the base of formal logic, Marxist-Leninists meant that in any formal system they are either assumed as axioms or follow from axioms, the latter having been so chosen that the three principles can be derived from them. Moreover, the three principles constitute the base of formal logic also in this sense that they are used as metalogical theorems. Thus, for instance, the so-called principle of bivalence corresponds to the logical principles of non-contradiction and of the excluded middle. The three logical principles are 'organically interrelated'; they are either materially or inferentially equivalent. They must either be accepted together or rejected together [42].

Formal logic accepts the three principles, Schaff argued, because they are considered to be self-evident and thus particularly well suited to constitute the base for the whole of formal logic. Besides this explanation, for which there is no evidence, Schaff mentioned another reason closer, though in a misleading fashion, to the prevailing views about the nature of logical and mathematical theorems. In his view, formalism fosters the tendency towards a-priorism, and a-priorism protects our preconceived ideas from the verification by experience. The three principles are considered by their supporters to be *a priori* truths (and thus universally valid). This last view is emphatically and quite rightly rejected by Marxist-Leninists [43].

Dialectics was supposedly not alone in its attempt to revise the foundations of logic. Seen against the background of the tendencies apparent in modern logic, dialectics, with its rejection of the law of non-contradiction, is nothing extraordinary. The logicians themselves have become aware that the old logic requires 'some generalisation and extension'. Aristotle considered the principle of non-contradiction as the 'firmest of all opinions', but was not convinced that it was an axiom immune from revision. Medieval philosophy killed what was strong and creative in Aristotle's thought; it replaced his moderation with 'absolute conceptions', which dominate the traditional way of thinking and its inclination to see phenomena as static and at rest. Only Łukasiewicz revealed what was Aristotle's authentic view on the principle of non-contradiction and threw doubt on its validity [44].

Schaff suggested that in many-valued logics a distinct step towards the revision of the traditional approach to the principle of non-contradiction has been made. Many-valued and intuitionist logics reject altogether the principle of the excluded middle, and consequently change their 'attitude to the principle of non-contradiction'. Thus, the restricted validity of traditional logic has been put into relief by investigations which, starting from different points of departure, have reached the same destination. The rejection of the principle of bivalence brings dialectics and formal logic closer together. In Schaff's opinion, we witness a revision of the fundamental laws of logic. A new viewpoint on the foundation problem of logic, to which dialectics contributes its share, is being formed [45].

The defence of the dialectical revision of logic was elaborate but ineffective, for most of its arguments rest on errors or misunderstandings. They are so numerous that not all of them can be dealt with. The exposure of the more fundamental ones is sufficient to make the whole case for dialectics collapse.

To begin with, there is the claim that the principles of identity, of the excluded

279

middle, and of non-contradiction are inferentially equivalent, that they constitute the base of all logic, that they have this role ascribed to them because of their being considered as *a priori* laws of thought, and that logic built on such assumptions is an unsound discipline, in need of a critical examination. This claim would have been justified, if its premises were correct. This, however, is not the case.

While in the so-called classical calculi the principles of identity, of the excluded middle, and of non-contradiction are inferentially equivalent, we face a different position on the ground of philosophical logic, which is that chosen by Schaff for his critical appraisal of logic. We cannot say, as Schaff did, that they are 'various formulations of one and the same fundamental principle, namely that of non-contradiction'. If someone rejects the formula

$$\sim (\varphi x \, . \, \sim \varphi x)$$

he may still accept that

$$\varphi x \, . \, \sim \varphi x \, . \supset . \, \varphi x \, . \sim \varphi x,$$

that is, recognise the law of identity. This was the case with thinkers like Heraclitus, Nicholas of Cusa, Hegel, and Engels who all rejected the principle of non-contradiction. Moreover, if we reject the principle of identity, as Kratylos did, all statements become false. For from the negation of $p \supset p$ we can infer $\sim p$. The rejection of the principle of non-contradiction implies that all statements are true. From p and $\sim p$ we can infer an arbitrary q. The two principles mean different things and carry different implications. They are not various formulations of the same law, the rejection of one of them does not imply the rejection of the other [46].

Nor are the principles of non-contradiction and of the excluded middle as closely bound up as Schaff suggested. To state that a certain object, *e.g.* a mathematical entity, is not contradictory, is not equivalent to the statement that it is determinate and that the principle of the excluded middle applies to it. This is exactly what the intuitionists claim in their dispute with the formalists over the sense to be associated with the existence of mathematical entities. We can, without inconsistency, respect the principle of non-contradiction and question the validity of the principle of the excluded middle. What is more, we can actually indicate the method of constructing a non-contradictory entity, *e.g.,* a number which is indeterminate in the sense that we are unable to show that it is either rational or non-rational, either real or non-real [47].

The opinion that in modern investigations on the foundations of logic and mathematics there is a return to Kant's a-priorism is not shared by Schaff alone [48]. It does not seem to be a case of an intentional distortion of the opponent's views in order to assail him with a seemingly devastating effectiveness. It appears to be a genuine misunderstanding, however difficult it might be to comprehend. The school to which the return to Kant's a-priorism is ascribed is, of course, logical empiricism with its division of all meaningful statements into empirical and analytic. To the latter group belong all statements which are true or false by virtue of their composition alone. They owe this distinction to the fact that they do not say anything about reality and are derived from arbitrarily laid down axioms and definitions by well-defined rules of transformation. Their origin explains their name – analytic or tautological statements. According to the theory of logical empiricism, logical and mathematical theorems are tautologies in the above indicated sense [49].

Whatever else we may say about this theory, it is clear that a tautology in the sense of logical empiricism is neither synthetic nor *a priori* in the Kantian sense. It is close to Kant's analytic sentences, which, like tautologies, are discovered by pure thought, without being identical with them. Kant's analytical sentences must have a subject and a predicate, and their analycity depends thereon. Analytic statements in the sense of logical empiricism are only seldom subject-predicate sentences. Most of them are functorial propositions, that is to say, they are propositions in which propositional functors occur and their analycity is closely bound up with this characteristic. Moreover, they are not extricated, as it were, from the mind itself, as are Kant's analytical sentences, but are transformations of more or less arbitrary axioms carried out by means of more or less arbitrary rules. Their truth and falsehood is recognisable by inspection in view of the fact that the criteria of logical truth refer to the notational features of statements. The more formalistic a logical system is, the less reason there is for the revival of Kant's division and the less room for *a priori* truths in his sense.

The view that the principles of identity, of the excluded middle and of non-contradiction constitute the base of logical systems is erroneous. It is true that they follow from the axioms in any complete calculus, which shows that they are logical laws as much as but not more than any other logical theorem proved in this calculus. Upon the publication of *Principia Mathematica* this view was universally accepted, for there is no reason for differentiating various logical laws once they are presented in axiomatic form. The choice of axioms is prompted by many considerations, one of them being that of the completeness of the system, and this objective is achieved when any meaningful expression within this system can be either proved or disproved. So far as the role of the principles of the excluded middle and of non-contradiction in the propositional calculus are concerned, it has been found, and caused much astonishment, that in spite of their fame they are only rarely used in proofs. Other less famous theorems are endowed with a much greater inferential power than the two principles in question.

History of logic has something to say on how the three principles have acquired the reputation of being the 'supreme laws of thought', a reputation they still seem to enjoy with some conservative philosophers. The law of identity is independent of all the other theses of Aristotle's syllogistic. If it is to be included in the system, it must be accepted axiomatically. Moreover, if a proposition in which the predicate is contained in the subject (an analytic proposition in the Kantian sense) is accepted as self-evident, the same, and *a fortiori*, applies to the law of identity. In the latter case the predicate is not only contained in but is also identical with the subject.

So far as the principles of the excluded middle and of non-contradiction are concerned, they play a considerable role in discussions and deductions in which the *reductio ad absurdum* provides a powerful instrument of inference. This seems to be the reason why Aristotle accorded to the latter an exalted position. Modern research in the history of logic suggests, however, that even Aristotle ceased to ascribe to the principle of non-contradiction its elevated rank when he realised that his syllogistic is independent of it [50].

The laws of identity, of non-contradiction, and of the excluded middle do not seem to have acquired the reputation of the 'supreme laws of thought' until the views of Leibniz, Kant, and Fichte became known. The reasons which prompted these thinkers to exalt them were mostly of an extra-logical nature and sprang from epistemological and metaphysical considerations. The 'supreme laws of thought' cannot be found in the English nineteenth century textbooks of logic, in J. S. Mill's *System of Logic*, W. S. Jevons' *Principles of Science*, J. N. Keynes' *Formal Logic* but they do appear in Überweg's *System der Logik* and Wundt's *Logik* [51]. It should be remembered that Überweg's textbook was Plekhanov's and Schaff's source from which they both drew their knowledge of logic.

Czeżowski suggested that in the absence of modern formal logic the three principles under discussion were fulfilling the function of a substitute for the non-existent propositional calculus. They seem to continue to fulfil this function in informal discussions. In such discussions the law of non-contradiction plays the role of the rejection rule which protects us from the acceptance of a pair of expressions from which any arbitrary expression may be derived. If that were possible, it would be no use to argue about anything.

There remains the question of the relation between the principle of bivalence and the notion of consistency of a formalised system on the one hand, the principles of the excluded middle and non-contradiction on the other. Schaff quoted Łukasiewicz as his authority to support the claim that on the ground of modern formal logic the principle of bivalence has restored the two principles to their elevated position of the 'supreme laws of thought' [52]. He failed to notice, however, that with the principle of bivalence we move to a more abstract level, that of metalogic. Łukasiewicz did not overlook this fact. He made it clear at that time that the principle of bivalence corresponds to the metalogical (and not logical) principles of non-contradiction and of the excluded middle, but he soon abandoned this view and later investigations confirmed that this was the right course to take [53]. The logical relations in various many-valued systems turned out to be more varied than it at first appeared and their study threw light also on the relation between the principles of bivalence, of non-contradiction, and of the excluded middle.

The formulation of the principles of bivalence and of the excluded middle makes it clear that they should be kept apart. While the first of these principles states that every proposition has one and only one of the two possible truth-values, the second lays down that of two contradictory propositions one must be true. The principle of bivalence is a metatheorem or a metaprinciple, characteristic of the so-called classical logical systems. In a bivalent system, in which negation of a false proposition is a true proposition, the negation of a true proposition is a false proposition and the alternative of p and q is true, if at least one of its arguments is true, the law of the excluded middle holds. In other words, the principle of the excluded middle follows from the law of bivalence and the matrices of negation and alternative. The difference between the two principles becomes still clearer if the three-valued propositional calculus is considered. In this calculus the laws of the excluded middle and of non-contradiction might or might not be valid and this depends on how the matrices are determined. The rejection of the bivalence principle does not necessarily imply that the laws of the excluded middle and of non-contradiction must be rejected too. It follows that the principle and the laws in question cannot be equivalent [54].

The concept of consistency and that of non-contradiction are concepts of different orders or levels. The latter is a logical, the former a metalogical concept. The law of non-contradiction may not be a theorem of a consistent theory. On the other hand, since an inconsistent theory includes all its meaningful expressions, the theorem of non-contradiction is a theorem of an inconsistent system. The sharp distinction between the metalogical principles of bivalence and consistency and the logical laws of the excluded middle and non-contradiction were firmly established at the time Schaff set out to revise the foundations of logic [55].

The consistency of a formal system might be defined without resorting to semantical concepts, that is to say, it might be given a definition syntactical in character, making no use of the metalogical principle of non-contradiction. But the requirement of consistency is prompted by semantical considerations; its objective is to exclude from the system pairs of propositions which cannot be true together. It offers the same kind of guarantee with respect to the whole system that outside it is provided by the law of non-contradiction. A deductive system which includes a pair of contradictory propositions would include any proposition whatsoever. All contradictory systems are, therefore, identical and their study would be of no interest. They would not help us in the search for truth by establishing valid forms of inference and by discovering the invalid ones. While it can be argued whether consistency is both the sufficient and necessary condition of the truth of logical and mathematical theories, the fact that it is a necessary condition is not questioned by any qualified person. To suggest, as Marxist-Leninists did, that the main obstacle to the acceptance of the dialectical principle of contradiction is force of habit and tradition, does not testify to the awareness of the issues involved, both in formal and non-formal reasoning [56].

The semantical principle of non-contradiction is indispensable in classical and non-classical logic, in formal and non-formal theories, it is a guidepost without which no advance of rational thought could be made and no argument about anything whatsoever could be carried on. In this sense Łukasiewicz called the semantical principle of non-contradiction an absolute principle [57]. Its indispensability includes also the discourse in which a Marxist-Leninist states that he does not accept its validity. He cannot say what he does unless he assumes that his statement and its denial cannot be true together. Only on this assumption is his statement meaningful and can its truth and falsehood be examined. What a

Marxist-Leninist denies in his theory he has to accept on the metatheoretical level, unless he speaks like an oracle, neither understanding himself nor expecting others to understand what he is saying.

To support the dialectical revision of formal logic Schaff referred to some modern developments in logic, which, as he thought, spoke in favour of dialectics. What Schaff said on this matter might be reduced to two main claims. First, that many-valued logics lead to the rejection or restriction of the principle of non-contradiction. Second, that many-valued and intuitionist logics deny the principle of the excluded middle and this denial affects in some way or other also the validity of the principle of non-contradiction.

The first of these claims needs a few introductory comments. We do not pass from the bivalued to the three- or many-valued propositional calculus by rejecting the principle of non-contradiction and of the excluded middle, but by rejecting the principle of bivalence, which states that every proposition is either true or false. For this purpose we accept the assumption that besides true and false propositions there are – to confine ourselves to the three-valued calculus – also propositions which are neither true nor false. In other words, instead of two we accept three truth-values which any statement may have, and thus we replace the current and intuitive true-false dichotomy by the trichotomy of true, false, and *tertium*. Every statement has one and only one truth-value, it is either true or false or *tertium*. *Tertium non datur* is replaced by *quartum non datur*.

The question arises whether we can construct a three-valued propositional calculus which is consistent, that is to say, in which no meaningful propositional formula α is both asserted and rejected. As is well known, this question has been answered affirmatively.

Three- and bivalued calculi are incomparable in view of the fact that different principles are assumed as their basis, and, consequently, their truth matrices are different. They both include only identically true formulae (tautologies), *i.e.* formulae which are true for all permissible substitutions. Not every formula valid in one system is, however, valid in the other, and conversely. Thus, there are formulae of the three-valued calculus which have no analog in the bivalued system and bivalued formulae which are no longer identically true formulae in the three-valued calculus. In particular, in Łukasiewicz's three-valued system the law of the excluded middle and of non-contradiction

$$p \lor \sim p, \qquad \sim (p \, . \sim p)$$

are no longer valid. If 'p' assumes the value of truth or falsehood their value is truth. But if 'p' is *tertium,* their value is *tertium*. Not being tautologies, the two laws do not belong to the three-valued propositional calculus. It would be an error, however, to infer that their negations are theorems or that two formulae like α and $\sim$ α may be true together. This is excluded by the consistency of the system.

Schaff's first claim is not, therefore, justified. The three-valued calculus does not make the contention of contradictory propositions being both true any more acceptable than it would have been without it. The fact that the law of non-contradiction is not a valid theorem of Łukasiewicz's calculus is a consequence of the trichotomy of truth-values and of the manner in which the truth matrices have been determined. Our inferences are bound to follow a different, though consistent, pattern if besides true and false propositions those which are neither true nor false are also accepted. Schaff's error seems to result from the confusion of the statement 'α is neither true nor false' with 'α and $\sim\alpha$ are true together'. Schaff assumed that the laws of the excluded middle and of non-contradiction are always materially or inferentially equivalent. This appears to have led him to the contention that many-valued logics, including intuitionist logic, throw doubt upon the universal validity of the law of non-contradiction, the reason being that the law of the excluded middle is not one of their theorems. It is true to say that in the two-valued propositional calculus the two laws are inferentially equivalent (with respect to De Morgan laws), and that if we reject one of them, we have also to reject the other. In many-valued logics this is no longer the case. Generally speaking, the position depends on how the truth matrices are determined and they might be determined in various ways without the risk of inconsistency. Thus, in Łukasiewicz's three-valued calculus neither the law of non-contradiction, nor that of the excluded middle are valid. On the other hand, in intuitionist logic the law of non-contradiction is a valid theorem and the law of the excluded middle is not.

It is misleading to say that intuitionist logic altogether rejects the law of the excluded middle. An intuitionist does not question its validity outside mathematics at all. For him as much as for anybody else two statements like 'this body is in motion' and 'this body is not in motion' cannot be both true. Intuitionist logic, wrote Heyting, concerns only mathematical propositions [58].

Not all objects, but only those which Brouwer called 'mental mathematical constructions' require a novel treatment. Upon being formalised, the formal system, of which intuitionist mental mathematical constructions provide a model, proves to have peculiar characteristics. Intuitionist logic is a part of mathematics. It grows out of the latter and is not something logically prior by means of which mathematics is constructed and which serves as its foundation. Moreover, within mathematics the principle remains valid as long as we deal with finite sets. The difficulty begins when we pass to the infinite sets or sequences of numbers. According to the intuitionists in these cases the principle is no longer admissible as a basis for existential inferences.

The principle of the excluded middle: $(p) . p \vee \sim p$, as it is understood by the intuitionists, demands a general method of solving every problem. To assert this principle means for them that they are able to prove by an actual construction either 'p' or '$\sim p$'. Since such a general method of construction does not exist, they refrain from asserting the principle of the excluded middle. A 'mathematical theorem', in the sense in which an intuitionist uses this term, refers to an empirical fact, that is, to the fact that a certain construction has been successful.

The issue between the intuitionists and other mathematicians does not, in fact, concern the validity of the principle of the excluded middle but the problem of mathematical existence, of what is really meant when the mathematician says 'there is such x that φx' and the range of the variable x is an infinite set. Let us assume that we try to prove that there exists a number x that fulfils a certain condition (φx). Let us further assume that we have found the proof which shows that the assumption 'there is no such x' results in a contradiction. A mathematician of the logistic or formalistic school of thought would then consider that by the law of the excluded middle he has proved the existence of a number such that φx. But an intuitionist would reject this conclusion. The negation of a general statement is an insufficient basis for proving the validity of an existential particular statement. To prove the latter we must be able to construct what in this particular statement is asserted to exist. An indirect proof does not allow us, as a rule, actually to construct a number x such that φx, and the truth of a mathematical theorem is determined by the law that enables the construction of the entities to which the theorem refers [59].

Intuitionist logic assumes, therefore, that besides true and false theorems there exist those unprovable, and thus rejects the principle of bivalence (which a formalist accepts, thus rejecting unprovable theorems). In other words, intuitionist logic accepts besides truth and falsehood at least one other truth-value, different from truth and falsehood [60]. This third value of the intuitionists is different from Łukasiewicz's *tertium*. While in Łukasiewicz's system the negation of *tertium* has *tertium* as its truth-value, the negation of the intuitionist's third value gives falsehood. On this account the law of non-contradiction is not valid in Łukasiewicz's system and is valid in intuitionist logic. Łukasiewicz's statements, whose value is *tertium,* can be described as statements which are neither true nor false; in intuitionist logic to say that a 'statement is unprovable' means the same as 'it is not false but it cannot be proved to be true'. In both systems the law of the excluded middle is not valid, but the lack of validity results from different considerations. Since an unprovable statement of intuitionist logic is not false, it is absurd to assume that the denial of the law of the excluded middle is true. While $p \lor \sim p$ is unprovable, the so-called law of the absurdity of the absurdity of the principle of the excluded middle

$$\sim \sim (p \lor \sim p)$$

is a valid theorem of intuitionist logic.

It turns out that Schaff's second claim is also based on error. Intuitionist logic does not deny the validity, as it were, of the elementary law of the excluded middle, in which dialectics is interested. Intuitionist logic considers the law as a theorem unprovable for certain classes of mathematical entities, but in these cases it assumes that its denial is absurd, and dialectics is concerned exactly with this denial. In fact, intuitionist logic is as much incompatible with dialectics as is the classic conception of logic that assumes the validity of *tertium non datur* without exception.

The discussion of the problems which have arisen from non-classical logic and from support of the claims of dialectics with which the principles adopted in the non-classical calculi allegedly provided dialectics has an air of unreality. A Marxist-Leninist should have refused to draw any advantages from the development of many-valued logics, even if there were any advantages to be drawn therefrom. In his opinion, any deviation from the principle of bivalence is incompatible with Marxist-Leninist philosophy and its theory of 'objective truth'. The theory of 'objective truth' is essentially the familiar one, known as the 'correspondence theory of truth'. Marxist-Leninists felt that this theory was perfectly capable of dealing with the problem of contingent propositions, which in Poland played a considerable role in the discovery and development of many-valued logics. A satisfactory solution of the difficulty presented by the contingent propositions would dispose of one of the most important reasons for the abandonment of the dichotomy of truth and falsehood. To achieve this purpose Schaff, in particular, adopted some of Kotarbiński's views concerning the truth value of statements in the future tense and, with slight modifications, incorporated them into what he called the 'materialist theory of truth'.

Kotarbiński distinguished two kinds of statements in the future tense, the one consisting of statements either true or false and the other of those neither true nor false. The statement 'Caesar crossed the Rubicon' is neither true nor false at any time preceding the moment of his crossing the Rubicon. The statement 'Halley's comet passed through the orbit of the Earth' is true at any time also prior to the time of its passing through the orbit of the Earth. The second statement is always true because the statement concerning the cause of the event is always true, its sufficient and necessary conditions are known. Statements in the future tense are either true or false if the events which they refer to are determined by the laws of Nature and neither true nor false otherwise [61].

Schaff accepted Kotarbiński's distinction and also his explanation why the first kind of statements in the future tense are either true or false. He disagreed, however, with Kotarbiński's opinion concerning the second kind of statements and followed Chwistek instead [62]. Chwistek felt that Łukasiewicz's views concerning the three-valued calculus were 'naive'. What Łukasiewicz wished to achieve by means of his three-valued calculus can be accommodated within the framework of two-valued logic by means of the calculus of probability. It is not quite clear whether Chwistek denied the existence of 'true' contingent propositions in Aristotle's sense. It cannot be doubted, however, that in his opinion whatever the status of these propositions might be, they do not require a different logic from that based on the dichotomy of truth and falsehood. This was also the view which Kotarbiński finally adopted under Leśniewski's influence.

Schaff argued as follows. If truth consists in the conformity of thought to reality, statements about the future which are predictions based on uniform regularities of Nature are either true or false as much as any other proposition. This view, which Schaff did not adequately explain, seems to imply that if a future event is predetermined by a cause or causes existing today – and this applies to events which are particular cases of a uniform regularity of Nature – the conformity of thought to reality can also be ascertained in advance. Predictions are verified in future but are true or false at present in so far as they do or do not correspond to what is the case, the case being determined by uniform regularities of events.

On the other hand, a statement about a future contingent event, e.g. 'John will be in the Soviet Union a year hence', is no prediction in the proper sense of this term; it is not a statement about a predetermined event and its truth or falsehood cannot be ascertained in the manner indicated above. It does not follow therefrom that it is neither true nor false. Such a statement cannot be qualified in terms of truth and falsehood, but only in those of probability. What is undecided at present, what may or may not happen, is not true or false, but probable, the probability being associated with the 'prediction' and not with the event to which it refers. The question whether it is true or false cannot be asked at all, and the answer, if given, is meaningless. A statement is true, if it corresponds to the facts of the case, and false, if it does not. Neither of these possibilities applies to a statement about a future event, since there are yet no 'facts of the case'. With one term of the correspondence relation missing, no correspondence relation can exist and be qualified as true or false [63]. Schaff would agree with what Professor Ryle said on this matter. As the adjectives 'deceased' and 'extinct' cannot be applied to people and mastodons while they exist, so 'true' and 'false' cannot be used with respect to statements in the future tense. In a way 'true' and 'false' are obituary or valedictory epithets [64].

Thinkers who consider the principle of bivalence to be an absolute truth may dispose of the counter-examples, intended to show that it is too narrow to account for the great variety of formal structures embedded in the discourse, in three different ways. They can say that every statement is either true or false irrespective of whether we are able to find out which is the case. Propositions in the future tense referring to matters not yet determined constitute no exception to this rule. This is the most common argument against many-valued logics, close to the views of Aristotle himself, represented by Leśniewski in Poland before the war and more recently by Greniewski [65].

Second, the supporters of the principle of bivalence can contend that the examples of statements neither true nor false are not genuine statements, but statement forms with free variables of time, place, and so forth. They must be bound before they can become statements. As soon as this is done, they turn out to be either true or false [66].

The third way of dealing with statements apparently neither true nor false – and this one deals specifically with statements in the future tense – is to point out that the question whether some of these statements are true or false is not an 'askable' one, since it is inappropriate to the circumstances and in this sense absurd. The sentence "'p' is neither true nor false" assumes that the question whether "'p' is false" can be resolved. This assumption is wrong and must be rejected with respect to some sentences in the future tense. We cannot discuss what a man yet unborn does or fails to do. Timeless shadows of events which have not yet been successful 'in the competition for actuality' cannot be made into 'surrogate contemporary things'[67]. This is the position which Schaff took. Statements referring to contingent events are right or wrong guesses. They can be dealt with, as Chwistek suggested, by means of the calculus of probability. The calculus of probability can be developed within the framework of two-valued logic and only two-valued logic is, in Schaff's opinion, compatible with the Marxist-Leninist conception of truth.

Schaff's position is not, however, consistent. While he rejects statements which are neither true nor false, he accepts those which are contradictory, *i.e.* statements both true and false. Moreover, he also accepts the existence of a class of statements which admit different degrees of truth and, being either more or less true than some other statements, are partly true and partly false. The latter are not, as he expressly stated, probability statements to be accommodated within two-valued logic. He seems to argue that the principle of bivalence both is and is not adequate to describe the structure of the universe [68].

Although one can be uncertain what Schaff's views on the principle of bivalence were, they were understood to mean a firm adherence to the dichotomy of truth and falsehood. The suggestion made earlier by a supporter of Marxism-Leninism that Marxism-Leninism should adopt the principle of the polyvalence of truth and falsehood, was never seriously considered [69]. The implications of such a step could not be easily foreseen and the idea of many-valued logic appeared not only bold, but also subversive with respect to the naive and uncritical conception of 'objective truth'. Moreover, some sound and good reasons against many-valued logics could be given. Statements which for specific reasons cannot be qualified as true or false provide a flimsy ground for the rejection of the principle of bivalence. In modal logic we encounter some stronger but not decisive reasons for questioning this principle [70]. Other examples of statements which might be interpreted in terms of three-valued logic find an adequate explanation also on the basis of the dichotomy of truth and falsehood. The principle of bivalence has served science well and is universally accepted in scientific investigations. No consideration important enough can be found to justify its rejection [71].

Marxism-Leninism, as interpreted in Poland, seems to agree with those who say: the fact that many-valued logics can be constructed does not entail that they are significant. They are purely abstract systems with no connection with reality. Consequently, many-valued logics might be didactically useful in reminding that no laws, be it even those of logic and mathematics, are immune from revision, but they have no other use [72]. This implies that nothing whatever that many-valued logics might have to say about the principle of non-contradiction is of any relevance to the issue of its validity. Marxist-Leninists failed to notice this implication. They should have insisted that the validity of the principle of non-contradiction is ultimately an ontological and not a formal problem to be solved in accordance with the 'empirical evidence' which might be brought in support of the claims of dialectics.

CHAPTER 14

CHANGE, MOTION, AND CONTRADICTION

Schaff put forward three arguments to support the dialectical thesis that the ontological principle of non-contradiction must be rejected. He considered them to be empirical and decisive.

Nature, Schaff argued referring to Engels, is the test of dialectics. Modern natural science, and physics in particular, has furnished a vast body of evidence which reveals contradictions inherent in natural phenomena. An 'objective contradiction' is something more than a unity of the opposites; the latter does not always involve a contradiction *sensu stricto*. Thus, an atom is a unity of positive and negative electric charges, a magnetic needle – of two opposite poles, the motion of a planet on its orbit – of the centrifugal and centripetal forces, society – of mutually exclusive class interests. In each case the unity of the opposites is real and 'objective', but a statement referring to it does not entail two contradictory propositions being both true. This is the case with respect to an 'objective contradiction'. An electron or a photon is both a particle and a wave; mass is and is not an attribute of matter. Since a contradiction *sensu stricto* is inherent in the nature of any particle of matter, an adequate description of a particle entails the truth of the conjunction

$$(\exists \varphi) \, . \, \varphi x \, . \sim \varphi x \, [73].$$

The second argument is stated very succinctly. It does not offer any proof, follows closely in Engels' footsteps, and is satisfied with awakening some intuitions at the back of the reader's mind, without examining their meaning and their logical implications. Any process of quantitative or qualitative change involves contradiction, any changing object is itself and not itself at the same time. Engels made the metaphysical mode of thought responsible for thinking in 'discontinuous antitheses'; Schaff put the blame on traditional logic. Logic encourages conceiving things as fixed and isolated objects instead of as events, which, while they change, pass through contradictory stages and are transformed into their opposites. We are referred to Hegel for examples and reminded that already the ancients knew that *summum ius est summa iniuria* [74].

Ajdukiewicz tried to extricate from this almost inarticulate argument some formal pattern of inference of which it makes use. Let us consider, he suggested, any process of change, for instance, a ripening fruit or a rising column of mercury in a thermometer. Let us then consider two distinct stages of the change, the green and the ripe fruit or the height of the mercury column as it indicates 20 and 21 centigrades. Let A and B stand for these states at different times. We often assume that if an object x passed from the state A to the state B there must have been a time t at which x was neither A nor B. This common assumption, which seems to be in agreement with our everyday experience, might be formulated as the principle of continuity. This principle requires that in any sufficiently small interval of time the rate of change occurring during this interval becomes arbitrarily small. In other words, a continuous change is a compact series of 'states'; no two 'states' are consecutive; between any two, however close to each other they might be, there are always others (this is a crude idea of continuity, but it is good enough for this purpose). The principle of continuity excludes the possibility that there should exist such an instant t during the time interval of the change from the state A to the state B that at the time t the object x is A and at every moment later than t the object x is B. It seems to follow that in the time interval of the change from A to B there must be contained such a sub-interval that within it the object x is neither A nor B.

If this premiss is accepted, a dialectical philosopher might infer his contention in the following manner. Let us consider the change of water (A) into steam (B). Water which is no longer in the liquid state might be described to be in the state non-A. In accordance with the principle of continuity there must have been such a time-interval when the considered portion of water was neither A nor non-A. But 'x is non-A' means the same as 'x is not A', and to say 'it is not true that x is not A' is equivalent to 'x is A'. It follows from the premiss

$$\sim (x \text{ is A}) \, . \, \sim (x \text{ is non-A})$$

that

$$\sim (x \text{ is A}) \, . \, (x \text{ is A}).$$

The principle of continuity leads to the conclusion that during a certain time-interval a changing object has contradictory attributes [75].

Schaff's third and final argument for the rejection of the ontological principle of non-contradiction is Zeno's time-honoured argument against motion. It was Hegel who in modern times revived Zeno's paradoxes and turned them to his own advantage, namely to prove that motion is a 'living contradiction'. Engels adopted Hegel's use of Zeno's arguments and Plekhanov made it prominent in his own presentation of dialectics. He also re-established the chain of ideas leading from Zeno through Hegel to Engels and passed it on to the Marxist-Leninist philosophy of our own times. Motion, wrote Plekhanov, is a 'contradiction in action', the moving body presents itself as an 'irrefutable argument' in favour of the 'logic of contradiction' [76].

Bertrand Russell observed a long time ago that Zeno's paradoxes have inspired practically all the theories concerned with the concepts of time, space, infinity, and continuity, and that they have acted as a powerful stimulus to the development of these concepts from Zeno's times to our own day. Marxist-Leninist philosophy is not interested in the theoretical aspect of Zeno's paradoxes. The interest of Marxist-Leninist philosophy in Zeno's arguments has been invariably limited to a single point, namely, to their usefulness in showing that contradictions *sensu stricto* exist 'objectively' in the phenomena of Nature.

Of all Zeno's arguments against motion Schaff considered only one, that of the 'arrow in flight'. In his opinion, it is not a paradox but a flawless argument [77].

It proves either that from the assumption 'the arrow is in flight' follows the conclusion 'the arrow is at rest', or that a moving body is at the same time in motion and at rest, it is at a given point and it is not there. In both cases the premiss that something moves entails a contradiction. We thus face the following alternative: either to deny the fact that motion is real, as Zeno did, or to accept Zeno's argument and the reality of motion. The latter course implies the conclusion that there are contradictions *sensu stricto* in Nature. Something must be given up, either the reality of motion or the laws of traditional logic. A Marxist-Leninist accepts the evidence of experience and rejects the laws of traditional logic 'Motion is a contradiction, a unity of contradictions'. Thus, to use Engels' words, he recognises that contradictions are 'objectively present in things and processes themselves', and, as it were, assume a 'corporeal form'[78].

Engels himself was probably all the more convinced that we actually cannot describe motion consistently, because in his opinion the differential and integral calculus is based on the 'contradiction that in certain circumstances straight lines and curves are identical' and yet the calculus produces 'correct results'[79]. This was no longer true when *Anti-Dühring* was published. The classical theory of functions of a real variable, which we learn today in elementary calculus – the definitions of limit and continuity, of derivative and definite integral, of convergence and continuous function – is fundamentally that of Cauchy published in the 'twenties of the last century. The exculpatory comment that Marx and Engels were misled by the mathematics of their time cannot be maintained[80]. If he wished, Engels could have known that motion may be described as a continuous function of time and that the concept of continuous function does not involve any contradiction.

Lenin was aware of this fact but dismissed it as a standard objection of Hegel's 'metaphysical' opponents. A mathematical analysis of motion describes the 'result of motion and not motion itself'; it disregards the 'possibility' (origin) of motion; and it constructs motion as a sum of stationary states, to escape the logical but not the dialectical contradiction. The latter is thus concealed at a deeper level, without being resolved.

Lenin's comment delighted some stubborn Polish adherents of 'real contradiction' and prompted them to add that the consistency of mechanics is relative, dependent on the consistency of the analysis. The analysis managed to 'overcome' the contradiction inherent in the concept of the infinitesimal to fall into new ones, arising from the concepts of class, infinite class and continuum. Thus Zeno's paradoxes are reproduced at a higher level of abstraction. Mechanics provides a conceptual tool by means of which a consistent description of motion can be given, but this description is 'banal', phenomenal and dependent on arbitrary assumptions. Real motion, its source and cause, remain as elusive and inexplicable as before[81].

Once the dialectical implications of the 'arrow in flight' are accepted, certain conclusions become inevitable. If the fundamental laws of formal logic require that there should be no contradiction in motion and motion does exhibit contradictory attributes, formal logic is shown to be a theory too narrow to account for the phenomena of Nature. The logic of 'either-or' must make room for a more comprehensive one that includes Plekhanov's formula 'yes is no and no is yes'. There are, therefore, two logics: formal logic which excludes contradictions and is concerned with things at rest, and dialectical logic which is a 'logic of contradiction' and applies to things in motion. The former is a special and marginal case of the latter [82].

We should accept, Schaff argued, the thesis of logical dualism formulated by Plekhanov in *Dialectic and Logic*. Plekhanov's thesis that dialectics does not suppress formal logic but 'merely deprives the laws of formal logic of the absolute value which metaphysicians have ascribed to them', is consistent with the teaching of Marx and Engels, basically true and to be accepted with some minor modifications [83]. The modifications are as follows.

The so-called classics of Marxism-Leninism did not subscribe to the view that every asserted proposition can be justifiably denied. Engels emphasised that consistency of thought helps to 'get over defective knowledge' and spoke disapprovingly of 'losing one's way in insoluble contradictions'[84]. The opinion that may be found in some Soviet textbooks and publications to the effect that 'formal logic does not make sense' can cause nothing but astonishment. There can be no question of dialectical logic ousting and supplanting formal logic altogether. Only the absolute monarchy of the latter must be abolished, and some kind of dual power, with priority accorded to dialectics, installed in its place [85].

If instead of the validity of the laws of formal logic being restricted, the laws of logic were altogether rejected, dialectics itself would not be immune from contradiction. Both the asserted and the rejected theorems of dialectics would then be valid and true. Dialectical logic recognises the objective existence of 'concrete contradictions', *i.e.* of objects which have contradictory attributes, but dialectics itself is not self-contradictory. Dialectics does not allow the acceptance of every pair of contradictory propositions, since this would invalidate 'correct thinking'. Dialectics being a 'logic of contradiction' remains a consistent system. It rejects theses which deny its own theorems and does not include theorems contradictory to each other [86].

Dialectical logic returns to formal logic the services which the latter renders to dialectics. Dialectics guards formal logic against the dangers of formalism and of losing touch with reality by abandoning itself excessively to abstractions. Dialectical logic formulates the important methodological rule that prescribes to 'split the unity' which conceals the opposites inherent in every object, to reveal and to get hold of them by means of appropriate procedures. 'To split the unity and to learn its contradictory factors', wrote Lenin, 'is the essence of dialectics'. This methodological rule is of particular importance in the social sciences, since it helps to lay bare the internal contradictions of bourgeois society and to guide to action conducive to the social development which results from the struggle and unity of the opposites. This is probably the main obstacle, Schaff suggested, to the acceptance of dialectical logic and accounts for the fact that the purely scientific dispute concerning the relation of formal logic to dialectics has degenerated into a distinctly political quarrel [87].

Thus, the relation between formal logic and dialectics turns out to be itself dialectic. On the one hand, they are interrelated and supplement each other. On the other, they are mutually exclusive and inconsistent. Marxist-Leninists did not seem to be able to decide which of the two possibilities applies and to be inclined to the view that both should be accepted. The urge for consistency, induced by the critical examination of Marxism-Leninism carried out by non-Marxist philosophers, is occasionally apparent but is ultimately overruled by extra-logical considerations [88].

The attempts at the reconciliation of formal logic and dialectics conceived as a 'logic of contradiction' was logically untenable, but in practice it had its advantages. The thesis of logical dualism has provided some protection for and made some concessions to the rights of formal and mathematical logic. It set restrictive limits to their study and applications, but within these limits logic could exist and survive.

Logical dualism prompted the extension of the so-called dialectical method to various fields of philosophical inquiry to the exclusion of any other method and reserved for dialectics a large place in the natural and social sciences, which led to something like total annihilation of some of them. On the other hand, logical dualism repudiated the intention of suppressing formal logic altogether and was explicitly committed to the recognition of its limited but real importance for scientific thinking.

The protection of logical dualism, which formal logic enjoyed, was reinforced by the results of the Soviet discussions on the subject-matter of formal logic and its relation to dialectics [89], and by Stalin's pronouncements, known under the collective title *Marxism and Problems of Linguistics*, first published in *Pravda* in June-August, 1950. Before Stalin's intervention the attitude of Marxist-Leninist philosophy to formal logic was, even in Poland, ambiguous and by no means provided a clear and safe assurance that Marxism-Leninism would recognise a further need for it. Upon Stalin's pronouncement, formal logic, like mathematics and grammar, could no longer be considered as a 'superstructure on the basis', the doubt as to its usefulness and the desirability of its continued development was precluded and could not be voiced by a faithful Party member [90].

To return to the discussion of the arguments in favour of the 'logic of contradiction', it should be observed that the first argument for the rejection of the ontological principle of non-contradiction has concerned matters highly controversial since the late 'twenties. Many theories have been formulated to explain them. They constitute problems to be solved by research and new explanations in the field of physics, for which a speculative short-cut is no substitute.

Schaff was quickly corrected in two essential respects. It is not true to say that an electron has simultaneously the characteristics of a particle and a wave, thus revealing contradictory attributes (in the logical sense of this term). No observation justifies this contention. Electrons do behave as if they were particles when they move in Wilson's cloud chamber, and as if they were waves when they pass through a crystal. These are, however, two different phenomena, the time and conditions of their occurrence are different. We cannot speak of the simultaneous but only of the successive duality of electrons. The successive duality of electrons is not inconsistent with the contradictory characteristics of atomic particles; however, it does not imply them. If it did, we would be unable to understand what we were saying [91]. For we know from the propositional calculus that if p implies $q \equiv \sim q$, p must be a falsehood

$$p \supset . q \equiv \sim q : \supset \sim p.$$

There are grounds to believe that the conditions under which the discussed phenomena occur (the recording apparatus) and the phenomena themselves are interrelated. This admits of various interpretations. None of them is a sufficient basis for implying that a statement describing the electron trail in the cloud chamber (the particle characteristic of electrons) and a statement describing the diffraction and interference pattern of a beam of electrons (the wave characteristic of electrons) should be considered as a conjunction of contradictory statements. There exists the puzzling problem of accounting for the wave-particle duality of electrons, but this is a question of physics and not of philosophy [92].

Moreover, the physicists were not on the side of the interpretation in terms of the 'logic of contradiction'. Both abroad and at home a great many of them were warning against reifying physical models of atomic particles and against the conclusion, drawn from their usefulness in describing the results of experiments, that something analogous, corresponding to the models, actually exists in Nature. What we know about the micro-objects makes it necessary to renounce the notion that they have a unique and precisely definable conceptual model or that their objective existence constitutes a definable whole, similar to that of large-scale phenomena, simultaneously and unambiguously accessible to observation. Those who refuse to accept the finality of this interpretation and the absolute validity of the indeterminacy principle would not consider for a moment an arbitrary assumption as a permissible way out of the difficulty [93].

Schaff was also corrected on the point concerning mass and matter and the transformation of mass and energy, governed by Einstein's equation, which in his opinion provided another striking instance of an objective contradiction in a 'corporeal form'. Mass and matter should not be identified. Like energy, mass is an attribute of matter, which can take the form of a particle or that of a field. In the former case physics speaks of mass as an attribute of matter, in the latter of its energy. Einstein's equation establishes the relation between two attributes of matter, or between the two forms that matter can take. There is again the problem of the field-particle duality of matter that so far defies a satisfactory solution and indicates our inadequate knowledge of facts. The problem involved belongs to physics and cannot be explained away by philosophical speculations [94].

The second argument, namely that every process of change involves the simultaneous emergence of contradictory attributes in the changing object, fared little better in discussions. Ajdukiewicz provided an intelligible formal pattern of inference which the argument seems to follow. When this was done, it became clear that it is unsound.

It should first be observed that the conclusion of the argument, that is to say, the statement to the effect that a changing object must at a certain instant display contradictory characteristics

$$\sim (x \text{ is A}) . (x \text{ is A})$$

is never confirmed by experience. Observation reveals that a changing object becomes different but it never verifies the contention that it exhibits contradictory attributes. This contention is an extrapolation; it refers to a possible state of affairs, which, being unconfirmed by experience and absurd in its implications, should be rejected [95].

Furthermore, there seems to be an error in the inference, by which the conjunction

$$\sim (x \text{ is A}) . (x \text{ is A})$$

is reached. The characteristic 'non-A' occurs in the inference as if it were a singular term, which is not in fact the case. Since 'non-A' denotes all states different from A, it is a general term. The principle of continuity is applicable to a process of change from a definite state A to a definite state B, when both 'A' and 'B' are singular terms. In the case when 'B' ('non-A') is the name of a class of states, the principle of continuity does not apply. The inference, therefore, by which the conclusion

$$\sim (x \text{ is A}) . (x \text{ is A})$$

was arrived at, is not valid [96].

Finally, and generally, Ajdukiewicz drew attention to the fact that our inability to decide in a particular case which of the incompatible predicates should be applied to a given object does not imply that both can be truly applied to this object, or that contradictory characteristics inhere in it at the same time. Sometimes our ignorance and sometimes the ambiguity of our language appear to suggest that two contradictory statements are both true. If we disregard these ambiguities we may easily reach the conclusion that Socrates who is turning old and bald is both old and young, both bald and not bald. This does not confirm the existence of contradictions in the external world, but indicates that the user of language has failed to specify the rules for the use of expressions, or to follow these rules, or to define the expressions themselves in relation to other expressions with a common 'fringe'. It is the use, or rather the misuse, of language that makes contradictions and inconsistencies possible. They serve as a warning that the meaning of the expressions has not been fixed and that it must be defined before it is descriptively applied. Limitations in the applicability of descriptive terms invalidate reasonings by means of which the existence of contradictions is inferred from the occurrence of ambiguous terms in our speech. A descriptive term which does not distinguish an object from what it is not, is more or less useless, and a sentence in which it occurs purports to say something though in fact it does not say anything at all [97].

Ajdukiewicz's explanations of elementary logic and logic of language had also some unintended implications, which might have impressed Marxist-Leninists. Ajdukiewicz showed that the emergence of contradictory attributes in the changing objects depends on the continuity of change. But for a Marxist-Leninist philosopher change is both a continuous and a discontinuous process, or a continuous process with 'breaks in continuity'. The principle of continuity explains the appearance of contradictory attributes; it also clashes with and undermines the 'theory of leaps', and that some time ago was pronounced to be a heresy [98]. The 'theory of leaps' explains by itself the emergence of new qualities and does not require the existence of 'corporeal contradictions'. In other words, one does not need to assume that every process of change involves a contradiction. It is enough to retain the Hegelian principle of the object being transformed into its opposite by the action of those polar forces which determine its existence. Instead of the contradictions, the polarity of the opposites provides a sufficient basis for the explanation of the spontaneous change and self-development of Nature. While the latter speculation is as arbitrary as the former, it is at least not incompatible with the fundamental requirements of logic and somewhat reduces the area of arbitrary and oracular thought.

Thus, however, the contradiction allegedly inherent in mechanical motion remains as the only mainstay left to support the contention that the law of non-contradiction is a relic of the metaphysical mode of thought, to be abandoned at the dialectical stage of the development of mankind. The question as to whether Zeno's analysis of the 'arrow in flight' can be maintained acquires crucial importance.

Ajdukiewicz subjected this matter to a thorough examination. His discussion of Zeno's paradoxes, in many respects novel, deserves close attention in view of the role his examination has played in the evolution of Marxist-Leninist philosophy in Poland [99].

Ajdukiewicz examined two possible interpretations of the flying arrow argument. Schaff seems to have used both of them in different places or in support of each other. The first of these interpretations starts with the assumption that the arrow is in flight and reaches the conclusion that if it is in flight then it is at rest. Since

$$(p) : p \supset \sim p . \supset \sim p,$$

the assumption must be rejected as self-contradictory. The argument proceeds by the following stages.

If the arrow is in flight during an interval T, then for every instant t of the interval T there is a position x in which the arrow is to be found (A). If there is a position in which the arrow is to be found at every instant t of its flight (T), then the arrow remains at rest throughout its flight (B). This implication makes use of the definition of rest by which a body is considered to be at rest during the interval T if there is a position in which it is to be found at every instant t of the interval T. From (A) and (B) follows the conclusion: if the arrow is in flight throughout T, then the arrow is at rest throughout T. The assumption that the arrow is in flight implies that the arrow is not in flight.

The inference seems to be a substitution of the following theorem of the propositional calculus

$$p \supset q \,.\, q \supset r : \supset \,.\, p \supset r \,.$$

This, however, is not the case. The sentences to be substituted for q in $p \supset q$ and in $q \supset r$ are not the same but two different propositions. The consequent of the first premiss is, 'for every instant t of the interval T there is a position x in which the arrow is to be found', and the antecedent of the second premiss runs, 'there is a position in which the arrow is to be found at every instant t of its flight (T)'. Symbolically expressed, the consequent in $p \supset q$ has the form

$$(t)\,(\exists x)\ \varphi x t \qquad (q_1),$$

and the antecedent in $q \supset r$

$$(\exists x)\,(t)\ \varphi x t \qquad (q_2).$$

The inference under discussion is, therefore, a substitution of a different theorem of the propositional calculus, namely of

$$p \supset q \,.\, s \supset r : \supset \,.\, p \supset r \,,$$

which is a valid formula if and only if $q \supset s$. But this is not so in our case, since q_1 does not imply q_2 (though q_2 does imply q_1). The rules which govern the use of quantifiers do not allow the inference

$$(t)\,[(\exists x)\ \varphi x t] \,.\, \supset \,.\, (\exists x)\,[(t)\ \varphi x t] \qquad (C).$$

A different example might make it clearer. The premiss 'for every x there exists such a y that $x < y$' does not imply 'there is such a y that for every x: $x < y$'. Similarly, from the fact that for every man there is a man who is his father does not follow that there is a man who is the father of every man. Since the antecedent of (C) is true and the consequent is false, (C) is not a valid formula. The inference on which Zeno's argument in its first interpretation is based is clearly fallacious [100].

The second, more common interpretation can be reduced to the following inference. If a body is in a definite position x at an instant t, then this body is at rest in x at the instant t (D). If the arrow in flight is in a definite position x at every instant of its flight, then the arrow is at rest at every instant of its flight (E). If the arrow in flight is at rest at every instant of its flight, then the arrow is at rest throughout its flight (F). [101].

The fallacy of Zeno's argument is twofold. The first depends on the ambiguity of the connective 'is'. The connective 'is' in the expression 'the arrow is in the position x' may mean the same as 'the arrow remains at x' (a). The connective 'is' may be also used, however, in the most general sense which does not specify the kind of relation between the arrow and its position, to mean 'it passes x' or 'leaves x behind' or 'reaches x' (b). If in the premiss (D) the first 'is' is used in the sense (b), the consequent of the premiss does not follow from the antecedent and the whole inference is destroyed. If, however, the connective 'is' in the antecedent of the premiss (D) has the meaning (a), it becomes a false statement, because a moving body certainly does not remain anywhere. Thus, there is no such meaning of 'is' in which the premiss (D) is true and the whole inference valid [102].

With the above distinction of meanings that the connective 'is' may have, Plekhanov's problem does not offer any difficulty. If we disagree with the thesis that 'a body in motion is at a given point, and at the same time it is not there', Plekhanov wrote, we will be 'forced to proclaim with Zeno that motion is merely an illusion of the senses'[103]. This is exactly the contention which made of the 'arrow in flight' the main argument for the existence of contradictions in the phenomena of Nature. The antecedent of Plekhanov's thesis is a perfectly true, though trivial proposition, if the first 'is' carries the meaning (b), and the second the meaning (a). We can agree with it without committing ourselves to the existence of 'corporeal contradictions'. On the other hand, if 'is' is differently interpreted, Plekhanov's antecedent becomes a false statement. We can disagree with it without being forced to admit that motion is illusory.

In order to know whether a body is in motion or at rest at an instant t, we must always consider what happens to this body at the instant earlier and later than t, i.e. we must consider a time interval that contains t [104]. Only then can we give exact definitions of what is motion, continuous motion, and rest. Zeno's argument goes astray at this point. If the arrow is where it is at a given instant, it does not follow therefrom that the arrow is then at rest. We cannot know whether it is in flight or at rest without considering its position at earlier and later instants. Where it is now does not presume where it was before or where it will be after, i.e. whether it is or is not in flight. There are obvious excuses for Zeno's paralogism; no physical definition of rest and motion was available at his time. Zeno cannot be blamed either for having made the assumption that there are consecutive instants and points. There are no such excuses for errors of the same kind when they are committed today [105].

To show that the alternative 'either motion is illusory or it involves contradiction' is invalid, since both its constituents are false, it is sufficient to apply the modern concept of mathematical continuity to Zeno's paradoxes. Motion consists in the occupation by the moving body B of different places at different times. When throughout an interval, however short it might be, different times are correlated with different places, B is in motion. Similarly, B is at rest, when throughout an arbitrary interval different times are correlated with the same place. This prompted Bertrand Russell to say that Weierstrass 'by strictly banishing all infinitesimal, has at last shown ...... that the arrow, at every moment of its flight, is truly at rest'[106]. By 'being at rest' Russell understands 'occupying a place equal to itself'. On this understanding Zeno was right in pointing out that an arrow in flight is at each instant where it is, irrespective of whether it does or does not fly. When the modern concept of continuity is applied, this does not imply that the arrow in flight is not at different places at different times throughout the interval of its flight.

CHAPTER 15

THE ABANDONMENT OF THE LOGIC OF

CONTRADICTION

The criticism of dialectical logic, of its relation to formal logic, and of the evidence produced in support of its claim that was raised on all sides in the years 1946–1948, put the Marxist-Leninist dialecticians into a philosophically untenable position. Dialectical logic appeared to be a huge misunderstanding, born of terminological ambiguities, ignorance of matters of fact, logical errors, primitive misconceptions and self-contradictory claims. Although Schaff stuck to his guns, he recognised that the relation of dialectics to formal logic was an 'extremely complicated question'. He pleaded for patience and suspension of judgement until some undisclosed logical and dialectical problems were solved. Self-contradiction, he stated, is self-destruction. Marxist-Leninists accepted the requirements of consistency, did not deny the importance of formal logic, and were only concerned with finding the limits of its validity [107].

After the lively discussions on the relation of dialectics to formal logic, which took place in the period 1946–1948, the next few years were marked by no significant developments. However, behind the scenes a slow-moving but decisive shift of opinion was taking place among the Marxist-Leninist dialecticians which finally resulted in the abandonment of the logic of contradiction by a considerable proportion of them. This happened in 1955 and the years 1955–1957 witnessed the revival of the discussions on the validity and role of the principle of non-contradiction.

With one exception, these discussions were conducted exclusively by Marxist-Leninist philosophers and were embarrassingly and solemnly elementary in character. Some Marxist-Leninists confessed their errors and fully accepted the position of logic and common sense. Others gave up the most glaring dialectical fallacies and retained only some residual and harmless opinions concerning not so much logic as its philosophical foundations. Finally, a small group refused to revise their views. This group also defended the old stand in a novel manner and tried, though unsuccessfully, to comply with the requirements of consistency.

Several factors contributed to the shift and to the final change of opinion. One of them was undoubtedly the results of the discussions on logic and dialectics in the Soviet Union. These results not only strengthened the hand of the logicians, but also set in motion new processes of thought among Marxist-Leninist philosophers. As Schaff put it, one cannot accept the validity of formal logic and contend that there are contradictions inherent in things and phenomena of Nature. Either the former or the latter must be rejected. *Hic Rhodus, hic Salta!* The times, he added, when M. B. Mitin (the leading Soviet philosopher of the 'thirties and still a man of considerable influence in the Soviet Union) could describe formal logic as 'fiddlesticks' and consider the matter closed, were over [108]. The fourth edition of the *Short Philosophical Dictionary* (1954) published in a Polish translation in 1955, expounded antiquated views on formal logic and spoke somewhat ambiguously on the difference between a 'logical' and a 'dialectical contradiction', but made a firm demand for the adherence to the laws of logic which are universally valid and absolutely necessary in all thinking [109]. About 1955 the logicians resumed the criticism of the view that dialectics follows a logic of its own, can do without the law of non-contradiction and is incompatible with formal logic. This view, they stated, rests on logical errors and fallacious thinking [110].

The alternative, formulated by Schaff, was not difficult to solve. Formal logic has proved its usefulness in the development of science and the alleged contradictions, to which the founders of Marxism-Leninism referred, turned out to be on closer examination only apparent contradictions, resulting from terminological inaccuracies, verbal confusions or the mistaken use of logical terms. These were the views which the logically trained philosophers presented in the discussions of 1946–1948 and which they continued to press and to spread in their teaching and other activities. They were increasingly accepted by the followers of Marxism-Leninism, although hardly anything of it transpired in print at that time [111].

There was yet another factor that seemed to have played a considerable role in the described development of events – the expurgation of Marxism-Leninism from Hegelian influences, to which reference was made in one of the preceding chapters. Schaff, who in 1946–1948 led the ineffective fight against the principle of non-contradiction and in the period 1955–1957 became the leading force among Marxist-Leninist philosophers for the abandonment of the logic of contradiction, belonged to the anti-Hegelian wing. The expurgation of Hegelian ideas from Marxism-Leninism was accompanied by a markedly increased respect for logic and common sense.

It was probably no matter of accident that while praising Stalin for correcting Engels in the formulation of the laws of dialectics and for having stopped 'coquetting Hegel', Schaff also extolled Stalin's 'iron logic', his precision and struggle against every kind of muddle-headedness and ambiguity. For Stalin, dialectics presupposed the respect for logic. Stalin also exposed the deviation which made dialectics and formal logic oppose each other and which denied that the latter possessed any significance. The rejection of formal logic, Schaff stated, turns dialectics into sophistry. Stalin, a true dialectician, restored the teaching of formal logic at secondary schools and universities, revived the interest in logic and showed that it does not possess superstructural character [112].

Waldemar Rolbiecki, a Marxist-Leninist of the younger generation, was the first to state the conclusions with respect to formal logic and the principle of non-contradiction, which resulted from a new appraisal of the relation between dialectics and logic [113]. Some of Rolbiecki's views were at once accepted by Polish Marxist-Leninists. Others were, however, challenged both from the viewpoint of orthodoxy and that of logical consistency.

Thus, Polish Marxist-Leninists split in two groups. One was led by Schaff, who came to the conclusion that he was wrong in his previous views on dialectics and formal logic, and that his opponents, Ajdukiewicz and Ossowski in particular, were right. The other section was led by Ładosz, who accused Schaff of yielding to the neo-positivist influence and of being guilty of serious misrepresentation of Marxism-Leninism [114]. These differences of opinion corresponded to a similar division among Soviet Marxist-Leninists. But while in Poland the stand taken by Schaff is supported by an overwhelming majority of Marxist-Leninists and Ładosz is almost isolated in his views, the position in the Soviet Union seems to be dissimilar. *Voprosy Filosofii* strongly supported the views defended by Ładosz in Poland, and condemned those of Schaff as well as the position, similar to Schaff's, taken by K. S. Bakradze and N. I. Kondakov in the Soviet Union. What seems to have been finally decided among leading Marxist-Leninists in Poland, still remains in the balance in the Soviet Union [115].

What all the Polish Marxist-Leninists seem to agree upon is the rejection of logical dualism. There is one and only one logic, whose importance for science and philosophy cannot be overestimated. The laws of logic apply universally, both to objects at rest as well as to those changing and in motion. There can be no consistency and, therefore, no science, if contradictory statements are accepted together, or if inferences from contradictory premises are accepted as valid. Dialectical logic is neither logic in the strict sense, nor formal; it does not deal with and does not provide rules of inference, which constitute the subject-matter of formal logic and which must be respected also by dialectics, if dialectics is to make sense. If the law of non-contradiction is rejected, anything may be asserted, anything follows from what we assert, all statements are equally valid, no principle and law remains true any longer [116].

Two explanations were offered to account for the fact that until recently a different view had prevailed in Marxist-Leninist philosophy, the validity of formal logic had been rejected or restricted, and a 'logic of contradiction' had to be put in its place. The first claimed that not Marx, Engels, Lenin and Stalin, but their followers should be blamed for this error. The founders of the doctrine never questioned the laws of logic, but only a particular and philosophical use made of them. What they said of logic did not refer to formal logic but to logic in the broad sense of this term, and above all, to the theory of knowledge. Even when Marx, Engels, or Lenin did speak of formal logic, they meant Aristotle's or Hegel's or traditional logic, which substantially differs from modern formal logic. What did apply to the former is not necessarily true with respect to the latter. The views of the present-day Marxist-Leninists on formal logic cannot justifiably claim the authority of the founders. Dialectics was never intended to be a science about the forms of valid inference, some kind of 'higher formal logic'. Plekhanov's logical dualism is a false conception of the relation between formal logic and dialectics, entirely foreign to the Marxist-Leninist doctrine [117].

For obvious reasons this opinion is unacceptable and it was rejected by Schaff and Eilstein. When the classical works of Marxism-Leninism are carefully examined, two things are perfectly clear. First, Marx, Engels and Lenin did recognise the validity of the law of non-contradiction and of the excluded middle whenever they were applied to some particular cases. They did not accept any view or argument which did not conform to these principles; if a view was contradictory or led to a contradiction, it was a sure indication of its falsehood. On the other hand, the founders of Marxism-Leninism did put restrictions on the validity of the principles in question. Both Engels and Lenin were convinced that the principle of non-contradiction and that of universal changeability were incompatible. However vague and inaccurate their use of the term 'contradiction' might have been, it must be recognised that in their view real and genuine contradictions *sensu stricto* were an essential feature of change and motion. They were convinced that an adequate description of natural, historical and social events could not be free from contradictions, for it had simultaneously to assert and to deny the same and in the same respect. Engels and Lenin found Hegel's opinion that an 'intelligent reflection . . . . . . consists in the understanding and enunciating of Contradiction' to be self-evident. Plekhanov tried to solve this paradox by his thesis of logical dualism and of the existence of the two realms of being to which dialectical and formal logic apply respectively. Plekhanov's thesis must be rejected on the ground of experience and of logical consistency.

It should be conceded that the founders of Marxism-Leninism denied the universal validity of the laws of logic. This error originated with Hegel, with his confusion of contradictories and contraries, and his belief that real contradiction is the root of all movement, change and life. From Hegel the error passed on to Engels, Lenin and to Marxist-Leninist dialectics in general. The founders of Marxism-Leninism were not infallible and to recognise that they committed an error does not mean that Marxist-Leninist philosophy is falling to pieces. The elimination of errors can only strengthen a doctrine in which they are discovered [118].

At this stage the point was reached where serious differences of opinion among Polish Marxist-Leninists began to loom large and two different theories were put forward. Their chief protagonists were Schaff and Eilstein on the one hand, Rolbiecki and Ładosz on the other.

According to Schaff and Eilstein, a sharp distinction should be made between a logical and a dialectical contradiction. The latter is a misleading term, if it is understood to carry a logical meaning. It does not imply that things and phenomena of Nature do and do not possess certain characteristics in the same respect and at the same time, *e.g.* that a moving body is and is not at a given place at the same instant or that motion is and is not continuous together. What dialectics calls a contradiction might have different meanings. It might refer to the inherence in the object of opposite forces or polar tendencies, or to the incompatibility between parts or aspects of a whole. The mutually exclusive interests of the proletariat and the bourgeoisie, the conflict between the productive forces and the relations of production within the capitalist system are the classical examples of dialectical contradictions. These are not contradictions *sensu stricto,* because opposite attributes do not involve a logical contradiction and do not entail a conjunction of contradictory statements to be true. We not only can but must speak consistently of dialectical contradictions.

In particular, motion is no contradiction. As Ajdukiewicz has shown, there are logical and semantical fallacies in Zeno's argument. Those who accept it in order to deny that motion is real or who accept it in order to claim that motion is a contradiction, commit a very similar error. This error is prompted by the metaphysical approach that constructs motion from static states.

The core of dialectics is the unity and struggle of the opposites and not the contradiction in the logical sense inherent as 'corporeal form' in the phenomena of Nature. The acceptance of the law of non-contradiction does not change the substance of Marxist-Leninist philosophy, makes it a consistent doctrine and reconciles dialectics with logic to the benefit of both [119].

Finally, it was suggested that the expression 'the unity and struggle of the opposites' is a metaphor which requires an interpretation before it can be applied to physical objects and processes. For a materialist the question why matter is in motion and what is its source has no definite meaning. He may and must, however, ask the question what are the causes which determine physical processes or events. The principle of the 'unity and struggle of the opposites' lays down that the causes should not be looked for outside but within matter itself, in its states, in other physical phenomena or in more elementary events. The principle in question also indicates that matter should not be conceived as consisting of homogeneous particles; matter reveals a differentiated structure and thus includes in itself the principle of motion, dynamic instability and qualitative change [120].

The appearance of contradictions, of antinomies and quasi-antinomies, of incompatible theories which are equally well justified at a given stage of knowledge, can be accounted for without resorting to the assumption of contradictions being inherent in the physical world. If the latter were truly there, we could not escape asserting conjunctions of contradictory statements as valid and true. But the progress of science invariably consists in showing that such conjunctions are invalid and are in fact eliminated by new techniques and the acquisition of new knowledge. The appearance of antinomies and incompatible theories is fully accounted for by the historical and social limitations of knowledge and by the presence of opposite tendencies in Nature [121].

The other Marxist-Leninist school of thought did not accept the view that the term 'dialectical contradiction' is a misnomer because it is not in fact a logical contradiction *sensu stricto*. In conformity with the Marxist-Leninist theory of knowledge, according to which knowledge is a reflection of the outside world, Rolbiecki argued that genuine logical contradictions, that is, other than those resulting from errors and ignorance, constantly eliminated and ever returning in a different form, are an indication of the 'dialectically contradictory character of reality' [122]. His views were elaborated and somewhat more systematically presented by Ładosz.

Ładosz's standpoint was essentially a reformulation of the traditional Marxist-Leninist doctrine. He treated lightly all efforts to eliminate or to resolve paradoxes, antinomies and contradictions by logical analysis. Logical analysis results in trivialities. It might achieve its purpose by some technical tricks or ingenuity, without, however, touching the heart of the problem. This was the case, in Ładosz's opinion, with Ajdukiewicz's analysis of Zeno's argument. It was an exercise in logical skill which blurred the real issue and left it unresolved. This real issue is that of the origin of change and motion. In agreement with the Hegelian-Marxian tradition, Ładosz assumed what others find so difficult to comprehend, namely that only logical contradictions *sensu stricto* make things change and move. On this account he dismissed logical analysis as a futile game and believed that dialectical, real contradictions *sensu stricto* are everlasting. They differ from purely logical contradictions just because they can never be 'overcome' or eliminated. There are, therefore, contradictory statements which are true together and the law 'one and only one of two contradictory statements is true' is generally false [123].

Real contradictions *sensu stricto* not only explain change and motion, but also the appearance of paradoxes and antinomies, as well as the whole course of the development of knowledge, progressing from one contradiction to another. In this respect Ładosz is a pure Hegelian and Leninist. 'The reflection of Nature in human thought', Lenin wrote, 'must be envisaged not as 'dead' or 'abstract' or static or free from contradiction, but as an eternal process of movement, in which contradictions are forever emerging and being resolved' [124]. They are 'dialectical contradictions of thought', corresponding to those in the outside world. The former are bound up with and inexplicable without the latter. On the other hand, real contradictions in Nature make it imperative that our concepts be kept vague and ambiguous, if they are to be descriptively useful and adequate to what they refer.

Ładosz ridiculed the idea that dialectical logic may be formalised to replace formal logic. The idea of a formalised dialectical logic does seem to be utterly unsound and fantastic. How could an inference whose validity is determined by its content be formally considered? How can a method that reconstructs the 'real movement' and follows the unfolding of contradictory relations, of which any particular content is made up, be formal? Above all, there is a more basic objection to 'formal dialectics'. Once Hegel's dialectics is turned upside down, 'dialectics of facts' is considered to be primary and the 'movement of thought' to be its reflection evolving in obedience to dialectic laws, the idea of dialectics codified into some kind of formal logic is in fact untenable. Whatever universality dialectics may claim, it cannot be that of logic. Since the emphasis on the dialectics of Nature is conspicuous in Marxism-Leninism, those anxious to uphold the orthodoxy can claim for dialectics only the universality of Nature or History, the universality of the 'laws of motion', which the unfolding of natural and historical events must obey.

While asserting that by the discovery and the 'overcoming' of objective and everlasting contradictions dialectics reveals the 'deep truth' about the world, Ładosz also thought highly of the cognitive value of formal and mathematical logic [125]. To reconcile this view with the recognition of the existence of contradictions *sensu stricto* he suggested that the binding force of logic, conceived as a system of inferential rules, remains unimpaired provided that it is supplemented by a rejection rule which forbids drawing inferences from contradictory

statements. It is not true to say, Ładosz argued, that the acceptance of contradictory statements being true together leads to falsehood and absurdities. Falsehood
results only from drawing inferences from such statements. The above mentioned
rejection rule 'constitutes the essence of the non-contradiction principle of formal logic' [126]. Thus, formal logic and dialectics can be reconciled without giving
up anything, either the traditional principles of dialectics or of formal logic.

Ładosz's solution is, however, apparent and does involve a 'dialectical contradiction of thought', or more plainly, it leads to a contradiction. The inconsistency of Ładosz's views on the relation between dialectics and formal logic
was shown by Kokoszyńska.

If the theorems of logic are conceived as rules of inference – among Polish
logicians this conception of logic had been investigated by Jaśkowski in the
'thirties and has been adopted by Suszko after the war – we might see in these
rules some kind of commands, either hypothetical or unconditional. The former
are incomplete, the latter complete expressions. A hypothetical command can
always be formulated in the indicative mood, which transforms an abbreviated
expression into a complete sentence. Thus, the imperative sentence 'do this or
that', interpreted as a hypothetical command, means 'if you wish to bring about
an identifiable state of affairs, you should do this or that'. The latter expression is
equivalent to an indicative statement 'the necessary condition of bringing about
an identifiable state of affairs is to do this or that'. Unconditional imperatives do
not admit of such interpretations. They must be considered as complete sentences
and cannot be reduced to an indicative expression which states that something
is the case. They invariably tell someone unambiguously to do something or to
make something the case.

If logical theorems are conceived as inferential rules, they offer a parallel to a
hypothetical command. As complete sentences they state: the necessary condition to assert only true sentences (with respect to some premises) is to reject a
certain sentence p, or: the necessary condition to reject only false sentences
(with respect to some premises) is to assert a certain sentence p. The former
corresponds to a forbidding, the latter to a prescriptive command. It is natural
to complete 'logical commands' in the described fashion, because science is
concerned with truth and falsehood and interested solely or mainly in how to
achieve the former and to avoid the latter [127].

To see what this conception of logic entails, another preparatory step must be
made. In any systematic examination we can distinguish five different levels of
discourse. First, the objects and their relations, investigated by a given science
(the objective level); second, the statements describing these objects and their
relations (subjective level); third, the statements concerning the truth and
falsehood of the second level statements (the metatheoretical or semantical
level); fourth, the rules of procedure acquired from the knowledge of the
investigated objects (the methodological level); fifth, the systematic order of
thought and the consistent adherence to the rules of procedure established in the
universe of discourse of which a given science makes use.

So far as logic is concerned, the distinction between the different levels of discourse has a long tradition. Aristotle distinguished the ontological and the logical principle of non-contradiction (corresponding to the first and second or third of the differentiated levels of discourse) and we are all well acquainted with its fourth level, since we follow the command 'Do not ever assert the conjunction of contradictory statements' [128].

The principle of non-contradiction can easily be formulated in terms of the first level, but to deal with other logical formulae in the same manner becomes awkward. As a rule, and for obvious reasons, we carry on logical investigations on the second and the third level. In principle, logical theorems can also be formulated in the language of methodology. This is what Ladosz suggested should be done. Then, however, certain conclusions become inevitable.

What is stated in methodological terms, determines the truth and falsehood of what is asserted at the lower levels of discourse. This is true as long as the 'logical commands' are conceived as incomplete hypothetical sentences. The rule: 'Accept every alternative of contradictory statements' would entail the truth of any such alternative. The rule in question expressed as a complete sentence means: the necessary condition of rejecting only false statements is not to reject any alternative of contradictory statements. It follows therefrom that if an alternative of contradictory statements is rejected, a true statement is rejected. Therefore, the alternative cannot be false, and not being false it must be true. The same reasoning applies to any other logical theorem conceived as a 'command' and reduced to a methodological rule.

In particular, the methodological rule of non-contradiction implies that no conjunction of contradictory statements is true. It cannot be true, therefore, that either the sentence 'motion is and is not continuous' is true, as Ladosz asserted, or, what is the case according to dialectics, that motion is and is not continuous. By declaring his adherence to the methodological rule of non-contradiction and asserting the above indicated sentence, Ladosz contradicts himself. Generally speaking, logic and dialectics are not thus reconciled, but exclude each other. What the former holds to be false, the latter declares to be true, and conversely. Ladosz's claim that he has produced a new theory of the relation between dialectics and formal logic, which is consistent and allows the adherence of both to their respective traditional principles, is not justified. The solution failed to achieve its purpose and the old conflict remains unresolved [129]

The contradiction can be avoided by conceiving 'logical commands' as unconditional. In this case the methodological rule of non-contradiction does not entail the conclusion that no conjunction of contradictory statements is true. A command might not be obeyed for some reason or other and the failure to follow it does not involve a contradiction, though it is exposed to the objection that such a behaviour is not consistent.

To adopt this attitude gives rise to some other important difficulties, which are extremely embarrassing to a Marxist-Leninist; they do seem to come into conflict with some of his other basic assumptions. How is the discrepancy between the nature of reality, which contains contradictions *sensu stricto,* and the requirements of thought, forbidding to accept contradictory statements and striving to eliminate them, to be explained? Is it not probable that if reality were as full of contradictions as Ładosz supposed it to be, the human mind would evolve a different logic from that which it actually adheres to? Furthermore, does not the acceptance of real contradictions *sensu stricto* lead to what Marxism-Leninism calls 'agnosticism'? To say that A is and is not B together implies that we have equally good reasons to assert both. Therefore, we do not know what A is. If we knew, we could decide whether it is or is not B. Thus, however, the irrationalistic solution of the relation between dialectics and formal logic is reinforced by agnosticism. While being able to give some explanation how antinomies and quasi-antinomies arise, Ładosz cannot account for the fact that the human mind strives for their solution or elimination. This striving is a Sisyphean and senseless toil, doomed to failure or trivialities, if we are to believe what Ładosz said. From his theories there emerges a world in which an existentialist, but not a Marxist-Leninist, might feel at home [130].

This criticism, to which no reply has been given, concludes the long-drawn battle between the logicians and the dialecticians about the meaning to be attached to the principles of dialectics, about the status of the law of non-contradiction and of formal logic in general. In the course of this discussion Polish Marxist-Leninists substantially changed their original ideas and, in fact, revised the classical Marxist-Leninist theory.

This restored peace between the logicians and Marxist-Leninist philosophers so far as the fundamentals are concerned. On this basis only a philosophical discussion becomes possible and other differences of opinion can be seriously examined instead of being simply dismissed by both sides, though for different and not equally well justifiable reasons.

NOTES TO PART IV

1. Lenin (4), 239.
2. Lenin (4), 81.
3. Engels (1), 135.
4. "T 'p' " stands for " 'p' is true".
5. Engels (2), 286; Marx-Engels (4), 519.
6. Łubnicki (7), 279–280.
7. Ossowski (5), 504; Ossowski (7), 11–12; Ossowski (8), 32–33; Ossowski (15), 142.
8. Strawson (1), 2.
9. Jaśkowski (7) and (8).
10. In the 'logic of discussion' '$p \supset q$' should be read '$(\Diamond\, p) \supset q$'.
11. See Jaśkowski (7), 69.
12. Pears (Ed.) (1), 164.
13. Jaśkowski (3), 68–70. Compare Chwistek (3), 29–30.
14. See, *e.g.*, Eilstein (6), 126; Schaff (7), 262.
15. Ajdukiewicz (15), 52; Kotarbiński (15), T. 2, 515–516.
16. Greniewski (5), 136–137, 204–206.
17. See, *e.g.,* Kotarbiński (6), 5–6; Ajdukiewicz (25), 51–58.
17a. Bocheński (9), 63.
18. Church (1), 1.
19. Engels (2), 58–59, Lenin (4), 64–65, 149, 165, 217.
20. Schaff (3), reprinted in Schaff (6), 109–143, with some significant omissions.
21. Schaff (3), 336–337. Schaff followed closely Engels (2), 285–286.
22. Lenin (3), 336; Lenin (4), 65–66, 68–69.
23. Engels (2), 296.
24. Schaff (3), 342, 345. Compare Lenin (3), 332–333.
25. Schaff (3), 340, 345; Schaff (14), 213–214; Lenin (3), 553. I do not think that Schaff would maintain to-day that vague and 'elastic' concepts are the best descriptive instruments of science. This doctrine still has supporters among Marxist-Leninists in Poland. See Ładosz (2), 132–133. Kokoszyńska made a sharp and trenchant criticism of this view. See Kokoszyńska (10), 144–149.
26. Hegel (1), Vol. 2, 66–70; Lenin (4), 110–116.
27. See, *e.g.,* Engels (1), 158; Engels (2), 271.
28. Białobrzeski (2), 37.
29. Other absurdities arising from the abuse of terms taken from physics and applied outside their proper field are discussed in Popper (3), 112–114.
30. Schaff (3), 351–352.
31. Engels (1), 135.
32. Kłósak (5), 75–77. Compare Suszko (7), 65.
33. See, *e.g.,* Popper (4), 162–163; Popper (5), 32–35.
34. Schaff (3), 332; Schaff (15), 40–41.
35. Schaff (3), 332. It was not unusual in those times to read in Soviet publications that to consider a logical or mathematical theory as 'an abstract hypothetico-deductive system without intrinsic content other than that implied by arbitrarily

prescribed sets of postulates' was prompted by the desire to further the cause of imperialism and capitalism. See Janowska (1), 6–7, who comments on Bell (1), 334.

36. See Jordan (3), 25–26; Łukasiewicz (18).
37. Ajdukiewicz (13) and (24).
38. See Mostowski (9), 16, 42; Suszko (5), 148–161; Grzegorczyk (6), 212–216.
39. This can be seen, for instance, by comparing Schaff's views with those of Kotarbiński or Ajdukiewicz. See Kotarbiński (16), 208–210; Ajdukiewicz (13) and (24).
40. Lenin (3), 334–335; Schaff (3), 342.
41. This view is taken from Soviet philosophy which has continued to adhere to it even when a little more enlightened opinions on logic could be heard in the Soviet Union. See Rozental-Judin (1), 338.
42. Schaff (3), 334–336, 349, 351.
43. Schaff (3), 336, 338, 347.
44. Schaff expresses these opinions without providing any evidence for either. Łukasiewicz (1), to which he referred, does not justify the view that Aristotle ever doubted the validity of the principle of non-contradiction and later research found no reason to modify this conclusion. See Bocheński (7), 40. As to Łukasiewicz's own views on this matter, Schaff's implied suggestion that Łukasiewicz questioned the validity of this principle is not justified. Łukasiewicz pointed out that the principle of non-contradiction requires a proof and that such a proof was not available at that time. Schaff did not seem to be aware of the fact that Łukasiewicz later modified his opinion on the principle in question.
45. Schaff (3), 335-336, 349; Schaff (7), 259, 263.
46. Czeżowski (9), 82; Czeżowski (22), 219; Kłósak (5), 96.
47. Heyting (1), 17; Czeżowski (9), 82–85; Zawirski (4), 188.
48. See, e.g., Suszko (5), 156. Such views were not shared by non-Marxist philosophers. See Ajdukiewicz (21), 45–49 or Kotarbiński (16), 210–211.
49. The theory of the analycity of logical and mathematical theorems has been criticised in Poland and is considered to be false and detrimental to the development of logic and mathematics. So far as Marxist-Leninists are concerned, they did not seem to distinguish the two possible meanings of the term 'tautology', that is, between statements true or false by virtue of their wording and tautologies in the sense familiar from formal logic. Thus, one of the axioms of the propositional calculus of Russell and Whitehead: $p \lor p. \supset p$, is known as the principle of tautology. It states that to assert p twice is to assert it just once. The two different meanings of 'tautology' seem to merge into one in the Marxist-Leninist language.
50. Łukasiewicz (20), 45, 149; Bocheński (7), 40–41.
51. Czeżowski (22), 222–227.
52. Łukasiewicz (10), 67–68.
53. Łukasiewicz (11), 63.
54. Czeżowski (11), 71; Kotarbiński (16), 136.
55. See, e.g., Mostowski (2), 273–274.
56. See Schaff (3), 329–330; Schaff (6), 115. Ossowski repeatedly criticised Schaff's view. See Ossowski (5), 504; (7), 11–12; (8), 33.
57. Łukasiewicz (18), 26. Compare Chwistek (3), 9, 109.
58. Heyting (1), 97.
59. Zawirski (4), 165–196.
60. I consider only the simplest case, namely the intuitionist propositional calculus based on the trichotomy of truth-values. Such a calculus is not complete. As was

shown by Gödel (1932) and later by Jaśkowski (1935), no finite truth-matrix adequately determines the intuitionist calculus. This can be only achieved, if matrices with an infinite number of truth-values are considered. See Zawirski (4), 204–222; Czeżowski (11), 76.

61. Kotarbiński (15), T. 1, 122–123, 129–130.
62. Chwistek (3), 131–132. Compare Mostowski (2), 42–43.
63. Schaff (14), 81–84.
64. Ryle (1), chapter 2; Pears (2), 232.
65. This is Becker's and Prior's interpretation of *De Interpretatione* 9 (Becker (1), Prior (1), 240–244). Łukasiewicz's view is to be found in Łukasiewicz (11), 75–76. See also Bocheński (7), 41; Bocheński (12), 73. According to Becker, Aristotle did not restrict the validity of the principle of the excluded middle and considered also the disjunction 'Either there will be a sea-battle tomorrow or there will not be' as true, although neither of its components is either true or false.
66. Rosser-Turquette (1), 3–5; Ryle (1), 25–27.
67. Pears (2), 235–236; Waismann (1), 457.
68. Schaff (14), 157–160, 165. In a recent publication Schaff was, therefore, rightly classified as a supporter of pseudo-bivalued logic (Greniewski (8), 91–93).
69. Wudel (1).
70. This contention cannot now be maintained. Łukasiewicz's investigations seem to have firmly established the fact that modal functors (as logical functors) have no interpretation in two-valued logic and that consequently every system of modal logic must be many-valued (Łukasiewicz (20), 166; Łukasiewicz (21), 111–113).
71. Greniewski (5), 207-212; Rolbiecki (1), 76–77; Eilstein (7), 116. An interesting example of statements which might be considered to be neither true nor false is given in Greniewski (5), 210–211.
72. Rosser-Turquette (1), 6; Greniewski (5), 212.
73. Schaff (3), 334, 341–342. The distinction between objects whose opposite characteristics do not and those which do require a conjunction of contradictory statements for their adequate description was important, because it paved the way for the final rejection of the existence of contradictory objects.
74. Engels (1), 27–28; Plekhanov (2), 94; Schaff (3), 333–334, 343–344.
75. Ajdukiewicz (15), 46–47.
76. Hegel (1), Vol. 2, 67; Engels (1), 135; Lenin (4), 244; Plekhanov (1), 112–113; Plekhanov (2), 92–94.
77. This opinion is still shared by some Marxist-Leninists in Poland. See Ładosz (2), 125–133. Outside Marxist-Leninist circles even their sympathisers were altogether unwilling to accept Schaff's views on Zeno's argument. See Greniewski (5), 352–353.
78. Schaff (3), 331, 339–341; Lenin (4), 243; Engels (1), 135.
79. Engels (1), 136, 151.
80. Schaff (23), 156.
81. Lenin (4), 244–245; Ładosz (2), 126–128.
82. Schaff (3), 340, 341, 343, 351–352.
83. Plekhanov (1), 118; Schaff (3), 349, 351. This appraisal of Plekhanov was never again repeated by Schaff and the phrase in question was deleted in Schaff (6). In Fomina (1), 283–285, we find the opinion that Plekhanov's views on dialectical logic are not faultless and that Plekhanov's 'dialectical opportunism', revealed in his political activities since 1903, originated from his views on the relation of dialectics to logic. Fomina's book, published in Russian in 1955, was severely censored

before publication and after its appearance in turn criticised for endorsing false opinions on Plekhanov. See Wetter (1), 108–109.

84. Engels (1), 28; Engels (2), 50. Schaff quoted Engels (1), 31 and 135, but the passages referred to above seem to better support Schaff's point.

85. Schaff (3), 347, 353. Also this passage was deleted in Schaff (6). Compare Suszko (3), 394.

86. Schaff (3), 346.

87. Lenin (4), 335; Schaff (3), 343, 345–346, 353.

88. Schaff (3), 349, 352.

89. Soviet discussions in *Voprosy Filosofii* (1950–1951) were summarised in *Dyskusja* (1) and Wróblewski (1), but they were of course available in the original and widely known. See, *e.g.,* Kokoszyńska (8), 186.

90. The logicians repeatedly took advantage of Stalin's pronouncements on linguistics to reassert their rights. See Stonert (1), 253; Kokoszyńska (8), 184, 186; Gregoro-wicz (1), 9–10. Stalin's pronouncement was emphatically endorsed by the leading Polish Marxist-Leninists. See Schaff (15), 40–41.

91. Białobrzeski (1), 169; Białobrzeski (7), 54–56.

92. Mehlberg (2), 97–98; Kłósak (5), 53–56.

93. See, *e.g.,* Szczeniowski (1), 33–34. The various possible views that a physicist may take of the dual nature of micro-objects are discussed in Bohm (1), 91–103.

94. Infeld-Sosnowski (1), 51; Szczeniowski (2), 185–186, 196–197.

95. Ajdukiewicz (15), 48; Łukasiewicz (1), 139. The same can be said of a moving body. The contention that it is at a given point and is not there at the same time is an extrapolation never to be actually observed (Kłósak (5), 71). See also Russell (3), 110–114, where an essentially similar argument is examined in a general manner.

96. Ajdukiewicz (15), 50.

97. Ajdukiewicz (15), 51.

98. Schaff (6), 103–108; Schaff (12), 97–102. A 'development by leaps, catastrophies, revolutions' was strongly emphasised by Lenin, who saw in this idea the revolutionary side of Hegel's philosophy. See, *e.g.,* Lenin (3), 23–25.

99. Ajdukiewicz's analysis of the 'race course' and 'Achilles and tortoise' arguments is omitted, because Marxist-Leninists never refer to them and Ajdukiewicz's exposition of Zeno's fallacy follows the familiar line (an infinite series might have a limit).

100. Ajdukiewicz (15), 39–40. This particular fallacy was analysed and explained in Ajdukiewicz (2), 205–206. See also Quine (2), 121–122. There can hardly be a better example of how the logical notation helps us to keep the distinction clear where ordinary speech signally fails.

101. I agree with Russell (3), 179, that the 'arrow in flight' assumes that finite segments of time and space consist of a finite number of instants (intervals) and points. This assumption should, therefore, be added to (E). Zeno's arguments against his adversaries who held that things were 'a many' proceeded on the assumption that segments of time and space consist either of a finite or an infinite number of instants and points. The 'arrow in flight' belongs to the first group of the *logoi* (Jordan (2), 40–43.).

102. Ajdukiewicz (15), 40–42. The two meanings of 'is' used in the statements about continuous motion and the difficulties arising therefrom are mentioned in Russell (3), 142. 'To be at a place' may carry different meanings according to whether we think in terms of instants or intervals.

103. Plekhanov (1), 112–113.
104. This is essentially Black's solution of the paradox. See Black (2), 140–147.
105. Ajdukiewicz (15), 42–45.
106. Russell (1), 347.
107. Schaff (7), 259, 269.
108. Schaff (31), 207–210.
109. Rozental-Judin (1), 338–340, 704–710.
110. Greniewski (5), 5; Grzegorczyk (8), 39–40; Ajdukiewicz (27), 75–78.
111. Rolbiecki (1), 63; Eilstein (7), 116. See also Ładosz (2), 107 and Schaff (21), 15, 29 where the discrepancy between the official doctrine and what more and more Marxist-Leninists thought to be the case was implicitly acknowledged.
112. Schaff (19), 69–70. The political motives, which initiated this trend, are analysed in Marcuse (1), 136–159.
113. Rolbiecki (1). This article appeared in print in 1955 but its substance was contained in a paper, written in 1953, which won the award in a competition organised by *Myśl Filozoficzna*. See Rolbiecki (1), 43, footnote.
114. Schaff (23), 143–144; Ładosz (2), 106.
115. Schaff (31), 201, 207–210. A slightly different appraisal of the position in the Soviet Union is given in Wetter (1), 243, 527–535. Schaff and Wetter are in agreement that Bakradze and Kondakov have probably more supporters than the public discussion in *Voprosy Filosofii* might suggest.
116. Rolbiecki (1), 49–62; Schaff (23), 157; Ładosz (2), 108–110, 123–134; Eilstein (6), 131, 143, 145.
117. Rolbiecki (1), 43–49. For a similar interpretation of Marx's views on formal logic see Calvez (1), 359–360.
118. Schaff (23), 144–147; Eilstein (6), 143–146.
119. Schaff (23), 148–158; Eilstein (6), 146–149.
120. Eilstein (6), 132–138. This answers another criticism of non-Marxist philosophers. See Łubnicki (1), 147; Łubnicki (7), 283–284; Kłósak (5), 78–79.
121. Schaff (31), 204–205; Eilstein (6), 138–143.
122. Rolbiecki (1), 72, 74.
123. Ładosz (2), 111, 125–127, 130–131.
124. Lenin (4), 168.
125. Ładosz (2), 107, 109.
126. Ładosz (2), 123.
127. Kokoszyńska (10), 131–133.
128. Kokoszyńska (8), 189–193; Kokoszyńska (10), 134–136.
129. Kokoszyńska (10), 136–139.
130. Kokoszyńska (10), 139–144.

PART FIVE

THE MATERIALISTIC THEORY OF KNOWLEDGE, THEORIES OF TRUTH AND OF UNIVERSALS

INTRODUCTION

Every sort of materialism involves epistemological realism, and Marxist-Leninist materialism is no exception to this rule. Although Marxism-Leninism is primarily metaphysics, and a theory of knowledge only by implication, the defence of epistemological realism is one of its constant and deep concerns.

Lenin discouraged even the use of the term 'realism' and applied 'materialism' or 'the materialist theory of knowledge' instead. 'Realism', he wrote, is a term usurped by the positivists and the other muddleheads who vacillate between materialism and idealism. It is an illegitimate and incorrect expression, by means of which idealist premisses are surreptitiously smuggled into materialism in the manner of Mach or Avenarius [1]. After some initial hesitation Lenin's followers in Poland have adhered to this terminology out of respect for his authority, and also because of necessity. For, speaking generally, not every realist is a materialist, and some of the staunchest opponents of Marxist-Leninist metaphysics, for instance, the Neo-Thomists, are epistemological realists. Marxist-Leninists being anxious to sever every kind of connection with these trends had to invent a distinctive name for themselves.

Since Lenin wrote *Materialism and Empirio-Criticism*, Marxist-Leninists had to define more and more sharply the difference between an epistemological and a materialist realist, as well as to devote their energy increasingly to the defence of their theory of knowledge. This theory was effectively criticised by materialist and non-materialist thinkers alike. On the other hand, epistemology has frequently provided the basis for the criticism of the Marxist-Leninist metaphysics. Marxism-Leninism could not ignore the existence of what Lenin called 'epistemological artifices', invented, as he thought, solely for the purpose of the struggle against materialism [2].

Marxist-Leninists often refer to scientific knowledge, and, in particular, to natural science as the most persuasive and the strongest epistemological justification of their metaphysical conjectures. They do not go as far and are not as consistent as Bertrand Russell is. Their mind is not dominated as much as Russell's by the world of astronomy, physics, and biology. They do not place as much reliance upon what science tells about the Universe as Russell does. They would disagree with him that scientific knowledge should be more trusted than any non-scientific or unscientific knowledge, unless 'scientific' is defined in such a manner that it would include what they hold to be true and exclude what they hold to be false. Finally, they would reject Russell's conviction that conscious and thinking life is restricted to a tiny fragment of space-time and constitutes only an inconsequential incident in the history of the Universe. The Marxist-Leninist approach to science is anthropocentric. Consequently, Russell's picture of the world is incompatible with their own which is concerned, above all, with the place and fate of man in the Universe and little with the Universe itself [3].

The epistemological support, which Marxist-Leninist philosophers expect to receive from natural science, should be sought for in what Lenin called 'natural scientific materialism' or the 'philosophically unconscious' materialist conviction shared and applied in research by an overwhelming majority of scientists. For it is a fact, inherent in scientific method, that all phenomena are investigated as if they were exclusively material. This method has proved to be extremely successful and has paved the way to ever new important discoveries. According to Lenin, the instinctively adopted standpoint of the materialist theory of knowledge gives all the required support to materialist metaphysics [4]. For Engels' and Lenin's attitude to the scientists was ambivalent: however respectful of their achievements, they were distrustful of their intentions. In the Marxist-Leninist tenet of the partisan character of science their mistrust has been raised to the status of a philosophical principle [5]. In general, Marxist-Leninist philosophy recognises scientific knowledge to be reliable as long as it helps to corroborate metaphysical materialism of a particular kind.

To say that scientific method presupposes materialism is a simplification, which is unlikely to find acceptance among scientists. For some of them would rejoin that science can do more than testify to a presupposition, and others that it fails to achieve even this purpose. The former might say that though neither materialist nor non-materialist metaphysics can be examined by scientific method, its conclusions can sometimes be investigated by it. For instance, vitalism and finalism in biology imply that certain material occurrences should be observed in the history of life. If such occurrences cannot be found, this would probabilify rather the materialist than the vitalist hypothesis. On this assumption, the choice between materialism, vitalism and finalism in biology would not be the result of a bias, inspired by the procedure of scientific method, but an inference based on the evaluation of scientific evidence [6].

Some other scientists would argue, however, that the success of scientific method does not justify any conclusions concerning the metaphysical nature of the Universe. From the fact that the method works, nothing else than it works can be inferred. Science is confined by its methodological conventions to material means of investigations and, consequently, its subject-matter cannot be but material phenomena. These methodological conventions are nothing more than regulative principles, which have been evolved by the method of trial and error. They decide what can be incorporated into the body of reliable knowledge at a given moment and are not invariant through time. There is nothing ultimate about them, they are themselves subject to the so-called 'principle of permanent control', that is, they are and should be the object of an endless criticism. Otherwise they could not remain a system of rules of empirical science. The inference, drawn from the procedure of scientific inquiry, that science confirms materialist metaphysics and imposes, as it were, materialism upon the Universe, is invalid. Methodological materialism of science does not imply materialist metaphysics and can never support it.

If the claim that science justifies one rather than another metaphysical creed about Nature and Man can be established at all, it requires something more than arguments of an elusive generality. The belief that there is an external world independent of the perceiving subject is a presupposition of natural science. But it is a presupposition and not a metaphysical point of view. The difference is of considerable importance. For a presupposition in this context means nothing more than a frame of reference accepted without inquiry into its implications, which remain disputable, and to-day, perhaps, more problematic than ever before. This is not what Lenin assumed. He believed that the frame of reference of natural science contains *in nuce* a philosophy of Nature which only needs to be made explicit to give birth to dialectic materialism [7].

Lenin was able to make his point by transforming the presupposition into a philosophical point of view, that is, by arguing in a philosophical manner that the presupposition of natural science is the correct one, since the world is material. The presupposition of natural science is compatible with this conclusion, but it does not logically imply it. For the meaning to be attached to the expression 'independent of the perceiving subject' or 'real ' is relative to physical theory and is defined in its terms. This becomes very clear when the classical and quantum mechanical description of reality are compared with respect to the kind of physical variables they involve. The confrontation of a physical theory of a high degree of universality with experience is accomplished as a last stage of theoretical analysis. The procedure, described by Carnap, makes it clear that the sense given to the term 'reality' appears as a conclusion to which there cannot easily be assigned a simple empirical meaning. 'Reality', as this term is understood in contemporary physics, is a word whose meaning is circumscribed by operations based on formal logic, methodology, and epistemology. Its relevance to the metaphysical reality of Lenin is indirect and doubtfull [8].

Ever since the end of the last century, when physics entered upon the path of its revolutionary development, arguments and counterarguments have constantly been produced to the effect that physics has demonstrated the existence within the physical universe of some spiritual elements or that nothing of that sort has actually happened and only a revision of the concept of matter and of laws of Nature has been accomplished. Numerous controversies of this kind took place in Poland in the post-war period between the Christian and the Marxist-Leninist philosophical journalists [9]. Such controversies have been inconclusive; neither side abandoned its claim to be supported by contemporary science. In Poland, as everywhere else, the dispute in question has been shown to be not about facts but about their interpretation, the differences in the interpretation being partly reducible to epistemological problems, *i.e.,* to what is knowledge, how we arrive at it, what degree of certainty we can ascribe to it, what is cognition and how it is related to the so-called empirical knowledge of matters of fact. The problems of cognition, which should be differentiated from the problems of epistemology, constitute the field investigated by the theory of knowledge in the narrower sense of this term. The views resulting from such investigations often provide important presuppositions in other branches of philosophical inquiry and in science. The theory of knowledge in the narrower sense has some peculiar difficulties of its own. They are questions of considerable complexity to which physics, physiology, psychology, and logic contribute their respective share and make of many of its issues a knot hard to disentangle. Marxist-Leninist philosophy has tried to consider them, though only marginally and reluctantly.

In the theory of knowledge we can follow two different lines of inquiry. We can consider the beliefs of common sense, such as that material things exist when they are not perceived, that they are known to us and are more or less such as they appear, as unwarranted under closer examination. Consequently, we are concerned with the questions: do material things exist when they are not perceived, and if they do, how can we know them in view of the fact that we do not know them directly.

On the other hand, we can accept the presuppositions of common sense as legitimate and more certain than their denial, and proceed to the examination of how we have come to the knowledge claimed. In the latter case we examine the theory explaining common sense knowledge and evaluate the measure of its adequacy. Engels and Lenin adopted the second approach and Marxism-Leninism has followed their lead. Lenin more than any body else has been responsible for making the naive beliefs of mankind the foundation of the materialist theory of knowledge [10].

While the Marxist-Leninist procedure, which starts with stating what we know and only later inquires into how we know, might be urged for various important reasons, the obligation of providing an explanation of the knowledge claimed to be in our possession cannot be ignored. A materialist outlook without a fully developed theory of knowledge is an unsatisfactory and highly vulnerable doctrine. Evidently, this aim cannot be achieved by the refutation of theories which are incompatible with materialism. If it is conceded that Lenin's objections against Machian phenomenalism are valid, this does not imply that Lenin's own views are valid. The refutation of phenomenalism has logically nothing to do with the justification of epistemological realism and its defence against possible objections. It is true that Lenin assumed that he was not refuting the views of this or that thinker, but what he called the whole Berkeleian and Humean line in epistemology. According to Lenin, there are two and only two possible standpoints in the theory of knowledge, corresponding to idealism and materialism, in the Marxist-Leninist sense of these terms. For we can assert either that there is 'no object without a subject' or that 'the object exists independently of the subject'. If the former is false, the latter must be true. This presupposition is both materially and formally fallacious. The two epistemological standpoints, singled out by Lenin, are not exclusive, for there are other possible intermediate standpoints. For instance, nothing that Lenin said against Mach refutes methodological phenomenalism, that is, the view that statements about physical objects are formally reducible or translatable into statements about sense-data. To assume that the materialist theory of knowledge is true, if epistemological idealism is false, is to show a defective grasp of logic. This particular error of

320

Lenin was implicitly recognised by Polish Marxist-Leninists [11]. They hesitated, however, for a long time before they moved further on to a more rational frame of mind and recognised that the existence of reasons sufficient for the rejection of Lenin's theories is incompatible with a continued adherence to them.

The chief aim of the materialist theory of knowledge is to provide a rational justification of the belief in the existence of the external world. If this belief is inadequately justified, the whole metaphysical structure is left hovering in the air. The first question to be examined is whether Marxist-Leninists can be credited with a theory of knowledge that achieves this aim and stands up to critical examination.

The second point to be considered concerns epistemology rather than the theory of knowledge in the narrower sense. Marxist-Leninists emphasise the social character and determination of knowledge. Although the emphasis of this assertion is laid upon socio-cultural thinking, in their view all knowledge should be related and ultimately reduced to its social source before its truth or falsehood can be established. Moreover, Marxist-Leninists maintain that the modern theory of knowledge has individualism as its sociological presupposition; this pattern set by Locke and Descartes has ruled ever since. The knower has been cut free from any connections with his social existence, and the influence of the social environment upon knowledge has acquired a negative significance. Since Bacon the social determination of knowledge has been regarded as a perverting influence from which the mind must be emancipated, if true and valid knowledge is to be reached. According to Marxist-Leninists, this doctrine itself perverts scientific objectivity and is a prime source of errors and falsehood.

This particular view has been already examined, including the manner in which its fallacy has been exposed by non-Marxist thinkers in Poland. There remains the question whether Marxist-Leninists tried to take advantage of it in their own epistemology and to show in what manner the social character and determination of knowledge secured true rationality and objectivity, unobtainable on the basis of an individualistically conceived epistemology.

In the following pages the question as to how the Marxist-Leninist theory of knowledge justifies its claims will be more closely examined. This inquiry has an intrinsic interest of its own, but it also throws light upon two other fundamental philosophical problems, to which Polish Marxist-Leninists devoted much attention, namely, the problem of truth and that of universals. These issues will be considered in the order indicated.

CHAPTER 16

ENGELS' REPRESENTATIVE REALISM AND LENIN'S
THEORY OF PERCEPTION

There is ample reason to agree with Durkheim that positivism was the most significant and important development in the philosophy of the nineteenth century. Durkheim showed that the idea originated with Saint-Simon who also gave an outline of the positive system of the sciences. The merits of Comte in working out in detail the great innovations brought about by positive philosophy in no way abolish the right of Saint-Simon to the honour, usually awarded to Comte, of being the father of positivism [12].

This fact is of some importance as far as Marxism-Leninism is concerned. For while even the name of Comte is anathema to the Marxist-Leninists, that of Saint-Simon is not. Marx, who early in his life came into contact with the Saint-Simonians and read Comte only much later, put it on record that he was opposed, naturally enough, to Comte's political and social doctrines, and that he had a poor opinion of his philosophy, only superior in detail but on the whole infinitely inferior to Hegel's. Marx and Engels found in Saint-Simon the 'breadth of view of a genius' and counted him among the 'three great utopians' – Fourrier and Owen being the other two – whose ideas, in Lenin's words, should be recognised as one of the three sources and component parts of the Marxian thought. Comte, Engels commented, had 'a series of brilliant thoughts', but they were all taken from Saint-Simon. In Comte's hands the magnificent conception of Saint-Simon was mutilated 'in philistine fashion to the best of his (Comte's) ability' [13]. Irrespective of whether Marx and Engels learnt about the idea of positive philosophy from the writings of Saint-Simon or those of Comte, there is no doubt that they were greatly impressed by it and assimilated it into their own system.

The impact of positive philosophy on Marx and Engels is already apparent in *The German Ideology*, but it finds its most pronounced expression in *Anti-Dühring* and *Ludwig Feuerbach*. For according to Engels the idea of positive philosophy could not have been implemented until idealism was driven from its last refuge and this was accomplished when Marx propounded the materialist conception of history. Historical materialism made it possible to transform history and the social sciences into positive disciplines, to merge all knowledge in the great body of positive sciences comprising Nature, human society and history, and thus to achieve the aspiration for the unity of knowledge. Philosophy conceived as a 'science of sciences', standing apart and above the positive sciences, with a separate subject matter of its own, came to an end. 'When reality is depicted', wrote Marx and Engels in *The German Ideology*, 'philosophy as an independent branch of activity loses its medium of existence'. There only remain the theory of the laws of thought, formal logic and dialectics, themselves a part of positive knowledge [14].

The main assumption of positive philosophy, as conceived by Saint-Simon and accepted by Engels, was to define knowledge as the totality of facts and of their interconnections, established by particular sciences. This leaves philosophy no separate realm of reality, for by definition everything that can be known belongs to some branch of scientific knowledge. There is no room left for philosophy but 'within the positive sciences'. Philosophy becomes an activity whose task is to systematise and to order knowledge into a picture of the world. Its validity must be established on the basis of the achievements of science available at the time, for philosophy has no other sources upon which it could draw. It is in the nature of scientific knowledge that it can never be completed; its accumulation knows no limit, each stage reached is provisional and far from perfect. Consequently, there is no exhaustive and final picture of the world. The latter must be constantly revised and adjusted to the progress achieved by particular sciences[15].

This is only an outline of the new conception of philosophy, which leaves many questions unanswered and lends itself to various interpretations. Thus, some time later, Engels' views were used to show that philosophy has after all a subject-matter of its own, namely, the most general laws of development, which applying to the world as a whole escape the grid of positive sciences. For Engels also said that philosophy, identified with dialectics, is the 'science of the general laws of motion and development of Nature, human society and thought'. Although philosophy cannot be practised apart from science, yet it is over and above science, since philosophy provides the latter with its epistemological and methodological foundation. It also paves the way for scientific progress by the formulation of laws of the highest generality, undiscoverable by any particular science, to which all phenomena are subject[16]. This interpretation is in keeping with the anti-positivistic trend initiated by Lenin in *Materialism and Empirio-Criticism* and continued with increasing vigour by Marxism-Leninism ever since.

For Lenin positivism lost its distinctive features to become a trend comprising a great variety of ideas. As he saw it, the 'broad current of positivism' included such diverse thinkers as Comte, Spencer, Mikhailovsky, some Neo-Kantians, Mach, and Avenarius. Lenin did not conceal his utter contempt for the currents of thought which came into prominence towards the end of the nineteenth century, for they lacked, in his opinion, originality and consistency whether they were called " 'positivism', 'realism', or some other professorial charlatanism"[17].

From the early 'thirties Marxism-Leninism has given great prominence to Lenin's views on positivism and vied in its hostility to logical positivism with that of Lenin to Mach and Avenarius. Philipp Frank's expectation, expressed in 1935, that some intellectual kinship between dialectical materialism and logical empiricism may possibly bring them closer together, did not materialise[18]. The pronounced anti-positivistic trend in Marxism-Leninism is combined with the confident claim that philosophy can acquire important and valid knowledge, unobtainable by any particular science. Philosophy is assigned a vantage point from which the whole of knowledge can be criticised, the true meaning of facts of experience revealed, and the laws of science reinterpreted or dismissed.

The important point to be noted in Engels' conception of philosophy is the fact that there is no place within it for a theory of knowledge. As a matter of fact, there is no evidence that Engels saw any need for it or that he attached any importance to epistemological problems.

Engels adopted the common sense, naively realistic standpoint in the theory of knowledge and thought that no serious attack could be made on it, least of all that an attack might be initiated and supported by science. He seemed to have been unaware of the subverting criticism based on Berkeley's approach, to which the common sense world might be subjected, and of the reinforcement with which the scientific study of the sense organs, of the nervous system and of the brain, from Johannes Müller onwards, might provide this line of attack. Engels considered Kant's philosophy as the most formidable obstacle that barred the path back to comprehending the real world in its sensuous immediacy, undiluted by Humean doubt and secure from transcendental analysis. Hegel helped to dispose of this obstacle, but at a heavy price, namely, by substituting the absolute concept for the world of Nature [19]. Once it was realised, however, that Hegel was wrong, and that the 'concepts in our head' are images of the real things instead of the latter being images of 'this or that stage of the absolute concept', all confusion seemed to disappear and the problem of how we come to know the objects of the external world presented no problem. There was no doubt that we know things as they actually are and not as they appear to us, for whatever we experience – feelings, thoughts, impulses, volitions – is the effect of the external world acting on the human brain. The thing-in-itself of the 'Neo-Kantian agnostics' is a figment of the imagination, which Hegel already saw through and dispelled. When we know the qualities of an object we know the object itself and since it is the cause of our perceptions we know also that it exists without us. Thus, Engels accepted the view common to all positivists and abhorred by all essentialists that things or bodies or matter are nothing apart from their attributes. In Marxism-Leninism only the negative part of Engels' idea, that is, that there is nothing unknowable in the world, has been accepted, and its positive assertion, directed against essentialism, has been ignored.

The realisation that there is no single thing that persists when its attributes change or are taken away in thought, inspired Engels with a vigorous optimism in man's unlimited capacity for knowledge, however limited and liable to errors it might be at each particular historical moment. We may have an imperfect knowledge of the external world but by manufacturing what we claim to know we can verify the truth of our knowledge. To know what albuminous bodies are is to be able to produce artificial albumen. The powerful and rapid progress of natural science and industry was an irrefutable argument against sceptical doubts about man's ability to acquire true knowledge about the external world.

Engels did speak of thoughts being reflections or images of material objects, but he contrasted this view with that of Hegel and not with those of Berkeley or Hume. For the metaphysical problem of the relation of Spirit to Nature occupied his mind more than the epistemological question concerning the relation of thought to reality. Engels did not conceive the idea, ascribed to him by

Lenin, who expounded his own theory of perception as if it were Engels', that sensations and concepts are 'copies, photographs, images, mirror-reflections of things'[20]. Engels was not concerned with the epistemological problems of perception and seemed to have felt that whatever difficulties they might raise they could simply and conclusively be disposed of.

An overwhelming majority of thinkers, Engels wrote and he counted himself as one of them, answers affirmatively the question whether our experience faithfully reflects the objects of the external world. The line of reasoning that questions the adequacy of our perceptions and denies that our senses give us correct representations of the objects we perceive through them, is hard to beat by mere argument. But such objections are philosophical inventions, not to be taken seriously, because experiment, practice, and industry are perfectly capable of dealing with them. There is no doubt that we do make false perceptual judgments and that actions based on false beliefs fail to achieve their purpose. If this happens, the cause of it should be sought for either in the perception being 'incomplete and superficial' or in 'defective reasoning'. There is no reason, however, to assert on this basis that there is an inherent discrepancy between what things seem to be and what they are. 'So long as we take care to train and use our senses properly, and to keep our actions within the limits prescribed by perceptions, properly made and properly used, so long shall we find that the result of our action proves the conformity of our perceptions with the objective nature of the things perceived'[21]. Engels did not realise that before he could speak of 'perceptions properly made and properly used' he would have to be in possession of the idea of what the world, causing all kinds of fleeting and evanescent sensations, is like. For in the absence of this idea the concept of properly made and properly used perception has no meaning and to define the world by means of this concept is to move in a vicious circle.

Engels' position can be described as that of naive realism: external objects are more or less as they seem. Our sensations are never wrong and errors begin only with the interpretation of sensational data. There are no illusions of the senses, though there are illusory inferences drawn from some perceptions. These errors are discovered by experiment, careful observation and putting our ideas about things to the test of practice. These views are supported by a rudimentary causal and representational theory of perception. The objects of the external world are causes of our perceptions and the latter are a reflection of the external world. The thesis that material objects appear to us disguised as their own effects (which also guarantees that they exist independently of us), and that these effects are a true reflection of material objects, is accepted as self-evident. Whatever proof might be provided must be produced by positive science. Philosophical perplexities are out of place; they raise doubts which science ignores. There are no specifically philosophical problems in the theory of perception or in that concerned with the objective validity of knowledge [22].

Engels adopted the attitude of the scientist of his time, who overlooked the fact that he himself is an observer, that he must finally rely on some immediate data of experience, and that he cannot start with ascribing to his findings the objectivity which they do not possess. The truths of physics and physiology are an inferred knowledge, based on direct records of experience. The physicist, stated one of the important conclusions reached by Mach, is always operating with sensations. His direct records of experience, however elaborate they might be, do not differ from observations of everyday life by means of which we verify a common sense statement. In both cases we record the occurrence of some sense-data. For this reason both science and common sense require a theory of know-ledge. To accept either in science or philosophy what common sense says on the matter, is to endorse bold and far-reaching metaphysical assumptions, made up as matters of fact. By his exposure of this common sense metaphysics Mach, Engels' contemporary, produced in his *Analysis of Sensations* and *Knowledge and Error* a decisive turning point in the philosophy of science. On the other hand, the view that science confirms the naive belief of mankind about the external world, is utterly mistaken. 'Naive realism leads to physics and physics, if true, shows that naive realism is false', wrote Bertrand Russell. For physics assures us that the green colour of grass or the hardness of stones are something very different from what we know in our own experience. 'Therefore, naive realism, if true, is false; therefore it is false'[23]. The objects, with which we are familiar in everyday life, must be, when unseen, quite unlike what they appear to be when seen. Science is not a continuation of common sense.

Lenin could not retain Engels' epistemological position in its initial form any longer. One of the important reasons for the readmission of the problems of knowledge into the philosopher's preserve was the fact that the causal theory of perception is compatible not only with naive realism but also with phenome-nalism, and phenomenalism was Lenin's main opponent. Moreover, while the causal theory of perception may be considered as supporting naive realism in the sense that it implies the belief, common to realism of all sorts, concerning the continued existence of material objects when they are not perceived, as well as accounting for mental images 'in our heads', it does not support it in another sense. For the causal theory of perception raises doubts as to whether things are exactly or even approximately as they seem and possess the qualities which we ascribe to things on perceiving them. This was already recognised by Helmholtz in 1866. To reinforce the position of naive realism, Lenin worked out his copy theory of perception, ascribed it, without much justification, to Engels, and retained the causal theory in the background as an auxiliary means of defence, used rather against subjective idealism than 'non-materialist' realism.

It is important to note that Lenin did restore to the theory of knowledge its philosophical character. He did not take this step in order to study the problems of knowledge on their own account but to protect materialist metaphysics against the criticism based on epistemological phenomenalism. This was recognised by the Marxist-Leninists in Poland. They emphasised that the content and formula-tion of the copy theory of perception cannot be properly understood unless it is related to the purpose it was to serve, that is, the refutation of idealist theories of knowledge[24].

Lenin's epistemology is pervaded by a boundless optimism which is based on two interrelated beliefs – his theory of perception that claims to have abolished the barrier between the phenomenon and the 'thing-in-itself' and the role ascribed to practice. The latter belief inspires him with the conviction that even to consider the possibility of any limitations inherent in human knowledge is a philosophical invention. There is nothing 'unknowable' in the world, knowledge is cumulative, the 'only difference is between what is known and what is not yet known'[25].

Lenin's opinion that science approximates more and more closely the 'true essence' of things rests on his theory of perception, according to which 'the objective reality.... is copied, photographed, and reflected by our sensations'. Lenin argued that not a 'single fact was or could be cited' to refute this view, 'which is shared by science to this day'[26]. Now, the opinion that sensations are true copies of the external objects is known in Poland, as everywhere else, under the name of 'naive realism' of a particular kind and is considered to be untenable and even meaningless. If our perceptions provide us with some kind of images, and this is granted for the sake of argument, the relation of the image to what it is an image of cannot be that of 'being its copy'. The perceptive image is supposed to be the content of the perception and by its very nature it cannot be either similar or dissimilar, a copy or a photograph, of something that is not a content of the perception. The theory implies either that the image itself is a physical object, which since Democritus and Epicurus nobody seems to be willing to accept, or that the relation is in fact not that between a portrait and a portrayed person[27].

A more serious error is, however, involved in the copy version of naive realism. What it says to be the case is either a metaphor, which cannot be actually applied in the theory of perception, or it assumes what it intends to prove, and what it assumes is unverifiable by any imaginable procedure. We know a portrait to be a portrait of the portrayed person, because we can perceive both and compare them with each other. This does not apply to our perceptions. If the copy theory is right, we perceive only images or copies of things and never the things themselves. We are unable, therefore, to compare the images with the perceived objects. If we are unable to do so, how can we say that these supposed images are 'true' or 'false', how can we say, at all, that they are images of the objects perceived? What the copy theory says might be right, but if it is right we could not know it. If it is right, we have no means to ascertain whether the images provide a good or bad likeness of the perceived objects with which, as the theory implies, we never come in direct contact. On closer examination the reflection theory of perception appears to be absurd[28].

According to Lenin, any deviation from the copy theory of perception, that is from the assumption that the 'thing in itself.... does not differ fundamentally from appearance' and the image from the thing, makes the existence of external objects subject to doubt. Just the contrary, however, seems to be the case. The metaphor of the sensation being a mirror-reflection of the outside world makes each of us a 'monad with no windows'. We can never pierce the veil of these mirror-reflections, be in direct communication with other individuals or in direct contact with any object of the outside world[29].

327

'Naive realism' is also the name of the view according to which things are what they appear to be; the sense-data belong to, or inhere in, or are a part of the perceived object. It can hardly be doubted that Lenin did believe in sense-data and that he held them to be a 'true' or an 'approximately true copy' of external objects. Moreover, if he thought that sensations are mirror-reflections of their objects and that the former can be actually compared with the latter, like a picture with its model, he was bound to accept the standpoint of naive realism in the second sense. Lenin's criticism of Helmholtz and, in general, of the 'theory of symbols' leaves little room for doubt that he was strongly opposed to any concession in favour of critical realism. Since critical realism introduces 'an entirely unnecessary element of agnosticism' and ultimately 'throws the door open for fideism', he clearly identified materialism with naive realism. This leaves him open to the objection that his philosophical concept of matter can hardly be reconciled with his naive realistic view in the theory of knowledge. According to the latter the bits and pieces of matter given us in sensation comprise the sensed colours, smells, flavours, and so forth, as their qualities. On the other hand, the philosophical concept of matter does not include in its connotation any of these sensual characteristics [30].

Lenin proved that if the copy theory of perception is true, phenomenalism cannot be right, but he failed to show that his own theory is a true one. He even failed to indicate how various facts, well known from the psychology of perception, can be accommodated within the copy theory, and failing this no theory of knowledge can provide a satisfactory account of what it intends to explain. One hardly needs to leave the ground of everyday experience to show that we have mental images of objects which do not exist, that we describe objects in a manner in which they do not appear, ascribe characteristics to them which they do not possess and which owe their existence merely to some peculiarity or psychophysical organisation of the perceiving subject. We have to recognise, therefore, that we do not always experience objects as they were or are and that we are aware of perceiving things when in fact we do not perceive them at all. These are no 'philosophical crotchets', produced, to use Lenin's picturesque language, by 'buffoons of bourgeois science', but facts of common experience to which Lenin himself frequently appealed to justify some of his views. The facts in question are troublesome if the standpoint of an unsophisticated realism is to be adhered to, but they cannot be overlooked or simply ignored. Thus, to give but one significant example, Lenin dealt firmly and summarily with the law of the specific energy of sensory nerves. Since the law implies that our sensations are not copies of objective reality, it cannot be true [31].

The apparent strength of Lenin's position in his criticism of the Machians does not result from the soundness of his own views but from his implied denial that some questions, which his opponents did put to themselves, could be asked legitimately. Lenin wished to bar certain questions from being raised and this aim was to be achieved by propounding a theory of perception within which they should not arise. But no philosophical question can be settled by an evasion or by refusing to notice questions that might and should legitimately be asked.

In Lenin's case, this refusal was prompted by the requirements of eliminating any possibility of deviation from 'absolute realism'. For Lenin was convinced that once the relativity of knowledge upon the cognising subject is recognised in any way whatever, one has to surrender to agnosticism (in the Marxist-Leninist sense of this term) or subjective idealism [32]. On the other hand, to defend the copy theory of perception was to defend materialist metaphysics, for, as Lenin saw it, they were beliefs logically equivalent. They can both function in the capacity of the 'fundamental premiss of materialism'.

Thus, judged by the criteria of factual evidence and logical consistency, Lenin's theory of knowledge faces considerable philosophical difficulties. On the one hand, Lenin was committed to an untenable theory of perception, on the other the falsehood of this theory implied, according to his own opinion, also the falsehood of materialist metaphysics. The copy theory is not a prop but a pitfall. If materialism is true, the copy theory cannot be maintained [33].

Under the impact of criticism made by non-Marxist thinkers, Marxist-Leninists in Poland recognised that the original version of the copy theory of perception could not be upheld. From the very beginning they showed a greater respect for facts than did Lenin. They recognised the dependence of sensations upon the nervous system and the state of the subject. Initially, however, they saw no reason, strange as it might appear, for rejecting the copy theory of perception, which alone – in this respect they followed Lenin faithfully – can prevent philosophy from falling an easy victim to Kantian agnosticism or subjective idealism. They were no more inclined to accept the implications of the recognised dependence of sense experience upon the perceiving subject than Lenin was, when he dismissed the law of the specific energy of sensory nerves. They were thus reduced to a theory [34] that denied in its conclusions what was stated in its premisses.

This position was as untenable as Lenin's and did not silence the criticism, which eventually compelled them to move a step further. While asserting that they were restoring to the copy theory its authentic meaning, they rejected its original version. Lenin's statement 'sensations are the true copy of the objective reality', repeated over and over again in *Materialism and Empirio-Criticism*, was never to be anything but an analogy or a metaphor. That it was nonsensical to interpret it as a literally true statement becomes plain if one tried to apply the metaphor to other sensations than those of sight. To say that our sensations reflect outside reality does not either assume or imply that there is the likeness, and still less the identity, between reality and its cognitive reflection. What is assumed is some kind of a correspondence relation between the two, by virtue of which the world is knowable. This implies that there are no 'things in themselves' and that our perceptions reflect 'more or less faithfully' the objective reality. The 'images' should be conceived as representations which accord in some way with their objects [35].

This accord is tested by practice. For if practice confirms the prediction made on the basis of perception, we can conclude that the representation is in accord with what it represents in the external world. The view that perception has a predictive function, confirmed or disconfirmed by subsequent action, is a characteristic feature of the materialist theory of knowledge (the idea was Helm-holtz's, later also adopted by his eminent pupil Heinrich Hertz, whose works on the subject were well known to Engels and Lenin, since both quoted them in *Dialectics of Nature* and *Materialism and Empirio-Criticism* respectively [36]). For if the criterion of practice is included in the theory of knowledge, this theory leads to materialism, that is, to the recognition that the external world reflected by the mind exists independently of the mind. This calls for the qualification that practice is only a partial criterion of the correspondence between the image and the thing imaged and that it provides the evidence for the correspondence being adequate on the whole and not in every respect and detail [37].

In non-Marxist terminology this is as much as to say that action provides an operational criterion of what it means that representations are in accord with their objects. From this it does not follow, however, that the predictive success proves anything more than that we are successful in making predictions.

It should be noted that no kind of practice can accomplish the feat of passing from the sensations conceived as mirror-like reflections of objects to the objects themselves once it is realised that on this assumption the percipient never has any access to the reality outside him. What he can gain by practice are ever new and more numerous 'reflections', whose relation to the 'model' must remain unknown to him. Practice alone does not transform naive realism in the first sense into critical realism and does not provide a direct access to the external objects. Lenin, and after him Polish Marxist-Leninists, must have been misled by the ambiguity of their own metaphor. When we observe reflections in the mirror we can turn our head or move about in the room to compare what is reflected with its mirror reflection. Practice, Lenin probably thought, plays the same role in life as our turning of the head and moving in the room. Here the simile goes astray. Whatever our perceptions are, we can, of course, move about and turn our head, but if the copy theory is right, we can never detach ourselves from the mirror; we have to look into it and never away from it, to compare the image with its model. We see only reflections in the mirror and, as the criticism of the causal theory of knowledge seems to show, we would even have no valid reason to infer from it the conjecture about something outside us being the cause of the apprehended reflections [38].

It is a moot point, therefore, whether practice and predictive success is by itself sufficient ground for claiming true knowledge. There can be little doubt, as Mach argued, that if predictive success separates knowledge from error, know-ledge would thus be proved to be a biologically useful psychological experience, which is a very valuable but by no means the final and the highest point of departure for inquiry [39]. Lenin expressly rejected this cautious interpretation. He maintained that nothing could be useful for the preservation of life and species, unless it reflects 'objective truth' independent of man. Marxist-Leninists in Poland, hard pressed by critics and opponents, gave unconditional support to Lenin's view and faith in the perfect rationality of the Universe [40].

The revision of Lenin's copy theory of perception, accomplished by Polish Marxist-Leninists, could be described as a return to Engels' broadly conceived 'representationism', with the exclusion of his naive realism, that is, of the view that things are as they seem. The revision in question has committed Polish Marxist-Leninists to the standpoint of critical – instead of the previous naive – realism in the theory of knowledge. This consequence has eagerly been endorsed by the Marxist-Leninists of the younger generation, who, unlike their elders, were fully aware of the inconsistencies in Lenin's original theory of perception[41]. Critical realism was not, however, examined. Its broad and general content was considered to be sufficient to justify the claim that we can know 'objective reality' and that our knowledge has a factual and material reference. Having stated that 'reflection' is not to be taken literally and to mean 'copy' or 'mirror-like reflection', implying likeness, resemblance or identity, Schaff wrote that the assertion of thoughts and perceptions being a reflection of reality is equivalent to a conjunction of three statements: reality exists independently of us; it is knowable, that is, it is adequately reflected in perception and conceptual thinking; cognition is not relative to the perceiving subject and progressively reveals the 'objective truth' about reality [42].

Does the theory of perception, to which Polish Marxist-Leninists adhere, justify the conjunction of these three statements? 'Representationism', either of Engels or of Lenin, excludes the possibility of some direct access to the objects of the external world, of knowing them otherwise than mediately via the interposed mental images. According to Engels and Lenin we are never in immediate contact with the outside world, material objects are always given to us by means of their reflections, whether these are conceived as true copies or representations of some other sort. One cannot assume that either Engels or Lenin conceived the data of sense experience as being a part of the object perceived, and, consequently, that whenever they spoke of perceiving an object this implied having knowledge that there was an object to which what was sensed belonged. This would be the 'line of subjectivism', expressly and vigorously criticised by Lenin, that is bound to result in identifying material objects with sensation-complexes. Lenin contrasted the 'subjective line' with the 'objective line', followed in Locke's footsteps, and accepted his epistemological dualism. What is immediately given is caused by the object, which is a source of sensations 'independent of humanity'. The object and the data of sense experience are two related but distinct entities.

A theory of knowledge which assumes the existence of sense-data, and Lenin's theory is one of them, cannot ignore the fact that the perceptual conditions which are necessary and sufficient to establish the existence of sense-data, are necessary but not sufficient conditions for the establishment of the existence of material objects. This means that the evidence for the existence of the former cannot be taken as the evidence for the existence of the latter. Furthermore, while the perceptual conditions under which the existence of sense-data can be established provide direct and, therefore, conclusive evidence for the existence of sense-data, no such direct and conclusive evidence can, in the very nature of the case, be ever available for the existence of material objects.

If we are never aware of objects except through the mediation of their representations, the existence of material objects is an inferred knowledge. The validity of this inference is not beyond doubt, for it is logically defective and questionable. The premisses speak of what is given to us directly, that is, of images and their content, and the conclusions refer to something else, to reflected or represented objects, which are not spoken of in the premisses. Such an inference does not yield a logically valid conclusion. This conclusion is not a substitution instance of a truth of logic, that is, it is not a logically true proposition in the wider sense of this expression. We can deny it without making a self-contradictory statement, what we assert might be true or false. The conviction that the conclusion is true provides a psychological justification for its acceptance, but adds nothing to the logical grounds for its validity. Psychologically the conclusion does not assert a simple fact of sense, but a belief causally or otherwise related to some other beliefs and is, to use Bertrand Russell's terminology, not a primitive but a derivative statement, supported not by a 'hard' but by a 'soft' datum. When its supposed obviousness, generated by habit and nurtured by familiarity, is recognised, what remains of the firm if not dogmatic assertion that the reality is knowable is merely a hypothesis, which it would be rash to reject off-hand but which is nothing more than a conjecture. The basic statement of the materialist theory of knowledge that the 'human mind reflects an objectively real external world' cannot be considered as satisfactorily proven beyond any reasonably held doubt.

Marxist-Leninists did not seem to have noticed that there is a gap between what, according to their own theory, is directly known – the perceptual world of the cognising subject, and what is not known in that manner and never directly experienced – the cognised object. In other words, they seem to be unaware of the fact that their theory of perception raises questions of how we can ever acquire knowledge of material things, if they are not directly given [43]. This gap can only be bridged by means of reasoning, either deductive or inductive. But in both cases the reasoning remains defective and the conclusion only a plausible one, accepted 'according to our inclination'. For we cannot make valid inferences from what is an experienced to what is an unexperienced entity.

This was clearly seen by Lenin when he criticised his opponents: "If the perceptual world is objective reality, then the door is closed to every other 'reality'" [44]. But what Lenin noticed in the views of his adversaries, he refused to acknowledge with respect to his own. Thus, he warned that the external object should not be identified with the sense-data, which are no part of it, 'for sense perception is not the reality existing outside us, it is only the image of that reality', to be found, as he emphasised elsewhere, 'within us'. Having made this distinction, Lenin denied, however, that there was any problem at all in accounting for the passage from the image within to the object without, or that the validity of this passage could be questioned and called illegitimate, if no plausible justification was forthcoming.

Confronted by this difficulty Lenin used to argue that to accept this point of view is to indulge in 'idealist aberration', unreconcilable with the natural sciences and to fly in the face of the evidence of our senses. The impassable gulf between the sense-data and the external object, the problem of the transcendence of the object, was according to Lenin an invention of priests and professors of philosophy. The transcendence of the object is an apparent problem, for the mental image and the imaged thing faithfully correspond to each other and this correspondence is an 'objective truth' acquired in experience. This truth can be doubted only by those who 'do not sufficiently trust the evidence of our sense-organs'. Lenin had more arguments than the confidence in this evidence to support his conviction, but he often spoke as if it were all we needed to dispose of the difficulty arising from the differentiation of the sense-data and the external objects [45].

There is, of course, a grain of common sense truth in what Lenin said, but this kind of truth is irrelevant so far as the demonstration of the existence of material objects is concerned. For Lenin did not provide any new arguments that would either logically justify the elimination of the transcendence problem or strengthen the validity of the step that bridges the gap between sense-data and objects. Confidence placed in the evidence of sense experience, to which Lenin over and over again appealed, is no logical but only a psychological argument from which nothing whatsoever can be inferred. From the fact that Lenin was convinced that what he said was true, it did not follow logically that it was true, for no conviction guarantees that what we are convinced of is true. A proposition might be true and disbelieved by some or everybody, as well as it might be false though believed to be true by a great many people. Convictions say something about those who share them. They provide, as Nagel put it, evidence for the biographies but no relevant evidence regarding their objects [46]. Few people would deny that we have strong psychological reasons for recognising the reality of the external world and its independent existence, in some meaning of this term, though hardly anyone would argue for it on the strength of the assumption that there is a unique correspondence between sense-data and objects. For even if it were the case, we could never verify the truth of this claim. The crux of the matter is, however, the logical reasons, not only the psychological ones, which would transform a subjective conviction into a logically true or a logically justifi-able proposition. These logical reasons Marxist-Leninist 'representationism' does not provide, and, furthermore, makes them perhaps more difficult to find than ever before.

The immediate knowledge given by sense experience need not be proved by argument – in this respect Lenin was quite right – but it contains much less than common sense supposes as a result of confusing psychologically primitive with psychologically derivative knowledge. By itself it cannot achieve the purpose which Lenin wished it to perform, that is, to provide proof for the existence of the external world. For various illusions, based on the evidence of the senses, exactly preclude the possibility of this evidence being invariably reliable. Although he never explicitly acknowledged it, Lenin must have been aware of the 'argument from illusion'. A rod dipped in water is visually crooked, but tactually and metrically straight. It does seem clear that there are many visual and tactual 'copies' of material objects which are not 'true copies' of the latter.

333

It follows that perceptual consciousness is not always a faithful reflection of the outside world; that it is at least sometimes erroneous; and that failing to mirror objective reality veridically, has not always an 'objective content'. Other facts reinforce the argument from 'abnormal copies'. Lenin must have known that we can see stars looking at them or by receiving a blow on the eye, we can see two tables instead of one when we press an eyeball. We have to differentiate, therefore, between the visual stars and tables and the real ones. The reason why Lenin preferred to speak of images instead of direct observations of material objects was the fact that statements about images do not imply that a material thing exists and is veridically perceived. If instead of images he spoke of direct observations he would be forced to admit that things are always exactly as they appear, which he wished to avoid, at least in some cases. For he was barred by his own assumptions from admitting, what Mach could have done, that nothing justifies us in dismissing some sensations as abnormal, all of them being only different or differently conditioned combinations of the 'elements'.

CHAPTER 17

THE CAUSAL THEORY OF KNOWLEDGE

From Lenin's viewpoint the evidence of our senses could not provide a convincing argument to demonstrate the existence of material objects and Lenin was determined to show that the existence of material objects is a demonstrable truth, open to no doubt whatsoever. It was not this evidence alone but sense experience combined with the causal theory of perception, which was to supply the missing link between mental images and the external world. For Lenin the causal theory was hardly distinct or in need of differentiation from the vague and complex body of direct and inferred knowledge, indiscriminately referred to as 'empirical knowledge'. What the causal theory seems to imply was merged in Lenin's thinking with the data of sense experience into an unanalysed whole that endowed the former with its supposed demonstrative power. The 'evidence of the senses', of which Lenin made use, is something more than what this expression usually conveys.

According to Lenin, the evidence of our senses can be trusted because our 'sensations are evoked in us by real objects'. This is proved by science and provides conclusive evidence of the objective existence of material objects [47]. The causal theory is presupposed in Lenin's definition of matter, which is conceived as that which acts upon our sense organs and produces sensations. This presupposition, which Lenin sometimes simply calls the 'standpoint of materialism', was explicitly endorsed by Polish followers of Lenin and singled out by them as an important component of the materialist theory of knowledge [48]. The causal theory of perception might appear to narrow or even to close the gap between the evidence and the conclusion about the existence of material objects. For it seems to provide what Lenin described as the 'connection between consciousness and the external world'. But in fact it does neither.

The causal theory of perception is really a part of physiology and physiological psychology. It was Helmholtz, Fechner and Wundt who formulated its basic assumptions and undertook on this basis to found a scientific psychology, capable of using the conceptual apparatus and methods of natural science in the investigations of mental phenomena. In the course of time the causal theory has been expanded and enriched with a mass of detailed findings. Scientists like Helmholtz used it to demonstrate the truth of epistemological realism as the simplest hypothesis, tested and verified in a very broad field of application. It vindicated the belief of science, instinctively accepted by many scientists, that our sensations, being effects wrought by external causes in our senses, are dependent on the external objects, while material things are causally independent of our observations of them. To regard the existence of physical objects as being in any way problematic could not, in Helmholtz's view, be reconciled with science. 'This is materialism', wrote Lenin referring to Helmholtz's exposition of the causal theory of perception [49].

According to the causal theory, the perception is the final stage in a long chain of events, physical and physiological, originating in the external world and terminating in the emergence of sensations – sense-data – above the threshold of consciousness. The perception is an end-product of a process that starts from and is determined by the external object. The object is regarded as one of the conditions which produce the perception of this very object, and perception, speaking metaphorically, is the object in a disguised form or its effect.

It should be observed that in the causal theory of perception the cognising subject is conceived as a material body, one external object among others. If physical objects consist of electrons, protons, neutrons, and other similar entities, the human body, the brain and the nervous system, the eye and the ear, must also be a structure composed of elements of this sort. The human body is a sensitive body, and we can, therefore, translate the cause-effect relation to that described in terms of stimuli and organic reactions, the latter being physical or physiological events. As G. F. Stout rightly emphasised, within the causal theory an experiencing individual should be treated 'as if he were only one group of phenomena, though of a very peculiar kind, within the general order of sequence and co-existence which it is the business of physical science to investigate' [50]. This is a necessary presupposition if the problem of perception is to be defined in terms of physics and its solution undertaken by methods of natural science.

The question arises, however, what are the implications of this legitimate and necessary presupposition when the causal theory is applied outside the province of natural science. The use made of it in the theory of knowledge is an instance in point. Mach pointed out that to regard all experiences as effects or extensions of an external world into consciousness is to make far-reaching metaphysical assumptions which lead to a tangle of difficulties, impossible to unravel. Mach's attempt to make a fresh approach to the problem of knowledge of the external world, that disregarded both 'representationism' and the causal theory of perception, has been followed by others. In Poland, the most notable achievement of this sort has been Kotarbiński's radical realism [51].

The causal theory has met much criticism from various quarters. Some say that this theory is a part of natural science and, as it stands, cannot function as its foundation, that is, as a theory of what perceptual observation is. For it is itself based upon observations of sense-organs, the nervous system and brain, lenses and retinae, physical media and objects, and assumes in its premises the theory which it is supposed to demonstrate. Translated into an epistemological account of observation it has an air of fundamental artificiality and implausibility, which a closer examination does not fail to confirm [52]. Others deny that the causal theory can be applied to the problems of knowledge at all. For it extends the concept of causality beyond the field of its significant applicability and results in the formulations of hypotheses for which there could be no valid evidence [53]. Moreover, the causal theory must also be examined as to its suitability to explain what it sets out to achieve in the theory of knowledge, namely, to account for the cognition of material objects in the act of perceiving them. It is this question which is of vital importance for the materialist theory of knowledge. For within

336

the latter the causal theory is to secure some kind of conclusive evidence concerning the existence of things outside and independent of our minds which the copy theory is unable to supply by itself.

At first glance it might appear that there is no problem here, that is, that the causal theory does close the gap between percept and object. If the external object is the cause and the sensation its effect, this causal relation explains both the appearance of the object to the senses and its cognisance by the senses. This was Helmholtz's view. Lenin and his supporters often suggested that only a fool could see any difficulty in a matter so simple and elementary. This opinion, however, cannot be accepted.

The reference of percepts ('images' in Lenin's terminology) to their physical and physiological causal conditions presupposes some prior knowledge of the existence of the external world [54]. This does not mean that the causal theory is bound to move in a vicious circle; what it requires is not a general knowledge of the existence of the external world, which inevitably is an inferred knowledge. What it cannot do without is some directly experienced connection between the perception as effect and the physical thing as its cause. If the search for this awareness of an external object in the perceptual process itself, as conceived by the causal theory, were successful, nothing would stand in the way of interpreting the stimulus-sensitive body relation as that of the cognising subject and the cognised object. We could then also assume that though the existence of the external world as a whole is an inferred and conjectural knowledge, the existence of particular material things is based on direct knowledge, as it were, a knowledge by acquaintance, secured in the very act of perceiving external objects.

It should be borne in mind, that on the basis of the causal theory of perception the cognising subject is a body as much external as any other external object. It neither could nor should be conceived as we know it from our internal experience. We are, therefore, barred from assuming any knowledge whatsoever that could be gained from this source and we are bound to examine ourselves as nothing but sensitive bodies.

If this limitation is accepted, and it is impossible to avoid it, it becomes clear that what happens to the sensitive body, affected by an external stimulus, cannot be apprehended as an effect of a cause. For, on the assumption of the theory, the perceptual experience of a sensitive body is just an event of perceiving and nothing else, distinct from the event which caused it as much as from any other with which it has no connection whatsoever. When the light from a distant star hits a photographic plate, a spot appears. Should a sensitive body replace the photographic plate, it would be aware of the event of perceiving a spot, but on the assumption of the causal theory this awareness does not point out, as it were, beyond itself, any more than the black spot on the photographic plate does, and without it there is no cognition called 'seeing the star'. The external causes can account for the fact of how the event of sensing or perceiving is brought about, but they are unable to explain how such events should be cognitions of anything outside them, of their causes in particular.

337

If the experience, of which a sensitive body is aware, is only the event of perceiving, nothing could be inferred from it either, unless the inference from effect to cause is identified with perceptual consciousness. But this begs the question and reverses the real order of thought. For the inference from effect to cause already presupposes some prior knowledge of the external world which a sensitive body is assumed not to possess. Not even a tentative thought of an external object could occur as a result of the action exercised by the objects on a sensitive body, if this action is restricted to the cause-effect relation. Moreover, according to the causal theory what happens to the sensitive body takes place inside it – Lenin's images 'exist within us' or even more specifically 'within the human head' – and the causal conditions are outside it. On this assumption, our inferred knowledge of the external objects turns out to be entirely inexplicable. For then, if the effect is within us and the cause that releases the chain of events outside us, we cannot arrive at this knowledge even by an inference from effect to cause. Why should the cause of the experienced effect be outside us? The antecedents of the perception are some occurrences in our nervous system, and the inference concerning the antecedents would have to place them inside and not outside our body. The causal theory by itself cannot transcend the bounds of sensations and events taking place within the sensitive body. This has been recognised by Bertrand Russell, who has drawn the conclusion therefrom that, for instance, the 'starry heaven that we know in visual sensation is inside us' and the 'external starry heaven that we believe in is inferred'[55].

If Lenin and his Polish followers came to a different conclusion and claimed that the causal theory of perception establishes the connection between the percept and the cognised object, this was probably due to the fact that he tacitly assumed in the premisses of the theory what it was intended to prove. It is easy to overlook that the concept of the cognising subject cannot be consistently accommodated within the causal theory and that to introduce it is to endow the sensitive body with a capacity that is exactly precluded because of what is assumed. The causal theory is a scientific theory which explains knowledge as a natural process without being able to establish that we actually have knowledge about the existence of physical objects. It is one thing to explain how sense-data are generated by the interaction of objects connected with each other by spatial, temporal, and causal relations, and a different one to justify the belief in the existence of physical objects. The former presupposes the latter, but the converse is not true. We may hold the belief in question and deny without self-contradiction the validity of the causal theory. This theory might be legitimately applied provided that we are already in possession of some knowledge about the existence of external objects and we make use of it to account for the manner in which we have acquired knowledge as a matter of fact.

Moreover, we can make use of it provided that we are ready to renounce naive realism in the sense that things are as they appear to be or that the 'thing-in-itself', as Lenin put it, 'does not differ fundamentally from its appearance'[56]. The causal theory does not seem to be compatible with this view. For it is very probable that the causes of our experiences, for instance, light or sound waves, do not resemble in any manner their effects, the experience of seeing colour or hearing a sound. It is, therefore, extremely doubtful that the objects which are the prime cause of our experience, the source of light and sound waves, should have any resemblance with the light and sound experience. The content of the latter might be like some of the intrinsic characteristics of the former, but it might also be totally different. There are no means available to find out which of the two possibilities applies and there are important reasons to believe that the second is the case. For we cannot even imagine what is the 'content' of any event unless it happens to us, and we do know, for instance, that the music caused by a gramophone record does not resemble the record itself. Lenin realised sometimes the implications of the causal theory, but most often firmly denied them [57].

If we are unable to justify our claim to the knowledge of the external objects in some other way, the causal theory does not provide any help in this respect. Either in conjunction with the copy theory or by itself, instead of bridging the gap between percept and object it severs the percipient body from the external object and leaves them both in their separate worlds. Engels and Lenin accused Hume and Kant of "fencing off 'the appearance' from that which appears, the perception from that which is perceived, the thing-for-us from the 'thing-in-itself' " [58]. This is exactly what the causal theory seems to do if it is mistaken for an epistemological theory. To accept the causal theory as a proof of the existence of material objects is to dogmatically assume the truth of physics. There is nothing wrong with this assumption provided that we do not try to misrepresent a scientific explanation as an epistemological one.

Whenever epistemological questions are discussed Marxist-Leninists assure us that the materialist theory of knowledge recognises the existence of a reality beyond the phenomena, of real objects outside and independent of us. If no logical justification is produced, the belief in the existence of physical things is no theory of knowledge but an epistemological dogma. Neither the causal nor the copy theory of perception provide the required justification. At most, they give an explanation of the manner in which we might possibly have acquired the knowledge claimed, but they do not justify knowledge that we claim to possess.

Marxist-Leninists are inclined to consider the distinction between these two different problems as a futile verbal evasion of what they regard as the main epistemological issue, namely, whether the existence of external objects independent of a cognising subject is accepted or rejected. To differentiate what is 'immediately' or 'factually given' from what is not, is to perform a masquerade in which an 'agnostic' disguises himself in a materialist's cloak, to befog and to sidetrack the main epistemological issue that divides materialism and idealism. Compared with this main issue, everything else – to use Lenin's inimitable style – is superfluous ballast of professorial erudition, muddleheaded tomfoolery and scholastic balderdash, which results in regarding 'gelehrtes (learned) fiction' as genuine philosophy. What Lenin considered as genuine philosophy does not seem to include the theory of knowledge and what he had in mind was metaphysical beliefs decked out in epistemological terms.

The materialist theory of knowledge is in a rudimentary state. It does not provide either an effective support for materialist metaphysics or the means of defence against the criticism of the latter based on a more elaborate theory of knowledge. The materialist theory of knowledge is hardly anything more than an accessory derived from the same first principles which underlie the Marxist-Leninist account of the Universe, an adventitious appendage of a deductive metaphysics.

CHAPTER 18

ANTHROPOLOGICAL REALISM

Lenin's theory of knowledge was part of orthodox Marxism-Leninism in Poland. But beside it another trend of thought had appeared among the younger generation of Marxist-Leninists, who were becoming increasingly dissatisfied with what the official doctrine had to say on the problems of knowledge. The leading spirits of this trend were Helena Eilstein, Zdzisław Kochański, and, above all, Leszek Kołakowski. Kołakowski's ideas have a considerable affinity with and are largely derived from the views of the young Marx, to be found in the unfinished manuscript *Nationalökonomie und Philosophie*. In Kołakowski's interpretation, the young Marx held a conception of knowledge radically different from the positivistic epistemology to which he and Engels later subscribed, and also from that prevalent in contemporary Marxism-Leninism, based mainly on Lenin's *Materialism and Empirio-Criticism*.

Kołakowski's views deserve attention for several reasons. They initiate a new trend of thought inspired by the Marxian tradition and are free from the stereotypes of Marxism-Leninism, which has precipitated a spate of sharp and sometimes angry rejoinders from the more traditionalistic supporters of the doctrine [59]. More specifically, Kołakowski makes the first attempt since the post-war Marxian revival in Poland to give a philosophical interpretation to the conviction that thinking is socially determined. In this attempt Kołakowski makes use of the general non-evaluative form of the total conception of ideology, formulated by Mannheim but applied by him exclusively to the analysis of the utopian political mentality.

Kołakowski has been the protagonist of the view that the whole development of modern philosophy suffers from the consequences of Descartes' reform of philosophy. Descartes set philosophy on a new course by his demand that the reflection on, and the criticism of knowledge should be put in the foreground and made the foundation for philosophical thinking. This demand has ever since prevented the relation of man to Nature and History to be seen in its true light. Moreover, it is also altogether unacceptable because it is prejudicial: on its basis an idealist solution of the problems of knowledge becomes inevitable. The conviction that this solution is entirely false, cannot prevail as long as Descartes' rule remains in force. If it is conceded at the very beginning that the cognising subject can be isolated from the community, of which he is a member, emancipated from historical and social determinations, as well as from the impact of scientific tradition, truth and reason are doomed to defeat and to all the irrational follies of subjectivism. An individual as conceived by Locke, Descartes, Berkeley or Hume never did and does not exist [60]. It is a fallacy to suppose that an abstract individual of the traditional epistemology could acquire any knowledge and that his acts of cognition would obtain objectivity and rationality. What the thinkers of the past regarded as a source of errors and bias are the very conditions without which no genuine cognitive act could be accomplished, no creative action and thought arise.

The question whether we can acquire any knowledge at all, frequently asked by modern philosophers, provides its own answer. If we could not gain any knowledge, we could not put the question either. *Ab esse ad posse valet consequentia.* What remains is the problem of the specific conditions under which the question, whether we can know anything, could have arisen. The question concerning the possibility of knowledge is settled by the fact that knowledge is inherent in the social life of man; for social life is a constant struggle to gain control over the environment and if this is not knowledge, what else might it be? The best proof that man is capable of doing something is that he does it. This was known to Marx when he pointed out that the question of the possibility of knowledge is not a question of theory but that of practice. It was also known to Engels when he quoted *Faust: Im Anfang war die That* [61].

It follows that not only the starting point of modern epistemology was wrong, but also that the materialist theory of knowledge is on the wrong track. For the latter, notwithstanding its protestations to the contrary, shares with the former its individualistic presupposition, tries to beat its opponent by inappropriate means, and has to pay the penalty for entering upon this course. The attempt of interpreting knowledge as a reflection of the 'objective reality' in the mind has encumbered the materialist theory of knowledge with 'rather embarrassing ambiguities' [62]. Both Engels and Lenin conceived knowledge as a more and more perfect picture or map of the world as it exists quite independently of the mind. But we could have no notion of what exists quite independently of us and the assumption that knowledge is a process similar to the reflection of objects in a mirror is simply untrue. Materialism is right when it asserts that the existence of the physical world is not dependent on the consciousness, but the knowledge of the physical world is relative to the mind. Both the biological constitution of man and social requirements produce definite reactions to definite stimuli and determine the manner in which the cognising subject organises the data of experience. The cognitive capacity of man is selective and not reflective; it is a product of the evolution of the human species and inheritance, of the totality of social circumstances and individual characteristics. It serves primarily the biological and social functions. If our perceptions inform us of things and relations existing in the outside world, these perceptions cannot be conceived as their images in the proper meaning of this term. For an image must display some resemblance to what it is an image of, and no resemblance can be demanded of perceptions. The external world exists independently of man and is not created by him in any sense of this expression. But the external world as it appears to man is a socially organised and construed reality, and the cognising subject is a social subject, whose concepts and categories are functionally or otherwise determined by the institutional structure of society, as well as by the biological and social evolution of the human species [63].

The views of the young Marx on the problems of knowledge were expounded in the form of critical observations on Hegel's system and his peculiar mode of thinking. The manuscript is unfinished, the elusiveness and imprecision of its style vies with Hegel's. It seems to be clear, however, that Marx subordinated 'pure reason' to 'practical reason' and thought that the problem of knowledge cannot even be formulated in terms of an abstract theory. Thinking and being are undoubtedly distinct, but they are intimately associated with each other. Marx's starting point differs from that of other historically known systems, including the materialist. This, one can add, was once emphasised by Bukharin. In Marx's theory of knowledge, Bukharin wrote, 'there is another object, another subject, and a different relationship between them'. In its essence his theory of knowledge is sociological [64].

From Marx's point of view the concept of reality-in-itself is devoid of any sense and cannot be rationally construed. There is never anything like a thing-in-itself, there are always only 'things for us'. The material world *an und für sich,* causally independent of man, does exist, but it is also entirely beyond his reach. Knowable is only the world that appears in man's experience, that is, divided into species and individuals, pieces and classes, articulated into objects and their relations, into things with a definite form, arrangement and structure, cut out from the chaotic mass of the pre-existing world as it persists by itself. This humanised world is knowable because it is a world determined by man. As a natural being man shapes the environment according to his needs, and the needs determine the articulation of the world into separate things and their connections. If the needs were different, the world would look differently, as it does to other animal species. The eye is not a mirror that faithfully reflects something outside it as it exists in itself, but a human eye, and the same applies to other senses. This means that the 'senses have..... become directly in their practice theoreticians', the objects become for man the objectification of himself, or, as Marx cryptically said, 'man himself becomes the object'. 'It is clear', Marx wrote, 'that thinghood..... is utterly without any independence, any essentiality *vis-à-vis* self-consciousness; that on the contrary it is a mere creature – something posited by self-consciousness. And what is posited, instead of confirming itself, is but a confirmation of the act as its product, seeming to give the de-posit – but only for a moment – the character of an independent, real substance' [65].

Language is a social product, used to provide names, concepts and categories. Its function is, as it were, to fix the socially shaped world and help to manipulate what is made by our needs into things and their interrelations. It provides no means of looking through and finding out what the world in itself is like. Language has no other uses than the familiar ones. It has got no concealed foundations beneath its surface, which some thinkers before and after Marx, from Kratylus to Wittgenstein, tried to discover.

The subjective world, articulated and determined in its structure by the powers of life, by man's needs, tendencies, impulses, and ability to suffer, is not an ephemeral world, ever becoming and passing away. For man is a natural being, that is, a member of an animal species, and a social being, destined to act with others. Man's individual and species life are not different, and the former, though it may not appear in the direct form of a communal life carried out together with others, is an expression of social life [66]. Man is not an individual but a social subject and his cognitive capacities and organising forms or categories of thought are social too. The subjective world is, therefore, socially subjective, and displays certain persisting qualities, corresponding to the durable characteristics of the human species. There are habits generated by repeated experiences, common to all members of the species; they induce what Bertrand Russell called 'animal inference', the spontaneous inclination to interpret sensations in a certain manner. Animal inferences endow the socially subjective world with some permanency, give man an initial store of regularities and laws, and guide him towards science [67].

The enlargement of the basis for an anthropologically oriented epistemology leads to several important conclusions. The barrier that in Engels' or Lenin's theory of knowledge fences off the percept from the perceived object disappears. For man's consciousness of himself is the correlate of the resistance in the environment, encountered by him as he tries, as a natural being, to appropriate from Nature what his needs require. Neither the self-consciousness nor the outside world, neither percept nor perceived object, can be apprehended separately from each other [68].

The idea is not peculiarly Marxian, though its formulation is. It was Kant who raised the presupposition contained in Marx's idea to the status of a general principle underlying his refutation of idealism. This general principle states that there is no self-knowledge prior and unrelated to the knowledge of other things, of spatio-temporal bodies in particular. In order to be known to itself, the self must be an experiencing individual and the experiencing must include that which is not-self. It follows that in our knowledge the self and the spatio-temporal world are inseparable. If either exists, the other must exist too.

Marx did not set the world as it appears to us over against the world *an und für sich,* which pre-exists every attempt to know it. The world of Feuerbach, Engels and Lenin that exists without and independently of us and yet is completely knowable, is for Marx a 'nullity', a 'nothing.... devoid of sense' or mere 'externality' [69]. Its existence is not problematic, but the question regarding the mode of its existence is no more significant than if we asked what the world would be like should our eyes be sensitive to wave frequencies different from those we can now perceive. An external world independent of the perceiving subject is a fiction beyond our comprehension and ability of rational construction, for all our concepts as well as our language are inevitably and exclusively related to the socially subjective world. It cannot even be said that the socially subjective world is a distorted picture of the real one. If 'distortion' were not a pejorative but a neutral term, it would still presuppose the correlative expression referring to what is not distorted and what functions as the model. Neither of the two Kantian distinctions between phenomena and things-in-themselves can be applied to provide this model. The world *an und für sich* is a nullity not only because it cannot be known through experience, but also be-

cause we cannot draw any nearer to it, whatever efforts we undertake and however extended in time our efforts are. There is nothing in the socially subjective
world that points beyond itself, to the transcendent world of the positivistically-
minded materialism [70].

There is a gulf, therefore, between the conception of a socially subjective
world and that of Aristotelian realism, based on the assumption that the conceptual apparatus can be brought into correspondence with the true and real
nature of things. Marxism-Leninism accepts the latter conception and stresses
its importance for science. From the viewpoint of anthropological realism this is
an illusion. For long before man began to reflect on the problems of knowledge,
the world as it can be known and the manner in which knowledge can be acquired had been biologically and socially determined. The biological and social
life had simultaneously determined the articulation of the external world into
separate objects and the conceptual apparatus whose primary function is to
help people to find their bearing in the environment [71].

There is a superficial similarity between anthropological realism and pragmatism,
for they both emphasise the primacy of human activity over reflection and
ascribe to things some kind of *esse concessum* or a 'posited substantiality' [72].
But there is no room in anthropological realism for the relativism of the pragmatists. Anthropological realism conceives both the outside world to be socially
constructed and the consciousness to be essentially a social product. Although
the so-called materialist definition of truth is inapplicable, the correspondence
theory of truth is perfectly compatible with the assumptions of anthropological
realism. Provided that 'Nature' is given the meaning of 'socially subjective world',
Lenin's definition of truth as the 'correspondence between the consciousness
which reflects Nature and the Nature which is reflected by consciousness'
remains valid [73].

Marx described his views as 'consistent naturalism and humanism', distinct
from materialism and idealism, and constituting the unifying truth of both [74].
This naturalism makes metaphysics, in a certain sense of this term, impossible.
For if humanised Nature is the only one that man can ever know, it is idle, futile,
and self-contradictory to speak of the world as it exists independently of man.
This is a pure speculative thought spun out by what Marx called the 'philosophic
mind' and which he defined as an 'estranged mind .... thinking within its
estrangement'. On the other hand, with the Marxian assumption we cannot
conceive scientific thinking as an activity that by its discoveries tries, as it were,
to reproduce imitatively the world as it exists *an und für sich* and to draw
nearer and nearer to some unconditional truth. 'The recognition of theory as a
copy, as an approximate copy of objective reality, is materialism' wrote Lenin [75].
This has been recognised by Marx as a self-contradictory thought. There can be
no question of hypotheses, which are at the base of scientific theories, being
regarded as accurate descriptions of the constitution of the Universe as it exists in
itself. The world accessible to man bears the imprint of human creativeness and
this creativeness continues to inform and direct scientific thinking [76].

Finally, the realisation that the world is created by man in the naturalistic and social meaning of this expression, faces the philosopher with a new task. Metaphysics is a wild goose chase. The theory of knowledge is not entirely impossible, but its terms of reference must be reformulated.

'Pure datum' is as elusive as the world of metaphysics and an epistemologist who in the fashion of an Avenarius undertakes the 'critique of pure experience' is as much off the track as a metaphysician. If anthropological realism is right, the capacity of man 'as such' to acquire knowledge cannot be investigated. The concept of universal man is either a biological concept, and thus belongs to natural science, or it is nothing at all. For the concept of man as a social thing is not a universal but essentially a historical notion which must always be related to definite circumstances in time and space. The social man is a creature of history, it has no unchanging essence, and to speak of the universal man in history is self-contradictory.

A general anthropological theory of knowledge is not impossible, but its content would be extremely poor and repetitious. It would have to restrict itself to the statement that knowledge functionally depends on historical development, on the social conditions, on class stratification and class conflicts, on man's relation to Nature. Such generalities lead nowhere, unless they are shown to apply to a definite historical, social, scientific, and philosophical context. But this would no longer be a general theory of knowledge and its conclusions would not be universal in character, for validity would have to be restricted in time and space.

Epistemology should be reduced, therefore, to the history of knowledge. Knowledge might be conceived *sensu largo,* and then the history of knowledge would merge with the history of philosophy, based on different assumptions from those traditionally accepted. It may also be understood *sensu stricto,* as scientific knowledge. In the latter case epistemology becomes a part of the history of science, dealing with the historical development of various descriptive schemes, their conceptual framework and underlying principles [77].

What remains for the philosophers to do cannot be easily and unambiguously described. There is no particular domain of facts or problems which is his own exclusive preserve. His interest is anthropological and this means that his inquiry is concentrated on the practical and human sense that any kind and part of knowledge might have. By definition, all the knowledge, as conceived by an anthropological realist, has this sense, but this might not always be apparent. Furthermore, the relative human importance and significance of a particular part of knowledge changes in time. It might be astronomy, as was the case at the time of the conflict between the Ptolemaic and Copernican systems, it might be physics and the issue of determinism, as is the case at present. It is not only the content but also the historical circumstances which decide what particular matter acquires philosophical relevance. From the anthropological standpoint, what is philosophically relevant is also morally important, it has an impact on human attitudes and conduct. For knowledge being biologically and socially determined has both a cognitive and regulative content, and the function of a philosopher is to discover and to explain their interdependence. It is important to emphasise both aspects of knowledge, if the exorcised follies of subjectivism, characteristic of the traditional theory of knowledge, are not to be supplanted by those of voluntarism, as happened, for instance, in some interpretations of the Marxian doctrine. Essentialism in theory and voluntarism in practice has produced a chimerical philosophical programme, inspired by a self-contented dilettantism [78].

Kołakowski did not go beyond the stage of programmatic statements. With one or two exceptions, he has expounded his views in a number of essays of a general and more or less popular form. His purpose was practical rather than theoretical, that is, he wished to modify the prevailing beliefs and attitudes of his contemporaries without offering a fully and systematically developed system [79]. His supporters have so far offered no more than some loose comments and marginal observations and have expressed clearly critical opinions of anthropological realism.

It should be borne in mind that Kołakowski's criticism of the individualistic presupposition accepted in modern epistemology is not as revolutionary and novel as it might appear at first glance. This criticism is implicit in some recent sociological theories as well as in some philosophical writings. Durkheim's studies on religion, which led to the conclusion that human conduct is primarily determined by social institutions, gave rise to the idea that social institutions provide the prevailing pattern of rationality and objectivity in general and that the individual's whole conceptual framework is of social origin. Mannheim's general theory of the total ideology and of epistemological relationism should be placed at the other extreme of Bacon's repudiation of the *idola fori*. Epistemological relationism is not only a methodological rule but also an epistemological assertion. Each socio-cultural perspective, to which individual thinking should be always related, far from being a source of errors and bias provides an insight into what must remain closed and inaccessible in another perspective [80].

Philosophers approached the same problem from a different direction. Dewey more than any other thinker emphasised the biological basis of human thought and its primary role as a means of adapting the organism to its environment. This implies that the conception of reason as an impartial power, immune from change and above time and history, is basically wrong. The faculties of reason are comprised in the flux of universal changeability, they contribute to and are affected by the process of biological and social adjustment. Cognitive experience originates within that of a non-cognitive sort, in which thought is a 'factor in action', an instrument in satisfying the needs of the human organism and the requirements of adaptation. The most refined devices of intellectual analysis are an evolutionary outcome of the activities that serve specific social and biological ends. The conception of experience and knowledge, initiated in the seventeenth century, that reduced experience and knowledge to 'subjective private consciousness set over against nature, which consists wholly of physical objects, has wrought havoc in philosophy'[81]. Dewey's own peculiar anthropological and psychological examinations of the methods of inquiry were to set philosophy on its right course again.

On the other hand, Philipp Frank emphasised that traditional epistemology and metaphysics are disguised social theories, which, being less respectable than the former have to appear made up in public. To say that sociological theories influence epistemological and metaphysical thinking or that the latter is a 'projection' of the former, does not imply that all thinking is socially determined. We come close to this assertion if we accept that the socio-cultural perspective is socially determined.

The belief that modern philosophy makes sociological individualism its foundation for the theory of knowledge seems to be right. The view that only an individual separated from his social and historical context is a rational being is a sociological theory. On the validity of this theory, accepted as self-evident and never so far examined or tested, hangs the validity and the relevance of much that modern epistemology has to say on the problems of knowledge.

The most doubtful part of anthropological realism is its consequences concerning scientific knowledge. That science can provide no adequate representation of the underlying realities, but only various generalised descriptive schemes, to be evaluated by other criteria than those of the correspondence theory of truth, is not a new belief in the philosophy of science. What is new in it, is its justification. But the arguments put forward by Kołakowski are far-fetched and elusive compared with those which, for instance, conventionalism or the instrumentalist and neo-positivistic conceptions of science can offer. For in the case of anthropological realism the view on scientific knowledge is simply a consequence deduced from the fact that the world is a socially subjective reality. If it is granted that this might be the case within certain limits, there remains the question of how wide these limits are. Do they include, to take some extreme examples, the reality revealed by radio astronomy, the electronic microscope, and atomic physics? More generally, the question can be asked: has the term 'reality' only one use? If it is not so, is not the arbitrary restriction of the use of the term to one meaning alone rather an invention foisted upon the facts than a discovery, whose claim to validity, though supported by some reasoned arguments, cannot, in the nature of the case, be based on hard facts? For what these facts could possibly be, is extremely difficult to see. Kołakowski's socially subjective reality within which we are for ever imprisoned recalls Eddington's two tables, the familiar and the 'scientific' one, immortalised in *The Nature of the Physical World*. The fallacy underlying Eddington's two tables theory has been cleared up by the observation that if something can be described in terms of two different languages, this fact does not imply that two ontologically different objects correspond to these manners of description. We can refer to the same object in different ways and this should not mislead us into believing that the object referred to is different in each case [82]. What the young Marx did was perhaps not to discover a new reality but a new language in terms of which reality can be described.

CHAPTER 19

THE MATERIALIST CONCEPTION OF TRUTH

The questions what does the truth of a belief consist in and how can we recognise that it is true, have given rise not only to various theories of truth but also to various philosophies. For as soon as the question of truth is raised, a whole intricate complex of issues appears in its wake and the examination of the concept of truth is transformed into a dispute between rival philosophical theories. Some of the most influential modern philosophical doctrines, for instance, the instrumentalist philosophy of Dewey or logical empiricism, have the criticism of the traditional concept of truth as their starting point.

Marxist-Leninist philosophy claims that it has a theory of truth of its own, the so-called (materialist) theory of objective truth. Its fundamental importance for the whole doctrine was emphasised by Lenin. 'To regard our sensations as images of the external world', Lenin wrote, 'to recognise objective truth, to hold the materialist theory of knowledge – these are all one and the same thing'[83]. Lenin could not have wished to say that all these beliefs are 'one and the same thing' in virtue of having the same meaning, for they do not mean the same. What he probably had in mind was the logical equivalence of the three views which being different in their respective meaning entail each other. Since according to Lenin the materialist theory of knowledge and materialism are also logically equivalent beliefs, these two together with the copy theory of perception and that of objective truth should be considered from the Marxist-Leninist viewpoint as a coherent whole in which each entails the other and none of which could be false if the other is true. This seems to be clear also from what Lenin's followers in Poland say on this matter [84].

In spite of the importance attached to the concept of truth in Marxist-Leninist philosophy, no larger work dealing with this concept ever appeared either in the Soviet Union or elsewhere. Schaff's study *Some Problems of the Marxist Theory of Truth*, published in 1951, should be, therefore, considered as by far the highest single achievement of the Marxist-Leninist school in Poland. It is the first and – its title notwithstanding – an exhaustive monograph on the subject, notable for its wide scope. It is half analytic and half polemical, the second half being concerned with the conception of truth of empirio-criticism, conventionalism, pragmatism and logical empiricism, including operationism[85].

There is very little in the works of Engels and Lenin which Schaff could draw upon in his examination of the materialist theory of truth (this might have been one of the reasons why no other monograph of this kind was published elsewhere), and he is heavily indebted to non-Marxist philosophy. In particular he made considerable use of various concepts and views worked out in Poland, above all, by Twardowski, Kotarbiński, Ajdukiewicz and Tarski.

Schaff did not adopt the achievements of the Warsaw school indiscriminately.

He subjected them to a scrutiny from his own viewpoint and adapted them to his own purpose. But even when this was not necessary and his direct philosophical debt is unmistakable, he was inclined to exaggerate the differences or to find them where there were none, for the Warsaw school thinkers were at that time condemned for their alleged idealism, conventionalism and other disreputable tendencies. His critical examination of and polemical observations on other people's views, those of foreign thinkers in particular, to whom he owes a great deal, do not always excel in fairness and objectivity. He often fails to acknowledge the value of the contributions made by thinkers with whom he disagrees and misconstrues in his account the views which he wishes to criticise. A harsh and self-righteous note of accusation pervades even criticism which is otherwise justified. Mach confessed in *Analysis of Sensations* that he never felt it necessary to insult people whose opinions differed from his own. In this matter, as in many others, Schaff felt differently from Mach [86].

Marxist-Leninist philosophy rests on what might be called the 'principle of dichotomy'. There are two and only two possible standpoints concerning the nature and constitution of the Universe, those of materialism and of idealism (in the Marxist-Leninist sense). There are two and only two possible standpoints in epistemology – the materialist and the idealist theory knowledge. In the Marxist-Leninist universe of discourse materialism or dialectical materialism and the materialist theory of knowledge are classes with a single element, and all the other possible views, whether like or unlike, comparable or incomparable, constitute their respective complementary classes. The materialist conception of truth also rests on the principle of dichotomy.

A theory of truth should provide a definition of the common property of true beliefs, that is, of some property which can be ascribed to all true beliefs without exception. If this condition is not fulfilled, a theory of this sort would be considered to be deficient in this respect. Schaff tacitly makes this assumption. From this viewpoint, all definitions of the common property which belongs to true beliefs can be divided into two main types, called, respectively, the correspondence or the materialist and the idealist conception of truth. Since the first one is derived from Aristotle's *Metaphysics*, in Poland it has also been called the classic, and the second, which does not make use of the correspondence relation, the non-classic definition of truth. Schaff often refers to the latter as the 'theory of subjective truth', set over against that of 'objective truth'. 'Subjective' and 'objective' are to indicate respectively that there is nothing beyond the belief in virtue of which a statement is true or false, or that there is something extraneous, as it were, on which the truth of the belief depends. In the first case what makes a belief true does, and in the second does not involve the mind of the individual who holds the belief, and, consequently, a statement is true irrespective of whether it has ever been actually made or is made by anybody at any time.

The materialist theory of truth assumes that there is a reality outside the mind and independent of it, which the mind can know, and the idealist theory does not need any of these assumptions. According to Schaff, the idealist theory of truth implies more than that. The common characteristic of the idealist conceptions of truth is their denial that objective reality is knowable or that it exists at all, and, consequently, they define truth as the conformity of thought with a principle or a norm. Some examples of the idealist conceptions of truth are provided by the theories which identify truth with self-evidence, *consensus communis*, coherence, economy of thought or utility [87].

The correspondence or materialist conception assumes that a belief is true if it agrees or accords with objective reality. The definition implies that there is an objective reality, that it existed before man appeared on the surface of the Earth and that it exists irrespective of whether anybody perceives it or not. This provides the criterion for distinguishing a pseudo-correspondence theory of truth from a genuine one. In Schaff's opinion, when this criterion is applied most of those who profess the correspondence theory turn out to be concealed adherents of the idealist conception of truth [88].

Thus, Aristotle's definition in *Metaphysics* is not an instance of the correspondence theory of truth *sensu stricto*, that is, a materialist theory of truth. Aristotle's definition is a brilliant intuition of a man of genius which in Marxism-Leninism has been raised to a higher level of rational perfection. The Thomist definition of truth verbally refers to Aristotle's formulation but it reduces the *adaequatio rei et intellectus* to the accord of man's thought with the thought of God. Most of the great thinkers of the past – Descartes, Leibniz, Kant – paid tribute to Aristotle but the manner in which they conceived what thought must correspond to in order to be true, led them away from the correspondence theory *sensu stricto*.

In modern philosophy thinkers who define correspondence as agreement of thought with facts must be distinguished from those who define it as agreement with experience. The latter adhere to idealism, for they are driven to the conclusion that only experienced events occur and that it is meaningless to speak of events which no one experiences. This imposes mutilating restrictions upon knowledge and identifies existence with cognition: *esse est cognoscendi*. On the other hand, those who speak of the correspondence of thought with facts, among whom are Kotarbiński, Ajdukiewicz and Tarski, respect the letter but not the essence of the materialist theory of truth. They are left somehow suspended between materialist truth and idealist error. Only the Marxist-Leninist conception provides a perfectly consistent definition of truth as well as a comprehensive theory that is able to give a completely satisfactory answer to every question concerning truth and falsehood. The materialist theory of truth comprises the claim of being itself an incontrovertible truth [89].

The superiority which the materialist theory of truth claims for itself is based on two arguments. A satisfactory solution of the question of what the truth of a belief consists in should define the terms between which the relation of correspondence holds. Moreover, the nature of the correspondence relation should also be defined. The supporters of the materialist theory of truth assert that they are able to accomplish both these tasks with a greater precision and material adequacy than any other theory.

So far as the terms of the correspondence relation are concerned, the materialist theory assumes that the predicates 'true' and 'false' refer primarily to beliefs, and derivatively to sentences in which they are expressed. Whatever a belief might be, it should not be considered as a psychological phenomenon (the act of believing). When a belief is said to be true or false, what is meant is that someone believes that something is or is not the case or that that which is believed is true or false.

The view that only beliefs are primarily true or false is not a new doctrine. In Poland it was held universally and specifically by Twardowski, Kotarbiński – by the latter with certain reservations – and Kokoszyńska, and abroad by numerous thinkers. The only difference between them and Schaff is that they accept the existence of some simple beliefs which are not necessarily expressed in words and Schaff does not [90]. Furthermore, the commonly accepted interpretation of the correspondence theory asserts that the property of truth and falsehood does not depend on any internal characteristic of beliefs, but on the relation of the beliefs to something else outside thought. About what this something else is, there are a number of views, as many thinkers, among them Marxist-Leninists also, rightly emphasise [91].

The most wide-spread opinion maintains that the truth and falsehood of beliefs depends on their relation to the events or states of affairs or facts. In Schaff's view, it depends on their relation to objective reality, which is an unambiguous expression, while the others are not. This is a moot point, if not a highly doubtful one (unless 'reality' simply means 'the sum of particular events and objects'). It is not more but less difficult to define the terms 'event', 'state of affairs' and 'fact' than 'objective reality'. If anything, the first three start with some advantage of concreteness which the fourth lacks. We can observe events and directly apprehend states of affairs and facts, but objective reality is an abstract term. Having recorded a measurement or a count, having applied any recognised empirical procedure or used the evidence of our senses, we cannot say that we have measured or counted or investigated objective reality. The intension of this concept might be more or less clear to us, but its extension is not. 'Objective reality' seems to be a term about which endless disputations have been carried on and are bound to continue in the future. For this reason it has been abandoned or avoided as much in Poland as abroad. It has not always been used in a metaphysical sense, but its metaphysical associations make it misleading.

The view according to which 'true' and 'false' are primarily predicated of beliefs and derivatively of sentences eliminates a certain metaphysical doctrine which for the sake of brevity will be called 'the hypothesis of propositions'. According to this hypothesis a proposition is not a linguistic entity, for it is not a part of any language at all, but a postulated or inferred entity, obtained by abstraction from language. This ideal entity is what a sentence in a given language and its translations into other languages have in common, the 'content of meaning' expressed by a declarative sentence whatever form the words used in it might have [92]. It is assumed that propositions do not exist in the way material objects

352

exist. Nevertheless, they are objectively real and are apprehended by the mind when the mind asserts or judges. These timeless entities, known only to some logicians, mathematicians and philosophers, are said to be in some cases – namely when the truths of mathematics and logic are considered – one of the terms between which the correspondence relation holds. On this view a sentence is true if it represents a true proposition, and false otherwise.

In Poland, it was Łukasiewicz and Ajdukiewicz who seemed to have supported the hypothesis of propositions without ever being committed to it. On the other hand, Leśniewski, Kotarbiński, Czeżowski and Tarski clearly rejected it. Kotarbiński devoted much of his energies to the criticism of this and similar hypotheses concerning the existence of abstract entities. Schaff mentioned Bertrand Russell as the chief contemporary supporter of the hypothesis of propositions, which is incompatible with the standpoint of materialism and, consequently, inadmissible for the materialist theory of truth [93]. He was not satisfied with its criticism from the viewpoint of nominalism, carried out in detail by Kotarbiński, for the nominalist approach is purely negative and barren. In general, nominalism is as much inadmissible as Platonic realism.

Kotarbiński rejected Frege's differentiation between particular judgments and their objective contents, between sentences as syntactical entities, series of printed or uttered signs, taken in abstraction from their meaning, and propositions which are named or represented by sentences. These distinctions separate what actually can be differentiated only in thought. For in fact there are no judgments or assertions either in the psychological or in the logical sense, there are only individuals who make judgments or assertions. When verbalised, the meaning of the latter is inseparable from the form of words or other symbols by means of which they are expressed. A sentence in Kotarbiński's sense is a series of sounds or inscriptions together with the meaning which they convey. Kotarbiński did not object to the use of the expression 'judgment' or 'sentence in the logical sense', provided that it was clearly understood that it was an abbreviated expression which did not name anything and by means of which the meaning of a sentence could be concisely referred to [94]. This is the present-day un-hypostatised use of the term 'proposition' which replaces the word 'sentence' whenever we are not concerned with a particular indicative sentence but with any sentence irrespective of the language in which it is expressed and which has the same meaning. Schaff rejected this kind of propositions too. It is not clear why he should have wished to dispense with them and to raise thereby almost insuperable difficulties in accounting for the existence of objective truths, *i.e.* propositions whose truth is not dependent upon the mind.

The hypothesis of substantial propositions is not the only theory which makes possible the objectivity and permanence of the truths of logic and mathematics, believed to be true before anybody thought of them and irrespective of whether anybody actually thinks of them or not. This time-independent meaning of the term 'true' is accepted by Marxist-Leninists. An objective or absolute truth is 'not dependent upon man and mankind' [95].

The objectivity of the truths of logic and mathematics does not require that these truths be independent of minds for their existence; there would be no propositions if there were no men to think of them and it is actually a matter of accident whether anybody happens to think of them or not. The essential point is that a proposition of logic and mathematics should not depend upon minds for its truth, that is, that what makes it true should not involve the mind which happens to think of it. We don't need the hypothesis of substantial propositions if some other theory would account consistently for the fact that though the propositions are created or constructed by man, their truth or falsehood is not. For such a theory can maintain that though propositions are mind-dependent, their truth-value does not depend on anybody's whim, and that there are true propositions which have not been thought and might never be thought by anyone.

A puzzling feature of the materialist theory of truth is its adherence to the objectivity and permanence of true propositions while it simultaneously asserts that only particular judgments or thoughts and sentences are true or false. For if only judgments made and uttered by particular persons at a particular time were true or false, objective truth would be unaccountable for. At every moment there are countless propositions of logic and mathematics which nobody happens to think. Consequently, the permanence of objective truth, its 'independence of man and mankind', would vanish. If only particular judgments are true and false, every true proposition is a mind-dependent truth.

Schaff follows Kotarbiński and assumes that judgements in the psychological sense are not entities of some sort but cognitive experiences of particular persons. Moreover, thinking is always done in sentences and to sever judgments from sentences is impermissible. We cannot really speak of judgments and sentences as separate units. There are only 'judgment-sentences'. We may speak of true and false sentences but the sentences are true or false in virtue of the judgments associated with them, which impart to the former their truth-value [96].

This, however, makes the acknowledgment of objective truth still more difficult to account for. What is judged, the content of judgment, becomes private to every mind and we have no means of finding out whether what one person thinks is also thought by another. If thoughts are to be exchanged between people, they must possess a modicum of verifiable identity. Apart from syntactical rules, the meaning of the sentences in which thoughts are expressed is usually considered to constitute the bridge of communication between private worlds of thought and experience. This bridge is destroyed if the understanding between people is said to be ultimately based on thoughts themselves, which are not public and directly accessible for comparison. The possibility of communication by means of language becomes extremely doubtful and incomprehensible if the common meaning of sentences that establishes the understanding is replaced by the putative identity of private thoughts.

The 'simple phenomenon of reflection' provides, according to Schaff, a satisfactory answer to those objections. The same objective reality is reflected by different minds and at different times; that which accounts for the identity of mental reflections lies outside the individual in the external world. In virtue of the common reference, thoughts have not the private character which is ascribed to them. The objective reality also safeguards the objectivity of truth, its independence of someone's happening to think it [97].

This seems to be, however, the same error as Engels' when he spoke of the 'properly made and properly used perceptions' as a means of finding out what the external world is like. The materialist theory of truth starts at the wrong end; what it is supposed to establish, it assumes as its premiss. The assumption is clearly not capable of being falsified. It can be maintained, if that is somebody's wish, but it is not a justifiable and rational assumption. The concepts of objective reality and mental reflection, as used in the materialist theory of truth, are metaphysical in the clearly pejorative sense of this term. They apply to objects and processes which we have never experienced and which in the nature of the case it is impossible that we should ever experience. Consequently, the explanation which they purport to provide is hollow in significance.

It is hard to see how the theory of reflection could account for the objectivity of truth. The difficulties might not be apparent if some simple singular 'judgment-sentences', like 'Warsaw is situated on the Vistula', are considered. But they become insuperable if the truth of such propositions as 'two times two makes four' or 'all men are mortal' is to be explained by means of the reflection metaphor. For objective reality does not include anything that these statements could possibly reflect. There is nothing in objective reality that would correspond to what they state in the same manner as the fact of the city of Warsaw extending on both banks of the Vistula corresponds to the singular statement 'Warsaw is situated on the Vistula'. In such cases the explanation in terms of reflections and objective reality not only lacks rationality, but also becomes meaningless. Moreover, if Lenin's assertion 'that an image cannot exist without the thing imaged and that the latter exists independently of that which images it' is taken seriously, the reintroduction of the rejected hypothesis of substantial propositions seems to become inescapable. There are some good reasons to doubt the justice of Schaff's claim that only the materialist theory of truth is capable of refuting the 'mysticism of abstract entities' [98].

The problem of the objectivity of truth cannot be more closely examined without inquiring into the second argument for the claim that the materialist theory of truth is superior to any rival theory. This argument asserts that only the materialist theory is capable of providing a satisfactory definition of the correspondence relation. According to the traditional definition, a judgment is truly made and a proposition is true if and only if there is an event or a state of affairs or a fact corresponding to what is judged or asserted, and false otherwise. Like many writers before him, Schaff points out that if the truth of a judgment or of a proposition consists in the correspondence of this kind, the term 'correspondence' should be defined. For neither this term nor any of its equivalents commonly used, such as 'agreement', 'accord', or 'adequacy', has a precise and sharply defined meaning; consequently, we are never sure whether it does or does not apply in a particular case.

It is Schaff's contention that the term 'reflection' has none of the ambiguities shared by the other relational expressions. Accordingly, the materialist theory defines the term 'true' in the following manner 'A judgment ('a judgment-sentence') is true if it faithfully reflects objective reality'. This definition, Schaff states, puts an end to all the imprecisions with which the traditional formulation of the classic definition of truth has been burdened since the time of Aristotle [99].

Attention has been drawn to the fact that this definition, understood literally, is a very ancient view, professed by the Greek atomists, and that the copy interpretation of the correspondence relation had been abandoned by Aristotle and Thomas Aquinas for the exact reason that it cannot apply in the literal sense [100]. It could not be said, for instance, that the proposition 'Warsaw is situated on the Vistula' is in the least like the state of affairs designated by the proposition. We can walk about the streets of Warsaw and take a swim in the Vistula, and obviously, we cannot do any of these things with the proposition. It is very odd to say that the terms in the proposition 'Warsaw is situated on the Vistula' are related in the same fashion as is Warsaw and the Vistula. What is reflected in the proposition stands for but is not itself a spatial relation that binds the objects denoted by the terms 'Warsaw' and 'the Vistula'. This is, however, to say that the mental reflection resembles what is reflected in one respect and not in another. But if 'reflecting' is a metaphoric relational expression and cannot be taken literally, it is not an unambiguous term and, in view of its misleading suggestions, not an unobjectionable one. The term 'correspondence' in an unspecified sense is as good as, if not better than, that of 'reflection' and if instead of the former the latter is applied it is self-deceptive to suppose that a step forward has been made.

This is the conclusion which Schaff had to accept, though only by implication and by using the old terminology in a new manner. He repudiated the suggestion that the 'theory of reflection' implies the identity of relations between elements in each term. It is enough to assume that the relations are 'analogous', and by this he probably meant what has just been said, namely, that they do resemble each other in some respects and do not in some others. This means, however, that so far as the definition of the correspondence relation is concerned the materialist theory of truth has nothing new to offer.

This is also made clear by Schaff's adherence to the semantical definition of truth which on the one hand offers a more precise form of the original Aristotelian formulation and, on the other, is neutral with respect to various epistemological attitudes. In Schaff's view the proposition 'a true (correct) judgment is a reflection of objective reality' is logically equivalent to " 'p' is true if and only if p" [101].

While recognising that the reflection relation is a metaphor, Schaff considered that the metaphor holds a strategically important position with respect to two problems: to the classic poser of true negative propositions and to the antinomies which arise from the use of self-referring sentences. There is apparently no adequate solution of these problems outside the materialist theory of truth.

A satisfactory theory of truth should be able to give an account of the opposite of truth, that is, of error. This condition has not always been fulfilled in the past and H. H. Joachim in *The Nature of Truth*, published in 1906, made use of this omission for the justification of the coherence theory of truth. Taking Joachim as his witness, Schaff assumed that a non-materialist theory of truth is incapable of accounting for false beliefs unless it postulates the existence of the non-existent facts, that is, unless it is self-contradictory. This conclusion is wide of the mark [102].

Truth and falsehood are correlative properties of beliefs; if there were no false beliefs, there would be no true beliefs either. To have both true and false beliefs, we need sentences and propositions on the one hand, events, states of affairs or facts on the other. This does not mean, however, that sentences or propositions name events, state of affairs or facts in a similar manner as proper names or predicates name something that is there. If a proposition were true in virtue of naming a fact, what would there be for a false or a true negative proposition to name? Sentences or propositions do not name but refer to or state, if true, a fact. The problem of what false sentences and true negative sentences are about largely arose from the confusion of the semantical relation of naming and referring.

G. E. Moore and Bertrand Russell realised a long time ago that if a theory of truth is to account for falsehood it must abandon the assumption of beliefs being a two term relation of the mind to a single object. The analysis of belief which reduces it to the relation between the believing person on the one hand, and what is believed (the fact or the proposition) on the other is incorrect. Consequently, Russell suggested that judging and believing should be conceived as a multiple relation which unites several terms into a complex whole. Sentences or propositions are constructed by the act of judgment. They are true, if to their relational complex whole there correspond events, states of affairs or facts which are also a relational complex whole. If the correspondence relation does not hold, the sentences or propositions are false and our beliefs or judgments are erroneous [103].

Russell's theory has been widely accepted, and it underlies Kotarbiński's and Ajdukiewicz's formulation of the correspondence theory of truth. Schaff's solution of the classic philosophical poser is in essence that of Moore, Russell, and the Polish philosophers, though their clarity and freedom from ambiguity is obscured in Schaff's exposition by the persistent idea that judgment is a mental reflection, in some sense of this term, of a single fact [104].

The idea that a judgment is a mental reflection of objective reality is claimed to provide an epistemological solution of the antinomies arising from the use of the term 'true' in colloquial language. Schaff argued that if the theory of reflection is accepted, the antinomies disappear, for statements like 'I am lying' or '*c* is not a true sentence' in Tarski's example [105] turn out to be no sentences at all but disturbances of air waves or patches of ink. On the other hand, if the theory of reflection is ignored, there is no valid reason simply to forbid the use of such sentences. Thus, we would be prevented from distinguishing truth from falsehood and the concept of truth in colloquial language would lose all significance. It has been already explained that this conclusion is fallacious and misinterprets the consequences of Tarski's investigations.

There is a basic difference between Schaff's and Tarski's approach to the problems of truth. For Schaff assumes that we can ignore the questions of language when we investigate 'objective reality' and that what reality is can be fixed in abstraction from and independently of the language adopted for its description. On the other hand, Tarski followed the path now familiar to contemporary thinkers: the answer to any question concerning reality depends upon reality itself, but also upon the language chosen for its description. Consequently, every question of fact has its linguistic aspect. The investigations of the structure of language, in which facts are stated, is a part of the investigations concerned with the facts themselves. This difference of approach was apparent in the whole Marxist-Leninist criticism of the Warsaw school, and it turns up again in the examination of the concept of truth.

Tarski's essay is largely concerned with the question of the bearing that the logical structure of language has upon the definition of the concept of truth. If all the results of his examinations had to be fully accepted, the concept of truth in colloquial language would still be not devoid of significance as much as that of a square circle. Apart from the knowledge provided by linguistic rules and definitions, there are other means by which true and false sentences can be distinguished. We have an intuitive knowledge of the concept of truth and in this sense we can be perfectly acquainted with it in spite of having failed to analyse it and to provide a satisfactory definition of a true sentence. Tarski never denied that we are familiar with the concept of truth and he drew upon our understanding of it in proposing his semantical definition of truth.

If by a proposition is meant anything that is believed or disbelieved, a sentence is a verbal expression of a proposition. Since Aristotle we assume that not every sentence expresses a proposition but only that which is either true or false. Sentences of this kind are usually called 'logical sentences'. Schaff's assertion is that not every logical sentence is a genuine logical sentence, and only the latter can be either true or false. A logical sentence is a genuine sentence if it expresses either directly or indirectly a mental reflection of objective reality. Some self-referring sentences, like 'I am lying' or 'c' in Tarski's example of 'c is not a true sentence', are not verbal expressions of a cognitive experience, and they do not express a judgment that reflects objective reality. Consequently, neither 'true' nor 'false' can legitimately be predicated of them. No antinomies arise if the use of 'true' and 'false' is restricted to sentences which express either directly or indirectly a judgment. For primarily only a judgment which does or does not faithfully reflect objective reality is true or false [106].

What Schaff has in mind is a hierarchy of mental reflections extending indefinitely upwards and downwards based solidly on reflections of what is there. The idea is exactly the same as that of a hierarchy of languages, formulated by Bertrand Russell [107]. A hierarchy of languages presupposes a language of the lowest type, called by Russell the 'object language' or the 'primary language'. What are the implications of this idea with respect to the truth and falsehood of sentences in the object language is best explained in Russell's own words:

"It is clear from Tarski's argument, that the words 'true' and 'false' cannot occur in the primary language; for these words, as applied to the sentences in the nth language, belong to the $(n+1)^{th}$ language. This does not mean that sentences in the primary language are neither true nor false, but that, if 'p' is a sentence in this language, the two sentences 'p is true' and 'p is false' belong to the secondary language. This is, indeed, obvious apart from Tarski's argument. For, if there is a primary language, its words must not be such as presuppose the existence of a language. Now 'true' and 'false' are words applicable to sentences, and thus presuppose the existence of language..... In the primary language, therefore, though we can make assertions, we cannot say that our own assertions or those of others are either true or false." [108]

If we had to express the same ideas in terms of a hierarchy of mental reflections, as Schaff suggested, we would at once be lost in confusion. We cannot imagine going indefinitely upwards from a reflection of a lower to that of a higher type, from a cognitive experience of the nth to that of the $(n+1)^{th}$ level. Confusion would creep in almost at the start and we would not know what we were talking about. This is not the case with a hierarchy of languages, for we have a symbolism ready at hand and the various languages can be neatly differentiated from each other. While no advantages are gained, clarity of thought is lost, if a hierarchy of mental reflections is substituted for Russell's hierarchy of languages.

The merits of the theory of reflection are in this case not only illusory, but in fact non-existent. We do not need to assume some kind of linguistic metaphysics, that is, to reduce thought and knowledge to the use of language, in order to consider the analysis of language and linguistic expressions as a fruitful approach to the examination of thought and knowledge [109]. Schaff probably felt that the latter cannot do without the former and came to the conclusion that Russell's hierarchy of languages must be expressed in terms of the theory of reflection to become acceptable to a Marxist-Leninist.

CHAPTER 20

THE TRUTHS OF LOGIC AND MATHEMATICS

The opinion that there is no sense of the term 'true' in which a belief may be true in spite of not corresponding to any fact and that the correspondence relation in which truth consists is that of reflection, meets with some difficulties in accounting for the truths of logic and mathematics. This is one of the reasons why the materialist theory of truth is firmly committed to the view that logic and mathematics have an empirical basis and express empirical generalisations of past experience. According to Lenin, this was 'proved' or 'brilliantly guessed' by Hegel. Marxist-Leninists in Poland accepted Engels' and Lenin's authority on this matter and felt that it provided a sufficient reason for dismissing any objections that have been raised against considering logic and mathematics as empirical science [110].

The belief that logic and mathematics have an empirical origin and that they are empirical science should not be confused. For we can be in general agreement with the former and reject the latter. Ernest Nagel rightly observed that a genetic account of logical and mathematical operations, highly speculative and dubious as it must be, contributes little or nothing at all to the understanding of the grounds of their present authority [111]. Nothing seems to follow from the observation of J. S. Mill, transformed by innumerable repetitions into a triviality, that experience and the requirements of social life have led to the development of logic and mathematics. It is even extremely doubtful whether what might be historically true, still applies at the present time.

According to the materialist theory of truth, logical and mathematical theorems reflect the external world in an abstract manner in virtue of which their validity is not necessarily established *a posteriori*. What an abstract reflection is and what it means has never been explained. Even in the very simple case of the sentence 'Warsaw is situated on the Vistula' it had to be conceded that this sentence reflects only metaphorically the fact of Warsaw being situated on the Vistula. When we pass to the theorems of logic and mathematics the reflection relation is said to be not only metaphoric but also abstract, and our power of understanding is strained beyond its imaginative and intellectual resources. Perhaps no important truth is lost, if, for instance, the assertion that Taylor's theorem reflects objective reality in an abstract fashion remains unexplored.

The view adopted in the materialist theory of truth that the abstract character of reflection provides logical and mathematical theorems with a certain measure of independence of experience is more significant, since it allows us, in fact, to disregard the reflection theory up to a certain point. This does not mean that logic and mathematics can be considered as independent structures, a free creation of the logician and mathematician, subject to one single law, namely, that their structures must be free from contradiction. Marxist-Leninists draw a sharp distinction between axioms and rules of transformations on the one hand and theorems on the other. Only the validation of the latter, but not of the former, is independent of experience. The empirical basis of logic, mathematics and, generally, of the deductive sciences, is preserved in their axioms and transformation rules which are invariably validated by an appeal to experience. Their choice is accomplished in accord with certain objective relationships, of which they are an image. The objective reference of axioms and transformation rules is inherited by theorems. It is, therefore, a fallacy to maintain that logic and mathematics are independent of experience, since their axioms are empirical hypotheses and the validity of their inference rules is based on empirical evidence. Not a single instance in support of this opinion has been given, nor has any attempt been made to substantiate the claim that the suggested method of empirical evidence was ever applied to validate logical axioms and rules of inference. One is reduced to a feeling of intellectual embarrassment when the assertion regarding the empirical character of logic and mathematics is considered to be conclusively established by a quotation from Lenin's *Philosophical Notebooks* to the effect that the figures of syllogism have acquired the 'permanence of preconceived ideas and an axiomatic character' on the strength of having been repeated millions and millions of times in man's practical activity [112].

Perhaps the principal source of the confusion, from which the argument in favour of logic and mathematics being an empirical science is drawn, is the ambiguity of the term 'practice'. The word 'practice' is a synonym of 'empirical evidence' in the Marxist-Leninist terminology. But 'practice' applied to logical and mathematical operations does not mean 'empirical evidence'. It is practice in some other sense, if it is practice at all, that establishes the validity of logical axioms and transformation rules by providing evidence that only materially true theorems can be deduced from a set of axioms by the application of the accepted rules of transformation which always yield true conclusions from true premises. If it were true that axioms and inference rules are validated in that manner, and this is not the case, it still would not follow that they are thus validated by recourse to empirical evidence. Moreover, if it were true that axioms and inference rules are empirical hypotheses or inductive generalisations, we should be able to indicate not only the confirming evidence, but also that which would falsify them and oblige us to reject them as unwarranted. For various reasons, which have been frequently explained in detail and need not be stated again, this course is not feasible, since no empirical procedure for testing the validity of logical and mathematical principles can be established.

One of the implications of the Marxist-Leninist view under discussion is the rejection of the conception originated by Wittgenstein and vigorously advanced by logical empiricism, according to which all meaningful statements are either analytic or empirical. Marxist-Leninists seem to be aware of the fact that an analytic statement is defined as a statement true or false in virtue of its wording [113]. Consequently, they should not confuse it either with Kant's *a priori* synthetic statement, since it continues to be true irrespective of what experience may reveal, nor with Kant's analytic statement, since it is not restricted to the class of subject-predicate sentences, discovered by 'pure thought', but is derived by arbitrarily fixed rules from arbitrarily fixed axioms and definitions. This expectation is not fulfilled. Although a-priorism should be understood to be the view which accepts synthetic *a priori* statements, and neither analytic nor empirical sentences are synthetic *a priori* statements, the distinction between analytic and synthetic truths is presented by the Marxist-Leninists as a revival of a-priorism and sometimes, oddly enough, also of conventionalism [114].

It is clear that if the existence of analytic statements is accepted and the theorems of logic, of pure mathematics, or of any axiomatic theory are conceived as systems of such statements, the materialist theory of truth in its present form cannot be maintained. For in this case not every true statement is a reflection of objective reality and some statements would have to be recognised as true in virtue of being in 'agreement with the accepted principles and inference rules', that is, their truth would depend solely upon language and not upon extra-linguistic facts, as required by the materialist theory. Because of this the supporters of the analytic character of the deductive sciences are singled out as particularly vicious opponents who endanger the materialist theory of truth and by the same token materialism as well [115].

The doctrine that logic and mathematics are of empirical origin constitutes a part of what has been known in Poland under the name of genetic empiricism [116]. Genetic empiricism can roughly be described as the belief that no part of our knowledge is psychologically independent of experience. Empiricism in the genetic sense should be differentiated from methodological empiricism, that is, from the view that no part of our knowledge can be validated *a priori*. The Marxist-Leninist standpoint concerning the nature of truths of logic and mathematics can be described as methodological empiricism of a narrow kind. Although it concedes that logical and mathematical theorems can be validated without recourse to experience, it maintains that this procedure is unobjectionable owing to the fact that accepted axioms and rules of transformation are validated *a posteriori*. The truth of axioms and the validity of inference rules, established by empirical evidence, provide the guarantee that theorems validated *a priori* are materially true propositions also. The class of analytic statements is an empty class, and all statements are factual or synthetic.

The elimination of propositions true by definition is a *tour de force* that overlooks some elementary facts of the case under examination. If by axioms are meant axioms of a formal axiomatic system, they differ from theorems in one single respect, significant only in relation to an inquiry, namely, they are logically prior to theorems. There is no reason to suppose that this fact alone should impart to axioms a different epistemological character from that possessed by theorems. What is an axiom in one formal system may be a proposition in another. Generally, an axiom is a relatively undemonstrable proposition, that is, undemonstrable in that system; there are no undemonstrable propositions in an absolute sense. The choice of axioms is subject to some restrictive rules, but these rules are concerned with the characteristics of the formal system itself. These facts are too familiar to deserve more than a passing mention.

362

The difference between a theorem and a rule of transformation is also relative and not absolute. Every theorem may be used as a rule of transformation. Provided that certain rules of inference are introduced axiomatically, all theorems can be reformulated in such a manner that they become rules of transformation. If Marxist-Leninists were right, this would mean that by a mere reformulation an analytic proposition in the restricted sense of this term, which they too recognise, becomes a proposition. validated *a posteriori*

If by axioms we do not mean axioms of a formal axiomatic system but what is popularly called so, that is, the laws of logic, such as the law of non-contradiction or the law of the excluded middle, they are not undemonstrable assumptions in the strict sense of this expression. In order not to confuse them with the latter, it is perhaps better to call them 'logical laws' or 'logical principles'. Marxist-Leninists considered these logical principles to be empirical laws, valid within certain relatively narrow limits, and invalid otherwise. Later they changed their opinion and have held them to be reliable and universally applicable empirical hypotheses. In this manner they wished to avoid not only the old-fashioned a-priorism and similar speculative vagaries, but also conventionalism, that is, to regard logical principles as arbitrarily made stipulations. Having safely sailed past Scylla, they have run into Charybdis. For if logical principles are empirical generalisations, they must also be subject to empirical refutation. This cannot, however, be justifiably maintained. There are no imaginable empirical circumstances which would invalidate the principles of logic. The empirical impossibility rests on the fact that the manner in which the principles are formulated excludes the logical possibility of any evidence inconsistent with them ever being admissible.

If in colloquial language the proposition 'nothing can both be so and so and not be so and so' is an axiom, the proposition 'every square has four sides' is an axiom too. For the ground on which they are acknowledged is the same. Marxist-Leninists seem to overlook the fact that every sentence must be formulated in some language, and every language is determined by rules which govern the acceptance of sentences. If there were no such rules, language would be no means of communication, which it can be provided that the use of expressions is not entirely arbitrary. On the other hand, the fact that language has some rules, which set restrictive limits to the ways in which its expressions are used, should not lead to the conclusion that all the rules of language can be exactly specified. This is the case in artificial languages, but not in natural ones. A special class of rules are those which can be regarded as implicit definitions of a particular expression or of a type of expressions. Ajdukiewicz called this class of rules 'axiomatic rules of meaning'[117].

The afore-mentioned instances of axioms are propositions whose acceptance is governed by axiomatic rules of language; no factual observation, experiment, or argument can provide a valid reason for their rejection; they hold, whatever might happen, as long as the rules hold. (The last qualification is necessary to avoid the impression that analytic statements are immune to revision). Analytic statements are accepted in virtue of the rules, in this case of the English language, that determine the use of the words, which they contain. They are accepted because these words are used in just that manner and we cannot apply them otherwise as long as we speak the English language. If the sentences in question are accepted in virtue of the rules of meaning, no experience can either confirm or refute them. They are true by definition and to call them hypotheses in need of validation by experience is not only idle but also misleading.

The rules of language are not absolute. They might be changed slowly and imperceptibly under the pressure of variable linguistic habits or deliberately revised to serve a definite purpose. This is the case in science, which adopts expressions of everyday language and defines them in accordance with its requirements. The use of scientific terms, such as 'atom', 'evolution', or 'axiom' is revised if factual observations or theoretical needs make it necessary. Since the rules of language change, the class of analytic statements in a given language is not fixed once and for all. We cannot speak of analytic propositions, if by a proposition is meant the meaning of a sentence and of its translations into different languages, but only of analytic statements. An analytic statement is not one 'true in all possible worlds', as Leibniz wished to define it. But analytic sentences are no invention; they are a linguistic matter of fact, which is just as impossible to ignore as any other non-linguistic matter of fact.

The elucidation of the relation between experience and variable linguistic habits, whether in everyday or scientific language, and the relation between the latter and the class of analytic sentences, presents a problem of enormous complexity. For the idea that we can neatly separate experience and language is utterly fictitious. Some language or other system of signs must be presupposed in order that we may speak of experience at all, and the mediation of language in describing matters of fact and 'objective reality' in general cannot be eliminated.

While probably all colloquial languages and all artificial languages so far constructed contain analytic sentences, there is no valid reason to regard them as a necessary part of every language. Suggestions of a limited scope for the elimination of some analytic sentences have been made in the past. Thus, for instance, it has been suggested that the development of a theory of certain sub-atomic phenomena requires a many- and not the two-valued logic. This implies that in such a theory a substitution of the law of non-contradiction or of the law of the excluded middle would not necessarily be an analytic but a factual sentence, to be tested, confirmed or disconfirmed by experience. In principle, a language could be constructed in which no sentence is accepted by virtue of an appropriate axiomatic rule. In such a language there would be no axiomatic rules of meaning and the laws of logic would become empirical hypotheses subject to confirmation by the evidence of experience [118].

The assertion of the materialist theory of truth that there are no analytic statements and that all statements are empirical, considered in relation to ordinary language, is a false statement. But it is not nonsensical. If a language were constructed in which there were no axiomatic rules of meaning, no sentence of this language would be analytic. Whether a language of this kind would offer any advantages in scientific inquiry is a question which cannot be settled *a priori*. Until it is actually constructed the existence of analytic sentences cannot be dismissed, for they are a part of the language of which all of us, including Marxist-Leninists, have to make use.

CHAPTER 21

ABSOLUTE AND RELATIVE TRUTH AND THE

RELATIVITY OF KNOWLEDGE

'Absolute truth' and 'relative truth' are ambiguous expressions. Furthermore, their meanings vary in different theories of truth. For the present purpose it is not necessary to distinguish all their meanings. Only those based on the correspondence conception of truth will be considered.

Adherence to this conception of truth does not commit its supporters either to the view that for every p, if 'p' is true, 'p' is absolutely true, or to its opposite, that for every p or for some p, if 'p' is true, 'p' is relatively true. Speaking freely and loosely, the first view asserts that if 'p' is once true it is always true, that is, that 'true' is a time-independent predicate. The second rejects this belief and contends that if 'p' is once or in some circumstances true, this does not imply that it is true at some other time or in some other circumstances, that is, that 'true' is a time-dependent predicate. William James contrasted them in *Pragmatism* as the belief in the 'immutability' and the 'mutability' of truths.

The question whether truths are or are not 'mutable' greatly preoccupied Polish thinkers. Twardowski's study *On the So-Called Relative Truths,* published in 1900, has exercised a powerful influence and his views have been widely shared ever since [119].

To establish the case that 'p' is relatively true it must be shown that p satisfies two conditions: with changing circumstances p changes solely in respect of its truth-value and p has different truth-values at different times. Twardowski's main argument against the relativity of truth was based on the observation that the first condition is never fulfilled and that all the sentences which might appear to be relatively true are in fact ambiguous or incomplete sentences. It is said, for instance, that the sentence 'Edward VII is King of England' was a true sentence in 1911 and is untrue to-day. But the sentence 'Edward VII is King of England' is an elliptic and ambiguous sentence. The complete sentence 'Edward VII is King of England in 1911' is no longer equivocal and it is true irrespective of whether it is uttered in 1911 or to-day or at any time in the future. Generally, it can be shown that all the instances of 'mutable' truths include, either implicitly or explicitly, egocentric particulars [120]. An essential feature of egocentric particulars is their reference to the speaker, to his experiences and his space-time position. Sentences which contain egocentric words are often equiform but not equipollent. They have a different meaning and, accordingly, might be true in some circumstances and untrue in others. This does not imperil the view that for every p, if 'p' is true, 'p' is absolutely true. For once the context in which p is stated is fully specified and, thus, the various meanings of the seemingly identical expressions are distinguished, we obtain two or more statements, no longer equiform, each of which, if true, is absolutely true [121].

There is little doubt that egocentric particulars play an important part in all arguments, based on the correspondence theory, for the relativity of truth. There is no evidence that these arguments could be produced if no such particulars were available in ordinary language. The supporters of 'absolute truths' get, therefore, some additional assistance from Bertrand Russell's investigations in which he found that in principle no egocentric particulars are needed in any part of the description of the world, and their use is solely a matter of convenience [122].

The formulation of the semantical concept of truth made it possible to differentiate more precisely the two understandings of truth. In the semantical definition of a true statement, 'true' is a complete predicate and is synonymous with 'absolutely true'. If 'true' means 'relatively true', this is not the case, that is, 'relatively true' is an incomplete predicate [123]. This is the most important difference between using 'true' in the relative and the absolute sense.

The relativity of truth should not be confused with the relativity of knowledge. The latter is a methodological and epistemological doctrine of modern origin, initiated by Saint-Simon and closely associated with the rise of positivism. The relative modernity of this doctrine conceals no mystery. 'The search for certainty', observed Reichenbach, 'had to burn itself out in the philosophical systems of the past before we were able to envisage a conception of knowledge which does away with all claims to eternal truth'[124]. On the other hand, epistemological absolutism, which identifies truth with perfect knowledge, final and eternal, is a doctrine of long antiquity. Parmenides and Plato conceived truth in this manner and they have been followed by many thinkers up to the present time.

According to epistemological absolutism it is possible to discover some ultimate truth or truths about the Universe. These truths make it possible to establish the *mathesis universalis,* to encompass and to order all knowledge in a systematic, connected and demonstrative manner. Its foundations are some perfectly certain assumptions, discovered by philosophers, from which all other knowledge, imperfect and doubtful as long as it stands by itself, can be derived deductively in a manner closely modelled on Euclid's *Elements.* The certainty of the assumptions is inherited by the inferred theorems, and, thus, perfect knowledge is fully achieved. In this conception which rather sets an ideal than formulates a method of investigation, knowledge is conceived as a system of incorrigible truths, for what is not an incorrigible truth is not knowledge at all, but a mere belief or opinion.

The doctrine of the relativity of knowledge rests upon a quite different conception. It starts from the assumption that knowledge of invariable truth in the traditional sense is unobtainable. The historical development of science makes it plain that the totality of scientific knowledge at any given time is never exhaustive and perfect. Human knowledge is a gradually expanding whole, never final and complete either in its totality or in any of its parts. Every proposition of an empirical science is corrigible, that is, only probable, every hypothesis is reversible, and, as a matter of fact, every one of them becomes sooner or later redundant, to be replaced by another. Since the truth of any empirical proposition can never be established with absolute certainty, to say that human knowledge can achieve invariable truth involves a contradiction in terms. These assumptions are codified in the methodological principle underlying scientific procedure which Felix Kaufmann called the 'principle of permanent control'. It stipulates that the 'system of rules of an empirical science must be so constructed that the elimination of any accepted proposition is rendered possible'[125].

It should be observed that the ideal of perfect knowledge does not necessarily imply belief in the absolute character of truth, nor is implied by the latter belief. As a matter of fact, the ideal of perfect knowledge has been more often combined with the coherence theory of truth than with the correspondence theory and the coherence theory involves the relativism of truth. This applies, for instance, to the Hegelian tradition and to the British idealists, above all to Bradley. On the other hand, the belief that every true proposition is an absolutely true proposition has been upheld by sober minds, by thinkers disinclined to indulge in speculative flights, represented by G. E. Moore in England or Twardowski in Poland. They combined this belief with that in the relativity of knowledge. Contrary to what is sometimes said, the two beliefs can both be true without contradicting each other. It is one thing to know that every true proposition is absolutely true and a different one to know whether a given proposition is true or not. Only if the former logically implied the latter, the existence of corrigible statements and the fact of 'true' being a complete predicate could not be consistently maintained. If we cannot decide with certainty whether a given proposition is true or false, and empirical propositions are of this sort, this is no reason for us to reject the belief in the absolute character of truth. For true beliefs depend upon the mind for their existence, but their truth is not mind-dependent.

There is a closer connection between the relativity of knowledge and the relativity of truth, though the connection is not of a logical nature and concerns other forms of the relativity of truth than that previously considered. For while some philosophers argued that the time-independent character of truth entails the view that nothing changes, others recognising that change does occur concluded that truth, at least in most cases, is not a time-independent property of true statements. This was one of the reasons why William James urged the view that truths are 'mutable' and that the opposite view is a result of the rationalistic prejudice which conceived 'reality complete and ready-made from all eternity'[126]. More recently, epistemological relativism was used in support of the view that the concept of absolute truth is dispensable or even not a genuine scientific concept. In the 'thirties a group of neo-positivists with Otto Neurath at their head suggested that the terms 'true' and 'false' should be avoided, since they cannot be predicated of any scientific statement. If we can never finally decide whether a statement of science is true in the absolute time-independent meaning of this term, the term 'true' becomes otiose and may be dispensed with. This was, as Schlick described it, a rather dogmatic formulation of positivistic principles and, though initially dominant, was later abandoned [126a].

Engels was greatly impressed by the doctrine of the relativity of knowledge and strongly supported it in *Anti-Dühring*. The anti-metaphysical orientation of epistemological relativism which became pronounced in Mach's philosophy of science, was not yet apparent in Engels' time. Simultaneously, Engels adhered to the concept of absolute truth. Engels felt, however, that while most or even all absolutely true propositions are either trivial or unimportant from the viewpoint of the progress of knowledge, most of the important ones, in the sense just indicated, are not absolutely true. Engels' emphatic epistemological relativism inspired some of his followers with the idea similar to that of the neopositivists of the 'thirties, that is, with the idea of rejecting the concept of absolute truth altogether.

Lenin combated this suggestion with his customary vigour and insisted, with much common sense, that this would be a serious error. Only insane people, Lenin argued, can doubt that some statements are absolutely true [127]. He made it quite clear, however, that what he wished to defend was the existence of absolutely true statements of a very particular kind. If the relativity of knowledge does not logically imply the denial of objective truth, it does not imply, either, that we cannot obtain true knowledge about the world. Lenin leaned more heavily upon Hegel than Engels did and upheld what Engels criticised as an inconsistency and weakness in the Hegelian philosophy. Engels considered that it was a contradiction on Hegel's part to 'dissolve all dogmatism' by the repudiation of the finality to be ascribed to any actually reached stage of knowledge and to declare Hegel's own system to be final and the absolute truth. For Lenin this was not necessarily an inconsistency, for human thought is capable of grasping 'absolute truth..... compounded of a sum-total of relative truths'. Each step in the development of science, Lenin argued, adds something to the sum of which absolute truth is made up and brings us closer to the Truth, that is, to the truth of materialism [128].

The relativity of knowledge, which is fully acknowledged in Marxism-Leninism, is inspired rather by the Hegelian dialectic, including the historically determined limits of knowledge, than by the logical and methodological examination of the principles of scientific procedure. In an empirical science we have to distinguish between the concept of 'true statement' and of 'confirmed statement'. If 'p' is true, it is absolutely true, and, consequently, it is inadvisable and confusing to use 'true' synonymously with 'confirmed'. For the concept of confirmed statement is time-dependent. To say, 'p is confirmed to such and such a degree by observation' is to make an incomplete statement, which requires a further specification 'at such and such a time'. Moreover, the concept of confirmation presupposes the definition of the concept of truth; the rules of the confirmation procedure make use of this definition. Neither 'true' nor 'confirmed' are dispensable and it is not possible to define the one in terms of the other. The relativity of knowledge rests on the fact that empirical knowledge consists of confirmed statements. On the other hand, we would not be able to establish any confirmed statement if we did not know in what the truth of a statement consists [129].

The relativity of knowledge in Marxism-Leninism is not supported by logical and methodological considerations of this sort. Its adherents argue sometimes very much like William James that if everything constantly changes thought must change too. On other occasions they inveigh, in the spirit of the idealist tradition from Hegel to Bradley, against the inherent artificiality of abstract thought. Bergson's exposure of the rationalistic illusions in the last chapter of *Évolution Créatrice,* which consists in supposing that we can think 'the unstable by means of the stable, the moving by means of the immobile'[130], is in essential agreement with the basic ideas of the Marxist-Leninist theory of knowledge. The negative part of Bergson's criticism could be accepted by every Marxist-Leninist with a clear conscience. He is convinced that only a 'moving thought' can be an adequate reflection of motion – this idea underlies the setting of 'dialectical thinking' against the 'metaphysical mode of thought' – and that if everything changes and moves, thoughts and truths must be 'mutable' too and relative in a certain sense. Thinking cannot be in accord with reality if it is not a process of the developing thought catching up with the developing reality [131].

To sum up the preceding discussion, it can be concluded that the materialist theory of truth rejects the relativity of truth, either in its radical or moderate form, that is, the view that either every or some true statements are relatively true. It recognises that the criticism of this doctrine, produced by non-Marxist thinkers, is valid although for some reasons it is not satisfactory [132]. It implicitly endorses the opinion that 'true' is a complete predicate, although it prefers a metaphoric description of this fact over the semantical definition of the concept of truth. The relativity of knowledge is an integral part of the Marxist-Leninist doctrine. But the acceptance of the relativity of knowledge in the materialist theory of truth has little, if anything, to do with the modern development in the methodology of empirical science [133]. It reveals some deep-rooted connections with the Hegelian tradition and strange similarities with anti-empirical and irrational philosophical trends, which it combats for other reasons. Over and above the idea that truth is something predicable of beliefs and sentences, there emerges the ancient conviction of the existence of one single Truth, no more a property of particular and fragmentary judgments but something inherent in and revealed by a whole coherent system of beliefs, however imperfect this system might be at a given moment. The metaphysical background and inspiration of the Marxist-Leninist view on Truth, absolute truths, and the relativity of knowledge comes out most clearly in the doctrine of partiality and concreteness of truths, which must now be considered.

CHAPTER 22

THE DOCTRINE OF PARTIALITY OF TRUTHS

According to the materialist theory of truth, a statement is absolutely true if it is a wholly true statement and reflects in some respect fully and faithfully either the totality of reality or any of its fragments. Such truths are 'immutable', 'eternal', and incorrigible [134]. The relativity of truth is an absurd doctrine for it leads to contradictions; if it were valid, the same statement could be both true and false, and this is absurd [135]. There are singular and general or universal wholly true statements, but the singular are probably more numerous and certainly easier to discover. Singular wholly true statements are often poor in content; for this reason Engels called them *Plattheiten*. Such statements as 'Napoleon died on May 5, 1821' or 'Paris was the capital of France in the nineteenth century' are absolutely or wholly true. They reflect a tiny bit of the objective reality, considered from a limited point of view [136].

Not every true statement is wholly true, there are also partially true statements, and the relation of the latter to the former constitutes the central problem in the understanding of an asymptotic progress towards absolute knowledge. Partially true statements are relative truths in some sense of this expression, for being neither wholly true nor wholly false they are corrigible and time-dependent. In the course of human practice they are constantly replaced by other and better partial truths. Since they are accepted at a given moment in virtue of the fragment of truth which they contain, they never become utter falsehood, though they might become otiose and pass into limbo [137].

It cannot be denied that the term 'true' is sometimes used in the manner suggested by Marxist-Leninists, that is, in the sense of 'being partially true'. This use is familiar from everyday language. Some philosophers also felt that it was not illegitimate to use the term 'true' in that sense. They argued that a partially false sentence is not true, but its not being true is not incompatible with its being partially true. Similarly, a partially true statement is not false, but its being partially false is not inconsistent with this fact. In recent times Bradley has been the most eminent protagonist of this view, which he supplemented with the belief that propositions possess different degrees of truth. This idea was, however, closely related in his case with what has been described as a rather extreme form of the coherence theory of truth [138]. On the other hand, partially true statements of the materialist theory are true clearly in the sense of the correspondence theory of truth. It is not easy to see, how a proposition can be true in this sense and yet be partially true or differ in its degree of truth from some other true proposition. For according to the correspondence theory what makes a statement true is the fact which it asserts, and no fact can together make and unmake a statement true or perform this function to a varying degree.

The Marxist-Leninist theory of partial truths and degrees of truth is in one respect superior to that of the British idealist. For while maintaining that a partially true statement is true in virtue of being a partial reflection of objective reality, the materialist theory of truth recognises the existence of wholly true and wholly false statements and thus escapes some obvious objections against the views of Bradley and Joachim. For Bradley maintained that all beliefs without exception are both partially true and also partially false, and no belief is wholly true or wholly false. Joachim included the coherence principle of truth, itself being a human product, among partial truths. G. E. Moore had no difficulty in refuting the view that all statements are partially true and partially false [139].

The materialist theory of truth does not explicitly maintain that a partially true statement is both partially true and partially false, though it is difficult to see how it could deny it. But the psychological reason for ignoring this fact is perhaps understandable. If a statement is not only partially true but also partially false, one cannot escape the impression that it must be wholly false (it will be shown that this impression is right). Its confusing impact would obstruct the road which otherwise the concept of degrees of truth might seem to have thrown open. For if some scale or scales of comparison between various partially true statements could be established, a method of assessing the degree of truth and of getting closer and closer to the Truth would have been found. Something similar was suggested by John of St. Thomas, a medieval scholar, a commentator of Thomas Aquinas, and author of *Ars Logica*. John of St. Thomas held a doctrine not unlike Schaff's. He also maintained that there are degrees of truth and tried to devise rules by means of which propositions containing truth and falsehood in different proportions could somehow be compared. Thus, for instance, he suggested that the proposition 'every European is a Moslem' is false to a higher degree according to quantity than 'every African is a Moslem', and 'trees are stones' is false to a lesser degree according to quality than 'the human spirit is a stone' [140]. As will be seen later, Schaff did think of some scale which would allow the grading of partial truths according to their approximation to absolute truth as their limit.

The semantical definition of truth makes it clear that the idea of finding a method of assessing the degrees of truth is unsound and that the concept of degrees of truth is incompatible with the correspondence theory of truth. According to the semantical definition of truth, 'true' is a one-place predicate, and, therefore, it cannot be said meaningfully that a proposition is true in some respect and untrue in some other. As long as the semantical definition of truth is adhered to, a statement is either true or false. This fact is obscured in the materialist theory of truth by the concept of reflection, for 'reflection' is a relational predicate as much as 'probable' or 'confirmed'. It is very likely that the doctrine of degrees of truth owes its existence to the obscurity and ambiguity of this concept.

It is, indeed, not easy to find out what Marxist-Leninists mean when they speak of a statement being partially true. The examples given by Engels, for instance Boyle's law, in which, as Engels puts it, a grain of truth is combined with a particle of error (for Boyle's law does not hold good in certain cases), seem to suggest that what Marxist-Leninists have in mind is the concept of the degree of confirmation. But a statement confirmed to such and such a degree cannot be said to be either partially true or partially false. Like any other statement it is either true or false, though we are unable to decide finally and with certainty which is the case.

Engels' argument was intended to make the position clear that the concept of confirmed statement is legitimate, though different from that of true statement. He emphasised the important place which statements approximately correct or correct within definite limits occupy in science, and exposed what he called 'empty phrasemongering' of some philosophers who from the fact that a statement cannot be shown to be true drew the inference 'therefore it is not a truth at all, therefore it is an error'[141]. The fallacy involved in this inference is obvious. No new concept is necessary to provide a safeguard against this kind of fallacy.

If 'partially true' is synonymous with 'confirmed', we can, in principle, dispense with the former expression and this seems to be advisable in view of its being misleading. The concepts 'true' and 'confirmed' must be clearly distinguished and the fact that they have no equiform part in common helps to keep this distinction clear. This is not the case with the concepts 'true' and 'partially true'. This increases the risk of confusion instead of eliminating it.

If 'partially true' does not mean 'confirmed' and is to apply to beliefs and sentences which are true in the sense of the correspondence theory of truth, though they cannot be said to be absolutely true, for like confirmed statements they are corrigible, the question arises whether the concept of partial truth, plausible as long as it remains unanalysed, does not involve contradiction. The fact that there are corrigible and incorrigible statements does not justify the distinction between partially and wholly true statements. For a confirmed statement is corrigible without being wholly or partially true in the sense of the correspondence theory of truth. Schaff makes it quite clear that a partially true statement is corrigible, but being partially true cannot simply consist in being corrigible. If the distinction between corrigibility and incorrigibility only were involved, the distinction between partially and wholly true statements would be redundant. The former must have some other property, apart from being corrigible, if they are to constitute a separate class, distinct from that of absolutely true statements on the one hand, and of confirmed statements on the other.

This property can only consist in the fact that there is a partial agreement with reality which does not belong either to absolutely true or to confirmed statements. But a partially true statement in this sense is at the same time partially false; otherwise it would be simply true. If this is the case, a partially true statement would be wholly false. For the statement " 'p' is partially true and 'p' is partially false" is true implies that " 'p' is partially false" is true too. But a sentence is true when there is a corresponding state of affairs, and is false when there is no corresponding state of affairs designated by this sentence. Consequently, since there is no state of affairs corresponding to 'p', the conjunction " 'p' is partially true and 'p' is partially false" must be false, or wholly false, in the Marxist-Leninist terminology. If the partial truth of a statement means its being in partial agreement with reality, as understood in the correspondence theory of truth, all partial truths are falsehoods [142]. This must have escaped the attention of those who wish to distinguish wholly and partially true statements, unless their understanding of the meaning to be attached to the expression 'partially true' differs from that assumed.

The concept of partially true statements which seems to be either redundant or self-contradictory or obscure, is not an isolated fragment of the materialist theory of truth. To use Richard Mises' expression, it is a connectable concept, whose ramifications reach far and wide to comprise much of what the materialist theory of truth has to say on the subject of truth in empirical science, on perfect knowledge, and on the validity of the whole Marxist-Leninist philosophy. It commands one of the central positions in the system of the Marxist-Leninist epistemology and theory of knowledge.

For instance, Schaff used it to dismiss summarily Twardowski's view that 'true' cannot be predicated of inductive generalisations, empirical laws, hypotheses and theories. According to Twardowski, whose opinions on this matter were shared by many scientists and philosophers, including Engels, and continue to be upheld up to the present day, the terms 'true' and 'false' do not apply to laws of empirical science. They are more or less probable, they describe in a manner more or less approximate the regularity of phenomena. In the case of universal empirical statements the crucial question is whether they hold or not, and if so, within what limits.

Schaff considered this view as unsatisfactory and, in the final analysis, absurd. For if the universal empirical statements are not true they must be false, and if they are false, practically our whole knowledge consists of falsehoods. But what we should call errors and false opinions, if Twardowski's view is accepted, has enabled engineers to take advantage of the forces of Nature to construct all kinds of machinery and to change the conditions of life on the Earth. This success of natural and technical science refutes the claim of the fallibility of empirical knowledge and of its being nothing but a collection of falsehoods. Since the consequences are absurd, the premiss, *i.e.* regarding natural laws as neither true nor false, must be rejected [143].

The fallacy of this reasoning, against which Engels warned, is transparent. If we cannot decide with certainty whether a statement is true and refrain from the assertion that it is true, that does not mean that it is not true and, therefore, that it must be false. The premiss does not imply, either, that if it is not possible to determine with finality the truth-value of empirical propositions, the whole history of science would consist exclusively of falsehood. Popper's methodological rule that it should be possible for an empirical scientific system to be refuted by experience does not mean that nothing but falsehood can be discovered in science. For to say that a system is confirmed with respect to a definite class of its verifiers is itself a time-independent statement and it does not become false in virtue of a falsifier of this system having been discovered. The pragmatical and semantical concepts of confirmed statements should not be confused. The allegedly absurd consequences of the view that 'true' and 'false' cannot be predicated of empirical propositions do not follow, if the distinction of these two concepts is made and applied [144].

The standpoint which Schaff himself adopted is that of Lenin. Schaff felt that many difficulties might be cleared up, if the concept of partial truth is accepted, universal empirical statements are recognised to be partially true and approximately faithful reflections of the regularities observed in the external world, gradually approaching objective truth. For truth admits of degrees and the concept of partial truth involves the concept of degrees of truth. Partial truths can be differentiated and ordered in accordance with a uniform scale, one partial truth being more or less true than some other partial truth (this does not imply that the degree of truth is a metrical concept no more so than that of the degree of confirmation, and Schaff does not make this claim). The corrigibility of empirical statements, the elimination and replacement of one by another, marks the progress from less to more true partial truths [145].

It has been already emphasised that if the concept of the degree of truth does not differ from that of the degree of confirmation, the advantage of using it is dubious. Marxist-Leninist thinkers see it otherwise. They say that the concept of the degree of truth serves an important purpose, namely, of bridging the gap between a wholly and a partially, between an absolutely and a relatively true statement (in the Marxist-Leninist sense) and reveals dialectic connections binding the opposites together [146]. If by this is meant that the degrees of truth (of confirmation) can be ordered on a continuous scale extending between the two truth-values of classic logic – truth and falsehood – this is an illusion. For when this suggestion was seriously taken up by Reichenbach and Zawirski with a view toward establishing probability logic as a generalised multi-valued logical system, it became clear that the differences between truth- and probability values did not disappear. An example may make clearer what this means. Let us assume that according to probability logic the degree of confirmation of a hypothesis H with respect to its evidence E can be calculated and is equal to a rational number m/n in the interval 0 and 1. This does not mean that the truth-value of H is equal to m/n. The hypothesis H still remains either true or false. Probability logic does not allow us to dispense with the dichotomy of truth and falsehood, but to measure the degree of confirmation and possibly to substitute definite probability values for its different degrees. Probability logic is not a generalised logic; it operates, as it were, within two-valued logic to provide a technique of dealing with statements which can only, if at all, be either confirmed or falsified and which remain either true or false irrespective of whether this is or is not known by anyone [147].

The function of the concept of partial truth is not only to provide the bridge between error and truth but also between ignorance and perfect knowledge. Marxist-Leninists argue very much like William James, with whom otherwise they radically disagree, that 'truth is largely made out of previous truths'[148]. This applies not only to the partial truths of to-day but also to the absolute truth as an ideal goal of the whole historical development of mankind. Perfect knowledge, which no further experience can ever alter or improve, is not something ready-made and waiting to be discovered all together and at once. It is rather like the limit of a converging series to which its partial sums approximate more and more. Perfect knowledge is something in the course of becoming; it is a process in virtue of which perfect knowledge itself is coming into being [149].

The metaphor of an infinite series, applied to the way in which knowledge is gained and extended, does more harm than good when it is taken literally. For we do not know the law in accordance with which the present partial truths are made out of previous partial truths and in the absence of this knowledge no series is determined. Similarly, the concept of limit and convergence has no meaning as applied to statements. The idea that each truth, as well as knowledge as a system of wholly true statements, is produced by the summation of partial truths, transformed from a metaphoric image into a descriptive phrase with factual implications and regarded as a faithful reflection of the actual process of acquiring knowledge, is bound, as will be seen, to make havoc of what reliable knowledge is.

CHAPTER 23

THE DOCTRINE OF CONCRETENESS OF TRUTHS

The assertion that absolute truths are the sum of relative or partial truths and that knowledge, the ideal goal of the search for Truth, is like the limit of a series to which its partial sums converge, should be considered against the background provided by the first law of dialectics. This law lays down that all things and phenomena of Nature are connected with, dependent on, and determined by each other. Consequently, to acquire knowledge about anything in the world we must examine it in its universal connections with everything else. For if any particular thing or phenomenon has relations to things or phenomena outside itself, and these relations 'make up' its nature, all things and phenomena become 'meaningless' outside the system to which they are related. The doctrine that maintains that relations constitute or affect the things they relate is known as the theory of internal relations. This theory had in Hegel its modern protagonist. From Hegel it passed to Marxist-Leninist philosophy.

If the theory of internal relations is accepted, it seems to follow that the only way of securing adequate knowledge of anything in particular is to specify all its relations with all other objects, that is, to consider the whole of reality from a particular space-time point of view. This conclusion is expressed by Marxist-Leninists in the assertion that there are no abstract truths, every truth is concrete. 'Concrete' here means 'relative to the circumstances, time and space in which the statement is made'. For in view of the fact that every event is related to every other event, there is no chance of ever making an absolutely true statement unless it is concrete in the indicated sense [150].

On the other hand, it should be observed that a concrete truth is an ideal point of destination, at which we cannot arrive, unless reality as a whole is included in it, which can never be the case. "Man", wrote Lenin, "is unable to embrace = to reflect = to mirror the whole of Nature in its fullness, in its 'immediate totality', he can only draw ever nearer to it". The means at man's disposal are concepts, judgments, generalisations, laws of nature, theories, and similar devices. But these devices sever the terms of relations from each other and the qualities from the subject, dismember the 'organic totality' into separate pieces. The reconstruction of reality in thought and in particular judgments by means of these distinct and separate mental constructs cannot be a faithful reflection of the original totality, but only an imperfect approximation to it. Cognition always contains a distorting factor. It immobilises what is changing, cuts up and dissects into fragments what is a complete and concrete fact within the totality of things and phenomena where everything is together with everything else [151]. The concept of concrete truth presupposes the contradistinction of 'abstract' and 'concrete' in some peculiar meaning of these terms.

Attention has been drawn to the fact that the use of the expressions 'abstract' and 'concrete' in Marxist-Leninist philosophy is closely related to Hegel's understanding of these terms and differs in some ways from that commonly accepted [152]. We speak of abstract concepts and thoughts and contrast them with the concrete, that is, with particular things in the external world. What is concrete for us was abstract for Hegel, and what was concrete for Hegel is abstract for us. Hegel's distinction concerned, of course, only thoughts, and not mental and physical objects respectively, but this difference from our use is not important in this context.

The essential point is the fact that Hegel qualified as abstract thoughts those which are closest to the world of physical objects and apply to particular things, such as the moon, trees, stones, and the like. According to Hegel, these thoughts were the product of crude common sense which maintains that 'thoughts are only thoughts', that is, they are mere forms unless sense perception endows them with substance and reality. They are abstract for they are one-sided and poor in their content, they do not grasp the essence, and are concerned with appearances. On the other hand, thoughts which we would call abstract, the highest categories comprising in themselves, according to Hegel, 'the full wealth of Particulars', were for Hegel concrete. A concrete concept is not self-contained, but it points and refers to something beyond itself. The unfolding of the content of concrete thoughts reveals in them what Hegel called 'concrete Universals'. When a concrete universal is predicated of an individual, the individual is at once shown to be embedded by its attributes and relational properties in the all-comprising whole, apart from which it is only an appearance [153].

Concrete thinking does not rest on the separation of the content and form of knowledge, assumed in 'ordinary consciousness'. For 'ordinary consciousness' makes its universals abstract, that is, void of content. A 'concrete universal' is full of content which is unfolded and differentiated by elucidations and deductions. This can be exemplified by the concept of concrete identity (similarly – concrete quantity, infinity, necessity, and so forth), which unlike the abstract identity of traditional logic and mathematics combines identity with difference within itself and, generally, by any 'fluid' or 'dialectical category' as opposed to a 'fixed' or 'rigid category'[154]. The co-existence of the polar opposites in 'dialectical categories' and the movement of thought revealing 'one pole already present in the other *in nuce*' by means of which mind 'gives itself its determinateness', lead to the apprehension of the unity of all things and of the internal connections which the abstract universality of common sense and science cannot grasp and express.

Hegel's thoughts were always thoughts of a thought; in the case of Marx and Engels they became thoughts of an object or of an aggregate of objects. In *Introduction to the Critique of Political Economy*, published posthumously by Karl Kautsky, Marx explained in what way his use of the terms 'abstract' and 'concrete' differs from Hegel's. Marx pointed out that Hegel mistook the 'movement of categories' for the real act of creation. 'Hegel', wrote Marx, 'fell into the error .... of considering the real as the result of self-coordinating, self-absorbed, and spontaneously operating thought, while the method of advancing from the abstract to the concrete is but a way of thinking by which the concrete is grasped and is reproduced in our mind as a concrete'. In a manner of speaking, it can be said that real objects, as comprehended objects, are a product of thought. But real objects, to which thought refers, have an independent existence 'outside of the head' before and after they have been grasped as 'concrete aggregates'. For Marx, 'concrete' and 'abstract' are predicates which apply to physical and mental objects respectively, and not, as for Hegel, to different varieties of thought.

But Marx retained Hegel's differentiation with respect to the mode of thinking and to the kind of concepts of which they make use. Thus, the concepts of population, capital, labour, money, are abstractions, and 'empty words' as long as they refer to a selected aspect of reality. The concept of population is an 'imaginary concrete' if it leaves out the social classes in the examination of the population. In their turn classes presuppose the consideration of wage-labour and capital, and the latter presuppose exchange, division of labour, value, and money. 'The concrete is concrete, because it is a combination of many objects with different destinations, *i.e.* a unity of diverse elements'. Unlike the abstract universality of natural science, criticised by Engels in *Dialectic of Nature*, which ignores the interconnections of phenomena, concrete thinking in Hegel's sense, advocated by Marx, leads to the knowledge that 'reproduces the concrete subject of judgment in the course of analysis and reasoning, and grasps objects as a rich aggregate of many conceptions and relations' within the totality of mutually related parts [155].

It is this concept of concreteness and the doctrine of thus conceived concrete truths which ultimately pave the way for raising the fundamental assumptions of Marxist-Leninist philosophy, in principle regarded as a 'sum of relative truths', from the status of relative to that of absolute truth. This cannot be achieved without an equivocation. For the concrete character of singular statements obviously differs from the alleged concrete character of universal statements in the Hegelian and Marxian meaning of the concreteness as qualifyingly applied to a mode of thinking. In the former case, 'concrete' means 'relative to time, space, and circumstances', and applies to statements about singular facts; in the latter, 'concrete' means 'revealing the interconnections of things and phenomena', and applies to general or universal facts. There is no easy passage from statements of the first kind to those of the second.

'Concrete truths' in the second meaning of this expression purport to be universal empirical statements. They must be empirical, for otherwise they would have to be analytic, and be regarded at best as true by convention, that is, as valid within a definite system of concepts. 'Concrete truths' of Marxist-Leninist philosophy are clearly non-analytic statements. But if they are non-analytic, they cannot raise an unconditional claim to truth.

If a statement is true at all, it is timelessly true. Non-analytic statements cannot, therefore, ever be true. They require verification by reference to what is found in particular cases and these cases of experience are infinite in number. No empirical statement is verified beyond the particular occasion of experience, it cannot be proved either conclusively true or conclusively false. For instance, if we assert: '(x) φ (x) $\supset$ ψ (x)' is true, we should be able to show that whatever value of 'x' is chosen, it is not the case that 'φ (x_n)' be true and 'ψ (x_n)' be false. This we are unable to accomplish, although we may frequently be 'practically sure' that it is so. In other words, we can possibly obtain psychological but not logical certainty. If we can establish that our belief is probable in a high degree, we are justified in holding this belief. A belief may be justified and rational without being conclusively certain and true.

There are insuperable difficulties in establishing the conditions under which universal empirical statements can be accepted as conclusively verified or true. For a Marxist-Leninist, armed with what Schaff calls 'dynamic analysis', there seem to be no difficulties. The assumption which underlies the smooth passage from the indubitable fact that some statements are absolutely true to the doubtful conclusion that some universal statements, such as the so-called laws of dialectics, are absolutely true, should be sought in the concept of concreteness in the Hegelian and Marxian sense. For this concept seems to justify the belief that nothing can be really and significantly true unless it is about the reality as a whole; the laws of dialectics are eminently universal statements of this sort. Should their truth be uncertain and subject to doubt, nothing whatever could be true and we would be at the mercy of complete relativism [156]. The *reductio ad absurdum* rests on the fallacy that whenever certainty is unobtainable the distinction between rational and irrational, credible and unjustifiable beliefs must fall to the ground.

It is in fact the Hegelian inheritance rather than that of Marx and Engels of which a Marxist-Leninist makes use in his claim of being in possession of irrefutable truths. Engels displayed a much greater caution and philosophical acumen than any of his Marxist-Leninist adherents with respect to the question whether there are any incorrigible truths, and, if there are, what sort of truths they are. Engels divided the whole realm of knowledge into three departments – exact sciences: mathematics, astronomy, mechanics, physics, and chemistry; biological sciences; historical sciences, including logic and dialectics. So far as the first department of knowledge, and particularly mathematics, is concerned, Engels thought that certain results obtained in it are final and ultimate truths. The more knowledge increases and expands, whether in mathematics, in astronomy and mechanics, physics and chemistry, the more rare, however, they become. In empirical science we have to rely on what is approximately correct and to which the polar concepts of error and truth do not apply.

No immutable truths, apart from platitudes, such as all men are mortal, all female mammals have mammary glands and the like, can be found in the second department of knowledge. In the realm of biology new discoveries constantly cause a complete revision of accepted views and theories. It would be unjustifiable to claim that any of them is final and incorrigible.

Eternal truths, Engels continued, are in an even worse plight in the historical group of sciences, though it is precisely in this sphere that claims are frequently made of the discovery of eternal and ultimate truths. The statement 'Napoleon died on May 5, 1821' is absolutely true, but statements of this kind were according to Engels commonplaces of the sorriest kind. We do not fare any better in dialectics and formal logic. In particular, ultimate truths are much more rarely encountered in logic than is commonly realised.

The scarcity of incorrigible truths, Engels commented, testifies to the constant advancement of knowledge and reflects the changeability of its object. To voice disappointment at the scarcity of ultimate truths is to confess one's ignorance of what science is and to assert that the scientist knows the absolute truth, is to claim an infallibility which no single individual can ever achieve. Engels advocated in these observations a thoroughly modern approach to scientific knowledge, which does not regard complete certainty as its distinguishing mark.

This certainty is desirable but unobtainable. Contemporary empiricism adopts this standpoint, maintains that probable and corrigible knowledge is the only one we can gain, and believes that the recognition of this fact confers upon science the reliability which we associate with it. For in this manner scientific knowledge includes in its assumptions the principle of self-corrigibility and of self-improvement, and safeguards its efficacy more securely than the elevated ideal of complete certainty compatible both with empiricism and speculative rationalism [157].

Lenin, and still more his successors, encountered insuperable difficulties in squaring their own views on what can be known with certainty and finality with those of Engels [158]. Lenin claimed that if the existence of absolute truths cannot be doubted, knowledge of incontrovertibly true empirical propositions ('objective truths') is obtainable. It is self-evident that this does not follow from the premiss, but it has been accepted as a valid conclusion in Marxist-Leninist philosophy. The Hegelian doctrine of the concreteness of truth is clearly the source and provides the justification of Lenin's claim.

According to Lenin, the truth of the dialectical laws and the dependence of any statement in respect of its significance and truth on the laws of dialectics, can be seen in analysing the simplest, most ordinary and common sentences. A subject-predicate sentence 'A is B' not only indicates that A is B, but also that A is not A, that is, in Hegel's words, that every finite thing strives for something other than itself, that it is incomplete, connected with other kinds of particular things, comprises the unity of the opposites – of the general and the singular. The nucleus of all the elements of dialectics are thus disclosed in any proposition, and on this fact the claim of dialectics being a property of all knowledge can be firmly and securely established [159]. The analysis of a simple subject-predicate sentence shows how the properties of every object, taken not in isolation but as it exists actually, as an aspect or moment in the development of the whole, dissolve into an extended network of relations in which it stands to everything else. Therefore, no particular thing can be comprehended unless it is examined in its universal connections and reproduced in thought by means of notions which reflect the structure and the movement of reality as a whole. The determination of particular things presupposes the knowledge of universal and 'concrete' principles, which are expressed in the dialectical method and the laws of dialectics.

Schaff referred to Lenin as his authority and tried to accomplish the impossible feat of combining Lenin's Hegelian ideas with the positivistic and empiricist approach of Engels. He distinguishes four classes of statements, which, if true, are absolutely true. The first class consists of singular historical statements. The second is made up of sentences referring to some linguistic facts. The sentence "the term *der Stuhl'* in the German language spoken in the first half of the twentieth century means 'the chair' in the English language spoken in the same period" is as absolutely true as the sentence 'Napoleon died on May 5, 1821'. The third class includes 'mathematical formulae' such as $2 \times 2 = 4$, the commutative law of addition, or arithmetical equalities. All the statements of these three classes have one common property, namely, they refer to some narrowly circumscribed state of affairs and the fact of their being absolutely true depends on this circumstance.

The fourth class of absolutely true statements is of a different sort. It consists of some general and universal statements, established by inductive generalisation or in another way, which the sentences 'all men are mortal' or 'motion is an inseparable property of matter' may exemplify. Generally, all empirical statements confirmed to the highest degree should be considered to be absolutely true. To build up an unbridgeable gulf between such statements and other absolutely true statements is sheer metaphysics [160].

It should be noted that whether we do or do not call it metaphysics, whatever this may mean in this context, the distinction of the terms 'true' and 'confirmed' saves us from contradiction. For while it is redundant, and possibly self-contradictory, to say "the statement 'p' is true to-day" (in the sense of the term 'true' accepted by the Marxist-Leninist), the statement " 'p' is confirmed to such and such a degree" is incomplete unless the time variable is implicitly assumed. There is no such thing as a conclusive verification of a universal proposition of physics or biology. If by verification is understood a definitive establishment of truth, no law of natural science can ever be verified, that is, accepted as true (although many empirical propositions are certain in the psychological sense). Instead, by testing its instances, we can obtain its confirmation. For these reasons we cannot say, "the confirmed statement 'p' is true". There would be no self-contradiction only if the semantical concept of confirmation were involved. But Schaff has clearly the pragmatical and not the semantical concept of confirmation in mind.

At the price of this contradiction Marxist-Leninist philosophy can claim that on the one hand its assumptions, for instance the laws of dialectics, are empirical generalisations or universal empirical statements, and that they are absolutely true on the other. This nobody else can achieve. Others have to be reconciled with corrigible beliefs, and only Marxist-Leninists are in possession of the immutable truth. In Poland this basic difference between Marxist-Leninist and other philosophical beliefs was used mostly in criticism of the latter; in the Soviet Union – in praise of the former. 'All the fundamental theses and an enormous number of lesser tenets of Marxist-Leninist philosophy, economic science, and the theory of socialism and the class struggle are absolutely true', wrote a Soviet philosopher [161]. There is an error in this statement. Not only an enormous number, but all lesser tenets of Marxist-Leninist philosophy are absolutely true. For from true premises only true conclusions can be derived. Thus, Marxist-Leninist philosophy, either as a whole or in any of its parts, consists solely of incontrovertible truths.

It is clear that the materialist theory of truth, and, in particular, the conception of the concreteness of truth (in the Hegelian sense), involves a definite doctrine of universals. The latter dovetails with the former and supports some of the claims on behalf of the theory of truth. Before the Marxist-Leninist doctrine of universals is examined, it may be advisable to make some general closing remarks on the method, by means of which the materialist theory establishes the absolute certainty of its own premises.

We say that q is presupposed by p, when p could not be true unless q were true. The truth of the latter is compatible both with the truth and falsity of its presupposition (its premiss), for a true proposition may be entailed by a false proposition. Marxist-Leninists seem to use the term 'presupposition' in a stronger sense, in which q is said to be presupposed by p when q could not be true unless p were true, that is, when p is not only a necessary but also a sufficient condition for q. It is in this sense that according to Marxist-Leninists the truth of any statement is presupposed by the truth of the dialectic laws or that the truth of a statement concerning a concrete thing or a particular part of reality is presupposed by the truth of some universal statements concerning the whole of reality. This belief and the procedure associated with it continue the philosophical trend called by Bertrand Russell the 'classical tradition' [162].

According to this tradition a general principle obtained by *a priori* reasoning can be more certain than any of its particular instances ascertainable by direct observation or inspection. Russell argued that the method of the classical tradition based on the inference from some general, 'higher' or 'better' principles to detailed or particular conclusions is bound to produce bewilderment rather than conviction because of the high likelihood of error liable to occur in abstract and involved arguments of this kind. It is a fact that by this method different thinkers reached mutually exclusive conclusions about the whole of reality and ascribed to them a greater certainty than they were inclined to concede to any piecemeal and detailed result of observation and analysis. Thus some said that reality is one and indivisible, timeless and changeless, others that it is the sum total of particular things engulfed in a continuous flux of change. In Russell's opinion it has been the empirical outlook that refuses to legislate what the Universe is that has thrust aside the classical tradition and the constructions of traditional metaphysics.

To this should be added the liberating effect upon philosophy exercised by the developments in logic. It has been logical analysis that cleared up a certain persistent misunderstanding concerning the relation between observational data or facts and theory that is to explain them. This misunderstanding arose in empirical science but its harmful effects could be particularly felt in philosophy, since it endowed speculative thought with a considerable power of resistance. It consists in the assumption that if it is possible to derive observational facts from theory by deductive inference, theory can be inferred inductively from observational facts. This is a fallacy, for the same set of observational facts can be, as a rule, derived from several different theories, or, more generally, one and the same conclusion may be inferred from different premisses. The inductive inference is not conclusive; it does not verify any of the alternative hypotheses, though it may confirm and throw some light on each and help to assess their respective probability and the measure of rational belief, which we can confer upon them. Consequently, a universal empirical statement cannot justify any of its particular instances and still less prove the falsehood of any unfavourable instance, for the truth of a particular instance is more certain than that of the universal principle, by means of which the truth or falsehood of a particular case is supposed to be established.

The rejection of the classical tradition in philosophy is ultimately based on the empirical outlook as well as on the rational attitude of mind which requires that the degree of certainty ascribed to a belief should be related to the degree of certainty of its evidence. Statements concerning the whole of reality, however important they might be for some reason or other, cannot be more certain than any particular statement which is said to be presupposed by some all-embracing principles. This applies equally to the laws of dialectics, one of the products of the classical tradition in philosophy. Ajdukiewicz emphasised that at most their degree of certainty is as strong as the degree of certainty conferred upon the established laws of Nature [163]. If the latter are not incontrovertible truths, the former are not such truths either. Whatever actual degree of certainty they possess, might be a matter of controversy, likely to remain unresolved, if the controversy is a concealed clash between mentalities affected by divergent inspirations, those of science and logic on the one side, of imagination and vision responsive to untestable generalities on the other.

CHAPTER 24

THE RELEVANCE OF THE PROBLEM OF UNIVERSALS AND

THE REJECTION OF THE THREE CLASSIC DOCTRINES

It is a point which has frequently been made by Bertrand Russell that the fortunes of metaphysics in modern times have been largely determined by the omission to consider any other but substantival and adjectival universals [164]. The failure to recognise that there also might be other kinds of universals led to the conclusion that all propositions can be regarded as attributing a property to a single thing. In particular, propositions expressing relations 'xRy' were reduced to subject-predicate propositions 'φx', where 'φ' is a name for the complex or relational property of 'having R to y'. This view had far-reaching consequences and lent support to monistic metaphysics. Since every object stands in some relations to outside things, nothing can be adequately described unless it is considered as a part of a whole and in its manifold relations to every other object. Moreover, nothing except the whole of reality is self-contained. Finally, no proposition is true unless it is entailed by propositions about reality as a whole. Some metaphysical views, which ascribe to reality otherwise unjustifiable fundamental characteristics, result from an incorrect logical analysis of language and an inadequate theory of universals.

There is another approach to the connection between theories of universals and metaphysics. In a sense, the question 'What are universals?' is not factual. For if it is assumed that whatever exists, exists somewhere and somewhen, universals have no real existence. We cannot answer the question about universals by pointing to something or by indicating it with a demonstrative phrase. It does not follow therefrom that the problem of universals not being factual must be purely linguistic and that once its metaphysical, *i.e.* its non-factual superstructure is exposed, it is actually reducible to a controversy over language. For the fact that a controversial problem can be stated in semantical terms does not entail that this problem is simply linguistic. We can make use of all kinds of general words and analyse the rules of their usage without seemingly leaving the realm of language, but we cannot make a reasoned choice among them, to advocate some and proscribe others, unless the ontological commitment, which we are ready to undertake, is explicitly stated. A theory of universals makes explicit this kind of commitment, and it should be evaluated by its ability to live up to its self-imposed standards. This is not a purely, or even mainly, linguistic problem, nor by any means an easy task to accomplish. For instance, everybody acquainted with the so-called nominalist programme is familiar with the magnitude of its difficulties. On the other hand, the answer to the question: 'What are universals?' undertaken without prior ontological restrictions on one's freedom of action might provide some useful linguistic and psychological clarifications, but would ultimately fail to face the issue. For sooner or later, to use Quine's simile, we are compelled to take the attitude of the parents who tell the Cinderella story, though they do not feel committed to admitting a fairy godmother into the circle of their acquaintances.

From this viewpoint the connection between some definite metaphysical views and some definite theory of universals should be examined by inquiring into the ontological commitments of the adopted discourse and conceptual framework, specified in the respective theory of universals and metaphysical beliefs, which claim the discovery of what is truly real and independent of the use of language. Marxist-Leninists often say that to inquire into the ontological commitments of language implies the conviction that the ontological state of affairs is not 'objective' and that it can be arbitrarily changed by a suitable choice of language. This conviction neither is nor should be assumed. For it is evident that what is real cannot be affected or be dependent in any manner upon linguistic stipulations, but the use of a definite language does involve ontological implications.

These implications are not absolute and the mere verbal references to entities which are excluded by accepted ontological beliefs do not necessarily involve an irresolvable conflict between language and ontology. For our language would become extremely cumbersome if its uses were always restricted to fit exactly the ontological scheme. The conflict between this scheme and the linguistic expressions becomes real, however, when no appropriate and recognised devices are available to show that an ontologically objectionable reference is an avoidable abbreviation. This method of avoiding conflicts between language and ontology was made known in Poland by Kotarbiński in the early 'twenties.

The question to be considered now can be stated as follows: is the Marxist-Leninist doctrine of universals consistent with materialist metaphysics or is it committed to an ontology that is incompatible with the latter? It will be useful to precede the examination of this problem by some general observations regarding the significance attached by Marxist-Leninist thinkers to the traditional problems of universals.

The distinction of two basic philosophic traditions, those of materialism and idealism, fundamental to Marxist-Leninist thinking, is supposed also to play a distinct and important role in adjudicating between various alternatives in the controversy over universals. The attitude taken in the all-pervasive dispute as to whether matter or thought is primary, co-determines the cleavage among the different points of view on universals. On the other hand, the problem of universals is said to be abstract and barren, unless it is related to and reflects the fundamental differences of philosophic outlooks [165].

It might be argued that idealism (in the Marxist-Leninist sense) is closely associated with realism, Platonic or Aristotelian, and that materialism is compatible only with nominalism. In its original form, Lenin observed, idealism consisted in recognising the existence of abstract entities, independent of minds, and this has remained the central and distinctive doctrine of all idealism, whether ancient or modern. Plato, Kant, or Hegel, each of them in his own way, held that the real is universal [166].

The logic of materialism, which found in Hobbes its modern embodiment, strives in the opposite direction. The universal is nowhere and 'nowhen' and to say this is to assert that the universal does not exist. 'An incorporeal substance', Marx commented upon Hobbes' nominalism, 'is just as much nonsense as an incorporeal body. Body, being, substance, are one and the same real idea'. It is a 'contradiction to say, on the one hand, that all ideas have their origin in the world of senses and to maintain, on the other hand, that a word is more than a word, that besides the beings represented, which are always individual, there exist also general beings'[167]. This was also the view that Engels took, though it appears that he adopted it with an important distinction. Like Marx, Engels maintained that 'qualities do not exist but only things with qualities' and that 'words like matter and motion are nothing but abbreviations . . . . . they are creations of thought and not sensuous objects'. But he also asserted in a manner reminiscent of Aristotle rather than of Hobbes or contemporary nominalism, that 'things always have certain qualities (properties of corporeality at least) in common' or that by means of general words, such as 'matter' or 'motion' we 'comprehend many different sensuously perceptible things according to their common properties'[168]. This is not nominalism unless the concept of common property, that occurs time and again in Engels' work, is explicated by means of the so-called Resemblance or Similarity theory. This is, however, an inadvisable, and in fact, unjustifiable course to take in view of the incompatibility of the Humean viewpoint on the one hand, the Marxian and the Marxist-Leninist viewpoints on the other in the theory of knowledge, and of the intellectual kinship between the latter standpoint and Aristotelian essentialism.

Historians of philosophical thought who represent the Marxian tradition and who have considered the controversy over universals in a larger context, that is, within the 'materialist-progressive' and the 'idealist-retrogressive' outlooks, have come to the conclusion that neither of these outlooks is uniquely associated either with nominalism or with realism. Marx did not conceal his admiration for Bacon and his dislike for Hobbes. Bacon's materialism, he said, might have been as full of inconsistencies as theology, but in his aphoristic doctrine 'matter smiles at man with poetical sensuous brightness'. Materialism systematised by Hobbes 'became hostile to humanity' by its rigid and ascetic logic of which nominalism was both an offspring and a driving force[169]. It cannot be denied that the nominalism of Hobbes, Spinoza, Helvetius, Feuerbach, and of all pre-Marxian materialist thinkers constituted an integral part of the materialist conceptual framework, favourable to the development of materialist thought. But nominalism in Paris and at Oxford in the fourteenth century had no connection with materialism. It testified to the rise of interest in natural objects and occurrences, it paved the way for methodological empiricism and was one of the ancestors of the idealist trend which found its protagonists in Berkeley and Hume, in the nineteenth century positivism and contemporary neo-positivism. Nominalism has nourished the development both of the materialist and idealist philosophy. It was nominalism that made available the tools for the liquidation of the concept of matter as a fictitious entity and for the establishment of the individualistic bourgeois society[170].

387

On the other hand, it could not be said that Platonic realism always provided an unequivocally retrogressive philosophic inspiration. It was the Platonic heritage that prompted John Scotus Eriugena towards pantheism and the abolition of the sharp distinction between God and the created world, characteristic of the Christian world picture. The far-reaching consequences of this idea were drawn only some three centuries later, when from Eriugena's premiss that God has no separate existence David of Dinant arrived at the conclusion that God must be the substance of all bodies and thus established materialist monism. Similarly, Platonic realism provided Averroes with arguments for his teachings on the mortality of the soul; this teaching contributed to the destruction of the faith in God's final judgment and proved to be a powerful weapon against theology, theocracy, and all the evils of organised religion. Non-nominalist doctrines of medieval thought should not be regarded as invariably retrogressive or anti-materialist [171].

Generally speaking, in no period of history can nominalism or realism be taken as an unambiguous criterion for differentiating materialist and idealist thought from each other. If the controversy over universals reflects the divergent tendencies of materialism and idealism, the reflection is neither clear nor unequivocal. In the course of time this conclusion led to the questioning of the relevance ascribed to the principle that the cleavage of the materialist and idealist traditions determines uniquely and in every respect the historical progress of philosophic thought. Before that happened it supported the belief that no historically established point of view regarding universals could be reconciled with the principles of Marxism-Leninism [172].

This conclusion puts the modern problem of universals in somewhat antiquated settings. For it not only ignores the fact that at present the old problem of universals is most hotly debated in a new field, namely, in the disputes on the foundations of logic and mathematics, but also refuses to recognise that some important contributions to the problem, as it had been discussed in the Middle Ages, have been made in modern times from the seventeenth century onwards. The modern version of the problem of universals, in particular as it emerged in the debate on the foundations of logic, had been discussed in Poland in the inter-war period and it was taken up again in some publications which appeared after the war. Marxist-Leninist writers ignored this development and showed no desire to become acquainted with it [173].

In their opinion the problem of universals in the present-day non-Marxist philosophy has not moved beyond the stage at which it had been left in the Middle Ages: it continues to debate the question whether universals exist independently of the mind, are mind-made entities or not even names of such entities. Since the fundamental issue of the problem of universals formulated in that manner had been solved a long time ago – no universals exist in the sense of Platonic realism – there is nothing of interest left for discussion. The present-day nominalists keep on producing arguments against Platonic entities and are unable to see the problem in any other but the scholastic form.

Marxist-Leninist thinkers are inclined to adopt a somewhat supercilious attitude to the problem of universals and to regard it as unworthy of serious attention. Once it was topical, since its realist solution buttressed a system of theology, of Christian ethics and metaphysics, while the nominalist trend provided a weapon against feudal medieval society and paved the way for empirical thinking oppressed by dogmas and speculative rationalism. At present the problem of universals is an unreal one, for it is concerned with an invention of religiously minded scholars. Nobody in his senses would to-day assert that abstract entities are real. In its scholastic formulation 'Are there universals?', the problem is so remote from the contemporary philosophic discussions that only a historian can take a genuine interest in it [174].

An account of the reasons for the rejection of all classic doctrines on universals may throw some light on what the Marxist-Leninist views on this matter are. E. A. Moody criticised Porphyry's account of Aristotle's teaching about universals for its failure to realise that the problem of universals is not only a metaphysical or an ontological problem, but also a logical one. The same applies to what Marxist-Leninists have to say on the problem of universals. They discuss it as if it were, above all, a metaphysical problem with implications for theology, sociology and the theory of knowledge. The logical questions are practically ignored. If mentioned at all, they were never examined in a competent manner.

In the opinion of Marxist-Leninist thinkers, the falsehood of Platonic realism is a matter of course, which does not need any justification. This applies equally to logicism, essentially the same doctrine, of which once Bertrand Russell and, at present, Alonzo Church are the most eminent supporters. Logicism, as defined by Quine, puts no restrictions on the use of bound variables and, consequently, accepts the existence or subsistence of some postulated or inferred abstract entities. Perhaps the main argument for this view is the fact that without the hypothesis of abstract entities logic and mathematics would become intolerably complex if not impossible. On their side, Marxist-Leninists argue that Platonic realism would destroy the material unity and homogeneity of the Universe. Therefore, a dialectic materialist must decisively reject it [175].

It might appear that for this reason nominalism should be the doctrine acceptable to materialist philosophy. There are grounds to believe that this was Marx's opinion. In Poland it has been represented by Kotarbiński. Kotarbiński believed that semantical reism, a particular sort of nominalism, supported by ontological reism (the world is the sum total of concrete particulars), is the only consistently materialist semantics. An aggregate of particulars and universals of some sort or another could not be an uniformly material world. It is not enough, Kotarbiński argued, to agree with the negative content of nominalism, that is, with its refutation of metaphysical realism. If a Marxist-Leninist rejects what nominalism asserts, namely, that only particulars exist, he initiates a platonising reaction and returns to Hegel's original position by again turning upside down the revision of the Hegelian standpoint accomplished by Marx [176].

Marxist-Leninist thinkers did not deny the merits of nominalism in so far as it has helped to refute Platonic realism. But they regard the negative side of nominalism, *i.e.* its criticism of other theories of universals, as its only valuable contribution to philosophy. They say that nominalism has won an undisputed victory over its medieval opponents and having achieved this purpose can be dismissed to oblivion. This opinion is right with respect to methodological nominalism in the natural sciences but is not corroborated by the present position in the dispute over universals. Nominalism in logic and mathematics is hard pressed by its opponents and numerically overwhelmed by supporters of realism and conceptualism. It is also threatened, as it were, at home by an increasing amount of penetrating criticism against its very foundation, the Resemblance or Similarity theory, with which it cannot dispense [177].

Having prematurely buried the opponents of nominalism, Marxist-Leninists seem to have a somewhat simplified and not entirely accurate idea of what the positive doctrine of contemporary nominalism actually is. For they are inclined to look at it as if it were a theory of how words can be used without any reference to non-linguistic occurrences. They assume that a nominalist must be a linguistic philosopher and a confirmed agnostic in ontology. They ignore the fact that nominalism as much as any other point of view on universals is committed to some ontological beliefs. They regard nominalism as an adversary of materialism, identified with dialectical materialism, and as a doctrine as objectionable as and more dangerous than Platonic realism [178].

There are several reasons, some tacitly admitted, some openly stated, which prompt Marxist-Leninist philosophers to take this attitude. The tacit reason is that no dialectical materialist could possibly be a nominalist, for the world, as he sees it, is an essentially stratified world, composed of ontological entities of different levels, irreducible to each other. Matter contains emergent characteristics, its constituents may form integrated systems of interaction which bring a new set of laws into operation. Therefore, statements about the whole, the systems of interactions, are not logically deducible from the statements about the parts of this whole, that is, about individuals. Consequently, speaking generally, biology is not reducible to physics and chemistry, and sociology is not reducible to biology. Marxist-Leninists assume that the irreducibility is not really an empirical problem to be decided by experiment and research, nor a logical question, since it involves something more than the impossibility of constructing appropriate theoretical systems. It results from the ontological or metaphysical characteristics of the Universe. Nominalism could not do justice to this fact, since it presupposes 'atomism' of some sort or another and has to reject non-additive wholes. The world of the nominalist, at least the world of Leśniewski and Kotarbiński, is ontologically uniform; it contains no other entities whatsoever except individuals of a certain sort. This might be described as an instance of the fallacy of misplaced concreteness. Marxist-Leninists share Whitehead's conviction that the scientific cosmology which presupposes the ultimate fact of an irreducible 'brute matter' is a false conception, born out of an intolerant use of 'formal abstraction'. Nature is a process in which nothing endures. 'Mechanistic materialism' refuses to recognise that the world is in a permanent change and evolution, and nominalism is the logical and semantical doctrine of 'mechanistic materialism'.

Furthermore, nominalism is unable to account for the universal interconnections of things and phenomena and being unable to account for them disrupts their universal interdependence. It sees only individuals and fails to notice that the singular and the general are internally bound together in the individual. In each particular thing the supposed polar opposites, the universal and the singular, are indissolubly merged and this fact testified to the truth discovered by Hegel and recognised by Lenin, 'the singular is the general . . . . . consequently, the opposites . . . . . . are identical' (we shall return to this statement later). If this were not the case, as nominalism asserts, our conceptual thinking would have no objective foundation in the external world and concepts would have no referents to reflect. To deny, as nominalism does, that conceptual thinking has an objective reference, reduces it to a shallow and one-sided empiricism, which, in Engels' words, 'as far as possible forbids itself thought' and 'precisely for that reason not only thinks incorrectly but also is incapable of faithfully pursuing the facts or even of reporting them faithfully, and which, therefore, becomes transformed into the opposite of true empiricism'[179].

Nominalism, which Marxist-Leninist thinkers criticise, includes views which clearly have been held only rarely, have not been shared by all nominalists, and have certainly not been supported by contemporary nominalism in Poland. For modern nominalism does not say that universals are *flatus vocis,* mere verbal utterances, or that things which are called by one name have only just this in common that they are called by the same name. The first of these views is ascribed to Roscelin and the second is sometimes discovered in the nominalism of Hobbes [180]. This extreme version of nominalism has found no adherents in contemporary philosophy.

There is also considerable simplification in the supposition that nominalism does not recognise any objective basis for applying the same word to a group of particulars. If this were true, the use of words, other than proper names, would be so arbitrary that language would cease to be a means of communication. Nominalism does not support a doctrine which flouts the fact that people do manage to exchange thoughts with each other.

It is true that a nominalist denies that a general word is a proper name for what is called 'common property' or, more generally, 'common character', for unlike an Aristotelian realist he does not believe that things have common, *i.e.* identical characters. But he does not deny that things can be grouped together or classified according to their similarity or resemblance. The nominalist asserts that similarities are empirically given and that he does not need the universal of similarity in order to be able to recognise a resemblance when he observes it. When a predicate 'φ' is ascribed to two or more objects, we do not say the same thing but similar things about them; this also applies to the sentences, in which the predicate 'φ' occurs. Consequently, he is not committed to the view that similarity is a 'true universal', which cannot be dispensed with – this is Bertrand Russell's opinion – or that things have a common property, something that being the same is simultaneously here and there. According to his logic, the Identity theory is self-contradictory.

A nominalist would insist that no property can belong to two different individuals and that every property is a particular property of one and only one individual. The fact that properties are as much particular as individuals is not incompatible with their being similar as a matter of fact or with their being described by means of general words. For general words and general sentences are an indirect manner of speaking about individuals, as will become clear later.

The objective basis for the use of general words is not immutable. Concepts, that is, the meaning of general words are not necessarily imposed by the given manifold of experience. They are devices to be evaluated according to their utility, open to change and adjustment if they prove their unsuitability or break down under the strain of the use to which they are put. It should be conceded, therefore, that for the nominalist language does contain a conventionalist element as its essential characteristic that cannot be overlooked in any language, irrespective of what particular philosophic purpose this language is to serve.

This is an outline of the doctrine of nominalism as it has been formulated by Leśniewski and Kotarbiński. The objection that it fails to recognise some objective basis for the use of general words and for distinguishing them from proper names does not apply in this case. Marxist-Leninist criticism flogged a dead horse.

Its implicitly and explicitly stated arguments against nominalism are neither unambiguous nor logically unobjectionable; they deal with elusive and equivocal generalities as well as shirk detailed analysis of specific expressions. The ontological frame of reference which underlies the criticism of nominalism remains undisclosed. But there is little doubt that it should be looked for in the presuppositions on which the truth of the laws of dialectics is based. It is the conceptual scheme of dialectics that justifies the rejection of nominalism, since this scheme cannot dispense with some abstract entities to whose admittance nominalism raises objections. If the laws of dialectics or the Marxian political economy were translated into the reistic language, stated one of the critics of nominalism, the essence of dialectics would disappear [181].

Although dialectical materialism considers conceptualism as a doctrine superior to its nominalist or Platonist rivals, it also repudiates conceptualism in the form given to it by Locke. For Locke is regarded as the primary source of what Marxist-Leninists call 'contemplative empiricism', the ancestor of the trend which radically divorces appearance from essence and theoretical thinking from practice. This trend has found in the philosophy of Berkeley and Hume, in positivism, neo-positivism, and linguistic philosophy its more extreme formulation [182].

The view expressed by a leading Polish Marxist-Leninist that dialectical materialism stands closest to an 'objectively interpreted conceptualism', has not been generally accepted [183]. Those objecting to this view take the attitude that the materialist doctrine of universals is something entirely novel and should not even be partially identified with any historically known point of view or presented as a perfected formulation of any of them [184]. To enhance the novelty of the Marxist-Leninist approach the use of the traditional expression 'the problem of universals' has been often discontinued and replaced by the cumbrous phrase 'the problem of the relation of the particular and the general'. The disagreement on this matter between Marxist-Leninist thinkers reflects their differences of opinion regarding the part which the Hegelian philosophy should be allowed to play in Marxist-Leninist philosophy.

CHAPTER 25

THE MARXIST-LENINIST THEORY OF UNIVERSALS

The Marxist-Leninist doctrine of universals is fragmentary, not always consistent and for the most part obscure [185]. The obscurity comes partly from Hegel, partly from other sources, and partly from itself. Besides Hegel, possibly Bradley's and certainly Whitehead's ideas have influenced Marxist-Leninist thinking on the subject [186]. Several threads of Whitehead's organic cosmology can be found in the Marxist-Leninist theory of universals: the rejection of any sort of atomism; the reduction of qualities to relations; the reincorporation of the knower into the world as its homogeneous constituent, acted upon and reacting to what is around him; the repudiation of the 'bifurcation of Nature'; the emphasis upon the internal relatedness and interfusion of events, as well as upon the whole as a determinant for its component parts. The powerful influence of Whitehead's metaphysics, abstracted from its intimate connections with science, above all, with mathematics and physics, which Marxist-Leninists ignore, will become clear in the further course of this account. For the moment another thread of the philosophic tradition which affects the Marxist-Leninist point of view on universals must be put into relief. For apart from the conspicuous upper layer of Hegelian origin, there is also an inconspicuous lower one of Aristotelian parentage. There is some truth in the assertion that dialectical materialism stands close to an 'objectively interpreted conceptualism'.

A mystifying element in the Marxist-Leninist doctrine of universals is its professed adherence to some assumptions of nominalism: only particulars exist, universals are a philosophic invention. But its professed repudiation of Platonic entities in the historical sense of this expression, of hypostatised genera and species, properties and other general words, does not mean that the Marxist-Leninist doctrine adheres to the rule that the quantified variable can take only names of individuals as its value. On the contrary, while denying the reality of universals, Marxist-Leninist thinkers are Platonist realists (in the modern sense of this term) in their discourse. It is clear, therefore, that their meaning of the term 'particular' must differ from that of a nominalist and that their confession of ontological faith, 'only particulars exist', cannot be taken at its face value. For instance, what they say makes it clear that the real world contains common properties, classes, and relations.

Marxist-Leninists reject emphatically the view according to which the statement 'Every red object is a coloured object' means '(x) if x is red, then x is coloured'. In the propositional schema the predicates 'red' and 'coloured' do not purport to name classes, but are used in reference to individuals in a particular context, outside which they have no meaning (such expressions belong to the semantical category called by Husserl 'syncategoramatic expressions', and this name was adopted in Poland). No extra-linguistic or extra-logical predicates need be assumed to make the sentences significant and true. According to Marxist-Leninists, the two quantified statements are not equivalent; the second leaves out some meaning which the first conveys. The truth of the first statement depends on whether there is some entity common to all the elements in virtue of which the class of red objects is not simply fabricated, to be reduced to Locke's 'workmanship of the understanding', but has an objective foundation and is included in the class of coloured objects. Thus, there are no universals in the sense of Platonic ideas and only particulars exist, but universals 'make up' or are involved in the conception of particulars. As Lenin put it, 'the singular is the general'. To say something of a class is not equivalent to a conjunction of statements about the elements of this class. The relations in which particulars stand to each other are of such a nature that they cannot be stated otherwise but by means of general statements, irreducible to singular ones. What is true to say about a class or a property might not be true to say about their elements or instances respectively. The existence of various levels of being, irreducible to each other, must be recognised. It is futile to argue that a class or a property, not being a thing in the reistic sense of this term, does not exist. For though it does not exist in this sense, it has an objective being [187].

So far there is seemingly nothing in the Marxist-Leninist solution of the problem of universals that goes beyond Aristotelian realism *sensu largo*. The position taken by a Marxist-Leninist is distinct, however, from that of a contemporary Aristotelian realist as defined by J. M. Bocheński, the eminent Thomist logician [188]. They share the so-called Identity or Common Property theory, which, unlike the Resemblance theory of the nominalist, appears to assume something more than empirically given similarities as the sufficient condition for attributing the predicate 'φ' to more than one instance. For to be ontologically justifiable the Identity theory cannot dispense with some unobservable entities, identically present in many individuals, and such entities are what is called universals *in re*. But Bocheński explicitly rejects the existence of classes in the external world and considers them to be mere constructions of the mind (unless the universe of classes is concealed behind the universal meanings)[189]. This is not the case in so far as a Marxist-Leninist is concerned. He is committed to the theory of reflection, and, consequently, he cannot treat what is mirrored in the mind and expressed in linguistic forms as mere constructions with no referent outside the mind and language. He cannot escape recognising the universe of classes and is driven by his own assumptions to positing their reality, reflected by concepts and depicted in the language by predicates.

The fact that Marxist-Leninists have been led by their various theories to the recognition of the universe of classes is obscured from their sight by their preoccupations with social problems and, in particular, the concept of social class [190]. A social class is a collection or a 'true aggregate of the persons composing it', according to Bukharin's definition. The term 'class' is in this case a genuine name, it names a certain real complex entity. But classes in the logical sense cannot be identified with any concrete objects or collections: a class of cows is not a herd of cows, a class of stones is not a heap of stones. The relation of part to whole differs from the relation of member to class in some important respects; the first is a transitive relation and the second is not. Moreover, 'to be part of' is a functor irreducible to logical terms, 'to be an element of' is a quasi-functor. 'Classes' in the logical sense are not genuine names, *i.e.* names of real objects. If they name anything, they must name abstract entities. 'We may call them aggregates or collections, if we like, but they are universals. That is, if there are classes' [191].

The distinction between classes and collections has been sharply drawn by Leśniewski and Kotarbiński, and the latter has also carefully analysed the philosophical implications of the essential difference which the concepts of class and of collection involve [192]. Leśniewski differentiated classes in the distributive sense from classes in the collective sense or the logical from the mereological concept of class. Originally Leśniewski developed his 'theory of collections' as a theory of sets (1916), but later he abandoned the idea that the whole theory of sets could be reconstructed on this basis and treated it as an independent theory of the whole-part relation, which has become known under the name of mereology. In mereology 'class' means 'collection' (of a special sort) and it is a genuine name, for it denotes a physical object and a class in this sense consists of parts or pieces, not necessarily contiguous (*e.g.* the fauna of the British Isles). A particular may be identified with the collection of its parts. Thus, a definite tree is the class (in the mereological sense) of its constituent cells. But a class in the mereological sense is not reducible to a class in the logical sense and the collection must be distinguished from the class of which the parts of the collection are members, in our example from the class of cells (in Leśniewski's system the calculus of classes is comprised in ontology). If this distinction is not observed, we are bound to fall into contradictions. For the tree in question can be said to consist of cells, or of atoms or of electrons, and the like. Therefore, if the tree as a collection is identified with the class of cells or with the class of some 'atomic units', each of which is distinct from the other, the tree is a self contradictory object. We can identify a particular with different collections of its parts, *i.e.* classes in the mereological sense, but no particular is identifiable with a class in the logical sense. Classes in the logical sense and particulars (collections) must be clearly distinguished from each other.

It appears that Marxist-Leninist thinkers might have been confused by the different meanings which the term 'class' may have. Their starting point was social classes, which are instances of classes in the mereological sense, *i.e.* objects as concrete as the individuals of whom they are composed. They seem to have been misled by this fact, and assumed that the term 'class' in the sense in which it is used in the logical analysis of language can also be identified with a collection, namely, the aggregate of its members, a complex but concrete object. For it is certain that they are unaware of the fact that by admitting classes in the logical sense into their discourse they have become committed to the existence of abstract entities, and one of the important sources of their deception is the mereological concept of class. They also feel that the definition of logical class in nominalistic terms necessitates the rejection of the mereological concept of class, and of social class in particular, as a fictitious entity to be explained away by verbal devices [193].

The kinship of the Marxist-Leninist doctrine of universals with Aristotelian realism is enhanced by the description of the process of abstraction as the apprehension of the essence of things. Aristotle believed that the process of generalisation and abstraction 'exhibits the Universal as implicit in the clearly known particular'. As a rough approximation this is also the Marxist-Leninist view. The essence, however, is not to be conceived as something fixed and immutable, shared by all particular things of a sort, in virtue of which they can be recognised as instances of one and the same species. Also essences are comprised by the evolutionary expansiveness of the Universe, by the development of what is potential, latent, and 'in itself' into what is actual, apparent, and 'for itself.' The essence endures and evolves, it is, as it were, growing and maturing, objectively and relative to human knowledge, in the progress of which deeper and deeper layers of essence can be discovered. This doctrine of abstraction is of Aristotelian origin, but the Aristotelian seed, as Marxist-Leninists themselves recognise, has clearly grown up in the Hegelian soil [194].

The process of abstraction by means of which the universals are apprehended and the essences of things discovered does not consist in generalising in the sense of Locke. It is not the operation of abstracting a core of qualities common to many particulars in order that this core may be used in a representative capacity for a whole range of particulars. If this were the only possible abstraction, its intension and extension would vary inversely; the less specific and poorer in content is the class defining property, the wider would be the class. There is a place in knowledge for this kind of abstraction, for generalisations providing economic abbreviations or devices for communication and facilitating thinking. But they have no cognitive value. For purely formal abstractions disrupt and destroy the connections and relations among concrete things, and cannot, therefore, reach their essence, which manifests itself in and is constituted by these connections and relations. Marxist-Leninist philosophy has never ceased echoing Hegel's dictum that there is no 'thing in itself', *i.e.* a thing unrelated to other things. Therefore, when its relations to other things, constitutive of its being, are disrupted, the thing itself is destroyed.

There is another sort of abstraction, different from the formal, which Marxist-Leninists call 'concrete abstraction'. No detailed account of the process by means of which concrete abstractions are obtained is available in the whole of Marxist-Leninist literature. It is always referred to in the most general terms, reminiscent of Lenin's observations on some aspects of dialectical thinking which is characterised by the endless process of deducing new relationships, by the passage from appearance to essence, and from 'superficial to deeper layers of being' [195]. It is certain that the activity of concrete abstraction differs totally from the process of generalising and abstracting which Locke, Berkeley or Hume tried to describe and analyse. For the British empiricists were solely concerned with formal abstractions and are among the main culprits responsible for leading the philosophy of mind astray. The evidence available seems to point to the conclusion that concrete abstraction is a methodological procedure involving operations known from the methodology of empirical science – inductive generalisations, formulation of empirical laws, derivations of their consequences, reformulation and readjustment of hypotheses and theories [196]. This complex methodological procedure seems to provide the scaffolding of concrete abstraction as a process, but remains distinct from what by using such devices the mind is able to apprehend.

Concrete abstractions in the sense of a product are probably concepts like those of matter, atom, evolution and similar ones, whose meaning cannot be apprehended and fixed once and for all in a definition, for they must be considered within the whole body of knowledge and theories of which they form a part, and this body is constantly changing and being improved upon. They are rather conceptual schemes than concepts in the accepted sense, or perhaps what Professor Kneale calls 'transcendent hypotheses'[197]. They mirror the unobservable but real interfusion of universal inner connections and mutual interdependence in the outside world, and reveal that a particular is not just an instance of a universal, but a knot in the network of interlocking universals. The discovery of the essence of an evolutionary complex whole precedes logically and epistemologically the discovery of the essence of any of its component parts [198]. The essence of an evolutionary complex whole seems to be Hegel's 'Universal which comprises in itself the full wealth of Particulars'. Schaff's description of concrete abstractions or, to avoid ambiguity, of concrete universals, echoes almost word for word Hegel's celebrated pronouncement: a concrete abstraction does not set the general against the particular but treats the general as comprising the whole rich content of the particular. He suggested that unlike the formal abstractions the concrete ones do not achieve comprehensiveness at the expense of the content, that is, the more general a universal is the more 'concrete' and comprehensive it becomes. Correspondingly, a particular is more and more transformed into a complex of universals [199].

The only example of concrete abstractions, to which Marxist-Leninists specifically refer, is the concept of capital as worked out by Marx. They add that Marx's method in *Capital* should not be regarded as an immutable standard procedure, for it has been devised for the social sciences alone, and what is suitable for the latter may fail in other domains of knowledge. Each particular science should try to formulate its own methodological pattern of concrete abstraction [200].

The concept of concrete abstraction introduces the notion of real aggregate or 'whole', a relatively stable, isolated or closed system of interaction. The latter is not simply a compound unit whose parts have no other relation to each other except that involved in being parts of one and the same whole. The concept of real aggregate refers to a whole which fulfils the following two conditions: firstly, the whole exhibits characteristics distinct from the properties of its component parts taken severally and collectively; secondly, the whole is determined by regularities irreducible to those to which each of its parts is subject when it is not a part of this whole. Only the aggregates which satisfy both these conditions are real aggregates in the Marxist-Leninist sense. Since the parts of an integrated system of interaction are supposed to display some important characteristics dependent upon their place in the system and are determined by the regularities which govern the whole, it is often said that it is the 'law' of an entire process (a system of interaction) or of the whole that determines the essence of a particular, *i.e.* a component part of the whole. A whole in the Marxist-Leninist sense includes, therefore, relations or relational properties, which cannot properly be called attributes of the parts, though they relate and qualify parts. If such wholes exist, they cannot be known or specified by the knowledge or by the enumeration of their parts. This raises the question of how we can know that a whole is a whole in the required sense. The only answer which Marxist-Leninists seem to be able to provide is that they are objectively given or found in the natural world. They subscribe to Whitehead's fundamental idea that Nature is not a mere aggregate of independent entities, each capable of isolation in virtue of being specified by the 'property of simple location'. The isolation of an entity in thought – the result of a formal abstraction in the Marxist-Leninist terminology – has no counterpart in Nature. 'An isolated event is not an event, because every event is a factor in a larger whole and is significant of that whole'. A contrary view has no foundation in Nature but substitutes for Nature the model invented by theoretical science [201].

It is claimed that the conditions which a compound unit should satisfy to be a whole in the Marxist-Leninist sense make more precise the notion of the whole-part relation wrapped in obscurity by its connections with idealist philosophy – *Gestalt* psychology, holism, vitalism, and the irrational trends originated by Dilthey and Bergson, and reduced to triviality by the formula 'the whole is more than the sum of its parts' [202]. The difference is perhaps not so considerable as Marxist-Leninists would wish it to be.

The concept of the whole, as defined above, attributes to a real aggregate two properties which a system of interaction of the sort investigated in natural science does not seem to possess. The whole cannot be constructed from simpler isolated elements by means of some well-defined composition rules derived from the laws to which the component parts are subject. Furthermore, the whole has some emergent characteristics, and consequently, its behaviour complies with some specific laws of its own. These are exactly the features which *Gestalt* psychology ascribes to the whole when it rejects the additive or associationist approach to mental phenomena and declares that 'the whole is more than the sum of its parts'.

The *Gestalt* psychologists, Wertheimer, Köhler, Koffka, have always emphasised that a whole is not an *Undverbindung* and that its behaviour is not determined by that of its particular elements, but, on the contrary, that the processes in which the parts are involved are themselves determined by the intrinsic nature of the whole. *Undverbindung* is a characteristic of compound units whose existence can be accounted for by some rules of composition, such, for instance, as the laws of association in psychology or the law of addition of velocities in dynamics. A statement about a compound unit of this sort is, therefore, equivalent to a conjunction of singular statements about its component factors. A genuine whole, a system of interaction or a real aggregate in the Marxist-Leninist terminology, is not an *Undverbindung* in either of these two senses.

The use of the terms *'Gestalt'* and 'whole' covers very much the same ground and their respective meanings are hardly distinguishable from each other. Moreover, they both play a double role, they are concepts of description, to be applied to what is found in the phenomenal world, and ontological concepts referring to the immanent functional interdependence in the natural world. In both these capacities the concept of *Gestalt* is more specific than the Marxist-Leninist concept of the whole. The former has also a wider factual empirical basis than the latter; it comprises psychology, physiology, physics, chemistry, and the theory of value, on which only the metaphysical superstructure is based. The *Gestalt* psychologists have worked out an alternative non-analytical approach to problems of science and their criticism of the traditional scientific methods, which they reject as inadequate, cannot simply be ignored.

This could not be said with full justice of the Marxist-Leninist use of the term 'whole' which, incorporating the characteristics of the whole put into relief by *Gestalt* psychology, still clings to its traditional connotation. The traditional connotation comprises a non-specific use of the word 'whole' and refers to the totality or to the total system of things including the properties and relations obtaining among its parts. This is an intuitive concept introduced to the study of history and society by Hegel. Since the operation with totalities of this sort engenders conflicts with the principles of rational and logical thinking, it is often associated with the denial or restrictions of the validity of logic, which is to be replaced by dialectics. The Hegelian concept of the totality has not been eliminated from Marxist-Leninist theories and it interfuses with that of *Gestalt*. This is clear from the fact that for Marxist-Leninists it makes sense to speak not only of the study of systems of interaction, which are wholes in the specific sense, but also of the study of the 'whole of society', the history of mankind as one single development or the world process 'as a whole', which involves the Hegelian concept of the totality.

The crucial point in the discussion to which the inquiry into the 'atomistic' and 'additive' approach in science has given rise concerns the emergence or unpredictability of some characteristics or entities, which Marxist-Leninists, in common with other supporters of holism, consider to be an immanent trait of the natural world. A property of a compound entity is called emergent if it cannot be inferred from the properties of its component parts. The existence of emergent characteristics or events or entities constitutes a controversial issue, which, in some form or another, has been debated from ancient times. The concept of *Gestalt* has revived the old controversy. For it follows from the definition of *Gestalt* that its specific properties are emergent and cannot be predicted, however exhaustive our knowledge of its parts is. If there are *Gestalten,* there must also be emergent properties, which should be attributed to them as a matter of fact and not only because of our imperfect knowledge. This is what is meant when it is said that wholes are subject to laws. The laws in question state that any entity constituted in such and such a manner has such and such an emergent property.

The issue at stake is not whether there are unpredictable characteristics of events or unpredictable phenomena, but what unpredictability in this context means. For according to the critics of holism 'unpredictable' is not an absolute term but a relative one and it requires a conceptual and factual framework with respect to which a given phenomenon can be said to be unpredictable. What is emergent in a system of interaction and cannot be predicted is relative to what factual information concerning its constituent elements is obtainable and what general laws and theories are available at any given time. Therefore, unpredictability alone provides insufficient reason for the recognition of the claim that emergence is a characteristic immanent in phenomena. Unpredictability gives an indication of the state of our knowledge at a given moment; whatever else is inferred from it remains a matter of considerable doubt and of little promise. The doctrine of absolute emergence encourages speculative thought but provides no avenues for exploration and scientific research [203].

The Marxist-Leninist concepts of the whole and emergence corroborates this opinion. Their introduction marks the point where a fully-fledge speculation decisively gains the upper hand in Marxist-Leninist philosophy.

The conceptual scheme of integrated systems or wholes, each of which contains less comprehensive integrated units and is contained in more comprehensive ones, is based on the doctrine of internal relations and on the monistic conception of relations. They are the logical presuppositions of this particular conception of the whole-part relation.

The monistic conception regards the proposition 'xRy' as a whole composed of x and y and R as an unanalysable property of this whole. Consequently xRy is irreducible to a conjunction of φx and ψy. This should not be understood to mean that there is no logical method of reducing relations to classes, but that this reduction is not feasible for ontological reasons, that is, relations constitute an independent ontological category. They cannot be explained away as some other logical constants. Unlike the latter, they are not only constituents of speech but also belong to the constitution of the Universe. The concept of the whole is, therefore, incompatible with nominalism. For while a nominalist is not unduly restricted in the selection of entities which he may admit as values of the variables of the lowest type, is not obliged to search for the 'ultimate atoms' of which the Universe is composed, and could choose wholes of some sort as individuals, he cannot accept wholes of an arbitrary order, since they are irreducible to individuals. The monistic conception of relations requires that the ontological validity of such wholes is recognised [204].

The monistic conception of relations is itself grounded in the doctrine of internal relations, derived from Hegel. For it was Hegel who conceived the idea that properties are no part of things; they are disguised effects of relations and indicate the capacity of being influenced by and of exercising influence on other things. As he put it, properties are determinate relations of one thing to another and it is in virtue of their being related that the terms of the relation are logically and causally 'posited'. 'Property is this very reciprocal relation and apart from it the thing is nothing; the mutual determination, the middle term of the Things-

401

in-themselves, which, as extremes, were supposed to remain indifferent as against this their relation, is itself that self-identical Reflection and Thing-in-itself which these extremes were supposed to be' [205].

One of the most puzzling features of the theory of internal relations is its claim that the relations in which things stand to each other modify or determine the nature of related terms. The argument is speculative for it derives its conclusion from the following definition: a relation is internal to a term when it cannot be changed without the thing itself being changed. This is supposed to be a common occurrence. For instance, the value of coal is determined by the regularities of social life; its value is not an intrinsic attribute of coal but that of coal as a product of exchange. Not an atom of matter enters into the composition of value, Marx wrote. It lies hidden behind the exchange relation of commodities and manifests itself in the social relations of one commodity to another. The same applies to other properties of things, whether mechanical, physical or chemical; they are effects of changes which terms undergo in virtue of being related in a certain manner determined by regularities and expressed in laws of Nature or laws of social life [206].

It is not easy to see what these assertions really mean. Are they intended to state something more than the fact that relational concepts enter into the description of systems of interaction and that processes of interaction, for instance, such as chemical reactions or gravitational behaviour investigated in the classical Newtonian physics, do occur? If they are not, there is no reason to speak of relations modifying the nature of related terms, for these processes of interaction can be described in sober terms. To describe the process, *i.e.* the sequence of events, which a system of interaction, let us say a system of gravitating bodies, undergoes, we need the concepts of mass, position and momentum. We must also know the law of gravitation which, given the initial conditions of the considered system, allows us to compute the values of the variables or the state of the system at any moment of time. What is called 'the system' is determined uniquely by the mass, the 'intrinsic' property of gravitating bodies. The system is closed if we do not need to consider any other variables outside its space to predict the gravitational behaviour of the system itself. The specification of other characteristics of the system as a system of interaction requires in addition the relational properties of position and momentum. The procedure, by means of which the state of the system at the time *t* is computed, is purely analytical or 'additive'. When it has been performed, there is nothing relevant left out in the analytical description of the process of interaction, and in this sense the description is complete. It is, of course, incomplete in an infinity of manners, but all of them are irrelevant in so far as the gravitational behaviour is concerned.

It is true that we frequently do not know all the relevant variables or that we lack the knowledge of the respective law. Both in and outside mechanics, even with respect to macroscopic phenomena, our knowledge of the laws of motion is insufficient to give an analytical description of every process of interaction. This, however, is clearly due to imperfect knowledge and not to any hidden occult qualities of the whole which prevents the description of its behaviour by analytical means.

It is also obviously true that no similar thing can be done with respect to the value of coal, and nobody would dream of deducing its value from its physical or chemical characteristics. The same applies the other way round: nothing relevant can be inferred about the physical or chemical constitution of coal from what we know about it as a commodity. This is self-evident and trivial. The value, *i.e.* the quantity or rather the 'socially necessary quantity' of labour contained in the commodity, as Marx defined it, is not a term in the vocabulary of physics or chemistry. It is, therefore, no wonder that nothing whatever is inferable about the value of coal from its fullest description in physical and chemical terms. To deal with the value of coal as a commodity we have to introduce new descriptive terms and those terms express relational concepts. It is extremely doubtful whether the best way of indicating this simple fact is to say that the nature of coal undergoes a change by being used as a commodity and thus becomes related to the social conditions of production.

It is clear that the belief ascribing to the relations the power associated with physical things, of causing changes or of inducing new properties, cannot really assert what it states unless it carries a figurative significance. G. E. Moore suggested that there is one perfectly natural sense in which a given relation may be said to modify the terms which it relates [207]. This happens, for instance, when we say that it was the relationship to the flame that melted a stick of sealing-wax put into a flame. We know what we mean thereby, though we do not wish to assert that it was the relationship that actually caused a stick of sealing-wax to undergo a change. Such an assertion would obviously be false. The perfectly natural and intelligible sense in which 'modify' is used in such contexts does not imply that the description in which it occurs is correct in any other but a metaphorical sense. For to admit the possibility that relationships may cause the related terms to undergo changes is either to confuse or to identify logical and causal relations.

Two somewhat different versions of the doctrine of internal relations are current among Polish Marxist-Leninists. According to a more moderate view, we can speak legitimately and significantly in some cases of individuals irrespective of the whole of which they are parts. There are relations external and internal not everything is dependent on everything else and can truly, though only partially be known apart from the whole. Besides the relational properties, particular things may have intrinsic attributes: Socrates is a man, some billiard balls are white and round. The intrinsic predicates may signify the recurrent and non-recurrent traits of individuals. In the first case they instantiate some universal characters, in the second they specify a particular object in its uniqueness. Finally, a thing with intrinsic properties is also a part of a whole, and, consequently, it should be said that there are no independent facts and separate things. It is only when they are given the place of a part in the whole and their properties determined by this position become apparent, when they are examined in their manifold and constantly changing interdependence, that we can

403

achieve a true knowledge and apprehend reality unaltered by the analytic dispositions of thought, by formal and artificial abstractions and, generally, by the metaphysical (in the Marxist-Leninist sense) mode of thinking [208].

The more extreme version of the doctrine of internal relations denies that there are any intrinsic properties or any external relations. There are no ultimate atoms of which the world is composed and only simple units could have intrinsic attributes; there are no ultimate properties common to particulars, for there are no particulars in the accepted sense; there are no ultimate regularities of Nature except those immanent in the Universe as an infinite system of interaction. Therefore, nominalism must fail to achieve its purpose; universals of any kind, whether *ante rem, in re,* or *post rem,* are useless; contradictions in thinking and science are inevitable and irrecoverable [209]. This is a purely Hegelian doctrine which presupposes that every unit is complex, that it is a mesh of relations, and that these relations rather than what they relate are the real constituents of the unit.

The dialectical theory, we are told, does not assume that we acquire concepts by grouping together in certain ways selected recurring elements of experience, to use them in a representative capacity and as principles of classification. A concept is created by the endeavour to discover the essence of an evolutionary totality which leads to a mental reconstruction of the concrete. This purpose can be achieved by transcending what is given in perception and discovering genetic and causal connections, structures and laws of change, which reveal the inner universal interdependence of things and phenomena [210].

The doctrine of internal relations, originated by Hegel and in more recent times held by F. H. Bradley, A. N. Whitehead and Brand Blanshard, is a component part of the tradition associated with philosophic idealism. It is in sharp conflict with the positivistic trend in science and with empiricism in philosophy. When a materialist adopts it, strange consequences are bound to follow.

The doctrine of internal relations has been analysed by G. E. Moore, Bertrand Russell, and Ernest Nagel [211]. They found it logically inadequate and factually false. There is no need to repeat their arguments or to add new ones, for those on record are sufficient for the rejection of the doctrine and have not been refuted by its supporters. It is important, however, to point out some of the implications involved in the doctrine of internal relations and to examine their role in Marxist-Leninist philosophy.

The point at issue between the pluralist and empiricist attitude on the one hand, the monistic and holistic on the other, is not whether particulars do or do not stand in manifold relations to and mutual dependence on each other. For an empiricist this is a matter of fact which he accepts as much as a Marxist-Leninist does. What is at stake between an empiricist and a monist is the question whether these manifold relations of dependence are or are not irreducible, that is, whether they are contingent connections or whether they indicate some necessary structure or a definite and all-inclusive pattern, comprising everything that happens. To consider the manifold relations as contingent does not imply that an empiricist would deny the existence of some recurrent systems of interaction in organic and inorganic matter, for they do occur in our experience.

404

What he does deny is that these recurrent patterns of order are reducible to some fundamental type of order which provides the Universe with a necessary structure and determines the mode of existence of everything that there is in the Universe. A monist accepts just what an empiricist rejects. He thus discovers a common basis for all knowledge, a body of primitive truths, concepts and methods, from which the essential characteristics and laws of partial, quasi-isolated systems, less comprehensive than that of reality as a whole, can be deduced and provisionally but rationally examined.

On this account a monist rejects as illegitimate and arbitrary any mode of inquiry that isolates any part of reality or considers it in some definite respect unless the fundamental artificiality of this procedure is clearly recognised. He may concede that we cannot deal with everything all at once and that to accept some limitations in our inquiries may be necessary. He will insist, however, that when this preliminary work is done, no true conclusion can be reached without restoring to its due place the principle that everything is related in some way to everything else. This means that the knowledge acquired must be shown to be derivable from the basic set of truths about reality as a whole and the artificial isolation of the investigated system must be demolished as a mere artifice of thought.

This general approach explains why Marxist-Leninists profess various theories incompatible with the empiricist and scientific attitude in philosophy, of which their views are claimed to be the most advanced embodiment. They say that fundamental truths about reality as a whole safeguard the possibility of acquiring knowledge about anything in particular, that 'wholes', and not classes of things or events, are the basic unit of inquiry and that the whole-part relation is the primary category of thought, all the others being either derivable from or subsidiary to the former; that no integrated whole is self-contained unless it is the whole of reality; that all artificial barriers between different realms of being must be broken and the traditional ways of thinking reconstructed if the correspondence between thought and reality is to be re-established.

The concessions which the moderate conception of integrated aggregates is ready to make to the common sense view and to the rules of scientific procedure do not modify substantially any of these theories. For both conceptions, the moderately and the radically monistic, assume that the world is not composed of particular simple elements which exhibit definite characteristics and stand in manifold external relations to each other. In fact there are only integrated systems or wholes in the natural world and the goal of science is to discover the evolutionary laws of these wholes. The better we understand the determinant for the whole, the more adequate is our knowledge of the particular, the part of this whole. We must know the whole before we can truly know its parts, the knowledge starts from the universal and reaches by stages the concrete particular, and not the other way round. 'An infinite sum of general concepts, laws, *etcetera,* construes the concrete in its fulness'[212]. No whole is self-sufficient. The ultimate ground of rational knowledge must be derived from the total process of the world in evolution [213].

Thus, in Marxist-Leninist language the terms 'universal' and 'particular' seem to acquire a different meaning from that usually accepted. 'Universal' seems to be synonymous with 'integrated whole'. Lenin's much quoted pronouncement 'The singular is the general' is obviously false if 'is' stands for class-membership, class-inclusion or identity. The interpretation according to which the sentence 'the singular is the general' is an abbreviated form of the sentence 'the property of being singular is a universal property' and implies nothing more than an Aristotelian variety of realism, has been explicitly rejected. 'The singular is the general' is not a metaphoric sentence; it is significant and literally true as it stands [214]. If 'is' means 'is part of' and 'general' is synonymous with 'integrated whole', the sentence under discussion may be significant in the literary sense.

If this interpretation renders faithfully what Marxist-Leninists have in mind, certain conclusions follow. It cannot be said that Marxist-Leninist philosophy has a theory of universals of its own, because it cannot dispense with universals in the traditional sense. According to Marxist-Leninists, an integrated whole is determined by a law of evolutionary development. But a law is a universal statement which states that every whole of a certain kind has such and such a property. To speak of integrated wholes we must be able, therefore, to say which of them are of the same sort or have a common property, and in general, to have at our disposal some principles of classification which cannot be derived from the whole-part relation. The latter is logically posterior to the theory of predicates, class concepts or propositional functions. The distinctions involved in using significantly the language in which the part-whole relation theory is expressed presupposes a theory of universals and does not itself provide it.

It cannot be said, therefore, that what Marxist-Leninists call their theory of universals offers a satisfactory and workable alternative to the existing ones concerned with universals in the phenomenal world. For should it be granted for the sake of argument what Marxist-Leninists profess, namely, that the phenomenal world displays a specific organization, systems of interaction, real aggregates in all degrees of complexity and articulation, there remains the fact that the holist confession of faith, to be stated at all, requires and has to make use of general words and principles of classification.

The second consequence concerns a point which has already been mentioned in passing, namely, the incompatibility of the theory of real aggregates with materialism. This point will now be considered in some greater detail.

CHAPTER 26

THE DANGER OF PLATONISM

The difficulties which Marxism-Leninism has encountered in connection with the problem of universals, as well as the platonising and idealist tendencies involved in the attempt to solve the problem in terms of the whole-part relation, can be reduced to a basic contradiction between materialist metaphysical assumptions and the theory of reflection. The theory of reflection implies that non-imaginative concepts, that is, supposed objects of a special sort in the mind, apprehended by pure intelligence, have an objective foundation in the natural world. This factual reference would not be satisfied if concepts were recognised to have only a representative capacity or symbolic character, and still less if they were defined as the meaning of certain expressions. For this would apparently lead to relativism, scepticism, idealism, and conventionalism. The concept must stand for something in the external world in a similar manner as 'John' or 'Fido' does. Lenin strongly insisted on the correspondence, in the literal, mirror- or copy-like sense, between thought and reality. Lenin's view has been fully accepted by Marxist-Leninists everywhere.

The same applies to the concept of law. Also laws must have a factual reference and an objective foundation, in the indicated sense, in the natural world. There must be some direct correspondence between the regularities in natural processes and their conceptual reflections expressed in the laws of science. Towards the end of his life Stalin emphasised the point that regularities of Nature cannot be changed or abolished by man and dwelt upon the difference of meaning in the use of the term 'law' in its descriptive and prescriptive sense, as much as upon the fact that they are faithfully reflected in the minds of men in a manner not dissimilar from the reflection of an object in a mirror. Stalin wrote for a didactic political purpose and did not feel any need to inquire into these trivialities and crudities. His followers in Poland accepted his view as a methodological discovery of the highest order; instead of a didactic simile they treated it as a literal truth. Natural regularities are in the real world in no metaphoric sense of this expression, and because they are there, the mind can discover and reflect them mentally. Since we do not acquire this knowledge through the senses but by means of intellectual and non-imaginative reflections in the mind, regularities are entities of the same ontological level as essences. 'The law', wrote Lenin, 'is a relation of essences', 'immanently present in the phenomenon'. He felt that this refuted 'the followers of Mach, as well as other agnostics and Kantians' [215].

This conception of natural laws differs radically from the positivist doctrine which defines natural laws as patterns of description or invariant formulae for making predictions. Laws are the work of man and successful predictions are the only criteria of causality and regularity in the world. For the confirmation of the prediction can be said to be the same as the empirical corroboration of the law. The presuppositions of this doctrine can be stated simply and concisely. We can observe the coexistence and succession of distinct things and events as well as compare the results of our observations. Laws formulate the observed correlations of coexistence and succession or the recurrent pattern of comparable observations.

According to Marxist-Leninists this is pure subjectivism, for it precludes the possibility of speaking about regularity and causality in the world. 'What shallowness of thought', exclaimed Engels, commenting on the viewpoint of positivism [216]. Law does exhibit something about the events themselves and shows that regularity and causality are immanent in things and phenomena. If it is a description at all, it is a description of the order of Nature; it expresses the uniformities by which things and events are bound up together, the objective principles of necessitation. Laws are not, therefore, patterns of description but descriptions of patterns in Nature. These patterns are a manifestation of the manner in which things are essentially and internally related to each other. Consequently, natural laws are as much descriptions as explanations, they describe what happens as much as explain why something happens.

There is yet another characteristic of the Marxist-Leninist concept of law by which it differs from the positivist doctrine. Since only matter remains eternally the same in all its transformations and everything else is eternally changing, the order of Nature changes accordingly. There are, therefore, no eternal laws of Nature, all of them are changeable, and are more or less impermanent. The opposite point of view results from the adherence to the geocentric standpoint accepted in natural science. It is true that some laws change relatively faster than others. For instance, social laws and laws of historical development are certainly more impermanent than natural laws. But essentially there is no difference between the two classes; every law is a 'historical presentation of the successive changes occurring in a system of the Universe from its origin to its passing away'. This idea, which Engels derived from Hegel, has acquired prominence in Marxist-Leninist philosophy, for it showed the way in which cosmology could dispense with God. Newton's Universe, though subject to eternal laws, could not have arisen out of chaos by itself, by the operation of the laws of Nature. It required God who imposed these laws and by his constant intervention kept the mechanism from disruption and going to pieces. The view which denies the permanence of the natural order and assumes the concurrent evolution of the Universe and its laws, could follow Laplace and has no need for Newton's theistic hypothesis [217].

The pictorial philosophy of the mind, which has just been summarised, is bound to come into conflict with the assumptions of materialism. For materialism leads to nominalism and nominalism denies the reality of universals in any form. On the other hand, the view regarding the nature of concepts and laws, based on the theory of reflection, implies the rejection of nominalism and the adoption of realism of some sort. Verbal evasive actions can dodge this consequence but are unable to escape from it. Marxist-Leninists seem to be bound by their viewpoint and theories to assign to concepts some existential, ontological

408

status in the natural world, to be committed to *universalia in rebus* or *inter res,* and to recognise the existence of non-material constituents as real as lumps of matter. In Marxist-Leninist philosophy metaphysics and the theory of knowledge seem to be at loggerheads and militate against each other.

Not all Marxist-Leninists are unaware of the fact that by failing to pay due attention to ontological, logical and psychological issues involved in the problem of universals, they have become entangled in contradictions. Also this minority, whose views have been presented by Kołakowski, is anxious to keep away from its traditional formulation, considered to be a congeries of pseudo-problems invented by theologians. The real issue is not the question 'What are universals?' but 'What is the subject-matter of abstract knowledge?'. It is the answer to this question that has committed Marxist-Leninist philosophy to views which actually are or might turn out to be incompatible with philosophic materialism [218].

To make this point clear, Kołakowski distinguishes two main types of conceptual and logical framework which can be adopted in science and which can be called by the traditional names of nominalism and realism. It will become clear that this is not an abuse of the traditional terminology, for the problem of universals has some methodological implications.This approach to the problem is legitimate, but it cannot avoid becoming involved in some questions of ontology and metaphysics. This also will become clear at once. Although the starting point of Kołakowski's examination is methodological, not only his conclusions but also some initial basic distinctions are of a metaphysical nature.

Methodological nominalism denies that the world contains any other entities but individuals and, consequently, refuses to acknowledge that universal statements have an 'independent cognitive value'. They are reports in a shorthand notation of what in principle can be fully described by a finite or an infinite conjunction of singular statements. Nominalism is a set of semantical, logical, and methodological rules of describing the world as composed solely of individuals. Properties and relations are inseparable from things to which they belong and are not independent ontological categories. The rules of nominalism do not imply, as some Marxist-Leninists suggested, that a nominalist must abandon the use of general words altogether. For the use of general words does not compel the nominalist to the acceptance of abstract objects whose existence he denies, if he can show that they are in principle expendable, that is, that they are introduced as convenient fictions or abbreviated manners of speaking.

In contradistinction to nominalism, methodological realism asserts that abstract knowledge has a subject-matter of its own. No universal statement is equivalent to any combination, finite or infinite, of singular statements, and general words are not an indirect manner of referring to particular things or events. Words are not merely arbitrary means of description and communication, for there are words proper to every thing which reflect its true nature. Methodological realism implies the acceptance of an independent realm of being, irreducible to the world of individuals. Realism may involve strict dualism, it may speak of two distinct and separate levels of existence. It may also do nothing of the

409

sort and, instead of following the Platonic, accept the Aristotelian moderate realism. In this case no separate existence of the universal constituents is assumed; their distinctiveness and independence are of a logical nature. The *intelligibile,* that is, the subject-matter of abstract knowledge, is distinct from but contained in matter and though inseparable from it in any other way than in thought remains a non-material constituent of reality [219].

The Marxist-Leninist philosophy of science is committed to some definite views concerning the object, nature, and method of scientific knowledge. These views involve certain ontological presuppositions which should be examined as to their compatibility with materialism. Five points in particular are worthy of attention. The Marxist-Leninist philosophy of science assumes that the laws of Nature are invariant and hold without exception. They form a hierarchical order in which laws of greater scope provide an explanation of those with a more limited scope. The laws state a necessary connection of events and the term 'necessary' is not intended to mean the same as the expression 'coincidence or succession admitting no exception'. The laws of Nature are true universal statements and refer to objects and events without regard to degree. They are, therefore, also an idealisation, for actual occurrences are more complex than their conditions assumed by the laws. Finally, scientific investigations are concerned not only with particular classes of occurrences and their interaction, but also with their real aggregates and emergent wholes. The latter are supposed to have properties irreducible to those attributed to their parts severally and are not, therefore, inferable from the characteristics manifested by their constituents in other circumstances. Yet these wholes are subject to laws and the laws of emergent wholes are constitutive of their parts whose nature they modify in a different manner in different combinations [220].

There seems to be a *prima facie* case for the supposition that the Marxist-Leninist philosophy of science operates with a realist and not a nominalist conceptual scheme. If that were true, the danger of Marxist-Leninist philosophy of science coming into conflict with its materialist assumptions would become apparent. The danger of Platonism appears on two levels, the ontological and the logical.

On the logical level the irreconcilability of the realist standpoint in the philosophy of science with that of materialism concerns mainly two points. They are the irreducibility of the laws of Nature to a conjunction of singular statements and the fact that causal laws being true statements are an idealisation, never fully satisfied by any observable instances, that is, they are true in general and, strictly speaking, false in every particular instance. To paraphrase a well-known saying: as far as natural laws refer to reality, they are not true, and as far as they are true, they do not refer to reality.

To examine more closely the first point it is advisable to introduce a distinction which was made by Popper. Two kinds of universal statements should be distinguished: the strictly universal and the numerically universal statements. The first claim to be true for any place and any time and are not, therefore, equivalent to a conjunction of certain singular statements; the second refer to a finite class (though possibly to a very large one) of specified elements to be found in a

410

restricted spatio-temporal region, and are equivalent to a conjunction of appropriate singular statements [221]. A simple example may be provided by the statement 'all men are mortal'. If the term 'men' is given an extensional definition or 'all' is referred restrictively to men who ever lived on the Earth, we have a numerically universal statement. On the other hand, if 'all men are mortal' is interpreted in the manner of modern logic as a statement about everything, free of spatio-temporal restrictions, it is a strictly universal statement.

Aristotle held that natural laws have a restricted validity; he was led to this view by the *a priori* argument that a denumerable infinite class is a self-contradictory entity. His opinion was revived by Whitehead in recent times for some different but also metaphysical reasons. Whitehead rejected the so-called property of simple location attributed to matter by modern science and wished to substitute for it what he called a 'community of occasions in a common space-time'. A somewhat similar view has recently been put forward in Poland [222]. Most scientists and philosophers have adhered to the other point of view and have regarded natural laws as strictly universal statements.

This is also the position adopted in Marxist-Leninist philosophy. It is argued that if natural laws are strictly universal statements they are not translatable into a conjunction of singular statements (which a nominalist cannot supposedly concede). Consequently, they cannot be said to be concerned with individual objects but with something of which the latter are only instances. In traditional terminology this means that laws of Nature involve universals of some sort. Otherwise their claim to universal validity would not be justified [223].

This argument is a little confused and not entirely faultless. The question as to whether a nominalist can accommodate strictly universal statements in his system does not depend on their reducibility to a conjunction of specified singular statements. For if that were the case, the nominalist could not expand them into his own language. This expansion is not to be identified, however, with establishing the equivalence in question, but with the use of bound variables. It is not clear, therefore, why the admittance of strictly universal statements should militate against the principle of nominalism [224].

Moreover, there is no apparent reason why laws of Nature should be regarded as strictly rather than numerically universal statements, though a logically-minded philosopher would support the former alternative [225]. If laws of Nature are regarded as strictly universal statements, this does not necessarily imply that they are existential assertions. For they can be expressed, in the manner of Popper, as prohibitions or proscriptions, to be given the form of non-existence statements, that is, of negations of strictly existential statements [226]. On the other hand, if they are regarded as schematic existential assertions, we are not obliged to admit the existence of universals. It is true that a natural and obvious way of avoiding this snare available for a nominalist is not available for a Marxist-Leninist who repudiates the interpretation of universal statements as propositional schemata. The criticism under discussion seems, therefore, to be justified with respect to his position. The interpretation given to universal statements in Marxist-Leninist philosophy commits it to the recognition of some sort of universals.

There is another confusion in this argument which is worth emphasising. It is said that a universal statement which does not establish an invariant repetition could not be considered a law of Nature. This is one of the reasons why Marxist-Leninists regard laws of Nature as strictly universal statements. Furthermore, they say that a causal law is not merely an assertion of an 'exceptionless' coincidence or succession but also states a necessary connection between cause and effect. Some of them realise that the idea, as Hume put it, of the real power in the objects or events, which we call causes, over their effects, making the effect follow the cause, is anthropomorphic and highly unsatisfactory. They insist, however, that the correlation of occurrences temporally and possibly locally connected should be distinguished from their necessary connection and the efficacious compelling nexus between cause and effect, irrespective of whether we can express the distinction in unambiguous terms. This view is one of the fundamental tenets of Marxist-Leninist philosophy, immune from revision for reasons which have nothing to do with the logical analysis of causality [227].

If laws of Nature are strictly universal statements, this insistence is no longer justifiable. For a strictly universal statement does not put any limitations on the correlation between occurrences to which it refers, but asserts that they follow each other always and everywhere. If a causal law states that the coincidence of occurrences is not only regular but also 'exceptionless', the addition that it is necessary seems to become redundant.

The second logical consideration which seems to put a Marxist-Leninist thinker under the obligation of accepting a Platonic realism of some sort can be stated as follows. If causal laws are true statements, as the Marxist-Leninist philosophy of science asserts, they must be about some ideal objects. For if they are about real entities, they cannot be true or even objectively significant, contrary to the assumption. This follows from the fact that with respect to individual objects causal laws are only approximately true or true within certain limits of probability. To accept such a conclusion would be inadmissible. It would imply that causal laws are not principles of necessitation, universally valid and invariant uniformities imposed by 'objective reality', but conceptual constructions, subjective and arbitrary, similar to Max Weber's ideal types, with a doubtful or non-existent reference to reality [228].

For Marxist-Leninist philosophy this is a major difficulty and no satisfactory suggestion as to how it could be explained away has so far been offered. A nominalist is not committed to the acceptance of ideal gases, levers in perfect equilibrium, or frictionless processes. He can reformulate contrary-to-fact laws as subjunctive conditionals. He is not obliged to regard natural laws as logical statements, either true or false. Since he assumes that existence is significantly predicable only of particulars he is not compelled to admit that causal laws state a connection of universals, which the Marxist-Leninist seems to be compelled to accept. There is a number of various nominalist theories regarding the nature of general statements in empirical science, closely linked with the so-called problem of demarcation, that is, with finding a reliable criterion of distinguishing a metaphysical from an empirical theoretical system. They have one

412

common feature, namely, they provide for the substitution of a probability implication for the implication of logic in the formulation of causal laws. Causal laws are if-then statements of the form 'For every x: if x is A then x is B'. They are empirically testable, confirmed to such and such a degree or eventually falsified, but never empirically verifiable, for their truth cannot be decided with certainty. Causal laws do not necessarily state that always p implies q. In some cases causal laws are probability laws and mean: p implies q to such and such a degree of probability. The degree of probability may be assigned either a metrical or a non-metrical measure, be assessed by the number and weight of reasons in its favour. A causal explanation of an event cannot be inferred from one or more universal laws alone. In addition some singular statements, called 'initial conditions', which describe the 'cause' of the event to be explained, must also be known. The variant initial conditions determine the degree of probability to be assigned to q when p implies q.

Probability logic provides no solution for Marxist-Leninists. They look with intense suspicion or outright disapproval at probability logic, unless it is clearly subordinated to some metaphysical presuppositions. For their approach is metaphysical and not logical or methodological; it is concerned with necessity and chance as metaphysical categories and their relation in the natural world established deductively, that is, by inference from metaphysical principles. The doctrine of chance and necessity in Marxist-Leninist philosophy in Poland is essentially that of Engels, hardly touched by any newer development in the methodology of empirical science. It recognises an 'objective foundation' both for chance and necessary events and involves the demand that the logic and methodology of empirical science should comply with the metaphysical postulates [229].

Engels thought that if chance events were denied altogether and 'only simple, direct necessity prevailed in Nature' (Engels, say Marxist-Leninists, had Laplace's strict determinism in mind), natural necessity would be degraded to the 'production of what is merely accidental' and become some sort of chance. What Engels wished to say is not quite clear. He might have meant that if every event is strictly determined, every event could be explained as an instance of a natural law. This would abolish the difference between an accidental and a necessary coincidence of events and discourage us from the search for laws. Engels seemed to have taken the position that if there were no chance events there would be no necessary events either, in the sense in which necessity is correlative to chance. Engels did not reject the conviction that determinism of some sort is an essential presupposition of science, and he probably believed that the search for laws would ultimately establish the fact that every event is an instance of a natural law or laws. What he objected to was the philosophical position taking for granted what remains to be shown. This becomes clearer perhaps if the Hegelian 'rational necessity' takes the place of Laplace's strict determinism, which, as a rule, is assumed to have been the target of Engels' criticism. For according to Hegel every fact is implied by every other fact in one all-inclusive system of interdependence, and Engels seemed to have aimed at this doctrine when he objected to the belief that the number of peas in a pod is preordained in the constitution of the solar system. This doctrine lays down as a truth of logic what cannot but be a statement of fact and imposes a frame of reference that could be said to leave no room for chance or to degrade necessitation to the level of chance.

This interpretation is consistent with another of Engels' beliefs, namely, that where necessary connection is absent, science comes to an end. For to have knowledge of an event is to know its causes, that is, the causal law under which it can be subsumed, and conversely, an event which cannot be incorporated into a natural law could not be known.

The absence of necessary connections in the case of a chance event cannot, therefore, mean the absence of a cause or causes. A chance event is not an uncaused event and a theory intended to explain it must assume the law of causality. This statement exposes the widespread error that the admission of chance is inconsistent with every kind of determinism and reflects credit upon Engels. But it sets a dilemma in the solution of which Hegel once again came to Engels' rescue. For it was Hegel who identified chance with the contingent, with what may or may not happen and what combines, as Hegel thought, the contradictory characters of the accidental and the necessary. The contingent is necessary in the sense of being causally conditioned, and it is not necessary in the sense of not being strictly causally determined (in the Hegelian terminology: it has its ground outside itself). A chance event occurs where there are alternative possibilities. It comes about as a cumulative effect of a number of causal chains, which happen to intersect and act in conjunction. On this account 'chance' is not an absolute but a relational term and a chance event is said to be something relative with respect to its causal antecedents. It could be different or no chance event at all if its causal antecedent were different [230].

From this viewpoint the introduction of the concept of probability to the logical analysis of causality must appear as inadmissible. It cannot be treated just as a new method of inference in empirical science, supplementing the classical nineteenth century methods of differential equations, which being 'exceptionless' could have been considered as a form of causal laws acceptable to Marxist-Leninist philosophy. Unlike the latter, probability logic contains a disintegrating element for it seems to undermine the validity of the law of causality and bring about the decline of causal laws in the traditional sense. In fairness it should be conceded that this is the claim of the contemporary methodology of empirical science. Without questioning the practical value of the concept of causality for everyday life and, within certain limits, for scientific activity, the view that this concept has outlived its usefulness and is no longer adequate for a precise description of natural phenomena has become prevalent among philosophers in close touch with the development of science.

Marxist-Leninist thinkers still accept the view of Engels that to give up the concept of causality is to repudiate science. For if there were no laws to discover, science would lose every reason for its existence, and scientific laws are always causal laws [231]. This view transformed into some kind of self-evident and incontrovertible truth did not reflect the prevailing opinions in science even at the

414

time of Engels. To-day, the unqualified assertion that genuine scientific knowledge is always knowledge of causes simply cannot be maintained without ignoring or repudiating a large field of science. It is certainly an error to assert that if natural phenomena are not subject to causal laws they are not subject to any laws at all. For causal laws are not the only or even the most important patterns of uniformities in Nature. As a matter of fact, they predominate at the less advanced stage of the development of science and once this stage is overcome the discovery of causes is no longer the main preoccupation in scientific inquiry. This has been recently recognised by some Marxist-Leninists in Poland, but only those of the younger generation; they are inclined to revise the conception of natural law still prevailing among their elders [232].

What is true in the Marxist-Leninist assertion is the historical fact that in the past the law of causality provided a compelling reason to search for universal laws. The law 'All changes take place according to the law of causality' methodologically meant just this 'To give a causal explanation of events is to discover natural laws'. This does not imply that causal explanations alone lead to the discovery of natural laws and that by abandoning the search for causes we abandon thereby the search for universal laws.

The paradoxical aspect of the Marxist-Leninist condemnation of the methodological trend, which regards the concept of causality as vague and inadequate, is the fact that this trend has been inspired by the idea close to the so-called first law of dialectics. The traditional conception of causality, said Mach, is a sort of pharmaceutical conception of the Universe. A dose of effect follows on a dose of cause. Since the natural connections are not often so simple, Mach suggested that the concept of cause should be replaced by that of function, by the conception of the dependence of phenomena on one another. The old concept of causality corresponds to the simplified picture of the world, dominated by the idea that there are isolated events which follow and are invariably connected with each other independently of all events [233].

The Marxist-Leninist view on chance and necessary events is not incompatible with the fact that some phenomena are subject to statistical laws. Although it does not exclude them, they can hardly be considered as genuine laws of Nature. Statistical laws are a makeshift and a temporary device rather than a true reflection of natural regularities, provisionally accepted until causal laws, underlying the statistical ones, are discovered [234]. In particular, causal laws cannot be conceived as limiting cases of statistical laws in which correlations between classes of events or objects with specific properties have a truth-frequency equal to unity. For a Marxist-Leninist is bound to insist that there is a qualitative – and not only a quantitative – difference between a causal and a statistical generalisation. In the former case one exception, that is, one single instance which satisfies the antecedent and falsifies the consequent is sufficient for the refutation of the generalisation. This is not true with respect to a statistical generalisation. For if 'p implies q' means 'p implies q in a certain percentage of instances', a single instance that turns the probability implication into a falsehood is not an exception.

For a Marxist-Leninist, restricted by his various inadequately analysed assumptions, the question 'What are causal laws about?' offers little scope for a satisfactory answer. He regards causal laws as strictly universal, true statements. They express some existential propositions and should be held to be false if there were no entities which they are said to describe. For instance, if the principle of conservation of mechanical energy is a strictly universal true statement, there must be frictionless processes to make it true and in their absence the principle would have to be declared false. Similarly, if Galileo's law about falling bodies is a strictly universal true statement, there must be a medium with no density, an ideal vacuum, in which all bodies fall with the same acceleration. A Marxist-Leninist has closed for himself all the ways of explaining away these existential implications. He cannot consider causal laws as descriptive summaries of observation, forming no essential part of inference, for these summaries do not describe anything observable, and, if they did, they could not be strictly universal, true statements. For a similar reason he cannot account for their contrary-to-fact character by reformulating them as conditionals 'if p were the case, q would be the case'. Neither can he treat them as prescriptions for the formation of predictions, or 'prohibitions', or some other kind of schemata for producing genuine statements. Finally, he cannot consider natural laws in the conventionalist manner as logical constructions and implicit definitions of terms which occur in their formulation. For according to all these interpretations causal laws are not assertive sentences, cannot be either true or false, and are, therefore, not genuine statements at all.

Causal laws cannot be strictly universal, true statements unless they describe some kind of ideal objects, processes and systems, supported by Platonic or Aristotelian realism. This has been clearly realised in the last forty years and prompted different attempts to reformulate universal empirical statements in such a manner that they would be free from ontological commitments to any kind of fictitious ideal objects [235]. These preoccupations are absent in the Marxist-Leninist philosophy of science and involve it in ontological presuppositions which possibly are not deliberately undertaken. An *ad hoc* repudiation of extra-linguistic universals would not remedy the position. For we cannot use a given discourse and simultaneously deny that we do not recognize the kind of objects which are presupposed in it. The discourse of the Marxist-Leninist philosophy of science precludes the possibility that universals are confined to the level of language and logical constructions. They are supposed to be discovered in the natural world as 'exceptionless' recurrences or relations between properties or kinds of events, and in this sense they are real. Engels seemed to have accepted this view. 'The form of universality in Nature', he said, 'is law' [236]. On this assumption it makes sense to say that natural laws are strictly universal, true statements, for this means that they assert connections of universals *in re*.

On the ontological level the conflict between materialism and the presuppositions of the Marxist-Leninist philosophy of science is even more apparent. Its origin is the concept of the whole whose acceptance is urged on ontological and metaphysical grounds as a trait said to be pervasive of reality. Whenever

Marxist-Leninists refer to this concept, they appeal to 'concrete experience', but they must use this expression in a manner different from that commonly accepted for they do not appeal to what can be intersubjectively tested. Their appeal is to what Whitehead called the 'primary article of metaphysical doctrine', to the supposition that 'thought can penetrate into every occasion of fact so that by comprehending its key conditions the whole complex of its pattern of conditions lies open before it'[237]. It is impossible to imagine how the whole could be declared constitutive of its parts, if this power of thought were not explicitly or implicitly recognised.

It is clear that experience alone is insufficient for the establishment of the concept of the whole in the capacity of the fundamental ontological category. It cannot be doubted that there are groups of objects (or sensations) which may be differentiated from their environment because they are more strongly connected with each other than with other elements given in experience. In this sense one can say that elements of such groups are not just a piece but a part of a whole. This was pointed out by Mach who at the same time emphasised the spurious nature of such composites. Although they assert themselves with elementary force, their practical importance not only for the individual but also for the species cannot seriously be doubted. To accept them as ultimate is to succumb to the force of habit. For the demarcation line dividing a whole from its environment is relative and not absolute, subjective and not objective, drawn according to some practical or theoretical requirements. A human being is either a part or a whole, and a part or a whole of a different kind, in accordance with various points of view – biological, demographic, anthropological, sociological, religious – from which we wish to consider him. To say that cohering wholes are natural and enduring structures given in experience would reveal an uncritical attitude of taking habits and points of view determined by theoretical interests for the basic structures underlying reality. The fact that entities and events are related or grouped into complexes does not imply that everything is related to everything else or that we cannot acquire knowledge about simple entities unless we investigate the whole of which they are parts. For there are empirical facts which are certainly causally or otherwise irrelevant to each other and we can examine various simple elements outside the whole which they may enter [238].

For a nominalist the ontological category of integrated units is a platonising ontology which is also devoid of the advantages of some other platonistic ontologies, that is, it does not simplify conceptually the account of any part of reality or of the total world picture. The fundamental point of the holistic philosophies of Hegel, Bradley, and Whitehead might be described as the wish to see the Universe as a 'unified and ordered and seamless whole'[239]. But this vision does not help us to know the Universe and to comprehend its structure. In this respect holistic philosophies are conspicuous by the absence of definite results and by the increase of confusion. For it may be true that the uniformities of Nature form one single intricate web, but if they do there is no other way of acquiring knowledge than by unravelling them and investigating each thread separately.

Some Marxist-Leninists are aware of the fact that their holistic ontology 'dangerously oscillates between the Scylla of physicalism and the Charybdis of Platonism'[240]. There is a Scylla of physicalism because the units or wholes are supposed to be material; in this sense the holistic ontology of Marxism-Leninism accepts the requirement of materialism. On the other hand, however, these material units reveal an internal structure which is not material. This structure is determined by the principle of emergence and modification, which is a property peculiar to wholes. The principle of modification – the internal relations holding between all the parts of the whole – influences the essence of subordinated and enduring, i.e. material entities. The relations are internal because the related terms are in virtue of being related different from what they would have been otherwise. On this account being a part of a whole means being causally changed by the 'laws' which determine this whole and acquiring a new mode of existence characterising the whole.

To accept the view that no terms, that is, lumps of matter (if the materialist is right), are independent of any of the relations (that is, of something which is certainly not material) in which they stand to other terms, and that these non-material constituents of the world qualify, modify and determine the related lumps of matter, is to accept a clearly idealist point of view. This applies equally to both doctrines of internal relations, to be found in Marxist-Leninist philosophy, to its moderate and extremist versions. Neither of them is compatible with materialist monism, both of them accept that the world is neither wholly nor essentially material, since its structure is determined or modified by its non-material constituents, namely, by an intelligible order of relations and interdependence which confers upon matter its emergent characteristics. It is obvious that these matter-modifying relations are not material. Neither are they solely mental. Like the terms they relate, they are supposed to be independent of thought. Being apprehended by and independent of thought, that is, not mind-made, they must be universals.

In the Marxist-Leninist doctrine these universals or complexes of relatedness do not constitute a realm apart (as Whitehead assumed), but are the constitutive element of the wholes of which matter is the other factor. Although universals are logically prior to matter, matter is primordial and irreducible to universals. Aristotelian dualism dilutes and tempers an essentially monistic and Hegelian version of philosophic idealism that the real is the universal.

The complexes of relatedness *in rebus* account for the fact that abstract knowledge has its own subject-matter, disregarded by the nominalist, as well as a significance and meaning, irreducible to a conjunction of singular statements. The object of abstract knowledge is the universals, which while subsisting *in rebus* or rather *inter res* do not constitute the common property of things, taken severally or collectively; neither are they principles of classifying things in arbitrarily selected groups. They are constitutive elements of wholes, subject to and expressed by the 'objective laws of Nature'[241].

According to Marxist-Leninist metaphysics the Universe contains only matter. If its ontological structure is not material, Marxist-Leninist philosophy can no longer be considered as unqualified materialist monism. This is the interpretation which has been suggested to explain Lenin's remarks that 'Nature is both concrete and abstract, both appearance and essence'[242]. The pervasive interconnection of the *intelligibile,* of logically independent constituents with matter, is close to Aristotle's dualism of matter and form. The principle of materialist monism is restricted but retained in virtue of the assumption that matter is primordial and the universal is emergent and evolutionary.

The dialectics of the whole-part relation, epitomised in the conclusion that nothing but the whole of reality or the evolutionary world process, considered as a totality, is ultimately knowable and that nothing can be wholly true unless it is about reality as a whole, has a streak of mysticism which it shares with idealist monism. Marxist-Leninists themselves have been anxious to emphasise another aspect of their venture: they have not offered anything more than some preliminary ideas and a programme of research, which is essentially of a logical and methodological nature [243]. This claim is not justified by what they say and do. The connections of their ideas and programme with logic and methodology are as illusory as in the case of Hegel's logic. Hegel's logic is quite different from what is commonly called logic; in fact, it is a honorific name for metaphysics. The concept of whole is clearly a metaphysical concept. It is not an analytic tool but a means by which the true vision of the world is supposed to be revealed.

Its acceptance implies that beneath the appearances there is concealed an order and structure accessible only to reason which eludes comprehension unless novel categories are applied to their understanding. The research programme, to which Marxist-Leninists refer, is in fact a proposal for a total reconstruction of familiar ways of thinking, based on logic and accredited rules of scientific procedure. As a reward for this reconstruction they promise to lay bare the latent structure and the true reality of thought and the Universe.

This is a classic gambit of all metaphysics, of which two basic types can be distinguished. There are the metaphysics inspired mainly by a theoretical purpose and that whose chief preoccupation is of a moral and social nature. For once the latent structure of reality is established, it is clear that in our moral and social actions we should be guided not by the 'phenomenal' but by the 'noumenal' order. The logical priority of metaphysics over social and moral philosophy does not necessarily mean that metaphysical conjectures also as a matter of fact precede definite moral and social convictions. The order of discovery differs from the order of exposition, and it is not implausible that the relation of metaphysical conjectures to moral and social convictions is no exception to this rule.

It is perhaps no accidental coincidence that in case of the Marxist-Leninist holistic metaphysics the discovery of the only genuine existence of the whole, as contrasted with that of an isolated thing, has been made in the field of the social sciences and history. It is certainly no chance coincidence that procedures adopted by some scholars in the examination of social and historical phenomena are practically the only exemplifications of the superiority conferred upon the method which considers the whole as primary and underivable instead of constructing a whole from separate pieces. The social sciences and history provide a rich hunting ground where the subject-matter itself seems to offer ample evidence that the whole is primary and the 'isolated' fact or event or thing is to be derived from the whole, which gives to its parts their meaning and determines their nature. The alleged fundamental difference between natural science and the humanities can be abolished by showing that the latter do not differ essentially in their subject-matter and method from the former. The unity of all sciences can, however, also be propounded by extending the concepts and methods of the historical and social sciences to the whole of knowledge. This seems to be the course adopted by Marx, who in this respect seems to have been followed by Marxist-Leninist philosophy.

NOTES TO PART V

1. Lenin (2), 48, 57–58. See also Kołakowski (6), 75.
2. Lenin (2), 348.
3. This accounts, for instance, for the invariable hostility shown to the second law of thermodynamics, 'the hypothesis of bourgeois physics', by Marxist-Leninists. See, *e.g.*, Eilstein (3), 125.
4. This is Lenin's argument, inspired by what Engels had already said on this matter. See Marx-Engels (3), Vol. 2, 94, 353. Lenin made much use of it in his polemics against Mach, Avenarius and their followers (Lenin (2), 353–363). Marxist-Leninists have transformed Lenin's argument into a standard justification of their claim that science supports the metaphysics of materialism or even dialectica materialism. See, *e.g.*, Schaff (14), 24.
5. See Engels (2), 279; Lenin (2), 349–350; Schaff (12), 57–58.
6. Simpson (1), 29.
7. Lenin (2), 319.
8. See Carnap (2), 63–64; Margenau (1). Polish physicists who have sympathised with the social and political ideology of Marxism-Leninism without surrendering their power of independent and critical judgement in matters of science and philosophy, supported this point of view, cautiously but firmly, also during the period of intellectual terror in Poland. See, *e.g.*, Infeld-Sosnowski (1).
9. The Christian point of view was expressed in numerous articles published in *Tygodnik Powszechny, Tygodnik Warszawski Dziś i Jutro* and *Znak*. The two main Marxist-Leninist publications are Krajewski (3) and Sejneński (1).
10. See Lenin (2), 48, 58, 62.
11. Schaff (14), 199.
12. Durkheim (2), chapter 6.
13. Marx-Engels (4), 218, 322, 559–560; Marx-Engels (3), Vol. 1, 58; Engels (1), 25, 286. See also Rozental-Judin (1), 69–70.
14. Marx-Engels (3), Vol. 2, 330–331, 362–363; Marx-Engels (1), 15; Engels (1), 31–33, 45, 155.
15. Engels (1), 45–46. Engels closely followed Saint-Simon's ideas. See Durkheim (2), 91–93.
16. Engels (1), 158; Schaff (12), 20.
17. Lenin (2), 203, 345.
18. Frank (1), 75–76.
19. Engels and Lenin frequently referred to Hegel's criticism of Kant's concept of thing-in-itself as one of Hegel's greatest contributions to philosophy. Hegel pointed out that since all knowledge is conceptual, to formulate concepts applying to a thing is to gain knowledge of that thing. Consequently, Kant's unknowable thing-in-itself is nothing unknowable; everything that Kant said about the *noumenon* only shows that he had knowledge of it. There is, therefore, nothing in the Universe that the mind cannot know. From this Hegel drew the conclusion that existence is the possibility of being known by the mind.
20. Lenin (2), 27–28, 232.

421

21. Marx-Engels (3), Vol. 2, 92–94, 335–336, 341, 349–350.
22. See Engels (1), 52–53.
23. Russell (6), 15.
24. Schaff (14), 39–40.
25. Lenin (2), 93.
26. Lenin (2), 47, 122.
27. Kotarbiński (3), T. 1, 109.
28. Kotarbiński (3), T. 1, 108; Ajdukiewicz (21), 18. Compare Paul (1).
29. Lenin (2), 195, 234–235; Schaff (6), 58, 63; Schaff (12), 195–196, 220–221. The criticism of Lenin's point of view is to be found in Łubnicki (7), 290. Łubnicki's objection was raised already in the past by Axel'rod. See Wetter (1), 151–152, 500.
30. Łubnicki (7), 290.
31. Lenin (2), 309.
32. See, e.g., Lenin (2), 45, 62, 121, 351–353.
33. Czeżowski (22), 309.
34. Schaff (6), 56–58, 63; Schaff (14), 180; Martel (1), 289.
35. Schaff (14), 36–47.
36. Helmholtz presented his views on the matter in *Die Thatsachen in der Wahrnemung,* which was translated (in extracts) into Polish by Ajdukiewicz, and Hertz in the introductory chapter to *Principles of Mechanics.*
37. Schaff (14), 127; Lenin (2), 136.
38. Compare Acton, H. B. (1), 38, 64; Lewis (1), 117–145.
39. Mach (1), 81.
40. Lenin (2), 133; Schaff (14), 106–107, 128–130.
41. See, e.g., Kołakowski (6), 87–88.
42. Schaff (14), 44–45.
43. This comes out very clearly in Schaff's observations on Łubnicki's argument against the copy theory of perception which pointed out the gap under discussion. See Schaff (14), 50–51.
44. Lenin (2), 351.
45. Lenin (2), 80, 105, 107–110, 118–122.
46. Nagel (2), 165.
47. Lenin (2), 295–296.
48. See, e.g., Lenin (2), 42, 80, 104, 140, 172; Schaff (14), 42, 47.
49. Lenin (2), 233.
50. Stout (1), 237.
51. Mach (1), 29, 35; Kotarbiński (3), T. 1, 122–133; Czeżowski (22), 36–38.
52. Price (1), 67, 99–102.
53. Ayer (1), 220–228. This point of view has been represented in Poland by Czeżowski. Czeżowski (22), 173.
54. Stout (1), 235.
55. Russell (10), 27.
56. Lenin (2), 195.
57. See, e.g., Lenin (2), 306–307, which, however, is incompatible with what he says of the relation between the image and the imaged material object elsewhere.
58. Lenin (2), 92.
59. Schaff (37); Fritzhand (8); Kuszko (1).
60. Compare Hampshire (1), chapter 1, where a similar attitude is taken, though the starting point is different.
61. Kołakowski (6), 135–137.

62. Kołakowski (19), 44.
63. Kołakowski (6), 87–88, 93, 159–160.
64. Bukharin (2), 23.
65. Marx (1), 107, 155.
66. Marx (1), 104–105.
67. Russell (8), 182.
68. Marx (1), 156–157; Kołakowski (19), 48. This view underlies the analysis of the labour process in *Capital*. See Marx (4), Vol. 1, 177–180.
69. Marx (1), 170.
70. Kołakowski (19), 52–53,56–57.
71. Kołakowski (19), 50–51.
72. The similarity is not as superficial as Kołakowski thinks, if instead of William James' views those of Dewey are considered. Kołakowski does not appear to be acquainted with Dewey's philosophy.
73. Lenin (2), 130; Kołakowski (19), 58–59.
74. Marx (1), 156.
75. Lenin (2), 267.
76. Marx (1), 148; Kołakowski (19), 53, 56.
77. Kołakowski (19), 54.
78. Kołakowski (12), 14–28.
79. Kołakowski (17), a work of considerable erudition and philosophical talent, is the most notable exception.
80. Mannheim (1), 244.
81. Dewey (1), 11.
82. Stebbing (1), 48.
83. Lenin (2), 122.
84. Schaff (14), 51, 100, 109, 131.
85. The last part of the polemical half of the book deals with the views of Wittgenstein, Neurath and Carnap, and was antiquated on the day of its publication, for it refers to the views of these thinkers as they were stated in the early 'twenties and 'thirties respectively.
86. See, *e.g.,* Schaff (14), 75, 225, 233, 249, 300, 324, 354.
87. Schaff (14), 27, 100–101, 107, 111. Brentano is one of those modern thinkers who revived the self-evidence theory of truth in recent times. Schaff contended that through Brentano and Twardowski this particular theory has established itself in the Polish philosophy of the inter-war period (Schaff (14), 103, 400). This claim falls under the category of interpretations intended to create a difference between Schaff's views and those of the Warsaw school, though in fact there is none in this respect. There is no evidence that any of the Warsaw school thinkers considered 'true' and 'self-evident' as logically equivalent terms. See Czeżowski (22), 82–87.
88. Schaff (14), 27–28, 35, 100, 109.
89. Schaff (14), 35–37, 107, 131, 379–380; Kołakowski (6), 106–118.
90. Schaff (14), 18–19; Kotarbiński (3), T. 1, 160–161; Kokoszyńska (4), 167–168. The view that belief is a pre-linguistic occurrence and that it does not need to be expressed in words to be held, is one of Bertrand Russell's reiterated convictions. See, *e.g.,* Russell (6), 227.
91. See Czeżowski (22), 68.
92. Church (1), 23–27; Church (2), 4–5; Carnap (5), 235–236.
93. Schaff (14), 20. Schaff refers the reader to Russell (1), 34–35, 47–49.

94. What Kotarbiński says on this matter in Kotarbiński (3), T. 1, 157–159, should be read in conjunction with Kotarbiński (6), 53–55. In his earlier writings he rejected the use of the expression 'judgement in the logical sense' since it suggested some hypostatised entities. – If the term 'sentence' applies merely to a given indicative sentence, to an individual physical thing, taken in association with its meaning, we may find it difficult to make statements about sentences which have the same meaning. For this reason Tarski preferred to understand by a sentence not an individual inscription but a class of such things which are of the same shape. See Tarski (5), 156.
95. Lenin (2), 125.
96. Schaff (14), 19.
97. Schaff (14), 21.
98. Lenin (2), 57; Schaff (14), 22.
99. Schaff (14), 36.
100. Czeżowski (22), 68; Ajdukiewicz (21), 18–19.
101. Tarski (3), 33–34; Schaff (14), 38, 40, 95, 98.
102. Schaff did not mention the criticism to which *The Nature of Truth* had been subjected by Bertrand Russell and G. E. Moore when it had been published in 1906.
103. Moore (2), 252–266; Russell (2), 193–203. Russell (2) was translated into Polish in 1913, reissued in the period between the two wars and well known to every Polish student of philosophy.
104. Schaff (14), 78–80.
105. Tarski (5), 158.
106. Schaff (14), 95–99.
107. Russell (6), chapter 4. Schaff refers to Russell (6) in connection with the paradox of the liar (Schaff (14), 399).
108. Russell (6), 63.
109. So far as I am aware, this idea was formulated as a methodological principle for the first time in Poland in Ajdukiewicz (3), 8.
110. Lenin (4), 154; Schaff (14), 56–58; Suszko (5), 146–147.
111. Nagel (2), 79; Fraenkel–Bar-Hillel (1), 343–344.
112. Schaff (14), 57–58, 62, 64; Lenin (4), 163, 189.
113. For a different definition of analytic statements see Ajdukiewicz (24), 292.
114. Schaff (14), 65–67.
115. Schaff (14), 65, 67–68, 333–335.
116. Kotarbiński (3), T. 2, 9.
117. Ajdukiewicz (5) and (6). Ajdukiewicz made use of the rules of meaning for the purpose of circumscribing the concept of analytic sentences in colloquial languages in Ajdukiewicz (24). There are some similarities between Ajdukiewicz's views and Nagel's operational interpretation of logical principles. See Nagel (2), 52–92.
118. Ajdukiewicz (24), 296–298.
119. See, *e.g.,* Kotarbiński (3), T. 1, 167–173.
120. 'Egocentric particulars' is a term introduced into the English language by Bertrand Russell. The semantic category of these expressions was first differentiated by Husserl in *Logische Untersuchungen,* Vol. 2. Husserl emphasised their essentially subjective character and called them *'okkasionelle Ausdrücke'.* In Polish they are known as 'occasional expressions' (occasional in the sense of being concerned with a particular occasion).

121. Kotarbiński (3), T. 1, 170.
122. Russell (6), 115.
123. Kokoszyńska (4).
124. Reichenbach (1), 49.
125. Kaufmann (1), 53; Czeżowski (22), 99–104.
126. James (1), 147.
126a. Neurath (1), 12-13; Carnap (3), 121–123, where the view under discussion is also critically examined; Russell (6), 139–149.
127. Lenin (2), 125.
128. Marx-Engels (3), Vol. 2, 328–329; Lenin (2), 127. Lenin's viewpoint has been fully supported by Polish Marxist-Leninists.
129. Carnap (3), 119–120, 124–125; Kokoszyńska (7), 105–112. See also Nagel (4), 2–4, where the impact of methodological developments on philosophical views is concisely discussed.
130. Bergson (1), 297.
131. Schaff (14), 139, 151.
132. Schaff (14), 172, 183; Schaff (35), 97–98.
133. Łuszczewska-Romahnowa tried to reconcile the Marxist-Leninist understanding of the relativity of knowledge with modern developments in the methodology of empirical science. But she did not distinguish Engels' views from those of Lenin and his adherents. See Łuszczewska-Romahnowa (4), 80–81.
134. Schaff (14), 137, 168–169, 191.
135. Schaff (14), 177. This argument is taken from Twardowski, but it is not quite convincing since it does not apply to a more carefully stated version of the relativity of truth. See Kokoszyńska (4), 171.
136. Engels (1), 103; Schaff (14), 172–173; Martel (1), 297.
137. Schaff (14), 137–138, 147.
138. Wollheim (1), 180.
139. Moore (2), 284.
140. Bocheński (2), 97.
141. Engels (1), 105.
142. Compare Moore (2), 284–286.
143. Schaff (14), 159, 169–171; Schaff (35), 95. The fallacy of Schaff's argument is recognised in Kołakowski (4), 341.
144. The distinction between the pragmatical and semantical concept of confirmation is implicitly contained in the conventionalist theory of science. See Czeżowski (22), 107. Czeżowski dealt with the two concepts under discussion in Czeżowski (19).
145. Schaff (14), 157–158, 171; Lenin (2), 314–319.
146. Schaff (14), 147.
147. Hosiasson (1); Carnap (4), 346–348.
148. James (1), 146. Lenin and Schaff use almost the same expression as James.
149. Schaff (14), 144, 195.
150. Schaff (14), 153–155.
151. Lenin (4), 156; Schaff (14), 151–152.
152. Wolniewicz (1).
153. Hegel (1), Vol. 1, 36, 69. Lenin commented upon this passage with approval and admiration. See Lenin (4), 71.
154. Engels (2), 270–321 is a commentary on this single subject and its importance for empirical science.

425

155. Marx (3), 292–300.
156. Schaff (35), 98.
157. Engels (1), 100–104.
158. See, *e.g.*, Lenin (2), 114–130; Schaff (14), 185–197.
159. Lenin (3), 335.
160. Schaff (14), 191–194.
161. Quoted by Wetter (1), 515.
162. Russell (3), 14–21.
163. Ajdukiewicz (33), 4–5, 11–12.
164. See, *e.g.*, Russell (2), 147–149; Russell (7), 758–760.
165. Nowiński (4), 14–15.
166. Lenin (4), 314.
167. Marx-Engels (2), 173.
168. Engels (2), 308, 312–313, 337.
169. Marx-Engels (2), 172–173.
170. Kołakowski (10), 127–129; Kołakowski (7), 134–137.
171. Kołakowski (10), 46–47, 77–78; Kołakowski (7), 138–139.
172. Schaff (2), 15; Schaff (4), 52; Nowiński (4), 50.
173. See, *e.g.*, Ajdukiewicz (21), 124–125; Czeżowski (22), 105–11; Czeżowski (4). In a public discussion in 1956 efforts were made by the non-Marxist thinkers to make their opponents familiar with the basic differences dividing contemporary nominalism and realism. See *Sesja* (3),188–191.
174. Kołakowski (10), 129; Kołakowski (7), 128–136; Greniewski (5), 410–411.
175. Quine (3), 14; Church (2), 9; Schaff (4), 53; Kołakowski (10), 129. Logicism, formalism and the views of logical empiricism are discussed in Suszko (5), without being differentiated from each other and without being related to the debate between nominalism and realism.
176. Kotarbiński (15), T. 2, 184–187; Kotarbiński (24), 13.
177. Quine (3), 127–129; Russell (6), chapter 25.
178. Kołakowski (7), 115. This view on modern nominalism underlies the criticism of Kotarbiński's semantical reism. See in particular Baczko (3), 43–45.
179. Engels (2), 152; Lenin (3), 334; Schaff (4), 53, 59; Schaff (22) 283; Baczko (3), 52–53.
180. Roscelin's and Hobbes' views are explicitly ascribed to the contemporary nominalist doctrine in Schaff (2), 11–12, 14; Baczko (2), 266. Nominalism or vulgar materialism, we are told, reduces concepts to 'empty words' and to verbal utterances, devoid of objective significance.
181. Baczko (3), 49-50.
182. Nowiński (4), 20-24.
183. Schaff (4), 54–59.
184. Nowiński (4), 35-36.
185. The fragmentary nature of the doctrine is recognised by its own supporters. See Schaff (4), 52; Kołakowski (10), 131; Nowiński (4), 17, 50. Its obscurity was deplored by some Marxist-Leninists and non-Marxist thinkers alike at a conference convened for the purpose of discussing it. See *Sesja* (3), 178, 195, 223.
186. The influence of Whitehead's philosophy of organism on Polish Marxist-Leninists is not only apparent in their views but also supported by explicit references to his works. So far as Bradley is concerned, no such evidence is available.
187. Schaff (4), 57–58; Baczko (3), 65.
188. Bocheński (10).

189. Bocheński (10), 40–44.
190. Popper has suggested that the social sciences have been the stronghold of methodological essentialism and that even philosophers who favour methodological nominalism in the natural sciences often remain essentialists in the social sciences. J. S. Mill provides perhaps the most striking instance of this fact. See Popper (3), 29-30; Popper (1), Vol. 1, 190. In the case of Marxist-Leninist philosophy the social sciences have been exercising a decisive influence in rejecting nominalism in favour of essentialism.
191. Quine (3), 115.
192. Leśniewski (3); Kotarbiński (3), T. 1, 16–20.
193. See Schaff (4), 57. The misunderstandings, to which the requirements of social theories and ignorance of elementary logic contribute their share, have recently been aired by Ossowski in Ossowski (17), 128–130.
194. Baczko (3), 56, 63; Nowiński (4), 74–82; Schaff (4), 54. The basic idea of this visionary scheme can be traced to Marx, but Marx did not apply it outside history and the social sciences. See, *e.g.*, Marx (2), 145.
195. Lenin (4), 194.
196. Nowiński (4), 86–100.
197. Kneale (1), 92–103.
198. Nowiński (3), 87.
199. Schaff (4), 58–59.
200. Nowiński (3), 88. Amsterdamski (1) and Reykowski (1) are studies of this sort. The first is, however, nothing more than a chapter from the history of the concept of chemical element and the second is veiled in obscurities and generalities which do not elucidate the psychological process of concrete abstraction.
201. Whitehead (1), 141–142.
202. Kołakowski (7), 154–157; Schaff (22), 286, 289. The concept of real aggregate plays a considerable role in Bukharin's sociology, where it is introduced as a structural principle underlying all natural processes. See Bukharin (1), 84–85.
203. The present state of the discussion on the concept of emergence is summarised in Hempel-Oppenheim (1), 331–337.
204. Kołakowski (7), 158–160; *Sesja* (3), 184–185.
205. Hegel (1), Vol. 2, 115–117, 119; Nowiński (4), 79.
206. Marx (4), Vol. 1, 47; Kołakowski (7), 151–153.
207. Moore (1), 278–279.
208. Kołakowski (7), 153–154; Schaff (22), 280–281, 284–286.
209. Nowiński (4), 52–53, 56; Rolbiecki (1), 74.
210. Nowiński (3), 86–87.
211. Moore (1), 276–309; Russell (1), 224–226; Russell (2), chapter 14; Nagel (3), chapter 15.
212. Lenin (4), 264.
213. Nowiński (3), 44.
214. *Sesja* (3), 262–263.
215. Stalin (3), 5–13, 93; Lenin (4), 125–127; Lenin (2), 150; Schaff (22), 32, 36; Modzelewski (1), 87; Michajłow (2), 114; Tomaszewski (3), 85–86; Ingarden, R.S. (1)–(3).
216. Engels (2), 307–308.
217. Engels (2), 54, 315–317; Stalin (3), 8; Schaff (22), 42–45; Michajłow (2), 123.
218. Kołakowski (7), 116, 159.
219. Kołakowski (7), 118–119, 124. Kołakowski's definition of nominalism probably

aimed at Kotarbiński's reism. His account of nominalism as a conceptual scheme underlying scientific theories was criticised from the non-Marxist viewpoint in Czerwiński (1).

220. Kołakowski (7), 141–159.
221. Popper (5), 62.
222. Whitehead (2), 45; Pelc (1), 30–40. Pelc has suggested that the universality of natural laws is restricted by their limitations to a definite space-time region but unrestricted with respect to the class of things or events to which natural laws apply.
223. Kołakowski (7), 141–143. See also Pelc (1), 25–27.
224. See Czeżowski (9), 134–135, where this objection is succinctly stated. Some logical empiricists once asserted that if natural laws are strictly universal statements they must be unverifiable, that is, meaningless. Consequently, they suggested that natural laws are not propositions but propositional schemata or proposition-forming instructions. Kołakowski appears to have confused the question of verifiability in its old, now antiquated formulation of logical empiricists, with that of the alleged existence of abstract entities, which in his view the acceptance of strictly universal statements implies.
225. In Grzegorczyk (6), 212–213, this choice is convincingly argued.
226. Popper (5), 68–69.
227. Schaff (6), 143–144; Kołakowski (7), 145–149. Schaff writes that one cannot dispense with the 'law of causality', in the sense of its being a principle of necessitation, unless one is ready to give up the scientific world outlook. 'Such attempts have been undertaken only by those who being anxious to preserve their class privileges at any price, are ready to sacrifice even science whenever science interferes in any manner with the means leading to this end' (Schaff (6), 152–153). Anthropomorphism consists in assigning human qualities to physical objects. When the law of causality confers efficacy upon natural causes this does not mean that a human quality is ascribed to them, as the idealist anti-anthropomorphism asserts, but that man is considered as a particular natural object instantiating an universal property of matter (Eilstein (9), 149).
228. Kołakowski (7), 149–150; Schaff (6), 147–148; Kryszewski (1), 228.
229. Schaff (6), 155–159; Schaff (22), 147–148; Krajewski (10), 103–175; Ładosz (1); Złotowski (1). For a concise characteristic of the concept of chance in Marxist-Leninist philosophy see Kotarbińska (1), 164–166; Szaniawski, K. (2), 79–80.
230. Engels (2), 288–293; Bukharin (1), 44–46.
231. Schaff (6), 144.
232. See Eilstein (9), 165–172.
233. Mach (1), 89; Mises (2), 152.
234. This is one of the important reasons why the Polish supporters of the 'materialist methodology' rejected the Copenhagen interpretation of the quantum theory. In their view the Copenhagen interpretation has 'identified probability with the absence of causality'. They welcomed the alternative interpretation of the quantum theory put forward by David Bohm and were in general agreement with the philosophic views of the Soviet physicists D. I. Blochincev and J. P. Terleckij. Blochincev and Terleckij suggested that the statistical treatment of the quantum theory would eventually be supplemented by a fuller account more in agreement with the conceptual framework of classical physics and the views on necessity and chance of dialectical materialism. See Plebański-Werle (1), Plebański (1), Eilstein (2). Simultaneously the biologists were warned against the application of statistical

methods, which frequently lead to 'arbitrary conclusions'. See *Statystyka* (1), 99.

235. Czeżowski (22), 105–111. Czeżowski refers to Ramsey (1), 237–255, who was the first to notice this implication.
236. Engels (2), 288–293.
237. Whitehead (2), 28.
238. Criticism along these lines can be found in *Sesja* (3), 198–199.
239. Wollheim (1), 282.
240. Kołakowski (7), 159.
241. Kołakowski (7), 160; Nowiński (4), 58–62.
242. Lenin (4), 180; Nowiński (3), 44. Lenin's comment should be read in conjunction with Hegel (1), Vol. 2, 429, to which it refers. There is another commentary of Lenin inspired by the chapter on *The Absolute Idea* in Hegel (1) which is very revealing in this context. 'The relationship of every thing (phenomenon, etc.)', Lenin wrote, ' is not only often manifold but also general, universal. Every thing (phenomenon, process, etc.) is connected with every other' (Lenin (4), 194).
243. Kołakowski (7), 159–160.

PART SIX

MARXIST-LENINIST HISTORICISM AND
THE CONCEPT OF IDEOLOGY

INTRODUCTION

The questions to be considered in this Part belong to critical rather than speculative philosophy of history [1]. Critical philosophy of history is a sober and modest kind of philosophical inquiry concerned with the examination of historical thinking, which was revived after the Second World War particularly in Anglo-Saxon countries. But since the Marxist-Leninist philosophy of history is mostly governed by problems of the speculative sort, it may not always be possible to keep within these limits.

According to Marxist-Leninists, the whole Universe and every part of it is in constant change, motion, transformation and development. Since any determinate existence has a history of its own, all knowledge is in fact historical. We cannot avoid inquiring into the temporal sequences of past events and must base knowledge of the present on knowledge of the past. Each branch of science and learning has a theoretical and a historical part and it is the latter that provides the key to the understanding of the former. It is history that helps us to understand the theoretical systems of science and learning and not conversely, as is commonly assumed.

This view emphasises the evolutionary character of reality and its laws and sets it against the eternal permanence supposedly ascribed to Nature and society by non-materialist philosophy. For instance, in Newton's physics and the political economy of the French physiocrats it is assumed that laws were fixed by the Creator for all time. The doctrine of eternal permanence supports the belief that the regularity of natural and social phenomena is established by divine legislation and kept in order by God's providence.

It was Hegel who began to resolve the doctrine of eternal permanence of order in Nature and society, but only Marx and Engels fully accomplished this task. We know only one science, they wrote, the science of history. One can distinguish in it the history of Nature and the history of man, but the distinction is analytic and not factual. For as long as men exist, the history of Nature and human history condition one another. History is the basic science to which every branch of knowledge must refer its findings for an ultimate explanation of their meaning and function in the sum total of man's experience. Without historical knowledge, comprising the entire life of society, that allows us to acquire an increasing mastery over the historical process itself, man would have no sense of direction and his destiny would continue to be governed by the operation of blind forces, some of which he himself created, without being able to control them and to make them work towards some man-determined ends. 'Science', wrote Deborin referring in fact to historical knowledge, 'gives men vision, lifts the curtain of the future and allows them to act consciously in a definite direction' [2].

Historical knowledge restricted to the history of man has, in Marxist-Leninist terminology, a wider scope than in the common usage. It absorbs much of the subject-matter of the social and cultural sciences, and also providis them with their basic premisses and rules of procedure. Any socio-cultural thinking should be related to the knowledge of the world historical process as a whole and be considered as its component part. Historical inquiry does not examine aspects of man's existence, various temporal sequences of past events, but has a distinctive subject-matter – the world historical process (the 'grand phenomenon' of Hegel, *la marche fondamentale du développement humain* of Comte), subject to its own internal laws of development, which hold sway 'both in history as a whole, and at a particular period and in particular lands'[3]. It is not, therefore, sociology, psychology, anthropology, economics, political science, art, or literature that provides the basis for the understanding of history, but it is historical knowledge that enables us to understand all the social sciences and man's cultural achievements. For the same reason a Marxist-Leninist is not satisfied to search for specific laws of social and cultural change but tries to discover the laws of history, *i.e.* the regularities to which the historical process conforms and which bring about the succession of its uniform patterns.

Like its immediate predecessor, the positivism of Saint-Simon and Comte, Marxian doctrine is a historical philosophy. It is permeated by the sense of growth, evolution, and, to some extent, of continuity brought into the world by man's action. Marx saw and examined the fundamental problems of life in terms of history and Marxism-Leninism has remained faithful to this inheritance. It is also a historical philosophy and this fact had some practical and significant effects. The belief that every work of the human hand and mind is a link in a chain that stretches back into the long past and points to the distant future has created, in principle, favourable circumstances for historical studies of every sort.

It should be clear from these observations that Marxist-Leninists reject the opinion that history is a distinctive procedure of inquiry into any subject-matter rather than a branch of knowledge with a distinctive subject-matter. These two radically different points of view have been named by a non-Marxist Polish historian the 'immanent' and the 'transcendent' interpretation of history respectively. The immanent interpretation sharply differentiates between history and meta-history or philosophy of history. History describes past events in terms of their own standards and values and from the perspective of men involved in described occurrences; meta-history is an attempt to go beyond actual happenings to the regularity or pattern concealed behind them. This demands the abandonment of the standpoint of the observer and the application of a theory of historical causation. The immanent interpretation of history is history *sensu stricto*, the transcendent interpretation abandons the historian's level of understanding and propounds theories, which, by the historian's standards of warranted knowledge, cannot claim scientific validity. For these theories rest on necessarily insufficient data and on unjustifiable generalisations [4].

The immanent interpretation of history is regarded by an overwhelming majority of historians as the historical outlook *par excellence*. It was given the name of *Historismus* in German historiography for which in the English language the term 'historism' has been suggested. It conceives the investigated historical process as one of growth and development, refrains from applying to any age or period standards which were foreign to them, and tries to do justice to each according to its own lights [5]. Historism implies the concern with particular events and sets itself limited aims. In this sense its method of investigation can be described as idiographic or individualising.

Historism does not subscribe, however, to the idiographic doctrine, a synthesis of the theories of Dilthey, Windelband and Rickert, according to which the subject-matter of history is the totality of unique or unrepeatable events. This doctrine implies, as has sometimes been said, that the historian applies only 'singular concepts' and abandons the use of general statements. A programme of this sort would clearly be unworkable and its starting point gives a false account of the historian's activity. Historism does not deny that historians make use of general concepts in their descriptions and of generalisations in their explanations of the sequence and connection of events. Historians only insist that however necessary and illuminating such general propositions and *obiter dicta* might be, they are not the essential purpose of their work. They want to 'find the truth about this or that', to establish which particular facts happened in the past, and to explain causally or otherwise singular events. [6] The supporters of the immanent interpretation of history in Poland, and that meant practically all the working Polish historians, did not regard history as an idiographic science in the so-called Rickertian sense [7].

Historism is essentially a methodological doctrine, but some ontological conclusions are sometimes drawn from it. It has been said that the plurality of histories points to ontological pluralism; that it supports the view that there is no such thing as one single historical process; and that history is not an 'efficient cause'. It has also been said that the temporal plurality of histories, *i.e.* the continual change of the principles of selections and perspectives applied to the same subject-matter, as well as the simultaneous multiplicity of different points of view which the historian can adopt, establishes the fact that history has no unique and universally valid meaning. If this conclusion is accepted, historical relativism acquires a new epistemological significance. For it gives a clearer understanding of the problems dominating every kind of historical research in which one has to take account of one's own situation to assess the significance of the results obtained. The recognition of our own active role in historical inquiry brings into relief the eternal gulf between 'history as it is' and our partial knowledge of it. This means progress in historical understanding and in self-awareness [8].

Whether this is or is not regarded as a valid argument against ontological and historical monism, the decision does not affect historism as a methodological doctrine. Historism is not a speculative philosophy of history, but a working historian's remedy for historiosophy. It came into being as a reaction to Hegel's philosophy of history and has continued to oppose similar attempts to substitute meta-history for history. (Geyl's criticism of Toynbee's *Study of History* is a recent instance). The approach to history as a rational whole with its distinct patterns and laws, by reference to which historical events acquire meaning, can be explained and predicted, has been named by Popper 'historicism' [9]. The irreconcilability of historism and historicism is manifested in their respective manner of inquiry (though, sometimes, the latter grew out of the former as a salvation from what Arnold Toynbee described as the 'nonsense view of history'), a point made perfectly clear by Popper's incisive critical analysis of historicism.

According to Marxist-Leninist historicism, the immanent approach deforms the subject-matter of history. It regards history as nothing but an assemblage of individual facts. It dissects the context, cuts the historical process into externalised parts, divorces one fact from another and makes it an abstraction linked with another abstraction by purely external relations of time, space, resemblance, causation, contiguity and the like [10]. In contradistinction to historism, or, as Marxist-Leninists say, historical immanentism, historicism conceives the subject matter of history as a whole whose various parts bear upon, overlap and interpenetrate each other. This presupposes belief in the historical world process, which gradually unfolds itself to successive generations of mankind, but whose dynamic factors and inner laws can be known to any man. This sets a historian a task different from that which historism wishes to perform. The historical process is not a sequential order of discrete facts to be described in their uniqueness, however desirable it might be for some limited purpose, but a stream of events growing organically out of and related to each other, to be shown as a unity or a potentiality striving for realisation. Moreover, if every event is an integral part of the world historical process, neither can its existence be apprehended, nor its nature known until the relations of this part to everything else have been considered and thereby its inner nature revealed in its true light. This can be achieved by subsuming it under historical laws, that is, by showing that it was brought about by the operation of forces which determine the pattern of change in conformity with historical laws.

There are two related but distinct strands in Marxist-Leninist historicism. The first is of Hegelian origin. When Engels introduced it in *Ludwig Feuerbach* he simply paraphrased a famous passage from Hegel's *The Philosophy of History* [11].

Historical events, wrote Engels, may appear to be governed by chance, for the spectacle which they offer is that of innumerable individuals, each of whom strives for his own desired ends. These ends cross and conflict with one another, or are incapable of realisation and have consequences quite different from those intended. And yet history being the 'resultant of these many wills operating in different directions and of their manifold effects upon the outer world' is governed by 'inner, hidden laws', in relation to which individual ends, motives and desires are only of secondary importance. For while people strive to gratify their interests, they thereby accomplish something else, latent in their actions, though not included in and transcendent to their designs. Their passions are

436

informed with general considerations and these are interrelated and interact to bring into existence the web of history, woven of constitutional and political forms, political, juristic, and philosophical theories, religious views and their development into systems of dogmas. Through the totality of these interrelated forms and events there asserts itself the necessity, 'forming the red thread which runs through them and alone leads to understanding' [12].

The discovery of the decisive movement that finally asserts itself in history as a whole shows how illusory 'empirical history' must remain and how futile and narrow-minded the academic erudition of a 'technical' historian is. For he treats historical facts as disjointed occurrences and pursues the hopeless task of discovering the truth by collecting humbly and patiently isolated facts, which, as such, cannot be an object of historical knowledge. The Hegelian idea of history exercised a powerful influence on the minds of Polish Marxist-Leninist historians of whom it might be said that they were Hegelians first and Marxist-Leninists second [13].

The other strand in Marxist-Leninist historicism is the Marxian theory of historical causation. It identifies the 'ultimate driving forces of history' with the productive forces of society and its mode of production which dynamically manifest themselves in the existence of classes and in the class struggle as the *modus operandi* of underlying historical factors. Together with the Hegelian idea of the universal interconnectedness and interdependence of historical events, it lays down the methodological rule that every social system and movement in history, every school of thought in the social sciences, philosophy, literature and art must be evaluated from the standpoint of the economic conditions which gave rise to them. 'For only such an approach', stated Stalin in one of his pronouncements, quoted frequently, 'saves the science of history from becoming a jumble of accidents and an agglomeration of most absurd mistakes' [14].

From the viewpoint of Hegelian historicism the immanent interpretation of history was solely a methodological error. The procedure chosen by its exponents was inadequate to its subject-matter and bound to result in misreadings of the historical process. The criticism based on Hegel's view of history would not take advantage of arguments different from those which, for instance, G.R. Collingwood used against positivistic historiography. Hegel's conception of historical process combined with the Marxian economic historicism, further simplified in Stalin's doctrine concerned with the relations between basis and superstructure, threw quite a different light on the immanent interpretation of history. There was no longer the question of a mere methodological error, but of a methodological error with an ideological significance and function to be revealed by relating it to the underlying class struggle.

The immanent interpretation of history does not start with the investigation of its subject-matter as it exists by itself, but sets up certain procedures, which, being arbitrarily chosen or determined by an ulterior motive, deform what they purport to describe. On the other hand, the Marxist-Leninist approach to history takes the historical process as its point of departure and formulates the principles of investigation in accordance with its specific traits.

437

Historical facts do not disclose anything by themselves, historical knowledge grows by the accumulations of solutions to problems raised. To ask questions we must be in possession of a conceptual scheme, and questions have a definite meaning within the framework of a theory. A historian cannot, therefore, investigate facts without the guidance provided by a theory. The question of which is the correct theory is to be decided on the ground of philosophical considerations. The criteria by means of which the relevance of the historian's conceptual categories and the validity of his theoretical assumptions, that is, their agreement with objective reality, can be established, are provided by philosophy. There is no divergence between Nature and history, the categories and laws that govern natural development also apply to the historical process. Since historical materialism is an extension of dialectical materialism in the study of social life and history, the dialectics of Nature provide the basis for the dialectics of history. Owing to this, the 'science of the history of society, despite all the complexity of the phenomena of social life, can become as precise a science as, let us say, biology' [15]. Philosophy helps us to establish the totality of laws to which the historical process conforms.

This is essentially a Hegelian idea. For according to Hegel what is a hypothesis in the domain of history can be demonstrated in philosophy. If Reason governs the world, it governs its history as well. Nothing less than Reason itself is required; for the 'fancies, in which an individual indulges, cannot be the model for universal reality' [16]. Marxist-Leninists claim empirical validity for their own manner of demonstrating the truth of historical materialism. In their opinion dialectical materialism is an empirically valid theory, and historical materialism is logically implied by dialectical materialism. Moreover, as Engels argued, modern developments have greatly simplified once concealed interconnections of events. At present to deny the assumptions of historical materialism on what are the ultimate driving forces of history and the laws of their operation, is to close one's eyes deliberately so as not to see the patent facts of the historical process [17]. Engels' appeal to the evidence provided by current political, social, and economic developments has been widely used ever since, though rather by statesmen and politicians than by philosophers and social scientists. The latter prefer to speak of the 'historical verification' of Marxist-Leninist theories [18]. This is hardly an improvement upon Engels' original idea, since it expresses a judgment by political sympathy and ideological affinity in neutral but misapplied scientific terms. A theory of such generality and abstractedness as historical materialism is not capable of verification in any simple or direct manner, whether historically or otherwise.

In the preceding pages attention has frequently been drawn to the fact that the source of various philosophical theories to which Marxist-Leninists adhere should be sought in their sociological ideas and political convictions. To justify the manner in which they try to change the world, Marxist-Leninists have formulated a picture of the world that in its all-pervasive traits, structures and laws is supposed to provide the warrant for their action. In the Marxist-Leninist 'socio-cosmic' conception of the Universe circular thinking is clearly involved.

But to its supporters it appears as a structure 'cast from a single piece of steel', from which 'you cannot eliminate one basic premiss, one essential part, without departing from objective truth' [19]. Lenin spoke more truly than he knew.

The philosophy of history is the nucleus of the Marxist-Leninist system; it is the starting point and the destination of the circular thinking by means of which the 'socio-cosmic' conception of the Universe comes into being and in turn lends its support to the views on history and society, as well as on what is worthy of man's efforts and devotion. For the dichotomy of matters of fact and matters of value is established by the rules of scientific procedure and is non-existent in thinking based on ideological premisses, in which values and ideas are interlocked. Marxist-Leninists have no difficulty in deriving recommendations and moral precepts from the 'analysis of facts', in bridging the gap between what is, could or might be, and what ought to be. The impervious crust of absolute certainty, which surrounds the Marxist-Leninist philosophy of history, results from its proximity to the total ideological attitude, underlying the doctrinal system, to its inherent value components and value-determined principles, which govern the arrangement of concepts, the organisation of evidence, and the construction of theories.

This will become clear in the course of the examination of Marxist-Leninist historicism and of the concept of ideology. The selection of these two problems has been prompted by the consideration that Polish Marxist-Leninists have made some contributions to their elucidation and elaboration which go beyond what can be found in Soviet Marxism-Leninism. Moreover, the evolution of the concept of ideology played an important role in the development of events leading to the rejection of dogmatism and the revival of critical inquiry in Poland. The closing part of the chapter will review the methodological premisses on which Marxist-Leninists wished to base and to rewrite the history of philosophy and the unexpected outcome of this undertaking.

CHAPTER 27

THE METHODOLOGICAL APPROACH

Since the last quarter of the nineteenth century, philosophers and historians have been involved in the controversy as to whether history provides knowledge *sui generis* or is a branch of science. Philosophers who support the latter alternative justify their view by a logical examination of the subject-matter and methods of history, which leads them to the conclusion that the reasons advanced for a sharp differentiation of history from science are untenable. This is also the view adopted by Marxist-Leninists but they reach it by a method of their own.

The Marxist-Leninist examination of historical thinking begins with laying down the conditions which it must satisfy to be a branch of scientific knowledge. The conditions are established by an *a priori* argument. To be a science history must recognise the existence of historical laws, make the search for these laws its chief preoccupation, and demonstrate that determinism rules supreme over the whole course of historical development. To recognise that the development of society and its history conforms to objective regularities and causal necessity, is to adopt the materialist standpoint. On the other hand, to deny that there are historical laws is to reduce history to the level of narration and explanation concerned with sequences of unique events. This is the idealist approach to history which either keeps historical inquiry at its pre-scientific stage or destroys it as a scientific activity. For scientifically valid and significant knowledge is always knowledge of laws. As Bukharin put it, the "Windelband-Rickert opposition of 'history' to 'theory' must be put away in the archives" [20].

This argument eliminates at a high level of abstraction any method of historical inquiry which does not consist in the discovery of laws. It does not reach its conclusion upon a prior examination of what principles underlie historical thinking and what a historian tries to do, but sets some standards of procedure as obligatory and tells historians what they ought to achieve. To suppose that one knows in advance what the right method with respect to a subject-matter is, is to commit oneself to an *a priori* conception of scientific method. The appropriateness and fruitfulness of a method cannot be proved *a priori* without running the risk of being led astray by false analogies or preconceived ideas. In the case of Marxist-Leninists, these preconceived ideas are written plain and large in what they say on the subject.

The first of them is the acceptance of the naive point of view that the historian can make a survey of the past and describe it as if it were there, for everybody to observe and to contemplate, with the same self-evident substantiality and existence independent of the mind as things of the common sense world have. This naive point of view prevailed in historiography until the establishment of modern historical scholarship in the nineteenth century, it ruled supreme in the philosophy of history, with the notable exception of Kant, and culminated in Hegel's idea of the 'grand phenomenon' of the world history. It was Hegel who in the introduction to his lectures on the philosophy of history informed his audience that what he was going to say would be a 'summary view' of the whole course of history which 'happens to be known to me because I have traversed the entire field' [21]. Marxist-Leninists often seem to vie with Hegel in this respect and they too make the claim to some kind of direct acquaintance with the world historical process. This claim is closely related to their adherence to the common sense view on the reality of the external world.

The hypostatisation of the subject of history, which has neither the spiritual subsistence of the Hegelian idea nor should be visualised in the image of Heraclitus' river, for its reality is apparent and created through man's constant effort to gain knowledge of his past, results from an implicit or explicit subordination of history to a philosophical principle, the *proton pseudos* of every speculative philosophy of history. The course advocated by Marxism-Leninism is precisely that which the founders of modern historical scholarship, Ranke or Burckhardt, had most emphatically repudiated as unhistorical and based on false premises.

Expressed in terms of contemporary methodology, Marxist-Leninists confuse two totally different questions. They rightly assume that historical inquiry cannot dispense with some heuristic constructs, generalisations, and universal laws, and that the latter are as indispensable in historical research as in natural science. This particular point, taken by them for granted, has been established by Max Weber and, more recently, by logical empiricists. It does not imply, as Marxist-Leninists seem to think, that the search for universal laws is the essential purpose of historical inquiry. Max Weber, perhaps more than anybody else, contributed to the realisation that in the historical sciences the knowledge of the universal and general is not valuable in itself, but merely as a means and a heuristic instrument for attaining a causal explanation and an interpretative understanding of the significance which a concrete constellation of reality has for us in certain individual situations. To give a causal explanation of historical events the historian refers to recurrent causal relationships of everyday experience and to universal laws. But no law, unless it is a value-judgment or a precept in disguise, can tell us anything about the significance of causally connected events. Their value-relevance is 'logically rooted' in the fact that men are cultural beings, endowed with the will and capacity to adopt a deliberate attitude towards the world and to confer significance upon it [22].

Weber's emphasis upon the value-interpretative approach and its priority in historical inquiry over psychological, sociological, economic and other kinds of explanations, reinforced the opinion that all knowledge of historical and cultural reality is always knowledge from a particular point of view, and, consequently, that it is never free from presuppositions and value-premisses. This does not imply that historical inquiry cannot establish any valid results and transcend the boundaries of the historian's arbitrary world. For once the choice, circumscribed by the values involved, is made, there is nothing subjective or arbitrary in the historian's procedure. He has to follow causal sequences, to submit to the evidence and universally valid rules of inference. On the other hand, Weber again put into relief the fact, which few historians ever questioned, that historical inquiry is concerned with the description of particular events. Although the historian cannot do without heuristic constructs, general and universal laws, his specific interest in singular events as such requires specific procedures. The logic of historical explanation can be only partly identified with the patterns applied in natural science. It also needs some methods of its own.

The Marxist-Leninist assumption that history would have no scientific significance if it did not search for laws which govern historical events is a survival of the times when the so-called principle of causality was regarded as a necessary presupposition of all scientific inquiry. The metaphysical belief in causality prompted the identification of scientific inquiry with the discovery of causal laws: *Scire est per causas scire*. For reasons of its own, nineteenth century positivism strongly fostered the belief that no inquiry is scientific unless it establishes laws. This prompted Durkheim to refuse history the name of science and to doubt whether it could ever gain this distinction [23]. From this viewpoint singular events were of no interest unless they provided particular instances to confirm or illustrate a generalisation or a law. The interest in singular events as such was outside the sphere of science and could not be reconciled with the nature and purpose of scientific inquiry.

Marxist-Leninists thought that this view, nowadays somewhat old-fashioned, could be supported by some fresh arguments. In their opinion, the results of the controversy over the subject-matter of history conducted more than fifty years ago and revived in the 'thirties in connection with the neo-positivistic programme of the unity of science supplied decisive evidence for the possibility of reducing history to a system of laws.

One of the difficulties obstructing the feasibility of the neo-positivistic programme was the dualistic conception of science, its division into *Naturwissenschaften* and *Geisteswissenschaften*, natural inquiries and human studies, which had a considerable following on the Continent of Europe in the first decades of this century. It was widely accepted that what was variously called historical, moral, or cultural sciences, human studies or the humanities, differed from natural science not only in their respective procedures, individualising in the case of the former, generalising in that of the latter, but also in their respective subject-matter. While natural science deals with recurrent or repeatable occurrences, the humanities are always concerned not only with specific and singular but also with unique and non-recurrent events. This view was challenged by logical empiricists. Uniqueness is not a distinctive characteristic of historical events. Every event is unique, if thereby all its characteristics are meant, and in this sense no event, whether natural or historical, repeats itself. But events which are unique in this sense can have some common or similar specific characteristics, and this applies equally to both categories of events. For instance, every battle is a unique combination of circumstances and differs from every other battle. But they have also some similar characteristics, because otherwise we could neither appreciate the uniqueness of each nor even refer to them by means of a common term [24].

Logical empiricists were content to disprove the assertion that 'unique' is a characteristic to be exclusively ascribed to historical events and that 'unique' is an absolute and not a relational predicate. For if 'unique' were an absolute predicate, no complete description of an event could be accomplished. Similarly, the past could not even be narrated. As Professor Butterfield observed, 'between a succession of absolutely unique particles there can be no thread that would hold a narrative together' [25]. The view that the variety of historical events surpasses in degree the variety of other events, but that all events are 'unique' in some sense of this term, which is compatible with attributing to them common or similar specified characteristics, gave an operational meaning to the unique individuality of historical events. We speak of recurrent or non-recurrent events in accordance with procedure, generalising in the first, individualising in the second case.

Logical empiricists did not deny or try to obscure the distinction between the historical and natural sciences, which indubitably exist. They only emphasised that the recognition of the distinction does not imply either an ontological difference in the subject-matter of the historical and natural sciences or a total incomparability of their respective procedures, comprising, in fact, some common elements, mixed up together in most branches of knowledge and applied in a pure form only in the two instances of the extreme opposites, in theoretical physics on the one hand and in a historical chronicle on the other [26].

This conclusion did not satisfy Polish Marxist-Leninists. They adopted the operational definition of uniqueness, established by logical empiricists, but rejected the opinion that an idiographic science, applying individualising methods, is either possible or desirable [27]. For if all events are recurrent relative to some specified characteristics, uniqueness or unrepeatability is only a cor-relative concept with no factual reference. There can be no science of the unique and non-recurrent; it would require an infinite number of statements to describe an event in its unique individuality. Consequently, historical inquiry cannot be concerned with specific singular events in so far as they are unique, but only with respect to some of their recurrent traits. Recurrence provides, however, a logical ground for the acceptance of generalisations and universal laws. This establishes the case that in historical inquiry the subject-matter itself imposes the task of searching for general and universal laws. As Engels has shown, the only alternative to the conception of history which ultimately faces an incoherent 'flux of disturbing fortuities' and has to give up the possibility of acquiring any kind of knowledge, is to base historical inquiry on the acceptance of historical laws and to explain the events by means of recurrent patterns governed by these laws. Marxism-Leninism adopts the second conception, which is supposed to provide the only basis for a scientific study of history [28].

There are some serious difficulties inherent in this point of view, discovered long ago and overlooked by Marxist-Leninists. Before they are considered, another point requires elucidation. When Marxist-Leninists say, 'There are historical laws', they do not mean, 'It is our conjecture that there are historical laws and for this reason we search for these laws and encourage others to follow in our footsteps'. The statement 'There are historical laws' means literally 'There are historical laws, for they have been discovered'. Because of this, the fact that historical events exhibit recurrent characteristics carries a logical significance, which it would not have otherwise. A recurrent sequence of events does not justify by itself the existence of universal laws, because a statement of recurrent sequence is not necessarily a universal law [29]. On the other hand, if there are historical laws, there must also be repeatable sequences of social elements or patterns which recur at intervals. There could be no such repeatable patterns, if historical events were unique. Therefore, the recurrence of events with specified characteristics, however different they may be in other respects, corroborates the existence of historical laws.

This argument involves the fatal flaw of circular thinking, which was exposed with painstaking thoroughness by Max Weber in his examination of analytical constructs, of ideal types in particular, and of their role in the logic of explanation in the historical and cultural sciences. The assumptions of historical materialism define a point of view or provide principles of selection, by means of which facts are construed and arranged, conceptual schemes are constructed, stages and periods are distinguished [30]. Weber emphasised that the clarity and explanatory power of such analytical constructs may produce the temptation to mix theory with history, 'ideas' with 'things', as Marx would have said, and to transform a point of view into a system of objectively valid laws. This would reverse the respective roles of facts and theoretical assumptions. The heuristic analytical instruments are framed for the purpose of serving historical knowledge and the confusion of theory and history with each other reduces historical knowledge to the role of evidence corroborating theory. The proof of the factual or metaphysical validity of the constructs cannot be achieved without inflicting distortions upon reality which is to be interpreted and explained. Weber criticised the Marxian theory from this point of view. He emphasised the soundness and fruitfulness of its socio-economic and developmental constructs as long as they are applied as ideal types and their perniciousness as soon as they are regarded as empirically and metaphysically valid 'transcendent hypotheses' concerning 'decisive forces' or 'tendencies' working with the necessity of a law [31].

The logic of the social sciences, as formulated by Weber, was the outcome of the failure suffered by the positivistic historiography. The collapse of the positivistic programme established the fact that no historical theory or point of view ever emerges by itself from the raw material of research. The theory must be brought, as it were, from the outside, to be in this sense *a priori*, to help to organise the material, to ask questions, and to raise problems. There are no facts in history apart from a point of view or a theory. For what counts as a fact is relative to a theoretical scheme of reference or to a tentative assumption of what are the essential features and connections in the sequence of events to be studied by the historian. Consequently, no historian can present a simple record and narrative of facts. A more objective study of history consists in the recognition of the limitations inherent in the historian's craft, in making explicit his implicit value premises and assumptions which define his specific point of view and provide him with his guiding rules of research.

Marxist-Leninists ignore this development, reject the methodology of historical relativism, and continue to define the task of historical inquiry in terms of nineteenth century positivism. Historical relativism is unacceptable to a Marxist-Leninist, for by its acceptance he would commit himself to the recognition of points of view other than his own. Moreover, as Lenin put it, the 'materialist' conception of history is no longer a hypothesis, but a scientifically demonstrated proposition', not 'a scientific conception of history' but 'the only scientific conception of history' [32]. It provides an absolutely objective frame of reference for the discovery of laws to which social relations and historical processes conform. It is self-evident that the claim of subjectivism – this term is used by Marxist-Leninists in preference to relativism – with its open admission of the limitations on objectivity to be accepted in historical inquiry is unjustifiable. While objectivity is unobtainable as long as we try to secure it by means of logic alone, it is achieved by the recognition of law, order, regularity, causality, and necessity in Nature capable of being faithfully reflected in the mind.

Lenin's restatement of the Marxian viewpoint bears no relevance to the issues raised by historical relativism. It should be noted that historical materialism did not originate in opposition to historical relativism but to the Hegelian or idealist conception of history which conceives history as the development of ideas and regards Reason as its ultimate metaphysical reality. Marx and Engels did not assert that their own interpretation was 'devoid of premises', but that these premises, formulated in terms of 'real individuals' and their activities in the material conditions under which they live, could be verified in a purely empirical way [33].

From the methodological point of view the historical materialism of Marx and Engels is a particular strand in the broad current of nineteenth century positivistic historiography, with its ideal of assimilating the process of history to a kind of natural process and history to natural science. Facts were to be ascertained and the laws framed by generalisations, inductive reasoning, the formulation and testing of hypotheses. This programme failed, for neither historical facts nor historical hypotheses are methodologically comparable with those of natural science. The nineteenth century model has become out-dated because it failed to solve the baffling problem of objectivity in history. The assumptions and the theoretical scheme of reference which the historian brings with him to his work and which results in conflicting historical interpretations of the same set of events, are not testable, either directly or indirectly, by observation, for there is no common body of evidence for these events recognised by all historians irrespective of their adopted point of view. Historical facts are relative to interpretations and thus they cannot confirm the adopted interpretation in the same manner as natural facts may test the validity of the proposed hypothesis.

While the Marxian conception of history provides an alternative to the idealist interpretation of history, it is not an alternative to historical relativism. It is not enough, as Lenin and his followers assume, to state the former to refute the latter. There are few historians to-day who would not make use of historical materialism as an analytical tool and as a principle of historical explanation. But historical materialism is a method of investigation or one hypothesis among many other possible points of view. This is more in keeping with Marx's own opinion of the role to be assigned to historical hypotheses than the current claim made by Marxist-Leninist philosophers and historians that one and only one of them is not arbitrary, is absolutely true and universally valid. There is no universal *passe-partout* to historical events, Marx wrote towards the end of his life. A particular historico-philosophical theory which explains everything explains nothing, and its supreme virtue consists in being super-historical [34].

CHAPTER 28

THE NATURE OF HISTORICAL LAWS

The Marxist-Leninist rejoinder to the criticism based on historical relativism makes use of the conception of natural and social laws which has already been mentioned. Laws are not products of man's perceptive and reasoning faculties, mere patterns of description or means of organising experience; they are factors of the external world, reflected with 'approximate fidelity' in man's mind. Any other view on this matter makes Nature a part of reason, instead of regarding reason as a part of Nature. Lenin devoted much space to the defence of 'objective law in Nature' and what he said is still accepted without major modifications. Polish Marxist-Leninists invariably refer to Lenin's idea of law and adopt it as their own [35].

This conception of law needs further elucidation, for its implications with respect to the historical and social sciences are by no means clear. When the construction of heuristic instruments, which Marxist-Leninists apply to the analysis of social action, is followed step by step, it becomes clear that the conception of 'objective law' leads to the reification of their conceptual scheme.

Lange's examination of the concept of law provides a suitable starting point for inquiring into the question as to where and how substances are found for the substantives and analytical constructs of the Marxist-Leninist discourse. "The economic laws", writes Lange, "are the 'exceptionless' recurrent relations between particular component factors of the economic process" [36]. At first it might appear that in Lange's definition the component factors of the economic process are patterns of institutionalised or group behaviour and that economic laws state the relations obtaining between them, relative to different objects and to a situation, which sets some definite limiting conditions to possible ways of interaction. We should, therefore, assume that action or interaction of individual actors is the basic unit of Lange's frame of reference. Since a system of such units is a relational concept – every action is oriented to various objects of the situation and its orientation is relevant to its description – economic inquiry should always distinguish two analytically different factors of its subject-matter. On the one hand, there is human action or rather the complexes of interaction between activities of many individuals, the product of human will dependent on the relations in which the individuals stand to each other. On the other, there is the objective situation, which human action tries to change and which confines the activities of many wills, setting the bounds to their outcome. The objective situation is a product of former activity, the sum total of the circumstances in which men find themselves, brought into existence and handed down to each generation by its predecessor. It is circumscribed by the productive forces, the relations of production, and, in general, the social forms of existence accumulated in the past. Although the objective situation is modified by each generation, it also exercises a restrictive power, prescribes the conditions of life, and provides the 'necessary forms' in which the activities of each generation are realised. This analysis of circumstances conditioning social action follows the lines familiar from *The German Ideology* or Marx's letter to Annenkov [37].

Further steps in Lange's analysis become more elusive. For it implicitly assumes that the objective situation constitutes something more than the limiting conditions for possible social action. If the restrictive conditions were endowed merely with passive powers of resistance, they would be unable to determine effectively the activities of men, whose energy would remain the real dynamic force in historical, social and economic development. This is implicitly denied by an additional premiss added at this stage of the construction. It is assumed that what men actually do matters little for out of their actions comes something quite different from what they intend. Objective social laws cannot, therefore, correspond with subjective aims, and they cannot be deduced from individual motivation or individual action analysed in terms of means-ends relations. This implies that society is not a sum of isolated individuals, united by some artificial and mechanical bonds, devised by the 'mathematical conception of society', but a specific whole. The 'efficient cause' and the principle of change, impelling social development, must lie elsewhere. They are found in the limiting conditions, transformed from passive into active factors, into historical, social or economic forces, to which the human will has to conform. These objective factors, and not what men actually do, are the really decisive elements [38].

'Everything which sets men in motion must go through their minds', Engels wrote, 'but what form it will take in the mind will depend very much upon the circumstances' [39]. The circumstances are the realm of economic relations independent of man's will, in which, contrary to appearances, the ultimate driving forces of history must be sought. Although productive forces and relations of production are technical, sociological or socio-economic concepts, they are hypostatised into effective forces operating behind actual events. They are assumed to have an objective existence 'in the world' and dynamic characteristics since they act as efficient causes. Heuristic constructs, reified into law-governed 'forces', work themselves out in social patterns, socio-economic formations and successions of historical events, in conformity with the universal laws of development.

The theory thus constructed, which is to provide an ultimate explanation of the economic, social and historical process, cannot be compared with the so-called transcendent hypotheses of natural science. For however abstract such hypotheses may be, they must remain testable, and this means that statements about perceptual objects must be derivable from them by logical deduction, to be confirmed or disconfirmed by actual experience. Otherwise they would have to be regarded as metaphysical theories. This condition is not satisfied by the hypothesis of abstract economic forces operating behind the historical scene, which from the start conflict with the elementary fact that reality consists of particular things and cannot be constituted by abstract entities.

The constructs intended to establish the basis for interpretative explanations of patterns of group behaviour acquire an independent existence over and above interacting individuals. This means that statements about social processes, in which these constructs occur, are no longer 'shorthand' descriptions referring to group behaviour of individuals in some definite situations. They refer to some socio-economic 'wholes' and their inner regularities from which the laws of group behaviour are derived as its 'necessary forms'. The latter determine, at least statistically, the behaviour of the individual within the group. The concepts and patterns of behaviour, primarily introduced for the descriptions of objective factors, which condition though not determine human action, become substantialised. They are supposedly discovered in the world as real and superior social entities, operating over men's heads and subject to laws of their own. These holistic laws are endowed with the power which determines the behaviour of individuals and their various groups. The empirically observable types of group behaviour of individuals, who act in an intelligible way, strive for definite ends and influence each other in a manifold manner, are relevant only with respect to appearances where accident holds sway. Behind these 'ideal driving forces' there are hidden their motive causes, which conform to 'inner general laws' and govern the course of social development.

This is also made clear by particular instances of historical or socio-economic laws. They are holistic laws, macroscopic with respect to the microscopic world of human individuals, that is, irreducible to regularities which govern group behaviour of individuals in definite situations. For instance, the two basic laws of Marxist-Leninist political economy state 'The relations of production must necessarily conform with the character of the productive forces' and 'The superstructure must necessarily conform to the economic basis'. The laws involve reified concepts as their variables and the relations obtaining between them are stated to be a faithful reflection of the regularities to which 'objective' social phenomena conform. Similarly, such constructs as 'feudalism', 'capitalism', and 'socialism' are not classificatory concepts or ideal types whose function in an empirical investigation is to provide a rational measure of comparison and a heuristic means of description of comprehensive thought and behaviour patterns. We are told that particular socio-economic formations – feudalism, capitalism, socialism – are not a 'semiotic product of an arbitrary scientific classification' but 'exist objectively' as real entities and 'wholes' which are not capable of interpretation in terms of their parts. Consequently, the claim is made that there is nothing arbitrary in the Marxist-Leninist classification, which reflects objective social facts and structures, each of which is unequivocally describable in terms of the inner laws governing its mode of existence and development [40].

According to the Marxist-Leninist doctrine, the social sciences, such as sociology or economics, are logically posterior to the general theory of historical materialism, which investigates the laws of the whole of social history. Sociology and economics deal with particular aspects of individual concrete wholes, the socio-economic formations. They have to assume the laws of historical development and build on this foundation.

The same applies to historiography which shares its subject-matter with sociology and differs from it in its method of inquiry and exposition. Both historiography and sociology investigate the whole tissue of social relationship in all its manifold interdependence. Society is not a self-contained whole, since it is only one aspect of objective reality or Nature. The principles of natural necessitation, in so far as they must be considered in the study of history and society, are included in the general theory of historical development (historical materialism). The assumptions of historical materialism protect particular historical and social sciences from distortions, which otherwise would arise because of the necessary limitations of historical or social inquiry to a partial aspect of the whole of reality.

The relation between historiography and sociology is similar to that between economic history and economic theory. The social scientist examines in logical order the same facts which the historian follows chronologically, in specific situations and temporal sequences, often disturbed by the interference of chance events. A sociological inquiry produces a corrected reflection of the 'real course of history itself', in that each factor is considered at the stage of its mature form [41].

Marxist-Leninists often say that one of the essential differences which divides the materialist and the idealist conception of history concerns the question of historical laws. The materialists do and the idealists do not recognise their existence. This statement is ambiguous and misleading. For those philosophers and historians who deny the existence of historical laws deny the existence of specifically historical laws, that is, of universal statements involving in their formulation specifically historical terms. Most of them would not deny, however, that the historian makes use of general laws to account for human action or to explain its outcome. These general laws are either taken over from other sciences or are assumed to be widely known as part of the common stock of life experience and wisdom. To establish the fact that historians refer in their explanations to some generalisations of everyday experience or to some universal statements of psychology, sociology, economics, and also biology and physics, does not mean that the existence of specifically historical laws has been established.

The application of the laws of science in a historical inquiry does not justify the claim that history conforms to laws. For this is commonly understood to mean that there is a set of laws which determine the course of human history. To maintain that the course of history is governed by laws and that these laws can be discovered is to adopt the viewpoint of historicism. Historicism is in fact rejected by a considerable number of philosophers and historians on account of the lack of supporting evidence in its favour [42].

It is incorrect to say that a Marxist-Leninist accepts and a non-Marxist refuses to accept the existence of historical laws. For both do not recognise the existence of specifically historical laws [43]. What does differentiate them is historicism, which a Marxist-Leninist accepts, and a non-Marxist, as a rule, rejects.

The Marxist-Leninist historicism is naturalistic, though to classify it in this manner requires certain qualifications. Marx, Engels, Lenin, Stalin, and the present-day Marxist-Leninists agree that social evolution is a 'process of natural history', a uniform law-governed natural process. Marx proclaimed that its successive stages cannot be cleared by 'bold leaps' and 'legal enactments'. A human society exists and changes under the laws of Nature. Marxist-Leninists do not subscribe to this thesis any longer; their historicism has become somewhat less naturalistic. They accept the possibility that the laws of Nature may, as it were, be suspended in their blind operation, be deflected and made use of for some consciously set purpose. Thus society becomes increasingly governed by its own laws. However wide a meaning is given to the term 'law of Nature', some of the laws of the Marxist-Leninist doctrine, for instance, those concerned with the relation of the superstructure to the basis, do not fall into this category. The retreat from the Marxian naturalism is concealed by the claim that the discovery of the objective laws governing the development of the system of social relations can be utilised for the purpose of directing social and economic activities, of framing programmes and policies on the basis of rational predictions [44].

The laws of social development are *sui generis*. They are neither of physical nor chemical nor of biological type, and they must be 'theoretically grasped' precisely in their specific character, in their 'new quality', which they manifest. "The overcoming of the "naturalist' point of view", Bukharin wrote, 'is far from implying an obligatory transition to the standpoint of idealist metaphysics. The idea of historicism is far from being the private property of the idealist tendencies in thought. Historical 'laws of movement' of society can in fact be discovered only by means of materialist dialectics" [45]. Historical laws exhibit the emergent qualities of highly organised matter and are the outcome of the dialectic process which brings a new set of laws into operation.

The laws of social development reveal the connections of social life with and its transcendence over Nature. The social process is both a natural and a socio-historical development and the corresponding laws bear the same character. On the one hand, they are as objective, *i.e.* independent of man's will, as natural laws. On the other, they have some specific characteristics and differ from laws of Nature in two respects. The laws of social development are impermanent, they apply to a definite historical period and in due course give place to new laws; moreover, they belong to the superstructure and have an ideological or class content. These are Stalin's formulations [46]. In Poland they were revised by Lange and made methodologically more acceptable.

The view that the social and historical sciences are ideological in character goes back to *The German Ideology*. The problems raised by the concept of ideology will be considered later. For the moment two points must be touched upon. In *The German Ideology* Marx emphasised that in the whole field of human studies the facts are not examined objectively owing to the interference of class-determined interests which are reflected in the prevailing ideas in metaphysics, the theory of knowledge, ethics, history, economics and jurisprudence. Together with the polemically advanced opinion that in these matters the questions of truth are obscured or distorted by implicitly accepted norms and valuations bound up with class interests, there is associated the conviction that this is not unavoidable. For true knowledge of the regular processes of 'real life' would reveal how the essential purposes of human activities and their norms emerge from the material conditions of life. Thus, facts may support and justify values. Marxism-Leninism has taken up this thread in the Marxian thought in its theory and practice. The other theme, which appeared in Marx's later works, is of a different nature. It implies the close relations between what we recognise as a matter of fact and our value premises, between our theories and our evaluative approach to social reality. This theme has been widely, if not universally, accepted and prompted a critical examination of the position prevailing in the social sciences.

There is an essential and vital difference between the natural and the social sciences. While in natural science we deal only with problems of fact, in the social sciences we are confronted by problems of fact and problems of value. To be more precise, in the social sciences factual and value-loaded concepts and assumptions interpenetrate each other and cannot be always satisfactorily disentangled from each other in the present state of knowledge. There might be differences of degree in the influence which value premises exercise on analysis of facts but their influence is universal and enters into every conceptual scheme in the social sciences. Although there is a grain of truth in what is often said, namely, that by realising how our apprehension of social phenomena is conditioned by some value presuppositions we can somewhat neutralise their effect, the question of objectivity in the social sciences constitutes a major methodological problem.

Very few Marxist-Leninists, and even then only at rare moments, are willing to accept these conclusions. Most of them adhere to the official doctrine which operates with two kinds of ideology. There is a mystifying and falsifying kind of ideology, and there is an ideology of another sort, which illuminates the phenomena of social life. While all the opponents of Marxism-Leninism are, consciously or unconsciously, dominated by the first kind of ideology, Marxist-Leninists alone enjoy the advantages of the second. In other words, Marxist-Leninists make use of the special conception of ideology in Mannheim's sense. They can recognise bias, prejudices, and aberrations in the point of view of others, but feel themselves immune from these common human failings. Thus, they are able to maintain both that the assertion 'The course of history is governed by laws' is an ideological statement (since to some it gives faith that they are on the side of History and discourages others by impressing upon them that History is not on theirs); that it is a true and valid scientific statement; and that whatever objections are raised against it, the refusal to accept the assertion is determined by ideological considerations in the pejorative sense of this expression [47].

The second distinguishing characteristic of the laws of social development is their lesser degree of permanence as compared with that of the laws of Nature. It should be remembered that according to Marxism-Leninism, which refers to Engels as its authority, natural laws are also historical, that is, they are valid with respect to a definite spatio-temporal region. Permanent is only matter in motion. At each stage in the history of the Universe different laws predominate, and none of them remains absolute and universally valid. It is not quite clear whether Engels and Marxist-Leninists wish to deny the validity of the so-called principle of the uniformity of Nature and maintain that regularities undergo some kind of transformation in the course of the evolution of the Universe, or whether they have something else in mind.

The postulate of the invariance of laws does not apply to the social sciences either. "To us", wrote Engels, "so-called 'economic laws' are not eternal laws of Nature but historical laws which arise and disappear". Consequently, economic laws older than modern bourgeois society express only those relations which are common to the conditions of all society based on class exploitation, and others are characteristic of modern bourgeois society alone [48]. More generally, economic categories are always the abstract expression of the existing relations of production and 'remain true' as long as these relations exist. Since the latter are transitory, economic categories cannot be more permanent than the relations which they express. Marx frequently ridiculed the 'eternal verity' of the doctrine of natural law, the postulated permanence of human nature, which always seeks satisfaction of the same needs and attainment of the same ends. He laughed at those supporting it for they recognise that 'there has been history, but there is no longer any' [49].

Stalin spoke with the self-assurance of the man who witnessed the realisation of Marx's prognosis of the bourgeois form of production being historical and transitory. He maintained that the majority of the laws of political economy sooner or later 'lose their validity owing to the new economic conditions and depart from the scene in order to give place to new laws... which arise from the new economic conditions' [50]. Stalin's pronouncement was, of course, universally acclaimed by his followers at the time it was made. But its main idea, which states that the generalisations and laws of economics are essentially historical, relative to certain historical conditions, as well as that outside these they lose relevance to the analysis of social reality, continues to be accepted [51].

There seems to be no reason to disagree with what Engels and Stalin said, if the permanence or invariance of laws is distinguished from their applicability. It is quite possible that some or most or all natural laws are applicable only in a cosmological period or in a particular region of the Universe in which definite physical conditions prevail. It is obvious and trivial to say that the laws of hydrostatics and hydrodynamics would not be applicable in an environment where there are no liquids. Changes in the physical environment might make a law no longer applicable, but they do not invalidate it. The difference is of vital importance.

To admit that laws are not invariant would make nonsense of science. We search for laws to explain change. Therefore, we might spare ourselves the trouble of searching for laws if the change of laws were admitted as an explanation of what we could not account for otherwise. Laws are or are not applicable relative to some definite conditions. Therefore, if the conditions change, laws might become no longer relevant to the analysis of phenomena. But this implies also that our theory breaks down and becomes redundant, unless there is a law which explains how the change of conditions came about by a law-governed process. This law would have to explain both the course of events by which the new conditions are brought about and the phenomena which previously were accounted for by the laws no longer applicable in the new conditions [52].

CHAPTER 29

THE TECHNOLOGICAL CONCEPTION OF HISTORY

The point that the impermanence of laws, whether natural or social, must be accounted for has been overlooked by Marxist-Leninists. They assume that it is enough to appeal to the change of social conditions – and these do change constantly – to account not only for the restricted applicability but also for the transitoriness of laws themselves, the 'disappearance' of the 'old' and the 'emergence' of the 'new' laws. This, however, is not the case. Suspicions have been aroused that there is something fundamentally wrong with the otherwise plausible view that the laws of economics are historical in character, limited to certain conditions of time and space [53]. In Poland it was Lange who realised that the point in question required elucidation and who tried to fill the gap in the theory by some provisions, which, without giving up the historical character of socio-economic laws, would account for the continuity of the evolutionary process.

Lange's contribution consists in putting Stalin's views, expounded in *Economic Problems of Socialism in the USSR*, in a systematic order. Lange is interested exclusively in historical materialism and its application to political economy, and he seems to regard historical materialism as a self-sufficient theory. It presupposes philosophical materialism but can do without the dialectics. In this respect Lange follows an independent line. Most Polish Marxist-Leninists adhere to Stalin's view and regard the laws of dialectics as the most fundamental assumptions of the theory of social development [54].

Lange distinguishes three categories of laws by means of which each socio-economic formation can be described [55]. To begin at the lowest level of generality, with which the shortest 'expectation of life' is associated, each of the various formations is governed by its own specific laws. They either refer to the characteristics of the economic basis and formulate laws of behaviour and patterns of interaction to which people, bound together by some definite relations of production, have to conform, or they express the effects brought about by the superstructure in the economic basis.

Among the specific laws the most important is the basic economic law of each formation. In the capitalist formation it is the law of the maximum capitalist profit, and in the socialist formation the law of the maximum satisfaction of needs of the whole of society. These laws are not only specific but also basic, because each of them determines a number of other laws specific for this formation, and thus confers upon it the character of a concrete whole and a distinct entity, existing 'in the world' independently of the will of man.

The laws resulting from the influence of the superstructure upon the basis might change more than once during the life-time of each formation. They are effects of the activity of the State which might pursue various policies with respect to foreign trade, money, foreign currency, and so forth. Such policies are economically relevant activities, they affect the web of relations constituting the economic basis and indirectly cause the emergence of new laws reflecting the changes in the basis.

These basic laws set some puzzling questions. For these laws are clearly normative in character and state the assumed social objectives to be pursued in the administration of economic resources. Once the objective is set, rules, including those concerned with the use of resources, can be formulated, which would be appropriate to the attainment of the pursued end. The rules would be relative to the available resources and the selected objective, and in this sense they are dependent on the basic law. It seems to follow that a socio-economic formation is determined by Aristotle's final cause. The description of the way in which a socio-economic formation operates has to make use of the logic of teleological explanation and to apply the means-ends model. This is hard to reconcile with that part of the Marxist-Leninist theory which states that economic laws prevail in Nature and are independent of man's will.

Moreover, the whole Marxist-Leninist conception of basic laws is hardly compatible with the belief that political economy is a value-free science, comparable with astronomy or physics. The basic law of capitalism or of socialism is clearly a normative principle binding upon practice. It makes a pronouncement which involves value judgments and standards of valuation. It is for the economists to decide whether they should admit such value-judgments into an economic theory. In this context it is sufficient to emphasise that it is misleading to suggest that the differences of opinion about ends can be resolved by economics as a positive science. It is also self-contradictory to proclaim that political economy is a neutral science and to admit a normative approach into political economy *qua* political economy.

The second main category consists of laws which hold in more than one socio-economic formation. For instance, the laws of money circulation hold in every formation in which money is used. The law of value, bound to appear in the wake of commodity production, held before capitalism existed and still holds after its overthrow. Its 'longevity' is associated with the fact that it may reflect some characteristics of the prevailing system of both production and distribution.

The third category of laws provides the basis for the continuity of social development. They are sociological in character and common to all formations. Two of these laws have already been mentioned: the laws of the necessary conformity of the relations of production and of the superstructure with the character of the productive forces and the economic basis respectively. There are also some universally valid purely economic laws. These are the so-called technical and accounting identities. They express the equality of certain sums of money or of certain uses of commodities in the economy. A simple example is provided by the statement that everybody's income is either spent or saved. It is obvious that such relations always remain true.

The two sociological laws are essentially forces of conservation. They constitute a self-corrective device which eliminates frictions and re-establishes the internal harmony of the formation. When, owing to the interference of some other forces, this self-corrective device ceases to operate, the required conformity can no longer be restored by other means but by a violent upheaval. This does not apply to a socio-economic formation from which antagonistic social forces have been eliminated. In a socialist formation the self-corrective device, resulting from the operation of the two sociological laws, can work smoothly and indefinitely. A formation of this kind is self-perpetuating, it knows no 'old age' and is immune from destruction. Its evolution follows a course of undisturbed and constant progress [56].

In the Marxian conceptual scheme the key to the dynamics of social evolution is provided by the role assigned to the relations of production. They may act as a principal mainspring impelling and stimulating the productive forces or as a brake upon them and a hindrance to any further development, which, speaking metaphorically, makes a revolutionary explosion both possible and inevitable. This is made clear in the celebrated passage of the preface to *A Contribution to the Critique of Political Economy* and even clearer in *The Communist Manifesto* and *Capital*. The relations of production play the role, ascribed to them by Marx, in the capitalist mode of production. In the whole course of the social evolution, however, the factor which is the 'most mobile and revolutionary force', which never stagnates and 'grows old', is the productive forces. Inventions and improvements of productive forces continually generate tensions and set problems, which must be solved by adjustments in the whole social fabric. The third fundamental sociological law (which, with the two previously mentioned, constitutes the foundation of the theory of historical materialism) states that there is a natural tendency for the productive forces to develop and improve [57].

It is the progressive development of the means of production that is the mainspring of change and social evolution. It gradually changes the conditions, makes the transformation of one mode of production into another inevitable, and acts as an impelling force of a limitless progress in the socialist formation. Engels' 'economic movement', which, in the last analysis, asserts itself decisively and necessarily, should be identified with the progressive development of productive forces.

Lange's views coincide with those of Bukharin. Referring to Marx and Plekhanov, Bukharin argued that technology, being a varying quantity, produces by its variations the changes in the relations between society and Nature. On the other hand, the development of the productive forces, which initiates the chain social reaction, consists precisely in the development of technology. It is the technological change which disturbs the external and internal equilibrium and thus maintains the evolutionary process. Consequently, Bukharin concluded, technology must constitute a point of departure in the analysis of social transformation. A contemporary American anthropologist expressed the same idea. Fundamentally, it is man's capacity to produce, or rather his technical skill, that evolves and progresses [58].

Lange takes up a strand of thought which is essential to Marx's way of thinking.

Franklin defined man as a tool-making animal and Marx adopted this definition. It is technology, Marx wrote, that enables us to distinguish different economic epochs, for technology supplies not only a standard of measurement, by means of which the degree of development attained by human labour can be established, but also serves as an indicator of its social conditions. If technology determines the development of material production, and material production is the 'basis of all social life', 'real history' in Marx's sense becomes indistinguishable from the history of technology. 'Technology discloses man's mode of dealing with Nature, the process of production by which he sustains his life, and thereby also lays bare the mode of formation of his social relations, and of the mental conceptions that flow from them' [59]. The view that technological knowledge provides the foundation on which society rests has a large number of supporters, not necessarily adherents of the Marxian school of thought.

The reduction of the materialist to the technological conception of history replaces a 'mere phrase', as Engels put it, an almost meaningless label, by a more precise and possibly testable hypothesis. It does not lend itself to large-scale constructions of the traditional Marxian kind, one of which is that of Lange himself. Productive forces are the tools together with human skill, experience, and knowledge of technological processes. Technique on which technology is based is not an independent branch of knowledge. It has grown up together with modern science and its continued growth is unimaginable without a steady scientific advancement on an ever widening front. Moreover, the progress of science is not dependent solely on the quantity and quality of intellectual ability engaged in scientific research. To say that the causes of social development are in the last resort technological is to assume a considerable number of variables which determine social progress.

To-day, we easily recognise that technology exercises a powerful influence, direct or indirect, upon social life, upon our intellectual and moral outlook. But the transformation of the economic structure and of the whole tissue of social relations through the application of science is an event of recent date. So far as the distant past is concerned, it is hard to say precisely, as a matter of fact and not as a surmise supported by a few isolated examples, what role science and technique played. The famous dictum in *The Poverty of Philosophy* that the 'hand-mill gives you society with the feudal lord; the steam-mill, society with the industrial capitalist' [60] is no substitute for what is required to transform an idea into a hypothesis corroborated by historical evidence covering all ages and places. Slave labour was the pivot of the economy of the Greek city-states and, up to the middle of the last century, of bourgeois economy in a large part of the world. Can the history of China or India be explained in terms of technological change? Generally speaking, it is difficult to answer the question whether in the past the effects of technological improvements on social life were negligible or whether they were real as to-day and only slower in relation to the life of a generation. For it is only in the present age that we have begun to move within a single lifetime out of one technological era into another and very different one.

There is a wide gap, therefore, between an intuitive understanding of the role of technology in social life and the assertion that it is the decisive factor that determines unequivocally social development in all its manifold manifestations. It is still less plausible to assume that technological advance is a necessary, inevitable, and predictable process. For there is no answer to the question why this should be the case. The cumulative character of knowledge makes it probable that our technological skill would continue to improve. Moreover, it has been suggested that the rate of technological growth increases with each increment of advancement. Consequently, technological progress makes more technological progress likely [61]. But to say that technological advance is inevitable is to ignore the fact that other factors, regular or irregular, may interfere or counteract technological growth, and to maintain that it can be predicted is to reveal one's ignorance of what a scientific prediction consists of. Neither historical knowledge about scientific development in the past nor the cumulative character of science provide the basis for predicting discoveries, inventions, and, in general, the development of science in the future. If we cannot anticipate the future state of knowledge, neither can we make a prognosis as to what its effects on social development would be. The technological conception of history is incompatible either with prophecies about the future, or, in general, with historicist conceptions which it is supposed to support.

CHAPTER 30

THE EMPIRICAL MEANING OF HISTORICAL
MATERIALISM

Lange's interpretation of historical materialism is an improvement upon the official Marxist-Leninist doctrine. He makes some of its concepts less vague and some of its premisses more articulate. But he follows in many respects the traditional speculative and ideological line. In particular, he is as careless as other Marxist-Leninists in his use of language. A modern philosopher would say that Lange does not use language for the purpose of formulating empirically significant possibilities, but with a pictorial intention. He is thus misled into assuming the existence of all kinds of abstract entities, which he regards as 'causes' or 'forces' responsible for social change.

An alternative, non-ideological and empirical approach to historical materialism has been worked out by Andrzej Malewski, a social scientist of the young generation, who studied logic and methodology under the teachers of the Warsaw school. Malewski is interested in historical materialism only as a complex of sociological statements. From this point of view the question whether they are empirically testable becomes the most important.

This problem is not capable of solution before an extensive preliminary analytical examination is undertaken. It is clear that some sociological statements of historical materialism can neither be proved nor disproved. When Engels writes that 'the ultimate cause and the great moving power of all important historic events (should be sought) in the economic development of society, in the changes in the modes of production and exchange' [62], we have not the slightest idea what 'the ultimate causes' or 'all important historic events' are. We do not know, either, what kind of relation is supposed to hold between the *explicans* and the *explicandum*. For sometimes the *explicans* is called 'cause' or '*primum agens*' and sometimes 'the basis'; sometimes it is said to 'determine' and sometimes to 'be in rebellion' against this or that. To refer to a statement like that just quoted as a 'law' suggests that it can be confirmed by available evidence. We are, however, unable to say how or even where to look for this evidence as long as the vagueness and ambiguity of expressions are not removed. Such a statement, honoured with the name 'law', has clearly no empirical meaning.

Historical materialism includes a cluster of various statements of a similar kind. We are told that 'the sum total of (definite) relations of production constitutes the economic structure of society – the real foundation on which rise legal and political superstructures and to which correspond definite forms of social consciousness'; that 'the history of all hitherto-existing society is the history of class struggle'; that the 'economic structure of society always forms the real basis from which, in the last analysis, is to be explained the whole superstructure of legal and political institutions as well as of the religious, philosophical,

460

and other conceptions of each historical period'. All these pronouncements cannot be regarded as either true or false until they are reformulated in such a manner that their empirical validity can either be confirmed or disconfirmed.

Malewski suggested that historical materialism involves three sets of hypotheses, or to be more precise, three theories [63]. The first concerns the regularities obtaining between the situation in which people live and their behaviour and beliefs. For instance, we could formulate the following hypotheses:

'If the acceptance of some definite ideology by a group would require giving up some of its privileges, the majority of its members would reject this ideology'.

'If there is a conflict between the interests and the ideology accepted by a group, its members will behave in conformity with their interests rather than with their ideology'.

'If there is a conflict between the interests and the ideology accepted by a group, the ideology will be modified and adjusted to what the interests require'.

Taking various formulations of historical materialism as a guide, a great number of hypotheses of this kind could be framed. Some of them would be statistical, others causal in character. Empirical research would probably require their further modification and particularisation. The tentatively formulated hypotheses indicate only the direction and procedure to be followed in the research that would decide whether, and if so, which empirical meaning could be attached to the celebrated dictum that 'social existence determines social consciousness'.

The second theory deals with society as a system of social and economic classes with conflicting interests. The hypotheses of this theory are more difficult to formulate in empirical terms. There is, for instance, Marx's assertion that in every class society there is the oppressor and the oppressed engaged in an uninterrupted hidden or open fight. Expressed in neutral terms this assertion states that there is always a conflict of interests between the owners of the means of production and those who do not own them with respect to the question as to how national income should be distributed. It is clear that the conflict concerns the relative share in the distribution. It should be assumed, therefore, that both groups are interested in increasing the absolute value of national income. There is further Marx's assertion that the economically exploiting class is also the politically dominant class or that the separation of society into an exploiting and exploited class coincides with that into a ruling and an oppressed class. The consequence of this assumption states that the government of a modern State is but a committee for managing the common affairs of the exploiters. The empirical sense of this assertion might be explicated in the following manner. 'If a group in society is 'stronger' than all the others taken together, and the existing legislation is not favourable to its interests, the legislation is either revised or not complied with'. This hypothesis could be supplemented by an inquiry whether a government actually acting contrary to the interests of the strongest group is forced either to resign or to become subservient to the wishes of the economically dominant group.

The third set of hypotheses, which can be disentangled from historical material-

461

ism is a theory of social change. It should be noted that this is not a general but a particular theory concerned with changes in the class structure of society. Its basic assumption is the close correlation between technological development and transformations in social stratification. Its two further assumptions state that if the prevailing legal and political system does not favour the interests of the class increasing in number and rising in power, this class will propagate an ideology justifying the revision of the existing legal and political system. In the struggle for power between different social classes, the victorious class is the one whose interests happen to coincide with the trend of economic progress.

The three theories and their various hypotheses may not give a full and satisfactory explication of the content of the Marxian historical and sociological doctrines. The important point in this approach is the recognition of the fact that historical materialism is a miscellany of deep insight, ideological oratory, devoid of empirical meaning, and clearly false conjectures. Into the two latter categories fall, for instance, such pronouncements as that the relations of production must conform with the character of the productive forces; that no social order ever disappears before all the productive forces, for which there is room in it, have been developed; that there will come the period of social revolution; that mankind always takes up only such problems as it can solve. The list of such pronouncements, perhaps important from the ideological viewpoint but not capable of empirical interpretation, could be continued [64].

The elusiveness of the precise content of the Marxian historical materialism has resulted in a variety of interpretations each of which claims to provide its 'only correct' understanding. Unlike a political scientist or a politician, a social scientist is interested in their empirical relevance and truth, and not in their conformity with some extra-logical requirements. Among the interpretations claiming validity on account of their agreement with Marx's genuine doctrine that of Marxism-Leninism deserves special attention because of its tangible relevance in the life of many people at the present time.

Marxism-Leninism goes in some respects beyond what Marx's statements warrant or what can be maintained without offending logic and truth. Thus, it maintains that in every State, where means of production are privately owned, the State is only a device for the protection of the interests of the propertied class; that every work of art serves the interests of only one class; that every class can be represented only by one political party; that with the abolition of private ownership of the means of production there disappears the exploitation of man by man of every sort, and the working classes gain an actual controlling influence on the way in which they are governed. These are clearly false assertions. Although they have some remote connection with what Marx and Engels said, they cannot be regarded as an interpretation or as implications of the Marxian historical materialism.

On the other hand, Marxism-Leninism fails to adopt some important component parts of the Marxian doctrine. These concern, above all, Marx's assertion that society is a system of social and economic classes with conflicting interests. It was maintained that this assertion no longer applies to post-capitalist socio-

462

economic formations. The Marxist-Leninist point of view was criticised on the ground that when national economy is nationalised the social stratification changes but does not disappear. Nor does it stop creating tensions and conflicts of interests of various groups.

In this respect Lange supports Malewski. According to Lange, the idea that in the socialist socio-economic formation tensions and conflicts of interests are entirely absent has no place in the sociology of historical materialism. It should be regarded as a hiliastic and eschatological survival of utopian socialism. In every formation the relations of production and the superstructure are conservative factors and the development of the relations of production always lags behind the development of the productive forces. Consequently, in the socialist formation also there appear social strata whose privileges are associated with a certain developmental stage of the relations of production or of superstructure. This gives rise to conflicts, which, however, in the absence of antagonistic social classes can be solved peacefully; though not without struggles, yet without revolutions [65].

CHAPTER 31

PREDICTION IN THE SOCIAL SCIENCES

If we knew the constituents of social, economic, and political systems and were successful in discovering and measuring their functional connections, we would have genuine knowledge of how the systems operate. Given the initial conditions, we would be able to predict the state of the system at any future time. Marxism-Leninism makes claim of having attained this kind of knowledge about social reality. Its predictive power with respect to social, economic, and political phenomena provides, therefore, a crucial test of the validity of this claim. If it is true, Marxism-Leninism as an applied science should be able to make predictions of the behaviour in some specified set of circumstances of various groups and of the outcome of complex social processes.

The predictive power of the social sciences is, however, still very limited. Even economics or political economy (Marxist-Leninists use the latter term, associated with the classical political economy and the theory of Marx, and leave the former to the present-day followers of what Marx called 'vulgar economy'), the most advanced among them, did not manage to become an applied science, that is, to predict fairly accurately the effects of alternative economic policies. An economist cannot be compared with a dam or bridge constructor who calculates with great precision the quantity and quality of materials required to carry out his work. Although political economy is apparently vastly superior to economics, it does not claim an advantage in predictive power over economics[66].

In spite of their lack of success in the most advanced of the social sciences, Marxist-Leninists contend that in social matters knowledge of the future is not beyond their power. Bukharin confidently stated that 'prediction is possible in the domain of the social sciences as well as in that of the natural sciences'. He qualified this statement by the proviso that since Marxism-Leninism does not claim to know the 'velocity of the social processes', it cannot predict the time of their occurrence but only their direction. Otherwise he had no doubt that the predictive power of the Marxian and Marxist-Leninist doctrines has been fully confirmed by the whole subsequent course of events. Deborin was even more confident than Bukharin. In his view, Marx created an 'absolutely new science' characterised by its ability to 'foresee the ways of future historical development'[67].

Popper defines historicism as an 'approach to the social sciences which assumes that historical prediction is their principal aim'[68]. Popper's definition applies perfectly to Schaff's approach. 'Historical prediction', Schaff wrote, 'is a component part of the science of history..... The laws of social development are not only objective, but also knowable. This is revealed by the practice of predicting social development, the prediction being based on the knowledge of historical laws'[69]. It is clear from Schaff's argument that in his opinion successful predictions concerning future social development were made in the past by applying the laws of historical materialism to this effect and that these successful predictions should be regarded as confirmation of the truth of historical materialism. There is a point in this argument which would win the support of numerous thinkers. The predictive success of a theory is widely considered as convincing evidence in its favour. The important condition to be satisfied is that the prediction has in fact been made by taking advantage of the theory in question.

We should distinguish a lucky guess in foretelling the future from a forecast and from a prediction. A lucky guess is saying in advance what happens to come true; it is not a prediction, for it is not based on evidence. Clairvoyance, prophecy and anticipation fall into this category. They are the province of visionaries and dreamers, but also of politicians and men of action. The latter foretell, as an act of faith, the course of distant events or state that the future will display a certain trait and realise a desired possibility, discerned more or less dimly as one among many courses the events might take.

Notwithstanding his historical materialism, Marx was aware of the fact that ideas and beliefs may pave the way for social realities. For men are urged into action by what they think to be the case and by what does not necessarily have to be the case. It sometimes happens, therefore, that something actually occurs because people think and act as if it were bound to occur. 'If men define situations as real, they are real in their consequences', stated the American sociologist W. I. Thomas. For the definition is in this case an integral part of the situation and consequently can influence the subsequent behaviour. Sociology has recently begun to study the effects of beliefs or acts of faith on the course of events and has reached the conclusion that they might be important causes as well as instruments of attaining long-range aims. They have been given the name of 'self-fulfilling prophecies'. A self-fulfilling prophecy 'is, in the beginning, a false definition of the situation evoking a new behaviour which makes the originally false conception come true'[70]. A sociological 'prophetic prediction' is itself a social fact, closely connected with action, and its power of creating what has been predicted is perhaps less mysterious than it might appear at first sight. This is even clearer in the case of a self-defeating prophecy, that is, of a prophecy which cannot be made without destroying the success of what is prophesied. The self-fulfilling and self-defeating prophecy clearly applies to what is within our control. However, the fact that it makes no difference whether anybody writes down a prediction of the sun's eclipse and that it might make a tremendous difference whether a sociological prophecy is made or not constitutes a puzzling problem when it is followed up and considered in detail.

Although a clairvoyant or a prophet or a man of action need not always be wrong, when he happens to be right he does not achieve anything more than a lucky guess. This is meant to indicate that no logical principle which implies what has been guessed is involved in foretelling the future.

A forecast is a conjectural estimate of future things, based on the analysis of a trend or a tendency. Meteorological or demographic forecasts provide the best examples of such conjectural estimates. They are genuine extrapolations based on the assumptions that certain specific initial conditions would persist. They

465

are, therefore, always subject to the proviso *rebus sic stantibus*. The more they are long-term estimates, the greater the probability that either the initial conditions change or some other unforeseen events interfere or some counteracting forces appear. There are always chances that other factors would make a difference, offset or affect the forecast effect and invalidate the conjectural estimate. The unreliability of forecasts based on trends results from our ignorance of the conditions on which a trend depends. Even if we know some of them, we can never be certain whether all its conditions have been considered, and in the absence of this knowledge we are unable to say whether and for how long it will continue to persist.

Prediction is extrapolation derived deductively from the discovery that certain events are regularly connected. Popper has shown that explanation and prediction have the same formal structure, in which three elements must be distinguished: universal statements or laws, initial conditions or *explicans*, and the prognosis or *explicandum*. To explain an event is to discover its initial conditions and to deduce the *explicandum* from the *explicans* and from some universal statements. To predict an event is to deduce a singular statement – the prognosis – from its known initial conditions and some universal laws. There are, therefore, some stringent restrictions attached to the procedure by means of which a prognosis can be established. If the law is not suitable or if the initial conditions cannot be ascertained or are not fully known, we can make no prediction. A law states a recurrent connection of certain conditions and subsequent events. If these conditions are not precisely defined by the law, the statement asserting a recurrent connection is not a law suitable for making predictions. On the other hand, if the antecedent conditions cannot be known, no law applies to them and no prognosis can be derived from universal statements alone.

A forecast is not a prediction. An estimate of future events depends on a trend, which is not unconditional, that is, it does not comprise either the sufficient or necessary conditions for the occurrence of events and is relative to some unspecified favourable circumstances. Therefore, it is not a universal law. Forecasts or guesses mistakenly regarded as predictions, such as, for instance, the supposed inevitability of progress, preached by Condorcet; or the inevitability of socialism resulting from the disappearance of the entrepreneurial stratum, foretold by Schumpeter; or the inexorable power of social evolution, impelled, according to Marx, by 'tendencies working with iron necessity towards inevitable results', confuse trends or alleged trends with laws. They assume that there are absolute trends, emancipated, as it were, from the restrictions of initial conditions, laws unto themselves, going on over men's heads to a predetermined consummation [71]. Such long-term and large-scale anticipations are closer to prophecies than to forecasts in the technical sense. Predictions and lucky guesses are still more widely apart than are scientific predictions and forecasts.

It is not always possible to say at the first glance whether a prognosis has been established as a lucky guess or by the scientific procedure of prediction. Should Western civilisation disintegrate, like so many others in the past, the historian of the future may admire Arnold Toynbee's predictive knowledge. His admiration

466

would not be justified. A historiosophic prophecy does not become a prediction on account of being formulated in terms of a historiosophic system. Speculative philosophies of history choose one of the present discernible possibilities to the exclusion of all others, regard it as decisive, and view the future as the actualisation of the selected potentiality. This choice might be prompted by an incisive insight into the 'logic of the historical situation' or by a sound feeling for what are important motives and ends of human action. If in this manner a more or less lucky guess is made – apart from clearly false prophecies such lucky guesses had been accomplished by Comte and Marx – it should not be called a prediction, but a prophecy or divination. For the philosophy of history, which provides the ostensible basis for foretelling the future, does not logically justify the prognosis about what happens to be rightly foreseen. The scientific way of predicting requires that the prognosis is logically inferred from some universal laws and specific statements describing the initial conditions [72].

The question whether a given 'prognosis', confirmed by actual observation, was a lucky guess, a forecast, or a genuine prognosis arrived at by means of the scientific way of prediction, is of considerable importance. For the procedure followed in predicting a specific event is also the procedure applied for the purpose of testing the validity of a theory. Successful predictions provide, therefore, relevant evidence of the soundness of the theory on which it was based. In the case of a forecast nothing more can be derived from its success than the conclusion concerning the continued persistence of the trend (this seems to suggest that trends are, in general, better suited for the purpose of explaining than for that of predicting). A lucky guess reveals just the fact that we were successful in making a guess.

When Schaff examines historical predictions, it is at once clear that he does not have scientific predictions in mind. He states explicitly that historical laws, that is, laws of social development, operate with the necessity of natural events. But he adds that no particular historical event can be predicted by means of these laws. What can be foreseen is the 'general direction of historical development and its result' [73]. What he probably had in mind was the view already stated by Bukharin, to which reference has been made: a social scientist may find out by inspecting a chain of events that there is a developmental process at work in it and that this process presses on to an outcome of which only the general character can be described. Just as Bukharin before him, Schaff failed to notice that such diagnoses are futile unless they are restricted by taking account of the counteracting factors. If the latter were known and the difference made by them could be assessed, the diagnoses could not have been made. On the other hand, if the counteracting factors are disregarded, the diagnoses must remain incomplete and the conclusions about the future, based upon them, cannot be held to be warranted. The feeling of confidence that something will happen is not a prediction or a forecast. Leonardo da Vinci was sure that it would become possible to fly. But his firm anticipatory belief was not a prediction in the relevant and important sense of this expression.

It should be noted that the impossibility of predicting historical events has no similarity to the impossibility of prediction which a natural scientist also would recognise in some cases. Eduard Meyer, the celebrated German historian, was of a different opinion [74]. He maintained that natural science can, for instance, assert that when dynamite is set on fire an explosion will occur, but it cannot predict what would happen in a specific instance, *e.g.* whether a particular person would be killed or not. This is not an absolute but a relative impossibility, that is, relative to the knowledge of the initial conditions. If these conditions are known, a prediction of what would happen to particular persons in a specific case of dynamite explosion can be made with a degree of probability dependent on the accuracy of our knowledge of the initial conditions. There is no analogy in this case between a scientist and a historian. The relative impossibility of prediction in the former is an absolute impossibility in the latter case. The historian has at his disposal no laws of the kind of which 'if dynamite is set on fire, an explosion will occur' is an instance.

As a matter of fact, no scientific prediction can be made on the ground of historical materialism. The law 'the relations of production must conform to the productive forces', or 'the superstructure must conform to the economic basis', or 'the productive forces must progressively improve', are not suitable for deducing any prognosis from them. The scientific way of predicting future events does not break down, it simply cannot be started.

A historical prediction in Schaff's sense is not a forecast either. 'What does it mean', he asks, 'that we make a prediction and that a historical development will take such and such course? It means that we discover the law of this development, and having discovered it, we succeed in determining the effect of a whole chain of development on the basis of a succession of causes and effects'. It is in that manner that Marx and Stalin predicted the inevitable destruction of the capitalist socio-economic formation. The 'models of scientific historical predictions' are provided by Marx's assertion in *The Communist Manifesto* and *Capital* that the fall of the bourgeoisie, the expropriation of the expropriators and the victory of the proletariat are equally inevitable or by Stalin's pronouncement of 1927 that in spite of some deflecting forces temporarily holding back the inevitable final destruction of capitalism, new economic crises, new periods of revolutionary upheavals, and new wars were drawing near [75].

A forecast is not arrived at by means of following up a chain of causes and effects of a whole developmental process. If this were the method of forecasting future events, no reliable forecast could ever be made. Moreover, if the rules of the 'composition of forces' are unknown and the 'forces' themselves are heterogeneous, it is impossible to have a clear idea of the cumulative effect of many distinct causes, even if each of them were an isolated system of conditions, which they are not. The different kinds of social 'forces' cannot be compared in terms of common standards and the resultant of their combination can be estimated only in a rough and ready manner. A forecast based on the estimate of the combined effect of heterogeneous social 'forces' is bound to be a lucky or a wrong guess. Marx's assertion that the introduction of labour saving machinery was bound to increase steadily the reserve army of the unemployed exemplifies the risks and the difficulties of the factor-combining procedure in the social sciences. It is now clear that Marx failed to consider all the relevant factors and to correctly estimate the respective share of those mentioned owing to the absence of a common measure of their comparison. Although Marx thought that he was drawing conclusions from a well established body of universal laws, he was actually involved in guess-work, which did not come off, on what would be the outcome of a number of interrelated but incomparable factors, none of which was either the sufficient or the necessary condition for the occurrence of the 'predicted' events. There is no easy and secure way of saying in advance which of the many factors carries more weight and is 'stronger' than any other or is 'decisive in the last analysis'[76].

In the case of a social evolutionary process the difficulty of applying the factor-combining procedure greatly increases owing to the circumstance that what is meant by 'development' is not the appearance of a simple observable characteristic, such, for instance, as can be recorded by measuring the position, velocity, or temperature of a physical body. 'Development' in the sense in which Schaff uses this term is a long chain of internal and structural changes, taking place 'from the inside outwards', which cannot be observed but are inferred from certain results obtained deductively by complicated and abstract reasoning. A good example of such 'inward transformations' is provided by Marx's demonstration that some characteristics of the capitalist mode of production turn 'every economic progress into a social calamity'[77]. The magnitude of such an undertaking clearly surpasses the power of any mind.

The other error involved in the assumption that events can be predicted by inspecting a chain of causes and effects extending into the distant future results from the misconception which has been inspired by Marx's analysis of the capitalist system. Marx assumed that a long succession of 'phases' or states of society conforms to a single fundamental law, that this law can be discovered and provide the basis for gaining a foresight into the future. This idea is explained in the preface to the first edition of *Capital* and is repeatedly applied throughout the work. The fallacy of this assumption has been exposed by Popper. While it is not unreasonable to suppose that any successive natural occurrences follow each other according to some laws of Nature, if periodical changes are excluded, practically no sequence of three or more causally connected occurrences takes place according to a single law. Popper concluded that though there might be singular hypotheses of evolution or development, each of them taking advantage of a number of natural laws, there is no law of evolution or development, which would have to be a universal statement [78]. A singular hypothesis does not provide us with what is needed to make a prediction. If what is foretold comes true, it is a lucky guess.

A forecast is not an estimate of a 'final effect', brought about by a chain of causes and effects. An estimate of future events makes the assumption, always subject to the clause *rebus sic stantibus,* that a certain configuration of causes would remain stable and produce a certain effect. Thus, a demographer makes the assumption that a set of causes determining the rate of deaths and births

469

would remain unchanged and produce only a slow rate of changeability in the ratio expressing the natural increase of the population. On this basis he evaluates the growth of a population in the years to come. He might be successful in his forecast if it is restricted to the near future. The narrow limits of safety are closely related to the ignorance of all the causes conditioning the trend. While this point might be ignored as long as the forecast remains short-term, the causes left unconsidered or unknown assert themselves in the long run and invalidate the presupposition on which the forecast was based.

Marx and Engels, Lenin and Stalin did make 'predictions', but neither they themselves nor their followers have so far succeeded in establishing the fact that these 'predictions' were warranted, that is, arrived at by means of the scientific procedure of prediction. If some of these 'predictions', as is the case with Marx, have turned out to be not entirely unsuccessful, they speak highly of Marx's foresight or his 'historical sense'. This is, however, a biographical characteristic which does not permit us to draw the conclusion that the laws of social development, formulated by Marx, have thus been confirmed. Only successful scientific predictions constitute evidence of the validity of the theory by means of which they are deduced.

'Predictions' of Marx and his successors were put in terms of and inspired by historical materialism. This was not the only source of their inspirations. They were made by great leaders of men, perhaps more anxious to change the world than to acquire a true knowledge of it. Their 'predictions' were to influence the course of events and become self-fulfilling prophecies. This factor has been put into relief by Bukharin and also by Schaff. 'The scientific analysis of the movement of capitalism', wrote Bukharin, 'is only a means of foreseeing, and foresight itself is only a means for practical activity'. Marx 'grasps the coming in order the more energetically, fully, actively and successfully to change the world' [79]. Schaff made similar observations. The problem of objectivity of historical laws and of predictions based thereon, he wrote, is not solved in the peace of the historian's study. It concerns, above all, political men of action and is decided in the tumult of the class struggle impelling the evolution of society. The most perfect kind of historical predictions is attained by men who combine the qualities of a theorist with those of a man of action. It requires the adoption of a partisan point of view and of the outlook of the progressive and revolutionary class, that is, of the proletariat [80].

These are clearly conditions for making a self-fulfilling prophecy which would encourage men to act in a certain way. To get men to act together, they must believe together and have confidence in the success of their action. The confidence that they are on the side of History and History on theirs has proved to be a powerful and effective motive of concerted and sustained effort (as well as a source of tragic and vicious delusions). Marx's foresight and feeling for the so-called historical forces are in fact reducible to his understanding of the role played by ideological motivation and normative value-permeated social theories in human destiny. Constructing his theories on this basis he managed to throw more light on the future than the scientific way of predicting would warrant [81]. In this manner, however, Marx's prophecies, in so far as they come true, contribute to the refutation of historicism and confirm the view that men alone bear responsibility for what happens in history. Although they are conditioned in their actions, their free choice plays a part in the making of history which is not governed by inexorable laws working with iron necessity towards inevitable results. If Marx's prophecies have come true, his basic assumptions must be false.

CHAPTER 32

THE REVISION OF THE THEORETICAL FRAMEWORK
OF HISTORICAL MATERIALISM

It has already been emphasised that the Marxist-Leninist doctrine of ideology is based on *The German Ideology* rather than on Marx's views expounded in his later work. This fact is of considerable importance. *The German Ideology* is a youthful study of Marx and Engels and polemical in character. It was written, as its authors later explained, to settle accounts with their former philosophic conscience. If this was their intention, the method adopted ill suited this undertaking [82].

The polemical purpose of the work and its narrow reference, limited to post-Hegelian philosophic trends in Germany, tended to enhance the iconoclastic rather than the cognitive function of the concept of ideology. While in his later historical and economic analyses Marx examined the relationship between knowledge and the social context in a general manner and came closer to the point of view of the sociology of knowledge, in *The German Ideology* he applied the special conception of ideology (in Mannheim's terminology). The primary concern of the special conception of ideology is to discredit the views of an adversary: to expose the 'worthlessness' of his point of view by providing an explanation of its genesis. The concept of ideology was adjusted to this purpose; it was applied as an 'intellectual weapon' and not as a conceptual construct. The special conception constitutes a part of eristics and not of theoretical knowledge.

In *The German Ideology* Marx was anxious to expose the causes which distorted thought in the human studies produced by post-Hegelian German thinkers. Their mystifying illusions about man and society resulted from their unsound and false philosophical point of departure, but this point of departure itself was a product of self-deception. They occupied themselves 'with thoughts as with independent entities, developing independently and subject only to their own laws'. To ignore the material determinants of thought, to consider it as evolving from other thoughts, to examine what is only mediated by thought as an independent history of political, juridical, philosophical, and theological ideas, is to indulge in an illusion or ideology, created by a 'process accomplished by the so-called thinker consciously..... but with a false consciousness'[83]. The principle of the primacy of thought or spirit, accepted by the Hegelians, was socially determined and grew out of the thinker's social context, which robbed him of the possibility of attaining the truth. The errors and ideological fictions, to which the Hegelians fell victims, can be laid bare by philosophical analysis, and their true meaning can be unmasked by exposing their social purpose. Ideology is a conscious or unconscious refusal to see reality as it is in order to justify the interests of the thinker's social class. It provides, therefore, a key to the understanding of its bearer's historical and social situation, but it is not a social theory, capable of attaining truth. This does not imply, however, that in human studies objective knowledge is impossible or that their social determination is always bound to produce conceptions as distorted as reflections in a concave mirror. Not every social theory is an ideology, *i.e.* a system of illusions, and thinking determined by the thinker's social position is not necessarily a source of error. This idea underlies *The German Ideology*. When the 'real basis of history' has been discovered, 'empty talk about consciousness ceases and real knowledge has to take its place'[84]. Valid and objectively true historical knowledge, which analyses the material determinants of human action and derives forms of consciousness from these determinants, is set against the 'phantoms of the brain' of the ideologist.

The least ambiguous formulation of this point of view is perhaps to be found in *The Poverty of Philosophy*, another early polemical work of Marx, in many ways superior to *The German Ideology*. In *The Poverty of Philosophy* also the assumptions of the materialist interpretation of history are expounded unsystematically and for the purpose of polemics, sometimes angry and disdainful, but they are stated in a clear and incisive manner. The theory, Marx wrote, which disregards the law manifested in the course of civilisation, must arrive at an idealised reality. The law of civilisation is, 'no antagonism, no progress'. In the dialectic movement of history the positive and the negative, the good and the bad sides should not be split asunder and neither of them should be abolished, for they both contribute to real history. 'The very moment civilisation begins, production begins to be founded on the antagonism of orders, estates, classes and, finally, on the antagonism of accumulated labour and actual labour ..... Till now the productive forces have been developed by virtue of this system of class antagonism'. The more the antagonistic character of each epoch comes to light, the more the theorists disagree among themselves and different schools of thought arise. Thus, the 'scientific representatives of the bourgeois class' became divided. There was the humanitarian and philanthropic school, to which Proudhon belonged, and which denied the necessity of antagonism. There were the fatalist economists, like Adam Smith and Ricardo, who were only interested in the production of wealth and the superiority of their own times over feudal society. Indifferent to poverty, they regarded it as 'merely the pang which accompanies every childbirth, in Nature as in industry'. On the other hand, there were the 'Socialists and the Communists ..... the theorists of the proletarian class'. They had to remain utopians as long as the productive forces of bourgeois society were not developed enough to reveal the material conditions necessary for the formation of a new society and for the emancipation of the proletariat. 'But in the measure that history moves forward and with it the struggle of the proletariat assumes clearer outlines, they no longer need to seek science in their minds; they have only to take note of what is happening before their eyes and to become the mouthpiece of this .... From this moment, science, produced by historical movement and associating itself with it in full recognition of its cause, has ceased to be doctrinaire and has become revolutionary'[85].

The line of division, which Marx seems to emphasise, runs between the utopias of the early Socialists and Communists and the ideologies of bourgeois humanitarians on the one hand, and the fatalist economists and the scientific representatives of the proletarian class on the other. While the former make an abstraction of the contradictions in actual reality and have a philosophic formula at their elbow as a remedy for every evil, the latter tackle hard facts and examine economic relations without embellishing them with phraseology, though from mutually exclusive viewpoints, corresponding to the antagonistic character of historical development.

The distinction drawn by Marx is of a logical nature. The contrast between utopian thinking and the apprehension of the 'real world' is finally reducible to the separation of factual statements and value judgments. While Marx emphasised the errors and illusions bound to arise from their confusion, he implied that there was a way of reuniting them by discovering the 'laws of the movement of history'. It should be observed that this Marxian belief in 'scientific politics' combined the Hegelian idea of history being reducible to a system of laws with the conviction of French positivism. It was Comte's belief that problems of conduct can be solved scientifically, once a science of morals is based on sociology and politics is transformed into an applied science of morals. This was the meaning of Comte's dictum that 'there is no liberty of judgment in astronomy or physics, and that there will be none in politics once sociology has been perfected'[86].

The Marxist-Leninist doctrine of ideology has codified the views of Marx expounded in or underlying *The German Ideology*. It accepts the thesis that all thinking about socio-cultural matters is socially or existentially determined. In the sociology of knowledge this is the premiss from which the conclusion is reached that all socio-cultural thinking has a relational structure; its assertions cannot be formulated absolutely, but only relatively, in terms of the 'perspective' of a given situation [87]. Marxist-Leninists deny this conclusion. Although the determination of thought by the social conditions of the thinker implies that the social sciences should be included in the sphere of superstructure rising over the material substructure, that is, in the sphere of ideology in the neutral sense of this term, the premiss fails to provide the criteria of validity and condemns the social sciences to a vicious relativism. There are qualitative differences in social and historical settings from which social reality is viewed. The qualitative differences in various perspectives and their corresponding outlooks result from the 'laws of motion', to which changes of the material determinants conform. While the perspective of a decaying class is bound to lead to diverse systems of illusions, conscious or unconscious falsifications, or ideology in the pejorative sense of this term, the perspective of rising classes leads to a scientific ideology, a faithful and objectively valid reflection of social reality. This is the essential point of the dual theory of ideology already mentioned, epitomised in the often repeated dictum that only Marxist-Leninst ideology, the ideology of the revolutionary class, is scientific.

The dual theory of ideology has some obvious logical flaws, which, for the moment, it is enough to mention in passing. To suppose that the conditions of the origin of an idea are decisive for even relevant to its logical validity and material truth is to commit the genetic fallacy. The dual theory of ideology cannot be upheld unless the genetic fallacy is ignored [88]. Furthermore, the theory is scientifically meaningless. A Marxist-Leninist insists that only he knows the truth and that only he has access to the criteria by means of which his claim can be evaluated. This means that he excludes and invalidates any criticism in advance and thus makes his statement unchallengeable by definition. There is no public evidence to support his view, and he does not need any. For the same reason his statement is scientifically meaningless. For in science all evidence is public. A statement untestable by public evidence forms no part of science. It can be said that in a certain sense the dual theory of ideology is anti-Marxian. For one of the constitutive ideas of Marxian thought was the identification of valid knowledge with scientific knowledge.

The dual theory of ideology was established by Lenin and made by Stalin into one of the official dogmas of Marxism-Leninism. Transplanted to Poland, it ruled supreme for a few years there, but at present it is no longer considered as a satisfactory solution of the problems raised by the social determination of socio-cultural thinking. The revision of the dogma has been initiated by the publication of Stalin's *Marxism and Problems of Linguistics*. To explain Stalin's unintended contribution to this particular revisionist trend in Marxism-Leninism, some peculiar features of the reception accorded to *Marxism and Problems of Linguistics* in Poland must be considered.

The peculiarity of the reception does not concern its manner, which was as adulatory as everywhere else. In accordance with the familiar ritual of the Stalinist period, representatives of practically every branch of knowledge, Marxist-Leninists of old standing and new converts, went on record to testify to the fact that *Marxism and Problems of Linguistics* was an epoch-making event in the field of their respective interests and of the theory and methodology of science in general [89]. By a strange coincidence, only the representatives of linguistics were conspicuous by their absence and the most eminent among them declared bluntly that Stalin's pronouncement was an internal Soviet affair without relevance to the study of language [90]. So far as Poland was concerned, this opinion turned out to be correct. Before Stalin's pronouncement the philologists managed to put up a successful resistance to the imposition of Marr's theories; the condemnation of 'Marrism' made no difference to their work. The repercussions caused by the publication of *Marxism and Problems of Linguistics* were wide, but they affected, above all, the position in those branches of scholarship where ideological issues loomed large, and linguistics were proclaimed by Stalin to be a non-ideological subject of study.

The general relevance and far-reaching implications of Stalin's intervention in the controversies of Soviet linguistics sprang from his remarks concerned with the economic basis, the superstructure, and their mutual relationship. According to Polish Marxist-Leninists, Stalin revised the whole theoretical framework for the analysis of the role of ideology on the basis of historical materialism. While

475

all of them were in agreement as to what these modifications were, there was considerable difference of opinion with respect to what they implied.

Also prior to the publication of *Marxism and Problems of Linguistics* it was assumed that the basis of socio-economic formations does not comprise all the diverse factors included in the complex of the material conditions of social life. The concept of material conditions has a wider scope. Material factors which remain relatively stable (*e.g.,* geographical environment) or which exercise an indeterminate influence on the course of social development (*e.g.,* the rate of population growth) form no part of the basis. The basis includes only highly variable material conditions which owing to their variability can determine in a unique fashion the character of each formation. These material factors were found in the mode of production, embracing the productive forces on the one hand and the relations of production on the other [91].

Polish Marxist-Leninists claimed that in *Marxism and Problems of Linguistics* Stalin excluded the productive forces from the basis. For the instruments of production cannot be regarded as the product of some one epoch. They are perfected by a gradual and continual accumulation of knowledge and the effort of all, they manifest a 'kind of indifference towards classes', and can serve different formations equally well. The growth of productive forces represents, therefore, the continuity in the social development. Like language, with which the instruments of production share a certain similarity, they should not be included either in the category of bases or in the category of superstructures.

On the other hand, the basis is characteristic for one formation only; it comes into being by the destruction of its predecessor, it changes and is eliminated to make room for its successor. Only the relations of production satisfy this condition. Consequently, and in agreement with what Marx said in the preface to *A Contribution to the Critique of Political Economy*, they are the 'real basis' that determines the economic structure of society at a given stage of its development. To identify the basis with the mode of production, wrote Schaff, is to open the door to vulgar Marxist conceptions and to economic materialism. The redefinition of the concept of the basis brings more clarity into the theoretical framework of historical materialism, since it allows us to differentiate the factors responsible for continuity from those accounting for revolutionary change. It also disposes of the crude notion according to which the superstructure was supposed to be a direct reflection of the processes of production [92].

The redefinition of the concepts of social consciousness and of superstructure is more extensive, less controversial, and much more important. What Stalin said on this matter, and, above all, the interpretation put on his pronouncements, gradually destroyed the whole Stalinist orthodoxy. At least, this was what happened to Marxism-Leninism in Poland in the course of the few years following the publication of *Marxism and Problems of Linguistics*.

The concept of social consciousness is an abstract notion. Marx used it synonymously with that of superstructure to denote the totality of various definite forms of social consciousness also called 'ideological forms' and 'superstructures' or, in general, any social phenomenon which 'rises over' or 'corresponds to' the economic basis. The concept of social consciousness was the widest possible notion that embraced the 'social, political, and spiritual processes of life'[93]. When the concept of economic basis was narrowed down and identified with the mode of production, the fundamental premiss of historical materialism stated that the mode of production determines social consciousness in the sense indicated above.

Towards the end of his life Engels – and after Engels, Plekhanov and Bukharin – was fully aware that in this formulation the fundamental premiss of historical materialism was obviously false. Engels insisted that the determination of the social consciousness by the economic substructure should not be understood too strictly; that it applied 'in the last analysis' and was only 'ultimately decisive'; that any particular phenomenon of the superstructure (in the Marxian sense) is endowed 'with a movement of its own' and 'with relative independence'; and that various ideological conceptions react upon the economic basis and 'may, within certain limits, modify it'. To deny this is to misinterpret the original meaning of historical materialism and to transform it 'into a meaningless, abstract, senseless phrase'[94].

Plekhanov and Bukharin fully accepted Engels' explanations or corrections and went beyond them. They both tried to analyse more closely the concept of material conditions of life [95] and that of superstructure or social consciousness. In particular, Plekhanov and Bukharin recognised that the social consciousness or superstructure in the Marxian sense is a complex entity in which diverse factors and structures can be distinguished: social and political institutions, science, the psychology of society and various ideological superstructures, differing in their degree of systematisation and abstractedness and separated from the basis by a considerable number of intermediate links. Social psychology embraces habits, manners, feelings, views, aspirations and ideals in their non-systematised and incoherent form in which they are experienced in everyday life. On the other hand, ideologies are systems of thought and rules of conduct and include the 'content' of various human studies. Plekhanov emphasised that the psychology of society is always subjected to the influence of other societies. Every society lives, therefore, in 'its own particular social historical environment' which influences its development and which 'may be, and very often is, in reality very similar to the historical environment surrounding other nations and peoples, but can never be, and never is, identical with it'. This introduces a powerful element of diversity into the whole process of social development. "As the economic movement of every society has a peculiar form in consequence of the peculiarity of the conditions in which it takes place", wrote Plekhanov, "there can be no 'formula of progress' covering the past and foretelling the future of the economic movement of all societies"[96].

It cannot be doubted that in *Marxism and Problems of Linguistics* Stalin adopted some ideas of Plekhanov and Bukharin. For various and sometimes incompatible reasons, however, Polish Marxist-Leninists read into Stalin's pronouncements more than they actually contained. In this undertaking Plekhanov was not their only guide [97].

For Plekhanov's ideas were known to them from the writings of Krzywicki, a Marxian scholar, who formulated them before Plekhanov published his *Development of the Monist View of History*. Krzywicki was perhaps a better guide than Plekhanov for he openly advocated a multifactorial approach to the analysis of social phenomena. Expressed in modern terminology, Krzywicki's basic assumption was that the economy is a differentiated and functional sub-system of the more inclusive society, itself a plurality of differentiated and inter-dependent sub-systems, subject to some definite relations of interdependence with other social sub-systems and the physical environment [98]. Consequently, social evolution cannot be simply reduced to economic change or growth, for economic growth itself, in the quantitative sense of this term, is never purely economic. The materialist character of this assumption is secured by the hypothesis that the economy, as a social sub-system, is in a regulatory, limit-setting relation to the growth and institutional change of other sub-systems within the total society. The modernised version of Krzywicki's interpretation of historical materialism brings out his cognitive interest in the materialist hypothesis, to which the politically minded Polish Marxist-Leninists have taken strong exception [99]. But Krzywicki's scholarly method of inquiry clearly impressed some Marxist-Leninists who were less prominent in the public eye and less vocal but more scientifically minded.

The main revision made by Stalin concerns the sharp distinction between the concepts of social consciousness and of superstructure. The former has a wider scope than the latter and embraces elements which cannot be regarded as super-structural in character. One of them is language. Stalin did not specify any other forms of the social consciousness to be excluded from the superstructure, but in the course of following discussions more and more of them were added, formal logic being the first to join language in its new capacity of a non-ideological form of social consciousness. The essential characteristic of this category of social phenomena is their 'indifference to classes'. They grow and develop throughout history, are a common heritage of a 'whole number of epochs', and serve every type of society as a whole, irrespective of whether this society is class-divided or classless, feudal, bourgeois or socialist.

The question whether a definite form of social consciousness belongs to the superstructure cannot be answered once and for all. Every basis has its own corresponding superstructure, which arises, changes and is eliminated together with the basis. The superstructure is a product of the basis not only in the sense that it uniquely corresponds to and reflects the basis, but also that it serves and assists the basis to 'take shape and consolidate itself'. This means that the superstructure provides society with systems of ideas and with institutions, as well as helps the basis to 'actively fight for the elimination of the old moribund basis together with its old superstructure'. Two conclusions followed from these characteristics of the superstructure, in the new and narrower sense of this term, and its relationship to the basis. The superstructure is an 'exceedingly active force' which may favour or retard the growth of the basis. Moreover, if a form of social consciousness renounces the auxiliary role and passes 'from a position of active defence of its basis to one of indifference towards it, to adopt an equal attitude to all classes . . . . . (it) ceases to be a superstructure'[100].

In view of the fact that the superstructure serves society only in so far as it assists the basis, the sphere of action of the superstructure is narrow and limited. On the other hand, non-ideological forms of social consciousness, such as language, enter into all kinds of man's activity. The distinction between the superstructure in the narrower sense and other forms of social consciousness results from the difference in their respective social functions. The former provides regulative and restrictive principles, the latter in some way or other assist material production [101].

These changes in the theoretical framework were accepted by all Polish Marxist-Leninists and acclaimed as a major contribution to the theory of Marxism-Leninism made by 'that genius of clear thinking'[102]. There arose, however, a serious disagreement as to which further and more detailed conclusions should be drawn from the accomplished revision. The difference of opinion concerned two points: where should the limit be set to the active role played by the superstructure in the 'consolidation' of its basis, and where the line of division should be drawn between ideologically-neutral and ideologically-active forms of social consciousness. The first point was largely a political matter, but the second was not. Stalin's definition of the superstructure in the narrower sense, according to which the superstructure is the common name for political, legal and other institutions as well as for political, legal, religious, artistic, philosophical views of society, corresponding to its economic structure, was of little help in deciding the question where the division line should be drawn. The prolonged discussion about this point was perhaps the most important single factor which entirely changed the intellectual scene in Poland and freed the country from the mental strait jacket. If it is remembered that it was Stalin himself who set this process in motion, we are reminded of the dictum of a great English historian about the place in the development of human destinies which should be accorded to the play of the contingent and the unforeseen.

CHAPTER 33

TWO INTERPRETATIONS OF THE ROLE OF IDEOLOGY

Among Marxist-Leninists in Poland there were two schools of thought as to what meaning should be attached to Stalin's revision of the theoretical framework of historical materialism. The difference between them was essentially that of the approach to historical materialism itself and concerned the question whether historical materialism should be regarded as a guide to action or as a guide to study.

The first interpretation laid emphasis upon those parts in *Marxism and Problems of Linguistics* which spoke of the active role of the superstructure with respect to the basis and tended to enlarge as much as possible the scope of the ideological elements of the social consciousness at the expense of those ideologically neutral. The other interpretation differentiated three categories of forms within the social consciousness: the ideological, idelogically-relevant and ideologically neutral elements, and tried to narrow down the scope of the first category to the advantage of the second and third [103].

According to Schaff, *Marxism and Problems of Linguistics* was a renewed reassertion of scientific socialism as an integral revolutionary theory. In his opinion, with which one can hardly disagree, Stalin's pronouncement was a further step in the long development initiated by Lenin in *What Is To Be Done?*.

One of the important issues in Lenin's controversy with the so-called Economists was the question of 'spontaneity' and 'consciousness' in the workers' movement (behind this question important differences of opinion on policy, organisation and the role of the Party were concealed). The Economists thought that the socialist consciousness arises spontaneously within the labour movement in the course of its struggle against poverty and misery. On the other hand, Lenin strongly believed that the reliance on its spontaneous growth can lead only to the subordination of the workers' movement to bourgeois ideology. For economic struggle means nothing more than the struggle for economic reforms, that is, for the perpetuation of the capitalist system and not for its overthrow. Consequently, if it is not possible to develop the class political consciousness of the workers from within the economic struggle, it should be brought to the workers from without, that is, by the Party, the most advanced section of the proletariat, armed with the socialist ideology [104]. Lenin's 'consciousness from without', with which his conception of a centralised and authoritarian party organisation was closely linked, marked the beginning of so-called 'revolutionary Marxism' or Marxism-Leninism, which placed an increasing emphasis upon the 'subjective factor in social development'. The final outcome of this trend was Stalin's dictatorship and the 'cult of personality', established after another battle was fought and won by the supporters of 'revolutionary Marxism' [105]. To this development of events corresponds the shift in ideology from determinism to voluntarism and the substitution of the political power of the Party for the 'laws of social development'. While lip-service was paid to the 'objective factors', they were dominated in practice by the subjective ones, the will and aims of the Party leaders, on whose decisions the dignity of verdicts based on the discovery of 'new laws' was conferred [106].

Schaff expressly referred to what he called Lenin's and Stalin's generalisations of the experiences in the international workers' movement which contributed to the defeat of the 'theories of spontaneity based on the vulgarisation of Marxism in the spirit of economic materialism', and regarded Stalin's pronouncement as a crowning achievement of the advance in this direction. If the productive forces do not constitute a component part of the basis and the latter comprises only the relations of production, it becomes clear that in a post-capitalist socio-economic formation it is no longer the basis that creates the superstructure, but it is the superstructure that brings the basis into existence. There is nothing inconceivable in the fact that the capitalist basis should spontaneously develop within the shell of the old society, to be finally set free from its feudal integument by a bourgeois revolution. But the socialist relations of production cannot arise in a capitalist society. Although under capitalism the productive forces expand and the material prerequisites of socialism grow mature, its victory requires the creation of the new superstructure and the new basis. It is the new superstructure, that is, the proletarian State, the proletarian Party, and the proletarian ideology, that sets up and develops its basis. Thus, with the overthrow of capitalism a new regularity begins to operate; the superstructure acquires a new quality; and the social development proceeds no longer spontaneously, blindly and destructively, but according to a plan and a consciously controlled purpose. This is clearly what Engels predicted when he spoke of the vast possibilities open to man by the knowledge of active social forces – their action, direction and effects – and of the gradual ascent of man from the kingdom of necessity to the kingdom of freedom [107].

There are certain practical conclusions to be drawn from the discovery of a new regularity which begins to operate after the overthrow of capitalism and secures the primacy of the superstructure over the basis. The countries which start the socialist construction – and Poland was among them – should take the utmost advantage of the powers inherent in the superstructure for the purpose of expanding and consolidating the new basis. This includes the elimination of the bourgeois society and its mode of thinking. The successful accomplishment of the socialist construction largely depends on the strengthening of the new superstructure [108].

In clear language this practical conclusion, derived from "Stalin's theoretical inquiry", amounted to the justification of the extreme forms of compulsion, of the imposition of the official creed by authoritarian enforcement, and of the suppression of every non-conformist thought. This was supposedly necessitated by the laws of development governing the socialist construction. Schaff was repeating Stalin's pronouncement of the 'thirties: the proletarian dictatorship is the mightiest of all governing powers that have ever existed and the highest development of its suppressive functions is a historical necessity, as much 'correct for its time' as Engels' formula that the State is bound to wither away is appropriate for a different period of history [109]. In Poland the events of the following years testified to the fact that the practical conclusions, on which Schaff insisted, were actually drawn.

The doctrine of the unity of theory and practice was applied to justify the unmasking and condemnation of every instance of intellectual non-conformity, of every 'erroneous' theory or methodological procedure as a politically hostile act. An opponent became an enemy who should be forced to surrender or be silenced. Ideas proved to be loaded with explosive materials, for they always carried social and political implications, and any error in this field was fraught with dangers for the success of the socialist construction. Not only theoretical views but also facts were scrutinised for their political implications and were challenged or denounced on political grounds.

The unlimited power of remaking the basis, ascribed to the superstructure, obliterated the distinction between ideological and ideologically neutral forms of social consciousness. Logic and mathematics, physics and chemistry, physiology and psychology, philosophy and sociology, all social and historical sciences, art and literature were declared to be ideological in character or to have a direct or indirect ideological significance. They were subjected, therefore, to political control. Particular theories were banned or imposed in the natural and social sciences, views which should be held in a given scientific field, a branch of scholarship or art, were enforced by decrees of the political authorities. An emotional and woolly ideological nebulosity descended upon all the manifestations of intellectual life, and the pressure of terror – another form of the superstructural force which was creating the basis – left little scope for the exercise of rational and critical thought.

The close connection between this course of events and the voluntarist interpretation of the relation between basis and superstructure was constantly stated and restated to enhance the alleged absence of any arbitrariness and the 'scientific' character of the policy pursued. It was History itself, its law-governed evolutionary process, that ordained the intensified revolutionary vigilance, the strengthening of the power of the State and the Party, the heightening of ideological struggle against bourgeois influences. In an appreciation of Stalin's contribution to the Marxist-Leninist doctrine, published after Stalin's death, Schaff wrote that Stalin's theory of the basis and the superstructure was like a 'floodlight that illuminated the road to revolutionary practice'. Three years passed by before Schaff confessed in a contrite mood that he was wrong in having advocated this disastrous course [110].

It has often been observed that in Marx a learned evolutionist was frequently at loggerheads with an ardent revolutionary. As an evolutionist Marx emphasised that the conquest of State power is the last act in the long chain of economic and social changes, and as a revolutionary he was inclined to advocate the reverse *ordre de bataille* – the overthrow of the capitalist economic structure by the application of State power, previously conquered by political action. The supporters of 'revolutionary Marxism' answered this charge by administering 'quotational shock treatment'. This was to remove any doubt that Marx had always regarded the conquest of political power as a necessary condition for the transformation of the relations of production. Although an impressive collection of Marx's statements of this kind can be piled up, it helps little towards the solution of the underlying theoretical issue. Being men of action, Marxist-Leninists simply appealed to practical considerations. It is self-evident, they announced, that the transition from one form of society to another is a political act. Although this is true, it needs qualification, for the transition in question is not only a political act. It is a complex phenomenon, which the Marxian economic monism does not allow for. The difficulty was finally removed by an inconsequential statement, hardly compatible with historical materialism, that economy is always determined by political action. For politics is an instance of the operation of the superstructural forces – political ideology and political power – upon its substructure, of which these forces are 'centralised expressions'.

But a moderate supporter of 'revolutionary Marxism' would also emphasise that superstructural forces do not have unlimited power. 'No force can transcend its limits', wrote Bukharin. 'The limits imposed upon the political power ..... are inherent in the existing state of economic conditions and therefore of the productive forces. In other words: the alteration in the economic conditions that may be attained with the aid of the political lever is itself dependent on the previous state of the economic conditions'[111]. Bukharin gave a theoretical elaboration of these views in his conception of internal and external equilibrium around which some fierce political battles, waged with abstract weapons, were fought in the Soviet Union in the years 1929–1930. Bukharin's conception of equilibrium located the origin of change in the environment, those who opposed him transferred it from the environment to the controlling power of man.

'Revolutionary Marxism' of the extreme sort disregards any limitations and thus lets a magical frame of mind gain ascendancy over rational thought and action. For magic has been defined as a 'body of purely practical acts, performed as a means to an end' or as an affirmation of "man's autonomous power of creating desired ends" without resorting to observation of Nature or to knowledge of its laws and capable of bringing about what Nature cannot produce [112].

It was William James who emphasised that there are cases where 'faith creates its own verification' and that in such circumstances it is the 'part of wisdom to believe what one desires'. This concerns ends whose realisation depends on a personal contribution, in turn conditioned by the willingness to exert oneself, this willingness being stimulated by the confidence in the success of the final outcome [113]. Such experiences may illustrate what Marxist-Leninists mean when they declare that the superstructure brings its own basis into existence.

Marxist-Leninists can safely assume that in some cases an attitude or a particular sort of behaviour is a necessary condition of a state of affairs being realised. Their error begins when this reasonable premiss is extended to cover all cases and when the appropriate attitudes and ways of behaviour are regarded not only as a necessary but also as the sufficient conditions for the realisation of the pursued objective. For this assumption prompts the belief, characteristic of magical practices, that it is enough to utter certain prescribed words of command or to perform certain prescribed actions to secure the achievement of the desired effect.

The period during which a magical frame of mind pervaded the Marxist-Leninist doctrine marked the point where activity becomes, as it were, the universal substance, and reality, at least social reality, is nothing but a correlate of the will. It was bound to and it did abolish the difference between illusion and reality, for it prompted the creation of 'idealist myths', and these were increasingly replacing rational beliefs in their function as guides to action [114].

Knowledge may be a form of adaptation to environment. The term 'adaptation' carries two meanings. It refers to adjustments to circumstances outside our control and to a purposeful action intended to produce change in the environment. Adaptation in both its meanings requires knowledge; the more detailed and accurate knowledge we have at our command, the better we can adapt ourselves. To assess truly the effectiveness of adaptive action, the inherent structure of environment must be clearly accepted, that is, the mind must submit to its inherent necessitations. For past experience has firmly established the belief that there are always certain things which happen, whatever we do. Moreover, there are always unwanted effects resulting from our action, which cannot be foreseen, however carefully our action is planned. Not all effects caused by human action can be known in advance and such unwanted effects give rise to unforeseeable and, sometimes, undesirable contingencies.

This means that however illuminating the criterion of success in assessing the manipulation of men, ideas and objects might be, a theoretical and empirical test of truth is not dispensable. The function of intelligence does not change when it is applied to the solution of practical problems: it should ascertain in an impartial, *i.e.* intersubjectively valid manner what the facts are in order that appropriate action may be planned and its results assessed. Unless this is done, we can never be sure that action which turns out upon trial to be successful in some respect has actually achieved its purpose. This applies, in particular, to action intended to change man. For by becoming aware of the actor's purpose, man's behaviour may be altered solely as a reaction to the action of which he is the goal.

The practical function of intelligence, divorced from its cognitive function, does not liberate man's power to change and shape reality from preconceived ideas, wish-determined illusions and the subtle deceit of emotion. Neither does it provide this power with any objective criterion by means of which the anticipated effects of action can actually be ascertained and assessed. If theoretical criteria of truth are abandoned, the man of action is left suspended in mid-air between his objectives, unrelated to reality, and a predefined state of affairs. For reality is assumed to be not what it is at any given time, but what it is to become as the result of action. When any limitations upon the possibility of directed changes are denied and the resistance of environment is regarded as non-

484

existent, the mind becomes an autonomous agent operating mysteriously in the surroundings which it spins out of itself. As environment does not stand in a regulatory relation to the course of action, practice provides no test of 'knowledge'. It is no longer action that is conditioned by reality, but reality is defined in terms of action, of its goal and anticipated effects, and conceived as dependent on what man intends to make of it.

The belief that the superstructure can remake or simply create the basis was the apogee of the voluntarist interpretation of Marxian thought. 'Revolutionary Marxism', drawing renewed strength from Stalin's pronouncement and pressed to its logical conclusion, reduced Marxian thought to a system of directives, subject to no restrictive conditions, for interfering with the social and historical process. The programme which started with the Baconian ideal of establishing the rule of science over the whole field of man's thought and action culminated in the destruction of the prerequisites of science.

Although the voluntarist exposition became the official Marxist-Leninist doctrine, another interpretation of *Marxism and Problems of Linguistics* was simultaneously put forward and gradually elaborated in the following years. It tried to restore to historical materialism its cognitive content and was, by implication, a criticism of the voluntarist exposition, which did not do justice to science by treating it as an instrument of technological and ideological change and simplified matters by regarding all branches of knowledge as equally ideological subjects.

The fact that in *Marxism and Problems of Linguistics* science was not included in the superstructure prompted the questions 'Where does science belong?' and 'Was it right to assume that science was class-determined?'. For there could be no doubt that all classes and socio-economic formations take advantage of scientific achievements. Without questioning the dogma that the expansion of science and scientific advance are closely associated with the conquest of political power by the 'ascending class', identified with the Communist Party, Berman urged the re-examination of the role played by ideology in particular branches of knowledge [115].

This approach was pursued by a number of Marxist-Leninist scholars. They analysed the concept of social consciousness into its component parts and pointed out that apart from the dominant superstructure in the narrower sense of this term the social consciousness embraces the relics of the preceding superstructure, the new superstructural elements in the process of formation, which rise over the new basis, and the ideologically neutral elements, which, like language, serve the whole of society and are not class-determined. Apart from language the fourth category includes logic, natural science, permanent cultural values, and social psychology in Plekhanov's and Bukharin's sense. Furthermore, it was claimed that not only natural science was ideologically neutral. The social sciences manifest to a great extent the same peculiarities which justify the exclusion of language from the superstructure. It would, therefore, be an error to include them in the superstructure in the narrower sense [116].

This direct attempt to 'rehabilitate' the social sciences was firmly rejected.

However, an alternative approach gradually evolved and, supported by an increasing weight of specific arguments, was more successful. It was suggested that besides the ideological and ideologically neutral component parts of the social consciousness there is yet a third category which in varying proportions combines the characteristics of both. For instance, the theory and history of literature combine ideologically neutral inquiries with those liable to ideological distortions. It would be unjustifiable to assume that the 'science of literature' is 'naturally and necessarily' class-determined. Facts did not corroborate this conjecture. There were numerous instances of important contributions to the 'science of literature' made by bourgeois scholars. The suggestion underlying this argument went further, for the argument actually assumed that any ideological bias, whether in the history of literature or any other branch of scholarship, is incompatible with scientific procedure. Such distortions do occur, and whenever they are discovered they should be exposed. Their occurrence is not due to any inherent characteristic of the history of literature but to the imperfections of methodology as yet unable to eliminate ideologically-loaded judgments disguised, with or without conscious intent, as statements of fact [117].

The distinction between ideological, ideologically neutral and ideologically relevant (and thus liable to ideological distortions) forms of social consciousness slowly gained ground and eventually could no longer be ignored by the representatives of the orthodox official standpoint [118]. This distinction favoured the emancipation of science and human studies from ideological tutelage and supported their claim for the right to conduct research free from outside control and ideological interference. The concessions made by the official conception of ideology were dictated by political rather than philosophical considerations. They testified to the disintegration of the prevailing authoritarian power system which was taking place at that time. The power vacuum, more and more extensive, created an opportunity for regaining the lost values of universalism and rationality, for the resumption of the practice of objectivity, for the respect of facts and rules of logic. An impressive and highly effective demonstration of this recovery was the re-examination of the whole position in the humanities during the Stalinist period, which was undertaken by Chałasiński and followed up by others [119]. Sociologists, philosophers, historians, economists, men of letters, pundits of all sorts stepped in to extend Chałasiński's criticism to the whole field of intellectual life. This was a period of flourishing and effective philosophical, sociological, economic and literary journalism, and of lively exchanges between the representatives of the non-Marxist and the Marxist-Leninist school of thought [120]. In the universal upsurge of critical thinking young Marxist-Leninists were settling accounts with their political and philosophical past [121].

Chałasiński dealt with two major issues closely connected with each other and with the voluntarist theory of the relationship between superstructure and basis. The first of them was concerned with the general conditions prevailing in the society and influencing the activities of scholars as members of this society. This was a study in the field of the sociology of science, which examined the

486

impact of the social environment upon the institutional structure and content of science. The second issue dealt specifically with methodological problems.

Chałasiński pointed out that the social conditions created by the authoritarian rule were not congenial to the development of scholarship. This view was not novel, but in the circumstances under which it was voiced it was an act pregnant with consequences. Its final outcome was the re-establishment of a large measure of freedom of thought.

Chałasiński argued that the prevailing social conditions were destroying the institutional values of science and scholarship [122], handicapped original work and rewarded intellectual conformity. They placed obedience to established authority above the requirements of rationality and subordinated the judgments of the scientist to the pronouncements of non-scientific authorities. There was no scope for independent inquiry, for it was bound to come into conflict with the imposed truth, values and ways of thinking. The lack of genuine achievements, the absence of individuality and the intellectual sterility, which characterised human studies in the preceding years, were inevitable concomitants of the existing social institutions and of the power and reward systems in the larger society (a corollary of this evaluative summary was that a theory which for a number of years did not produce concrete results could not possibly be sound). They created a 'hollow man', a type of scholar whose reputation was not based on his high achievements, but on his usefulness to the fighting creed and on the good opinion of those in authority [123].

The transmission of scientific procedure and beliefs is effected by example; the scientist who performs his professional duties is simultaneously a bearer of a tradition and of some vital social values. His social role is closely bound to his primary obligation of refusing all obedience in his thinking to any authority. It is the performance of his professional duty that secures for him the social reputation of being guided by respect for truth alone. In the field of creative thinking society has a need of and is sustained by persons for whom their commitment to what they believe to be true comes first. Men who respect truth, that is, consistently try to subordinate themselves to conscience, uphold thereby justice, tolerance, reasonableness, human fellowship and other moral beliefs contributing to the well-being of society. If by some means or other a scientist is induced to misuse his professional authority, to subordinate his activities to the transitory requirements of expediency or to social self-advancement, his failure to act in accordance with his professional and social function has wide social implications. He deprives himself of his social authority and the society of the values of science. He also destroys the tradition, without which science cannot prosper. When the esteem enjoyed by a scientist or a scholar is not commensurate with the significance of his contribution to knowledge, but with the political significance of his opinions and activities, the difference between scientific competence and incompetence is abolished. Science and scholarship cannot flourish unless their moral and intellectual values are recognised, respected and maintained throughout society. In circumstances in which scientific reputations instead of being made by scientific merit are based on commonplace or fanciful achievements, compromises with the truth for reasons of political expediency and favours of the constituted power, the advance of knowledge is bound to suffer. For such circumstances undermine in others the urge to search for truth, that is, to inquire into new problems and to try to find their correct solution [124].

The corrosive effectiveness of the conditions prevailing in all spheres of social life assumed a particularly destructive form in the field of science and scholarship because of their sensitivity to the interference by non-scientific authority. The politician or the man of action has no interest in the advancement of knowledge as such, in so far as it goes beyond the area of its practical application. A characteristic feature of the plans for the development of science, imposed by the authoritarian enforcement in the preceding years, was their utilitarianism. Science was conceived as a means which was to serve the attainment of certain economic ends and the setting up of a superstructure controlled by a bureaucratic organization of political scholars. The task assigned to science not only reflected the intention of establishing a centralised institutionalised control over scientific activities, but also the popular social idea of science, in which the primary value of science is its ability to produce practical results. When the man of action, who is not competent to judge what the scientist does, gains control over the direction to be followed by science, he acts on the assumption that applied science is sufficient unto itself. The control of a non-scientific authority over science favours the instrumental or technical function of knowledge to the detriment of its cognitive ends. This is bound to become a factor counteracting the advancement of knowledge and, from the practical point of view, a self-defeating measure in view of the dependence of applied science on pure research [125].

The man of action is dimly aware of the wider implications of pure science. Habits of thought, which pure science creates – its ethos of rationality and universalism and its detached scrutiny of facts, where facts involve values held to be unquestionable and sacred – exercise an all pervasive influence upon the accepted ideological, social and philosophical ideas. They foster a critical attitude and produce 'upsetting effects' in society at large either for good or for ill [126]. The centralisation of institutional controls over science and its integration into the wider authoritarian society was one of the remedies for the undesirable influence of scientific activity in the larger society. This remedy was strengthened by the establishment of the 'monopoly of a single school', of an institutionalised monopoly of Marxism-Leninism, with its exclusive claim to truth and validity. This was a mechanism of political control over the direction, content and dissemination of scientific knowledge. But the institutionalised monopoly of Marxism-Leninism was bound to affect the rate of advancement of science. For it made it practically impossible to take advantage of what others have achieved, and it corrupted the standards of objectivity. These standards cannot be applied and respected, if the rules of scientific procedure and criticism are laid down arbitrarily and specifically exclude the possibility of questioning the soundness, rationality and fruitfulness of the institutionalised monopoly of a single school. Elaborate ideologies or myths were required to conceal the lack of congruence between the social organisation and the organisation of science, the contrast between propagandist homages paid to science and the absence of conditions favourable to its advancement [127].

On the methodological level, the extension of the concept of ideology, accomplished in the voluntarist interpretation of the relationship between superstructure and basis, sanctioned lack of competence and specialised knowledge, distortion and falsification of facts. It did not encourage original studies, new lines of inquiry and the examination of social and cultural phenomena in all their complexity. The assumption that all processes of spiritual life are ideological, class-determined, and intended to promote the interests of one class against those of another, narrowed the scope of human studies and left them with one question to answer. The past and its achievement were not examined for their own sake, but solely from the viewpoint whether they promoted 'progress' or 'reaction', contributed to the bourgeois or to the proletarian culture. The sole purpose of human studies dealing with a work of art, literature or thought was to attach to it one of these labels. The directives of Marxist-Leninist methodology produced inquiries restricted to elusive generalities, barren of results and liable to stretch and whittle the facts, to fit them to the Procrustean bed of the doctrine. The doctrine provided a student of culture with a scheme of pigeon-holes into which he was expected to put suitably selected and adjusted facts. It ignored the important truth that there is continuity in the development of culture, in the accumulation of knowledge and values, recognised in all historical epochs and increasingly shared by all classes and nations. Although particular conceptions and values may be class-determined in their origin, this genesis is not relevant to their meaning, validity and truth. To approach the work of an artist, a writer, or a thinker with questions formulated in advance and with some 'retroactive criteria' of evaluation is to tear him away from his times. To assume that what men believe in a particular matter is subordinated to what they believe on the whole is to view them through the spectacles of sectarianism. Historical materialism loses its scientific significance, if it is to support the claim that politics inspires and pervades every human thought and experience, and that the class struggle is the decisive factor of scientific and cultural development. It becomes a metaphysical political doctrine, devoid of scientific value and unjustifiable on sociological grounds [128].

Chałasiński's re-examination of the whole position in the humanities and of the destructive influence which Marxist-Leninist methodology exerted in social and historical inquiry was followed by a long public discussion [129]. The supporters of the orthodoxy (Schaff, Żółkiewski, Suchodolski) were ready to recognise that some errors were committed in the past, though the basic approach, laid down by Marxism-Leninism, was the only valid, fruitful and 'objectively true' one. But the defenders of the orthodoxy themselves became diffident of the justice of their cause and no longer sure that 'scientific politics' can successfully replace scientific procedure, criteria of truth and individual judgment. They fought a rear-guard action and were more and more isolated, for this was the period when freedom of speech and thought was being regained in

489

Poland. Under these conditions the claim that the 'priority of politics over science' and the monopoly of Marxism-Leninism were beneficial to scientific advance became untenable. The orthodoxy disintegrated and its former supporters hastened to confess that they no longer wished to uphold the 'errors and distortions of the past period'[130].

CHAPTER 34

THE REAPPRAISAL OF THE DUAL THEORY OF
IDEOLOGY

The disintegration of the orthodox doctrine of ideology presented the supporters of Marxism-Leninism with the question of what remained of their theory of ideology and in what respect they differed from other scholars who recognised the importance of existential, ideological or valuational factors in socio-cultural thinking [131]. It soon became clear that Marxist-Leninists continued to reject the universalistic approach of the sociology of knowledge. In their opinion the basic assumption of the sociology of knowledge, namely that the inherent situational determination and the relational structure of certain types of knowledge must be universally recognised, is an absurd and false view. They argued that if this conjecture is accepted, every ideology becomes 'false consciousness', *i.e.* a system of illusions, and the qualitative difference between various ideological systems, determined by their class origin, is abolished [132]. For some obvious extra-theoretical reasons Marxist-Leninists refused to accept this conclusion. Thus, they were forced to uphold the dual theory of ideology and maintain that while generally systems of social and moral beliefs are conditioned by and serve the interests of some social class and are, therefore, deceptive and mystifying, their own ideology is scientific. The old contradiction remained unresolved, though its sharp edge was somehow blunted by the renunciation of the claim to absolute truth. Marxist-Leninists regarded their own ideology as a 'relatively true' reflection of social reality, capable of being improved upon. Its supposed superiority resulted from its inherent and specific quality which favours a gradual and more and more adequate approximation to true knowledge. This point of view was reaffirmed by Marxist-Leninist writers who dealt with this matter after 1956 [133].

If ideologies are defined as beliefs or systems of beliefs whose acceptance is not governed by scientific procedure, a scientific ideology is a self-contradictory expression. The above definition is certainly inadequate, but it is not arbitrary, devised for the purpose of making nonsense of the Marxist-Leninist concept of scientific ideology. For it is widely, if not universally held that ideologies are accountable on extra-logical grounds and that they are rationalisations or expressions of some individual or collective motives, to be derived from some psychological or social substructure. Marxist-Leninists themselves use the term 'ideology' in this sense when they speak of the ideologies of which they disapprove. Ideologies in this sense are not cognitive but expressive and deceptive functional products, to be interpreted in terms of the substructure by which they are supposed to be determined. These systems of beliefs do not raise the question 'Are they valid?', but 'How do they happen to be held?' and 'What are their implications for or relevance to action?' [134].

Marxist-Leninists are anxious to use the expression 'scientific ideology' without self-contradiction. While in some contexts they apply the term 'ideology' synonymously with 'systems of illusions' (ideology$_1$), and do not try to sharpen its vague outlines and blurred meanings, they have also another concept of ideology. Ideology in the second sense (ideology$_2$) denotes non-systematised beliefs as well as systems of beliefs whose subject-matter is ideological. 'Ideological' is a predicate attributed to each or all subject-matters such as philosophy, social philosophy, history, ethics, aesthetics, jurisprudence, economics, political science. This list is not complete, but the subject-matters enumerated are the most frequent instances of knowledge with ideological significance. The term 'knowledge' in the expression 'knowledge with ideological significance' has a meaning as broad and vague as in the sociology of knowledge [135]. The concept is ambiguous and is bound to give rise to inconclusive disputes whenever any general statement concerning ideology$_2$ is examined and discussed.

It might appear that ideology$_2$ is a neutral descriptive concept, but this is not the case. For whatever its subject-matter a system of beliefs is not an ideology$_2$ unless it is shared by the members of a collectivity, bound together by social and economic interests, that is, unless it is a class-determined system of beliefs. The class determination of ideology$_2$ implies two entire social theories. It is assumed that there is a 'correspondence' between the social position of a class and the beliefs held by this class, the correspondence being the result of the pressure exercised by the needs, causally dependent on the relation to the means of production, which 'give rise to' or 'produce' or 'find reflection in' appropriate beliefs. Moreover, these beliefs are not only class-determined in their content, but also in their capacity as means for the attainment of definite goals, which also arise out of or reflect the class situational determination of their bearers. Ideology$_2$ assists or serves one and only one class [136].

The social theories underlying the second characteristic of ideology$_2$ make it clear that ideology$_2$ contains value-judgments or value-loaded statements. It is actually widely recognised that in ideologies$_2$ evaluative interest takes precedence over cognitive interest in ideas; that they involve a moral commitment to beliefs and an obligation to accept the latter as the basis of action on the part of those who subscribe to ideologies$_2$; that in ideologies$_2$ the conviction of truth and the sense of being morally right are inseparably merged; and that ideologies$_2$ justify and recommend a certain value-orientation and value-selection in the solution of action-dilemmas [137]. This is only rarely recognised by Marxist-Leninists who either ignore or avoid stating clearly the primacy of the evaluative content in ideologies$_2$ [138]. Value-judgements may be rationally justified and supported by various arguments, but they cannot be held on the grounds of their conformity to scientific procedure. It is not possible, therefore, to speak of a scientific ideology$_2$, unless 'scientific' is used as self-congratulatory qualification, intended to impress the uninstructed and the unwary.

The definition of ideology$_2$ is not immune from serious difficulties. It is one thing to say that ideologies$_2$ should be analysed in terms of their social functions and related to a particular social perspective, and quite another to give criteria by means of which the appropriateness of some ideological beliefs (ideology$_2$)

with respect to the underlying class interests can be assessed. Both Marx and Lenin emphasised that the class appropriateness of ideological beliefs cannot be established by discovering the class origin of the thinker. There are bourgeois and proletarian ideologists who are of bourgeois origin. In spite of his contempt for intellectuals Lenin conceded that without them there would be no theory of socialism and without socialist theory workers would remain ideologically enslaved to the bourgeoisie [139]. It is rather the thinker's identification with a particular class – his theoretical comprehension, as Marx put it, of the historical movement as a whole – that makes him an ideologist of this class, and his social location should be established by the examination of his views. But this results either in circularity of reasoning or in reaching the decision by *fiat,* as has actually been the case in 'revolutionary Marxism', first Lenin and later Stalin having been the authoritative legislator [140]. It is no matter of accident that the formulation of the dual theory of ideology by Lenin coincided with the beginnings of sharp polemics, mounting in volume and virulence, against the corruption, opportunism, reformism and revisionism in the workers' movement, which prevented it from recognising that Marxism-Leninism was the appropriate ideology$_2$ of the working classes. Since there were no objective criteria of distinguishing which beliefs were and which were not appropriate, the deviations could not have been accounted for by errors in thinking, but had to be denounced in moral terms as due to the venality of some leaders and to the depravity of some sections of the workers. In 'Imperialism' Lenin established a new 'inner law' of capitalism which related the so-called opportunism in the labour movement to the features of capitalism in the epoch of finance capital and of monopolies [141].

For the Marxist-Leninist theory of ideology the concept of appropriateness of ideological beliefs with respect to class determined situational perspective is of crucial importance. It is this appropriateness which justifies the claim of Marxist-Leninist ideology$_2$ to objective validity, to being an 'adequate' or 'truest' reflection of social reality. But the appropriateness itself has not been established in a satisfactory manner. It remains a matter of faith or a wish-determined belief.

Should this point be conceded on the ground that though faith and rational belief differ essentially, faith need not necessarily be wrong, there remains another major difficulty. The Marxist-Leninist theory of ideology assumes that the appropriateness of ideological beliefs guarantees their objective validity provided that they reflect the historically and situationally adequate class-determined social perspective. This raises a new problem, namely, under which conditions class-determined social perspective can be regarded as historically and situationally adequate. The fact that the functional relation between substructure and superstructure, described by various terms (some of them clearly metaphorical, others implying some kind of causal relation), should produce either an ideology$_1$ or an ideology$_2$ requires explanation.

The Marxist-Leninist answer does not make use of causal agents or empirically discoverable features of social life, nor does it appeal to the criteria of validity applied in scientific procedure, but invokes the verdict of History. It is History itself, which once granted to the bourgeoisie and now grants to the proletariat the perspective that allows it to acquire an undistorted knowledge of social reality. In each of its major periods History vouchsafes this privilege to the class which is the rising and progressive one. The further advanced a class is and the higher stage in historical development it holds, the better it is situated and equipped to know reality. Thus, the socialist society creates more favourable conditions for the progress of knowledge than its predecessor, and the proletarian class in the socialist society approaches truth more closely than the bourgeois class in capitalist society. These premises once justified the tenet that *partijnost'* is a necessary condition of objectivity, or, more crudely, that whatever serves the interests of the suitably defined proletariat is true or promotes the discovery of truth.

This is a chapter from social mythology rather than the methodology of the social sciences. To say that the situation or position of the class within the social structure is the sufficient condition for the adequacy and validity of its ideological beliefs presupposes some kind of omniscience on the part of those who make this claim. For it has no meaning unless the outlooks reflecting various situationally determined perspectives at a given stage of historical development could be compared with each other and with the outlook that does in fact adequately reflect social reality at that stage. Such an outlook would have, however, to be socially undetermined, free from the limiting conditions, which, according to the Marxist-Leninist theory, are never absent from the thinker's thought about social reality.

Our vision of outside objects is subject to the laws of perspective. We cannot say that an object viewed from a particular angle is seen more adequately than it would be from another. For this would mean that we know what the object undistorted by the laws of perspective looks like. We can only say that the same object looks different when viewed from different directions and in different conditions. In each case we learn about this object something new and peculiar to the perspective in which we view it.

Marxist-Leninists claim a kind of knowledge which in the nature of the case it is impossible to obtain. It is no wonder that they have to resort to verdicts of History. Verdicts of History cannot be disproved. They can be invoked whatever empirical data are available, and no set of such data could ever falsify them. The hypothesis supposedly explaining the situational adequacy of class-determined perspectives is not empirically significant. It may be true or may be false, but logically it is a myth. For the mere situational position within the social structure provides no logical reason whatsoever (and still less the sufficient reason) for claiming validity of the outlook corresponding to or determined by this position.

Finally, there is a striking omission in all Marxist-Leninist investigations dealing with ideology$_1$ or ideology$_2$. Marxist-Leninists assume that ideology$_1$ and ideology$_2$ are socially and class-determined, or, more generally, that 'knowledge' is determined by the existential, material conditions of life. They do not

494

specify, however, the kind of relations obtaining between 'knowledge' and material conditions. It is certain that they do not wish merely to establish a one-to-one correspondence based on empirically observable correlations between two distinct sets of phenomena. Thought is supposed to be actually and objectively determined by extra-theoretical and material factors. Mannheim made the same assumption and was faced by the same difficulty: what meaning should be attached to the expression 'existential determination of knowledge' and how various forms of thought are to be derived from existential conditions. Having rejected the idea that 'determination' means 'a mechanical cause-effect sequence', he left the meaning of the term open and ambiguous and never found a satisfactory solution of the problem. Neurath, who was suspicious of the 'cause-effect phraseology' and despaired of the possibility of precision in the social sciences at this stage, preferred, in accordance with his idea of 'aggregational analysis', vague expressions like 'to grow out of' or 'to arise from' over 'to be determined by', which commits us to beliefs at present unjustifiable. But Neurath was also anxious to eliminate the 'superstructure-substructure phraseology' from the language of the social sciences [142].

In the case of Marxism-Leninism the difficulty under discussion is even more baffling than that of Mannheim. For in its conceptual framework there is nothing to mediate between the material factors in social change and the ideas which form part of the superstructure. The latter directly rises over or is brought into existence by the basis. Mannheim introduced a third heuristic concept, that of perspective. 'The social context to which Mannheim relates ideas is mental, not material; it is a system of human relations, not a physical object' [143]. The style of thought in Mannheim's sense is not, therefore, determined directly by the existential conditions but is mediated by the perspective and existential ideas, the peculiar manner in which the individual realises or describes his position with respect to non-human and human environment, to an external reality and other social actors. The existential determination of knowledge does not put us under the obligation of deriving ideas from material objects, from entities of a different realm of being, but of relating one class of ideas to another class of ideas [144]. This does not solve all the difficulties but removes one major obstacle to the formulation of the Marxian theory in an empirically significant language.

If the concept of ideology$_1$ is accepted, the possibility of social science should be denied. Marx who initially seemed to have used the term 'ideology' in the sense of ideology$_1$, did not follow this course. On this account he is sometimes accused of inconsistency, of having denied by implication the possibility of social science excepting his own social theories [145]. There are some reasons for raising this objection, since Marx, as everybody else, was not immune from conceptual confusions and terminological ambiguities. There is, however, little ground for asserting that Marx set the concept of ideology$_2$ against that of ideology$_1$ and believed that while others fell victims to illusions he managed to produce a scientific ideology$_2$ [146]. Marx rather believed that though human studies are liable to ideological distortions (in the sense of ideology$_1$), a positive

495

science about ideological subject-matters is possible. In other words, Marx believed that it is possible to differentiate the ideological or evaluative and cognitive content in human studies. In terms of present-day knowledge, Marx asserted that sociological relationism in human studies does not imply epistemological relativism, and that in spite of the conscious or unconscious distortions in which social knowledge is wrapped, a true and scientifically valid social knowledge can be obtained. This was a common belief of nineteenth century positivism of which Marx was an adherent.

The distinction between the cognitive and ideological (evaluative) content in human studies was rejected by Marxist-Leninists in the past and is still rejected to-day. However, the basic disagreement is now narrower than it used to be. The present version of the dual theory of ideology has dropped some of its more extreme views, in which it took pride in the past. It lost its former glib finality, which tends to emphasise the disparity between liberal and authoritarian habits of mind. It stopped using invidious epithets in order to dispose of views disliked or difficult to refute, equating such views with advocacy and advocacy with deliberate lies. The intention to impose the dual theory of ideology by an *a priori fiat* is absent. There is a semblance of an argument offered to justify the theory and its claims are stated in moderate, sometimes tentative terms, as well as qualified by various restrictive conditions.

It is not always quite clear whether Polish Marxist-Leninists distinguish three possible different meanings which the dual theory of ideology may have. The first of them is based on the idea due to Mannheim. Mannheim suggested that the historical and social genesis of an idea is not as irrelevant to its ultimate validity as the genetic fallacy argument claims. In his view, social conditions, under which a perspective emerges, have some effects on the content and form peculiar to this perspective. Perspectives differ qualitatively in their conceptual frameworks, the meaning attached to concepts, ontological commitments, models of thought, levels of abstraction, patterns of argument, kinds of inferences made in controversies [147]. Mannheim claimed that the social position infiltrates, as it were, into the investigator's method and results of inquiry and reveals otherwise unobservable aspects of social reality. Each perspective contains, therefore, new cognitive elements which must remain unnoticed to the investigator, who is himself determined by different social conditions. Mannheim's anticipatory assertion, unobjectionable as long as it is accepted as a programme of inquiry or a hypothesis to be tested, has been assimilated into the dual theory of ideology as a well-established fact [148].

Mannheim's idea that each perspective contains new cognitive elements is linked with a quite different assertion, namely, that knowledge provided by different perspectives differs in adequacy and that perspectives determined by the social position of 'progressive' and 'revolutionary classes' are more adequate than any other. It is assumed as self-evident that a 'perishing class' can produce only an ideology$_1$ as a means of disguising the real nature of a social and historical situation, the recognition of which would not serve its interests. This is the second meaning which can be attributed to the dual theory of ideology. In contradistinction to the past, Marxist-Leninists no longer claim absolute validity and truth for ideologies₂ developed by 'rising classes'. Since the perspective of a rising class reflects the direction of social development, knowledge arising out of its social conditions is more adequate or closer to truth than any other that might be obtained at that stage [149].

This modification has further been restricted by the recognition that neither social theories held by 'progressive classes' are immune from falling victim to ideological distortions (ideology₁), nor are those produced by the representatives of other classes a mere collection of errors and illusions. The social sciences are liable to ideological myth-producing conceptions, irrespective of the investigator's class location. The cognitive content of the social sciences should be distinguished from their ideological coefficient, and the criteria of validity from those of social significance. The elimination of ideologically distorted knowledge depends on the improvement of the methods of social inquiry and on our knowledge of how ideological rationalisations operate to cover up the real situation by a protective web of fictitious ideas. The position of a class within the social structure does not by itself validate or invalidate its conceptions. The fact that ideological ingredients, that is, rationalisations of interests and practical aims, characteristic for particular classes or groups within them, are a universal feature of thinking, makes the differentiation of the Marxist-Leninist and the bourgeois sociology untenable. What can be fairly presumed is only the fact that proletarian ideological inspiration is more fruitful for progress in social research than any other [150].

The change in the meaning of the term 'ideology', which is thus accepted, could be described as a shift towards the particular conception of ideology in Mannheim's sense [151]. Since the particular conception differs fundamentally from the total conception, involved in the first of the above given interpretations of the dual theory, this theory clearly contains incompatible views. The particular conception of ideology recognises that the opponent's thought does not always need to be ideological (ideology₁) and that some of his assertions may be valid and true. This implies the recognition of what the total conception of ideology denies, *i.e.* the existence of common and universal criteria of validity, accepted and shared by individuals who are 'ideological' adversaries. An ideological controversy becomes essentially a disagreement on the evaluative level. Although it may involve disagreements concerning matters of fact, these differences of opinion can be separated from the evaluative controversies and resolved by the accepted rules of scientific procedure. This leaves open the question what is the source, the mechanism and relative significance of diverse evaluative approaches.

This touches upon the third possible meaning of the dual theory of ideology. All Marxist-Leninist writers, who took part in the revision of the concept of ideology, have referred to it, but it has most clearly been expounded by Lange. Lange has always held that value- and socially-determined ideas ('ideological elements') pervade all kinds of thinking, whether in social or natural sciences [152]. He has recognised the force of the genetic fallacy argument and never seriously believed that the criteria of validity could be formulated in terms of alleged social significance. At the same time, he has rejected the view that ideological motivation must always impede scientific research and place the scientist at a disadvantage in reaching universally valid results. If 'ideological elements' are inherent in all thinking, the ideal of thinking entirely emancipated from ideological motivation is unobtainable and unreal. Instead of denouncing them we mus tlearn how to live with and make the best possible use of them [153].

For it is an error to suppose that ideological motivation can never stimulate the development of science. Veblen observed a long time ago that the factors of psychological, social and mental inertia are not equally distributed throughout society. Classes which are sheltered from the impact of environment tend to retard the process of social transformation, to perpetuate their ways of life and thinking. Unlike the leisured classes inclined to conservatism, those exposed to the strain and stresses of the environment show the liveliest interest in and awareness of newly arising possibilities of reconstructing the traditional scheme of life [154]. Gunnar Myrdal, who is far from being under the influence of the Marxian school, has been fascinated by the 'fusion' of the cognitive and evaluative elements in the social sciences and by the selective or constitutive role played in them by 'ideological ingredients' [155]. Lange's approach to the valuational coefficient in thinking combined the strands inherent in Marxian teaching with the tendencies and conclusions reached by some contemporary non-Marxist scholars.

Lange's formulation of the dual theory of ideology removes the theory from the methodology to the psychology and sociology of science. There is a conservative and a progressive ideological attitude. The former tends to disfavour and the latter to favour the advance in the social sciences. For 'love of freedom', 'hatred of injustice' or 'desire for social betterment' spur the undertaking of new lines of research and, generally, stimulate the spirit of inquiry and inventiveness, which are a prerequisite of the growth of knowledge. The conservative ideological attitude is motivated by the desire to maintain the established social order and acts as a stimulus to the inquisitiveness of the mind only so far as new facts can thereby be discovered that help to perpetuate the existing institutions. Generally speaking, the conservative ideological attitude tends to mystify and the progressive one to illuminate social reality. For the latter, being free from any inhibition to the discovery of the 'whole truth' about social reality, is bound to be favourable to scientific progress [156].

The conservative and the progressive ideological attitudes are theoretical constructs which admit intermediate attitudes between the two extremes. The latter combine a confusing motivation in one field of study with an exploratory inspiration in another field. In fact, the conservative and the progressive attitudes seem to be ideal types in Max Weber's sense, never actually realised in a pure form. For Lange accepts the fact that the conservative attitude may also stimulate a limited but real scientific advance, as well as that the progressive attitude may produce mystifications. Utopian pre-Marxian socialism, revisionist deviations from scientific socialism, the period of dogmatism and the 'cult of personality' in recent years provide examples of distorted knowledge and biased conceptions in the workers' movement, which would have to remain unaccountable, if the progressive and the proletarian ideological attitude guaranteed automatically an adequate reflection of social reality.

Two things remain vague or even ambiguous in Lange's interpretation of the dual theory of ideology. The first concerns the question whether the ideological attitude has merely a selective significance or whether it may also determine the content of thought (though not its validity, which should be established solely by means of scientific procedure). The selective function of ideological attitudes is widely accepted by historians and social scientists and it does not raise any serious problems concerning the objectivity of social knowledge. While value-judgments contribute to the delimitation of the subject-matter at the initial stage of inquiry, they do not penetrate into inquiry itself, which proceeds in accordance with the rules of scientific procedure [157]. The view that value-determined principles of selection underlying scientific inquiries are bound to distort their results is based on a misunderstanding. The misunderstanding arises when what is found to be the case under certain conditions or with respect to some definite assumptions is regarded as universally valid, irrespective of the accepted assumptions and limiting conditions. Such fallacies, which can be exemplified by Marx's law of the progressive and inevitable pauperisation of the masses or Malthus' theory of population, are not due to the underlying evaluative assumptions, but to unwarranted extrapolations or to an error of logic and not to the contamination of thinking by partial and biased conceptions.

On the other hand, the possibility of separating evaluative and non-evaluative sentences is highly doubtful, if Mannheim's conjecture is accepted, that is, if ideological attitudes exercise not only the selective role but also determine the content of thought as well as patterns of inference and logical rules of inquiry. Mannheim's conjecture has not been tested by observational material, and it is far from certain that it is a tenable hypothesis. It is a tentative surmise, to be regarded with due caution until a considerable effort is made to analyse in detail the alleged differences in styles of thought and in logic [158].

The second ambiguity involves the problem whether ideological attitudes should be regarded as psychologically or class-determined. The difference is important. For in the latter case ideological attitudes can no longer play a purely selective role. They become a constitutive factor or a style of thought in Mannheim's sense, characteristic for particular classes of which the individual is a member. In the thinking of the individual the class-determined style of thought becomes explicit and articulated. Consequently, thought is regarded as wholly a function of a definite social position. To presume this and to assert that there is some necessary relation between particular ideological attitudes and particular classes is to readmit a fruitful source of ideology₁, which in the past culminated in conferring some kind of infallibility upon the proletarian class and some kind of perverse blindness to truth upon all the other classes. It also led to the establishment of the sharp distinction between bourgeois science, inevitably fraudulent and tendentious, on the one hand, and proletarian science, inevitably objective on the other, a distinction to-day repudiated by most Marxist-Leninists in Poland. Both the premiss and the conclusion manifest a style of thought which is rooted in the habit of avoiding questions about the evidence which supports these sweeping and untested assertions.

There is an understandable but important omission in the account of the relation between science and ideology, in both meanings of this term, given by Polish Marxist-Leninists. For they never mention institutionalised ideologies, integrated with the power system in society, which world play a considerable role in the contemporary. Either indirectly, that is, by modifying the social structure of the larger society, or directly, by interfering with the institutional structure of science, institutionalised ideologies are the factor which at present probably most strongly inhibits the advancement of knowledge. In this respect favourable or unfavourable ideological attitudes seem to be of a secondary import as compared with the crucial significance to be attached to definite conditions in the structure of the society. Recent history has finally invalidated the belief that while science exercises a powerful influence upon the social structure, science is exempt from the impact of the processes in the wider society upon its institutional structure. Science advances in various social systems, but its development may proceed at a different rate determined by its interaction with a whole series of social variables. One important determinant of the rate is the social environment of science [159]. Social scientists have done much to elucidate the interdependence of science and the social structure as well as to reveal the reasons why in an authoritarian society the latent tension between scientists and scholars on the one hand, politicians and men of action on the other, present in all social structures, assumes an acute form [160]. In Poland Chałasiński and Ossowski tried to give a sociological analysis of the mechanism by means of which the centralisation of institutional controls over science and its integration into a monocentric power system resulted in limitations of the scope for scientific activity, slowed down or even halted in some cases scientific advance. The institutionalised ideology and its authoritarian enforcement thwarted and frustrated all kinds of ideological attitudes, including those which Lange calls progressive. If the latter are actually as favourable to scientific achievements as they are said to be, the state of science in Poland has provided no confirmatory evidence to this effect. Compared with the pressure exercised by an institutionalised ideology, they have proved to be powerless.

Ossowski's fortunes in the past and Chałasiński's recent experiences have illustrated this fact. Chałasiński's studies were greatly resented by the constituted power, and he was finally severely penalised for inquiring into the connection between science and social structure in Poland [161]. One of the tenets of the institutionalised ideology in Poland is the belief that the present social structure is more favourable to the advancement of knowledge than it had ever been, and the questioning of this belief impinged upon the protected values of the official creed.

In conclusion it is only fair to emphasise the considerable amount of intellectual energy which Polish Marxist-Leninists had to spend on clarifying the inherited doctrine of ideology and on extricating themselves from the entangling web of transparent fallacies and gross errors, some of which still haunt Marxist-Leninist thinking [162]. The paucity of positive results is out of proportion to the expended effort.

The sociology of knowledge is a field of study which is clearly Marxian in origin. If it can claim, however, some progress since the times when Marx became its founder, all the major contributors to this development were without exception non-Marxist scholars: Max Weber, Émile Durkheim, W. F. Ogburn, Karl Mannheim, Florian Znaniecki, and at the present time, P. A. Sorokin, R. K. Merton, and Talcott Parsons. Judged by their achievements, Polish Marxism-Leninism, as for that matter Marxism-Leninism elsewhere, has contributed nothing of interest to the common fund of knowledge in this field of study and remains at the stage where Marx left it. This in itself is a fact which requires an explanation in terms of the sociology of knowledge and the sociology of science.

It has been suggested that a social scientist or a social philosopher, irrespective of whether he takes part in or turns away from politics, cannot help to influence his environment by the knowledge acquired in his inquiries. Social knowledge is a form of a critical consciousness of social reality; it does not take for granted the prevailing social concepts and views, the existing social order and institutions. On the other hand, an authoritarian or totalitarian social system cannot maintain itself, if it allows people to question its wisdom and judgment or to spread the awareness of the current and perennial social problems. The conflict is inevitable and so is its outcome in the short-run. The stagnation of social thought is a phenomenon concomitant of the domination of politics over science [163].

CHAPTER 35

THE NEW PRINCIPLES OF THE HISTORY OF PHILOSOPHY

AND THEIR REVISION

It was the history of philosophy that during the Stalinist period attracted the greatest number and the most enterprising minds of the younger generation of Marxist-Leninists [164]. This was an understandable development, related to a widespread tendency among scholars to escape from the present to the past. Unlike the Marxist-Leninist theory of knowledge, metaphysics, philosophy of science or social philosophy, the history of philosophy was an area relatively unchartered by the established doctrine and thus offered to independent minds some allurements denied to the former. Although a Marxist-Leninist could never forget that the philosophical past was, on the whole, a record of errors and intentional or unintentional misconceptions occasionally interspersed with anticipatory ray of philosophical comprehension, the vindication of truth could not have been achieved without a glimpse beyond the restricted ground of the established doctrine.

On the other hand, the intimate contact with an immense mass, variety and complexity of historical facts had a chastening and liberating effect on the young Marxist-Leninist historians of philosophical thought. The impact of the subject-matter on their views was enhanced by the wide historical knowledge which some of them had acquired. The dissatisfaction with and the propensity to revise the methodological principles of Marxist-Leninist historiography, laid down from above, made an early appearance among the young historians of philosophical thought. Having learnt the skill of exposing the befogging effect of class interests inherent in the thinker's social and intellectual location or the limitations imposed by his theoretical viewpoint, they began to wonder whether for a historian it was at all possible to remain unaffected by man's involvement in history. This prompted the question whether there were no blind spots and preconceived ideas in their own minds, by which they were led astray into believing themselves exempt from this universal human characteristic.

This realisation came only later. At the beginning the young Marxist-Leninist historians had no doubt that whatever had been done before them had little, if any value at all, showed no really scientific understanding of historical facts and, generally, was useful solely as source-material for illustrating the decay and ideological collapse among the bourgeoisie. The main characteristic feature of the bourgeois histories of philosophy, as exemplified by Windelband's *Lehrbuch der Geschichte der Philosophie*, Überweg's *Grundriß der Geschichte der Philosophie*, Bréhier's *Histoire de la philosophie*, or Tatarkiewicz's *History of Philosophy*, was to treat philosophy in abstraction from its social and political context and to reduce its history to a motley mass of information about various thinkers, bound together by the filiation of ideas and mutual influence of one mind upon another. The history of philosophy was thus transformed into an encyclopaedic reference book which lists names and titles, summarises philosophical systems, enumerates concepts and problems. Since it ignores the existence of historical laws and historical progress, bourgeois historiography dissects the stream of events, which is in fact all of one piece, into discrete unrelated elements and replaces an agglomeration of atomic facts for the progressive movement of thought. The dissection results in misjudging the relative importance of particular thinkers and misconstruing their intentions, in an unjust dismissal of some philosophers to oblivion and an unwarranted elevation of others to an exalted position, generally, in an unforgivable lack of discrimination between what is of primary and what only of secondary significance. Having cut up the progressive movement of ideas by sharp lines into individual facts and separated them from their context, the bourgeois history of philosophy proceeded to the construction of its schemes into which ready-made facts were to be fitted. The clear-cut distinction between materialism and idealism vanished in such constructions, and philosophy turned out to be a striving for the establishment of values which make capitalism the sacred and everlasting achievement of mankind. In particular, as a result of such constructions Marxism-Leninism was no longer a revolutionary upheaval in the history of philosophy. It was reduced to the stature of a philosophical current comparable with Spencer's evolutionism, Neo-Kantianism, or neo-positivism. Its existence was not disregarded, but its distinctive features were discounted. For it was treated as one of the numerous schools of thought, that comes into being, continues to exercise influence and is bound to be forgotten eventually. Marxism-Leninism was presented as if it were to share the fate of all the other schools of thought in the past which come and go [165].

A history of philosophy that is unaware of its important role in the political and ideological struggle degenerates into a useless register of events and 'instead of being an effective weapon of social progress becomes an inventory of relics laid up in archives' [166]. Philosophy is an ideology, a theoretical worldoutlook, whose function it is to direct and to influence man's beliefs and attitudes. Kant referred to this function of philosophy in *Kritik der reinen Vernunft* and called it 'the cosmical conception'. Philosophy, Marxist-Leninists argued, has a therapeutic value, it is, in Avicenna's words, the 'science about how to cure the soul'. It liberates humanity from the weight of superstitions, awakens trust in science and reason, teaches faith in life and in the effectiveness of human exertions. Philosophy should contribute to man's happiness by showing him the true values, those which by reflecting the course of progress increase the well-being of the individual and improve his social conditions. The history of philosophy is, therefore, the 'collective memory' of the age-long struggles for a scientific worldoutlook that emerges from the unceasing conflict between materialism and idealism and leads to the discovery of Marxism-Leninism [167].

This vital function of the history of philosophy is ignored, obstructed or endangered by the bourgeois historians, who, by 'falsification and distortion', try to deprive Marxism-Leninism of its historical ancestry and to invalidate its claim to being the inheritor of every progressive idea in the history of mankind. There is hardly a single materialist thinker whose views were not misinterpreted in order to appropriate his reputation and to assimilate his contribution into the tradition of idealism. Democritus is presented as a supporter of empirio-criticism, Lucretius of existentialism, Spinoza of irrationalism and mysticism; Descartes is a continuator of St. Augustine and Thomas More is a martyr of the Church. French materialists of the Enlightenment are mere agnostics; the Renaissance is an inept attempt to continue the achievements of the Middle Ages, which have remained as the unsurpassed heights of philosophical understanding. Some materialist philosophers such as those of the Renaissance period or Gassendi or the Russian revolutionary democrats are totally ignored [168]. On the other hand, the bourgeois historians glorify thinkers who represent the most reactionary philosophical tradition, hostile to science and social progress, for instance, Thomas Aquinas, Berkeley, Hume, and Malthus. At the same time, the history of philosophy is made to fit the cosmopolitan categories of European culture. A geographical division of the world is supplanted by that of different spheres of cultural influence, and Marxism-Leninism is presented as an outgrowth of a civilisation essentially different from that of the Western world [169].

As the Marxist-Leninists saw it, the different conceptions of history, underlying the immanent and their own historicist interpretation of the political, economic, social or philosophical thought, were not only to be differentiated from the theoretical and methodological standpoint, but also evaluated in terms of truth and falsehood, to be totally rejected or totally accepted. Again, as in the case of sociology, the ground was swept clear of everything that had been done before and the history of philosophy, particularly of philosophy in Poland, was to be entirely rewritten [170]. Its guiding principles were formulated in a general but unambiguous manner.

The basic methodological principle of the Marxist-Leninist history of philosophy is the Hegelian assumption of the interconnectedness and interdependence of all historical events. Philosophy is no autonomous development but only one form of social consciousness, dependent on and being influenced by its other forms and ultimately determined by the material conditions of life. But to relate philosophical ideas, philosophical problems and solutions to a definite social-economic context means to examine philosophy as an ideological expression of definite class relations and interests, which it serves and perpetuates. There are various laws, therefore, which govern philosophical development and which reveal coherence and progress in the concourse and sequence of seemingly fortuitous circumstances [171].

Kroński's *Lectures on the History of Ancient Philosophy* provides a fair example of what this assumption implied. Kroński regarded the slave system as the key to the understanding of the ancient Greek and Roman philosophy and the struggle between the *demos* and the aristocracy as the driving force of its development. These two classes, he argued, produced two doctrines or two traditions which can be named after Democritus and Plato and which reflected their political interests and goals. The doctrines of a spontaneous naive materialism and of various sorts of idealism alternated, surged forward and declined.

Finally, they both disappeared for neither of them represented the slaves, the exploited class and the human economic basis of the system. As soon as this basis was eliminated, its superstructure had to vanish too. The institution of slavery acted as fetters on the progress of scientific and materialist thought and, generally, held back philosophical development. This accounts for the fact that ancient philosophy has made no appreciable contribution to the advancement of knowledge. Kroński followed Farrington whose *Greek Science* was translated into Polish and justly, though inordinately, admired. It is Farrington's view that the aristocratic contempt for manual work made the advance of many branches of science impossible in Greece and produced 'an ideal of science . . . . . which was largely verbal and unrelated to practice'[172].

Although the materialists and the idealists of modern times have referred to the tradition of Democritus and Plato respectively, materialism and idealism of the capitalist era are totally different from their initial forms in the ancient world. There is no genuine continuity. Modern philosophy is free from the limitations inherent in the slave system or in the feudal mode of production. The similarities are superficial and the revival of ancient theories, whether those of Democritus or of Plato and Aristotle, is in fact their reformulation, determined by the requirements and intended to assist the consolidation or transformation of the capitalist basis [173].

The account of particular philosophical systems and views is as schematic as the above described structure, mystifying in its terminology, in the distribution of the relative significance and the selection of material. Thus, the time-span from Thales to Plotinus is divided into three epochs: the period of the growth of the slave society, the times of the democracy of slave owners, and those of its decay. To the first period belong the 'naive, spontanoeus materialists (Thales and the Milesian school), the dialectician-materialist Heraclitus, and the reactionary idealist philosophers – Pythagoras and the Eleatics'. Plato is presented mainly as a political philosopher, who has always provided the chief ideological requisites for the struggle against the working classes. He gets less space than Epicurus and Lucretius. Socrates was an enemy of democracy who was sentenced to death by its defenders; he was made into some kinds saint by bourgeois historians. The bourgeois tradition has also invented the myth of the Greek miracle to justify the imperialist conquest of coloured peoples and to protect the purity of its civilisation from racial contamination. These are a few glimpses at the picture of Greek antiquity, drawn by the Marxist-Leninist historian. The picture would not become more impressive by adding more details.

Kroński's *Lectures on the History of Ancient Philosophy* was received as a valuable methodological guide to ancient philosophy and as a truly educational work of a scholar 'conscious of the justice of his cause'. But praise was mixed up with some anxious misgivings as to whether this synopsis did justice to the philosophy of Greece and Rome [174]. Kołakowski's *Lectures on Medieval Philosophy* [175], another synopsis conceived on similar lines but vastly superior to the former by its erudition and relieved by flashes of originality, could have

505

caused the same apprehensions. They both appeared at the time when Tatarkie-wicz's learned and erudite *History of Philosophy* was withdrawn from circulation and Adam Krokiewicz, the leading Polish historian of ancient philosophy, was unable to publish some of his works [176].

There could have been little doubt that the conspectuses, which were replacing the works denounced for their alleged ideological distortions and factual inadequacies, were themselves ideological tracts for the edification of the ignorant. As instances of historical inquiry they exemplified the error peculiar to pragmatical history, known later under the name of 'presentism'. Presentism is historiography written backward. On the one hand, as Hegel pointed out, it takes the 'occurrence out of the category of the Past and makes it virtually Present', on the other it 'brings the past to bear upon the present conditions of things' [177]. To write history backward we have to abandon the narrative and resort to the scissor-and-paste history [178]. This is a method favoured by those who view history as nothing but a preparation, in this case, a preparation for the advent of Marx, Engels and Marxism-Leninism.

The particular type of the scissor-and-paste history, which the Marxist-Leninist historians cultivated, was cognate to the historiography of the French Enlightenment [179]. *Voltaire,* wrote Montesquieu, *écrit pour son couvent,* by which he meant that for Voltaire historiography was a way of crusading for the victory of Reason. The fit substance of history must be selected from the collection of innumerable facts according to a plan and purpose imposed from without. Voltaire's purpose was to show how the barbarian uncouthness of the past has been slowly transformed into the civility, blessings and good fortune of his own times and how in general *le monde avec lenteur marche vers la sagesse.* The pragmatical or didactical purpose prevented Voltaire and the writers of the Enlightenment to 'lift history above the level of propaganda' [180]. This also happened to the Marxist-Leninist historians of philosophy, who by an appropriate selection of evidence tried to demonstrate the soundness of certain historiosophic principles and to show that Marxism-Leninism was the consummation of all philosophic thought in the past.

But the Enlightenment not only bequeathed to the young Marxist-Leninist historians the pragmatical conception of history, the lack of sympathy for and understanding of the 'dark ages' prior to the appearance of Reason, and the superficial to absurdity idea of historical causation; it also inspired them with its peculiar fervour and disruptive spirit that permeates its historical, literary and philosophic writings. There was in the Enlightenment a force which redeemed its fanaticism. The Enlightenment turned against every dogma, including, finally, its own; it contained a self-corrective device that was bound to abolish the limitations and prejudices so conspicuous at its initial stage. In the course of time this influence of the French Enlightenment also made itself felt and deeply affected the young men who regarded themselves as in many ways the successors of the *philosophes.* At first, however, its spirit of a holy war, in which history was a weapon, was uppermost in their mind and joined hands with the crudities of Zhdanov's passionate militancy and intellectual arrogance.

The idea that philosophical systems are solely an ideological expression of definite class interests provided the basis for the establishment of two fundamental 'laws' of the history of philosophy. Both of them were formulated by Zhdanov and accepted by all Marxist-Leninist historians in Poland.

If the disputes of various philosophical schools reflect the class struggle taking place in an antagonistic society, and if the main line of class division in such a society always differentiates two classes, those of the exploiters and of the exploited masses, there are also two main philosophical schools of thought struggling with each other throughout the ages, those of idealism and materialism. Furthermore, since social progress is the process of change that leads from a class-ridden to a classless society and the struggle for the abolition of classes is bound up with the development of the materialist outlook, the 'scientific history of philosophy', that truly and adequately reflects the historical process, is the 'history of the birth, rise and development of the materialist world outlook and its laws'. So far as materialism grew and developed by constant disputes with various idealist trends, the 'history of philosophy is at the same time the history of the struggle of materialism with idealism'[181].

This assumption is neither a matter of convention nor a mere classification of philosophical currents, comparable to any other classificatory division, but the 'fundamental historical law of philosophical development'. This can be seen from the fact that the solution of many particular philosophical problems is supposedly determined in advance by the thinker's choice between materialism and idealism [182].

The second 'law' of the scientific history of philosophy regards the teaching of Marx as a philosophical revolution. It has resulted in the creation of a new philosophy 'differing qualitatively from all previous philosophical systems, however progressive they were'. Consequently, there are two epochs in the development of philosophy: the period prior and posterior to Marx and Engels whose life work forms the great divide [183].

From these two fundamental laws of philosophical development three subsidiary methodological rules were derived. The first and most important extended the class determination of philosophy from schools of thought to particular thinkers and to their particular views. A 'concrete interpretation' requires the assignment to any philosopher of a definite position with respect to the class struggle of his time, the description of his share in the consolidation or destruction of the existing economic basis and its ideological superstructure. Any ascertainable philosophical deviation in the thinker's views from the prevailing ideological patterns should be reduced to socio-economic causes, to strains and stresses within the social class, to which he belonged, and to the shift in class relations[184].

The second methodological rule recommended that advantage should be taken of the results obtained by the application of the first directive to assess the relative importance of a given thinker for the development of the scientific materialist world outlook. In this manner Marxist-Leninist methodology gains an objective and universal criterion by means of which it can make the right selection of facts and order them according to their relative significance. This establishes the third rule which enjoins the historian to trace the direction of progress in philosophy and to assign to particular thinkers a place in it in accordance to whether they managed, in the specific conditions of their times, to discover and to resolve problems that promoted the objectively ascertainable course of social progress [185].

The three methodological rules had some direct and far-reaching implications. First, they made havoc of the relative independence of philosophical thought with respect to the material conditions of life, recognised by Engels in his old age and nominally endorsed by Marxist-Leninists, including Zhdanov. Second, they ascribed a high rank of philosophical importance to various writers, who so far have only been marginally considered in the history of philosophy (though they have a place in the history of social or political thought). The history of philosophy, wrote Kroński, has to give an extensive account of the 'great plebeian thinkers', such as Thomas More, Winstanley, Mably and Morelly; of the ideologists of the bourgeois revolution, *e.g.* Milton, and the precursors of socialism – Robert Owen and the French utopian socialists. According to the same criteria, Herzen, Belinsky and, generally, the so-called Russian revolutionary democrats, assume the most important place in the period between Hegel and Marx. This ran counter to the opinion of Marx and Engels who, understandably, assigned this rank to Feuerbach [186]. As far as the history of philosophy in Poland was concerned, the methodological rules of Marxist-Leninist historiography implied an upheaval and a complete revaluation of the prevailing tradition. In particular, Edward Dembowski, a Polish revolutionary democrat (according to the Marxist-Leninist classificatory categories) and the leader of an abortive peasant rising in 1846, to which Marx and Engels referred in laudatory terms [187], was to be given, jointly with Herzen and Belinsky, the most elevated rank, for they all, in Kroński's opinion, rose to the greatest philosophical heights in the period prior to Marx [188].

The scissor-and-paste history of philosophy, combined with Zhdanov's peremptory instructions, was firmly established in Poland by 1952. Its methodological rules were applied, above all, in a large-scale effort to adjust as much as possible the pattern of social, ideological and philosophical developments in nineteenth century Poland to that in Russia, as established by Soviet historians. The most cursory and commonplace references to Poland, made by Marx and Engels, every sentence, however trivial, of Lenin and Stalin concerned with the approach to historical inquiry or with the ideological development in the past, were scrutinised with reverence and the utmost care to serve as an unconditionally accepted guidance for historical research [189]. Two of Lenin's short contributions, *In Memory of Herzen* and *Two Utopias,* were of particular importance [190]. The main historical categories – those of revolutionary nobles, bourgeois democrats, and revolutionary democrats – which served to differentiate various political and ideological movements in nineteenth century Poland, were taken from *In Memory of Herzen.* They were applied and adjusted to Polish conditions in a great number of contributions that appeared in the years 1952–1956. The ideological transformations in Russia and Poland in the pre-Marxian period were described as essentially similar. They ran parallel to and interacted with each other. To show in detail that this had actually been the case and that the reception of Marxism-Leninism in Poland had proceeded in a 'correct manner' became the objective which was moved by the taskmasters of historical inquiry to the centre of interest [191].

The task assigned by Zhdanov to the historian of philosophy turned out to be extremely burdensome and difficult, if not impossible to accomplish. For the extension of what had to be considered in a historical-philosophical inquiry was expanded to an unmanageable size. It included not only ontology, the theory of knowledge, methodology, logic and ethics, but also, and above all, aesthetics, the theory of art, historiosophy, social philosophy, philosophy of religion, politics, science, economics, and ideology. At any rate, these were the problems which a historian of the nineteenth century philosophy in Poland, as it was conceived by Marxist-Leninists, should have investigated. The same applied to other periods [192]. Generally, the conception of philosophy as a world outlook and of its history as a synoptic vision comprising political, social, economic, and philosophical thought, cultural trends and artistic currents, disregarded the accepted distinctions and self-imposed limitations. It also abolished the difference between philosophers at one extreme, philosophical journalists and polemical writers of political tracts for the times at the other. It resulted in insuperable difficulties of which, at first, Marxist-Leninist historians were unaware and which they regarded as a sign of their superiority over the traditional historian of philosophy [193].

There is a passage in Lord Acton's *Inaugural Lecture on the Study of History* in which he pointed out the confusion ensuing from a study of history, if it does not display in its course specific and distinctive characteristics of its own. Mastery, he argued, is acquired by resolved limitations a historian is a master of detail, without which his synthesis loses itself in the realm of fantasy. At the time when Marxist-Leninists were embarking upon their new course Tatarkiewicz gave the same advice to the historian of philosophy: he should not try to do everything at once; self-imposed limitations and principles of selection are unavoidable in his inquiry [194]. Marxist-Leninists discovered the justice of this view when from making plans they passed on to their implementation. For they were unable to retain control over their all-inclusive subject-matter; they got lost in the tangle of the sum total of views on man, society, history, religion, politics, literature, morals, and the like. They became trapped in trivialities and generalities unsupported by the study of detailed and concrete facts. On the other hand, the assumption that the history of philosophy can be represented as a mere response to socio-economic needs and the corollary of this assumption that an alleged social and political significance should be imputed to every philosophical view, overreached the evidence. The historian's attention, focussed at the wrong place, impeded the progress of his study. Since the examination of particular facts was neglected, a typical Marxist-Leninist historical contribution contained very little of interest to the history of philosophy in the specific meaning of this term.

There was yet another difficulty no less formidable than the first. For their methodology put Marxist-Leninists under the obligation of relating the phenomena of the superstructure to those of the basis. This presupposed the existence of an economic and social history with a wealth of detailed material, generalisations and syntheses. But economic and social history as advanced as the philosophic programme required was non-existent.

This does not mean that no economic history of Poland was available. On the contrary, Franciszek Bujak (1875–1953) and Jan Rutkowski, mentioned before, have created thriving schools of research, and the latter produced the first comprehensive *Economic History of Poland*[195]. This work did not, however, satisfy the requirements of Marxist-Leninists, for, in their opinion, it was based on entirely false theories and could be used only as a source of materials [196]. Strange as it may appear, economic history as a specialised branch of historical inquiry was suppressed during the Stalinist period, since such a specialisation was considered to be harmful [197]. A short essay that discussed various views on and succinctly described some aspects of the development of capitalism in Poland in the first half of the nineteenth century was practically all that was made available to the historian of philosophical thought [198]. Although a Marxist-Leninist historian should have had a wide and detailed command over the history of economic and social development, he was left entirely to his own resources with practically no help from economic historians.

To acomplish his assigned task, a historian of philosophy had first to change into an economic and social historian, and, as he was not equipped and prepared to perform this role, what he did was to make a short-cut of an impermissible sort. Over and over again he turned in a vicious circle. First, he deduced his economic and social data from various historical material at hand and later related the inferred state of affairs largely to the same material from which he started. This procedure was either actually displayed before the reader's eyes or made apparent by stereotype descriptions as much alike as if they came from the same mould[199]. Moreover, it has been said that the influence of ideology shows nowhere more strongly than in economic history. Marxist-Leninist economic history affords a striking instance of the justice of this observation. When the historians finally recognised the amateurishness and irresponsibility of their procedure, they also confessed that it always filled those who had to resort to it with an unconcealed dismay [200].

THE REVISIONIST TREND

Those were some of the reasons which explain the fact that hardly were the rules of Marxist-Leninist methodology and the plan of historical-philosophical inquiry announced, when the soundness of the rules and the feasibility of the plan were brought into question. The first misgivings and suggestions concerning the advisability of methodological revisions appeared in print towards the end of 1954. The following year the unsatisfactory state of inquiries on the history of philosophy in Poland was brought into the open, and its causes were analysed. Finally, about the middle of 1956 the retreat was publicly sounded, for it was recognised that without an extensive modification of the methodological principles laid down in 1952 no useful progress could be made.

The defences of the scissors-and-paste history of philosophy were breached by the simple observation that while philosophical doctrines may serve as an instrument in the class struggle, they are not exclusively a class weapon. They contain some knowledge about the world, which is not determined by the class struggle but by the stage reached in the development of science.

The question whether a philosophical system is an adequate reflection of the world is not decided by ascertaining the class origin of its author. For the pressure of the class consciousness determines only the urge for knowledge and not its content. Moreover, if the thinker's class origin were to be considered as a decisive factor, a historian of philosophy could hardly make any use of it. It should be remembered, for instance, that the founders of modern philosophy were 'an escaped monk, a state-chancellor, a cobbler, a nobleman, a proscribed Jew, a learned diplomat, independent men of letters and journalists'[201].

To say that Marx's teaching has been a turning point in philosophy does not mean that he has solved every possible philosophical problem and brought the development of philosophy to its final destination beyond which no further progress can be made. Such interpretations would militate against the very essence of Marx's mode of thinking. The great service rendered by Marx to philosophy is the complete emancipation of human thought of every illusion, whether ideological or religious, which precisely removes all obstacles to an unimpeded progress of science and philosophy [202].

If philosophical doctrines are not determined solely by the class struggle, it is impermissible to treat their history as a constant advance of materialist systems gradually approximating true knowledge, the progress of which is obstructed or disrupted by the interference of idealist thinking. If that were the case, Duns Scotus, Averroes, Giordano Bruno, Descartes and many other thinkers would have to be dismissed as having contributed nothing to philosophy. Marxism-Leninism would succumb to the spirit of a sectarian narrow-mindedness and to falsehood, if it denied the patent fact that thinkers of all classes and of all kinds, including the idealists, can make a contribution to the development of the scientific world outlook. It should be observed that prior to Marx the protagonists of materialism came always from the progressive groups of the propertied classes; that the systems of Leibniz and Hegel are purely idealist and yet without them scientific socialism would be unthinkable; and that the various plebeian movements, however much they might have contributed to the scientific world outlook, combined, as a rule, ideological radicalism with irrationalism, religious ideas and mysticism.

Any philosophical opinion of the past should be examined from the viewpoint of its role in the development of philosophical thought. In a certain superficial sense of this term, the *Cogito* of Descartes and Spinoza's ontological proof of

God's existence are idealist. But what Descartes and Spinoza wished to and did accomplish by these means was to emancipate philosophy from the tutelage of theology. They took advantage of them to show the autonomy of Reason and the independent existence of Nature. To be rightly assessed, the particular achievements of Descartes or Spinoza or any other thinker should be viewed in relation to their other opinions, examined against the background of the past ages and in the light of the conclusions drawn by their successors. For it will then be found that *cum duo faciunt idem, non est idem.* Bacon's reliance on perception is the point of departure for the assertion that empirical knowledge is not only possible, but the only fruitful and valuable one. When Thomas Aquinas speaks of the priority of knowledge through the senses he embarks upon the proof that was to show the limitations of natural knowledge and its need for supernatural enlightenment [203].

The criticism of the methodological rules was soon extended to what was initially called the 'fundamental historical law of philosophical development' – the division of all systems into two mutually exclusive classes of idealist and materialist philosophies. This division was to be coextensive with another and equally important one, namely, that of progressive and retrograde or reactionary doctrines. It was, however, clear that they were not coextensive. For Hobbes is a materialist and Hegel an idealist, but, according to Marxist-Leninists, neither the former is a progressive nor the latter a retrograde thinker [204]. Still greater difficulty arises when a particular question and its various solutions of fundamental importance in philosophy are to be evaluated. The problem of universals provides an instance in point. Nominalism, already considered in the preceding pages, is often associated with materialism and was its first harbinger in modern times. It does not follow from this, however, that nominalism has always played a progressive role and that the anti-nominalistic solutions have obstructed the progress of philosophy. Sometimes just the opposite has been the case. Not every doctrine, even an important one, can be unambiguously described as either idealist or reactionary [205].

The initial methodological rules have thus been considerably revised. First and foremost the distinction has been made between the ideological and cognitive function of philosophical ideas. More generally, the inference that the content of philosophical ideas is exclusively social, since it might be given a causal social and historical explanation, has been rejected. This clearly implied the re-establishment of the relative independence of philosophical thought and its examination in relation to what its predecessors handed down, to contemporary scientific knowledge, and to its internal order and coherence. This restored the immanent interpretation of history to its rightful position in historical inquiry from which it had been previously banished. Contrary to the initial wholesale condemnation, there was no longer the question of denying that bourgeois historical studies may have some value. While a Marxist-Leninist disagrees with many important findings and the general direction of the traditional history of philosophy, he is not duty-bound to dismiss as worthless nonsense every result obtained by traditional methods [206].

512

The difference between a Marxist-Leninist and a non-Marxist historian does not consist in the fact that the former rejects and the latter accepts the immanent interpretation of history. They both accept it but with one difference. For a Marxist-Leninist historian does not consider the immanent interpretation as self-sufficient and applies to the history of philosophy as a whole and to the actual research work the rules of procedure provided by historical materialism. In this sense the historian's immanent approach is restricted by being considered as a first stage of historical inquiry whose results are subject to another interpretation of a higher order.

The revised methodology has been finally and universally accepted in 1956, and the occasion was provided by the publication of Lenin's *Philosophical Notebooks* in a Polish translation. Kroński, once the leading exponent of the scissor-and-paste history of philosophy, acknowledged that Zhdanov's principles produced a 'vulgarised historiography' and a 'false picture of the development of philosophy'. The revision of the methodological rules, once again restated with a flourish, characteristic for this *Sturm und Drang Periode,* was supported by Lenin's authority, whose original ideas on 'scientific history of philosophy' could be rediscovered upon the publication of *Philosophical Notebooks.* In Kroński's opinion, it paved the way for the return to Hegel's historicism after the 'ruthless and brutal retrogression from Hegelianism' in Marxist-Leninist thinking during the past years [207].

The reference to the rediscovery of Lenin's original ideas was clearly a face-saving formula. *Philosophical Notebooks* were widely available in the original and, since 1949, in German translation [208]. Zhdanov's standpoint could have been as profusely supported by quotations from Lenin's writing as its criticism, made by the disenchanted supporter of Zhdanov's line.

Whether Hegel can teach common sense, respect for facts and logic is a moot question. There is no doubt, however, that interest in and respect for Hegel is no longer concealed and that this revival has at present a beneficial effect upon Marxist-Leninist historiography [209]. Whether this influence would remain beneficial in the long-run is by no means a foregone conclusion. For while in the past Hegel has inspired fruitful lines of approach to the history of law, political institutions, art, moral and philosophical ideas, his historicism has exercised a baleful influence. His use of Spinoza's principle: *omnis determinatio est negatio,* has produced a method of thinking which is as empty as it is arbitrary. Practically every preconceived idea, every prejudice or superstition can be 'rationally' established by applying Hegel's dialectic mode of thinking. The present revival of the Hegelian philosophy in Polish Marxism-Leninism is not associated, however, with Hegel's historicism, but with his historism. Hegel's greatness, wrote Kroński, should be seen in his rising above the horizon of thought of his own epoch and in making it possible for others to follow in his footsteps [210]. The liberating effect of the Hegelian philosophy, which its admirers at present experience, rests upon its interpretation as an anti-dogmatic historical philosophy, denying the finality of any intellectual achievement.

THE REVALUATION

It has already been mentioned that the high rank assigned to history by the Marxist-Leninist doctrine has promoted interest in and enlarged the scope for historical inquiry of every kind. With some signal exceptions – economic history, to which reference has been made, is an instance in point – and under certain conditions – historical inquiry had to be restricted to the national culture and be free from cosmopolitan influences as defined in Chapter 8 – the expansion of the existing and the initiation of new lines of historical studies were encouraged by Polish Marxist-Leninists in every possible way. A considerable and steadily rising number of research workers were engaged in the history of art, literature, education, technique, social and natural sciences, logic, mathematics, law, economic, social and political thought. The history of philosophy has also benefited from this stimulus. If the number of contributions only were considered, the history of philosophy could be described as flourishing in the last few years. In general, a definite and sometimes a considerable advance in many domains of historical inquiry has been achieved and the interest in the historical approach to knowledge has been greatly and fruitfully stimulated.

The encouragement given to historical inquiry was, however, prescriptive, and this spoiled much effort and harmed many results. The insistence that 'cosmopolitism' should be eliminated, narrowed down the boundaries of the historian's outlook or even reduced it to parochial proportions. Under the inescapable methodological guidance of the Marxist-Leninist doctrine historical inquiry was often deflected from its cognitive end and served didactic or ideological purposes. Some definite directives were imposed from above and were strictly enforced. The main task of the historian was laid down once and for all. He had to differentiate between two main trends in the national culture, the progressive and the reactionary, and to show how the former has grown throughout the ages to reach its culmination point in Marxism-Leninism, the inheritor of everything that was healthy, vital, great and revolutionary in the national tradition. This approach to the past, inspired by one of Lenin's polemical and marginal remarks, was obligatory for every historian, whatever his particular subject of study.

Thus, Marxist-Leninist historiography came into conflict with well-established facts, for its assumption and objective could not have been substantiated without inflicting violence on the silent material of the past. The history of nineteenth century philosophical thought in Poland may provide an example of how this conflict was resolved.

The first half of the last century was dominated by the so-called national philosophy, which arose under the influence of the Hegelian system and, as Engels would have said, of its conservative rather than revolutionary side. 'The tradition of all the dead generations', wrote Marx, 'weighs like a nightmare on the brain of the living'. In the opinion of Marxist-Leninist historians, the nightmare that haunts the minds of the Polish people at the present time is still the national philosophy of the last century with its insistence on the worth of the individual, social solidarity, supremacy of the moral values, national independence as a prerequisite of the individual's self-fulfilment, and the rule of Christian providence in history. To remove this weight would accomplish a twofold task. It would establish the bond between theory and practice in the field of the history of philosophy, that is, it would relate the history of philosophy to the current ideological and political struggle for the acceptance by the people of the Marxist-Leninist outlook. Second, to reveal the reactionary character of the national philosophy would be the first step toward its replacement in the social consciousness by the democratic and revolutionary trend, which, in the past, was overshadowed and concealed by the national philosophy. Marxist-Leninists argued that this programme did not infringe upon objectivity, since objectivity presupposes a close bond between history and the struggle for progress. The victory of the scientific world outlook of Marxism-Leninism in the mind of the people would represent the resumption of the sway of progress over the forces of darkness and superstition [211].

Consequently, the national philosophy was made to appear as an ideological expression of the fear of the revolution experienced by the propertied classes. These classes – the feudal gentry and aristocracy, later transformed into capitalist landowners – cherished no illusions but that a revolution would have deprived them of their privileged position in the community. The national philosophy was an ideology anti-national in character, socially and morally cynical and prompted by the hatred of progress which it tried to oppose [212].

Parallel to the reactionary trend in the national tradition the progressive one has made its way, in the past obstructed and stifled by the furies of private interests and doomed to oblivion in historiography by revengeful class-inspired scorn and forgetfulness. The progressive tradition was represented by the revolutionary nobles, the bourgeois democrats and, above all, the revolutionary democrats; the latter were the most advanced incarnation of pre-Marxian philosophical thought. Their guiding idea was to combine the struggle for national independence with a wide programme of social reforms or with a social revolution.

Marxist-Leninist historians concentrated all their efforts on the second thread in the cultural tradition and accomplished a complete reshuffle in the order of relative importance. The national philosophy, morally condemned and neglected, receded into the background to leave the intellectual scene for the representatives of the progressive and revolutionary trend.

The error of Marxist-Leninist historiography did not consist in recalling the existence of trends and aspirations in nineteenth century Poland which could not be accommodated within the tradition of the national philosophy, but in assigning to them a role that the available facts did not warrant. Whatever we may feel about the two trends, the fact remains that the national philosophy was dominant and the revolutionary democrats were a weak force. For instance, Edward Dembowski, the leading revolutionary democrat, not only failed to exercise a wider intellectual influence on his contemporaries in general, but also was entirely ignored by those who, according to Marxist-Leninists themselves, continued his programme [213]. Moreover, it is hardly possible to differentiate the representatives of the revolutionary and the national trends from the philosophical viewpoint. The former were not materialists and the latter idealists in the Marxist-Leninist sense; they were all idealists. The differences between the two trends hardly touched any philosophical issue apart from those which in a very loose sense of these terms could be called problems of social philosophy and historiosophy. The real differences concerned the questions of political programmes and ideologies [214].

The revolutionary democrats were ranked among the forerunners of Marxist-Leninist materialism for reasons which have nothing to do with materialism in the accepted sense. They were described as harbingers of the materialist outlook for they formulated the ideology of the exploited masses, contrasted the existing social system with a utopian socialist ideal, voiced atheism or rejected religious inspirations in their thinking on social matters, and did not see in the individual but in the masses of the people the decisive force in history [215]. They did not discuss these problems in a general and systematic manner, and their views had to be disentangled from their books and articles concerned with political, literary and ideological issues of the day.

There is considerable doubt whether their writings are of any philosophical interest, which does not mean that they are of no interest whatsoever. The advance of philosophy has been mainly dependent on the advance of science, and a close relation with the latter has a decisive, beneficial and fruitful influence upon philosophy. It should be recognised, however, that in the past other influences were often at work. Conceptions growing out of the religious, moral, artistic, political, and social life also affected philosophical thinking and in the popular social image they are philosophy *par excellence*. On this account there are, in principle, some reasons in the past philosophical tradition for the inclusion of the revolutionary democrats into the history of philosophy. But both the nature of what was uppermost in their minds and the manner in which they presented their views seem to justify the opinion that they were, above all, political writers. They were little interested in formulating theoretical views on reality unless they were clearly relevant to the practical direction of social and political life.

The history of philosophy which assigns to them the rank of the most important representatives of philosophical thought of the period necessarily becomes the history of political and social thought. This actually was the case with the Marxist-Leninist contribution to the history of the nineteenth century philosophy in Poland. It was no longer a history of philosophical ideas and problems, but a history of various political attitudes, political parties and groups, their programmes and ideologies [216].

There was a cleavage or discrepancy between the Marxist-Leninist reconstruction of history and its ascertainable course. As the Marxist-Leninist historians of philosophy went along with their studies, the cleavage widened, and no amount of abuse showered on bourgeois historiography for its distortions of the objective historical truth could bridge this abyss. For they began to realise that the spirit of crusade and the sitting in judgment over the past was producing a history which was superficial and patently tendentious. The initial certainty of knowing all the truth and of having the inner light that was to enable them to see through the darkness of human destinies grew dim under the impact of the historical picture created by their own efforts. The feeling of intellectual uneasiness, apparent practically from the very outset, became ultimately transformed into the awareness that they must retrace their steps and start again. They were led to believe, Kołakowski explained, that they would converse with the great demiurge of History. The demiurge turned out to be a figment of the imagination created by a secular eschatology, cultivated under the name of scientific history.

The conclusion that was drawn by the Marxist-Leninist historians of philosophy from their experiences was the dissociation of the idea of progress from the concept of historical process. Progress may be real, but it is not inevitable. History may have a meaning and purpose, but they cannot be read out of the historical process as if they were the inner side of events, discernible to every unprejudiced mind. It is an error to face historical events and past epochs with a standard of right and wrong, truth and falsehood, which were not their own, or to rely on Hegel's cunning of reason to bring about the golden age, or to believe that what is historically progressive is also morally good. Thus myths are created, and fallacies and self-deceptions are let loose upon the world to deprive the human mind of its power of understanding, of seeing clearly and fearlessly, of ever extending its imaginative and comprehensive range. To express one's feelings towards the past or to turn history into an ideological holy war for the instruction and benefit of its contemporary participants is something different from trying to discover the truth about the past, that is, what the available evidence obliges the historian to assert [217].

What Kołakowski tried to impress upon the historians who thought of their subject-matter in philosophical terms was an emphatic reminder that the supreme task of the historian's craft is to disentangle myth and reality. This means that a historian must approach history with all the tolerance, reverence, reasonableness, and ingenuity that he can master, if he wishes to do justice to the past. Kołakowski followed his own advice in his study on Spinoza [218]. It remains to be seen whether the others will discard the old assumptions as thoroughly as he did.

NOTES TO PART VI

1. See W. H. Walsh, *An Introduction to Philosophy of History*, Hutchinson's University Library, 1951, pp. 13–15,
2. Deborin (1), 91
3. Marx-Engels (3), Vol. 2, 356.
4. Górski, K. (1), 9, 23. Górski is a Catholic historian and the lecture in which he propounded these views was delivered at the Catholic University of Lublin. He dismissed every kind of historiosophy, not only that of inevitable progress or of historical materialism, but also theological historicism. He made it quite clear that a Catholic historian should draw a sharp distinction between accepting the teaching of the Church and making use of it in describing and explaining the actions and motives of men.
5. Geyl (1), 31–33; Geyl (2), 11. Paul Kecskemeti, the translator of Mannheim (2), used 'historicism' for the German '*Historismus*'.
6. Bullock (1), 293–296.
7. Polish Marxist-Leninists thought otherwise and accused Polish historians of supporting the 'idiographic creed'. This also applied to Górski and his views presented above. See Schaff (22), 184–186.
8. Randall (1), 39, 46; Aron (1), 160; Aron (2), 66.
9. Historism and historicism are confused with each other by many Marxist-Leninist and non-Marxist writers in Poland. See Baczko (11), 54–55; Kula (4), 31, 141; Borucka-Arctowa (1), 280–284; Kroński (9), 256.
10. Schaff (22), 138–155.
11. Hegel (2), 22, 27–28.
12. Marx-Engels (3), Vol. 2, 354–355, 443, 458.
13. See, *e.g.*, Kroński (3), 251–254; Kołakowski (16).
14. Stalin (1), 574.
15. Stalin (1), 578.
16. Hegel (2), 9–10, 25, 35.
17. Marx-Engels (3), Vol. 2, 356.
18. Lange (5), 277.
19. Lenin (2), 332.
20. Schaff (22), 8–10, 22, 155, 188; Bukharin (2), 43.
21. Hegel (2), 10.
22. Weber (1), 178–181. The logical priority of the value interpretative approach to historical inquiry, together with the assumption that this approach is consciously or unconsciously class-bound and class-determined, was used by Polish Marxist-Leninists for the purpose of refuting methodological individualism in the social sciences and of defending historicism against Popper's criticism in Popper (3). See Żółkiewski (12), 280–286. Popper's critic made his task easy by ignoring the last chapter of Popper (1), a work to which he referred but failed to take into account. Methodological individualism does not exclude the interpretative approach.
23. Aron (2), 68.

24. Mises (2), 209–215; Hempel (1), 460–461; Hempel-Oppenheim (1), 326–327; Zilsel (1), 720–721.
25. Butterfield (2), 102.
26. See Mises (2), 215; Popper (1), Vol. 2, 250–252; Popper (3), 143–147.
27. Schaff (22), 100–111. The distinction of the absolute and relative sense of the term 'unique' and of 'recurrent' or 'non-recurrent events' are accepted in Schaff (22), 277–283, without reference to the contribution of logical empiricists whose essays are quoted in a different context and dismissed for they 'deny' the laws of history. See Schaff (22), 133–138. Popper's views are evaluated in extremely sharp language. They are said to represent "the very heights of ignorance which shocks even when judged by the 'more solid' standards of bourgeois science". Compare Żółkiewski (12), 278. Schaff also misunderstood the views of Rickert. See Lazari-Pawłowska (1), 19–21.
28. Schaff (22), 283–293.
29. See Popper (5), 420.
30. This comes out clearly also in Schaff's inquiry. At one point in his argument he speaks of the 'objective laws of development' providing the criterion of distinguishing which characteristics should be regarded as singular or general, recurrent or non-recurrent (Schaff (22), 283). But this is soon forgotten, and the recurrent characteristics, given irrespective of adopted viewpoint, are considered as corroborating evidence for the acceptance of laws (Schaff (22), 289).
31. Weber (1), 204–205. The Marxist-Leninist criticism of Weber's methodological theories is to be found in Schaff (22), 239–246; Kryszewski (1). Schaff saw in them only a collection of 'false and reactionary conclusions' drawn from the erroneous premiss that abstract concepts have no factual reference. Schaff's peremptory condemnation was in turn criticised in Lange (5), 99. The role of 'typological concepts' in the humanities is examined in Lazari-Pawłowska (2). This is a scholarly essay, whose task is to re-examine the whole problem in the light of recent developments provided, above all, by C. G. Hempel and P. Oppenheim, *Der Typusbegriff im Lichte der neuen Logik* (Leiden, 1936) and Polish inquiries in the domain of sociology, history of art and literature.
32. Lenin (1), Vol. 1, 84–85.
33. Marx-Engels (1), 6–7, 14–15, 30.
34. Quoted in Berlin (2), 121–122.
35. See, *e.g.,* Schaff (22), 34, 37–38; Lange (5), 51.
36. Lange (5), 51.
37. Marx-Engels (1), 28–29; Marx-Engels (3), Vol. 2, 401–402.
38. Lange (5), 55–56.
39. Marx-Engels (3), Vol. 2, 356.
40. Lange (4), 30–32; Lange (5), 67, 97–99.
41. Schaff (22), 298–307. Schaff closely follows Engels. See Marx-Engels (3), Vol. 1, 338–339 and also Bukharin (1), XI–XV, 49.
42. For more specific arguments against historicism see Popper (3).
43. According to Schaff, historical laws are laws of social development. See Schaff (22), 51, 307.
44. Schaff (22), 24–31.
45. Bukharin (2), 33.
46. Stalin (3), 8, 10–11.
47. Schaff (22), 12–14.
48. Marx-Engels (4), 208.

49. Marx (2), 102; Marx-Engels (3), Vol. 2, 404–405, 407–408.
50. Stalin (3), 8.
51. Lange (4), 22–23; Schaff (22), 42–45.
52. Popper (3), 102–103; Popper (5), 252–254.
53. Robbins (1), 79–83.
54. See Schaff (22), 52.
55. Lange (4), 23–30; Lange (5), 58–70.
56. Lange (5), 44–47, 79–81.
57. Stalin (3), 71, 75; Lange (5), 38–43.
58. Bukharin (1), 120–129, 148; Goldschmidt (1), 108.
59. Marx (4), Vol. 1, 372–373, 180. See also Marx-Engels, (3), Vol. 1, 83–84.
60. Marx (2), 92.
61. Goldschmidt (1), 112–113.
62. Marx-Engels (3), Vol. 2, 94.
63. Malewski (2), 63–74.
64. The analytical and empiricist approach to the traditional formulation of histori-
    cal materialism aroused strong objections on the part of the supporters of Marx-
    ism-Leninism not only of the 'old school' but also those of the younger generation.
    See, *e.g.*, Kossak (1). The publication of Malewski (2) was followed by a long and
    sometimes heated exchanges of views. See Wiatr (2) and (3), and the reply of
    Malewski in Malewski (4) and (6). The main objection against Malewski's ap-
    proach was that historical materialism constitutes a coherent sociological system
    and that a greater precision in its formulation should not be accomplished at the
    expense of disrupting its coherence and comprehensiveness.
65. Malewski (2), 77–79; Lange (5), 46–47, 81–82, 291.
66. See Lange (2), 746.
67. Bukharin (1), 49; Deborin (1), 91.
68. Popper (3), 3.
69. Schaff (22), 350.
70. Merton (1), 423. See also Neurath (1), 29; Goldschmidt (1), 103.
71. Popper (3), 128.
72. Hempel (1), 466–467.
73. Schaff (22), 354.
74. See Weber (1), 220.
75. Schaff (22), 367, 351–353.
76. An attempt to establish some formal criteria by means of which causal factors
    can be 'weighted' in respect to their degree of importance is to be found in Nagel
    (1), 696–700.
77. Marx (4), Vol. 1, 486–488.
78. Popper (3), 109–117.
79. Bukharin (2), 64–65.
80. Schaff (22), 350–351, 376.
81. See Northrop (1), 262–263. Northrop makes some illuminating comments along
    the lines indicated.
82. See Mehring (1), 111.
83. Marx-Engels (3), Vol. 2, 360, 451.
84. Marx-Engels (1), 15. Similarly, in *The Communist Manifesto* Marx sharply
    differentiated his own conclusions from the ideas or principles invented by would-
    be reformers as well as from the prejudices of the bourgeoisie, its views on law,
    morality, or religion 'behind which lurk in ambush just as many bourgeois in-

terests'. While the latter are dismissed as ideologies, the conclusions of Communism 'merely express, in general terms, actual relations springing from an existing class struggle, from a historical movement going on under our very eyes' (Marx-Engels (3), Vol. 1, 42, 44).

85. Marx (2), 53, 104–107.
86. Aron (2), 83.
87. Mannheim (1), 254.
88. Some Marxist-Leninists, *e.g.,* Schaff (33), 18–25, seem to derive comfort from the fact that Mannheim's conception of the general total ideology, which should not be identified with the sociology of knowledge, leads to epistemological relativism and its familiar antinomies. See Merton (1), 502–508. Mannheim's relativistic fallacy is, of course, no remedy which would relieve Marxist-Leninists of their own fallacy.
89. It can be noted as an amusing incident that Stalin's pronouncements on linguistics and socialism were also found to contain a great wealth of thought for those interested in the theory and history of music. See Lissa (1).
90. *Życie Nauki* (1), 73.
91. Stalin (1), 581–584.
92. Berman (1), 222; Schaff (13), 242–243; Lange (3), 31–32. Lange carefully avoided saying clearly that he disagreed with Berman and Schaff, though he could not have endorsed their interpretation, which was probably based on Stalin (2), 7–8, 25, 48.
93. Marx (3), 11–12.
94. Marx-Engels (3), Vol. 2, 443, 447–448.
95. This applies, first of all, to Plekhanov (1). Stalin's observations on this matter were a disguised criticism of Plekhanov.
96. Bukharin (1), 207–208; Plekhanov (2), 205–207, 224, 300.
97. Plekhanov's works were published in Polish and easily available. Bukharin's *Historical Materialism* was translated into Polish in the 'thirties and, of course, not republished after the war. But he was probably studied as much in secret as he is now studied and commented upon in public.
98. Parsons-Smelser (1), 27.
99. Schaff (12), 367–376, where Krzywicki is criticised for having divorced his scientific activity from the struggle for the dictatorship of the proletariat and for having abandoned the partisan attitude. See also Kowalik (1), 337–341.
100. Stalin (2), 8–10.
101. Stalin (2), 14–15.
102. Dembowski (3), 30; Berman (1), 223–224; Schaff (13), 244–246; Lange (3), 32–33.
103. It is strange to note that the chief exponent of the first interpretation was Schaff, a Marxist-Leninist philosopher, and that of the second Jakub Berman, a politician and *éminence grise* of the Communist Party, the prototype of Doctor Faul in K. Brandys' story *The Defence of Granada*, translated into English and published in the collection *The Broken Mirror* (New York, Random House, 1958). A few years later Berman was expelled from the Party and Schaff emerged as one of the spokesmen for its liberalising wing.
104. Lenin (1), Vol. 1, 175–178, 203–204. It has been observed that Lenin's contention concerning the working class inability to rise by itself above the 'trade-union consciousness' amounts to the recognition of the fact that in some cases class-determined ideas may be antagonistic to the interests of that class. (Bauer (1), 105).
105. This was the fight against the so-called 'right wing deviation in the C.P.S.U.'. It should be remembered that Gomułka was accused of the same deviation in 1948.

106. See Stalin (1), 509–510.
107. Marx-Engels (3), Vol. 2, 137, 140–141; Schaff (13), 247–249. Schaff was supported by the economist Brus. See *Życie Nauki* (1), 73–74.
108. Schaff (13), 249.
109. Stalin (1), 249–257; Stalin (2), 64–66.
110. Schaff (19), 55; Schaff (28), 10–35.
111. Bukharin (1), 264–265.
112. Malinowski (1), 70, 75–76; Marcuse (1), 88.
113. James (2), 97.
114. The concept of idealist myth played a key role in the criticism of Marxism-Leninism in the years 1955–1957. The magical frame of mind enhanced three tendencies in the voluntaristic interpretation of the Marxian thought: its abandonment of methodological empiricism, of epistemological realism and of ontological materialism.
115. Berman (1), 225.
116. Lange (3), 32; Markiewicz (1), 356–357; Markiewicz (2), 44; Budzyk (1); Krajewski (4).
117. Budzyk (1), 396–398; Markiewicz (1), 360.
118. See, *e.g.,* Żółkiewski (9) and (10).
119. The whole discussion is reviewed in Kurowski (1), 177–256. The most influential contributions were Kotarbiński (14); Ossowski (14), 78–99; Szczepański (9), 94–101; and some of the essays reprinted in Kołakowski (12).
120. Some of this journalism was later republished in book form: Bieńkowski (1), Lipiński (2), Kula (4), Kurowski (1), Markiewicz (3).
121. See Baczko (8) and (9), Eilstein (5), Kołakowski (11), (12), (13), (15).
122. The primary function of institutions in the sociological sense of this term is to regulate the actions of individuals, groups or collectivities in their interaction with each other. This regulative function is exercised by defining institutional objectives and norms of conduct, conducive to their achievements. The institutional values of science and scholarship are these regulative and normative principles, inherent in science and scholarship as a social institution. They are also known under the non-technical name of the 'ethos of science'. Merton dealt with them in his illuminating studies concerned with the sociology of science and distinguished four primary institutional values of science: universalism, communism, disinterestedness and organised scepticism. See Merton (1), 550–561.
123. Chałasiński (27), 147–148; Chałasiński (28), 136–139.
124. Ossowski (12), 20–22.
125. Chałasiński (32), 14–18. The narrow utilitarianism, which followed the abolition of the autonomy of science and its subordination to political authorities, was widely criticised in the years 1956–1957. Among the most vocal critics were political scholars. See *Sesja* (2), 20–21, 92–95.
126. This is one of the main sources of the hostility to science manifested by totalitarian political parties as well as by the public at large. Dictatorships have often exploited this public hostility for their own purposes. See Merton (1), 545–548; Parsons (1), 338–339.
127. Chałasiński (27), 144–146; Chałasiński (29) and (34).
128. Chałasiński (25) and (26).
129. Most of the contributions to this discussion appeared in *Przegląd Kulturalny* in the period September,1955–March, 1956.
130. One of the fullest statements of this kind is Schaff (28).

131. See, *e.g.,* Ossowski (15), 140–151.
132. Hoffman (2), 57–58; Schaff (33), 10, 33 (Schaff (33) is a slightly revised version of Schaff (27)). Most of Schaff's critical observations on Mannheim's sociology of knowledge were forestalled and answered by Mannheim himself. In particular, Mannheim answered those objections of relativism on which Schaff laid great emphasis. See, *e.g.,* Mannheim (1), 269–270.
133. Schaff (33); Lange (5), chapter 7; Wiatr (4), chapter 7.
134. See Mannheim (1), 62.
135. See Merton (1), 496–498.
136. Schaff (33), 30; Markiewicz (1), 354.
137. See, *e.g.,* Parsons (1), 348–352; Naess-Christophersen-Kvalø (1), 161–165.
138. Wiatr (4), 279, who does not seem to see the difficulties created by this recognition.
139. Lenin (1), Vol. 2, 170, 177; Marx's view in Marx-Engels (3), Vol. 1, 41–42.
140. This difficulty was emphasised by the critics of Marxism-Leninism in Poland. See Ossowski (14), 72–73. Max Weber suggested in *The Protestant Ethics and the Spirit of Capitalism* that the theoretical problem involved is insoluble by the Marxian historical method and that the comparative method should be used instead.
141. Lenin, *Imperialism,* chapter 8.
142. Mannheim (1), 239–240; Neurath (1), 20–22. See a detailed analysis of Mannheim's difficulty in Merton (1), 498–502.
143. Aron (2), 57.
144. See Mannheim (1), 229; Parsons (2), 23–24.
145. See, *e.g.,* Schumpeter (2), 354.
146. This view is ascribed to Marx in Schaff (33), 31, and Wiatr (4), 269–270, 277–278. Both these writers agree, however, that the concept of 'scientific ideology' is due to Lenin rather than to Marx.
147. Mannheim (1), 243–244.
148. Schaff (33), 34–35.
149. Schaff (33), 30–31.
150. Wiatr (4), 287–294.
151. See Mannheim (1), 49–53, 57–62, where the particular and the total conceptions of ideology are described.
152. Lange would probably agree that the role of ideological elements in natural science is not comparable with that in the social sciences, for they do not affect, as is the case in the latter, the structure but the acceptance of a theory. There is nothing extraordinary or sinister when one social fact – an ideological belief – influences another social fact, that is the acceptance or dissemination of some scientific opinions. Some social scientists are inclined to a more extreme view on this matter. See Merton (1), 498.
153. Lange (2), 750–751. Compare Schumpeter (2), 358–359; Myrdal (2), chapter 10.
154. Veblen (1), 192–196, compare Neurath (1), 43.
155. Myrdal (1) and (2).
156. Lange (5), 281–287. Similar views were voiced by Max Adler. See Aron (2), 53.
157. We owe this distinction to Max Weber. Schumpeter (2) is one of the clearest recent statements of this point of view.
158. See Naess-Christophersen-Kvalø (1), 206–208.
159. These problems are touched upon in Hirszowicz (2), 65–66.
160. Merton (1), chapter 15 and 16; Parsons (1), 335–345.
161. In November, 1959, following the publication of Chałasiński (34), Chałasiński was removed from the Praesidium of the Polish Academy of Science. The Institute

of Sociology and History of Culture, of which he was director, was closed down and he lost the editorship of some periodicals published under the auspices of the Academy.

162. Schaff (33) and Martel (3) provide a good example of the still prevailing conceptual confusion.

163. Ossowski (7), 4–16; Ossowski (15), 167–170; Szczepański (3), 15–33; Chałasiński (16), 459–464. Compare Aron (2), 122.

164. Historians of philosophy who did not accept Marxism-Leninism will not be considered in this survey, for they could not be active in the period under review.

165. Kroński (3), 251–254, 256–257, 260, 264; Legowicz (3), 181. What Kroński said about the treatment of Marxism-Leninism by the bourgeois history of philosophy referred to Tatarkiewicz (5), Vol. 3, 353–363. Scathing references to Tatarkiewicz's work continued for several years.

166. Baczko-Kołakowski (1), 77.

167. Kołakowski (3), 54; Baczko-Kołakowski (1), 77–78.

168. The Russian revolutionary democrats in question are Belinsky, Chernyshevsky, and Dobroljubov, who, according to the Marxist-Leninist history of philosophy, represent the most advanced stage of materialist thought prior to Marx and Engels. Tatarkiewicz was criticised for the omission of the Russian revolutionary democrats in his *History of Philosophy,* and this omission was ascribed to his cosmopolitism. In fact, they are mentioned (Tatarkiewicz (5), Vol. 3, 17), for in Tatarkiewicz's opinion their writings contain a contribution to aesthetics. Since, however, Tatarkiewicz (5) does not include the history of aesthetics, the author did not pay attention to them apart from a cursory remark.

169. Baczko-Kołakowski (1), 80–82. The last sentence refers to Wetter (1) and Bocheński (13), which were criticised elsewhere with an abusive and malicious vehemence. See Kołakowski (5).

170. Schaff (15), 29, 39, 45; Kroński (3), 251; Baczko-Kołakowski (1), 81.

171. Kroński (3), 251, 257, 271–272.

172. Farrington (1), 150. It has often been observed that Farrington himself provided evidence which undermines his general thesis.

173. Kroński (7), 5–7, 77–78.

174. Legowicz (3).

175. Kołakowski (10).

176. In spite of its banishment Tatarkiewicz (5) was widely read and studied by a large number of people, including Marxist-Leninists, and was for the philosophers the main source of historical knowledge. Krokiewicz published some articles in journals of classical scholarship, but Krokiewicz (7) ready for print in 1950 did not appear until 1958 because of the refusal of the Communist authorities. Legowicz, a medieval scholar and a sympathiser of Marxism-Leninism, published little. See Legowicz (1) and (2).

177. Hegel (2), 6–7.

178. This is Collingwood's expression.

179. The high regard in which the historiography of the Enlightenment was held can be seen from Serejski (2), 11–41. Serejski is the leading Polish historian of historiography.

180. Collingwood (1), 81.

181. Zhdanov (1), 79.

182. Baczko-Kołakowski (1), 83.

183. Zhdanov (1), 80; Kroński (3), 270.

524

184. Kroński (3), 255; Kroński (5); Baczko-Kołakowski (1), 83; Śladkowska (2), 105–106.
185. Kroński (3), 268.
186. Apart from Engels' *Ludwig Feuerbach* the importance of Feuerbach was emphasised in Marx-Engels (2), 124–127. Kroński argued that in Feuerbach there were many flaws and a considerable amount of narrow-mindedness which reduced his stature and made of his system an anachronism. See Kroński (4) and Kroński (9), 141–156.
187. See, *e.g.*, Marx-Engels (3), Vol. 1, 61, and a detailed account in Bobińska (5), 61–72.
188. Kroński (3), 256, 269; Śladkowska (4), 388. A more cautious evaluation of the Russian revolutionary democrats described them as 'thinkers with philosophical abilities of genius' which could not, because of the censorship, find expression in any other form except that of literary criticism. See Walicki (1), 124. Dembowski's collected works appeared in 1955 and apart from numerous articles two books dealing with his life and views were published, namely, Śladkowska (3) and Przemski (1).
189. Examples are provided by Bobińska (1), (2), (3), (5) and (6); Baczko (4).
190. Lenin (1), Vol. 1, 533–538, 556–559.
191. Baczko (4), 247–254, 273–280; Baczko (7), 28–64.
192. Baczko (11), 45–67; Kołakowski (9), 25–34; Suchodolski (7), 10, 45.
193. Kroński (3), 255–257; Krajewski (6), 232–235.
194. Lord Acton (1), 27; Tatarkiewicz (10). Tatarkiewicz's observations were received with the scathing remark that they testified to their author's patent anti-historism (anti-historicism was actually meant) and anti-scientific tendencies. See Kroński (3), 255.
195. Rutkowski (5). A short survey of the history of economic historiography in Poland is to be found in Tymieniecki (1), 120–123.
196. Kula (1).
197. Kula (3), 159–160.
198. Kula (2).
199. Baczko (4), 251; Kołakowski (9), 14; Kroński (6), 122; Poniatowski (1), 173–175; Śladkowska (1), 114–118.
200. Baczko (5) 214, 239; Kołakowski (9), 43.
201. Windelband (1), Vol. 1, 7.
202. Baczko-Kołakowski (1), 84.
203. Baczko-Kołakowski (1), 87–93.
204. Engels wrote of Hobbes that he was the first modern materialist in the eighteenth century sense and an absolutist in a period 'when the fight of absolute monarchy *versus* the people was beginning in England'. Engels referred to Hobbes as an example of how economic influences under a political disguise ultimately dominate philosophical thinking. See Marx-Engels (3), Vol. 2, 449.
205. Kołakowski (7), 134–139; Kołakowski (17), 619–620.
206. Kołakowski argued this point against Kroński (3), 269–272, in Kołakowski (9), 41.
207. Kroński (9), 243–244. See also Serejski (1).
208. Wetter (1), 119.
209. Baczko (10); Kroński (9), 59–139. Hegel's *Lectures on the Philosophy of History* in Polish translation were again published in 1958, Deborin (2) appeared in 1959.
210. Kroński (9), 119.

211. Marx-Engels (3), Vol. 1, 225; Baczko (5), 214–216; Baczko (7), 9–11.
212. Kroński (5), 121–138; Poniatowski (2), 11–13.
213. Baczko (11), 66; Bobińska (6), 115–117.
214. In a Marxist-Leninist contribution to the history of philosophy in the nineteenth century the examination of philosophical problems filled a tiny proportion of the space, most of it being devoted to extra-philosophical matters. Poniatowski (2) provides a good instance, for he dealt with the most philosophically minded representative of the progressive trend, and yet out of 135 pages in Poniatowski's book some 25 at most are concerned with philosophy. The same applies to contributions dealing with other periods. See, *e.g.*, Suchodolski (7).
215. This understanding of the expression 'materialist outlook' is common to all Marxist-Leninist historians of the nineteenth century philosophy, but is particularly apparent in Baczko (4), Śladkowska (2) and (4).
216. This was recognised in Baczko (6), which is a critical evaluation of the state of studies on Polish philosophical thought in the nineteenth century.
217. Kołakowski (16).
218. Kołakowski (17).

CONCLUSIONS

There remain a few words to say about the most recent developments in Polish philosophy and about the effects which Marxist-Leninist ideology and academic philosophy exercised upon each other.

'Institutional Marxism-Leninism' disintegrated in Poland in 1956 or, to provide the event with a convenient fixed date, in October 1956. The disintegration of 'institutional Marxism-Leninism' was not a direct outcome of its criticism by philosophical argument; more powerful factors had to come into play to turn the scale. Philosophical arguments were conducive to the final outcome by releasing a chain reaction, which they precipitated by awakening a critical frame of mind among Marxist-Leninist philosophers themselves. In the preceding pages their revisions of fundamental assumptions and intellectual retreat have been illustrated in a number of examples.

The relinquishing of the dogma also took the more tangible form of a progressive relaxation of the monopoly of a single school and of the slow re-emergence in public of other philosophical trends. Towards the end of 1955 there appeared Kotarbiński's *A Treatise on Good Work*, the first non-Marxist philosophical book since 1949. Ever since, the signs of a steady return to normality have been multiplying, the progress being sometimes checked by and never free from outside interference. Notwithstanding the intellectual and moral disaster it suffered, Marxist-Leninist philosophy continues to be protected by the constituted power, and this includes occasional relapses into the practices of the past and restrictive measures imposed upon non-Marxist philosophers. This factor, threateningly concealed in the background, must be reckoned with whenever the future of philosophy in Poland is envisaged.

The considerable advance towards normality since 1956 is undeniable and in many ways striking. The ban on certain books withdrawn from circulation has been lifted, suppressed manuscripts have been published, access to world philosophical literature and contacts abroad have been restored, philosophers and sociologists denounced as unfit to teach in the People's Poland have regained their chairs, freedom of teaching and discussion has reasserted itself. Perhaps nothing better exemplifies the spirit of the new and happier period than the philosophers' public homage to the memory of Twardowski, on the occasion of the twentieth anniversary of his death (February, 1959), or the tribute of the sociologists to Znaniecki's contributions to sociology in Poland and abroad (February, 1959). Marxist-Leninists participated in the official gatherings to commemorate the hundredth anniversary of Krzywicki's and the ninetieth anniversary of Lenin's birth (June, 1959, and February, 1960 respectively). They no longer felt that attendance at the former conflicted with their due respect for Lenin.

The production of philosophical books is considerable. Some notable new publications have already been mentioned: *A Treatise on Good Work* (1955) and *Lectures on the History of Logic* (1957) by Kotarbiński, *Bourgeois Morality* (1956) by Maria Ossowska, *Class Structure in Social Consciousness* (1957) by Stanisław Ossowski. To these should be added Krokiewicz's *Socrates* (1958), Znamierowski's *Principles and Trends in Ethics* (1957), and *Philosophical Fragments* (1959), a commemorative volume of essays offered by Kotarbiński's pupils to their teacher. Two works of A. M. Krąpiec published since 1956 – *Realism of Human Knowledge* (1959) and *The Theory of Metaphysical Analogy* (1959) – are considered as noteworthy contributions to Christian philosophy. Many books banished during the Stalinist period have been republished. They include works of Chwistek, Czeżowski, Ingarden, Kotarbiński, Łukasiewicz, Ossowska, Ossowski and Tatarkiewicz as well as Witwicki, Baley, Petrażycki and Lande.

Myśl Filozoficzna, the militant Marxist-Leninist periodical, ceased to appear and has been replaced by *Studia Filozoficzne.* With the exception of Christian philosophy, which has a periodical of its own, *Studia Filozoficzne* does not exclude any point of view. Its columns are open to discussion and criticism, unhindered by extraneous considerations. The publication of *Ruch Filozoficzny* was resumed. It reports freely on philosophical publications and developments in Poland and abroad, both in the East and in the West.

Sociologists are again free to teach, to publish their own periodical *Przegląd Socjologiczny* (discontinued in 1949), and to launch various research projects. Among the most important is a large scale research on the changes in the social structure carried out by Szczepański with a large group of assistants.

The present philosophical scene in Poland is varied and lively. The interest in philosophy and sociology is widespread, and the number of young thinkers and research workers of ability is considerable.

Although Marxist-Leninists have not renounced the very real benefits and privileges secured by the Communist State administration, they are also reconciled, within certain limits, to being only one school of thought among others. They are now anxious to achieve by persuasion and free discussion what they failed to do by compulsion. Their difficulty is that they do not know themselves what they want to persuade the others of.

The collapse of 'institutional Marxism-Leninism' not only disrupted the union of definite practices and obligatory beliefs but also left unanswered the question of whether any, and if so which, of these beliefs continue to be obligatory. To-day a Marxist-Leninist is thrown back upon his own resources. Consequently, it is hardly possible to say that there is a definite and unique Marxist-Leninist doctrine in Poland. There is a cluster of various views and ideas marked with the imprint of their Marxist-Leninist provenance, but whose unity and inner coherence is a matter of considerable doubt. Marxist-Leninists differ from each other less than from the scientifically and logically minded philosophers, but among themselves they differ considerably and do not seem to subscribe to the same body of views. Different orientations are apparent among them and they oscillate uneasily between denounced orthodoxy and perilous revisionism, between the cherished illusion of being explorers in the new lands of philosophical thought and the concealed anxious desire to equal their adversaries in skill, knowledge and methodological refinement. There is the Hegelian and the anti-Hegelian tendency as well as the positivistic and the anti-positivistic wing. 'Positivism' is used here in its nineteenth century meaning and refers to the form in which it can be found in some writings of Marx and Engels in contradistinction to those of Lenin or Stalin. No trend has prevailed and no hard core of views emerged to differentiate a Marxist-Leninist from a non-Marxist in the philosophical sense of these terms. The turmoil precipitated by the collapse of 'institutional Marxism-Leninism' has not subsided and the debate over the content of Marxist-Leninist philosophy continues unabated.

In Poland Marxist-Leninist philosophers differ essentially from the scientifically minded philosophers both in their method of thinking and in the range of their interests. Their method has remained traditionalistic, unaffected by the development of modern logic, methodology and philosophy of language. Their main concern continues to be problems of the view of the world or ideology, that is, beliefs that offer a synoptic understanding of the Universe, society and man's place in his natural and human environment. They are inhibited by the belief that the antiquated or oracular pronouncements of their founders and other extra-scientific authorities constitute sacred truths, which cannot be reformulated and adjusted to the requirements of contemporary knowledge for they would thus be relinquished. In consequence, they cannot emancipate themselves from the view that some vague intellectual intuitions and untestable speculative conjectures are superior to knowledge based on scientific procedure. Their opinions on the application of this procedure to philosophy are very close to those held by the traditionalistic philosophers of the inter-war period.

In general, the methodological similarity between them is considerable. Like the pre-war traditionalistic philosophers, Marxist-Leninists of to-day are not ethically and politically neutral; they are staunch conservatives in their conception of philosophy, are given to irrational beliefs, and regard loyalty to a dogmatic standpoint preferable to reliance upon tested methods of science.

While Marxist-Leninists have left their basic methodological assumptions unrevised and their profuse philosophical production displays all the old characteristics of amateurism, a contrary tendency is also noticeable. For Marxist-Leninists have shown an increasing readiness to recognise the requirements of common sense and consistency, to respect facts and to consider particular issues on their own merit. There is a progressive renunciation of the more extravagant claims and of wild speculations, an evolution towards a more reasonable frame of mind, a growing willingness to enlarge the scope of the subject and improve the techniques bequeathed by the so-called classics of Marxism-Leninism. In their criticism and controversie with other philosophers Marxist-Leninists no longer resort to invective and offensive vocabulary. They now accept the view that a dispassionate approach is favourable to discussion and that objectivity is not a vice but a prerequisite of philosophical inquiry.

529

Present-day Marxist-Leninist philosophy in Poland is exposed to mutually exclusive pressures which push and pull its supporters in opposite directions. It also suffers from the dual role and the conflicting functions it is expected to perform. On the one hand, Marxist-Leninist philosophy is the official doctrine of the ruling Party on the other; it is supposed to be a genuine and independent school of philosophical thought. A Marxist-Leninist philosopher is constantly subjected to the tension between political and philosophical ideas and must try to reconcile their irreconcilable or discrepant claims. By subscribing to the view that there exists a close relationship between philosophy and politics he is doomed to move in a circle from which there is no breaking out.

The dual role of Marxist-Leninist philosophy is the prime source of its various defects, of which the less sophisticated of its supporters are unaware and which the others are reluctant to bring out. This is not the case with Leszek Kołakowski, the only outstanding and original thinker produced by Marxism-Leninism in Poland. He gained a certain fame or notoriety in and outside Poland for his outspoken and incisive criticism of Marxist-Leninist ideology. His clear statement of the general position was at first acclaimed by other Marxist-Leninists, but his conclusions drawn from his critical assessments were denounced as a revisionist heresy. Kołakowski has continued his search for an alternative distinctive outlook to the rejected ideology. He can best be described as a philosopher of life, rooted in the Marxian tradition, who regards philosophical systems as disguised moral and social doctrines on a grand scale and philosophical beliefs as situational convictions, that is, as convictions bound with and determined by the historical and social context of the thinker.

The encounter of philosophy and ideology affected not only the latter but also the former. In the case of philosophy two changes are most conspicuous. The realistic attitude and the anti-irrationalistic outlook were the characteristic features of the Warsaw school in the past. While sustained and fruitful efforts were made to consider the linguistic aspect of philosophical problems, there was never any serious danger of mistaking or substituting the inquiry of language for philosophical investigations. This was due partly to the close links between philosophy and science and partly to considerable advances in philosophy of language made in Warsaw at an early stage. But the accusations of idealism, fideism or conventionalism, which were indiscriminately bandied about by Marxist-Leninists against all and sundry, tended to invigorate all these tendencies. The philosophers had to concentrate upon the basic issues, to restate and re-examine the reasons why they did not regard the world as an illusion, placed confidence in science, relied on logic, refused to accept views, whether ideological or philosophical, conflicting with what the empirical sciences and common sense reveal. In particular, they had to redefine their point of view on matters concerning the relation between a linguistic and a philosophical inquiry, and this led to the explicit rejection of 'linguistic philosophy'. Polish philosophers would not regard as philosophy an inquiry restricted to the investigation of the complexities, functioning and usages of language, and pursuing the study of language for its own sake or for the purpose of explaining away philosophical puzzles as due merely to misuses and abuses of language. A systematic study of language is valuable if it constitutes a part of our efforts to understand the world, that is, if it elucidates the question of how thinking is related to the nature of the world. 'Linguistic philosophy', pure and simple, is recognised as generally arid and misleading in some cases, considered to be erring in its restrictive practices and leading to a blind alley because of its estrangement from the problems of science.

Ideology might also have been partly responsible for the shift of interest in the methodology from the deductive to the empirical sciences. The concern with rigour and refined technical devices does not need justification when applied to logical and philosophical problems of physics, chemistry or biology. The methodology of empirical science also seems to offer the opportunity for advancing scientific knowledge, joins logic and science, philosophy and cosmology in a more satisfactory manner than the speculative metaphysics of Marxism-Leninism. It is probably no accident that the younger generation of philosophers consists mostly of methodologists of empirical science. This particular change might have been reinforced by the division of logic into two branches of formal and mathematical logic, the latter comprising methodological investigations on the deductive sciences. Mathematical logic has acquired the status of a highly specialised subject, and it has become extremely hard to combine philosophical inquiry with research in mathematical logic.

The second transformation of philosophy, caused by its encounter with ideology, goes deeper and may have some more far-reaching effects. The sharp contrast in the nature and scope of interests displayed by ideology and philosophy respectively drove home the realisation that the line dividing philosophical problems and those of *Weltanschauung* was, after all, historically unjustifiable, partly didactic in purpose, and arbitrary in the sense of being based on a methodological decision. The considerable expansion of historical studies provided or seemed to provide some evidence that philosophy, even when pursued for a clearly cognitive purpose, may have some unintended general implications (this was brilliantly shown by Kołakowski in his study on Spinoza). Moreover, although the Marxist-Leninist technique of debunking philosophical views and outlooks by exposing their alleged ideological purpose was fanciful and unjustifiable, there was a point in it not to be easily dismissed. It is not unreasonable to assume that social conditions determine in some way and to some extent philosophical inquiry. A thinker may make blunders because his logic is wrong, but he may also be led astray by the particular social conditions prompting the formulation and examination of the problems, with which he is concerned. Social conditions may restrict the scope of philosophical inquiry or draw into the focus of attention some definite problems because of their value-relevance. This assumption is not unreasonable in view of the fact that scientific inquiry is also social activity and as such is exposed to the influence of its social environment. The capacity for abstract thought does not immunise the thinker from the impact of social circumstances. There is a case for the point of view that philosophy has some general implications for society at large and that the conceptual framework of philosophy need not be value- or ideologically-neutral. To admit this possibility does not imply or support the belief that the validity and truth of definite views are socially determined; that to relate them to a social context is to provide their confirmation or refutation; or that they should be evaluated solely in terms of their social significance. There arises, however, the need to look at what the philosopher does from a new angle and to consider the advisability of extending the scope of his subject.

It remains to be seen what concrete effects this shift in attitude and outlook will have for philosophical practice. It is hard to see how the enlargement of the scope of philosophical inquiry could be accomplished without reducing or even abandoning its established standards of performance. At present, there is no question of sacrificing the requirement of rigour, clarity and precision or of surrendering scientific procedure as the only reliable route to warranted knowledge. There is a dilemma here which the young generation of philosophers will have to face.

Mach observed in one of his lectures that it is most difficult to persuade strangers to science that the 'grand universal laws of physics' are not essentially different from descriptions. It is equally hard to persuade strangers to philosophy that philosophy is not essentially different from analysis, explications of concepts and elucidations of the logical structure of beliefs. A philosopher can try to think impartially as long as he pursues philosophical analysis. He is bound to lose his neutrality as much as everybody else, when he sees his proper function in the examination of the problems of *Weltanschauung*. He is unable to carry over his scientific habits of mind from philosophical analysis to the examination of ideological convictions, and what he loses in the process of crossing the line dividing philosophy and ideology is an irretrievable loss. For philosophical detachment provides a salutary counterbalance against the impatient certainties of the ideologist. The philosopher strives for truth conceived as warranted assertibility, the ideologist for 'truth' emanating from the persuasive power of a total experience. The inner tension between them is inevitable. But neither the ideologist nor society at large would be any better if the philosopher abandoned his search for what can be justifiably asserted and what protects us from falling victim to irrational beliefs and inordinate fancies. For the philosopher to hold aloof from discussions of subjects irrelevant to the pursuit of philosophical truth is to perform a vital cognitive and social function which no ideologist dealing with the so-called great issues could ever discharge.

There need be no apprehensions that the world would ever be short of men of letters or of philosophers of a certain type eager to debate inconclusively and to write in an exciting emotional style about the so-called great issues, that is, issues ill-defined or not defined at all or essentially undecidable at the present state of knowledge. But the world has always been short of those rare and precious minds who do not shirk hard analytical work, are anxious to reach a clear and fearless vision of the world, and strive for an intellectual catharsis by means of rigorous reasoning and a precise mode of expression.

London, 15 July, 1960.

BIBLIOGRAPHY

ABBREVIATIONS USED IN THE BIBLIOGRAPHY

ACIPHS-Paris   Actes du Congrès International de Philosophie Scientifique, Sorbonne, Paris, 1935, Vol. 1–8. Actualités Scientifiques et Industrielles, No. 388–395. Paris, Hermann et Cie, Éditeurs, 1936.

AHFMS   Archiwum Historii Filozofii i Myśli Społecznej

AK   Ateneum Kapłańskie

ASMP   Annales de la Société Polonaise de Mathématique

AUMCS-SF   Annales Universitatis Mariae Curie-Skłodowska, Sectio F

AUMCS-SG   Annales Universitatis Mariae Curie-Skłodowska, Sectio G

CM   Colloquium Mathematicum

CRSSLV-C3   Comptes Rendus de la Société des Sciences et des Lettres de Varsovie, Classe 3

FM   Fundamenta Mathematicae

IBL   Instytut Badań Literackich

IEUS   International Encyclopedia of Unified Science

JSL   Journal of Symbolic Logic

KF   Kwartalnik Filozoficzny

KH   Kwartalnik Historyczny

KIW   Książka i Wiedza

KP   Kwartalnik Psychologiczny

KS   Kultura i Społeczeństwo

ŁTN   Łódzkie Towarzystwo Naukowe

MF   Myśl Filozoficzna

MSD   Materiały do studiów i dyskusji z zakresu teorii i historii sztuki, krytyki artystycznej oraz metodologii badań nad sztuką

MW   Myśl Współczesna

ND   Nowe Drogi

NK   Nowa Kultura

NP   Nauka Polska, PAN

NPL   Nauka Polska, jej potrzeby, organizacja i rozwoj. Wydawnictwo Kasy Im. Mianowskiego

PAN   Polska Akademia Nauk

PAU   Polska Akademia Umiejętności

PF   Przegląd Filozoficzny

PFz   Postępy Fizyki

PH   Przegląd Historyczny

PICPHA   Proceedings of the Tenth International Congress of Philosophy, Amsterdam, August 11–18, 1948. North-Holland Publishing Company, Amsterdam, 1949

PICPHB Proceedings of the Eleventh International Congress of Philosophy, Brussels, August 20–26, 1953. Amsterdam, North-Holland Publishing Company, 1953
  PIW Polski Instytut Wydawniczy
   PK Przegląd Kulturalny
   PL Pamiętnik Literacki
 PNHS Przegląd Nauk Historycznych i Społecznych
   PP Przegląd Powszechny
  PPR Państwo i Prawo
   PS Przegląd Socjologiczny
 PTPN Poznańskie Towarzystwo Przyjaciół Nauk
 PWN Państwowe Wydawnictwo Naukowe
 PZWS Państwowe Zakłady Wydawnictw Szkolnych
 RCZF Roczniki Filozoficzne
  RF Ruch Filozoficzny
 RPAS Review of the Polish Academy of Science
 RPTN Rocznik Polskiego Towarzystwa Naukowego na Obczyźnie (London)
 RUW Rocznik Uniwersytetu Warszawskiego
SCZP-PAN Sprawozdania z Czynności i Prac, PAN
  SF Studia Filozoficzne
 SFB Science and Freedom. A Bulletin of the Committee on Science and Freedom
  SL Studia Logica
SMDNP Studia i Materiały z Dziejów Nauki Polskiej
 SPAU Sprawozdania PAU
 SPH Studia Philosophica
SPTPN Sprawozdania PTPN
SSST-SA Studia Societatis Scientiarum Toruniensis, Sectio A (Mathematica-Physica)
STNKUL Sprawozdania TNKUL
 STNT Sprawozdania TNT
TNKUL Towarzystwo Naukowe Katolickiego Uniwersytetu Lubelskiego
 TNT Towarzystwo Naukowe w Toruniu
  TP Tygodnik Powszechny
TWCSA Transactions of the Third World Congress of Sociology, Amsterdam, August 22–29, 1956. London, International Sociological Association, 1956
TWCSS Transactions of the Fourth World Congress of Sociology, Milan and Stresa, September 8–15, 1959. London, International Sociological Association, 1959
WRTN Wrocławskie Towarzystwo Naukowe
 WŻ Wiedza i Życie
 ŻM Życie i Myśl

ZMT   Zastosowania Matematyki
ŻN   Życie Nauki
ZNIO   Zakład Narodowy im. Ossolińskich we Wrocławiu
ZNKUL   Zeszyty Naukowe Katolickiego Uniwersytetu Lubelskiego
ZPNP   Zeszyty Problemowe Nauki Polskiej, PAN
ZWFUW   Zeszyty Wydziału Filozoficznego Uniwersytetu Warszawskiego

BIBLIOGRAPHY

Apart from the writings discussed or mentioned in the text, the following list includes a number of books and articles which seem to be representative of the period considered or which helped the author to write this study.

1. ABEL, TH.: Sociology in Postwar Poland. American Sociological Review 15, 1950 (1), 104–106.
1. A. B. S.: Konwersatorium metafizyczne. ZNKUL 1, 1958 (3), 132–136.
1. ACTON, H. B.: The Illusion of the Epoch. Marxism-Leninism as a Philosophical Creed. London, Cohen and West, 1955, 278 pp.
1. ACTON, LORD: Essays on Freedom and Power. Selected, with a new introduction, by Gertrude Himmelfarb. A Meridian Book. London, Thames and Hudson, 1956, 350 pp.
1. ADLER, E.: Partyjność filozofii i nauki. NP 1, 1953 (2), 248–250.
1. AJDUKIEWICZ, K.: Założenia logiki tradycyjnej. PF 29, 1926, 200–229.
2. Główne zasady metodologii nauk i logiki formalnej. Skrypt autoryzowany. Zredagował M. Presburger. Warszawa, Nakładem Komisji Wydawniczej Koła Matematyczno-Fizycznego Słuchaczów Uniwersytetu Warszawskiego, 1928, 304 str.
3. Logiczne podstawy nauczania. Odbitka z Encyklopedii Wychowania. Warszawa, 'Nasza Księgarnia', 1934, 79 str.
4. W sprawie 'uniwersaliow'. PF 37, 1934, 219–234.
5. Sprache und Sinn. Erkenntnis 4, 1934 (2), 100–138.
6. Das Weltbild und die Begriffsapparatur. Erkenntnis 4, 1934 (4), 259–287.
7. O stosowalności czystej logiki do zagadnień filozoficznych. PF 37, 1934, 323–327.
8. Der logistische Antiirrationalismus in Polen. Erkenntnis 5, 1935 (2), 151–161.
9. Die syntaktische Konnexität. SPH 1, 1935, 1–27.
10. Problemat transcendentalnego idealizmu w sformułowaniu semantycznym. PF 40, 1937, 271–287.
11. O tak zwanym neopozytywiźmie. MW 1946, 6–7, 155–176.
12. Co to jest wolność nauki. ŻN 1946, 6, 417–426.
13. Logika a doświadczenie. PF 43, 1947 (1–4), 3–21.
14. Konwencjonalizm w nauce. WŻ 16, 1947 (4), 304–313.
15. Zmiana i sprzeczność. MW 1948, 8–9/27–28, 35–52.
16. Epistemologia i semiotyka. PF 44, 1948 (4), 336–347.
17. Epistemology and Semiotic. PICPHA 1, 607–609.

18. AJDUKIEWICZ, K.: Kazimierz Twardowski jako nauczyciel filozofii. Ex: Rutkowski, J. (Red).: Z zagadnień dydaktycznych wyższego szkolnictwa. Praca zbiorowa. Poznań, PTPN, 1948, 55–60.

19. Propedeutyka filozofii. Dla liceów ogólnokształcących, wyd. 3 poprawione. Wrocław-Warszawa, Książnica Atlas, 1948, 216 str.

20. Metodologia i metanauka. ŻN 1948, 31–32, 4–15.

21. Zagadnienia i kierunki filozofii. Teoria poznania i metafizyka. Warszawa, Czytelnik, 1949, 235 str.

22. The Scientific World-Perspective. Ex: Feigl, H., Sellars, W. (Ed.): Readings in Philosophical Analysis. New York, Appleton-Century-Crofts, Inc., 1949, 182–188.

23. On the Notion of Existence. SPH 4, 1949–1950, 7–22.

24. Logic and Experience. Synthese 8, 1950 (6–7), 289–299.

25. Logika, jej zadania i potrzeby w Polsce Ludowej. MF 1951, 1–2, 50–67.

26. W sprawie artykułu prof. A. Schaffa o moich poglądach filozoficznych. MF 1953, 2/8, 292–334.

27. Zarys logiki, wyd. 2. Książka pomocnicza dla nauczyciela. Warszawa, PZWS, 1955, 208 str.

28. Klasyfikacja rozumowań. SL 2, 1955, 278–300.

29. Sprawa planu prac badawczych w zakresie logiki. SL 2, 1955, 267–276.

30. W sprawie programów logiki usługowej. MF 1956, 2/22, 126–136.

31. Okres warunkowy a implikacja materialna. SL 4, 1956, 117–134.

32. O wolności nauki. NP 5, 1957 (3), 1–20.

33. On the Freedom of Science. RPAS 2, 1957 (1–2), 1–19.

34. Zagadnienie racjonalności zawodnych sposobow wnioskowania. SF 1958, 4/7, 14–29.

35. Trzy pojęcia definicji. SF 1958, 5/8, 3–16.

36. Le problème du fondement des propositions analytiques. SL 8, 1958, 259–272.

37. Pozanaukowa działalność Kazimierza Twardowskiego. RF 19, 1959 (1–2), 29–35.

1. AMSTERDAMSKI, S.: Rozwój pojęcia pierwiastka chemicznego. Ex: Światopoglądowe i metodologiczne problemy abstrakcji naukowej, T. 2. Warszawa, PWN, 1957, 3–81.

1. ANTONIEWICZ, W.: Zadania i organizacja szkół akademickich. ŻN 1947, 19–20, 9–26; 1947, 21–22, 103–123; 1947, 23–24, 265–274.

1. ANTOSZCZUK, S.: Stanisław Krusiński. MW 1950, 1/44, 3–25.

1. ARON, R.: Relativism in History. Ex: Meyerhoff, H. (Ed.): The Philosophy of History in our Time. An Anthology. New York, Doubleday and Company, Inc., 1959, 153–162.

2. German Sociology. Translated by Mary and Thomas Bottomore. London, Heinemann, 1957, 8 and 141 pp.

1. ASSORODOBRAJ, N.: W sprawie kryterium postępowości w historii historiografii. KH 60, 1953 (4), 150–186.

2. Życie i dzieło Stefana Czarnowskiego. Ex: Czarnowski, S.: Dzieła, T. 5.

Warszawa, PWN, 1956, 105–156.

1. AUGUSTYNEK, Z.: Szczególna teoria względności a przyczynowość. MF 1956, 1/21, 164–175.
2. O obiektywnym charakterze definicji równoczesności. Ex: Światopoglądowe i metodologiczne problemy abstrakcji naukowej, T. 2. Warszawa, PWN, 1957, 83–113.
1. AUGUSTYNEK, Z., MAJEWSKI, Z.: Problem obiektywności czasu i przestrzeni w świetle teorii względności. SF 1958, 3/6, 103–120.
1. AYER, A. J.: The Foundations of Empirical Knowledge. London, Macmillan 1940, 10 and 276 pp.
2. Philosophical Essays. London, Macmillan, 1954, 9 and 289 pp.
3. Meaning and Intentionality. Ex: Relazioni introductive. Atti del XII Congresso Internazionale di Filosofia. Firenze, G. C. Sansoni Editore, 1958, 141–153.
1. A. Z.: Sprawozdanie Myśli Filozoficznej na Radzie Naukowej Instytutu Filozoficznego UW. MF 1953, 1/7, 350–354.

1. BACHULSKI, A.: Nauki historyczne w Związku Socjalistycznych Republik Radzieckich. NPL 20, 1935, 290–302.
1. BACZKO, B.: Prawo retrospekcji przewrotowej Kelles-Krauza. MW 1949, 8–9/39–40, 58–68.
2. O poglądach filozoficznych i społeczno-politycznych Tadeusza Kotarbińskiego. MF 1951, 1–2, 247–289.
3. O poglądach filozoficznych i społeczno-politycznych Tadeusza Kotarbińskiego. Instytut Kształcenia Kadr Naukowych przy KC PZPR, Katedra Materializmu Dialektycznego i Historycznego. Warszawa, KIW, 1951, 133 str.
4. W sprawie etapów rozwoju polskiej postępowej przedmarksowskiej myśli filozoficznej i społecznej XIX w. MF 1953, 2/8, 247–282.
5. Głos w dyskusji w sprawie liberalizmu. MF 1954, 4/14, 213–239.
6. W sprawie dróg kształtowania się światopoglądu w polskiej demokratycznej myśli społecznej połowy XIX wieku. MF 1955, 4/18, 62–95.
7. Poglądy społeczno-polityczne i filozoficzne Towarzystwa Demokratycznego Polskiego. Warszawa, KIW, 1955, 412 str.
8. O stylu filozofowania. MF 1956, 4/24, 3–28.
9. Drogi i bezdroża. NK 7, 1956, 48/348, 1 i 7.
10. Hegel, Marks i problemy alienacji. SF 1957, 1, 36–58.
11. Niektóre węzłowe problemy rozwoju polskiej myśli społeczno-politycznej i filozoficznej XIX w. Ex: Baczko, B., Assorodobraj, N. (Red.): Z dziejów polskiej myśli filozoficznej i społecznej, T. 3. Warszawa, KIW, 1957, 9–67.
12. Kryptoproblemy i historyzm. SF 1958, 3/6, 76–102.
1. BACZKO, B., KOŁAKOWSKI, L.: Tradycje naukowego socjalizmu i zadania marksistowskiej historiografii filozoficznej. MF 1954, 4/14, 78–103.

1. BALEY, S.: Kazimierz Twardowski a kierunki psychologii współczesnej. PF 41, 1938 (4), 339–344.
2. Psychologiczna problematyka wieku dojrzewania. MW 1950, 7/50, 25–43.
3. Marksizm a psychologia społeczna. SPAU 51, 1950 (9), 593–594.
4. Nauka Pawłowa a psychologia. ŻN 1952, 6, 43–64.
5. Wprowadzenie do psychologii społecznej. Warszawa, PWN, 1959, 226 str.
1. BARBER, B.: Science and the Social Order. London, Allen and Unwin, 1953, 288 pp.
2. Sociology of Science. A Trend Report and Bibliography. Current Sociology 5, 1956 (2), 91–153.
1. BARNES, H. E., BECKER, H.: Social Thought from Lore to Science, 2d ed, Vol. 1–2. Washington, Harren Press, 1952, 1178 pp.
1. BARTOSZEWSKI, W.: Socjologia w czasie okupacji niemieckiej. PS 8, 1946, 210–212.
1. BAUER, R. A.: The New Man in Soviet Psychology. Cambridge, Harvard University Press, 1952, 23 and 229 pp.
1. BAUMAN, Z.: O przezwyciężenie dezintegracji filozofii marksistowskiej. MF 1956, 6/26, 133–140.
2. O potrzebie socjologii partii. MF 1957, 2/28, 3–26.
1. BAUMAN, Z., WIATR, J.: O roli mas w historii. MF 1953, 4/10, 69–99.
2. Marksizm a socjologia współczesna. MF 1957, 1/27, 3–23.
1. BECKER, O.: Bestreitet Aristoteles die Gültigkeit des 'Tertium non datur' für Zukunftaussagen? (Zum 9. Kapitel der Aristotelischen Hermeneutik). ACIPHS-Paris 6, 69–74.
1. BELL, E. T.: The Development of Mathematics, 2d ed. New York, Mc-Graw-Hill Book Company, Inc., 1945, 11 and 637 pp.
1. BERGMANN, G.: The Metaphysics of Logical Positivism. New York, Longmans, Green and Co., 1954, 10 and 341 pp.
1. BERGSON, H.: Creative Evolution, in the authorized translation by Arthur Mitchell. The Modern Library. New York, Random House, 1944, 25 and 453 pp.
1. BERLIN, I.: Historical Inevitability. Auguste Comte Memorial Lecture No. 1. London, Oxford University Press, 1954, 78 pp.
2. Karl Marx. His Life and Environment, 2d ed. London, Oxford University Press, 1956, 280 pp.
1. BERMAN, J.: O bazie i nadbudowie w świetle prac J. Stalina o języko-znawstwie. MW 1950, 11–12/54–55, 220–229.
1. BETH, E. W.: Les fondements logiques des mathématiques, 2e éd. Collection de logique mathématique, Série A. Paris, Gauthier-Villars, 1955, 15 et 241 pp.
1. BIAŁOBRZESKI, Cz.: Czym jest materia. Nauka i Sztuka, 1, 1945 (2–3), 147–174.
2. Fizyka wobec materializmu i idealizmu. PP 225, 1948 (1), 37–41.
3. Synteza filozoficzna i metodologiczna nauk przyrodniczych. NPL 25, 1947, 37–45.

4. BIAŁOBRZESKI, Cz.: O interpretacji ontologicznej podstaw fizyki świata atomowego. SPAU 51, 1950 (6), 364–365.
5. Fizyka przed pół wiekiem a dziś. Kraków, PAU, 1950, 16 str.
6. Problem uwarstwienia rzeczywistości. SPAU 52, 1951ʿ(3), 184–185.
7. Podstawy poznawcze fizyki świata atomowego. PAN, Komitet Fizyki. Warszawa, PWN, 1956, 362 str.
1. BIBLIOGRAFIA prac Jana Łukasiewicza. SL 5, 1957, 9–11.
1. BIEŃKOWSKI, W.: Rewolucji ciąg dalszy. Warszawa, KIW, 1957, 171 str.
1. BIERUT, B.: O nauce, kulturze, oświacie w Polsce Ludowej. ŻN 1951, 5–6, 483–519.
1. BIOLOGIA I POLITYKA. Materiały narady biologów zorganizowanej przez 'Po Prostu'. Biblioteczka 'Po Prostu' 9. Warszawa, KIW, 1957, 160 str.
1. BLACK, M.: Language and Philosophy. Studies in Method. Ithaca, Cornell University Press, 1949, 13 and 264 pp.
2. Problems of Analysis. Philosophical Essays. London, Routledge and Kegan Paul, 1954, 11 and 304 pp.
1. BOBIŃSKA, C.: Stanowisko Marksa i Engelsa w 1848 roku wobec sprawy polskiej. MW 1948, 11–12/30–31, 15–32.
2. Stalin a węzłowe zagadnienia nauk społecznych. MW 1949, 12/43, 257–270.
3. Marks o emigracja polska w okresie wojny krymskiej. MF 1953, 3/9, 44–63.
4. Spór a ujęcie pozytywizmu i historyków pozytywistów. KH 61, 1954 (1), 178–204.
5. Marks i Engels a sprawy polskie do osiemdziesiątych lat XIX wieku, wyd. 2 uzupełnione. Warszawa, KIW, 1955, 251 str.
6. Ideologia rewolucyjnych demokratów polskich w latach sześćdziesiątych XIX wieku. Warszawa, PWN, 1956, 119 str.
1. BOCHEŃSKI, J. M.: Tradycja myśli katolickiej a ścisłość. Ex: Myśl katolicka wobec logiki współczesnej. Studia Gnesnensia 15. Poznań, Księgarnia Św. Wojciecha, 1937, 27–34.
2. O 'relatywiźmie' logistycznym. Ex: Myśl katolicka wobec logiki współczesnej. Studia Gnesnensia 15. Poznań, Księgarnia Św. Wojciecha, 1937, 87–111.
3. La philosophie. Ex: Pologne 1919–1939, Vol. 3, Vie intellectuelle et artistique. Neuchâtel, Editions de la Baconnière, 1947, 229–260.
4. Europäische Philosophie der Gegenwart. Sammlung Dalp, B. 50. Bern, A. Francke AG. Verlag, 1947, 304 SS; 2. A. Bern 1951.
5. La logique de Théophraste. Collectanea Friburgensia, Nouvelle Série, Fasc. 32. Fribourg en Suisse, Librairie de l'Université, 1947, 138 pp.
6. L'État et les besoins de l'histoire de la logique formelle. PICPHA 1, 1062–1064.
7. Ancient Formal Logic. Studies in Logic and the Foundations of Mathematics. Amsterdam, North-Holland Publishing Company, 1951, 6 and 122 pp.

8. BOCHEŃSKI, J. M.: Die Zeitgenossischen Denkmethoden. Dalp Taschen-bücher, B. 304. München, Lehnen Verlag, 1954, 150 SS.

9. Die Entwicklung der Formalen Logik. Ex: Eisermann, G. (Red.): Wirtschaft und Kultursysteme. Erlenbach-Zurich und Stuttgart, Eugen Reutsch Verlag, 1955, 61–75.

10. The Problem of Universals. Ex: The Problem of Universals. A Symposium. Notre Dame, University of Notre Dame Press, 1956, 35–54.

11. Contemporary European Philosophy. Translated from the German by Donald Nicholl and Karl Aschenbrenner. Berkeley and Los Angeles, University of California Press, 1956, 321 pp.

12. Formale Logik. Sammlung Orbis. München, Verlag Karl Freiburg, 1956, 15 und 639 SS.

13. Der Sowjet-Russische Dialektische Materialismus (Diamat). Dalp Taschenbücher, B. 325. München, Lehnen Verlag, 1956, 150 SS.

1. BOEHNER, PH.: Medieval Logic. An Outline of its Development from 1250 to c. 1400. Manchester, Manchester University Press, 1952, 17 and 130 pp.

1. BOHM, D.: Causality and Chance in Modern Physics. Foreword by Louis de Broglie. London, Routledge and Kegan Paul, 1957, 11 and 170 pp.

1. BORKOWSKI, L.: Über analytische und synthetische Definitionen. SL 4, 1956, 7–60.

2. Z nowszych badań nad rachunkiem zdań. SL 5, 1957, 13–26.

3. Systems of the Propositional and of the Functional Calculus Based on One Primitive Term. SL 6, 1957, 7–55.

4. O terminach modalnych. SL 7, 1958, 7–37.

5. On Proper Quantifiers. SL 8, 1958, 65–128.

6. Reduction of Arithmetic to Logic Based on the Theory of Types without the Axiom of Infinity and the Typical Ambiguity of Arithmetical Constants. SL 8, 1958, 283–295.

1. BORKOWSKI, L., SŁUPECKI, J.: A Logical System Based on Rules and Its Application in Teaching Mathematical Logic. SL 7, 1958, 71–106.

2. The Logical Works of J. Łukasiewicz. SL 8, 1958, 7–56.

1. BORNSTEIN, B.: Teoria absolutu. Metafizyka jako nauka ścisła. ŁTN, Wydz. 1, Nr. 2. Łodź, ŁTN, 1948, 130 str.

1. BORUCKA-ARCTOWA, M.: Prawo natury jako ideologia antyfeudalna. Warszawa, PWN, 1957, 330 str.

1. BROMBERG, A.: Książki i wydawcy. Ruch wydawniczy w Polsce Ludowej w latach 1944–1957. Warszawa, PWN, 1958, 273 str.

1. BRUS, W.: Niektóre zagadnienia metody dialektycznej w świetle 'Kapitału' Marksa. Warszawa, KIW, 1951, 48 str.

1. BUCZYŃSKA, H.: Pare informacji o semantyce ogólnej. SF 1958, 2/5, 232–236.

1. BUDZYK, K.: O trwałe wartości w nauce. PL 42, 1951 (2), 388–405.

2. Nauka a partia. ND 1956, 11–12/89–90, 131–136.

3. Z problematyki naukowo-wydawniczej. NP 5, 1957 (1), 124–129.

1. BUKHARIN, N. I.: Historical Materialism. A System of Sociology.

Authorized translation from the third Russian edition. New York, International Publishers Co., Inc., 1928, 15 and 318 pp.

2. BUKHARIN, N. I.: Marx's Teaching and its Historical Importance. Ex: Bukharin, N. I., Deborin, A. M., Uranovsky, Y. M., Vavilov, S. I., Komarov, V. L., Tiumeniev, A. I.: Marxism and Modern Thought. Translated by R. Fox. London, Routledge and Sons, 1935, 1–90.

1. BULLOCK, A.: The Historian's Purpose: History and Metahistory. Ex: Meyerhoff, H. (Ed.): The Philosophy of History in Our Time. An Anthology. New York, Doubleday and Company, Inc., 1959, 292–299.

1. BUTTERFIELD, H.: History and Human Relations. London, Collins, 1951, 254 pp.

2. Man on His Past. The Study of the History of Historical Scholarship. Cambridge, Cambridge University Press, 1955, 17 and 237 pp.

1. BYCHOWSKI, B.: Marazm współczesnej filozofii burżuazyjnej. ND 1947, 5, 80–99.

1. BYSTROŃ, J. S.: Rozwój problemu socjologicznego w nauce polskiej. Archiwum do Badania Historyi Filozofii w Polsce, T. 1, cz. 2. Kraków, Nakładem Akademii Umiejętności, 1917, 189–260.

2. Socjologia. Wstęp informacyjny i bibliograficzny, wyd. 3 uzupełnione. Warszawa, Książnica Polska, 1947, 196 str.

1. CALVEZ, J.-Y.: La pensée de Karl Marx. Paris, Edition du Seuil, 1956, 664 pp.

1. CARNAP, R.: The Logical Syntax of Language. Translated by A. Smeaton (Countess von Zeppelin). London, Kegan Paul-Treuch-Trubner and Co., 1937, 16 and 352 pp.

2. Foundations of Logic and Mathematics. IEUS, Vol. 1, No. 3. Chicago, University of Chicago Press, 4 and 71 pp.

3. Truth and Confirmation. Ex: Feigl, H., Sellars, W. (Ed): Readings in Philosophical Analysis. New York, Appleton-Century-Crofts, Inc., 1949, 119–127.

4. The Two Concepts of Probability. Ex: Feigl, H., Sellars, W. (Ed.): Readings in Philosophical Analysis. New York, Appleton-Century-Crofts, Inc., 1949, 330–348.

5. Introduction to Semantics and Formalization of Logic. Two Volumes in One. Cambridge, Harvard University Press, 1959, 14 and 259, 15 and 159 pp.

6. Introduction to Symbolic Logic and Its Applications. Translated by William H. Meyer and John Wilkinson. New York, Dover Publications, Inc., 1958, 15 and 241 pp.

7. Meaning and Necessity. A Study in Semantics and Modal Logic. Enlarged edition. Chicago, University of Chicago Press, Phoenix Books, 1958, 8 and 258 pp.

1. CHAŁASIŃSKI, J.: Młode pokolenie chłopów. Procesy i zagadnienia

kształtowania się warstwy chłopskiej w Polsce, T. 1–4. Z przedmową Floriana Znanieckiego. Warszawa, Państwowy Instytut Kultury Wsi, 1938, 90 i 326, 553, 601, 556 str.

2. CHAŁASIŃSKI, J.: Społeczna genealogia inteligencji polskiej. Prace Polskiego Instytutu Socjologicznego, Studium Problemów Chłopskich i Robotniczych, 1. Warszawa, Czytelnik, 1946, 81 str.

3. Socjologiczne założenia reformy wychowania. MW 1946, 1, 5–24.

4. Tworzenie legendy i naukowe zadania historii. MW 1946, 6–7, 126–154.

5. Zasadnicze stanowiska we współczesnej socjologii polskiej. PS 8, 1946, 4–39.

6. Historia i socjologia. PS 9, 1947, 302–308.

7. Zagadnienia historyczno-socjologicznej samowiedzy inteligencji polskiej. MW 1947, 5/12, 141–174.

8. Współczesne reformy szkolne a idea narodu i socjalizmu. MW 1947, 11/18, 398-425.

9. Problemy demokracji. Odrodzenie 4, 1947, 14–15/123–124, 8–9.

10. Pedagogika personalizmu i pedagogika socjalizmu? Kuźnica 3, 1947, 4/74, 1–2.

11. O społeczny sens reformy uniwersytetów. Kuźnica 3, 1947, 24/93, 3–6.

12. Idea narodu i idea socjalizmu w dziejach Europy nowoczesnej. MW 1948, 2–3/21–22, 189–208.

13. Trzydzieści lat socjologii polskiej, 1918 do 1947. PS 10, 1948, 1–54.

14. Z kongresu intelektualistów. Po światowym kongresie intelektualistów w obronie pokoju we Wrocławiu. PS 10, 1948, 355–380.

15. Instytut Socjologiczny Uniwersytetu Łódzkiego. PS 10, 1948, 576–589.

16. Porządek myślowy w socjologii. MW 1948, 6–7/25–26, 457–464.

17. Społeczeństwo i wychowanie. Socjologiczne zagadnienia szkolnictwa i wychowania w społeczeństwie współczesnym. Warszawa, 'Nasza Księgarnia', 1948, 431 str.; wyd 2, Warszawa, PWN, 1958, 335 str.

18. Socjologia polska w latach międzywojennych a prądy społeczne i umysłowe. MW 1949, 1–2/32–33, 11–40.

19. O socjalistyczną ideę uniwersytetu. PNHS 1, 1950, 11–47.

20. Z zagadnień metodologii badań społecznych. MF 1951, 1–2, 75–105.

21. Uczeni w walce o pokój i socjalizm. ŻN 1951, 5–6, 543–562.

22. Rzecz z powodu 'Humanistyki bez hipostaz'. MF 1952, 2/4, 303–314.

23. Humanizm socjalistyczny a podstawowe prawo ekonomiczne socjalizmu. MF 1953, 2/8, 102–132.

24. Problem nauki i roli uczonego w społeczeństwie. NP 1, 1953 (1), 164–185.

25. Z zagadnień historii kultury polskiej pierwszej połowy XIX wieku. NP 2, 1954 (1), 81–121.

26. Jeszcze jedno nieporozumienie wokół liberalizmu. NP 2, 1954 (3), 266–280.

27. Inteligencja ludowa. Naukowy pogląd na świat. Upowszechnienie wiedzy i kultury. NP 2, 1954 (4), 130–148.

28. Zagadnienia kultury współczesnej w humanistyce polskiej. Szkoły w nauce. Instytuty naukowe. NP 3, 1955 (2), 125–146.

29. CHAŁASIŃSKI, J.: Spór o rozumienie kultury. PK 1955, 39, 1–2.
30. Kultura umysłowa i jej autorytety. PK 4, 1955, 41, 1 i 4–5.
31. Polski Instytut Socjologiczny. NP 4, 1956 (4), 202–205.
32. Drogi i bezdroża socjalizmu w nauce polskiej. KS 1, 1957 (1), 7–43.
33. Przeszłość i przyszłość inteligencji polskiej. Warszawa, Ludowa Spółdzielnia Wydawnicza, 1958, 209 str.
34. Sociology and Social Mythology in Post-War Poland. TWCSS 1, 139–146.

1. CHMAJ, L.: Bracia polscy. Ludzie, idee, wpływy. Warszawa, PWN, 1957, 506 str.

1. CHOJNACKI, P.: Filozofia tomistyczna i neotomistyczna. Poznań, Instytut Wydawniczy 'Kultura', 1947, 177 str.
2. Podstawy filozofii chrześcijańskiej. Warszawskie Studia Teologiczne 27. Warszawa, Pax, 1955, 200 str.
3. Kierunki rozwoju i kryteria humanizmu. ZM 1956, 4–5, 23–31.

1. CHURCH, A. : Introduction to Mathematical Logic, Vol. 1. Princeton, Princeton University Press, 1956, 9 and 376 pp.
2. Propositions and Sentences. Ex: The Problem of Universals. Notre Dame, University of Notre Dame Press, 1956, 3–11.

1. CHWISTEK, L.: Antynomie logiki formalnej. PF 24, 1921, 164–171.
1a. The Theory of Constructive Types. Principles of Logic and Mathematics. ASPM 2, 1924, 9–48; 3, 1925, 92–141.
2. Granice nauki. Lwów-Warszawa, Książnica Atlas, s.a. (1935), 24 i 264 str.
3. The Limits of Science. Translation of Chwistek (2) with introduction and appendix by H. Ch. Brodie. London, Kegan Paul-Trench-Trubner and Co., 1948, 57 and 347 pp.
4. Überwindung des Begriffsrealismus. SPH 2, 1937, 1–18.
5. New Foundations of Formal Metamathematics. JSL 3, 1938 (1), 1–36.
6. La méthode générale des sciences positives. L'esprit de la sémantique. Actualités Scientifiques et Industrielles, No. 1014. Paris, Hermann et Cie, 1946, 46 pp.

1. CHOYNOWSKI, M.: Nauka wobec społeczeństwa. ŻN 1946, 1, 3–18.
2. 'Życie Nauki' przed sądem. ŻN 1946, 11–12, 322–334.
3. Czy filozofia jest nauką. PF 44, 1948 (1–3), 198–217.
4. O sytuacji w psychologii polskiej. NP 4, 1956 (4), 175–179.
5. O wyjście z zastoju w psychologii polskiej. KS 1, 1957 (1), 64–83.

1. CIEŚLAK, T.: Nowy okres w pracach PAN. NP 5, 1957 (1), 111–123.

1. COLLINGWOOD, R. G.: The Idea of History. Oxford, Clarendon Press, 1946, 26 and 339 pp.

1. CSORBA, H: Na marginesie edycji klasyków. NP 4, 1956 (1), 115–116.

1. CZARNOWSKI, S.: Le culte des héros et ses conditions sociales. Saint-Patrick, Héros national de l'Irlande. Travaux de l'Année Sociologique publiés sous la direction de M. É. Durkheim. Paris, Alcan, 1919, 94 et 369 pp.
2. Społeczeństwo – Kultura. Prace z socjologii i historii kultury. Warszawa, Biblioteka Socjologiczna, 1939, 98 i 558 str.

3. CZARNOWSKI, S.: Dzieła, T. 1–5. W opracowaniu N. Assorodobraj i S. Ossowskiego. Warszawa, PWN, 1956, 224, 250, 278, 255, 224 str.

1. CZERWIŃSKI, Z.: W sprawie walki z nominalizmem. MF 1956, 4/24, 160–169.

2. Zagadnienie 'całości'. Problem sprowadzalności twierdzeń o zbiorach do twierdzeń o elementach (częściach) tych zbiorów. ZPNP 12, 1956, 130–135.

3. Jeszcze raz o nominaliźmie. MF 1957, 1/27, 220–225.

4. Zagadnienie probabilistycznego uzasadnienia indukcji enumeracyjnej. SL 5, 1957, 91–103.

5. O paradoksie implikacji. SL 7, 1958, 265–271.

6. On the Relation of Statistical Inference to Traditional Induction and Deduction. SL 7, 1958, 243–260.

1. CZEŻOWSKI, T.: Główne zasady nauk filozoficznych. Wydawnictwo Uniwersytetu Mikołaja Kopernika 2, wyd. 2. Toruń, Księgarnia Naukowa T. Szczęsny i Ska, 1946, 198 str. Wyd. 3, poprawione i rozszerzone, Wrocław, ZNIO, 1959, 240 str.

2. O uniwersytecie i studiach uniwersyteckich. Biblioteka Toruńska 3. Toruń, Księgarnia Nakładowa T. Szczęsny i Ska, 1946, 68 str.

3. Kazimierz Twardowski as Teacher. SPH 3, 1939–1946, 13–17.

4. Quelques problèmes anciens sous la forme moderne. SPH 3, 1939–1946, 101–113.

5. O naukach humanistycznych. Biblioteka Powszechnych Wykładów Uniwersytetu Mikołaja Kopernika 3. Toruń, Księgarnia Nakładowa T. Szczęsny i Ska, 1946, 20 str.

6. Twierdzenia ogólne w teorii naukowej. ŻN 1947, 17–18, 302–308.

7. Przyczynki do analizy rozumowania. PF 44, 1948 (1–3), 66–76.

8. Perspektywy światopoglądowe. RF 16, 1948 (3–4), 138–140.

9. O metafizyce, jej kierunkach i zagadnieniach. Wydawnictwo Uniwersytetu Mikołaja Kopernika 5. Toruń, Księgarnia Naukowa T. Szczęsny i Ska, 1948, 143 str.

10. Trzy postawy wobec świata. WŻ 17, 1948 (6–7), 567–571.

11. Logika. Podręcznik dla studiujących nauki filozoficzne. Warszawa, PZWS, 1949, 273 str.

12. Etyka jako nauka empiryczna. KF 18, 1949 (2), 161–171.

13. Kilka uwag o racjonaliźmie i empiryźmie, STNT 3, 1949, 89–92.

14. O rozumowaniu prawdopodobieństwowym. STNT 4, 1950, 83–88.

15. Zagadnienie istnienia świata w świetle przemian metodologicznych. SPAU 52, 1951 (8), 685–688.

16. De la vérification dans les sciences empiriques. Analyse logique. Revue Internationale de Philosophie 5, 1951, 3–4/17–18, 243–250, 347–366.

17. Identyczność a indywiduum i jego trwanie. STNT 5, 1951, 109-113.

18. Uwagi o klasycznej definicji prawdy. Księga Pamiątkowa 75-lecia TNT. Toruń, TNT, 1952, 35–41.

19. On Certainty in Empirical Sciences. PICPHB, Vol. 6, 126–129.

20. CZEŻOWSKI, T.: O metodzie opisu analitycznego. STNT 7, 1953, 114–118.
21. On Certain Peculiarities of Singular Propositions. Mind 64, 1955 (255), 392–395.
22. Odczyty Filozoficzne. TNT, Prace Wydziału Filologiczno-Filozoficznego, T. 7(1). Toruń, PWN, 1958, 323 str.
23. Wkład Kazimierza Twardowskiego do teorii nauki. RF 19, 1959(1–2), 4–9.

1. CZUBALSKI, F.: I. P. Pawłow jako badacz i myśliciel. Kraków, PAU, 1950, 16 str.

1. CZUJ, J.: Patrologia. Poznań, Pallotinum, 1953, 218 str.; wyd 2, uzupełnione, Poznań, 1954, 311 str.

1. DĄMBSKA, I.: L'Homme anonyme. SPH 3, 1939–1946, 115–149.
2. O rodzajach sceptycyzmu. KF 17, 1948(1–2), 79–86.
3. Czterdzieści lat filozofii we Lwowie 1898–1938. PF 44, 1948 (1–3), 14–25.
4. W sprawie tzw. nazw pustych. PF 44, 1948 (1–3), 77–81.
5. Z filozofii imion własnych. KF 18, 1949 (3–4), 241–261.
6. Z genealogii ideałów życiowych: Platoński ideał filozofa. Meander 4, 1949 (7), 325–334.
7. Ze współczesnej teorii poznania fizykalnego. SPAU 52, 1951(5), 328–329.
8. O dwoistości w aspekcie bytu i poznania i o tendencji do przezwyciężenia tej dwoistości jako podstawie kierunków i stanowisk filozoficznych. SPAU 53, 1952(7–10), 472–476.
9. Sceptycyzm filozoficzny a metoda naukowa. STNT 8, 1954, 79–81.
10. Podział logiczny a definicja. STNT 8, 1954, 81–82.
11. Review of Kotarbiński (8). SL 5, 1957, 145–149.
12. Sceptycyzm francuski XVI i XVII wieku. TNT, Prace Wydziału Filologiczno-Filozoficznego, T. 7(2). Toruń, 1958, 89 str.

1. DEBORIN, A. M.: Karl Marx and the Present. Ex: Bukharin, N. I., Deborin, A. M., Uranovsky, Y. M., Vavilov, S. I., Komarov, V. L., Tiumeniev, A. I.: Marxism and Modern Thought. London, Routledge and Sons, 1935, 91–135.
2. Wstęp do filozofii materializmu dialektycznego. Tłumaczył z rosyjskiego Jakub Wachtel. Warszawa, KIW, 1959, 98 and 348 str.

1. DEMBOWSKI, J.: O nowym pojmowaniu dziedziczności. MW 1950, 3/46, 361–373.
2. Prezydent Bierut a nauka polska. MF 1952, 2/4, 13–25.
3. Science in New Poland. London, Lawrence and Wishart, 1952, 59 pp.
4. Kierunki rozwoju i badań Polskiej Akademii Nauk w latach 1956-1960. NP 3, 1955(4), 1–10.
5. Rozwój i funkcja nauki polskiej w ustroju demokracji ludowej. Ex: Dziesięć lat rozwoju nauki w Polsce Ludowej, PAN, Komitet Historii Nauki. Warszawa, PWN, 1956, 9–19.

1. DEMBOWSKI, J., OLEKIEWICZ, M.: Prawidłowość i przypadkowość. Warszawa, KIW, 34 str.

1. DEWEY, J.: Experience and Nature. New York, Dover Publications, 1958, 14 and 443 pp.
1. DOBROSIELSKI, M.: Logika a retoryka. ZWFUW Nr. 4. Warszawa, PWN, 1957, 15 str.
1. DOROSZEWSKI, W.: Uwagi o semantyce. Z dyskusji logiczno-lingwistycznej. MF 1955, 3/17, 83–94.
1. DREWNOWSKI, J.: Nauka a państwo. MW 1948, 1/20, 179–186.
2. Planowanie w nauce. MW 1950, 8–9/51–52, 189–205.
1. DREWNOWSKI, J. Fr.: Neoscholastyka wobec nowoczesnych wymagań. Ex: Myśl katolicka wobec logiki współczesnej. Studia Gnesnensia 15. Poznań, Księgarnia Św. Wojciecha, 1937, 49–57.
2. Czy metafizyka i religia wytrzymują krytykę naukową. RCZF 1, 1948, 83–97.
1. DURKHEIM, E.: The Elementary Forms of the Religious Life. Translated from the French by J. W. Swain. London, Allen and Unwin, 1957, 11 and 456 pp.
2. Socialism and Saint-Simon. Edited with an Introduction by A. W. Gouldner. Translated by Ch. Sattler. London, Routledge and Kegan Paul, 1958, 29 and 240 pp.
1. Dyskusja o logice w Związku Radzieckim. MF 1952, 2/4, 360–362.

1. EILSTEIN, H.: W sprawie artykułu 'O rozwoju pojęcia materii w fizyce'. MF 1952, 4/6, 198–209.
2. Leninowskie pojęcie materii a idealizm fizyczny. MF 1953, 4/10, 183–221.
3. Rozwój jako przechodzenie do stanów jakościowo wyższych (cz. 1). MF 1955, 3/17, 119–135; cz. 2, MF 1955, 4/18, 178–193.
4. Szczeble odbicia a etapy poznania. MF 1955, 5–6/19–20, 219–226.
5. O stanie filozofii krytycznie. Artykuł dyskusyjny. ND 1956, 2/80, 45–66.
6. Problem logiki w świetle marksistowskiej teorii poznania (cz.1). MF 1956' 5/25, 124–149.
7. Problem logiki w świetle marksistowskiej teorii poznania (cz. 2). MF 1956, 6/26, 116–132.
8. Szkic o sensach pojęcia odbicia. MF 1957, 1/27, 78–107.
9. Laplace, Engels i nasi współcześni. Uwagi o determiniźmie na tle dyskusji w fizyce. SF 1958, 1/4, 143–174.
10. Laplace, Engels i nasi współcześni. Cz. 2: Laplace przepołowiony. SF 1958, 2/5, 36–50.
11. O stylu filozofowania Leszka Kołakowskiego tudzież o 'młodo-marksowskiej' i 'engelsowsko-leninowskiej' teorii poznania. SF 1959, 6/15, 157–201.
1. EILSTEIN, H., KOCHAŃSKI, Z.: O projekcie programu materializmu dialektycznego. MF 1956, 3/23, 147–165.
1. ELZENBERG, H.: La personalité créatrice de l'artiste. PICPHA 1, 520–522.
2. Stoicyzm historyczny i 'stoicyzm' w rozumieniu potocznym. RF 17, 1949–1950 (1–3), 44–46.

3. ELZENBERG, H.: L'Idéalisme de Berkeley est-il un idéalisme immanent? PICPHB, Vol. 13, 78–86.

1. ENGELS, FR.: Herr Eugen Dühring's Revolution in Science (Anti-Dühring). Translated by E. Burns. London, Lawrence and Wishart, s.a., 6 and 356 pp.

2. Dialectics of Nature. Moscow, Foreign Languages Publishing House, 1954, 496 pp.

1. Entretiens philosophiques de Varsovie. Les rapports de la pensée et de l'action. 17–26 Juillet 1957. ZPNP 15, Wrocław-Warszawa, ZNIO, 1958, 202 pp.

1. E.S., B.K.: XI kongres filozofii burżuazyjnej. MF 1954, 1/11, 228–240.

1. FARBER, M.: Experience and Subjectivism. Ex: Sellars, R. W., McGill, V. J., Farber, M. (Ed.): Philosophy for the Future. The Quest of Modern Materialism. New York, Macmillan, 1949, 591–632.

1. FARRINGTON, B.: Greek Science. Its Meaning for Us. London, Penguin Books, 1953, 320 pp.

1. FOMINA, W. A.: Filozoficzne poglądy Plechanowa. Tłumaczył W. Głuchowski. Warszawa, KIW, 1957, 15 i 340 str.

1. FRAENKEL, A. A., BAR-HILLEL, Y.: Foundations of Set Theory. Studies in Logic and the Foundations of Mathematics. Amsterdam, North-Holland Publishing Company, 1958, 10 and 415 pp.

1. FRAGMENTY FILOZOFICZNE. Księga pamiątkowa ku uczczeniu piętnastolecia pracy nauczycielskiej w Uniwersytecie Warszawskim profesora Tadeusza Kotarbińskiego. Warszawa, Nakładem Uczniów, 1934, 214 str.

2. Fragmenty filozoficzne. Seria druga. Księga pamiątkowa ku uczczeniu czterdziestolecia pracy nauczycielskiej w Uniwersytecie Warszawskim profesora Tadeusza Kotarbińskiego. Warszawa, PWN, 1959, 330 str.

1. FREGE, G.: Translations from the Philosophical Writings of Gottlob Frege. Edited by P. Geach and M. Black. Oxford, Basil Blackwell, 1952, 10 and 244 pp.

1. FRANK, PH.: Logisierender Empirismus in der Philosophie der U.S.S.R. ACIPHS-Paris 8, 68–76.

2. Einstein, Mach, and Logical Positivism. Ex: Schilpp, P. A. (Ed.): Albert Einstein: Philosopher-Scientist. New York, Harper and Brothers Publishers, Harper Torchbooks/Science Library, 1959, Vol. 1, 271–286.

3. Philosophy of Science. The Link between Science and Philosophy. Englewood Cliffs, Prentice-Hall, Inc., 1957, 22 and 394 pp.

4. Present Role of Science. Ex: Atti del XII Congresso Internazionale di Filosofia. Firenze, Sansoni Editore, 1958, 5–17.

1. FRITZHAND, M.: Na manowcach idealizmu obiektywnego w etyce. MW 1951, 9/64, 222–259.

2. Prawo i moralność w teorii Petrażyckiego. PPR 7, 1952, 8–9/78–79, 220-244.

BIBLIOGRAPHY

3. FRITZHAND, M.: O sytuacji w etyce polskiej. MF 1952, 3/5, 131–162.
4. O zagadnieniu wolności i konieczności. MF 1953, 4/10, 100–125.
5. Instytut Filozoficzny UW. MF 1953, 1/7, 332–339.
6. O elementarnych normach moralnych. MF 1956, 1/21, 3–28.
7. Etyka a walka klas. Ex: Ateizm a religia. Wykłady wygłoszone na centralnym kursie aktywu partyjnego, maj 1957. Warszawa, KIW, 1957, 318–334.
8. Spór o spuściznę filozoficzną młodego Marksa. ND 1960, 1/128, 91–103.

1. GARDNER, M.: Fads and Fallacies: In the Name of Science. New York, Dover Publications, 1957, 10 and 355 pp.
1. GAWECKI, J.: Czym jest filozofia. WŻ 15, 1946(6), 535–543.
2. O wyrażaniu myśli. WŻ 15, 1946 (8), 785–793.
3. Pojęcie nauki. WŻ 16, 1947 (5), 415–422.
4. Metoda nauk przyrodniczych. WŻ 16, 1947 (6), 511–519.
5. Pięćdziesiąt lat filozofii w Krakowie. PF 44, 1948 (1–3), 26–37.
6. Zygmunt Zawirski. PF 44, 1948 (4), 436–443.
7. Władysław Heinrich (1869–1957). RF 18, 1958 (1–3), 2–10.
8. Zarys realizmu ewolucyjnego. SF 1958, 5/8, 81–100.
1. GEYL, P.: Use and Abuse of History. New Haven, Yale University Press, 1955, 6 and 97 pp.
2. Debates with Historians. The Hague, Martinus Nijhoff, 1955, 8 and 241 pp.
1. GIEDYMIN, J.: Model historyzmu prof. K. Poppera. SF 1958, 3/6, 205–214.
2. Uogólnienie postulatu rozstrzygalności hipotez. SF 1959, 5/14, 139–160.
1. GIEROWSKI, S.: Realizm krytyczny i pozytywizm. KF 18, 1949 (1), 1–29.
1. GIERULANKA, D., POŁTAWSKI, A.: O istnieniu i strukturze dzieła literackiego. SF 1958, 5/8, 142–157.
1. GINSBERG, M.: Essays in Sociology and Social Philosophy. Vol. 1: On the Diversity of Morals. London, Heinemann, 1956, 14 and 329 pp.
1. GOLDSCHMIDT, W.: Understanding Human Society. London, Routledge and Kegan Paul, 1959, 253 pp.
1. GOODMAN, N.: A World of Individuals. Ex: The Problem of Universals. A Symposium. Notre Dame, University of Notre Dame Press, 1956, 15–31.
1. GORDON, M.: Czynna rola abstrakcyjnego myślenia w systemie Ernsta Cassirera. SF 1958, 1/4, 175–208.
2. Zagadnienie powtarzalności jako cechy prawidłowości koegzystencjalnych i przyczynowych w ujęciu Papa i Philippa Franka. SF 1958, 4/7, 54–88.
1. GÓRSKI, J.: Na marginesie książki 'Wprowadzenie do teorii marksizmu'. ND 1948, 7, 291–301.
2. Na marginesie książki 'Wprowadzenie do Socjologii'. MW 1948, 6–7/25–26, 464–471.

1. GÓRSKI, K.: O interpretacji i wartościowaniu w historii. TNKUL, Wykłady i przemówienia 31. Lublin, TNKUL, 1948, 30 str.

1. GREGOROWICZ, J.: Zarys logiki dla prawników, wyd. 2. Warszawa, PWN, 1957, 134 str.

1. GRENIEWSKI, H.: Functors of the Propositional Calculus. VI Zjazd Matematyków Polskich. Dodatek do ASMP 22, 1950, 78–80.
2. On Some Systems of Propositions. CM 2, 1951, 69–71.
3. Arithmetics of Natural Numbers as a Part of the Bi-Valued Propositional Calculus. CM 2, 1951, 291–297.
4. Próba 'odmłodzenia' kwadratu logicznego. SL 1, 1953, 276–286.
5. Elementy logiki formalnej. Warszawa, PWN, 1955, 492 str.
6. Elementy logiki indukcji. Warszawa, PWN, 1955, 90 str.
7. Milla kanon zmian towarzyszących. SL 5, 1957, 109–126.
8. 2^{n+1} wartości logicznych (cz. 1). SF 1957, 2, 82–116.
9. 2^{n+1} wartości logicznych (cz. 2). SF 1957, 3, 3–28.
10. Refleksje na marginesie 'Wykładów z dziejów logiki' Tadeusza Kotarbińskiego, SF 1958, 3/6, 165–184.

1. GRENIEWSKI, H., BOCHENEK, K., MARCZYŃSKI, R.: Application of Bi-Elemental Boolean Algebra to Electronic Circuits. SL 2, 1955, 7–75.

1. GRENIEWSKI, H., BOGUSŁAWSKI, S., SZAPIRO, J.: Dialogi o cybernetyce. MF 1954, 4/14, 158–212.

1. GRENIEWSKI, H., WOJTASIEWICZ, O.: From the History of Chinese Logic. SL 4, 1956, 241–244.

1. GROMSKA, D.: Philosophes polonais morts entre 1938 et 1945. SPH 3, 1939–1946, 31–97.
2. Poglądy etyczne Kazimierza Twardowskiego. RF 19, 1959 (1–2), 9–17.

1. GROMSKA, D., MOSTOWSKI, A.: Bibliographie des travaux de Jan Łukasiewicz. FM 44, 1957, 7–11.

1. GRZEGORCZYK, A.: Próba ugruntowania semantyki języka opisowego. PF 44, 1948 (4), 348–371.
2. Un essai d'établir la sémantique de langage descriptif. PICPHA 1, 776–778.
3. The Pragmatic Foundation of Semantics. Synthese 8, 1950–51, 6–7, 300–324.
4. Some Classes of Recursive Functions. Rozprawy Matematyczne 4, 1953, 1–45.
5. Konferencja logikow. MF 1953, 1/7, 340–349.
6. Uwagi o rozumieniu praw logiki. MF 1955, 1/15, 206–221.
7. The System of Leśniewski in Relation to Contemporary Logical Research. SL 1955, 77–95.
8. Logika popularna. Przystępny zarys logiki zdań. Monografie Popularno-Naukowe, Matematyka. Warszawa, PWN, 1955, 131 str.
9. Uwagi z historii logiki. MF 1957, 1/27, 164–176.
10. Zagadnienia rozstrzygalności. Warszawa, PWN, 1957, 142 str.
11. O pewnych formalnych konsekwencjach reizmu. Ex: Fragmenty Filozoficzne (2), 7–14.

12. GRZEGORCZYK, A.: Analiza filozoficzna, kontemplacja, wartościowanie. SF 1959, 5/14, 161–173.
1. GURVITCH, G., MOORE, W. E.: Twentieth Century Sociology. New York, The Philosophical Library, 1945, 7 and 754 pp.

1. HAMMER, S.: Historia filologii klasycznej w Polsce. PAU, Historia Nauki Polskiej w Monografiach. Kraków, PAU, 1948, 92 str.
1. HAMPSHIRE, S.: Thought and Action. London, Chatto and Windus, 1959, 276 pp.
1. HEGEL, G. W. F.: Science of Logic, Vol. 1–2. Translated by W. H. Johnston and L. G. Struthers. London, Allen and Unwin, 1951, 404 and 486 pp.
2. The Philosophy of History. With prefaces by Charles Hegel and the translator, J. Sibree, and a new introduction by Professor C. J. Friedrich. New York, Dover Publications, 1956, 16 and 457 pp.
1. HEINRICH, WŁ.: Zarys historii filozofii. T. 1, cz. 1: Filozofia grecka. Warszawa, Gebethner i Wolf, 1925, 8 i 206 str.; T. 1, cz. 2: Filozofia średniowieczna. Warszawa, Gebethner i Wolf, 1930, 11 i 231 str.
1. HEMPEL, C. G.: The Function of General Laws in History. Ex: Feigl, H., Sellars, W. (Ed.): Readings in Philosophical Analysis. New York, Appleton-Century-Crofts, Inc., 1949, 459–471.
2. On the Nature of Mathematical Truth. Ex: Feigl, H., Brodbeck, M. (Ed.): Readings in the Philosophy of Science. New York, Appleton-Century-Crofts, Inc., 1953, 148–162.
1. HEMPEL, C. G., OPPENHEIM, P.: The Logic of Explanation. Ex: Feigl, H., Brodbeck, M. (Ed.): Readings in the Philosophy of Science. New York, Appleton-Century-Crofts, Inc., 1953, 319–352.
1. HERTZ, A.: Ludwik Krzywicki jako historyk rozwoju społecznego i kultury. Ex: Ludwik Krzywicki. Praca zbiorowa poświęcona jego życiu i twórczości. Warszawa, Instytut Gospodarstwa Społecznego, 1938, 49–87.
1. HEYTING, A.: Intuitionism. An Introduction. Studies in Logic and the Foundations of Mathematics. Amsterdam, North-Holland Publishing Company, 1956, 132 pp.
1. HIŻ, H.: Filozofia w Stanach Zjednoczonych 1939–1947, Wstęp-Logika. PF 44, 1948 (1–2), 234–249.
2. Orzeczach. Ex: Fragmenty Filozoficzne (2), 15–24.
1. HIRSZFELD, L.: Historia jednego życia. Kraków, Czytelnik, 1946, 369 str.
2. Rola dydaktyki w życiu i twórczości uczonego. KS 1, 1957 (1), 44–63.
1. HIRSZOWICZ, M.: Ideologia a nauka. MF 1956, 6/26, 3–30.
2. Ideologia i nauka. Próba wstępnej analizy. SF 1959, 4/13, 49–72.
1. H. M., Dyskusja o pojęciu materii. MF 1955, 2/16, 235–241.
1. HOCHFELD, J.: O znaczeniu marksizmu. Artykuł dyskusyjny. MW 1948, 4/23, 70–94.
2. O naukowe uogólnianie doświadczeń budownictwa socjalistycznego w Polsce. ŻN 1951, 5–6, 604–610.

3. HOCHFELD, J.: O niektórych aspektach przeciwstawności materializmu historycznego i socjologii burżuazyjnej. MF 1951, 1–2, 106–154.

4. W 40-lecie pracy Stalina 'Marksizm a kwestia narodowa'. MF 1953, 2/8, 162–196.

5. Filozofia współczesnego socialimperializmu. MF 1953, 3/9, 224–241.

6. Z dziejów rozwoju marksistowskiej teorii państwa. MF 1954, 4/14, 264-290.

7. O niektórych aspektach kwestii narodowej w obecnej fazie ogólnego kryzysu kapitalizmu. MF 1955, 4/18, 3–25.

8. On the Programme of Research on the Formation of New Worker Milieus in People's Poland. TWCSA, Vol. 7, 121–129.

1. HOCHFELD, J., NOWAKOWSKI, S.: Uwagi o wykorzystaniu pamiętników do badań nad świadomością proletariatu. MF 1953, 4/10, 242–268.

1. HOFFMAN, P.: Legenda Stanisława Brzozowskiego. ND 1947, 2, 103–135.

2. Filozofia orężem walki klasowej. ND 1949, 4/16, 50–63.

1. HOLLAND, H.: Legenda o Kazimierzu Twardowskim. MF 1952, 3/5, 260–312.

1. HOOK, S.: The Hero in History. A Study in Limitation and Possibility. London, Secker and Warburg, 1945, 184 pp.

1. HORNOWSKI, B.: Pojęcie i struktura światopoglądu. SPTPN 1956, 3, 9–11.

2. Nowy etap w psychologii polskiej. NP 5, 1957(2), 133–139.

1. HOSIASSON, J.: La théorie des probabilités est-elle une logique géneralisée? Analyse critique. ACIPHS-Paris 4, 58–64,

1a. Why Do We Prefer Probabilities Relative to Many Data? Mind 40, 1931 (157), 23–36.

2. On Confirmation. JSL 5, 1940 (4), 133–148.

3. Induction et Analogie: Comparaison de leur fondement. Mind 50, 1941 (200), 351–365.

4. Postęp wiedzy z punktu widzenia poznawczego. PF 44, 1948 (1–3), 59–65.

5. Theoretical Aspect of the Advancement of Knowledge. Synthese 7, 1948–1949 (4–5), 253–261.

1. HUSSERL, E.: Ideas. An Introduction to Pure Phenomenology. Translated by W. R. Boyce Gibson. London, Allen and Unwin, 1931, 465 pp.

1. INDAN, F.: Sądy wartościujące w etyce Durkheima. PF 45, 1949 (3–4), 363–383.

1. INFELD, L.: On the Structure of Our Universe. Ex: Sellars, R. W., McGill, V. J., Farber, M. (Ed.): Philosophy for the Future. The Quest of Modern Materialism. New York, Macmillan, 1949, 173–187.

2. Leonardo da Vinci and the Fundamental Laws of Science. Science and Society 17, 1953(1), 26–41.

3. Rola teorii względności w nauce. PFz 5, 1954(3), 355–367.

4. Kilka uwag o teorii względności. MF 1954, 1/11, 70–79.

5. Znaczenie prac Kopernika dla rozwoju fizyki. SMDNP 2, 1954, 33–53.

6. INFELD, L.: Historia teorii względności. PFz 6, 1955(5), 489–499.
7. Moje wspomnienia o Einsteinie. Warszawa, Iskry, 1956, 148 str.
8. Albert Einstein. Jego dzieło i rola w nauce. Warszawa, PWN, 1956, 188 str.
1. INFELD, L., SOSNOWSKI, L.: O rozwoju pojęcia materii w fizyce. MF 1952, 2/4, 42–55.
1. INGARDEN, R.: Bemerkungen zum Problem 'Idealismus-Realismus'. Ex: Festschrift Edmund Husserl zum 70. Geburtstag gewidmet. Ergänzungsband zum Jahrbuch für Philosophie und Phänomenologische Forschung. Halle a. d. Saale, Max Niemeyer Verlag, 1929, 159–190.
2. Niektóre założenia idealizmu Berkeleya. Ex: Księga Pamiątkowa Polskiego Towarzystwa Filozoficznego we Lwowie. Lwów, 1931.
3. Logistyczna próba nowego ukształtowania filozofii. PF 37, 1934 (4), 335–342.
4. L'Essai logistique d'une refonte de la philosophie. Revue Philosophique 120, 1935 (7–8), 137–159.
5. Vom formalen Aufbau des individuellen Gegenstandes. SPH 1, 1935, 29–106.
6. Das literarische Kunstwerk. Eine Untersuchung aus dem Grenzgebiet der Ontologie, Logik und Literaturwissenschaft. Halle (Saale), Max Niemeyer Verlag, 1931, 14 und 389 SS.
7. Czy zadaniem filozofii jest synteza nauk szczegółowych. KF 13, 1936, 195–214.
8. Esencjalne zagadnienia formy i jej podstawowe pojęcia. KF 16, 1946 (2–4), 101–164.
9. Quelques remarques sur la relation de causalité. SPH 3, 1939–1946, 151–166.
10. The Scientific Activity of Kazimierz Twardowski. SPH 3, 1939–1946, 17–30.
11. Szkice z filozofii literatury, T. 1. Łodź, Spółdzielnia Wydawnicza 'Polonista', 1947, 203 str.
12. Spór o istnienie świata, T. 1. Kraków, PAU, 1947, 296 str.; T. 2, Kraków, PAU, 1948, 848 str.
13. O poznawaniu cudzych stanów psychicznych. KP, 13, 1947, 1–26.
14. Z dziejów teorii dzieła literackiego. KF 17, 1948 (1–2), 135–172.
15. Uwagi o względności wartości. PF 44, 1948 (1–3), 82–94.
16. Les modes d'existence et le problème 'idéalisme-réalisme'. PICPHA 1, 347–350.
17. Zagadnienie przypadku. SPAU 49, 1948 (4), 195–200.
18. Ze studiów nad zagadnieniem formy i treści dzieła sztuki. PF 45, 1949 (1–2), 65–86.
19. O sądzie warunkowym. KF 18, 1949 (3–4), 263–308.
20. O przedmiocie historii filozofii. SPAU 53, 1952 (5), 273–279.
21. Über die gegenwärtigen Aufgaben der Phänomenologie. Archivio di Filosofia 1957, 229–241.

22. INGARDEN, R.: Studia z estetyki, T. 1. Warszawa, PWN, 1957, 9 i 439 str.;
    T. 2, Warszawa, PWN, 1958, 478 str.
23. Wspomnienie o Stanisławie Ignacym Witkiewiczu. Ex: Kotarbiński-
    Płomieński (1), 169–176.
24. The Hypothetical Proposition. Philosophy and Phenomenological
    Research 18, 1958 (4), 435–450.
25. O dziele literackim. Badania z pogranicza ontologii, teorii języka i
    filozofii literatury. Warszawa, PWN, 1960, 489 str.
 1. INGARDEN, R. S.: Descartes a fizyka nowożytna. KF 19, 1950 (1–2), 71–
    148.
 2. Mikołaj Kopernik i zagadnienie obiektywności praw naukowych.
    Warszawa, PIW, 1953, 81 str.
 3. Buridan i Kopernik: Dwie koncepcje nauki. SMDNP 1, 1953, 51–63.
 1. IWANICKI, J.: Powojenna filozofia sowiecka. AK 48, 1948 (5), 500–507.
 2. Dedukcja naturalna i logistyczna. Warszawa, Nakładem Polskiego
    Towarzystwa Teologicznego, 1949, 16 i 164 str.
 3. Problematyka filozoficzna w ciągu ostatniego 50-lecia w Polsce. AK 58,
    1959 (1–3), 255–293.

 1. JABŁOŃSKI, H.: Osiągnięcia Polskiej Akademii Nauk w pierwszych
    trzech latach jej działalności. NP 3, 1955 (4), 11–40.
 2. Polska Akademia Nauk – autonomiczna organizacja uczonych. NP 5,
    1957 (1), 3–37.
 3. Polska Akademia Nauk a aktualne warunki rozwoju nauki w Polsce.
    NP 6, 1958 (3), 6–46.
 1. JAMES, W.: Pragmatism and Four Essays from The Meaning of Truth.
    Meridian Books. New York, The Noonday Press, 1955, 269 pp.
 2. The Will to Believe and Other Essays in Popular Philosophy. New York,
    Dover Publications, 1956, 17 and 332.
 1. JANICZAK, A.: A Remark Concerning Decidability of Complete Theories.
    JSL 15, 1950, 277–279.
 2. Undecidability of Some Simple Formalized Theories. FM 40, 1953,
    131–139.
 3. On the Reducibility of Decision Problems. CM 3, 1954–1955 (1), 33–36.
 1. JANION, M.: Jeszcze jedno nieporozumienie wokół liberalizmu. Z
    powodu publikacji prof. Chałasińskiego. PL 45, 1954 (3–4), 112–142.
 1. JANOWSKA, Z.: Idee Łobaczewskiego w walce z idealizmem w matematy-
    ce. Przełożył z wydania rosyjskiego (1950 r.) A. Kosiński. Warszawa,
    PWN, 1953, 87 str.
 1. JARNUSZKIEWICZ, H.: Czy początek nowego okresu w pracach Polskiej
    Akademii Nauk? NP 4, 1956 (4), 147–169.
 2. Aktualne zadania nauki w Polsce. NP 6, 1958 (3), 152–169.
 1. JAROSZYŃSKI, M.: Jeszcze o autonomii szkoły i nauki. Kuźnica 3, 1947,
    21/90, 8–9.

2. JAROSZYŃSKI, M.: Nowy etap organizacji szkolnictwa wyższego. ŻN 1952, 1–2, 39–59.
1. JASINOWSKI, B.: Les bornes de la mathématique grecque et ses fondements spéculatifs. ACIPHS-Paris 8, 9–19.
1. JAŚKOWSKI, S.: Recherche sur le système de la logique intuitioniste. ACIPHS–Paris 6, 58–61.
2. Międzynarodowy Kongres Filozofii Naukowej. NPL 22, 1937, 275–279.
3. Zagadnienia logiczne a matematyka. MW 1947, 7–8/14–15, 57–70.
4. Trois contributions au calcul des propositions bivalent. SSST-SA 1, 1948 (1), 3–15.
5. Sur les variables propositionelles dépendantes. SSST-SA 1, 1948 (2), 17–21.
6. Sur certaines groupes formés de classes d'ensembles et leur application aux définitions de nombres. SSST-SA 1, 1948 (3), 23–35.
7. Rachunek zdań dla systemów dedukcyjnych sprzecznych. SSST–SA 1, 1948 (5), 57–77.
8. O koniunkcji dyskusyjnej w rachunku zdań dla systemów dedukcyjnych sprzecznych. SSST-SA 1, 1949 (8), 171–172.
9. On the Modal and Causal Function in Symbolic Logic. SPH 4, 1949–1950, 71–92.
10. O interpretacji zdań kategorycznych Arystotelesa w rachunku predykatów. SSST-SA 2, 1950 (3), 77–90.
1. J. K., Szkoły wyższe na przełomie. ŻN 1947, 17–18, 342–346.
1. JØRGENSEN, J.: The Development of Logical Empiricism. IEUS 2, No. 9. Chicago, The University of Chicago Press, 1954, 3 and 100 pp.
1. JORDAN, Z.: Próba analizy zdań psychologicznych Prof. T. Kotarbińskiego. Psychometria 2, 1935.
2. O matematycznych podstawach systemu Platona. Z historii racjonalizmu. PTPN, Prace Komisji Filozoficznej T. 6. Poznań, PTPN, 1937, 6 and 326 str.
3. The Development of Mathematical Logic and of Logical Positivism in Poland between the Two Wars. Polish Science and Learning No. 6. London, Oxford University Press, 1945, 47 pp.

1. KACZOROWSKI, S.: Logika tradycyjna. Zarys dziejów, wyd. 2. Licealna Biblioteczka Filozoficzna T. 2. Łódź, Księgarnia Naukowa, 1946, 24 str.
2. Logika matematyczna. Cz. 1, Algebra logiki. Zarys dziejów, wyd. 2. Licealna Biblioteczka Filozoficzna T. 6. Łódź, Księgarnia Naukowa, 1946, 26 str.
3. O niektórych przekształceniach podziału. ŁTN, Wydz. 1, Nr. 7. Łodź, ŁTN, 1949, 127 str.
1. KALINOWSKI, J.: Teoria reguły społecznej i reguły prawnej Leona Duguita. Problem podstaw mocy obowiązującej prawa. Studium filozoficzno-prawne. TNKUL, Rozprawy Wydziału Nauk Społecznych 4. Lublin, TNKUL, 1949, 183 str.

2. KALINOWSKI, J.: Teoria zdań normatywnych. SL 1, 1953, 113–146.
3. Polskie skrypty i podręczniki logiki dla prawnikow od 1947 do 1954. SL 4, 1956, 266-272.
4. Arystotelesowska teoria sprawności intelektualnych czyli o dwu pojęciach mądrości. RCZF 5, 1955–1957 (4), 45–65.
5. Interpretacja prawa a logika zdań normatywnych. RCZF 5, 1955–1957 (2), 151–169.
6. O istocie i jedności filozofii. RCZF 6, 1958 (1), 5–17.
1. KAMIŃSKI, S.: Fregego logika zdań. RCZF 5, 1955-1957 (2), 31–64.
2. Rola Locke' a i Condillaca w dziejach teorii definicji. RCZF 5, 1955-1957 (4), 67–101.
3. Hobbesa teoria definicji. SL 7, 1958, 43–65.
4. O początkach indukcji matematycznej. SL 7, 1958, 221–239.
5. W sprawie liczby konkludujących trybów sylogistycznych. SL 8, 1958, 165-174.
6. Gorgonne'a teoria definicji. Lublin, TNKUL, 1958, 142 str.
1. KAUFMANN, F.: Methodology of the Social Sciences. London, Thames and Hudson, 1958, 8 and 272 pp.
1. KELLER, J.: Etyka a nauka moralności. STNKUL 1952 (4), 11–13, 18–20.
2. Etyka. T. 1: Zagadnienia etyki ogólnej. Warszawa, Pax, 1954, 219 str. T. 2: Etyka katolicka. Warszawa, Pax, 1957, 390 str.
1. KLEMENSIEWICZ, Z.: Stan i potrzeby językoznawstwa w Polsce. Ex: Dziesięć lat rozwoju nauki w Polsce Ludowej. Warszawa, PWN, 1956, 181–192.
1. KŁÓSAK, K.: Materializm dialektyczny a fizyka współczesna. Znak 2, 1947 (7), 719–732.
2. Metafizyczna i filozoficzna zasada przyczynowości wobec relacji niedokładności W. Heisenberga. RCZF 1, 1948, 198–213.
3. Dialektyka a tradycyjna teoria ewolucji. Znak 3, 1948 (4), 316–325.
4. Teoria indeterminizmu ontologicznego a trójwartościowa logika zdań prof. Jana Łukasiewicza. AK 49, 1948 (3), 209–230.
5. Materializm dialektyczny. Studia krytyczne. Kraków, Wydawnictwo Mariackie, 1948, 106 str.
6. Konieczność wyjścia poza logikę dwuwartościową. AK 50, 1949 (2), 105–116.
7. O. Jacek Woroniecki. PF 45, 1949 (3–4), 437–440.
8. Dialektyczne prawo jedności i walki przeciwieństw. PP 228, 1949 (9), 161–168.
9. Dialektyczne prawo wszechzależności rzeczy i zjawisk. PP 228, 1949 (10), 203–213.
10. Dialektyczne prawo przechodzenia ilości w jakość. PP 228, 1949 (7–8), 69–79.
11. Podział kierunków filozoficznych u diamatyków. Znak 6, 1951 (2), 126–140.
12. Jak pojąć w neoscholastyce przedmiot i metodę filozofii przyrody. RCZF 4, 1954, 1–28.

13. KŁÓSAK, K.: W poszukiwaniu pierwszej przyczyny. Argumentacja za istnieniem Boga z początku trwania czasowego wszechświata i z początku życia organicznego. Warszawskie Studia z Zakresu Filozofii Chrześcijańskiej 1. Warszawa, Pax, 1955, 262 str.; cz. 2: Argumentacja za istnieniem Boga z zależności treściowej poznawanych przez nas prawd, z porządku panującego w biokosmosie, z przygodności rzeczy oraz z ruchu, jaki występuje w przyrodzie. Warszawskie Studia z Zakresu Filozofii Chrześcijańskiej 2. Warszawa, Pax, 1957, 303 str.

14. Próba oceny. ŻM 1956 (3), 82–91.

1. KŁÓSAK, K., USOWICZ, A.: Konstanty Michalski (1879-1947). Kraków, Analecta Historica Congregationis Missionis Prov. Polonorum, Nr. 3, 1949, 249 str.

1. KMITA, J.: W sprawie funkcji semantycznych języka literatury. SF 1959, 5/14, 175–190.

1. KNEALE, W.: Probability and Induction. Oxford, Clarendon Press, 1952, 8 and 264 pp.

1. KOCHAŃSKI, Z.: W sprawie wydania 'Idei ewolucji w biologii' Nusbauma-Hilarowicza. MF 1953, 3/9, 294–297.

2. Nauka Pawłowa – przyrodnicze potwierdzenie marksistowsko-leninowskiej teorii poznania. Materiały i Sudia, T. 3, Seria Filozoficzna. Warszawa, KIW, 1955, 151–183.

3. Poznanie jako subiektywne odbicie obiektywnej rzeczywistości. MF 1956, 5/25, 48–66; MF 1956, 6/26, 68–79.

1. KOKOSZYŃSKA, M.: Syntax, Semantik und Wissenschaftslogik. ACIPHS-Paris 3, 9–14.

1a. Nauka o supozycji terminów według Piotra Hiszpana. PF 37, 1934, 235–261.

2. Über den absoluten Wahrheitsbegriff und einige andere semantische Begriffe. Erkenntnis 6, 1936, 143–165.

2a. Bemerkungen über die Einheitswissenschaft. Erkenntnis 7, 1939 (5–6), 325–335.

3. O różnych rodzajach zdań. PF 43, 1947 (1–4), 22–51.

4. What Means 'Relativity of Truth'. SPH 3, 1939–1946, 167–176.

5. On a Certain Condition of a Semantical Theory of Science. PICPHA 1, 773–775.

6. O pewnym warunku semantycznej teorii wiedzy. PF 44, 1948 (4), 372–381.

7. A Refutation of the Relativism of Truth. SPH 4, 1949–1950, 93–149.

8. W sprawie stosunku logiki do dialektyki. SL 3, 1955, 184–203.

9. O 'dobrej' i 'złej' indukcji. SL 5, 1957, 43–64.

10. Krytyka niektórych poglądów na stosunek logiki do dialektyki. SF 1957, 3, 118–151.

1. KOKOSZYŃSKA, M., KUBIŃSKI, T., SŁUPECKI, J.: Zastosowanie pojęć logiki matematycznej do wyjaśniania niektórych pojęć przyrodoznawstwa. SL 4, 1956, 155–205.

1. KOŁAKOWSKI, L.: Metodologia ks. Kłósaka. Felieton filozoficzny. MF 1951, 1–2, 315–322.

2. KOŁAKOWSKI, L.: M. Cornforth: Nauka przeciw idealizmowi. MW 1951, 11–12/66–67, 304–311.

3. Avicenna – lekarz dusz i ciał. MF 1952, 3/5, 36–55.

4. Filozofia nieinterwencji. Głos w dyskusji nad radykalnym konwencjonalizmem. MF 1953, 2/8, 335–373.

5. Nauka przed sądem Ciemnogrodu. MF 1953, 2/8, 374–388.

6. Szkice o filozofii katolickiej. Warszawa, PWN, 1955, 265 str.

7. Aktualność sporu o powszechniki. Ex: Światopoglądowe i metodologiczne problemy abstrakcji naukowej, T. 1. Warszawa, PWN, 1957, 113–160 = MF 1956, 2/22, 3–32.

8. O łatwości rozstrzygnięcia problemu nominalizmu. MF 1956, 5/25, 150–155.

9. Problematyka historii polskiej filozofii i myśli społecznej XV-XVII w. Ex: Kołakowski, L. (Red.): Z dziejów polskiej myśli filozoficznej i społecznej, T. 1. Warszawa, KIW, 1956, 9–43.

10. Wykłady o filozofii średniowiecznej. Warszawa, PWN, 1956, 140 str.

11. Intelektualiści a ruch komunistyczny. ND 1956, 9/87, 22–31.

12. Światopogląd i życie codzienne. Warszawa, PIW, 1957, 205 str.

13. Aktualne i nieaktualne pojęcie marksizmu. NK 8, 1957, 4/357, 2 i 7.

14. Permanent and Transitory Aspects of Marxism. Ex: Mayewski, P. (Red.): The Broken Mirror. A Collection of Writings from Contemporary Poland. New York, Random House, 1958, 157–174.

15. Sens ideowy pojęcia lewicy. Po Prostu 1957, 8/423, 1–2 i 4.

16. Odpowiedzialność i historia. Cz. 1: Spisek pięknoduchów. NK 8, 1957, 35/388, 1–2 i 11. Cz. 2: Narkotyk wielkiego demiurga. NK 8, 1957, 36/389, 4–5. Cz. 3: Sumienie i postęp społeczny. NK 8, 1957, 37/390, 4–5. Cz. 4: Nadzieja i materia historyczna. NK 8, 1957, 38/391, 4–5.

17. Jednostka i nieskończoność. Wolność i antynomie wolności w filozofii Spinozy. Warszawa, PWN, 1958, 630 str.

18. Światopogląd XVII stulecia. Ex: Filozofia XVII wieku. Francja-Holandia-Niemcy. Wyboru dokonał, wstępem i przypisami opatrzył L. Kołakowski. Warszawa, PWN, 1959, 7–44.

19. Karol Marks i klasyczna definicja prawdy. SF 1959, 2/11, 43–67.

20. Determinizm i odpowiedzialność. Ex: Fragmenty Filozoficzne (2), 25–43.

1. KOMITET FILOZOFICZNY Polskiej Akademii Nauk. MF 1954, 4/14, 388–389.

1. KONFERENCJA LOGIKÓW. SCZP–PAN 3, 1955 (1), 38–52.

1. KONORSKI, J.: Conditioned Reflexes and Neuron Organisation. Translated from the Polish MS under the author's supervision by S. Garry. Cambridge Biological Studies. Cambridge, Cambridge University Press, 1948, 14 and 267 pp.

2. Podstawy fizjologiczne pamięci. MW 1948, 5/24, 215–232.

3. I. J. Pawłow, jego życie i dzieło. MW 1949, 12/43, 343–352.

4. Kierunki rozwoju fizjologii mózgu. NP 5, 1957 (3), 33–56.

1. KONRAD, P.: Marksizm bez przyłbicy. Odrodzenie 4, 1947, 14–15/123–124, 10–11.

2. KONRAD, P.: Marksizm nie przedawniony. Odrodzenie 4, 1947, 23/132, 2.

1. KORCIK, A.: Gottlob Frege jako twórca pierwszego systemu aksjoma-
tycznego współczesnej logiki. RCZF 1, 1948, 138–164.

2. Teoria sylogizmu zdań asertorycznych u Arystotelesa na tle logiki
tradycyjnej. Studium historyczno-krytyczne. TNKUL, Rozprawy
Wydziału Historyczno-Filologicznego, Sekcja Filozoficzna T. 2. Lublin,
TNKUL, 1948, 87 str.

3. Geneza pomysłu Sheffera dotyczącego redukcji pięciu stałych logicznych
do pewnej stałej różnej od nich. RCZF 2–3, 1949–1950, 423–428.

4. Przyczynek do historii rachunku zdań. SL 1, 1953, 247–252.

5. Teoria sylogizmu Hospiniana i Leibniza. RCZF 4, 1954, 51–70.

6. O tak zwanych naczelnych prawach rozumowania i zależnościach
między nimi. RCZF 5, 1955–1957 (2), 183–191.

1. KOSSAK, J.: Kontynuacja czy negacja. ND 1959, 2/116, 106–120.

1. KOTARBIŃSKA, J.: Analiza pojęcia przypadku. Przyczynek do słownika
filozoficznego. Ex: Fragmenty Filozoficzne (1), 161–179.

2. Janina Hosiasson-Lindenbaumowa. PF 42, 1946 (3–4), 324.

3. Ewolucja Koła Wiedeńskiego. Pozytywizm, empiryzm, fizykalizm. MW
1947, 2/9, 145–160.

4. Le physicalisme et les étapes de son évolution. PICPHA 1, 636–639.

5. Definicja. SL 2, 1955, 301–321.

6. Pojęcie znaku. SL 6, 1957, 57–143.

7. Tak zwana definicja dejktyczna. Ex: Fragmenty Filozoficzne (2), 44–74.

8. On Ostensive Definitions. Philosophy of Science 27, 1960 (1), 1–22.

1. KOTARBIŃSKI, T.: Zasady dobrej roboty. MW 1946, 1, 25–41.

2. Principes de bon travail. SPH 3, 1939–1946, 177–189.

3. Elementy teorii poznania, logiki formalnej i metodologii nauk, T. 1–2.
Warszawa, Akademicka Spółdzielnia Wydawnicza, 1947, 344 i 305 str.
(Mimeographed, first published 1929).

'4. Sur l'attitude réiste (ou concrétiste). Synthese 7, 1948–1949 (4–5), 262–273.

5. Les valeurs techniques de l'activité. SPH 4, 1949–1950, 151–169.

6. Kurs logiki dla prawników. Warszawa, PWN, 1955, 215 str. (1st ed.:
Warszawa, Gebethner i Wolf, 1951, 255 str.).

7. W sprawie artykułu 'Legenda o Kazimierzu Twardowskim'. MF 1952,
4/6, 356–357.

8. Traktat o dobrej robocie. ŁTN, Wydz. 1, Nr. 18. Łódź, ZNIO, 1955, 360 str.

9. The Fundamental Idea of Pansomatism. Mind 64, 1955 (256), 488–500.

10. Kryzys logiki. MF 1955, 1/15, 223–228.

11. Pojęcie 'istoty rzeczy'. MF 1956, 3/23, 135–146.

12. Treść i zakres pojęcia metodologii. MF 1956, 4/24, 97–105.

13. Sprawność i błąd. Z myślą o dobrej robocie nauczyciela. Warszawa,
PZWS, 1956, 102 str.

14. Sprawy sumienia. Biblioteczka 'Po Prostu' 1. Warszawa, KIW, 1956, 43 str.

15. Wybór pism, T. 1. Warszawa, PWN, 1957, 733 str.; T. 2, Warszawa,
PWN, 1958, 936 str.

16. KOTARBIŃSKI, T.: Wykłady z dziejów logiki. ŁTN, Wydz. 1, Nr. 28, Łódź, ZNIO, 1957, 251 str.

17. Filozofia St. I. Witkiewicza. Ex: Kotarbiński-Płomieński (1), 11–20.

18. Niektóre problemy etyki niezależnej. Ex: Ateizm a religia. Cykl wykładów. Warszawa, KIW, 1957, 300–317.

19. Filozof. SF 1957, 1, 4–16.

20. O pojęciu metody. Warszawa, PWN, 1957, 15 str.

21. La philosophie dans la Pologne contemporaine. Synthèse 12, 1957 (137), 29–38.

22. Zasady etyki niezależnej. SF 1958, 1/4, 3–13.

23. Myśli o nauce. KS 2, 1958 (1), 13–23.

24. Fazy rozwojowe konkretyzmu. SF 1958, 4/7, 3–13.

25. Próba redukcji poznania psychologicznego do ekstraspekcji. SF 1958, 5/8, 138–141.

26. La logique en Pologne. Ex: Klibansky, R. (Ed.): Philosophy in the Mid-Century. A Survey. Firenze, La Nuova Italia Editrice, 1958, Vol. 1, 45–52.

27. La philosophie dans la Pologne contemporaine. Ex: Klibansky, R. (Ed.): Philosophy in the Mid-Century. A Survey. Firenze, La Nuova Italia Editrice, 1959, Vol. 4, 224–235.

28. Styl pracy Kazimierza Twardowskiego. RF 19, 1959 (1–2), 1–4.

29. La logique en Pologne. Son originalité et les influences étrangères. Accademia Polacca di Scienze e Lettere. Biblioteca di Roma, Fascicolo 7. Roma, Angelo Signorelli, 1959, 24 pp.

1. KOTARBIŃSKI, T., PŁOMIEŃSKI, J. E.: Stanisław Ignacy Witkiewicz. Człowiek i twórca. Księga pamiątkowa. Warszawa, Państwowy Instytut Wydawniczy, 1957, 407 str.

1. KOTT, J.: Postęp i głupstwo, T. 1–2. Warszawa, PIW, 1956, 388 i 365 str.

1. KOWALIK, T.: O Ludwiku Krzywickim. Studium społeczno-ekonomiczne. Warszawa, PWN, 1959, 382 str.

1. KOWALSKI, S.: Socjologiczna teoria wychowania Floriana Znanieckiego. Studia Pedagogiczne 7, 1959, 7–78.

1. KRAJEWSKI, W.: Materia i materializm w świetle fizyki współczesnej. MW 1948, 6–7/25–26, 330–349.

2. Dialektyka fizyki współczesnej. MW 1949, 3/34, 206–228.

3. Materializm dialektyczny w świetle fizyki współczesnej, wyd. 2. Warszawa, KIW, 1950, 70 str.

4. O charakterze i roli nauk przyrodniczych. ŻN 1951, 5–6, 590–603.

5. O właściwą ocenę charakteru nauk przyrodniczych. ND 1951, 2/26, 133–140.

6. Marian Smoluchowski jako filozof-materialista. MF 1952, 4/6, 232–248.

7. O dialektyce marksistowskiej. Warszawa, Wiedza Powszechna, 1952, 78 str.

8. Uwagi o prawach dynamicznych i statystycznych. MF 1954, 3/13, 225–239.

BIBLIOGRAPHY

9. KRAJEWSKI, W.: O prawie negacji negacji czyli rozwoju po spirali. MF 1955, 5-6/19-20, 191-218.
10. Światopogląd Mariana Smoluchowskiego. Warszawa, PWN, 1956, 247 str.
11. O przedmiocie filozofii marksistowskiej i innych sprawach spornych. SF 1958, 2/5, 172-185.
12. Główne zagadnienia i kierunki filozofii. Cz. 2: Ontologia. Warszawa, PWN, 1959, 150 str.
1. KRAJEWSKI,W.,TEMKIN, H.,HEKKER,R.: O materializmie historycznym. Warszawa, Wiedza Powszechna, 1953, 151 str.
1. KRASSOWSKA, E.: Planowanie w nauce. MW 1948, 1/20, 160-165.
2. Perspektywy nauki polskiej. Odrodzenie 6, 1949, 10/223, 1-2.
1. KRASZEWSKI, Z.: Logika stosunków zakresowych. SL 4, 1956, 63-87.
1. KRĄPIEC, M. A.: Egzystencjalizm tomistyczny. Znak 6, 1951 (2), 108-125.
2. Zdrowy rozsądek a filozofia. Znak 7, 1952 (3), 185-201.
3. Zdrowy rozsądek a krytyka poznania. Znak 9, 1957 (4), 291-305.
4. Matematyczny i filozoficzny interpretacjonizm materii. ZNKUL 1, 1958 (3), 9-30.
5. Zagadnienie jednostkowienia bytów materialnych. RCZF 6, 1958 (1), 97-148.
6. Teoria materii. Ujęcie fizykalne i filozoficzne. ZNKUL 2, 1959, 2/6, 3-48.
7. Realizm ludzkiego poznania. Poznań, Pallotinum, 1959, 652 str.
8. Teoria analogii bytu. TNKUL, Rozprawy Wydziału Filozoficznego 9. Lublin, TNKUL, 1959, 400 str.
1. KREUTZ, M.: Główne kierunki współczesnej psychologii, wyd. 2. Przedruk z Encyklopedii Wychowania. Warszawa, Instytut Wydawniczy 'Nasza Księgarnia', 1946, 80 str.
2. Podstawy psychologii. Studium nad metodami i pojęciami współczesnej psychologii. Warszawa-Kraków, Czytelnik, 1949, 402 str.
1. KROKIEWICZ, A.: Heraklit. KF 17, 1948 (1-2), 1-46.
2. Geneza atomizmu. Meander 3, 1948 (1), 10-26.
3. Tales i narodziny filozofii greckiej. PH 37, 1948, 83-91.
4. O logice Stoików. KF 17, 1948 (3-4), 173-197.
5. Protagoras i Gorgiasz. Ex: Kumaniecki, K., Sokołowski, F., Michałowski K., Krokiewicz, A., Winniczuk, L., Lorentz, S.: Epoka Peryklesa. Biblioteka Meandra 10. Warszawa, PZWS, 1949, 65-86.
6. Etyka Demokryta. SPAU 53, 1952 (3), 114-118.
7. Sokrates. Warszawa, Pax, 1958, 187 str.
1. KRONIKA POLSKA. Z ruchu filozoficznego. PS 9, 1947, 461-464.
1. KROŃSKI, T.: Rozkładowe kierunki filozofii i estetyki burżuazyjnej i ich oddziaływanie na gruncie polskim. MSD 1950, 2, 32-60.
2. Świat w klamrach ontologii. MF 1952, 1/3, 318-331.
3. O 'Historii Filozofii' W. Tatarkiewicza. MF 1952, 4/6, 249-272.
4. Ludwik Feuerbach i 'Wykłady o istocie religii'. Ex: Feuerbach, L.:. Wykłady o istocie religii. Przekład E. Skowrona i T. Witwickiego.

Wstępem poprzedził T. Kroński. Biblioteka Klasyków Filozofii. Warszawa, PWN, 1953, IX–XVIII.

5. KROŃSKI, T.: Reakcja mesjanistyczna i katolicka w Polsce połowy XIX wieku. MF 1954, 3/13, 120–149.

6. Walka wokół Kanta w Polsce pierwszych dziesięcioleci XIX wieku. MF 1954, 4/14, 120–149.

7. Wykłady z historii filozofii starożytnej. Grecja i Rzym. Warszawa, PWN, 1955, 81 str.

8. Hegel i problemy filozofii historii. SF 1958, 3/6, 42–75.

9. Rozważania wokół Hegla. Warszawa, PWN, 1960, 499 str.

1. KRYSZEWSKI, W.: Teoria 'typów idealnych' M. Webera jako subiektywno-idealistyczne wypaczenie marksistowskiej problematyki abstrakcji konkretnej. ZPNP 12, 1956, 155–161.

1. KRZYWICKI, L.: Primitive Society and Its Vital Statistics. Warsaw, J. Mianowski Institute for the Promotion of Science and Letters, 1934, 13 and 589 pp.

2. Studia socjologiczne. Wybrał i wstępem poprzedził A. Schaff. Warszawa, PIW, 1951, 460 str.

3. Idea a życie. Z wczesnej publicystyki (1883–1892) Wyboru dokonał, przedmową i przypisami opatrzył H. Holland. Warszawa, PWN, 1957, 98 i 614 str.

4. Dzieła. T. 1: Pierwociny więzi społecznej. Warszawa, PWN, 1957, 806 str.; T. 2: Artykuły i rozprawy 1880–1886. Warszawa, PWN, 1957, 606 str.

5. Wspomnienia, T. 1–3. Warszawa, Czytelnik, 1957–1959, 450, 626, 543 str.

1. KRZYŻANOWSKI, A.: Chrześcijańska moralność polityczna. Warszawa-Kraków, Wydawnictwo E. Kuthana, 1948, 230 str.

1. KUBIŃSKI, T.: O pewnej metodzie tworzenia logik modalnych. SL 4, 1956, 213–235.

2. Nazwy nieostre. SL 7, 1958, 115–174.

1. KUDEROWICZ, Z.: Polemika w sprawie poglądów filozoficznych młodego Marksa. MF 1957, 3/29, 210–218.

1. KULA, W.: Przedmowa. Ex: Rutkowski, J.: Historia gospodarcza Polski do 1864 r. Warszawa, KIW, 1953, V-XII.

2. Kształtowanie się kapitalizmu w Polsce. Warszawa, PWN, 1955, 135 str.

3. W sprawie naszej polityki naukowej. KH 63, 1956 (3), 151–166.

4. Rozważania o historii. Warszawa, PWN, 1958, 296 str.

1. KURATOWSKI, K.: Państwowy Instytut Matematyczny. ŻN 1948, 31–32, 64–67.

1. KUROWSKI, S. J.: Szkice optymistyczne. Warszawa, Pax, 1957, 382 str.

1. KUSZKO, E.: W sprawie artykułu L. Kołakowskiego 'Karol Marks i klasyczna definicja prawdy'. SF 1959, 5/14, 222–229.

1. KUZIŃSKI, S.: Teoria społeczna E. Abramowskiego. MW 1950, 1/44, 26–60.

BIBLIOGRAPHY

1. LANDE, J.: O ocenach. Uwagi dyskusyjne. KF 17, 1948 (3-4), 241-315.
2. Studia z filozofii prawa. Warszawa, PWN, 1959, 1005 str.
1. LANGE, O.: Ludwik Krzywicki jako teoretyk materializmu historycznego. Ex: Ludwik Krzywicki. Praca zbiorowa poświęcona jego życiu i twórczości. Warszawa, Instytut Gospodarstwa Społecznego, 1938, 91-120.
2. The Scope and Method of Economics. Ex.: Feigl, H., Brodbeck, M. (Ed.): Readings in the Philosophy of Science. New York, Appleton-Century-Crofts, Inc., 1953, 744-754.
3. O twórczym rozwoju teorii marksistowskiej. ŻN 1951, 1-2, 24-34.
4. Zagadnienia ekonomii politycznej w świetle pracy J. Stalina 'Ekonomiczne problemy socjalizmu w ZSRR'. Warszawa, PWN, 1953, 160 str.
5. Ekonomia polityczna. T. 1: Zagadnienia ogólne. Warszawa, PWN, 1959, 302 str.
1. LAZARI-PAWŁOWSKA, I.: Idiograficzna koncepcja historii. SF 1958, 1/4, 14-41.
2. O pojęciu typologicznym w humanistyce. SF 1958, 4/7, 30-53.
3. Tworzenie pojęć nauk humanistycznych według koncepcji Leona Petrażyckiego. Ex: Fragmenty Filozoficzne (2), 102-114.
1. LEGOWICZ, J.: 'Dialogi filozoficzne' Aureliusza Augustyna w walce z naukowym poglądem na świat. MF 1954, 3/13, 168-202.
2. Tomasz z Akwinu i narodziny postawy naukowej w filozofii XIII wieku. MF 1955, 5-6/19-20, 146-190.
3. Kilka uwag o 'Wykładach z historii filozofii starożytnej'. MF 1956, 4/24, 181-186.
4. Metodologiczne założenia recepcji arystotelizmu u Bonawentury. SF 1957, 1, 116-144.
5. Humanizm dialektyki, metody i myślenia u Heraklita. RUW 1, 1958, 9-39.
1. LEJEWSKI. Cz.: O pojęciu istnienia w logice. RPTN 1953-1954, 15-17.
2. A Contribution to Leśniewski's Mereology. RPTN 1954-1955, 43-50.
3. A New Axiom of Mereology. RPTN 1955-1956, 65-70.
4. On Leśniewski's Ontology. Ratio 1, 1958 (2), 150-176.
5. A Re-Examination of the Russellian Theory of Descriptions. Philosophy 35, 1960 (1), 14-29.
1. LENIN, V. I.: The Essentials of Lenin. In Two Volumes. London, Lawrence and Wishart, 1947, 758 and 855 pp.
2. Materialism and Empirio-Criticism. Collected Works of V. I. Lenin, Vol. 13. London, Lawrence and Wishart, 1938, 7 and 384 pp.
3. Marx-Engels-Marxism, 4th ed. Moscow, Foreign Languages Publishing House, 1951, 580 pp.
4. Zeszyty Filozoficzne. Polish translation from the 1947 Russian edition. Warszawa, KIW, 1956, 483 str.
1. LESZCZYŃSKI, J.: Teoria świata w ujęciu Hansa Corneliusa. KF 1949 (2), 73-160; 1949 (3-4), 173-240.
2. Wartość logiczna zdań o przyszłości. SPAU 53, 1952 (7-10), 480-482.

3. LESZCZYŃSKI, J.: Filozof metafizycznego niepokoju. Ex: Kotarbiński-Płomieński (1), 93-118.

1. LEŚNIAK, K.: Filodemoja traktat o indukcji. SL 2, 1955, 77-111.

2. Epikureizm jako doktryna socjologiczna. MF 1956, 1/21, 85-107.

3. Stoicyzm i etyka Marka Aurelego. SF 1958, 2/5, 128-152.

1. LEŚNIEWSKI, S.: Krytyka logicznej zasady wyłączonego środka. PF 16, 1913 (2-3), 315-352.

2. Czy klasa klas nie podporządkowanych sobie jest podporządkowana sobie. PF 17, 1914 (1), 63-75.

3. O podstawach matematyki. PF 30, 1927, 164-206; (2), PF 31, 1928, 261-291; (3), PF 32, 1929, 60-105; (4), PF 33, 1930, 77-105; (5), PF 34, 1931, 142-170.

4. Grundzüge eines neuen Systems der Grundlagen der Mathematik, §§ 1-11. FM 14, 1929, 1-81.

5. Über die Grundlagen der Ontologie. CRSSLV-C3 24, 1932, 111-132.

1. LEŚNODORSKI, B.: Szkoły wyższe i nakazy życia. ŻN 1947, 23-24, 241-264.

2. Dobre i złe tradycje nauki polskiej. Ich wyraz w publicystyce Jana Rutkowskiego. ŻN 1950, 5-6, 333-343.

1. LEŚNODORSKI, B., OPAŁEK, K.: Z zagadnień historii nauki. Nauka zjawiskiem społecznym. ŻN 1951, 5-6, 611-631.

1. LEWICKA, H.: Przeciw idealistycznym i mechanistycznym teoriom fonemu. MF 1951, 1-2, 188-201.

1. LEWICKA, H., STRELCYN, S.: Językoznawstwo na nowym etapie. MW 1950, 11-12/54-55, 295-305.

1. LEWIS, C. I.: Mind and the World Order. Outline of a Theory of Knowledge. New York, Dover Publications, 1956, 14 and 446 pp.

1. LIDER, J.: Pogadanki o dialektyce i materializmie, wyd. 6. Warszawa, PIW, 1951, 254 str.

1. LIPIŃSKI, E.: Studia nad historią polskiej myśli ekonomicznej. Warszawa, PWN, 1956, 536 str.

2. Rewizje. Warszawa, PWN, 1958, 167 str.

1. LISSA, Z.: O obiektywności praw w marksistowskiej historii i teorii muzyki. MSD 1953, 1/13, 121-165.

1. LITWIN, J.: Przegląd Socjologiczny. MW 1950, 1/44, 158-173.

2. Uwagi o świadomości klasowej proletariatu. MF 1952, 2/4, 266-302.

3. Przyczynek do genezy materializmu historycznego. Warszawa, KIW, 1953, 116 str.

4. O roli czynnika demograficznego w rozwoju społecznym. MF 1953, 2/8, 389-400.

1. LUKÁCS, G.: Existentialism. Ex: Sellars, R. W., McGill, V. J., Farber, M. (Ed.): Philosophy for the Future. The Quest of Modern Materialism. New York, Macmillan, 1949, 571-590.

1. LUTYŃSKI, J.: Ewolucjonizm w etnologii anglosaskiej a etnografia radziecka. Uniwersytet Łódzki, Prace z Historii Myśli Społecznej i z Badań Społecznych T. 6. Łódź, ZNIO, 1956, 350 str.

2. LUTYŃSKI, J.: Posłowie. Ex: Krzywicki (4), T. 1, 781–804.
3. O wartościowaniu i manichejskiej postawie w naukach społecznych. KS 2, 1958 (4), 18–44.
1. LYSENKO, T. D.: Soviet Biology. A Report to the Lenin Academy of Agricultural Sciences, Moscow, 1948. London, Birch Books Limited, s.a., 51 pp.

1. ŁADOSZ, J.: O obiektywnym znaczeniu prawdopodobieństwa. Materiały i Studia, T. 3, Seria Filozoficzna. Warszawa, KIW, 1955, 111–150.
2. O sprzecznościach logicznych i dialektycznych. MF 1956, 4/24, 106–135.
1. ŁOŚ, J.: Próba aksjomatyzacji logiki tradycyjnej. AUMCS-SF 1, 1946 (3), 211–228.
2. Podstawy analizy metodologicznej kanonów Milla. AUMCS-SF 2, 1947 (5), 269–301.
3. Logiki wielowartościowe a formalizacja funkcji intenzjonalnych. KF 17, 1948 (1–2), 59–86.
4. O matrycach logicznych. Prace WRTN, Seria B, Nr. 19. Wrocław, WRTN, 42 str.
5. An Algebraic Proof of Completeness for the Two-Valued Propositional Calculus. CM 2, 1951, 236–240.
6. On the Categoricity in Power of Elementary Deductive Systems and Some Related Problems. CM 3, 1954–1955 (1), 58–62.
7. On the Axiomatic Treatment of Probability. CM 3, 1954–1955(2), 125–137.
8. The Algebraic Treatment of the Methodology of Elementary Deductive Systems. SL 2, 1955, 151–212.
1. ŁUBNICKI, N.: Teoria poznania materializmu dialektycznego. AUMCS-SF 1, 1946 (2), 121–186.
2. Zagadnienia teoriopoznawcze materializmu dialektycznego. PF 43, 1947 (1–4), 60–86.
3. Witalizm i mechanizm. MW 1947, 12/19, 538–543.
4. Indywidualizm i demokracja. PF 44, 1948 (4), 402–417.
5. Individualisme et democratie. PICPHA 1, 144–147.
6. Vitalisme et mécanisme. PICPHA 1, 879–881.
7. Epistemological Problems of Dialectical Materialism. Synthese 7, 1948–1949 (4–5), 274–296.
8. Radziecka myśl filozoficzna lat ostatnich. PF 45, 1949 (3–4), 400–411.
9. Descartes a nowoczesny materializm. AUMCS-SF 8, 1953 (1), 1–37.
10. Myślenie a działanie. SF 1957, 2, 117–144.
11. Ewolucja światopoglądu A. Herzena. AUMCS-SF 11, 1957 (1), 1–84.
12. Poglądy filozoficzne Adama Mahrburga. SF 1958, 1/4, 61–85; 2/5, 51–79.
1. ŁUKASIEWICZ, J.: O zasadzie sprzeczności u Arystotelesa. Studium krytyczne. Kraków, Akademia Umiejętności, 1910, 210 str.
2. Die logische Grundlagen der Wahrscheinlichkeitsrechnung. Kraków,

Akademie der Wissenschaften, 1913, 75 SS.
3. ŁUKASIEWICZ, J.: O pojęciu wielkości. PF 19, 1916, 1–70.
4. Treść wykładu pożegnalnego wygłoszonego w sali Uniwersytetu Warszawskiego dnia 7 marca 1918. Pro Arte et Studio 11, 1918. Reprinted: Wiadomości (London) 10, 1955, 45/501, 4.
5. O logice trójwartościowej. RF 5, 1919–1920, 170a–171a.
6. Logika dwuwartościowa. PF 23, 1921, 189–205.
7. O logice Stoików. PF 30, 1927, 278–279.
8. O metodę w filozofii. PF 31, 1928, 3–5.
9. O znaczeniu i potrzebach logiki matematycznej. NPL 10, 1929, 604–620.
10. Elementy logiki matematycznej. Skrypt autoryzowany. Opracował H. Presburger. Warszawa, Komisja Wydawnicza Koła Mat.-Fiz. Studentów Uniwersytetu Warszawskiego, 1929, 200 str. Wyd, 2, Warszawa, PWN, 1958, 98 str.
11. Philosophische Bemerkungen zu mehrwertigen Systemen des Aussagenkalküls. CRSSLV-C3 23, 1930, 51–77.
12. O nauce. Biblioteczka Filozoficzna 5. Lwów, Polskie Towarzystwo Filozoficzne, 1934, 40 str.
13. Z historii logiki zdań. PF 37, 1934, 417–437.
14. Znaczenie analizy logicznej dla poznania. PF 37, 1934, 369–377.
15. Zur Geschichte der Aussagenlogik. Erkenntnis 5, 1935, 111–131.
16. Co dała filozofii współczesna logika matematyczna. PF 39, 1936, 325–326.
17. Logistyka a filozofia. PF 39, 1936, 115–131.
18. W obronie logistyki. Ex: Myśl katolicka wobec logiki współczesnej. Studia Gnesnensia 15. Poznań, Księgarnia Św. Wojciecha, 1937, 22 str.
19. Die Logik und das Grundlagenproblem. Les Entretiens de Zurich sur les fondements et la méthode des sciences mathématiques 6–9 Décembre 1938. Exposés et discussions publiés par le Président des débats F. Gonseth. Zurich, Editeurs S.A. Leemans frères et Cie, 1941, 82–108.
20. Aristotle's Syllogistic from the Standpoint of Modern Formal Logic, 2nd ed. Oxford, Clarendon Press, 1957, 13 and 222 pp.
21. A System of Modal Logic. Journal of Computing Systems 1, 1953 (3), 111–149.

1. ŁUKASIEWICZ, J., TARSKI, A.: Untersuchungen über den Aussagenkalkül. CRSSLV-C3 23, 1930, 1–21. English text in Tarski (5), 38–59.

1. ŁUSZCZEWSKA-ROMAHNOWA, S.: Wieloznaczność a język nauki. KF 17, 1948 (1–2), 47–58.
2. Kartezjański ideał wiedzy. KF 19, 1950 (1–2), 25–38.
3. Analiza i uogólnienie metody sprawdzania formuł logicznych przy pomocy diagramów Venna. SL 1, 1953, 185–213.
4. Indukcja a pradopodobieństwo. SL 5, 1957, 71–86.

1. MACH, E.: The Analysis of Sensations. Translated by C. M. Williams, revised and supplemented by S. Waterlow. New York, Dover Publica-

tions, 1959, 42 and 380 pp.

1. MALEWSKI, A.: Postulaty praktycznej użyteczności a rozwój nauk społecznych. Zeszyty Naukowe Uniwersytetu A. Mickiewicza Nr. 5, Filo-
zofia-Psychologia-Pedagogika Z. 1. Poznań, PWN, 1956, 3–13.

2. Empiryczny sens teorii materializmu historycznego. SF 1957, 2, 58–81.

3. ABC porządnego myślenia, wyd. 2. Warszawa, PZWS, 1958, 164 str.

4. O rozbieżnościach w poglądach socjologicznych i o rozbieżnościach w
pojmowaniu nauki. SF 1958, 2/5, 186–205.

5. Zagadnienie idiograficzności historii. KH 65, 1958 (2), 464–479.

6. W sprawie artykułów o empirycznym sensie teorii materializmu historycznego – po raz ostatni. SF 1958, 5/8, 158–163.

1. MALEWSKI, A., TOPOLSKI, J.: O wyjaśnianiu przyczynowym w historii.
KH 64, 1957 (2), 3–35.

2. Metoda materializmu historycznego w pracach historyków polskich.SF
1959, 6/15, 129–156.

1. MALINOWSKI, B.: Magic, Science and Religion and Other Essays. New
York, Doubleday and Company, Inc., 1955, 274 pp.

1. MANNHEIM, K.: Ideology and Utopia. London, Kegan Paul, Trench,
Trubner and Co., 1946, 31 and 318 pp.

2. Essays on the Sociology of Knowledge. London, Routledge and Kegan
Paul, 1952, 8 and 322 pp.

1. MARCHLEWSKI, J.: Pisma wybrane, T. 1. Warszawa, KIW, 1952, 27 i 682
str.; T. 2, 1956, 35 i 817 str.

1. MARCHLEWSKI, T.: W sprawie pewnej dyskusji naukowej. MW 1950,
3/46, 385–390.

1. MARCUSE, H.: Soviet Marxism. A Critical Analysis. London, Routledge
and Kegan Paul, 1958, 271 pp.

1. MARCZEWSKI, E.: Rozwój matematyki w Polsce. PAU, Historia Nauki
Polskiej w Monografiach 1. Kraków, PAU, 1948, 46 str.

1. MARGENAU, H.: Einstein's Conception of Reality. Ex: Schilpp, P. A.
(Ed.): Albert Einstein: Philosopher-Scientist. New York, Harper and
Brothers Publishers, Harper Torchbooks/Science Library, 1959, Vol. 1,
245–268.

1. MARKIEWICZ, H.: O specyficznych cechach literatury jako formy świadomości społecznej. PL 42, 1951 (2), 353–361.

2. O marksistowskiej teorii literatury. IBL, Studia Historyczno-Literackie T.
14. Wrocław, ZNIO, 1952, 126 str.

3. Tradycje i rewizje. Kraków, Wydawnictwo Literackie, 1957, 362 str.

1. MARTEL, K.: O marksistowsko-leninowskiej teorii poznania. MF 1953,
1/7, 281–303.

2. Marksistowski naturalizm a filozoficzna koncepcja człowieka społecznego. Warszawa, KIW, 1958, 86 str.

3. Ideologia a nauki społeczne. ND 1959, 5/119, 36–50.

1. MARX, K.: Economic and Philosophic Manuscripts of 1844. Moscow,
Foreign Languages Publishing House, 1959, 208 pp.

2. MARX, K.: The Poverty of Philosophy. London, Lawrence and Wishart, 1941, 214 pp.

3. A Contribution to the Critique of Political Economy. With an Appendix Containing Marx's Introduction to the Critique Recently Published among His Posthumous Papers. Translated by N. I. Stoke. Calcutta, Bharati Library, s.a., 314 pp.

4. Capital, Vol. 1–3. Moscow, Foreign Languages Publishing House, 1957–1959, 807, 546, 923 pp.

1. MARX, K., ENGELS, F.: The German Ideology. Part 1 and 3. London, Lawrence and Wishart, 1940, 214 pp.

2. The Holy Family or Critique of Critical Critique. Moscow, Foreign Languages Publishing House, 1956, 299 pp.

3. Selected Works. In Two Volumes. Moscow, Foreign Languages Publishing House, 1951, 615, 483 pp.

4. Selected Correspondence. Moscow, Foreign Languages Publishing House, 1956, 623 pp.

1. MARKS I ENGELS w Polsce. Materiały do bibliografii 1842–1952.Warszawa, Biblioteka Narodowa, 1953, 111 str.

1. MAZIERSKI, S.: Problem substancjalizmu u podstaw rzeczywistości fizycznej. RCZF 4, 1954, 87–104.

2. Uogólnienie pojęcia przyczynowości. RCZF 5, 1955–1957 (4), 153–171.

3. Obraz świata w oczach fizyka i historyka. RCZF 6, 1958 (3), 99–118.

4. Zasada przyczynowości w aspekcie fizykalnym i metafizycznym. ZNKUL 1, 1958 (4), 27–42.

5. Pojęcie konieczności w filozofii św. Tomasza z Akwinu. TNKUL, Rozprawy Wydziału Filozoficznego T. 8. Lublin, TNKUL, 1958, 119 str.

1. MEHLBERG, H.: Positivisme et science. SPH 3, 1939–1946, 211–294.

2. Idealizm i realizm na tle współczesnej fizyki. KF 17, 1948 (1–2), 87–116.

3. O sprawdzalnych założeniach nauki. PF 44, 1948 (4), 319–335.

4. Les hypothèses invérifiables dans la science empirique. PICPHA 1, 627–628.

5. The Idealistic Interpretation of Atomic Physics. SPH 4, 1949–1950, 171–235.

1. MEHRING, F.: Karl Marx. The Story of His Life. Translated by E. Fitzgerald. London, Allen and Unwin, 1948, 21 and 575 pp.

1. MERTON, R. K.: Social Theory and Social Structure. Revised and Enlarged Edition. Glencoe, The Free Press, 1957, 18 and 645 pp.

1. MICHAJŁOW, W.: Na pierwszym etapie rozwoju nowej biologii w Polsce. ND 1949, 3/15, 123–133.

2. Wnioski z pracy Stalina 'Ekonomiczne problemy socjalizmu w ZSRR' dla biologii. MF 1953, 3/9, 111–137.

1. MICHALSKI, K.: Le problème de la volonté à Oxford et à Paris au XIV-e siècle. SPH 2, 1937, 233–365.

2. Ks. Jan Salamucha. TP 2, 1946, 2/43, 2.

1. MICHAŁOWSKI, W.: Zagadnienia nazw pustych w sylogistyce w świetle 'Ontologii' Leśniewskiego. RCZF 5, 1955–1957 (2), 65–95.

BIBLIOGRAPHY

1. Miciński, B.: Portret Kanta. Znak 2, 1947 (6), 621–647.
1. Milbrandt, M.: Filozofia egzystencjalna Gabriela Marcela. PF 43, 1947 (1–4), 137–147.
1. Mirek, F.: Zarys socjologii. Lublin, TNKUL, 1948, 745 str.
1. Mises, R.: Probability, Statistics and Truth. Translated by J. Neyman, D. Scholl, and E. Rabinowitsch. London, W. Hodge, 1939, 16 and 323 pp.
2. Positivism. A Study in Human Understanding. Cambridge, Harvard University Press, 1951, 11 and 404 pp.
1. Modzelewski, Z.: Znaczenie pracy Stalina 'Ekonomiczne problemy socjalizmu w ZSRR' dla rozwoju nauki. MF 1953, 2/8, 86–101.
2. Wybór pism. Warszawa, PWN, 1956, 350 str.
1. Moore, G. E.: Philosophical Studies. London, Kegan Paul, Trench, Trubner and Co., 1922, 8 and 342 pp.
2. Some Main Problems of Philosophy. London, Allen and Unwin, 1953, 12 and 380 pp.
1. Morawski, S.: Estetyczne królestwo Ingardena. NK 9, 1958, 27/432, 8 i 11.
1. Mostowski, A.: O zdaniach nierozstrzygalnych w sformalizowanych systemach matematycznych. KF 16, 1946 (2–4), 223–277.
2. Logika Matematyczna. Polskie Towarzystwo Matematyczne, Monografie Matematyczne T. 18. Warszawa-Wrocław, Polskie Towarzystwo Matematyczne, 1948, 8 i 388 str.
3. Sur l'interprétation géométrique et topologique des notions logiques. PICPHA 1, 767–769.
4. A Classification of Logical Systems. SPH 4, 1949–1950, 237–274.
5. On Models of Axiomatic Systems. FM 39, 1952, 133–158.
6. Sentences Undecidable in Formalised Arithmetic. Studies in Logic and the Foundations of Mathematics. Amsterdam, North-Holland Publishing Company, 1952, 125 pp.
7. O geometrycznej interpretacji wyrażeń logicznych. SL 1, 1953, 254–269.
8. O tzw. konstruktywnych poglądach w dziedzinie podstaw matematyki. MF 1953, 1/7, 230–241.
9. The Present State of Investigations on the Foundations of Mathematics. PAN, Instytut Matematyczny. Warszawa, PWN, 1955, 47 pp.
10. L'oeuvre scientifique de Jan Łukasiewicz dans le domaine de la logique mathématique. FM 44, 1957, 1–7.
11. Organizacja i prace naukowe Instytutu Matematycznego Uniwersytetu Warszawskiego. RUW 1, 1958, 261–268.
1. Moszczeńska, W.: O sprzecznościach wewnętrznych 'programowego' subiektywizmu. W sprawie książki H. I. Marrou. KH 65, 1958 (2), 440–463.
1. Myhill, J. R.: Review of L. Chwistek's 'The Limits of Science'. JSL 14, 1949 (2), 119–125.
1. Myrdal, G.: The Political Element in the Development of Economic Theory. Translated by P. Streeten. London, Routledge and Kegan Paul, 1955, 17 and 248 pp.

2. MYRDAL, G.: Value in Social Theory. A Selection of Essays on Methodology. Edited by P. Streeten. London, Routledge and Kegan Paul, 1958, 46 and 269 pp.
1. MYŚL FILOZOFICZNA: Od redakcji. MF 1951, 1–2, 7–15.
2. Od redakcji. MF 1952, 2/4, 331–337.
3. W sprawie artykułu 'Legenda o Kazimierzu Twardowskim'. MF 1952, 4/6, 357–358.

1. NÆSS, A., CHRISTOPHERSEN, J. A., KVALØ, K.: Democracy, Ideology and Objectivity. Studies in the Semantics and Cognitive Analysis of Ideological Controversy. Oslo, University Press, 1956, 346 pp.
1. NAGEL, E.: The Logic of Historical Analysis. Ex: Feigl, H., Brodbeck, M. (Ed.): Readings in the Philosophy of Science. New York, Appleton-Century-Crofts, Inc., 1953, 688–700.
2. Logic without Metaphysics and Other Studies in the Philosophy of Science. Glencoe, The Free Press, 1956, 18 and 433 pp.
3. Sovereign Reason and Other Essays in the Philosophy of Science. Glencoe, The Free Press, 1954, 315 pp.
4. Principles of the Theory of Probability. IEUS 1, No. 6. Chicago, The University of Chicago Press, 1958, 3 and 80 pp.
1. NARBUTT, O.: O pierwszym polskim podręczniku logiki. Z rozważań nad filozofią Oświecenia. ŁTN, Wydz. 1, Nr. 33. Łódź, ZNIO, 1958, 146 str.
1. NEURATH, O.: Foundations of the Social Sciences. IEUS 2, No. 1. Chicago, The University of Chicago Press, 1954, 3 and 51 pp.
1. NORTHROP, F. S. C.: The Logic of the Sciences and the Humanities. New York, Meridian Books, Inc., 1959, 14 and 402 pp.
1. NOWAKOWSKI, S.: Socjologia i marksizm. NP 4, 1956 (2–3), 326–329.
1. NOWIŃSKI, Cz.: Formalna i normatywna teoria prawa i państwa. PPR 2, 1947, 3/13, 3–11.
2. Reakcyjne oblicze pozytywizmu i pragmatyzmu. MF 1952, 4/6, 273–298.
3. Problematyka stosunku tego to jednostkowe i tego co ogólne w świetle 'Zeszytów Filozoficznych' Lenina. ZPNP 12, 27–90, 256–279.
4. To co jednostkowe i to co ogólne. Ex: Światopoglądowe i metodologiczne problemy abstrakcji naukowej, T. 1. Warszawa, PWN, 1957, 5–112.

1. OBRADY podsekcji filozofii i nauk społecznych I Kongresu Nauki Polskiej. MF 1951, 1–2, 351–367.
1. OGONOWSKI, Z.: Filozoficzna i społeczna ideologia Braci Polskich. MF 1955, 1/15, 69–113.
2. Z zagadnień tolerancji w Polsce XVII wieku. Warszawa, PWN, 1958 350 str.
1. OLSZEWICZ, B.: Lista strat kultury polskiej. Warszawa, Wydawnictwo S. Arcta, 1947, 16 i 336 str.

BIBLIOGRAPHY

1. OPAŁEK, K.: Badania nad historią nauki, ich charakter, zakres, organizacja. SMDNP 1, 1953, 5–28.
2. Stan badań nad nauką polskiego Oświecenia. SMDNP 6, 1958, 63–79.
1. OPAŁEK, K., WOLTER, W.: Nauka filozofii prawa i prawa karnego w Polsce. PAU, Historia Nauki Polskiej w Monografiach. Kraków, PAU, 1948, 39 str.
1. ORTHWEIN, K.: Zjazd ekonomistów polskich. ŻN 1951, 1–2, 94–103.
1. OSIADACZ, A.: U początków myśli marksistowskiej w Polsce. MF 1952, 3/5, 334–348.
2. W sprawie monografii o Bronisławie Białobłockim. MF 1954, 4/14, 240–254.
1. OSSOWSKA, M.: O dwóch rodzajach ocen. KF 16, 1946 (2–4), 273–292.
2. Les problèmes d'une science de la morale. SPH 3, 1939–1946, 259–304.
3. Wzór obywatela w ustroju demokratycznym. Biblioteka Oświaty Robotniczej. Warszawa, Towarzystwo Uniwersytetu Robotniczego, 1946, 20 str.
4. Inteligent polski na tle grup towarzyskich Europy Zachodniej. MW 1947, 5/12, 129–140.
5. Podstawy nauki o moralności. Warszawa, Czytelnik, 1947, 380 str.; wyd. 2, Warszawa, PWN, 1957, 416 str.
6. Egoizm i altruizm a typy stosunków społecznych. PS 9, 1947, 63–72.
7. Qu'est ce qu'un jugement de valeur? PICPHA 1, 443–444.
8. Co to jest ocena? PF 44, 1948(4), 425–427.
9. Motywy postępowania. Z zagadnień psychologii moralności. Warszawa, KIW, 1949, 325 str.; wyd. 2, Warszawa, KIW, 1958, 327 str.
10. Oceny i normy. KF 18, 1949 (3–4), 313–320.
11. Uwagi o strukturze systemów etycznych. SPAU 52, 1951(4), 325–326.
12. Moralność mieszczańska. ŁTN, Wydz. 1, Nr. 22. Łódź, ZNIO, 1956, 326 str.
13. Changes in the Ethics of Fighting in the Course of the Last Century. TWCSA, Vol. 6, 81–86.
14. O pewnych przemianach etyki walki. Biblioteczka 'Po Prostu' 12. Warszawa, KIW, 1957, 41 str.
15. Zagadnienie powszechnie uznanych norm moralnych. SF 1957, 3, 80–96.
16. Norma prawna i norma moralna u Petrażyckiego. Fragmenty Filozoficzne (2), 75–85.
1. OSSOWSKA, M., OSSOWSKI, S.: Nauka o nauce. NPL 20, 1935, 1–12.
1. OSSOWSKI, S.: Nauki humanistyczne a ideologia społeczna. NPL 22, 1937, 1–24.
2. Stefan Czarnowski (1879–1937). PF 41, 1938, 301–303.
3. Analiza socjologiczna pojęcia ojczyzny. MW 1946, 2, 154–175.
4. Socjologia w świecie powojennym. Kuźnica 2, 1946, 25/43, 1–2.
5. Doktryna marksistowska na tle dzisiejszej epoki. MW 1947, 12/19, 501–513.
6. Ku nowym formom życia społecznego. Warszawa, Wiedza, 1947, 65 str.;

wyd. 2, Biblioteczka 'Po Prostu'. Warszawa, KIW, 1956, 74 str.
7. OSSOWSKI, S.: Teoretyczne zadania marksizmu. Szkic programu. MW 1948, 1/20, 3–18.
8. Na szlakach marksizmu. MW 1948, 8–9, 19–34.
9. Więź społeczna i dziedzictwo krwi, wyd. 2. Warszawa; Spółdzielnia Wydawnicza 'Książka', 1948, 287 str.
10. U podstaw estetyki, wyd. 2, Warszawa, Czytelnik, 1949, 318 str.; wyd. 3, opracowane na nowo i rozszerzone, Warszawa, PWN, 1958, 362 str.
11. Changing Patterns in Modern National Ideology. International Social Science Bulletin 3, 1951(2), 247–253.
12. Tactics and Truth. SFB 1956, 7, 17–24.
13. Old Notions and New Problems: Interpretations of Social Structure in Modern Society. TWCSA, Vol. 3, 18–25.
14. Marksizm i twórczość naukowa w społeczeństwie socjalistycznym. Artykuły z lat 1947–56. Biblioteczka 'Po Prostu' 11. Warszawa, KIW, 1957, 99 str.
15. Struktura klasowa w społecznej świadomości. ŁTN, Wydz. 2, Nr. 21. Łódź, ZNIO, 1957, 186 str.
16. Social Conditions and Consequences of Social Planning. TWCSS, Vol. 2, 199–222.
17. Wielogłowy Lewiatan i grupa społeczna. O perypetiach pojęciowych w socjologii. SF 1959, 5/14, 101–138.

1. PARSONS, T.: The Social System. Glencoe, The Free Press, 1952, 18 and 575 pp.
2. Essays in Sociological Theory. Revised Edition. Glencoe, The Free Press, 1954, 459 pp.
1. PARSONS, T., SMELSER, N. J.: Economy and Society. A Study in the Integration of Economic and Social Theory. London, Routledge and Kegan Paul, 1956, 21 and 322 pp.
1. PASTUSZKA, J.: Materialistyczna a katolicka koncepcja człowieka. PF 43, 1947 (1–4), 105–118.
2. Idea człowieka we współczesnych prądach filozoficznych. Poznań, Wydawnictwo 'Kultura', 1947, 45 str.
3. Psychologia ogólna. TNKUL T. 35–36. Lublin, TNKUL 1946–1947, 414 i 412 str.; wyd. 2 zmienione, Lublin, TNKUL, 1957, 355 i 375 str.
4. Trwałe wartości filozofii chrześcijańskiej na tle nowoczesnych prądów filozoficznych. RCZF 1, 1948, 1–41.
5. Wydział filozofii chrześcijańskiej – nowy ośrodek studiów filozoficznych. RCZF 1, 1948, 270–277.
6. Charakter człowieka. Struktura, typologia, diagnostyka psychologiczna. Lublin, TNKUL, 1959, 427 str.
1. PAUL, G. A.: Lenin's Theory of Perception. Ex: MacDonald, M. (Ed.): Philosophy and Analysis. Oxford, Basil Blackwell, 1954, 278–286.

BIBLIOGRAPHY

1. PAWŁOWSKI, T.: Z logiki pojęć przyrodoznawstwa. SF 1957, 1, 145–168.
2. Klasyfikacja sztuczna a klasyfikacja naturalna w biologii. Ex: Fragmenty Filozoficzne (2), 115–141.
1. PEARS, D. F.: Universals. Ex: Flew, A. G. N. (Ed.): Logic and Language, Second Series. Oxford, Basil Blackwell, 1955, 51–64.
2. Time, Truth, and Inference. Ex: Flew, A. (Ed.): Essays in Conceptual Analysis. London, Macmillan, 1956, 228–252.
1. PEARS, D. F. (Ed.): The Nature of Metaphysics. London, Macmillan, 1957, 6 and 164 pp.
1. PELC, J.: Prawa nauki. Ex: Pelc, J., Przełęcki, M., Szaniawski, K.: Prawa nauki. Trzy studia z zakresu logiki. Warszawa, PWN, 1957, 7–44.
2. O istnieniu i strukturze dzieła literackiego. SF 1958, 3/6, 121–164.
3. Szkic analizy znaczeniowej terminu 'ideologia dzieła literackiego'. Ex: Fragmenty Filozoficzne (2), 142–177.
1. PERRY, R. B.: Present Philosophical Tendencies. New York, G. Braziller Inc., 1955, 15 and 383 pp.
1. PETRAŻYCKI, L.: Law and Morality. Translated by H. W. Babb, with an Introduction by N. S. Timasheff. 20th Century Legal Philosophy Series: Vol. VII. Cambridge, Harvard University Press, 1955, 46 and 335 pp.
2. Wstęp do nauki prawa i moralności. Podstawy psychologii emocjonalnej. Opracował J. Lande, wstępem opatrzył T. Kotarbiński. Warszawa, PWN, 1959, 492 str.
3. Teoria prawa i państwa w związku z teorią moralności, T. 1. Opracował J. Lande. Warszawa, PWN, 1959, 451 str.
1. PETRUSEWICZ, K.: Mechanizm i witalizm a materializm dialektyczny. MW 1951, 3–4/58–59, 396–426.
2. O problemie powstawania gatunków. MF 1954, 1/11, 80–100.
1. PIECH, T.: Zarys historii fizyki w Polsce. PAU, Historia Nauki Polskiej w Monografiach 3. Kraków, PAU, 1948, 46 str.
1. PIETER, J.: Wstęp do teorii zjawisk moralnych. PF 42, 1946 (3–4), 273–298.
2. Psychologia jako nauka. Wstęp do psychologii, cz. 1. Kraków, Wiedza-Zawód-Kultura, 1947, 288 str.
1. PIETRZKIEWICZ, T.: Idealizm contra realizm w różnych odmianach tych pojęć. KF 16, 1946 (2–4), 351–370.
1. PIOTROWSKI, W.: Zagadnienia nauki i szkolnictwa wyższego. PS 10, 1948, 490–496.
1. PIWOWARCZYK, J.: Filozofia marksizmu. TP 1, 1945, 31, 1; Teologia marksizmu. TP 1, 1945, 32, 2; Etyka marksizmu. TP 1, 1945, 34, 2; Socjologia marksizmu. TP 1, 1945, 35, 2; Własność w systemie Marksa. TP 1, 1945, 37, 2; Jeszcze marksizm. TP 2, 1946, 3/44, 4.
2. Dwie oceny marksizmu. TP 3, 1947, 39/132, 4.
1. PLAMENATZ, J.: German Marxism and Russian Communism. London, Longmans Green and Co., 1954, 23 and 356 pp.

1. PLEBAŃSKI, J.: Dyskusja nad możliwością kauzalnej interpretacji mechaniki kwantowej. NP 2, 1954 (4), 85–129.
1. PLEBAŃSKI, J., GAJEWSKI, R.: O materialistycznej treści fizyki Alberta Einsteina. MF 1955, 5–6/19–20, 32–67.
1. PLEBAŃSKI, J., WERLE, J.: O interpretacjach mechaniki kwantowej. MF 1954, 2/12, 39–78.
1. PLEKHANOV, G.: Fundamental Problems of Marxism. Translated from the second Russian edition, published at Moscow, 1928, by Eden and Cedar Paul. London, Lawrence Ltd., s.a., 14 and 145 pp.
2. The Development of the Monist View of History. Moscow, Foreign Languages Publishing House, 1956, 410 pp.
1. POGONOWSKI, J.: Metoda nauki językoznawczej w porównaniu z metodą nauk przyrodniczych. KF 1946 (2–4), 293–350.
1. POINCARÉ, H.: The Value of Science. Authorized Translation by G. B. Halsted. New York, Dover Publications, 1958, 3 and 147 pp.
1. POLANYI, M.: The Magic of Marxism and The Next Stage of History. A Special Supplement to the SFB, November, 1956, 24 pp.
1. PONIATOWSKI, Z: Społeczno-filozoficzne poglądy Henryka Kamieńskiego w okresie Przedwiośnia 1848 roku. MF 1952, 2/4, 172–212.
2. O poglądach społeczno-filozoficznych Henryka Kamieńskiego. Warszawa, KIW, 1955, 149 str.
1. POPPER, K. R.: The Open Society and Its Enemies, Vol. 1–2. London, Routledge and Sons, 1945, 268, 352 pp.
2. Three Views Concerning Human Knowledge. Ex: Lewis, H. D. (Ed.): Contemporary British Philosophy. Personal Statements. London, Allen and Unwin, 1956, 357–388.
3. The Poverty of Historicism. London, Routledge and Kegan Paul, 1957, 14 and 166 pp.
4. Philosophy of Science. A Personal Report. Ex: Mace, C. A. (Ed.): British Philosophy in the Mid-Century. London, Allen and Unwin, 1957, 155–191.
5. The Logic of Scientific Discovery. London, Hutchinson, 1959, 479 pp.
1. POSIEDZENIE RADY REDAKCYJNEJ 'Myśli Filozoficznej'. MF 1952, 1/3, 336-338.
2. Posiedzenie Rady Redakcyjnej 'Myśli Filozoficznej'. MF 1952, 2/4, 363–365.
1. POZNAŃSKI, E. Operacjonizm po trzydziestu latach (1927–1957). Ex: Fragmenty Filozoficzne (2), 178–218.
1. POZNAŃSKI, E., WUNDHEILER, A.: Pojęcie prawdy na terenie fizyki. Ex: Fragmenty Filozoficzne (1), 97–143.
1. PRICE, H. H.: Perception. London, Methuen, 1954, 9 and 332 pp.
1. PRIOR, A. N.: Formal Logic. Oxford, Clarendon Press, 1955, 9 and 329 pp.
2. Łukasiewicz's Contributions to Logic. Ex: Klibansky, R. (Ed.): Philosophy in the Mid-Century. A Survey. Firenze, La Nuova Italia Editrice, 1958, Vol. 1, 53–55.

BIBLIOGRAPHY

1. PRZEŁĘCKI, M.: O tzw. definicjach operacyjnych. SL 3, 1955, 125–149.
2. Logiczna analiza rozwoju pojęcia pierwiastka chemicznego. SF 1957, 1, 169–178.
3. Prawa a definicje. Ex: Pelc, J., Przełęcki, M., Szaniawski, K.: Prawa nauki. Trzy studia z zakresu logiki. Warszawa, PWN, 1957, 47–70.
4. W sprawie terminów nieostrych. SL 8, 1958, 313–317.
5. Postulaty empiryczności terminów przyrodniczych. Ex: Fragmenty Filozoficzne (2), 219–248.
1. PRZEMSKI, L.: Edward Dembowski. Warszawa, PIW, 1953, 257 str.

1. QUINE, W. V. O.: Mathematical Logic. New York, W. W. Norton and Company, Inc., 1940, 13 and 348 pp.
2. Methods of Logic. London, Routledge and Kegan Paul, 1952, 19 and 264 pp.
3. From a Logical Point of View. Cambridge, Harvard University Press, 1953, 6 and 184 pp.
4. Truth by Convention. Ex: Feigl, H., Sellars, W. (Ed.): Readings in Philosophical Analysis. New York, Appleton-Century-Crofts, Inc., 1949, 250–273.

1. RAMSEY, F. P.: The Foundations of Mathematics and Other Essays. London, Kegan Paul, Trench, Trubner and Co., 1931, 18 and 292 pp.
1. RANDALL, J. H., JR.: Nature and Historical Experience. Essays in Naturalism and in the Theory of History. New York, Columbia University Press, 1958, 8 and 326 pp.
1. RASIOWA, H.: Axiomatisation d'un système partiel de la théorie de la deduction. CRSSLV-C3 40, 1947–1948, 22–37.
2. Sur un certain système d' axiomes du calcul des propositions. Norsk Matematisk Tidsskrift 31, 1949, 1–3.
3. Algebraic Treatment of the Functional Calculi of Heyting and Lewis. FM 38, 1951, 99–126.
4. Algebraic Models of Axiomatic Theories. FM 41, 1955, 291–310.
5. O pewnym fragmencie implikacyjnego rachunku zdań. SL 3, 1955, 208–222.
1. RASIOWA, H., SIKORSKI, R.: A Proof of the Completeness Theorem of Gödel. FM 37, 1950, 193–200.
2. A Proof of the Skolem-Löwenheim Theorem. FM 38, 1951, 230–232.
3. Algebraic Treatment of the Notion of Satisfiability. FM 40, 1953, 62–95.
1. REICHBACH, J.: Über den Alternative und Negation aufgebauten Aussagenkalkül. SL 1, 1953, 13–18.
2. O pełności węższego rachunku funkcyjnego. SL 2, 1955, 213–228.
3. On the First-Order Functional Calculus and the Truncation of Models. SL 7, 1958, 181–216.

1. REICHENBACH, H.: The Rise of Scientific Philosophy (Paper-bound edition). Berkeley and Los Angeles, University of California Press, 1956, 11 and 333 pp.

1. REUTT, J.: Akademia Nauk ZSRR. O potrzebach i organizacji nauki sowieckiej. NPL 22, 1937, 257–260.

1. REYKOWSKI, J.: Uwagi o fizjologicznej podstawie i specyfice pojęć. Ex: Światopoglądowe i metodologiczne problemy abstrakcji naukowej, T. 2. Warszawa, PWN, 1957, 115–187.

2. Marksizm a psychologia w ujęciu amerykańskich krytyków. SF 1957, 3, 214–220.

1. ROBBINS, L.: An Essays on the Nature and Significance of Economic Science, 2nd ed., revised and extended. London, Macmillan, 1949, 18 and 160 pp.

1. ROLBIECKI, W.: Niektóre zagadnienia logiki formalnej w świetle teorii marksizmu-leninizmu. MF 1955, 2/16, 43–78.

1. ROSSER, J. B., TURQUETTE, A. R.: Many-Valued Logics. Studies in Logic and the Foundations of Mathematics. Amsterdam, North-Holland Publishing Company, 1952, 124 pp.

1. ROZENTAL, M., JUDIN, P. (Red.): Krótki słownik filozoficzny. Przekład z czwartego uzupełnionego i poprawionego wydania rosyjskiego. Warszawa, KIW, 1955, 1955, 756 str.

1. RUDNIAŃSKI, S.: Die erkenntnistheoretischen Grundlagen des französischen Materialismus. Archiv für Geschichte der Philosophie 35, 1923, 3–12.

2. Podaganki filozoficzne. Przewodnicy ludzkości. Warszawa, KIW, 1958, 274 str.

3. Z dziejów filozofii. Warszawa, KIW, 1959, 278 str.

1. RUSSELL, B.: The Principles of Mathematics, Vol. 1. Cambridge, University Press, 1903, 29 and 534 pp.

2. The Problems of Philosophy. London, William and Norgate, s.a., 8 and 255 pp.

3. Our Knowledge of the External World. London, Allen and Unwin, 1926 (revised), 251 pp.

4. Mysticism and Logic and Other Essays. London, Allen and Unwin, 1949 (8th impr.), 6 and 234 pp.

5. The Analysis of Matter. London, Allen and Unwin, s.a., 408 pp.

6. An Inquiry into Meaning and Truth. London, Allen and Unwin, 1940, 352 pp.

7. History of Western Philosophy. London, Allen and Unwin, 1946, 916 pp.

8. Human Knowledge. Its Scope and Limits. London, Allen and Unwin, 1951, 538 pp.

10. My Philosophical Development. London, Allen and Unwin, 1959, 279 pp.

1. RUSSELL, L. J.: Belief and Action. Ex: Lewis, H. D. (Ed.): Contemporary British Philosophy. Personal Statements. London, Allen and Unwin, 1956, 403-423.

BIBLIOGRAPHY

1. RUTKOWSKI, J.: Prace zespołowe i instytuty badawcze w naukach humanistycznych. ŻN 1946, 4, 243–254.
2. Zagadnienia planowania w nauce. ŻN 1946, 11–12, 363–374.
3. O zadaniach kół naukoznawczych. NPL 25, 1947, 303–309.
4. Uwagi o uspołecznieniu warsztatów pracy naukowej. ŻN 1948, 33–34, 161–168.
5. Historia gospodarcza Polski, T. 1–2. Poznań, Księgarnia Akademicka, 1946–1950, 370 i 512 str.; wyd. 2, skrócone, Warszawa, KIW, 1953, 568 str.

1. RUTSKI, J.: Doktryna Hume'a o prawdopodobieństwie. TNT, Prace Wydziału Filologiczno-Filozoficznego T. 1, Z. 1. Toruń, TNT, 1948, 55 str.

1. RYBICKI, M.: O postęp na wyższych uczelniach. ND 1949, 4/16, 33–49.

1. RYLE, G.: Dilemmas. Cambridge, The University Press, 1954, 129 pp.
2. The Theory of Meaning. Ex: Mace, C. A. (Ed.): British Philosophy in the Mid-Century. London, Allen and Unwin, 1957, 239–264.

1. SALAMUCHA, J.: Logika zdań u Wilhelma Ockhama. PF 38, 1935, 208–239.
2. Die Aussagenlogik bei Wilhelm Ockham. Franziskanische Studien 31, 1949, 97–134.
3. Zestawienie scholastycznych narzędzi logicznych z narzędziami logistycznymi. Ex: Myśl katolicka wobec logiki współczesnej. Studia Gnesnensia 15. Poznań, Księgarnia Św. Wojciecha, 1937, 35–48.
4. O możliwościach ścisłego formalizowania dziedziny pojęć analogicznych. Studia Gnesnensia 15. Poznań, Księgarnia Św. Wojciecha, 1937, 122–153.
5. Pojawienie się zagadnień antynomialnych na gruncie logiki średniowiecznej. PF 40, 1937, 68–89, 320–343.
6. The Proof 'Ex Motu' for the Existence of God: Logical Analysis of St. Thomas' Arguments. The New Scholasticism 32, 1958 (3), 334–372.

1. SANDLER, S.: U początków marksistowskiej krytyki literackiej w Polsce. Bronisław Białobłocki. IBL, Studia Historyczno-Literackie T. 21. Wrocław, ZNIO, 1954, 152 str.
2. O brązownictwie i antybrązownictwie. W sprawie monografii o Bronisławie Białobłockim. MF 1955, 2/16, 122–148.

1. SAWICKI, F.: Pojęcie i zagadnienie nicości u Heideggera. RCZF 4, 1954, 125–137.

1. SCHAFF, A.: Ks. Piwowarczykowi w odpowiedzi. Kuźnica 1, 1945, 15, 3–4; Kuźnica 1, 1945, 16, 4–5.
2. Pojęcie i słowo. Łódź, Książka, 1946, 218 str.
3. Zasada sprzeczności w świetle logiki dialektycznej. MW 1946, 3–4, 328–353.
4. Problem powszechników w świetle materializmu dialektycznego. PF 43, 1947 (1–4), 52–59.
5. Klasowy charakter filozofii. Kuźnica 4, 1948, 47/168, 4–5.

6. SCHAFF, A.: Wstęp do teorii marksizmu. Warszawa, Książka, 1948, 290 str.
7. Marksizm a rozwój nauki. MW 1948, 6–7/25–26, 245–263.
8. Ludwik Krzywicki a filozofia marksistowska. MW 1949, 8–9/39–40, 3–28.
9. Kazimierz Kelles-Krauz. ND 1949, 1, 147–164.
10. Kosmopolityzm – ideologia imperializmu. MW 1949, 11/42, 135–151.
11. Zarys rozwoju filozofii marksistowskiej w Polsce. SPAU 50, 1949 (10), 597–599.
12. Narodziny i rozwój filozofii marksistowskiej. Warszawa, KIW, 1950, 403 str.
13. O niektórych zagadnieniach filozoficznych w pracach Stalina o językoznawstwie. MW 1950, 11–12/54–55, 230–249.
14. Z zagadnień marksistowskiej teorii prawdy. Warszawa, KIW, 1951, 406 str.
15. Zadania frontu filozoficznego w świetle uchwał I Kongresu Nauki Polskiej. MF 1951, 1–2, 16–49.
16. Poglądy filozoficzne Kazimierza Ajdukiewicza. MF 1952, 1/3, 209–256.
17. Metoda dokumentów osobistych a społeczne badania terenowe. MF 1952, 3/5, 221–259.
18. Zagadnienie obiektywności praw historycznych. MF 1953, 1/7, 3–37.
19. Stalinowski wkład w filozofię marksistowską. MF 1953, 2/8, 43–85.
20. W sprawie oceny poglądów filozoficznych K. Ajdukiewicza. MF 1953, 3/9, 201–223.
21. Dziesięć lat walki o zwycięstwo filozofii marksistowskiej w Polsce Ludowej. MF 1954, 3/13, 3–33.
22. Obiektywny charakter praw historii. Warszawa, PWN, 1955, 412 str.
23. Dialektyka marksistowska a zasada sprzeczności. MF 1955, 4/18, 143–158.
24. O badaniach kultury i o szkołach w nauce. PK 4, 1955, 37, 1 i 4.
25. Marksizm a rozwój polskiej humanistyki. PK 4, 1955, 44, 1 i 4.
26. O pozytywny program badań społecznych. PK 4, 1955, 45, 1–2.
27. Mannheima 'socjologia wiedzy' a zagadnienia obiektywności prawdy. MF 1956, 1/21, 116–134.
28. Aktualne zagadnienia polityki kulturalnej w dziedzinie filozofii i socjologii. Warszawa, PWN, 1956, 97 str.
29. Z czym walczymy i do czego dążymy występując przeciwko 'kultowi jednostki'. ND 1956, 4/82, 18–29.
30. W sprawie partyjnego kierowania nauką. ND 1956, 6/84, 12–23.
31. Jeszcze raz o dialektyce i zasadzie sprzeczności. SF 1957, 1, 201–213.
32. Filozoficzny aspekt procesu porozumiewania się. SF 1958, 2/5, 3–35.
33. Ideologia w ujęciu Mannheima. Warszawa, KIW 1958, 35 str.
34. Spór o zagadnienie moralności. Warszawa, KIW, 1958, 176 str.
35. Główne zagadnienia i kierunki filozofii. Cz. 1: Teoria poznania. Warszawa, PWN, 1958, 148 str.
36. Aktualne zagadnienia nauk społecznych. ND 1959, 6/120, 28–39.

37. SCHAFF, A.: O studiach nad młodym Marksem i istotnych wypaczeniach. Na marginesie artykułu L. Kołakowskiego pt. 'Karol Marks i klasyczna definicja prawdy'. ND 1959, 13/127, 16–29.

1. SCHAFF, A., BRUM, L.: Pogadanki ekonomiczne, wyd. 3. Łódź, Książka, 1947, 123 str.

1. SCHUMPETER, J. A.: Capitalism, Socialism, and Democracy. London, Allen and Unwin, 1943, 10 and 381 pp.

2. Science and Ideology. The American Economic Review 39, 1949 (2), 345–359.

1. SEJNEŃSKI, H.: Polska myśl katolicka a fizyka współczesna 1945–1955. Warszawa, PWN, 1956, 168 str.

1. SEREJSKI, M. H.: O właściwy stosunek do tradycji naukowej. Zeszyty Naukowe Uniwersytetu Łódzkiego Seria 1, Nauki Humanistyczno-Społeczne Z. 4. Łódź, PWN, 1956, 5–10.

2. Koncepcja historii powszechnej Joachima Lelewela. Warszawa, PWN, 1958, 429 str.

1. V SESJA zgromadzenia ogólnego PAN. SCZP-PAN 4, 1956 (1), 3–114.

2. VI Sesja zgromadzenia ogólnego PAN. SCZP-PAN 4, 1956 (3), 3–184.

3. Sesja naukowa poświęcona 'Zeszytom Filozoficznym' W. I. Lenina. ZPNP 12, 1956, 279 str.

1. SIMPSON, G. G.: The Meaning of Evolution. A Mentor Book. New York, The New American Library, 1951, 192 pp.

1. SKOWRON, S.: Krytyka chromozonowej teorii dziedziczności w zjawiskach rozwoju zarodkowego. MW 1950, 3/46, 427–443.

1. SKOWRON, S., WRÓBLEWSKI, R.: Zagadnienie żywej substancji. MF 1952, 3/5, 106–130.

1. SŁONIEWSKA, H.: Filozofia i pogląd na świat. Śladami myśli K. Twardowskiego. Zeszyty Wrocławskie 2, 1948 (3), 55–63.

2. Kazimierz Twardowski w psychologii polskiej. RF 19, 1959 (1–2), 17–24.

1. SŁUPECKI, J.: Der volle dreiwertige Aussagenkalkül. CRSSLV–C3 29, 1936, 9–11.

2. Kryterium pełności wielowartościowych systemów logiki zdań. CRSSLV-C3 32, 1939, 102–109.

3. Dowód aksjomatyzowalności pełnych systemów wielowartościowych rachunków zdań. CRSSLV-C3 32, 1939, 110–128.

4. Uwagi o sylogistyce Arystotelesa. AUMCS-SF 1, 1946 (3), 187–191.

5. Pełny trójwartościowy rachunek zdań. AUMCS-SF 1, 1946 (3), 193–209.

6. Czym jest logika. Warszawa, Wiedza-Spółdzielnia Wydawnicza, 1948, 71 str.

7. Z badań nad sylogistyką Arystotelesa. Prace WRTN, Seria B, Nr. 6. Wrocław, WRTN, 1948, 30 str.

8. O właściwych regułach inferencyjnych. KF 18, 1949 (3–4), 309–312.

9. On Aristotelian Syllogistic. SPH 4, 1949–1950, 275–300.

10. Über die Regeln des Aussagenkalküls. SL 1, 1953, 19–43.

11. St. Leśniewski's Protothetics. SL 1, 1953, 44–112.

12. SŁUPECKI, J.: System logiczny bez operatorów. SL 3, 1955, 98–108.
13. S. Leśniewski's Calculus of Names. SL 3, 1955, 7–71.
14. Towards a Generalised Mereology of Leśniewski. SL 8, 1958, 131–154.
15. O pewnych fragmentarycznych systemach rachunku zdań. SL 8, 1958, 177–185.
16. Funkcja Łukasiewicza. Zeszyty Naukowe Uniwersytetu Im. B. Bieruta, Seria B, Nr. 3, 1959, 33–40.

1. SMOLUCHOWSKI, M.: Pisma, T. 1–3. Z polecenia PAU zgromadzone i wydane przez Wł. Natansona i J. Stocka. Kraków, Drukarnia Uniwersytetu Jagiellońskiego, 1924–1928, 612, 654, 348 str.

1. SOBOCIŃSKI, B.: O kolejnych uproszczeniach aksjomatyki 'Ontologii' prof. St. Leśniewskiego. Ex: Fragmenty Filozoficzne (1), 144–160.
2. An Investigation of Protothetic. Cahiers de l'Institut d'Etudes Polonaises en Belgique, No. 5. Brussels 1949, 5 and 44 pp.
3. L'Analyse de l'antinomie russelliènne par Leśniewski, Methodos 1, 1949 (1), 94–107; (2), 220–228; (3), 308–316; Methodos 2, 1950 (2), 237–257.
4. Z badań nad aksjomatyką prototetyki Stanisława Leśniewskiego. RPTN 1953–1954, 18–20.
5. Studies in Leśniewski's Mereology. RPTN 1954–1955, 109–114.
6. On well Constructed Axiom Systems. RPTN 1955–1956, 54–70.
7. In Memoriam. Jan Łukasiewicz (1878–1956). Philosophical Studies 6, 1956, 3–49.
8. Jan Salamucha (1903–1944): A Biographical Note. The New Scholasticism 32, 1958 (3), 327–333.

1. SOBOCIŃSKI, W.: Wstęp do teorii marksizmu. ŻN 1948, 29–30, 429–435.

1. SOKORSKI, W.: Organizacja nauki i szkół wyższych. Odrodzenie 4, 1947, 20/129, 2.
2. Prawda obiektywna czy prawda objawiona. Na marginesie dyskusji o szkołach wyższych. Odrodzenie 4, 1947, 27/136, 2.
3. Istota reformy ustrojowej wyższego szkolnictwa. MW 1948, 1/20, 144–152.

1. SOŚNICKI, K.: Początki logiki. Toruń, Księgarnia Naukowa T. Szczęsny i Ska, 1948, 151 str.
2. Działalność pedagogiczna Kazimierza Twardowskiego. RF 19, 1959 (1–2), 24–29.

1. SPIRA, Z.: Uwagi nad metodologią i teorią poznania Poppera. KF 16, 1946 (2–4), 371–403.

1. SPIRAŁO, A.: Logika Jana Spangenberga. SF 1958, 2/5, 80–96.

1. SPRAWOZDANIE Z III posiedzenia prezydium Polskiej Akademii Nauk. SCZP-PAN 1, 1953 (3–4), 3–16.

1. STALIN, J.: Problems of Leninism. Moscow, Foreign Languages Publishing House, 1947, 642 pp.
2. Marxism and Problems of Linguistics. Moscow, Foreign Languages Publishing House, 1954, 71 pp.

3. STALIN, J.: Economic Problems of Socialism in the USSR. Moscow, Foreign Languages Publishing House, 1952, 104 pp.
4. Works, Vol. 1. Moscow, Foreign Languages Publishing House, 1954, 21 and 426 pp.
1. STATYSTYKA jako metoda poznawcza. Materiały konferencji problemowej PTP im. Kopernika. Warszawa, 1956, 237 str.
1. STEBBING, L. S.: Philosophy and the Physicists. London, Penguin Books, 1944, 219 pp.
1. STEINHAUS, H.: Prawdopodobieństwo, wiarogodność i możliwość. ZMT 1, 1953–1954 (3), 149–171.
2. O prognozie. ZMT 3, 1956 (1), 1–6.
3. Wnioskowanie indukcyjne. MF 1956, 5/25, 26–47.
1. STONERT, H.: Sprawozdanie z I Konferencji logików. SL 2, 1955, 251–265.
2. Analiza logiczna teorii atomistycznej w klasycznej chemii. Ex: Fragmenty Filozoficzne (2), 270–290.
1. STOUT, G. F.: Mind and Matter. Cambridge, The University Press, 1931, 14 and 325 pp.
1. STRAWSON, P. F.: Introduction to Logical Theory. London, Methuen, 1952, 10 and 266 pp.
1. SUCHODOLSKI, B.: O wielorakości i jedności egzystencjalizmu. PF 43, 1947 (1–4), 39–61.
2. Uspołecznienie kultury, wyd. 2. Warszawa, Trzaska-Ewert-Michalski, 1947, 449.
3. Polskie tradycje demokratyczne. Kraków, Wiedza-Zawód-Kultura, 1947, 183 str.
4. La vie de l'esprit. SPH 3, 1939–1946, 305–408.
5. W sprawie klasyfikacji i krytyki nowożytnych prądów pedagogicznych. MW 1950, 1/44, 61–75.
6. Krytyka niektórych kierunków pedagogicznych w dziełach K. Marksa. MW 1951, 1/56, 43–74.
7. Rozwój i problematyka filozofii Oświecenia w Polsce. Ex: Suchodolski, B. (Red.): Z dziejów polskiej myśli filozoficznej i społecznej, T. 2. Warszawa, KIW, 1956, 7–71.
8. U podstaw materialistycznej teorii wychowania. Warszawa, PWN, 1957, 403 str.
9. Katedra pedagogiki w latach 1945–1955. RUW 1, 1958, 229–249.
1. SUCHODOLSKI, W.: Na marginesie konferencji krakowskiej w sprawie potrzeb i organizacji nauki w Polsce. ŻN 1946, 3, 169–172.
1. SUSZKO, R.: W sprawie logiki bez aksjomatów. KF 17, 1948 (3–4), 199–205.
2. O analitycznych aksjomatach i logicznych regułach wnioskowania. PTPN, Prace Komisji Filozoficznej T. 7, Z. 5. Poznań, PTPN, 1949, 59 str.
3. Logika matematyczna i teoria podstaw matematyki w ZSRR. MW 1949, 12/42, 390–396.
4. Canonic Axiomatic Systems. SPH 4, 1949–1950, 301–330.

5. SUSZKO, R.: Aksjomat, analityczność i aprioryzm. MF 1952, 4/6, 139–161.
6. Czy logika znów pod znakiem zapytania. MF 1955, 1/15, 229–234.
7. Logika formalna a niektóre zagadnienia teorii poznania. Cz. 1: MF 1957, 2/28, 27–56; Cz. 2: MF 1957, 3/29, 34–67.
8. Formalna teoria wartości logicznych. SL 6, 1957, 145–237.
9. Zarys elementarnej składni logicznej. W sprawie antynomii kłamcy i semantyki języka naturalnego. Warszawa, PWN, 1957, 55 str.
10. Syntactic Structure and Semantical Reference. (I): SL 8, 1958, 213–243; (II): SL 9, 1960, 63–91.

1. SZACKI, J.: Pragmatyzm – filozofia która się opłaca. MF 1954, 3/13, 240–259.
2. Marksizm i polityka kulturalna. MF 1956, 6/26, 31–42.

1. SZANIAWSKI, I.: Posłowie. Ex: Rudniański (2), 267–271.

1. SZANIAWSKI, K.: Morał bajki dydaktycznej. PF 45, 1949 (3–4), 384–399.
2. Prawo, prawidłowość statystyczna, prawdopodobieństwo. Ex: Pelc, J., Przełęcki, M., Szaniawski, K.: Prawa nauki. Trzy studia z zakresu logiki. Warszawa, PWN, 1957, 73–85.
3. Z teorii nauk empirycznych. SF 1957, 1, 214–221.
4. O indukcji eliminacyjnej. Ex: Fragmenty Filozoficzne (2), 203–209.

1. SZANIAWSKI, K., MORAWSKI, S.: Książki o etyce marksistowskiej. PF 45, 1949 (3–4), 430–436.

1. SZCZENIOWSKI, SZ.: Budowa jądra atomowego. Warszawa, PZWS, 1947, 102 str.
2. Pojęcie pola i cząsteczki w fizyce dzisiejszej. MF 1952, 4/6, 184–197.
3. Wpływ Kopernika na rozwój fizyki. PFz. 5, 1954(3), 239–266.
4. Próby nowej interpretacji mechaniki kwantowej. MF 1955, 5–6/19–20, 68–91.
5. Nowe fakty dotyczące cząstek elementarnych i ich znaczenie dla zagadnienia struktury czasoprzestrzeni. SF 1958, 5/8, 52–80.

1. SZCZEPAŃSKI, J.: Interpretacja i rozumienie ludzkiego zachowania. MW 1946, 6–7, 177–189.
2. Epistemologiczne zagadnienia socjologii. PS, 9, 1947, 323–325.
3. Socjologia, ideologia i technika społeczna. PS 9, 1947, 15–33.
4. Użytkowanie dokumentów osobistych w psychologii społecznej. PS 10, 1948, 55–80.
5. Metodologiczne tendencje w socjologii współczesnej. MW 1948, 5/24, 186–197.
6. Zagadnienia metodologii badań społecznych w niektórych pracach Marksa i Engelsa. MF 1952, 2/4, 228–265.
7. Teoria społeczeństwa we współczesnej socjologii amerykańskiej. PNHS 3, 1953, 187–219.
8. Kryzys koncepcji uniwersytetu liberalnego. PS 11, 1957, 53–92.
9. Inteligencja i społeczeństwo. Biblioteczka 'Po Prostu' 15. Warszawa, KIW, 1957, 110 str.
10. Poland. Ex: Rose, A. M. (Ed.): The Institutions of Advanced Societies,

Minneapolis, University of Minnesota Press, 1958, 235–273.
1. SZUMAN, S.: Poważne i pogodne zagadnienia afirmacji życia. Katowice, J. Nawrocki, 1947, 134 str.
1. SZUMOWSKI, W.: Dzieje filozofii medycyny. Jej istota, nazwa i definicja. PAU, Prace Komisji Historii Medycyny i Nauk Matematyczno-Przyrodniczych, T. 2, 1949, 91–149.
2. La philosophie de la médicine, son histoire, son essence, sa dénomination et sa définition. Archives Internationales d'Histoire des Sciences 1949, 9, 1097–1139.

1. ŚLADKOWSKA, A.: Poglądy polityczne Edwarda Dembowskiego. MF 1952, 2/4, 112–171.
2. Stosunek polskiej filozofii połowy XIX wieku do klasycznej filozofii niemieckiej. MF 1954, 4/14, 104–119.
3. Poglądy społeczno-polityczne i filozoficzne Edwarda Dembowskiego. Warszawa, KIW, 1955, 295 str.
4. Rozwój ideologiczny Edwarda Dembowskiego. Ex: Baczko, B., Assorodobraj, N. (Red.): Z dziejów polskiej myśli filozoficznej i społecznej, T. 3. Warszawa, KIW, 1957, 336–388.
1. ŚREDZIŃSKA, I.: Logika i nowa metodologia Adama Burskiego. MF 1954, 2/12, 188–216.
1. ŚWIEŻAWSKI, S.: Tomistyczna a kartezjańska koncepcja człowieka. PF 43, 1947 (1–4), 87–104.
2. Centralne zagadnienie tomistycznej nauki o duszy. PF 44, 1948 (1–3), 131–189.
3. U źródeł konfliktu nowożytnego przyrodoznawstwa z filozofią scholastyczną. RCZF 1, 1948, 42–63.
4. Byt. Zagadnienia metafizyki tomistycznej. TNKUL, Rozprawy Wydziału Historyczno-Filozoficznego, Sekcja Filozoficzna T. 1. Lublin, TNKUL, 1948, 360 str.
5. Kultura umysłowa wieków średnich. TNKUL, Wykłady i Przemówienia Nr. 33. Lublin, TNKUL, 1949, 30 str.
6. O niektórych przyczynach niepowodzenia tomizmu. Znak 9, 1957 (6), 490–508.

1. TARSKI, A.: Pojęcie prawdy w językach nauk dedukcyjnych. Prace Towarzystwa Naukowego Warszawskiego, Wydział 3, Nr. 34. Warszawa, Towarzystwo Naukowe Warszawskie, 1933, 7 i 116 str.
2. Der Wahrheitsbegriff in den formalisierten Sprachen. SPH 1, 1935, 261–405.
3. The Semantic Conception of Truth and the Foundations of Semantics. Ex: Linsky, L. (Ed.): Semantics and the Philosophy of Language. A Collection of Readings. Urbana, The University of Illinois Press, 1952, 13–47.

4. TARSKI, A.: Introduction to Logic and to the Methodology of Deductive Sciences, 2d ed. revised. Translated by E. Helmer. New York, Oxford University Press, 1946, 18 and 239 pp.

5. Logic, Semantics, Metamathematics. Papers from 1923 to 1938. Translated by J. H. Woodger. Oxford, The Clarendon Press, 1956, 14 and 471 pp.

1. TARSKI, A., MOSTOWSKI, A., ROBINSON, R. M.: Undecidable Theories. Studies in Logic and the Foundations of Mathematics. Amsterdam, North-Holland Publishing Company, 1953, 11 and 98 pp.

1. TATARKIEWICZ, WŁ.: Zygmunt Łempicki. PF 42, 1946 (3–4), 329–330.

2. Mieczysław Milbrandt. PF 42, 1946 (3–4), 342–344.

3. Two Chapters on Happiness. SPH 3, 1939–46, 409–447.

4. O szczęściu. Kraków, Wiedza-Zawód-Kultura, 1947, 507 str.; wyd. 2, 1949.

5. Historia Filozofii, T. 1–3. T. 1, wyd. 3, Kraków, Czytelnik, 1946, 415 str.; T. 2, wyd. 3, 1947, 354 str.; T. 3, 1950, 602 str. Wydanie nowe, przejrzane i uzupełnione, Warszawa, PWN, 1958, 436, 341, 605 str.

6. Pięćdziesiąt lat filozofii w Warszawie 1898–1948. PF 44, 1948 (1–3), 3–14.

7. Morale et bonheur. PICPHA 1, 188–189.

8. Sciences nomologiques et typologiques: Essais d'une classification des sciences. PICPHA 1, 621–623.

9. Skupienie i marzenie. Kraków, Wydawnictwo M. Kot, 1951, 140 str.

10. O pisaniu historii filozofii. SPAU 53, 1952 (3), 141–147, 155–160.

11. Vouloir et pouvoir en histoire de la philosophie. PICPHB, Vol. 12, 14–19.

1. TAYLOR, E.: Rozwój ekonomiki a światopogląd. Ex: Opuscula Casimiro Tymieniecki Septuagenario Dedicata. Poznań, PTPN, 1959, 305–317.

1. TEZY DYSKUSYJNE. ŻN 1946, 2, 97–102.

1. TOMASZEWSKI, T.: W sprawie klasowego charakteru psychologii polskiej. MW 1950, 7/50, 3–24.

2. Kryzys metodologiczny w psychologii. Przegląd Psychologiczny 1952, 1, 1–35.

3. Uwagi o obiektywności praw nauki. MF 1953, 3/9, 84–110.

1. TYMIENIECKA, A. T.: Essence et existence. Etude à propos de la philosophie de Roman Ingarden et Nicolai Hartmann. Paris, Aubier, Edition Montaigne, 1957, 249 pp.

1. TYMIENIECKI, K.: Zarys dziejów historiografii polskiej. PAU, Historia Nauki Polskiej w Monografiach 19. Kraków, PAU, 1948, 141 str.

1. USOWICZ, A.: Ks. Konstanty Michalski. PF 44, 1948(4), 428–435.

1. VEBLEN, TH.: The Theory of the Leisure Class. London, Allen and Unwin, 1949, 6 and 404 pp.

BIBLIOGRAPHY

1. **Wagner, O.**: O dialektyce marksistowskiej. Warszawa, KIW, 1953, 179 str.
1. **Waismann, F.**: How I See Philosophy. Ex: Lewis, H. D. (Ed.): Contemporary British Philosophy. Personal Statements. London, Allen and Unwin, 1956, 447–490.
1. **Wajsberg, M.**: Aksjomatyzacja trójwartościowego rachunku zdań. CRSSLV-C3 24, 1931, 5–24.
1. **Walicki, A.**: Poglądy etyczne W. Bielińskiego. MF 1954, 2/12, 124–156.
2. Osobowość a historia. Warszawa, PIW, 1959, 488 str.
1. **Wallis, M.**: On Some Cases in Which Investigations Alter the Object Investigated. PICPHA 1, 647–648.
2. O przypadkach w których badanie zmienia przedmiot badany. PF 44, 1948 (4), 382–388.
3. Polish Contributions to Aesthetics and Science of Art before 1939: A Selective Bibliography. Journal of Aesthetics and Art Criticism 7, 1948–1949 (1), 51–53.
4. Koncepcje biologiczne w humanistyce. Ex: Fragmenty Filozoficzne (2), 307–330.
1. **Ważyk, A.**: W stronę humanizmu. Warszawa, KIW, 1949, 154 str.
1. **Wąsik, W.**: Stefan Rudniański. PF 42, 1946 (3–4), 325.
2. Benedykt Bornstein. PF 44, 1948 (4), 444–451.
3. Historia filozofii polskiej, T. 1. Warszawa, Pax, 1958, 424 str.
1. **Weber, M.**: Gesammelte Aufsätze zur Wissenschaftslehre. Tübingen, Verlag J. C. B. Mohr (Paul Siebeck), 1951, 7 und 687 SS.
2. The Theory of Social and Economic Organization. Being Part I of Wirtschaft und Gesellschaft. Translated from the German by A.R. Henderson and T. Parsons. London, W. Hodge and Company, 1947, 404 pp.
1. **Werfel, R.**: Miejsce intelektualistów – komunistów – w ramach partii. ND 1956, 9/87, 32–53.
1. **Wetter, G. A.**: Dialectical Materialism. A Historical and Systematic Survey of Philosophy in the Soviet Union. Translated from the German by P. Heath. London, Routledge and Kegan Paul, 1958, 12 and 609 pp.
1. **White, L. A.**: Ethnological Theory. Ex: Sellars, R. W., McGill, V. J., Farber, M. (Ed.): Philosophy for the Future. The Quest of Modern Materialism. New York, Macmillan, 1949, 357–384.
1. **Whitehead, A. N.**: The Concept of Nature. Cambridge, The University Press, 1930, 8 and 202 pp.
2. Science and the Modern World. A Mentor Book. New York, The New American Library, 1954, 212 pp.
1. **Wiatr, J.**: Bezdroża socjologii amerykańskiej. MF 1954, 4/14, 318–325.
2. O interpretacji materializmu historycznego. SF 1958, 1/4, 209–227.
3. Jeszcze o interpretacji materializmu historycznego. SF 1958, 3/6, 185–204.
4. Zagadnienia rasowe w socjologii amerykańskiej. Warszawa, PWN, 1959, 295 str.
1. **Wiegner, A.**: Zagadnienie poznawcze w oświetleniu L. Nelsona. PTPN,

Prace Komisji Filozoficznej 1, Z. 5. Poznań, PTPN, 1925, 70 str.
2. WIEGNER, A.: O istocie zjawisk psychicznych. PTPN, Prace Komisji Filozoficznej 4, Z. 2. Poznań, PTPN, 1934, 57 str.
3. Filozoficzne znaczenie teorii postaci. SPTPN 1948, 1, 26–28.
4. Elementy logiki formalnej. Poznań, Księgarnia Akademicka, 1948, 180 str.
5. W sprawie nowej klasyfikacji rozumowań. SL 7, 1958, 274–275.
1. WILKOSZ, W.: Liczę i myślę. Jak powstała liczba. Wydanie nowe opracowane przez I. Wilkoszową. Warszawa, PZWS, 1951, 140 str.
1. WILLMANN GRABOWSKA, H.: Stanisław Schayer. PF 42, 1946 (3–4), 317–320.
1. WINDELBAND, W.: A History of Philosophy, Vol. 1–2. New York, Harper and Brothers Publishers, Harper Torchbooks, 1958, 690 pp.
1. WITKIEWICZ, S. I.: Pojęcia i twierdzenia implikowane przez pojęcie istnienia. Warszawa, Wyd. Kasy im. Mianowskiego, 1935, 182 str.
2. O idealiźmie i realiźmie. PF 42, 1946 (3–4), 235–272.
1. WITWICKI, WŁ.: Pogadanki obyczajowe. Warszawa, PWN, 1957, 158 str.
1. WNIOSEK POLSKIEGO INSTYTUTU SOCJOLOGICZNEGO DO UNESCO· PS 8, 1946, 240–241.
1. WOJCIECHOWSKA, M.: PTPN po drugiej wojnie światowej. Księga Pamiątkowa w stulecie PTPN. Roczniki Historyczne 23, 1957, 509–542.
1. WOJTASIEWICZ, O.: Metajęzyki i metateorie a nauki humanistyczne. NP 5, 1957 (3), 146–149.
1. WOLFE, B. D.: Three Who Made a Revolution. London, Thames and Hudson, 1956, 10 and 661 pp.
1. WOLLHEIM, R.: F. H. Bradley. London, Penguin Books, 1959, 288 pp.
1. WOLNIEWICZ, B.: Pojęcie abstrakcji u Hegla i w marksiźmie. RF 18, 1958 (4), 172–175.
1. 'Woprosy Filosofii' o 'Myśli Filozoficznej'. MF 1953, 2/8, 418–423.
1. WORONIECKI, J.: Lubelskie środowisko filozoficzne. PF 44, 1948 (1–3), 50–56.
2. Katolicka etyka wychowawcza, T. 1–2. Kraków, Wydawnictwo Mariackie, 1948, 420, 476 str.
1. WRÓBLEWSKI, J.: Logika formalna a dialektyka. ŻN 1951, 3, 292–301.
1. WUDEL, W.: Powstanie logiki wyższej. MW 1947, 3/10, 343–367.

1. ZAWIRSKI, Z.: Les rapports de la logique polyvalente avec le calcul des probabilités. ACIPHS – Paris 4, 40–45.
1a. Stosunek logiki wielowartościowej do rachunku prawdopodobieństwa. PTPN, Prace Komisji Filozoficznej T. 4. Poznań, PTPN, 1934, 155–240.
1b. Über das Verhältnis der mehrwertigen Logik zur Wahrscheinlichkeitsrechnung. SPH 1, 1935, 407–442.
2. L'Évolution de la notion du temps. Kraków, PAU, 1936.
3. Międzynarodowy Kongres Jedności Nauki w Kopenhadze w r. 1936. NPL 22, 1937, 279–284.

4. ZAWIRSKI, Z.: Geneza i rozwój logiki intuicjonistycznej. KF 16, 1946 (2–4), 165–222.

5. Joachim Metallmann. PF 42, 1946 (3–4), 320–323.

6. Leon Chwistek. PF 42, 1946 (3–4), 330–334.

7. O współczesnych kierunkach filozofii. Kraków, Wiedza-Zawód-Kultura, 1947, 31 str.

8. Observations sur la méthode des sciences de la nature. PICPHA 1, 803–805.

9. Uwagi o metodzie nauk przyrodniczych. PF 44, 1948 (4), 315–318.

1. ZEIDLER, F.: Mechanizm i witalizm. SPTPN, 1945–1946, 2, 162–164.

2. O różnych interpretacjach epistemologicznych fizyki kwantowej. SPTPN 1948, 1, 28–30.

1. ZHDANOV, A. A.: On Literature, Music and Philosophy. London, Lawrence and Wishart, 1950, 112 pp.

1. ZIEMSKI, S.: Z zagadnień logiki polskiej doby Odrodzenia. MF 1953, 4/10, 58–68.

1. ZIEMSKI, S., SPIRAŁO, A.: Logika Mikołaja Mościckiego. Z badań nad logiką polską doby Odrodzenia. AHFMS 1957, 1, 43–69.

1. ZILSEL, E.: Physics and the Problem of Historico-Sociological Laws. Ex: Feigl, H., Brodbeck, M. (Ed.): Readings in the Philosophy of Science. New York, Appleton-Century-Crofts, Inc., 1953, 714–722.

1. ZŁOTOWSKI, I.: O prawidłowościach statystycznych w przyrodzie. MF 1954, 2/12, 79–87.

1. ZNAMIEROWSKI, Cz.: Analiza oceny moralnej. MW 1946, 3–4, 302–327.

2. Elita i demokracja, wyd. 2. Poznań, Narodowy Instytut Postępu, 1946, 42 str.

3. Potrzeby życia a nauki społeczne. ŻN 1947, 17–18, 289–301.

4. Normy grupy wolnej. MW 1947, 9–10/16–17, 171–199.

5. Prolegomena do nauki o państwie, wyd. 2. Poznań, Księgarnia Z. Gustowskiego, 1947–48, 271 str.

6. Rodzaje ocen. KF 17, 1948 (1–2), 117–132.

7. Ocena. PF 44, 1948 (1–3), 95–113.

8. Norma aksjologiczna. PF 45, 1949 (3–4), 327–344.

9. Zasady i kierunki etyki. Warszawa, PWN, 1957, 157 str.

10. Oceny i normy. Warszawa, PWN, 1957, 628 str.

1. ZNANIECKI, E. M.: Polish Sociology. Ex: Gurvitch-Moore (1), 703–717.

1. ZNANIECKI, F.: Wstęp do socjologii. PTPN, Prace Komisji Nauk Społecznych T. 2. Poznań, PTPN, 1922, 467 str.

2. The Object-Matter of Sociology. American Journal of Sociology 32, 1927 (4), 529–584.

3. Socjologia Wychowania, T. 1–2. Warszawa, Książnica Atlas, 1928–30, 312, 372 str.

4. Potrzeby socjologii w Polsce. NPL 10, 1929, 486–498.

5. The Method of Sociology. New York, Rinehart and Company, Inc., 1934, 12 and 338 pp.

6. ZNANIECKI, F.: Ludzie teraźniejszości a cywilizacja przyszłości. Lwów-Warszawa, Książnica-Atlas, 1935, 380 str.
7. Znaczenie socjolcgiczne badań Ludwika Krzywickiego nad społeczeństwami niższymi. Ex: Ludwik Krzywicki. Praca zbiorowa poświęcona jego życiu i twórczości. Warszawa, Instytut Gospodarstwa Społecznego, 1938, 219–248.
8. The Social Role of the Man of Knowledge. New York, Columbia University Press, 1940, 212 pp.
9. Social Organization and Institutions. Ex: Gurvitch-Moore (1), 172–217.
10. Cultural Sciences. Their Origin and Development. Urbana, University of Illinois Press, 1952, 8 and 438 pp.

1. ŻÓŁKIEWSKI, S.: O pozytywny program kulturalny. Odrodzenie 2, 1945, 37, 1–2.
2. Głos marksisty. Odrodzenie 2, 1945, 51, 1.
3. Przechadzka filozoficzna po księgarniach londyńskich. Kuźnica 1, 1945, 16, 1–3.
4. Kronika kulturalna. ND 1947, 1, 153–156.
5. Ze wspomnień polskiego inteligenta. Kuźnica 3, 1947, 3/72, 5–6; 4/73, 12–14.
6. Nad książką antynaturalisty. Kuźnica 3, 1947, 24/93, 8–10; 25/94, 8–9.
6a. Adam Schaff. Odrodzenie 5, 1948, 51–52/212–213, 5.
7. Badania nad literaturą polską. Dorobek, stan, potrzeby. Z powodu I Kongresu Nauki Polskiej. Warszawa, PIW, 1951, 103 str.
8. Z zagadnień organizacyjnych Polskiej Akademii Nauk na tle doświadczeń radzieckich. NP 1, 1953 (4), 26–40.
9. O aktualnych dyskusjach literackich. ND 1955, 6/72, 16–37.
10. Niektóre zagadnienia rozwoju nauk społecznych w Polsce. ND 12/78, 3–23.
11. Przemiany metodologiczne i organizacyjne nauki polskiej w minionym dziesięcioleciu. Ex: Dziesięć lat rozwoju nauki w Polsce Ludowej. PAN, Komitet Historii Nauki. Warszawa, PWN, 1956, 37–84.
12. Kultura i polityka. Warszawa, PIW, 1958, 290 str.
13. O dziele literackim. NK 11, 1960, 15/524, 2.
1. ŻYCIE NAUKI: U progu obrad I Kongresu Nauki Polskiej. ŻN 1951, 5–6, 529–542.

INDEX OF NAMES